FOURTH EDITION

3

Series Director: **Diane Larsen-Freeman**

Grammar Dimensions

Form • Meaning • Use

Lesson Planner

Suzanne Mitri

HEINLE
CENGAGE Learning™

Australia • Brazil • Japan • Korea • Mexico • Singapore • Spain • United Kingdom • United States

HEINLE
CENGAGE Learning™

Grammar Dimensions 3: Form, Meaning, and Use

Series Director: Diane Larsen-Freeman

Author: Suzanne Mitri

Publisher: Sherrise Roehr

Acquisitions Editor: Tom Jefferies

Editorial Assistant: Cécile Bruso

Executive Marketing Manager: Jim McDonough

Product Marketing Manager: Katie Kelley

Senior Content Project Manager: Maryellen Eschmann-Killeen

Senior Print Buyer: Mary Beth Hennebury

Production Project Manager: Chrystie Hopkins

Production Services: PrePress PMG

Interior Design: Lori Stuart

Cover Design: Studio Montage

Cover Image: © Digital Vision/Getty/RF

ISBN 13: 978-1-4240-0358-7

ISBN 10: 1-4240-0358-X

Heinle
25 Thomson Place
Boston, Massachusetts 02210
USA

Cengage Learning products are represented in Canada by Nelson Education, Ltd.

Visit Heinle online at **elt.heinle.com**
Visit our corporate website at **cengage.com**

Printed in the United States of America.
1 2 3 4 5 6 7 8 9 10—12 11 10 09 08

CONTENTS

Unit 14   Present Perfect
Describing Past Events in Relation to the Present   230

Unit 15   Future Time
Using Present Tenses, Using *Will* Versus *Be Going To* Versus *Shall*; Adverbial Clauses in Future   244

Unit 16   Modals of Prediction and Inference   256

A Word from Diane Larsen-Freeman, Series Editor

Before *Grammar Dimensions* was published, teachers would ask me, "What is the role of grammar in a communicative approach?" These teachers recognized the importance of teaching grammar, but they associated grammar with form and communication with meaning, and thus could not see how the two easily fit together. *Grammar Dimensions* was created to help teachers and students appreciate the fact that grammar is not just about form. While grammar does indeed involve form, in order to communicate, language users also need to know the meaning of the forms and when to use them appropriately. In fact, it is sometimes not the form, but the *meaning* or *appropriate use* of a grammatical structure that represents the greatest long-term learning challenge for students. For instance, learning when it is appropriate to use the present perfect tense instead of the past tense, or being able to use two-word or phrasal verbs meaningfully, represent formidable challenges for English language learners.

The three dimensions of *form*, *meaning*, and *use* can be depicted in a pie chart with their interrelationship illustrated by the three arrows:

How is the grammar structure formed? (accuracy)

form

What does the grammar structure mean? (meaning)

meaning

use

When or why is the grammar structure used? (appropriateness)

Helping students learn to use grammatical structures accurately, meaningfully, and appropriately is the fundamental goal of *Grammar Dimensions.* It is consistent with the goal of helping students to communicate meaningfully in English, and one that recognizes the undeniable interdependence of grammar and communication.

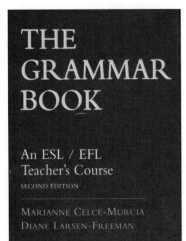

To learn more about form, meaning, and use, read *The Grammar Book: An ESL/EFL Teacher's Course,* Second Edition, by Marianne Celce-Murcia and Diane Larsen-Freeman. ISBN: 0-8384-4725-2.

To understand more about teaching grammar effectively, read *Teaching Language: From Grammar to Grammaring* by Diane Larsen-Freeman. ISBN: 0-8384-6675-3.

Enjoy the Fourth Edition of *Grammar Dimensions*!

Welcome to *Grammar Dimensions,* Fourth Edition!

The **clearest**, most **comprehensive** and **communicative** grammar series available!
The fourth edition of *Grammar Dimensions* is more **user-friendly** and makes
teaching grammar more **effective** than ever.

GRAMMAR DIMENSIONS IS COMPREHENSIVE AND CLEAR.

Grammar Dimensions systematically addresses the three dimensions of language—
form, meaning, and use—through clear and comprehensive grammar explanations
and extensive practice exercises. Each unit methodically focuses on each students'
dimension and then integrates what they have learned in end-of-unit activities.
In addition, grammatical structures are recycled throughout the series allowing
students to practice and build upon their existing knowledge.

GRAMMAR DIMENSIONS IS COMMUNICATIVE.

Grammar Dimensions includes a large variety of lively communicative and
personalized activities throughout each unit, eliciting self-expression and personalized
practice. Interactive activities at the start of each unit serve as diagnostic tools directing
student learning towards the most challenging dimensions of language structure.
Integrated activities at the end of each unit include reading, writing, listening, and
speaking activities allowing students to practice grammar and communication in
tandem. New research activities encourage students to use authentic Internet resources
and to reflect on their own learning.

GRAMMAR DIMENSIONS IS USER-FRIENDLY AND FLEXIBLE.

Grammar Dimensions has been designed to be flexible. Instructors can use the units
in order or as set by their curriculum. Exercises can be used in order or as needed by
the students. In addition, a tight integration between the Student Book, the
Workbook, and the Lesson Planner makes teaching easier and makes the series more
user-friendly.

GRAMMAR DIMENSIONS IS EFFECTIVE.

Students who learn the form, meaning, and use of each grammar structure will be able
to communicate more accurately, meaningfully, and appropriately.

New to the Fourth Edition

- **NEW and revised grammar explanations** and examples help students and teachers easily understand and comprehend each language structure.

- **NEW and revised grammar charts and exercises** provide a wealth of opportunities for students to practice and master their new language.

- **NEW thematically and grammatically related Internet and *InfoTrac*®** *College Edition activities* in every unit of books 2, 3, and 4 develop student research using current technologies.

- **NEW Reflection activities** encourage students to create personal language goals and to develop learning strategies.

- **NEW design, art, and photos** make each activity and exercise more engaging.

- **NEW Lesson Planners** assist both beginning and experienced teachers in giving their students the practice and skills they need to communicate accurately, meaningfully, and appropriately. All activities and exercises in the Lesson Planner are organized into step-by-step lessons so that no instructor feel overwhelmed.

SEQUENCING OF *GRAMMAR DIMENSIONS*

In *Grammar Dimensions* students progress from the sentence level to the discourse level, and learn to communicate appropriately at all levels.

Grammar Dimensions Book 1	*Grammar Dimensions* Book 2	*Grammar Dimensions* Book 3	*Grammar Dimensions* Book 4

Sentence level → Discourse level

	Book 1	**Book 2**	**Book 3**	**Book 4**
Level	High-beginning	Intermediate	High-Intermediate	Advanced
Grammar level	Sentence and sub-sentence level	Sentence and sub-sentence level	Discourse level	Discourse level
Primary language and communication focus	Semantic notions such as *time* and *place*	Social functions, such as *making requests* and *seeking* permission	Cohesion and coherence at the discourse level	Academic and technical discourse
Major skill focus	Listening and speaking	Listening and speaking	Reading and writing	Reading and writing

Guided Tour of *Grammar Dimensions* 3

Unit goals **provide a roadmap** for the grammar points students will work on.

"**Opening Task**" can be used as a **diagnostic warm-up** exercise to explore students' knowledge of each structure.

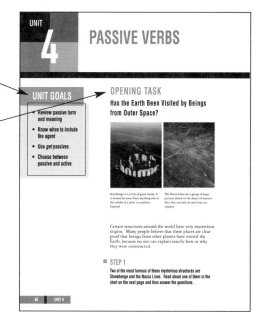

UNIT 4 **PASSIVE VERBS**

UNIT GOALS

- Review passive form and meaning
- Know when to include the agent
- Use *get* passives
- Choose between passive and active

OPENING TASK

Has the Earth Been Visited by Beings from Outer Space?

Stonehenge is a circle of giant stones. It is located far away from anything else in the middle of a plain in southern England.

The Nazca Lines are a group of huge pictures drawn in the desert of western Peru that can only be seen from an airplane.

Certain structures around the world have very mysterious origins. Many people believe that these places are clear proof that beings from other planets have visited the Earth, because no one can explain exactly how or why they were constructed.

STEP 1

Two of the most famous of these mysterious structures are Stonehenge and the Nazca Lines. Read about one of them in the chart on the next page and then answer the questions.

46 UNIT 4

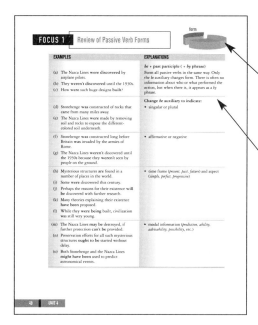

FOCUS 1 Review of Passive Verb Forms

EXAMPLES	EXPLANATIONS
(a) The Nazca Lines were discovered by airplane pilots. (b) They weren't discovered until the 1930s. (c) How were such huge designs built?	*be* + past participle (+ *by* phrase) Form all passive verbs in the same way. Only the *be* auxiliary changes form. There is often no information about who or what performed the action, but when there is, it appears as a *by* phrase.
(d) Stonehenge **was** constructed of rocks that came from many miles away. (e) The Nazca Lines **were** made by removing soil and rocks to expose the different-colored soil underneath.	Change *be* auxiliary to indicate: • singular or plural
(f) Stonehenge **was** constructed long before Britain **was** invaded by the armies of Rome. (g) The Nazca Lines **weren't** discovered until the 1930s because they **weren't** seen by people on the ground.	• affirmative or negative
(h) Mysterious structures **are** found in a number of places in the world. (i) Some **were** discovered this century. (j) Perhaps the reasons for their existence **will** be discovered with further research. (k) Many theories explaining their existence **have** been proposed. (l) While they **were** being built, civilization was still very young.	• time frame (*present, past, future*) and aspect (*simple, perfect, progressive*)
(m) The Nazca Lines **may** be destroyed, if further protection **can't** be provided. (n) Preservation efforts for all such mysterious structures **ought to** be started without delay. (o) Both Stonehenge and the Nazca Lines **might** have been used to predict astronomical events.	• modal information (*prediction, ability, advisability, possibility, etc.*)

48 UNIT 4

"**Focus**" sections present the **form, meaning,** and/or **use** of a particular structure helping students develop the skill of "**grammaring**"—the ability to use structures accurately, meaningfully, and appropriately.

Clear grammar charts present rules and explanation preceded by examples, so teachers can have students work inductively to try to discover the rule on their own.

EXERCISE 13

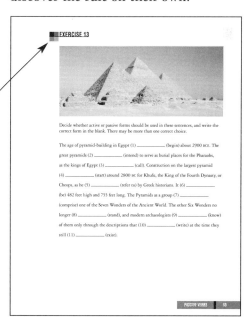

Decide whether active or passive forms should be used in these sentences, and write the correct form in the blank. There may be more than one correct choice.

The age of pyramid-building in Egypt (1) _____ (begin) about 2900 BCE. The great pyramids (2) _____ (intend) to serve as burial places for the Pharaohs, as the kings of Egypt (3) _____ (call). Construction on the largest pyramid (4) _____ (start) around 2800 BC for Khufu, the King of the Fourth Dynasty, or Cheops, as he (5) _____ (refer to) by Greek historians. It (6) _____ (be) 482 feet high and 755 feet long. The Pyramids as a group (7) _____ (comprise) one of the Seven Wonders of the Ancient World. The other Six Wonders no longer (8) _____ (stand), and modern archaeologists (9) _____ (know) of them only through the descriptions that (10) _____ (write) at the time they still (11) _____ (exist).

Purposeful exercises provide a wealth of opportunity for students to practice and personalize the grammar.

PASSIVE VERBS 49

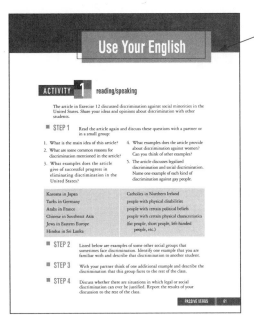

"Use Your English" (fondly known as the purple pages) offer communicative activities that **integrate grammar with reading, writing, listening, and speaking skills.** Communicative activities consolidate grammar instruction with enjoyable and meaningful tasks.

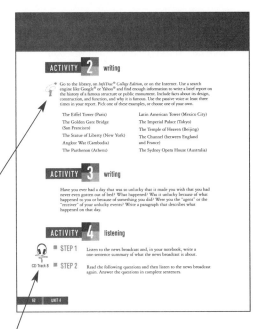

Research activity using *InfoTrac® College Edition* and the Internet encourages students to read articles on carefully selected topics and use this information to reflect on a theme or on information studied in each unit. *InfoTrac® College Edition*, an Online Research and Learning Center, appears in Grammar Dimensions 2, 3, and 4 and offers over 20 million full-text articles from nearly 6,000 scholarly and popular periodicals. Articles cover a broad spectrum of disciplines and topics—ideal for every type of researcher. Instructors and students can gain access to the online database 24/7 on any computer with Internet access.

Engaging listening activities on audio cassette and audio CD further reinforce the target structure.

Reflection activities help students understand their learning style and create learning strategies.

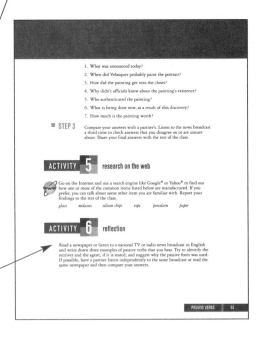

Supplements

These additional components help teachers teach and student learn to use English grammar structures accurately.

The Lesson Planner

The lesson planner facilitates teaching by providing detailed lesson plans and examples, answer keys to the Student Book and Workbook, references to all of the components, and the tapescript for the audiocassette activities. The Lesson Planner minimizes teacher preparation time by providing:

- Summary of main grammar points for the teacher
- Information for the teacher on typical student errors
- Step-by-step guidelines for every focus box, exercise, and activity
- Suggested correlations between exercises and activities in the Use Your English pages
- Suggested timing for each exercise and each lesson
- Lead-in suggestions and examples for focus boxes
- Suggestions for expansion work follow most exercises
- Balance of cognitive and communicative activities
- Explanation for the teacher of the purpose of each activity, in order to differentiate cognitive from communicative emphasis
- Occasional methodology notes to anticipate possible procedural problems.

Assessment CD-ROM with ExamView Pro Test Generator

The Assessment CD-ROM allows instructors to **create customized quizzes and tests** quickly and easily from a test bank of questions. Monitoring student understanding and progress has never been easier! The answer key appears with instructor copies of each quiz or test created.

Audio Program

Audio cassettes and CDs **provide listening activities for** each unit so students can practice listening to **grammar structures.**

Workbook

Workbooks **provide additional exercises** for each grammar point presented in the student text. Also offers editing practice and questions types found on many language exams.

Web site

Features additional grammar practice activities: elt.heinle.com/grammardimensions.

Empirical and Experiential Support for the *Grammar Dimensions* Approach

Opening Task Activities

The approach to teaching grammar used in the *Grammar Dimensions* series is well-grounded empirically and experientially. The Opening Task in each unit situates the learning challenge and allows students to participate in and learn from activity right from the beginning (Greeno 2006). In addition, students don't enter the classroom as empty vessels, waiting to be filled (Sawyer 2006). By observing how students perform on the Opening Task, teachers can analyze for themselves what students know and are able to do and what they don't know or are not able to do. Teachers can thus select from each unit what is necessary for students to build on from what they already bring with them.

Consciousness-Raising Exercises and Focus Boxes

Many of the exercises in *Grammar Dimensions* are of the consciousness-raising sort, where students are invited to make observations about some aspect of the target structure. This type of activity promotes students' noticing (Schmidt 1990), an important step in acquiring the grammar structure. The Focus Boxes further encourage this noticing, this time very explicitly. Explicit formulations of the sort found in the Focus Boxes can lead to implicit acquisition with practice (DeKeyser 1998). Moreover, certain learners (those with analytic learning styles) benefit greatly from explicit treatment of grammar structures (Larsen-Freeman and Long 1991).

Productive Practice and Communicative Activities

However, noticing by itself is insufficient. In order to be able to use the grammar structure, students need productive practice (Gatbonton and Segalowitz 1988; Larsen-Freeman 2003). Therefore, many of the exercises in *Grammar Dimensions* are of the output practice sort. Furthermore, each unit ends with communicative activities, where attention to the grammar is once again implicit, but where students can use the grammar structure in "psychologically authentic" or meaningful ways. Psychological authenticity is very important in order for students to be able to transfer what they know to new situations so that they can use it for their own purposes (Blaxton 1989) and so they are not left to contend with the "inert knowledge problem," (Whitehead 1929) where they know about the grammar, but can't use it.

The Three Dimensions of Grammar: Form, Meaning, and Use

Finally, applied linguistics research (Celce-Murcia and Larsen-Freeman 1999) supports the fundamental premise underlying *Grammar Dimensions*: that knowing a grammar structure means being able to use it accurately, meaningfully, and appropriately. Form focus or meaning focus by itself is insufficient (Larsen-Freeman 2001); all three dimensions—form, meaning, and use—need to be learned.

References

Blaxton, T. (1989). Investigating dissociations among memory measures: Support for a transfer-appropriate processing framework. *Journal of Experimental Psychology: Learning, Memory, and Cognition 15 (4): 657–668.*

Celce-Murcia, M. and D. Larsen-Freeman. (1999). *The grammar book: An ESL/EFL teacher's course.* Second Edition. Boston: Heinle & Heinle.

De Keyser, R. (1998). Beyond focus on form: Cognitive perspectives on learning and practicing second language grammar. n C. Doughty and J. Williams (eds.), *Focus on Classroom Second Language Acquisition.* Cambridge: Cambridge University Press, 42–63.

Gatbonton, E. and N. Segalowitz. (1988). Creative automatization: Principles for promoting fluency within a communicative framework. *TESOL Quarterly 22 (3): 473–492.*

Greeno, J. (2006). Learning in activity. In R. K. Sawyer (ed.), *The Cambridge handbook of learning sciences.* Cambridge: Cambridge University Press, 79–96.

Larsen-Freeman, D. (2001). Teaching grammar. In M. Celce-Murcia (ed.), *Teaching English as a Second or Foreign Language.* Third edition. Boston: Heinle & Heinle, 251–266.

Larsen-Freeman, D. (2003). *Teaching language: From grammar to grammaring.* Boston: Heinle & Heinle.

Larsen-Freeman, D. and M. Long. (1991). *An introduction to second language qcquisition research.* London: Longman.

Sawyer, R. K. (2006). Introduction: The new science of learning. In R. K. Sawyer (ed.), *The Cambridge handbook of learning sciences.* Cambridge: Cambridge University Press, 1–16.

Schmidt, R. (1990). The role of consciousness in second language learning. *Applied Linguistics 11 (2), 129–158.*

Whitehead, A. N. 1929. *The aims of education.* New York: MacMillan.

Acknowledgments from the Series Director

This fourth edition would not have come about if it had not been for the enthusiastic response of teachers and students using all the previous editions. I am very grateful for the reception *Grammar Dimensions* has been given.

I am also grateful for all the authors' efforts. To be a teacher, and at the same time a writer, is a difficult balance to achieve . . . so is being an innovative creator of materials, and yet, a team player. They have met these challenges exceedingly well in my opinion. Then, too, the Thomson Heinle team has been impressive. I am grateful for the leadership exercised by Jim Brown, Sherrise Roehr, and Tom Jefferies. I also appreciate all the support from Anita Raducanu, Amy Mabley, Sarah Barnicle, Laura Needham, Chrystie Hopkins, Mary Beth Hennebury, and Abigail Greshik of Pre-Press Company. Deserving special mention are Amy Lawler and Yeny Kim, who never lost the vision while they attended to the detail with good humor and professionalism.

I have also benefited from the counsel of Marianne Celce-Murcia, consultant for the first edition of this project, and my friend. Finally, I wish to thank my family members, Elliott, Brent, and Gavin, for not once asking the (negative yes-no) question that must have occurred to them countless times: "Haven't you finished yet?" As we all have discovered, this project has a life of its own and is never really finished! And, for this, I am exceedingly grateful. Happy Grammaring all!

A Special Thanks

The series director, authors, and publisher would like to thank the following reviewers whose experienced observations and thoughtful suggestions have assisted us in creating and revising *Grammar Dimensions*.

Michelle Alvarez
University of Miami
Coral Gables, Florida

Edina Pingleton Bagley
Nassau Community College
Garden City, New York

Jane Berger
Solano Community College,
California

Mary Bottega
San Jose State University

Mary Brooks
Eastern Washington University

Christina Broucqsault
*California State Polytechnic
    University*

José Carmona
Hudson Community College

Susan Carnell
University of Texas at Arlington

Susana Christie
San Diego State University

Diana Christopher
Georgetown University

Gwendolyn Cooper
Rutgers University

Julia Correia
Henderson State University
Arkadelphia, Arkansas

Sue Cozzarelli
EF International, San Diego

Catherine Crystal
Laney College, California

Kevin Ccross
University of San Francisco

Julie Damron
*Interlink at Valparaiso
    University, Indiana*

Glen Deckert
Eastern Michigan University

Eric Dwyer
University of Texas at Austin

Nikki Ellman
Laney College
Oakland, California

Ann Eubank
Jefferson Community College

Alice Fine
UCLA Extension

Alicia Going
*The English Language Study
    Center, Oregon*

Molly Gould
University of Delaware

Maren M. Hargis
San Diego Mesa College

Penny Harrold
Universidad de Monterrey
Monterrey, Mexico

Robin Hendrickson
Riverside City College
Riverside, California

Mary Herbert
*University of California, Davis
    Extension*

Jane Hilbert
*ELS Language Center,
Florida International
University*

Eli Hinkel
Xavier University

Kathy Hitchcox
*International English
Institute, Fresno*

Abeer Hubi
Altarbia Alislamia Schools
Riyadh, Saudi Arabia

Joyce Hutchings
Georgetown University

Heather Jeddy
*Northern Virginia
Community College*

Judi Keen
*University of California,
Davis,* and *Sacramento
City College*

Karli Kelber
*American Language Institute,
New York University*

Anne Kornfield
*LaGuardia Community
College*

Kay Longmire
*Interlink at Valparaiso
University, Indiana*

Robin Longshaw
Rhode Island School of Design

Robert Ludwiczak
Texas A&M University
College Station, Texas

Bernadette McGlynn
*ELS Language Center, St.
Joseph's University*

Billy McGowan
Aspect International, Boston

Margaret Mehran
Queens College

Richard Moore
University of Washington

Karen Moreno
*Teikyo Post University,
Connecticut*

Gino Muzzetti
*Santa Rosa Junior College,
California*

Mary Nance-Tager
*LaGuardia Community
College, City University of
New York*

So Nguyen
Orange Coast College
Costa Mesa, California

Karen O'Neill
San Jose State University

Mary O'Neal
*Northern Virginia
Community College*

Nancy Pagliara
*Northern Virginia
Community College*

Keith Pharis
Southern Illinois University

Amy Parker
*ELS Language Center, San
Francisco*

Margene Petersen
*ELS Language Center,
Philadelphia*

Nancy Pfingstag
*University of North
Carolina, Charlotte*

Sally Prieto
*Grand Rapids Community
College*

India Plough
Michigan State University

Mostafa Rahbar
*University of Tennessee at
Knoxville*

Dudley Reynolds
Indiana University

Dzidra Rodins
DePaul University
Chicago, Illinois

Ann Salzman
*University of Illinois at
Urbana-Champaign*

Jennifer Schmidt
*San Francisco State
University*

Cynthia Schuemann
*Miami-Dade Community
College*

Jennifer Schultz
*Golden Gate University,
California*

Mary Beth Selbo
*Wright College, City Colleges
of Chicago*

Mary Selseleh
American River College
Sacramento, California

Stephen Sheeran
*Bishop's University,
Lenoxville, Quebec*

Kathy Sherak
*San Francisco State
University*

Sandra E. Sklarew
Merritt Community College
Oakland, California

Keith Smith
*ELS Language Center, San
Francisco*

Helen Solorzano
Northeastern University

Jorge Vazquez Solorzano
*Bachillerato de la Reina de
Mexico*
S. C., Mexico, D. F.,
Mexico

Christina Valdez
Pasadena City College
Pasadena, California

Danielle Valentini
Oakland Community College
Farmington Hills,
Michigan

Amelia Yongue
Howard Community College
Columbia, Maryland

Welcome to the Grammar Dimensions Lesson Planner!

To the Teacher

This newly revised Lesson Planner for *Grammar Dimensions* (4th edition) provides the teacher with a comprehensive guide to using the Student Book. Its aim is to facilitate lesson planning by suggesting step-by-step guidelines for each task, focus chart, exercise, and activity. It also provides suggestions for extra supplementary exercises. Throughout the text, teachers will find methodology tips and background to language and grammar points that may help to answer questions often asked by students. In addition, there are unit-by-unit examples of typical student errors for each grammar point that may be used by the teacher to predict student problems, to identify areas of difficulty, and to create supplementary materials.

The Lesson Planner is *not* intended as a blueprint to be followed closely in every detail. We hope that as you use *Grammar Dimensions*, you will continue to explore and discover new ways of adapting the material to suit the needs of your students, as well as your own teaching style. It is hoped, however, that by providing more detailed teachers' notes, the Lesson Planner will help in two ways. First, we hope to provide a useful and informative guide for those teachers who are using *Grammar Dimensions* for the first time. Also, we want to provide additional ideas for those teachers who are already familiar with the *Grammar Dimensions* series and who are looking for fresh ways to present and review the material.

OPENING TASK

Each unit starts with an Opening Task. The aim of this task is to help you find out what your students know and don't know. This information will enable you to target the material in the unit. You may decide to omit sections of the unit material that are already well understood by your students. You may decide to add extra exercises or practice to the sections that present difficulty. This Lesson Planner will help you do both. The best way to find out the extent to which your students are able to use a particular structure correctly is to put them into a situation where they need to use it. This is the aim of the Opening Task. Each task has been constructed so that students will need to use the target structures in order to complete it successfully. Their mastery (or need for further practice) should become immediately evident after completing this section.

Diagnostic Tool

When using these tasks, we ask you to focus students' attention on understanding and completing the task. They should not feel that this is a test of their linguistic knowledge. Indeed the students should not be aware that this first section of each unit functions as a diagnostic tool for you, their teacher. While their attention is focused on completing the task, you will be able to listen and take notes on their language use. This diagnostic approach is quite different from communicative tasks that are used to practice a given structure. The purpose here is to allow students the opportunity to make mistakes as well as to use the target structures correctly. Only by allowing them the freedom to communicate with their peers freely, will you be able to understand which aspects of the grammar point cause difficulty and which aspects of *meaning*, *use*, and *form* need most attention. Should students struggle with the Opening Task, you may decide to come back to the Opening Task, once the targeted grammar point has been studied in more detail, and use this task to practice the given structures again.

TEACHER OBSERVATION

The Opening Tasks are designed so that, after initially setting up the task and explaining the steps, they may be carried out by students independently in pairs or groups. This will allow you to circulate among the students with your notebook, "eavesdropping" on their conversations, and taking notes of problems in *meaning*, *form*, or *use* that will be useful for you later in the unit. While you are listening, try to visualize the *form*, *meaning*, and *use* pie chart in your mind and see if you can determine where students firmly grasp a point, and where they need help.

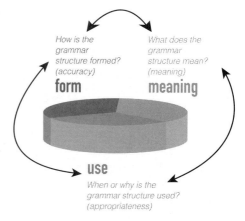

Error Correction

At this point, it is best if you avoid error correction. The Opening Tasks are intended to encourage students to work meaningfully and without concern that they will be interrupted, evaluated, or corrected. The only exception might be the need to remind students to work in English if they are using another language.

Extra Review

In this new edition, we have recognized the importance of allowing some time for students to become familiar with the topic of the task. Some topics may be culturally unfamiliar—for example, the topic of traditional people living in the United States such as the Inuit and the Amish (Unit 5). On rare occasion, the vocabulary may need reviewing—for example, words for types of people (Unit 8, page 129). In these cases, it is worth spending a little time talking around the topic in order to generate increased motivation for the task. We hope that the pictures in the Opening Tasks will also help to engage students visually. (You may wish to supplement them by bringing in more pictures of your own.) In general, however, if students seem comfortable with the topic and the vocabulary, we recommend moving on to the next step as soon as possible.

Final Step

In this new edition of *Grammar Dimensions*, we have tried to focus more explicit attention on the target structure in the final step of the task. This final step can be used to make sure all students have recognized the link between the target language and the task. If some students have been using the target structures successfully, they can share this knowledge with the class. If no one has been able to use the structures, the teacher may use this opportunity to bridge to the first focus.

In some cases, the Opening Task is referred to at later points in the unit. If you collect examples of students' performance in the Opening Task, you may also find yourself referring back to these examples as you reach the relevant explanation or practice exercise later in the unit. For this reason, we do not recommend omitting the Opening Task. But, if you are short of time, you might want to shorten or omit the final step.

FOCUS CHARTS

The Focus charts present the *form, meaning*, and use of the target structure with examples and explanations that are appropriate for the level. Each aspect of the unit grammar is presented separately and is followed by exercises providing controlled practice. The Focus charts allow students to develop step-by-step a better understanding of, and an ability to use, the structure accurately, meaningfully, and appropriately. The pie chart at the top of the Focus indicates whether the chart focuses on the *form, meaning*, and *use* of the target structure.

Step-by-Step Guidelines

A new feature of this revised teacher's edition is the step-by-step guidelines for using the Focus charts. As with all suggestions in this Lesson Planner, they are intended for guidance only. Teachers will use the Focus charts in different ways depending on the needs of their students and their own teaching style.

Lead-in Suggestions

The notes for each Focus start with a Lead-in suggestion. We have tried to include a variety of presentation styles in the Lead-in, such as using student examples, using diagrams or pictures, creating information gap practices, and other ideas that may help to vary the presentation format of the chart. We hope that you will experiment with different ideas and find the best way to present each grammar point, noting only that any student (and teacher) may get tired of repeatedly using the same presentation format.

Understanding Through Examples

In some cases, we have suggested asking students to look at the examples and try to work out the rules. You may find this takes longer, but the increased engagement of the learner and the greater time investment involved may result in greater retention. The examples allow students to make observations about how the use of language changes and thus avoid memorizing "the rules." Students who engage in the study of grammar and are cognitively engaged are far more likely to retain knowledge of how the grammar works than those who simply memorize rules.

If you prefer a more deductive approach, you may ask students to read the information in the chart and come up with further examples of their own. A variation on this is to ask students individually or in pairs to present the information in a Focus chart to another pair of students, or even to the whole class, adding a few new examples of their own. Teaching something to others is a great way to learn!

Alternative Approach

Another possible way of using the Focus chart is not to present them at all, but rather to assign students the exercises that go along with them. The Focus charts can be used for reference purposes as the students work their way through the exercises. In this way, the material becomes more meaningful to students because they will need to understand it in order to complete the exercise.

EXERCISES

At least one exercise follows each Focus. There is a wide variety of exercises in *Grammar Dimensions*. Comprehension exercises work on students' awareness and understanding. Production exercises develop students' skill in using the structures. The step-by-step teacher's notes for each exercise begin with an introductory sentence explaining which grammar point is being practiced and whether the purpose is to practice the form or use of the target structure.

Some exercises continue the theme of the Opening Task and some introduce students to new themes and vocabulary in order to provide variety and to foster students' ability to transfer their learning to new contexts. There are also many personalized exercises, in which students use their own background knowledge or opinions to answer questions.

Exercises and Class Length

As with the Focus charts, there is a variety of ways in which you may decide to use the exercises. Depending on your class length, you may decide to set some exercises for homework and go over the answers in class. You may do the exercises in class using pairs or groups, perhaps assigning one section of the exercise to one set of groups or pairs, and another section of the exercise to the others. You may do the exercise orally in class and ask students to write the answers for homework.

Exercises and Lesson Length

In this new edition, we have made suggestions for the estimated time needed for each exercise. This time length will vary depending on the degree of difficulty your students have with this structure, whether they have previewed the exercise for homework, and other factors. The time length given is only a rough estimate of the minimum time needed to complete the exercise in class. For your convenience, we have divided each unit into two lessons. Each lesson is intended to help lesson planning by indicating which exercises may most easily be omitted if necessary, and which may be used as extension exercises for classes that meet for a longer time period each week. Correlations with the *Grammar Dimensions* Workbook are also provided for further practice.

Exercise Corrections

There are also many options for how exercise answers can be checked. For example:

1. You can circulate while students are doing an exercise in class and spot-check.
2. You can go over the exercise afterwards as a whole class with each student being called on to supply an answer.
3. Exercises can be done individually and then pairs of students can get together to check their answers with each other. Where a difference of opinion occurs, you (or another pair of students) can act as a referee.
4. Different students, pairs, or groups of students can be assigned different parts of an exercise. For example, the first group does #'s 1–3, the second group does #'s 4–6, etc. The groups post their answers on newsprint or butcher block paper and everyone circulates at the end noting the answers and asking questions.

5. A variation of number 4 in this list is to have one student from each group get together and present to the other students the exercise answers that his or her group came up with.
6. You can prepare a handout with the answers, and each student corrects his or her answers individually.
7. You can collect the written work, and make a list of common errors. You can put the errors on an overhead transparency and show it to the students during the next class and have them correct the errors together.

Many exercises require students not only to choose the best answer, but also to explain the reasons for their choices. We believe that this ability to justify and explain the reasons for grammatical choices will enhance students' ability to use grammar accurately, meaningfully, and appropriately. In other words, engaging the students in this decision making process will help students make the grammar knowledge their own.

USE YOUR ENGLISH ACTIVITIES

The "Use Your English" activities section of each unit offer a range of activities where students can apply the language discussed in the unit to wider contexts and integrate it with the language they already know. Many activities give students more freedom than the exercises do to assert their own experiences and offer them more opportunities to express their own points of view across a range of topics. Most of the activities lend themselves to being done or coordinated with structures covered in the unit, but many activities do not absolutely require that they be done along side a particular focus or exercise.

Activity Options

The activities section is also designed to give instructors a variety of options. As you may probably not have time to do all the activities, you might select the ones you think would be most beneficial, or ask your students to choose ones that they would prefer. Perhaps different groups of students could do different activities and then report on their experience to the whole class. We suggest that the activities should be interspersed throughout the unit (as well as at the end of the unit) in order to provide variety and also to allow you to assess students' ability to use the target structures in natural contexts. In the teacher's notes, therefore, we have suggested correlations between the exercises and the activities, keeping in mind that these are entirely optional. Also, it may be useful to go back to a previous unit periodically and use an activity for review purposes. This is especially useful at the beginning of a new, but related, unit.

Activity Skills

Each activity in the Use Your English section is labeled with the skill or skills that it focuses on depending on the steps involved. For example, an activity which promotes group discussion followed by an individualized written summary would be labeled speaking/writing. If you are teaching in a skill-based program, you might want to collaborate with your colleagues and distribute the activities among yourselves. For example, the writing teacher could assign the activities that involve a written report, the teacher of listening could work on the listening activities during his or her class periods, or the teacher of speaking could work with students on activities where students are supposed to make an oral presentation.

Diagnostic Activities

The activities are an integral part of each unit because they not only provide students with opportunities to stretch their language use, but as with the Opening Task, they also provide you with the opportunity to observe your students' language use in action. In this way, activities can be informal holistic assessment measures encouraging students to show you how well they can use the target structures communicatively. Any problems that still exist with a grammar concept, or with its application within one of the four skills areas, can be noted for follow-up at a later time when students have opportunities and appropriate time to review them.

Internet Activities

This new edition includes a "research on the Web" activity at the end of each unit. The purpose of this activity is to provide a natural context for using the target grammar. An additional purpose is to encourage students to share strategies for finding information on the Internet. Internet search engines are suggested but instructors are encouraged to assist students in looking for information in a discriminating manner. We also recommend that instructors provide specific keywords, previewing the resulting Web sites, to assist students in finding and interpreting level-appropriate articles and information.

Reflection Activities

Also new to this edition is the addition of a reflection activity that provides an opportunity for students to use the target structures of the unit while reflecting on their language learning. In the past, teachers controlled the knowledge of how students were progressing. In this section, we hope that students will gain an understanding of their own progress and a way to express what they know about language.

Many of these activities can be done as pair or group activities in class or as homework. You may wish to ask students to keep a learning journal. As well as providing you with firsthand feedback on your students' progress, it also encourages reflection and self-evaluation that can facilitate language learning. Here are some additional suggested topics to include in a learning journal:

- Which grammar points do you find difficult, confusing, or easy—and why?
- Which grammar points are similar to or different from your native language?
- Which learning activities did you enjoy most in this unit, and why?
- Which learning activities would you like to do more of or less of?
- What aspect of your learning did you feel most proud of when doing this unit?

As you can see, *Grammar Dimensions* is meant to provide you with a great deal of flexibility so that you can provide quality instruction appropriate for your class. We encourage you to experiment with different aspects of the material in order to best meet the needs of your unique group of students.

OVERVIEW OF THE ENGLISH VERB SYSTEM
Time and Tense

UNIT GOALS

- Review the English verb system
- Keep tenses in the same time frame
- Change the time frame correctly within a passage

OPENING TASK
Comparing Past, Present, and Future

▪ STEP 1

Work with a partner: Student A, look at the following information about Bob Lee, a typical American college student. Student B, look at the information on the next page about Bob's grandfather, Robert Lee. Student A, tell Student B about Bob's life. Student B, tell Student A about Robert's life.

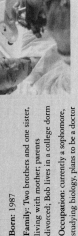

BOB LEE

Born: 1987

Family: Two brothers and one sister, living with mother; parents divorced; Bob lives in a college dorm

Occupation: currently a sophomore, studying biology, plans to be a doctor

Regular activities: school, part-time job in the library, time with girlfriend, visiting family some weekends and during school vacations

Hobbies or favorite sports: basketball, skiing, computers, music, TV

Visits to foreign countries: Mexico (once), Canada (twice)

Special skills or abilities: computers, university chorus

Probable activity at this moment: studying for biology midterm

ROBERT LEE

Born: 1930 **DIED:** 1992

Family: Five brothers, four sisters; only one sister and brother survived childhood; father died of tuberculosis when Robert was 14 years old

Occupation: factory worker, never finished high school

Regular activities: job (12-hour days); helping mother; family life, church

Hobbies or favorite sports: radio, baseball (on factory team)

Visits to foreign countries: none

Special skills or abilities: baseball, harmonica playing

Probable activity when Bob was born: working at the factory

▪ STEP 2

Now work together to create a story for Roberta, Bob's granddaughter. Fill in some information below and then tell another pair of students about how you think Roberta's life will be.

ROBERTA CHONG-DAVIS

Born: 2035

Family: _____

Occupation: _____

Regular activities: _____

Hobbies or favorite sports: _____

Visits to foreign countries or planets: _____

Special skills or abilities: _____

Probable activity at this moment 100 years from today: _____

OVERVIEW OF THE ENGLISH VERB SYSTEM

LESSON PLAN 1

UNIT OVERVIEW

Unit 1 provides an overview of the English verb system, explains when to keep tenses in the same time frame, and demonstrates when to change time frame within a passage.

GRAMMAR NOTE

Verbs in the English verb system fall into the present, past, and future time frames. **Aspect** (simple, progressive, perfect, perfect progressive) defines how the verb relates to the time. Time combined with aspect creates **tenses**. In the English language, a tense shows the time when the action of a verb occurred. This concept may be difficult for students whose languages use markers other than verb form to suggest the time of a verb. Also, many students have difficulty keeping passages in a consistent time frame and recognizing under what conditions to change time frame.

UNIT GOALS

Some instructors may want to review the goals listed on Student Book (SB) page 0 after completing the Opening Task so that students understand what they should know by the end of the unit. These goals can also be reviewed at the end of the unit when students are more familiar with the grammar terminology.

OPENING TASK [30 minutes]

The purpose of this task is to create a context in which students must use different time frames to talk about people. The problem-solving format is designed to show the teacher how well the students can produce the target structure implicitly and spontaneously when they are engaged in a communicative task. For a more complete discussion of the purpose of the Opening Task, see To the Teacher, Lesson Planner (LP) page xxii.

Setting Up the Task

Divide the class into pairs. Student A will look at the information on SB page 0. Student B will look at the information on SB page 1.

Conducting the Task

STEP 1

Tell students to look at their information carefully and decide which time frame they will use to talk about the different categories of the person's life. Then have them talk about the person in the picture with their partner.

STEP 2

1. Tell pairs that they will create a story together and then share it with another pair. Circulate as pairs work. Make sure that students understand that the person in the picture has not been born yet and that they are imagining what her life will be like.

2. While students work in pairs, you can circulate and listen to get an idea of students' current use of the various time frames and corresponding tenses. Do not correct; accuracy is not important at this stage.

3. Take notes of typical errors of form, meaning, confusion, and inappropriate use. This way you'll know what to select and focus on for the remainder of the unit.

4. Take notes of correct uses of time frames and tenses. You can use them when you debrief the task.

5. Invite students to write some of their sentences on the board. Leave these on the board for reference in Focus 1.

Closing the Task

1. As a class, draw the following chart on the board:

Present	Past	Future

2. Call on volunteers to state the verbs they used in their descriptions. Invite a volunteer to act as a secretary and list the verb forms under the corresponding time frame. Do not go into explanations at this stage.

3. Use these points to lead into Focus Chart 1 on SB page 2.

GRAMMAR NOTE

Typical student errors (form)

- Recognizing the time frame and aspect of a verb:—e.g., *have started* is in the present time frame, perfect aspect.
- Omitting auxiliaries: * *He studying French next year.*
- Making errors with irregular verbs forms: * *catched* * *quitted*
- Misspelling the past tense form or the past participle form: * *sleeped* * *forgotten*

Typical student errors (use)

- Failing to keep tenses in the same time frame. (See Focus 2.)
- Not changing time frame within a passage when necessary. (See Focus 3.)

FOCUS 1

Overview of the English Verb System

The form of any verb in English is made up of two things: time frame and aspect.

form

meaning

Time frame tells when something took place. There are three basic time frames: **present, past,** and **future.**	**Aspect** tells how the verb is related to that time, or gives some other information about the quality of the action. (See Unit 2.)

There are four kinds of aspect, and each one has a basic meaning.

ASPECT	MEANING
simple	at that time
progressive	in progress during that time
perfect	before that time
perfect progressive	in progress during and before that time

When we combine the three time frames and the four aspects, we get twelve possible combinations of forms. These forms are called **tenses**, and the name of each tense tells which time frame and which aspect are being used. The charts in Appendix 1, on pages A-1 to A-4, show in more detail the three basic time frames and the tenses that are used in each.

ASPECT ▶ Time Frame ▼	SIMPLE	PROGRESSIVE	PERFECT	PERFECT PROGRESSIVE
			TENSES	
Present	*simple present* study/studies give/gives	*present progressive* am/is/are studying am/is/are giving	*present perfect* has/have studied has/have given	*present perfect progressive* has/have been studying has/have been giving
Past	*simple past* studied gave	*past progressive* was/were studying was/were giving	*past perfect* had studied had given	*past perfect progressive* had been studying had been giving
Future	*simple future* will study will give	*future progressive* will be studying will be giving	*future perfect* will have studied will have given	*future perfect progressive* will have been studying will have been giving

EXERCISE 1

Read the following numbered passages and identify the time frame of each. Is it present time, past time, or future time?

1. (a) Matt had a terrible headache. (b) His tongue was dry, and his eyes were burning. (c) He had been sneezing constantly for nearly an hour. (d) He hated springtime. (e) For most people spring meant flowers and sunshine, but for Matt it meant allergies.

2. (a) I really don't know what to do for vacation. (b) My vacation starts in three weeks, and (c) I'm trying to decide what to do. (d) I've been to Hawaii and New York. (e) It's too early in the year to go camping in the mountains. (f) I've been working hard at the office and I really need a break. (g) I've saved enough money to have a really nice trip. (h) I just can't decide where to go or what to do.

3. (a) The changing world climate will mean changes in food production. (b) Scientists think that summers throughout North America will become much hotter and drier than they are now. (c) Crops that require a lot of water will be less economical to grow. (d) Society will have to develop different energy sources, (e) since fossil fuels, such as coal and oil, may have become depleted by the end of the next century.

4. (a) "Social Darwinism" was a popular theory of the nineteenth century. (b) It compared social and economic development with biological evolution. (c) According to this theory, competition between rich people and poor people was unavoidable. (d) The poor were like dinosaurs who were dying out because they had lost the battle for survival—economic survival.

5. (a) Scientific research often has an important social impact. (b) In recent years scientists have discovered that Vitamin B can prevent certain kinds of childhood blindness. (c) As a result, programs have been established that provide education and dietary supplements to children in developing countries.

EXERCISE 2

Choose three of the passages in Exercise 1, and underline each complete verb phrase (the verb plus any auxiliary—*have, do, is,* etc.—that shows the tense of the verb). Name the tense of each verb phrase you have underlined.

EXERCISE 3

Check your knowledge of irregular verb forms by completing the chart on page 4. You may work with others students. When you finish, check your work using Appendix 6, Irregular Verbs, on page A-10.

ANSWER KEY

Exercise 1 1. past 2. present 3. future 4. past 5. present

Exercise 2 Verbs underlined above. Verb tenses include: 1. (a) simple past (b) simple past; past progressive (c) past perfect progressive (d) simple past (e) simple past; simple past 2. (a) present; simple present simple present (b) simple present (c) present progressive (d) present perfect; simple present simple present (e) present perfect progressive; simple present (f) present perfect progressive; simple present perfect perfect (g) present perfect (h) simple present; simple present; simple present; simple present (c) simple present; simple future (d) simple future (e) future perfect 4. (a) simple past (b) simple past (c) simple past (d) simple past; past progressive; past perfect 5. (a) simple present (b) present perfect; simple present (c) present perfect; simple present

Exercise 3 Answers are shown on LP page 4.

FOCUS 1 [15 minutes]

1. **Lead-in:** Write the following sentences on the board.

   I live in Cairo.
   I lived in Cairo last summer.
   I will live in Cairo some day.

   Ask students what the difference is between these sentences. (*they are in different time frames*)

2. Read the examples and explanations in the focus chart. Have students look at the sentences on the board from the Lead-in. Ask what aspect each verb is. (*simple*) Invite students to experiment with putting the sentences into different aspects (e.g., *I have lived in Cairo.*—perfect aspect; *I was living in Cairo when I met my husband.*—progressive aspect; *When I graduate, I will have been living in Cairo for five years.*—perfect progressive aspect).

3. Ask student to suggest sentences for each tense shown in the focus chart at the bottom of SB page 2. Write some examples on the board using real information about your students. For example:

   Present simple: *Sheila does her homework on the train.*

   Past progressive: *Leo was text messaging in class today.*

4. Review the list of sentences on the board from the Opening Task.

5. Ask students to identify the tense used in each sentence. Help students to infer the time frame and aspect.

EXERCISE 1 [10 minutes]

1. Ask students to read the passages individually and identify if they are in the present, past, or future time frame. If they have difficulty, refer them to Focus Chart 1 on SB page 2.

2. Have students compare answers with a partner. See answers on LP page 2.

EXERCISE 2 [10 minutes]

This exercise has students focus on the aspect of verb phrases and then identify tenses.

1. In pairs, have students choose three passages and underline the verb phrases. Then have them name the tense of each verb phrase. Refer them to the focus chart on SB page 2 if they need help.

2. To extend this activity, have pairs name the tenses in the passage they did not choose.

3. Bring the class together and go over the answers. See answers on LP page 2.

[workbook] For more practice, use *Grammar Dimensions 3* Workbook page 1, Exercise 1 and Exercise 2.

EXPANSION 1 [15 minutes]

You may want use Activity 2 (listening) on SB page 9 to practice listening for different time frames and tenses.

EXPANSION 2 [15 minutes]

The following exercises can be used to practice identifying time frames and tenses.

1. Read these sentences and have students identify the time frame and tense of the verb in each sentence. Repeat as needed.

   Richard has been studying Chinese for five years. (present perfect progressive)
   I take the bus to work on Fridays. (simple present)
   Meredith worked for a software company last summer. (simple past)
   Next year, Deborah will have been a graduate student for ten years. (future perfect)
   Our research group had hoped to publish the article by next summer. (past perfect)
   I will be traveling through Asia next summer. (future progressive)
   The weather is getting warmer and warmer. (present progressive)
   The students have been preparing for the exam for a long time. (present perfect progressive)
   I have seen that documentary before. (present perfect)
   I will volunteer at the local shelter this year. (simple future)
   Joe was talking on his cell phone when he heard the loud noise. (past progressive)
   Tomorrow, I will have been writing this essay for two weeks! (future perfect progressive)

2. Bring the class together and go over the answers. Discuss any questions students might have.

VARIATION [15 minutes]

Instead of reading the sentences in Expansion 2, have students make up the sentences in groups, and then exchange their sentences with another group to identify the time frame and tense of each verb.

EXERCISE 3 [15 minutes]

1. Remind students that irregular verbs have special past tense and past participle forms, while the past tense and past participle of regular verbs are created by adding *-ed* or *-d* to the base form.

2. Have students work in pairs or in groups to complete the chart. Students can skip answers they don't know and return to them later.

3. Either have pairs check answers using Appendix 6 (SB page A-10) or bring the class together to go over the answers.

4. To extend this activity, invite students to write sentences using the past tense form or the past participle form of the different verbs.

Note: The complete set of irregular verbs is listed in Appendix 6. Make sure that students don't just copy the verb forms from that list.

meaning

use

FOCUS 2

Keeping Tenses in the Same Time Frame

In general, we choose a particular time frame and then choose from among the tenses within that time frame in order to describe events.

EXAMPLES

(a) My roommate Charley **had** a dance party last Friday night. I **was working** that night, so I **didn't get** home until 10:00, and by then everyone **had** already **started** dancing.

(b) My roommate Charley **has** a dance party every Friday night. I **work** on Friday nights, so I **don't get** home until 10:00, and by then everyone **has** already **started** dancing.

(c) My roommate Charley **is going to have** a dance party next Friday night. I **will be working** next Friday night, so I **won't get** home until 10:00, and by then everyone **will** already **have started** dancing.

EXPLANATIONS

Use past tenses to describe things that happened at a specific time in the past.

Use present tenses to describe things that are happening now, are related to now, or happen again and again.

Use future tenses to describe events that are going to happen at some time in the future.

EXERCISE 4

Decide what time frame each of these passages should be written in, and then write the appropriate verb form in the blanks.

1. I hear we (a) ___will be___ (be) playing games at Charley's party next week. I hope there (b) ___will be___ (be) dancing as well! I (c) ___will have completed___ (have completed) my dance class by then.

2. Jeff (a) ___had___ (have) an interesting experience yesterday afternoon. As he (b) ___was walking___ (be walking) from his house to the grocery store, he (c) ___saw___ (see) someone he (d) ___had gone___ (have gone) to high school with.

(Exercise 4 is continued on LP page 6.)

OVERVIEW OF THE ENGLISH VERB SYSTEM Time and Tense   5

ANSWER KEY

Exercise 4   *Verbs are written above. Verb forms include: 1. future   2. past*

BASE FORM	PAST TENSE FORM	PAST PARTICIPLE FORM	BASE FORM	PAST TENSE FORM	PAST PARTICIPLE FORM	BASE FORM	PAST TENSE FORM	PAST PARTICIPLE FORM	BASE FORM	PAST TENSE FORM	PAST PARTICIPLE FORM
become	became	become	become	became	become	go	went	gone	sing	sang	sung
begin	began	begun	bend	bent	bent	grind	ground	ground	sink	sank	sunk
bet	bet	bet	bet	bet	bet	grow	grew	grown	sit	sat	sat
bind	bound	bound	bleed	bled	bled	hang	hung	hung	sleep	slept	slept
bite	bit	bit	blow	blew	blown	have	had	had	slide	slid	slid
bleed	bled	bled	break	broke	broken	hear	heard	heard	speak	spoke	spoken
bring	brought	brought	bring	brought	brought	hide	hid	hidden	speed	sped	sped
build	built	built	bought	bought	bought	hit	hit	hit	spend	spent	spent
buy	bought	bought	catch	caught	caught	hold	held	held	split	split	split
catch	caught	caught	choose	chose	chosen	hurt	hurt	hurt	spread	spread	spread
choose	chose	chosen	come	came	come	keep	kept	kept	spring	sprang	sprung
come	came	come	cost	cost	cost	know	knew	known	stand	stood	stood
cut	cut	cut	cut	cut	cut	lead	led	led	steal	stole	stolen
dig	dug	dug	do	did	done	leave	left	left	stick	stuck	stuck
do	did	done	draw	drew	drawn	lend	lent	lent	sting	stung	stung
draw	drew	drawn	drink	drank	drunk	let	let	let	strike	struck	stricken
drink	drank	drunk	drive	drove	driven	make	made	made	swear	swore	sworn
drive	drove	driven	eat	ate	eaten	mean	meant	meant	sweep	swept	swept
eat	ate	eaten	fall	fell	fallen	meet	met	met	swim	swam	swum
fall	fell	fallen	feed	fed	fed	put	put	put	swing	swung	swung
feed	fed	fed	feel	felt	felt	quit	quit	quit	take	took	taken
feel	felt	felt	fight	fought	fought	read	read	read	teach	taught	taught
fight	fought	fought	find	found	found	ride	rode	ridden	tear	tore	torn
find	found	found	fit	fit	fit	ring	rang	rung	tell	told	told
fit	fit	fit	fly	flew	flown	rise	rose	risen	think	thought	thought
fly	flew	flown	forbid	forbade	forbidden	run	ran	run	throw	threw	thrown
forbid	forbade	forbidden	forget	forgot	forgotten	say	said	said	understand	understood	understood
forget	forgot	forgotten	forgive	forgave	forgiven	see	saw	seen	wake	woke	woken
forgive	forgave	forgiven	freeze	froze	frozen	seek	sought	sought	wear	wore	worn
freeze	froze	frozen	get	got	gotten	sell	sold	sold	weave	wove	woven
get	got	gotten	give	gave	given	send	sent	sent	weep	wept	wept
give	gave	given				set	set	set	win	won	won
						shake	shook	shaken	wind	wound	wound
						shine	shone	shone	write	wrote	written
						shoot	shot	shot			
						shine	shone	shone			
						shut	shut	shut			

LESSON PLAN 1

FOCUS 2 [10 minutes]

Focus 2 addresses a common problem students face in written and spoken English: keeping tenses in a consistent time frame when describing events.

1. **Lead-in:** Write the following sentences on the board:

   I attended an interesting lecture last night. It is about the effect of pollution on the environment. Students will ask the professor a lot of questions. Unfortunately be didn't have time to answer all of them.

2. Ask students if there are any problems with this passage, and if so, what they are and how they can be fixed. (*The passage has too many different time frames and tenses. It should be in the past time frame, and the tenses should be consistent. Corrections: It was about . . . ; Students asked . . .*)

3. Call on volunteers to read the examples and explanations in the focus chart.

4. Ask students what time indicators are used in the example passages. (*a. last Friday night, that night; b. every Friday night; Friday nights; c. next Friday night*) Point out that such words, combined with tenses, help determine the time frame of a passage.

GRAMMAR NOTE

A common problem for students is not being consistent in tense use. Whether writing a short paragraph, an essay, or a lengthier research paper, students often lose track of tenses when expressing their thoughts. A good self-editing technique is to have students underline all the verbs once they have finished a piece of writing. Then they should think carefully about the time frame and aspect to make sure they have used the appropriate tense with each verb.

EXERCISE 4 [15 minutes]

This exercise has students look at the context of passages in order to determine the time frames and fill in blanks with appropriate verb forms.

1. Have students do the exercise in pairs or individually.

2. Encourage them to look for clues about time frame in the sentences (e.g., 1. *next week, by then*; 2. *As . . .*). Circulate and assist as needed.

3. Review answers as a class. Encourage students to mention any time indicators that helped them decide which time frame to use in the passage. See answers on LP pages 4 and 6.

For more practice, use *Grammar Dimensions 3* Workbook page 2, Exercises 3 and 4.

EXPANSION 1 [20 minutes]

You may want to use Activity 4 (writing/speaking) on SB page 10 for further practice using appropriate verb forms.

EXPANSION 2 [50 minutes]

You may want use Activity 3 (speaking/writing) on SB page 10 as a homework assignment to practice keeping tenses in the same time frame.

EXPANSION 3 [20 minutes]

This exercise allows students to practice keeping tenses in the same time frame.

1. Individually, have students write a couple of sentences about a news item they heard on TV or radio, or read about in a newspaper or online. Tell them to use either the present, past, or future time frame consistently.

2. Then have pairs read each other's sentences and identify the time frame. Tell students to make sure their partners kept tenses in the same time frames. Encourage them to suggest corrections if they note mistakes. Circulate and assist as needed.

3. Bring the class together and have volunteers read their sentences to the class. Invite students to respond to the news item if they heard about it as well. Listen to make sure that they use the correct time frame. Make corrections as needed.

GRAMMAR NOTE

Tell students that they can consult a dictionary if they are ever uncertain if a verb is regular or irregular, or if they don't know what the correct irregular form is. A dictionary lists irregular forms.

EXPANSION 4 [15 minutes]

The following exercise provides further review of irregular verb forms. It is appropriate for classes where students may need more practice with irregular verbs.

1. Divide the class into two teams.

2. Use Appendix 6 on SB page A-10 to select verbs. Then interchangeably ask teams one of the following questions.

   What is the base form of [verb]?
   What is the past participle form of [verb]?
   What is the past tense form [verb]?

For each correct answer, grant a team a point and ask another question. The team with the most points wins.

(Exercise 4 is continued on LP page 6.)

use

FOCUS 3

Changing the Time Frame Within a Passage

Although the time frame often stays the same within a passage, an author sometimes changes the time frame.

EXAMPLES	EXPLANATIONS
	The author does this in order to:
(a) There are many examples in history of increasing military power causing a decreasing standard of living. Rome was unable to feed both its army and its population. Great Britain **declined** steadily from its economic position in the early part of this century.	move from a general statement to specific examples.
(b) **One hundred years ago** the life expectancy in the United States **was** about 65. **Nowadays**, it **has increased** by an average of ten years. **In the next century**, if current trends continue, people **should be able to live** until their nineties. Interestingly enough, however, **a hundred years ago** the number of people who were over 100 **was** less than 1 percent of the population. That figure **has not changed** substantially, even today.	show contrast between one time and another.
(c) I saw an elderly lady yesterday. **You don't see her kind much anymore.** She was wearing a black dress and she was carrying an umbrella. **Most elderly ladies I know don't carry umbrellas, and pants are more common than dresses.** As she walked down the street, I thought about how much life has changed since she was my age.	make a statement of general truth.

EXERCISE 5

Mark the following passages with a slanted line (/) to show where the time frame changes. The first one has been done for you as an example.

1. My brother <u>called</u> me up yesterday. / I always <u>know</u> he <u>needs</u> to borrow money when he <u>calls</u>, because I never <u>hear</u> from him at any other time. / We <u>spoke</u> about this and that for a few minutes. He asked about my job and my family. We <u>talked</u> about his problems with his boss. / These <u>are</u> typical topics before he finally <u>asks</u> for a loan. / This phone call <u>was</u> no exception. He <u>needed</u> fifty dollars "until pay day." / Somehow, when payday <u>comes</u> he never <u>remembers</u> to pay back the loan.

---

3. Matt (a) ___ *has* ___ (have) a terrible time getting to work every day. When he (b) ___ *is driving* ___ (be driving) to work he often (c) ___ *gets* ___ (get) caught in terrible traffic jams. Even though he only (d) ___ *lives* ___ (live) a few miles from the office, it sometimes (e) ___ *takes* ___ (take) nearly an hour to get to work.

4. The Imperial City of Rome (a) ___ *was* ___ (be) badly damaged by fire during the first century AD. At the time it (b) ___ *was believed* ___ (be believed) that the Emperor Nero (c) ___ *was playing* ___ (be playing) a violin while the city (d) ___ *burned* ___ (burn) to the ground.

5. Scientists (a) ___ *are* ___ (be) worried that the world climate (b) ___ *is changing* ___ (be changing). They (c) ___ *believe* ___ (believe) this change (d) ___ *has resulted* ___ (have resulted) from an increase in the amount of carbon dioxide (CO$_2$) in the earth's atmosphere. Whenever "fossil fuels" such as coal or oil (e) ___ *are burned* ___ (be burned), the amount of CO$_2$ (f) ___ *causes* ___ (cause) the atmosphere to retain more heat. There (h) ___ *is* ___ (be) proof that this process already (i) ___ *has begun* ___ (have begun). Scientists (j) ___ *have discovered* ___ (have discovered) that the average temperature of the world's oceans (k) ___ *has risen* ___ (have risen) by one degree in the last twenty years.

(g) ___ *increases/is increased* ___ (increase). This

6. John (a) ___ *will leave* ___ (leave) for Paris on Tuesday. He (b) ___ *will be staying* ___ (be staying) with a local family for the first few weeks. After that, he probably (c) ___ *will find* ___ (find) a small apartment of his own.

ANSWER KEY

Exercise 4 (*Continued from LP page 4.*) 3. present 4. past 5. present 6. future

OVERVIEW OF THE ENGLISH VERB SYSTEM

LESSON PLAN 2

FOCUS 3 [10 minutes]

This focus chart gives different examples of situations when an author might change time frame within a passage.

1. **Lead-in:** Have students close their books, and ask them to think of examples of when an author might have to change time frame in a passage. Write student thoughts on the board.

2. Call on volunteers to read each example and explanation. Focus on the shift in time in each passage and ask what the time frame is of each sentence and what time frame it shifts to. Then have students notice time indicators in the passages (e.g., one hundred years ago, nowadays, in the next century, etc). Point out that these phrases help indicate when a time change will occur.

3. Compare the examples and explanations in the chart to those proposed by students in the lead-in.

EXERCISE 5 [15 minutes]

The goal of this exercise is for students to identify where time frame changes occur in a passage.

1. Focus on the first passage as a class. Call on a volunteer to read the sentence(s) before each slanted line. After each sentence/set of sentences ask students what time frame was used.

2. Have students work individually to mark the shifts in time frame in the remainder of the exercise. Circulate and assist as needed. See answers on LP page 8.

work book

For more practice, use *Grammar Dimensions 3* Workbook page 2, Exercise 5.

EXPANSION [20 minutes]

This exercise has students write a passage with changing time frame.

1. Draw the following chart on the board:

Past	Present	Future

As a class, brainstorm how Internet technology has changed over the years (e.g., *Past: in the 1990s few people had Internet access and email addresses; Present: people are very dependent on the Internet for everyday use*). Then make predictions of what Internet technology will be like in the future (e.g., *cities will be wireless and people will have Internet access everywhere*).

2. For homework, have students use the notes from the chart to write a passage about Internet technology. Encourage them to make appropriate changes in time frame.

3. Collect assignments and give individual feedback.

Use Your English

ACTIVITY 1 speaking/writing/listening

STEP 1 Work with a partner. Describe a typical day in your life. Tell your partner about the things you do, where you go, and how you typically spend your time. Mention at least five regular activities.

STEP 2 Next, describe a typical day in your life five years ago. Mention at least five activities that you did on a regular basis.

STEP 3 Your partner should use this information to decide what three things in your life have changed the most in the last five years, and report this information to the rest of the class. Make a similar report to the class about the changes in your partner's life.

ACTIVITY 2 listening

Listen to these descriptions about two people—one who is no longer living and one who is still alive. Based on the time frame and verb tenses used in the descriptions, decide which person is still living and which person is deceased.

CD Track 1

---

2. I'll be really happy when the summer is over./ I don't like hot weather, and I can't stand mosquitoes. There's a lot of both of those things in the summer./ Last summer I tried to escape by going on a trip to Alaska. The heat wasn't bad, but the mosquitoes were terrible!/ Next year I think I'll consider a vacation in Antarctica./ I understand it's really cold there in July.

3. For more than fifty years scientists around the world have all used a single system to measure the strength (or "magnitude") of earthquakes./ The Richter Scale was developed by Charles Richter in 1935. It was designed so scientists could compare the strength of earthquakes in different parts of the world. It was not designed to measure damage in earthquakes, but only intensity./ This is because a less powerful earthquake in a heavily populated area can cause more damage than a stronger earthquake in an unpopulated area.

EXERCISE 6

Discuss each change of time frame that you found in Exercise 5 with a partner. Why did the author change the time frame? There may be more than one reason. Share your explanation with the rest of the class.

EXERCISE 7

Underline the complete verb phrases (verb plus auxiliaries) in the passages in Exercise 5 and name the tense of each verb phrase.

Exercise 6 Answers will vary. Possible answers are: 1. general truth/movement to specific example/general truth/movement to specific example/general truth 2. general truth/clear time marker or specific example/clear time marker/general truth 3. movement from general statement to specific example/statement of general truth

Exercise 7 See LP page 6 and above for underling. Verb tenses include: 1. simple past; simple present; simple present; simple present; simple past; simple past; simple past; simple present; simple present; simple past; simple present; simple present; simple past; simple present 2. simple future; simple present; simple present; simple past; simple past; simple past; simple past; simple present; simple future; simple present; simple present 3. present perfect; simple past; simple past; simple past; simple past; simple present; simple present

Activity 2 Dr. Deborah Jones is alive. Dr. Sally Smith is dead.

LESSON PLAN 2/USE YOUR ENGLISH OVERVIEW OF THE ENGLISH VERB SYSTEM

EXERCISE 6 [10 minutes]

1. Have pairs discuss the shifts in time frame that occurred in each passage. Refer them to the explanations in Focus Chart 3 on SB page 7.

2. Bring the class together and go over the answers.

EXERCISE 7 [10 minutes]

1. Have students work in pairs to underline the verb phrase and identify the tenses. Refer them to Focus 1 on SB page 2. Point out that some sentences use modal forms, and some are in the passive voice.

2. Bring the class together and go over the answers. See answers on LP page 8.

work book

For more practice, use *Grammar Dimensions 3* Workbook page 3, Exercise 6.

EXPANSION 1 [20 minutes]

1. Bring in newspapers and magazines to class, or have students bring them in.

2. In pairs, have students select a passage in an article and mark any changes in time. Then have them discuss reasons for the change in time. Circulate and assist.

EXPANSION 2 [20 minutes]

You may wish to assign Activity 1 (speaking/writing/listening) on SB page 9 for a review of the unit contents—keeping tenses in the same time frame and changing time frame within a passage.

EXPANSION 3 [15 minutes/homework]

You may want to assign Activity 6 (language strategy/reflection) on SB page 11 as homework after Exercise 7. This activity provides a good opportunity for review of the material covered in the unit by

having students evaluate their accomplishments in English language learning thus far, and set goals and strategies for further learning.

UNIT GOAL REVIEW [10 minutes]

Ask students to look at the goals on the opening page of the unit again. Refer to the pages of the unit where information on each goal can be found.

ExamView® Test Generator

For assessment of Unit 1, use *Grammar Dimensions ExamView®*.

USE YOUR ENGLISH

The Use Your English activities contain situations that should naturally elicit the structures covered in the unit. For a more complete discussion of how to use the Use Your English activities see To the Teacher on LP page xxii.

ACTIVITY 1 speaking/writing/listening [20 minutes]

You can use this activity at the end of the unit after Exercise 7 on SB page 8 to review all the material covered in the unit.

■ STEP 1   Tell pairs to take notes as they listen to their partners' typical daily activities. Remind students to use the correct tense as they speak.

■ STEP 2   Have pairs take notes as they repeat Step 1, this time speaking to each other about a typical day in their life from five years ago.

■ STEP 3

1. Have pairs combine the information they got from their partner to decide what three things

have changed in the last five years. Tell them to use time indicators such as *today, nowadays, in the past, five years ago.*

2. Have students report information about their partner to the rest of the class.

3. Take notes while students speak and then give feedback as necessary at the end of the reports.

VARIATION

1. Tell pairs to ask each other how they think their lives will be different in five years.

2. Have students take notes and then write a paragraph combining this information with the information about the present and past gathered in Activity 1. Remind them to make necessary shifts in time frame in their paragraphs.

ACTIVITY 2 listening [15 minutes]

CD Track 1

You can use this activity after Exercise 2 on SB page 3.

1. Before playing the audio, ask:
   What time frame will be used to talk about the person still living? (present)
   What time frame will be used for the person no longer living? (past)

2. Have students listen to the descriptions. Tell them to write down the name of each person. Then have them listen again and take notes about the two people.

3. In pairs, have students identify which person is still living, and which person is deceased. Encourage them to give examples of tenses they heard in the description that revealed the time frame. See answers on LP page 8.

4. To extend this activity, have students write a paragraph about each of the people described in the audio. Remind students to use the appropriate time frame and tenses.

ACTIVITY 3 speaking/writing

Congratulations! You've just won a million dollars in a lottery. BUT . . . you have to spend all the money in a single week. AND . . . you can't spend more than $50,000 for any single purchase. (In other words, you can't just buy a million-dollar house. You have to make at least twenty separate purchases.) If you don't spend it all, you won't get any of it.

■ STEP 1   What are your plans? In a brief essay, or in an oral presentation, answer this question: **How you will spend the money?**

■ STEP 2   It's the end of the week. How did you spend your money? Change the verb tenses of your essay or presentation to answer this question: **How did you spend the money?**

ACTIVITY 4 writing/speaking

Newspaper headlines represent a special kind of English. They usually omit a lot of important grammatical information. Test how well you know the basic sentence elements of English by "translating" these headlines into complete sentences. Compare your "translations" to those of another student.

Example: BABY FOUND IN BUS STATION
A baby has been found in the bus station.

STOCK MARKET CRASHES   TEST SCORES IMPROVING IN
U.S. POPULATION MOVING WEST   PUBLIC SCHOOLS
NEW BUDGET TERMED "DISASTER"   LINK FOUND BETWEEN DIET AND
U.S. TO PROTEST NUCLEAR TESTING   HEART DISEASE
PRESIDENT TO VISIT CHINA   CANCER REPORTED INCREASING
DROUGHT EXPECTED TO WORSEN   MAJOR DECREASE IN
BIG WHITE HOUSE SHAKE-UP   INTERNATIONAL STUDENTS IN U.S.
NEW PLAN TO IMPROVE BUS
SERVICES

ACTIVITY 5 research on the web

In Activity 3 you were asked to imagine how you would spend a million dollars. How do you think your choices compare to real people who won that kind of money?

■ STEP 1   Log onto *InfoTrac® College Edition* and do a keyword search of "lottery winners' behavior". There are several articles in *People Weekly* (for example) that tell what happened to real lottery winners after their good fortune. How did their real life experiences compare to the way you imagined yours would be? Compare two or three winners' stories to your own.

■ STEP 2   With a partner or in a small group name three things that lottery winners typically do with their winnings. Name two or three disadvantages to becoming suddenly wealthy.

ACTIVITY 6 language strategy activity/reflection

Now that you have finished this first unit and have some ideas about your areas of strength and weakness, look briefly through all the units of this book and the Table of Contents on pp. iii–xi in order to identify:

* one unit you would like the whole class to study.
* one unit you would enjoy studying by yourself.
* one unit you think you could study together with another student in the class.
* one unit you feel you already understand well enough to explain to another student.

ANSWER KEY

Activity 4   Answers will vary. Possible answers are: The stock market has crashed./ The U.S. population is moving west./ The new budget was termed a disaster./ The United States will protest nuclear testing./ The President will visit China./The drought is expected to worsen./ There has been a big shakeup at the White House./ There is a new plan to improve bus service./ Test scores are improving in the public schools./ A link has been found between diet and heart disease./ Cancer is reported to be increasing./ There has been a major decrease in the number of international students in the United States.

USE YOUR ENGLISH

ACTIVITY 3 — speaking/writing [50 minutes/homework]

You may wish to assign Activity 3 as homework after Exercise 4 on SB pages 5 and 6. The goal of this activity is to practice using the future and past time frames.

■ STEP 1

1. Make sure students understand the rules of the contest. Call on volunteers to share examples of how they will spend the money.
2. Tell students that they will write a short essay for homework describing their plans for spending the money. Remind students to choose the correct time frame and keep all tenses in this time frame.

■ STEP 2

1. Instruct students to imagine that they have spent the money and have them rewrite their essay, changing the tenses. Remind them to keep the tenses consistent in the new time frame. You may wish to do this step in class in pairs, once students have done the Step 1 essays for homework.
2. Collect essays and provide individual feedback.

EXPANSION [20 minutes]

This role-play activity can be used for speaking practice in a variety of time frames.

1. Have students work with a partner to role-play an interview between the contest winner described in Activity 3 and a TV reporter. The interview will take place at the end of the week, after all the purchases have been made.
2. As a class make up questions the interviewer could ask and write them on the board (e.g., *How did you spend your money? Which purchase was the most expensive? Did you make any purchases for someone else? How has your life changed since you won the money?*)
3. Have pairs role-play the interview. Circulate and listen for correct usage of tenses and shifts in time frame.
4. Bring the class together and offer feedback on errors you may have heard.

ACTIVITY 4 — writing/speaking [20 minutes]

You may wish to assign this activity after Exercise 4 on SB pages 5 and 6. This activity tests students' understanding of tenses by having them transfer the meaning of newspaper headlines into full sentences.

1. Have students scan the headlines. Explain vocabulary as needed. Ask a volunteer to read the example out loud. Answer any questions.
2. Divide the class into groups of three or four and have them "translate" the headlines. Tell them to think carefully about the time frame and tense they think should be used. Refer students to Focus 1 on SB page 2. Point out that more than one "translation" may be possible in some cases.
3. Bring the class together and call on groups for their interpretations. Discuss any difficulties students may have had.

EXPANSION [15 minutes]

This activity provides students with additional practice writing in specific time frames, shifting them when necessary, and using different tenses. It can be used as a homework assignment.

1. Tell students to choose one of the headlines from the newspaper and make up an article to follow it. Encourage students to choose topics that interest them, but tell them the content does not have to be true.
2. Have students write the articles for homework, paying attention to tenses and any necessary shifts in time frame.
3. Collect the work and give feedback.

ACTIVITY 5 — research on the web [50 minutes/homework]

1. For homework, have students complete Step 1 of this activity in conjunction with Activity 3 on SB page 10.
2. Have students print out articles to share with other students in class.
3. After discussing their findings with other students, have students note advantages and disadvantages to becoming wealthy suddenly in two columns on the board.

ACTIVITY 6 — language strategy activity [15 minutes]

You can assign this activity at the end of the unit so that students familiarize themselves with the contents of the remainder of the book.

Have students skim the Table of Contents and the units of the book, and then respond to the bullet points. Call on volunteers to share their answers. Student feedback can be helpful to you, the teacher, when creating the syllabus for the course. For example, you might choose to skip or briefly review a unit or content that most students feel they know quite well.

OVERVIEW OF THE ENGLISH VERB SYSTEM

Aspect

OPENING TASK
A Picture Is Worth a Thousand Words

STEP 1
With a partner, discuss each of these photographs and together write sentences about them. Your sentences should answer these questions.

- What has just happened? Why do you think so?
- What is happening now? Why do you think so?
- What is going to happen next? Why do you think so?

STEP 2
Once you have described all the pictures, compare your descriptions with two other pairs of students. Do you all agree? Did you use the same verb tenses in your descriptions?

STEP 3
Report any interesting similarities and differences to the rest of the class.

LESSON PLAN 1

UNIT OVERVIEW

Unit 2 reviews aspect in English verbs by first going over simple tenses and then demonstrating the differences between simple, perfect, progressive, and perfect progressive aspects in context.

GRAMMAR NOTE

Verbs in English are marked not only by time (the present, past, and future), but also by aspect (simple, perfect, progressive, and perfect progressive). **Aspect** gives information beyond the time something happens to describe ideas such as the relationship between verbs (e.g., which happened first) or the manner in which a verb happens (e.g., habitual).

UNIT GOALS

Some instructors may want to review the goals listed on Student Book (SB) page 12 after completing the Opening Task so that students understand what they should know by the end of the unit. These goals can also be reviewed at the end of the unit when students are more familiar with the grammar terminology.

OPENING TASK [30 minutes]

The aim of this activity is to give students the opportunity to work with the form, meaning, and use of a variety of verb forms. The problem-solving format is designed to show the teacher how well the students can produce the target structures implicitly and spontaneously when they are engaged in a communicative task. For a more complete discussion of the purpose of the Opening Task, see To the Teacher, Lesson Planner (LP) page xxii.

Setting Up the Task

The Opening Task assists instructors to diagnose not only accuracy, but meaningfulness, and appropriateness, too.

▪ STEP 1

1. Divide the class into pairs and ask them to look at each of the four pictures on SB pages 12 and 13.
2. Ask students to first discuss each picture with their partner and determine what has happened, what is happening now, and what is going to happen next.
3. Next, ask the pairs to work together to write about each picture. Their sentences should answer the questions listed in Step 1 on SB page 13.

Conducting the Task

1. While students are working together, make note of any difficulties students are having. Do not correct student errors at this point. Let students negotiate meaning now and leave the form for later.
2. Offer vocabulary to pairs when appropriate and take a moment to write any new vocabulary on the board.
3. As you circulate, get an idea of students' current use and familiarity with the various aspects. This can be seen from how they respond to each of the questions in Step 1. Are the students sticking with simple and progressive aspects? Do they attempt to use the perfect aspects? Note any common errors in verb form or use to bring up later.
4. Look for examples which may be of use when debriefing and filling in the chart below.

▪ STEP 2

1. As pairs finish up their sentences, ask them to compare their work with other pairs.
2. As some pairs or groups of pairs finish the activity early, invite individuals to write a sentence or two on the board to share with the class. Encourage a wide variety of sentence types.

Suggestion: You may want to scan students' sentences first and ask students to put specific sentences on the board in order to highlight either a common error or a good variety of the proper use of aspect.

Closing the Task

Draw the following chart on the board:

	Simple	Progressive	Perfect	Perfect Progressive
Present				
Past				
Future				

▪ STEP 3

1. As a class, share descriptions along with any interesting differences found between groups.
2. Draw the class' attention to any new vocabulary in the sentences on the board (from Step 2). New vocabulary can be put into a vocabulary notebook. You may want to find ways to reuse these words throughout the unit to encourage vocabulary development.
3. Ask students who wrote sentences on the board to read them out loud to the class and state the verb(s) they used. Record these verbs in the corresponding column of the chart shown above.
4. Ask volunteers to read their other sentences to the class and state the verb(s) they used. Record these verbs in the corresponding column of the chart. Do not go into explanations at this stage.
5. Use this chart to lead into Focus 1 on SB page 14.

EXPANSION [15 minutes]

You may want to use Activity 2 (writing) on SB page 25.

FOCUS 1

Overview of Aspect

The basic aspect meanings listed on page 2 in Unit 1 indicate the time relationship between one verb and another.

ASPECT	MEANING		EXAMPLE
simple	at that time	(a)	The police **arrested** the protesters at 2:45 P.M.
progressive	**in progress during** that time	(b)	They **were blocking** the street when they were arrested.
perfect	**before** that time	(c)	They **had stopped** traffic for over an hour.
perfect progressive	**in progress during** and **before** that time	(d)	They **had been protesting** the president's decision when the arrests started.

We also use aspect to describe additional distinctions about an action or situation:

EXAMPLES

(e) The protester **disrupted** the politician's speech.

(f) Protesters **have been disrupting** politician's speeches as long as politicians **have been making** them.

(g) The police **are arresting** the protester, but perhaps he'll escape.

(h) The police **have arrested** the protester, so he won't be able to escape.

(i) Shopkeepers **are storing** some of their breakable items on the floor until the threat of earthquake aftershocks has passed.

(j) Shopkeepers in earthquake areas **store** expensive, breakable items on the lower shelves in order to lessen the possibility of damage.

EXPLANATIONS

Aspect indicates whether the action or situation:
- happens just once

OR

- happens continuously or repeatedly

- is still happening

OR

- is completed

- is temporary

OR

- is permanent

EXERCISE 1

Analyze one of these paragraphs with a partner. Identify the basic time frame. Then say which meaning is expressed by the aspect in the underlined verb phrases.

future time frame

1. By the time John gets on Flight 53 to Paris the day after tomorrow, he <u>will have moved out</u> of the apartment where he has been living for the last couple of years. He <u>will have said</u> some long, sad good-byes. He <u>will have been living</u> for the last couple of years. He <u>will have said</u> some long, sad good-byes. He <u>will certainly be thinking</u> about all the friends he <u>will no longer see</u> every day.

past time frame

2. When the earthquake hit San Francisco in 1989, Jeff <u>was</u> still at his office. He <u>had been working</u> on it for over a week, and he <u>was</u> almost done. He <u>was just making</u> some final changes when the building started to move. When the quake <u>started</u>, he quickly <u>got</u> under his desk. He <u>was</u> glad that he <u>had once read</u> an article on what to do in earthquakes. He <u>had studied</u> the article carefully, so he <u>knew</u> exactly what to do.

present time frame

3. Denise <u>is</u> quite a stylish dresser. She <u>thinks</u> that it <u>is</u> important to be neat and well-dressed, and she always <u>wants</u> to look her best. Every morning before she <u>leaves</u> for work, she <u>looks</u> at herself in the mirror. She <u>checks</u> to make sure that she <u>has combed</u> her hair and <u>hasn't put</u> her makeup on too heavily. She <u>makes sure</u> that she <u>is wearing</u> makeup colors that <u>go</u> nicely with the clothes she <u>is wearing</u>. She <u>checks</u> to see that her slip <u>isn't showing</u>, and her stockings <u>are</u> straight. She <u>makes sure</u> that the shoes she <u>has chosen</u> match the color of her dress and her coat. She <u>likes</u> feeling confident and attractive, and she <u>feels</u> that taking an extra minute in front of the mirror <u>is</u> worth the time.

Exercise 1 Time frames are listed above in Exercise 1. The meanings for each underlined verb phrase are as follows: **1.** will have accomplished: before that time; will have moved out: before that time; has been living: in progress during and before that time; will have said: before that time; will certainly be thinking: at that time; will no longer see: after that time   **2.** was: at that time; had been trying: in progress during and before that time; had been working: in progress during and before that time; was: at that time; was just making: in progress during that time; started: at that time; got: at that time; was: at that time; had read: before that time; had studied: before that time; knew: at that

3. is: at that time; thinks: at that time; is: at that time; wants: at that time; leaves: at that time; looks: at that time; checks: at that time; has combed: before that time; hasn't put: before that time; makes: at that time; is wearing: during that time; go: at that time; is wearing: during that time; checks: at that time; isn't showing: during that time; are: at that time; makes sure: at that time; has chosen: before that time; match: at that time; likes: at that time; feels: at that time; is: at that time

FOCUS 1 [15 minutes]

Focus 1 introduces students to the concept of aspect and gives general examples of how aspect can show the time relationship between one verb and another, and show distinctions, duration, or manner of an action.

1. **Lead-in:** Write the following sentences on the board:

   *The children **played in** the field.*

   *They **were playing** when it began to rain.*

   *They **hadn't finished** their games when it began to rain.*

   *They **had been playing** for only a short time when it began to rain.*

   Ask the students what time frame these sentences are set in. (*they are all in the past tense*)

   Ask students what the difference between these sentences is. (*different aspects: first sentence: simple, second sentence: progressive, third sentence: perfect, fourth sentence: perfect progressive*)

2. Tell the students that this chapter will focus their attention on the various meanings of these four different **aspects** in English.

3. Read the examples and explanations in the top part of the focus chart on SB page 14. Ask students to suggest other example sentences for each aspect. Draw their attention again to the chart you made in the Opening Task and add more verbs from these new sentences to this chart. As you gather student sentences, try to reiterate the meaning of each aspect (e.g., simple = at that time, progressive = in progress during that time, perfect = before that time, perfect progressive = in progress during and before that time).

4. Review the list of sentences on the board from the Opening Task and ask students to identify the aspect used in each sentence.

5. Ask students to look at the second part of the focus chart on SB page 14. Go over the examples and the explanations for the distinctions between these sentence pairs.

GRAMMAR NOTE

Typical student errors (form)

- Omitting auxiliaries: * *She putting on makeup.* * *He has working there for two years.*
- Making errors with irregular verb forms: * *catched* * *quitted*
- Misspelling the past tense form or the past participle form: * *tryed* * *begining*

Typical student errors (use)

- Using the progressive aspect for stative verbs: * *He is wanting a new car.*
- Confusing different tenses when showing the relationship between two verbs: * *They haven't finished packing when the taxi arrived.*
- Misusing the past tense and past participle forms: * *She has took the train before.*

EXERCISE 1 [10 minutes]

This exercise asks students to identify basic time frames and explain the meaning expressed by the aspect of the verbs.

1. Put students into pairs again and either assign a paragraph to each pair or ask them to choose one of the three paragraphs on SB page 15.

2. Have students identify the basic time frame of their paragraph.

3. Next ask students to refer to Focus 1 on SB page 14 and choose which aspect meaning is expressed by each of the underlined verb phrases within their paragraph.

4. As pairs finish, ask them to work on another paragraph. Compare answers as a class and answer any questions. See answers on LP page 14.

For more practice, use *Grammar Dimensions 3* Workbook page 4, Exercise 1.

EXPANSION [20 minutes]

You may want to use Activity 3 (reading) on SB page 25 to encourage further work on the time relationship between verbs.

FOCUS 3 Progressive Aspect

use

Progressive tenses (present progressive, past progressive, and future progressive) are made by using forms of

Be + Verb + -ing

EXAMPLES	EXPLANATIONS
	Use progressive aspect instead of simple aspect to describe:
(a) Other people **are** always **waiting** when Jeff **gets** to the bus stop. (They're already waiting **before** he gets there.)	• actions already in progress versus actions that happen afterwards
(b) Jeff **reads** the morning paper when he **gets** to the bus stop. (He reads his paper **after** he gets there.)	
(c) When Denise **entered** the room, the other employees **were working**, but when she left the room, they **laughed**. (They were working **before** she entered, but they laughed **after** she left.)	
(d) Victor **studies** English, but he **is not studying** at the moment.	• actions at a specific time (**now** or **then**) versus habitual or recurring actions
(e) John **lived** in France for a year, but he certainly **wasn't living** there when they had the election.	
(f) Those protesters **are** always **asking** for changes in the government.	• repeated actions
(g) Denise **is** still **working** to finish the report.	• uncompleted actions
(h) Those protesters **are being** very noisy, but they **are** angry, so I guess it's understandable.	• actions rather than states

FOCUS 2 Simple Tenses

use

EXAMPLES	EXPLANATIONS
	Use simple tenses:
(a) Social psychology **is** the study of the factors that **influence** group behavior.	• to express general ideas, relationships, and truths
(b) The people of ancient Rome **spoke** Latin.	
(c) A criminal **will** always **return** to the scene of the crime.	
(d) Denise always **checks** her appearance in the mirror before she leaves for work.	• to describe habitual or recurrent actions
(e) James Fennimore Cooper **wrote** for three hours every day except Sunday.	
(f) People **will commute** to the moon by spaceship at the end of the next century.	
(g) Scientists **report** that they have identified the cause of AIDS.	• to establish time frame
(h) When the protesters **decided** to disrupt the meeting they had already heard about the president's decision.	
(i) Roberta Chong-Davis **will visit** the moon someday.	
(j) Denise **worries** that she won't look professional.	• to describe mental perceptions or emotions
(k) One hundred years ago many people **felt** that a woman's place was in the home, not the office.	
(l) If Bob is late for dinner, his mom **will worry** about him.	
(m) Bob **has** two brothers and a sister.	• to express possession or logical relationship
(n) Robert's hobbies **consisted** of playing baseball and the harmonica.	
(o) Roberta's job **will require** regular travel to the moon.	

EXERCISE 2

Work with the same partner that you did for the Opening Task of Unit 1. But instead of describing Bob Lee and his family, describe your own lives, and those of your grandfathers and what may be true for your granddaughters. Each of you should write at least two sentences that describe the lives of each generation.

ANSWER KEY

Exercise 2 Answers will vary. In general, sentences describing the students' lives should be in present time frame, those describing grandparents' lives should be in past time frame, and those describing grandchildren should be in future time frame. Ask students to identify sentences that are in simple aspect and explain why they chose that particular tense. Most will be, because they are describing habitual or recurrent actions, general ideas, etc.

FOCUS 2 [15 minutes]

1. **Lead-in:** Divide the board into three areas and write each of the following questions in one area of the board.

   When do we use the simple present tense?

   When do we use the simple past tense?

   When do we use the simple future tense?

2. Ask the students to close their books and work in pairs or small groups to answer the three questions as best they can.

3. Bring the class together and call on groups to volunteer their answers. Write key words down in response to each question in the corresponding areas. Leave these columns on the board. They will be used again in Exercise 4.

4. Next, have students open their books to SB page 16 and call on volunteers to read the examples and explanations in the chart for Focus 2.

5. As you go through the chart, ask students if they can suggest other example sentences to illustrate each of these five general uses of the simple tenses.

GRAMMAR NOTE

The **simple tenses** are generally used to express truths, such as facts of nature, or a habitual situation.

The simple present tense can also be used to express the future when referring to things that are scheduled or events that are planned as in the following: *The train leaves at 6:00 tonight* OR *My birthday is on Saturday.*

EXPANSION 1 [20 minutes]

This "Who Am I" activity allows students to use the simple present tense to ask questions about facts.

1. Decide on a category for the game: animals, jobs, cities, etc.

2. Create a deck of index cards with the name of one thing in your category on each card (e.g., animals = wolf, gorilla, alligator, panda, etc.)

3. Put a card on the back of each student without letting that student see what the card says.

4. Tell the students what the category is and that they should show the card on their back to other students in the class. Then they can ask only yes/no questions about the habits or traits of their card. (*Do I have fur? Do I eat meat?*)

5. When they think that they know who they are, they can continue mingling with the other students and answering questions until everyone is finished or the time is up.

EXPANSION 2 [20 minutes]

1. Once students have guessed their card, have them write a paragraph describing the habits or traits of the category on their card.

2. Have students report back to the class and share their information in small groups or as a class.

EXERCISE 2 [10 minutes]

1. Have students get together with their original partner from the Opening Task for Unit 1. This time they will be describing their own lives. Students should write at least two sentences for each generation they are describing.

2. Looking at the three columns from the Focus 2 lead-in, label them as follows: present/me, past/my grandparents, future/my grandchildren. Ask students who finish early to put one of their sentences on the board in the corresponding area.

work book

For more practice, use *Grammar Dimensions 3* Workbook page 4, Exercise 2.

FOCUS 3 [10 minutes]

1. **Lead-in:** Contrast the present progressive and the simple present by talking about the class. Use examples of students' regular habits versus what is happening today. For example, *Ernest brings a red backpack to class. Today, Tanya is wearing boots. Cristo sits by the window.* Ask students to share other observations about their classroom or classmates. Have students suggest explanations for when to use progressive and when to use the simple aspects based on these examples.

2. Now write these two sentences on the board:

   He was speaking Spanish when she came into the room.

   He spoke Spanish when she came into the room.

3. Ask students if they think the sentences have the same meanings, and if not, what the difference is, and why. (*In the first sentence, the activity was already in progress when she came in. In the second sentence, the activity began after she came in.*)

4. Now ask students to look at the chart for Focus 3 on SB page 17. Have students volunteer to read the example sentences and go over the explanations together.

EXPANSION [20 minutes]

Depending on the number of students in your class, make a handout with a list of sentence pairs. Here are a few sentence pairs to you may start with:

1. (a) Peter was reading a magazine when Denise began talking.
   (b) Peter read a magazine when Denise began talking.
2. (a) Whenever Maria sees John, he is smiling.
   (b) Whenever Maria sees John, he smiles.
3. (a) Anna was singing when Fred arrived.
   (b) Anna sang when Fred arrived.

Have students get together with a partner to practice acting out these sentence pairs together. Then discuss as a class how the two acts differed from each other. Invite pairs to come to the front of the classroom and act out a pair of sentences.

use

FOCUS 4 | Perfect Aspect

Perfect Tenses (present perfect, past perfect, and future perfect) are made by using forms of:

Have + Verb (past participle usually ends in *-ed* or *-en*)

The basic meaning of the perfect aspect is this: the action described using the perfect aspect began before another action or another point in time, and it continues to have influence.

EXAMPLES	EXPLANATIONS
	Use perfect aspect instead of simple aspect to describe actions:
(a) Peter **had finished** the project when Denise **talked** to him. (The project was finished before she talked to him.)	• that happen before another action
(b) Peter **finished** the project after Denise **talked** to him. (She talked to him first, and then he finished the project.)	
(c) He has a report to present tomorrow. He **has reviewed** the figures, but he **hasn't prepared** the PowerPoint presentation yet.	• that focus on whether they are completed or uncompleted
(d) I **have finished** my work so now I'm watching TV.	• that are related to the present moment
(e) I **have just had** a snack, so I don't want any dinner.	
(f) Robert Lee **has worked** in a factory for thirty-five years. (He still works there.)	• that began in the past but still continue now
(g) Robert Lee **worked** in a factory for thirty-five years. (He doesn't work there anymore.)	

EXERCISE 3

Why is progressive aspect used in these sentences? There may be more than one possible reason.

Example: He is studying for an examination now.

action in progress now; uncompleted action

1. Peter was reading a magazine when Denise saw him.
2. Don't call Jeff after 10:00 PM because he will be sleeping.
3. They were selling Girl Scout cookies from house to house yesterday afternoon.
4. Whenever I see John, he is always reading a book.
5. Matt will be visiting friends all over the country during the summer.
6. Denise was thinking about a solution to her problem, so I didn't interrupt her.
7. Charley was living with his cousin for a while.
8. Are you having trouble with this assignment?
9. Our teacher will be staying at the Bates Motel during the conference.
10. I am trying to explain this, so please pay attention.

EXERCISE 4

Decide whether simple or progressive aspect should be used in these sentences. Both choices may be correct.

1. Please turn down the radio. I _____ (study) for a test.
2. Peter _____ (read) the newspaper when the phone rang.
3. I'm afraid those demonstrators might (a) _____ (get) in trouble with the police because they (b) _____ (march) without official permission.
4. Bambang still _____ (not study) as much as his parents want him to.
5. Rebecca _____ (speak) Russian. I wonder where she learned it?
6. Columbus (a) _____ (look) for a shorter route to Asia when he (b) _____ (think) it (discover) the New World by mistake.
7. When Columbus (a) _____ (reach) Cuba, he (b) _____ (think) it was India.
8. I _____ (try) to help you. Please listen carefully.
9. I (a) _____ (study) in the library when I (b) _____ (hear) the news about the latest suicide bombing.
10. Matt will probably _____ (sleep) if you wait until midnight to try to call him.

ANSWER KEY

Exercise 3 1. action in progress; uncompleted action 2. action already in progress 3. repeated action 4. repeated action 5. temporary situation 6. temporary situation 7. temporary situation 8. action in progress/temporary situation 9. action happening at a specific time in the future 10. action already in progress

Exercise 4 1. am studying (simple) 2. was reading (progressive) 3. get (simple); are marching (progressive) 4. doesn't study/is not studying (simple/progressive) 5. speaks (simple) 6. was looking (progressive); discovered (simple) 7. reached (simple); thought (simple) 8. am trying (progressive) 9. was studying (progressive); heard (simple) 10. be sleeping (progressive)

EXERCISE 3 [10 minutes]

This exercise asks students to think about when and why the progressive aspect is used.

1. Look at the example sentence together as a class. Ask a volunteer to read the example sentence.
2. Ask the class why the progressive aspect was used here. Then ask students to check Focus Chart 3 on SB page 17 to see other examples of using the progressive to show an *action in progress now* and an *uncompleted action*.
3. Have students work individually to complete the exercise with the help of the explanations from the focus chart. Circulate and help students.
4. Finally, ask students to compare their answers with a partner. Ask them to explain their reasons to their partner. Remind them that more than one reason may be correct. Go over the possible answers as a class. See answers on LP page 18.

EXERCISE 4 [15 minutes]

In this exercise, students will need to choose the simple or progressive aspect for the verb given in parenthesis. In some cases, both the simple and the progressive aspect are possible. Remind students that a shift in aspect changes the meaning of the sentence.

1. Have students work individually to complete the exercise and fill in the blanks with the verb in either the simple or the progressive aspect. Remind them to check the sentence meaning for the correct tense when choosing an aspect for each verb.
2. As you circulate, occasionally ask students to explain their answers. You will learn whether they are simply conjugating verbs or making choices based on meaning.
3. Have students check their answers with a partner.
4. Go over all possible answers as a class. Call on volunteers to explain their choices. See answers on LP page 18.

LESSON PLAN 2

FOCUS 4 [10 minutes]

Focus 4 presents the **perfect tenses** and explains that the perfect aspect is used to describe actions that happen before another point in time and continue to have some meaning on the later point in time. The perfect tenses are formed by using a form of *have* with the past participle of the verb.

1. **Lead-in:** Write the following sentences on the board:

   Max finished his homework when his mom came home from work.

   Max had finished his homework when his mom came home from work.

2. Next, ask students what differences they can see between the sentences. (*different aspect or different meanings*) Next, ask students in which sentence Max finished the homework first. (*he finished first in sentence 2*)
3. Explain to students that the perfect aspect is used to show that one action happened before another.
4. Write the following sentences on the board:

   Marta has eaten at that restaurant for many years.

   Marta ate at that restaurant for many years.

5. Now ask the students again what differences they see between the sentences. (*different aspect*) Also ask them if they can identify which sentence says that Marta still eats at the restaurant and which sentence says that she no longer eats there. (*sentence 3 says that she still eats there and sentence 4 says that she no longer eats at the restaurant*)
6. Explain to students that the perfect aspect is also used to show that an action is uncompleted or still continues until now. This aspect can mean the difference between *I have lived in five different countries* and *I lived in five different countries*, where the first sentence implies that the speaker may yet move again and the second sentence implies that the speaker does not plan to move around anymore.
7. Write the formula on the board for creating the perfect tenses:

   Have + Verb (past participle usually ends in -ed or -en)

8. Ask volunteers to read the example sentences and discuss the explanations as a class.

   Suggestion: You may wish to write the key words for these four different explanations on the board now in preparation for Exercise 5 on SB page 20.

   happened before another action

   uncompleted

   related to the present moment

   began in the past but still continues

GRAMMAR NOTE

The perfect aspect relates one action in time with another point in time. This can cause confusion when students are trying to decide which action happened first in time. Because the perfect tenses use the past participle of the verb, you may want to review these participles. The irregular past participles can be difficult for learners to remember because they are used less frequently than other verb forms. Students may use the wrong form of the verb: * *They have went to bed already.* * *I hadn't saw that movie before.*

FOCUS 5

Perfect Progressive Aspect

use

Perfect progressive tenses (present perfect progressive, past perfect progressive, and future perfect progressive) are made by using forms of:

$$Have + Been + Verb + \text{-}ing$$

EXAMPLES

(a) Peter **has been working** on that project all day. He still hasn't finished it.

(b) Peter **has worked** on that project for three hours. Now he can do something else.

(c) You **have been talking** for the last hour. Please give someone else a chance to use the phone.

(d) Denise **has talked** to Peter several times about his lack of effort.

EXPLANATIONS

Use perfect progressive aspect instead of perfect aspect to describe:

• actions that are uncompleted (a) instead of completed (b)

• actions that are continuous (c) instead of repeated (d)

EXERCISE 5

Why is perfect aspect used in these sentences? There may be more than one reason.

1. Please don't take my plate. I haven't finished my dessert.

2. You are too late; the doctor has just left the office.

3. He had forgotten to leave a key, so we couldn't get into the office.

4. She will already have left before you receive her farewell letter.

5. I've done my homework for tomorrow.

6. Biff hadn't even finished high school when he joined the Army.

7. The teacher has canceled the grammar test, so we won't need to study tonight.

8. It has rained every January for the last ten years, so I don't think it's a good idea to plan a picnic.

EXERCISE 6

Decide whether perfect or simple aspect should be used in these sentences.

1. John _____ (say) goodbye to his classmates at school when he started packing for his trip.

2. Jonas Salk _____ (conduct) many unsuccessful experiments when his efforts finally resulted in the discovery of a vaccine for polio.

3. The United States _____ (have) the same form of government for more than two hundred years.

4. Bob _____ (visit) Mexico five times so far. He really likes traveling there.

5. When Bambang (a) _____ (come) to the United States, he (b) _____ (not be) away from his parents for more than a few days.

6. By the time Roberta Chong-Davis is 50 years old, she will probably _____ (travel) to the moon several times.

7. I _____ (not sleep) well since those noisy people moved into the apartment next door.

8. Columbus (a) _____ (complete) three voyages to islands in the Caribbean when he (b) _____ (realize) that the islands (c) _____ (not be) part of India.

9. We _____ (live) in this house since 1986.

10. Victor _____ (study) very hard for the TOEFL* test, so I hope he does well!

*TOEFL is a registered trademark of the Educational Testing Service (ETS). This publication is not endorsed or approved by ETS.

EXERCISE 7

Decide whether perfect or perfect progressive aspect should be used in these sentences. More than one answer may be correct.

1. It _____ (rain) ever since we got here. I wish it would stop!

2. Matt _____ (work) on that computer virus for nearly a year before he realized that nothing could destroy it.

3. I'm very pleased. I _____ (find) the picture you mentioned in the newspaper.

4. Lately John _____ (find) life without Mary more and more difficult.

5. Gladstone _____ (cook) all afternoon. I hope the food will be as delicious as it smells.

6. Jeff (a) _____ (look) for his car keys for over an hour, when he realized that he (b) _____ (leave) them in the car.

7. I _____ (try) to solve the problem for over an hour. I give up!

8. Next January 31, Jeff and Matt _____ (live) together as roommates for five years.

9. The protesters (a) _____ (come) to city hall once a year ever since I (b) _____ (move) here.

10. I _____ (try) to reach him several times by phone, without success.

Exercise 5 1. action is related to present moment 2. action happens before another event; action is related to the present moment 3. action happened before another event 4. action happened before another event 5. action is related to present moment 6. sentence focuses on whether the action is completed or uncompleted 7. action is related to the present moment 8. action is related to the present moment

Exercise 6 1. had said/said (perfect/simple) 2. had conducted (perfect) 3. has had (perfect) 4. has visited (perfect) 5. came (simple); had not been (perfect) 6. have traveled (perfect) 7. haven't slept/don't sleep (perfect/simple) 8. had completed (perfect); realized (simple); weren't (simple) 9. have lived (perfect) 10. has studied/studied (perfect/simple);

Exercise 7 1. has been raining (perfect progressive) 2. had worked/had been working (perfect/perfect progressive) 3. have found (perfect) 4. has been finding/has found (perfect progressive/perfect) 5. has been cooking/has cooked (perfect progressive/perfect) 6. had been looking/had looked (perfect progressive/perfect); had left/left (perfect/simple) 7. have been trying/have tried (perfect progressive/perfect) 8. will have lived/will have been living (perfect/perfect progressive) 9. have been coming/have come (perfect progressive/perfect); have moved (perfect) 10. have tried (perfect)

LESSON PLAN 2

OVERVIEW OF THE ENGLISH VERB SYSTEM

EXERCISE 5 [10 minutes]

This exercise gives students the opportunity to check their understanding of when the perfect aspect is used as listed in Focus Chart 4 on SB page 19.

1. Have students work together to first underline the uses of the perfect aspect in each sentence.

2. Then have them decide together why the perfect aspect is used in each case. You can have them refer either to Focus 4 or to the list of key words you just put on the board from the Lead-in exercise.

3. Invite volunteers to explain their answers to the class. See answers on LP page 20.

EXERCISE 6 [10 minutes]

This exercise asks students to make a choice between the perfect or simple aspect. Students will need to look carefully at each sentence and consider how the missing verb fits in with the rest of the sentence.

1. Have students work individually to complete the sentences by using the verb in either the perfect or simple aspect.

2. You may want to have students try the first two sentences quickly on their own and go over those as a class before they continue on with the rest of the sentences.

3. See answers on LP page 20.

For more practice, use *Grammar Dimensions 3* Workbook page 5, exercise 3, and page 6, Exercise 4.

FOCUS 5 [10 minutes]

Focus 5 illustrates the uses of the perfect progressive aspect in contrast to the perfect aspect (see Focus 4). The perfect progressive is used to show uncompleted or continuous actions.

1. **Lead-in:** Write the basic formulas for making both the perfect and the perfect progressive tenses on the board:

   Perfect Aspect   **Perfect Progressive Aspect**
   have + verb *-ed/-en*   *have + been + verb -ing*

2. Come up with some example sentences for your class using the perfect and perfect progressive to describe things that you have done or experienced as a class this term. For example, *We have taken two quizzes. We have been studying verb aspects. It has snowed once. It has been snowing since yesterday. We have had one holiday so far. We have been meeting twice a week this term.*

3. Have students get into pairs or small groups and make a list of things they have done during this term so far.

EXERCISE 7 [10 minutes]

This exercise asks students to make a choice between the perfect and the perfect progressive aspect. Students will then need to form the verb correctly. You may want to remind students again of the basic formulas you put on the board in the Lead-in.

1. Have students try the first few sentences on their own before checking together as a class and going over the reasons for each correct choice.

2. Let students finish up the exercise individually. Have them discuss their choices with a partner when they are finished.

3. Go over the answers as a class. See answers on LP page 20.

For more practice, use *Grammar Dimensions 3* Workbook page 6, Exercise 5.

EXERCISE 10

Rewrite the paragraph in Exercise 8 in a future time frame. Keep the time relations between the verbs the same by maintaining the same aspect differences as in the paragraph in Exercise 8.

My roommate Charley (1) _is going to have_ (have) a dance party next Friday night. He has done this so often that I think I know exactly what's going to happen. I (2) _will be working_ (work) next Friday night, so I (3) _won't get_ (not get) home until 10:00. By the time I (4) _get_ (get) there, I'm sure that everyone (5) _will have started_ (start) dancing already. When I (6) _walk_ (walk) into the room everybody (7) _will shout_ (shout) "Welcome home!" because I (8) _will have just arrived_ (just arrive), but they probably (9) _will keep_ (keep) dancing. I probably (10) _will go_ (go) into the kitchen to find something to eat, and undoubtedly there (11) _will be_ (be) several other people in the kitchen. They (12) _will be sitting_ (sit) by an open window. If next Friday is like most of these parties, we (13) _will talk_ (talk) and (14) _laugh_ (laugh) for a while, and just when I (15) _am_ (be) ready to start dancing myself, there most likely (16) _will be_ (be) a knock at the door. I (17) _will go_ (go) to answer it, and (18) _will discover_ (discover) our neighbor. He (19) _will complain_ (complain) about the noise, and (20) _will ask/ask_ (ask) us to turn the music down. We (21) _will obey_ (obey), of course. Although the party (22) _will get_ (get) a little quieter, we undoubtedly still (23) _will have_ (have) fun.

EXERCISE 11

Work with a partner. Compare the tenses you used in Exercises 8, 9, and 10. Did you use the same aspect for each verb in all three exercises? What does this tell you about how tenses work together in a particular time frame? Discuss these questions with your partner, and report your ideas to the rest of the class.

EXERCISE 12

Talk about your own life. Complete these sentences with true information about yourself. Compare your answers with other students. Did you all use the same verb forms?

1. Until I came to this country, I . . .
2. I often think about my problems when . . .
3. I had never seen . . . before I . . .
4. The next time I see my family they . . .
5. I am usually unhappy if . . .
6. When I was growing up, I . . .
7. I have been studying English since I . . .
8. Lately, I . . .
9. Once I have completed my education, I . . .
10. I have never . . . but I plan to do it someday.

EXERCISE 8

Write the appropriate form for the verbs in the following paragraph. The first three have been done for you as examples.

My roommate Charley (1) _had_ (have) a dance party last Friday night. I (2) _was working_ (work) that Friday night, so I (3) _didn't get_ (not get) home until 10:00. By the time I (4) _got_ (get) there, everyone (5) _had started_ (start) dancing. When I (6) _walked_ (walk) into the room, everybody (7) _shouted_ (shout) "Welcome home!" because I (8) _had just arrived_ (just arrive), and they (9) _kept_ (keep) dancing. I (10) _went_ (go) into the kitchen to find something to eat. There (11) _were_ (be) several other people in the kitchen. They (12) _were sitting_ (sit) by an open window. We (13) _talked_ (talk) and (14) _laughed_ (laugh) for a while. Just when I (15) _was_ (be) ready to start dancing myself, there (16) _was_ (be) a knock at the door. I (17) _went_ (go) to answer it and (18) _discovered_ (discover) our neighbor, who (19) _was complaining_ (complain) about the noise. He (20) _asked_ (ask) us to turn the music down. We (21) _obeyed_ (obey), of course. And although the party (22) _got_ (get) a little quieter, we still (23) _had_ (have) fun.

EXERCISE 9

Rewrite the paragraph in Exercise 8 in a present time frame. Keep the time relations between the verbs the same by maintaining the same aspect differences as in the paragraph in Exercise 8.

My roommate Charley (1) _has_ (have) a dance party every Friday night. I (2) _am working_ (work) Friday night these days, so I (3) _don't get_ (not get) home until 10:00. On most Fridays, by the time I (4) _get_ (get) there, everyone (5) _has started_ (start) dancing. When I (6) _walk_ (walk) into the room everybody (7) _shouts_ (shout) "Welcome home!" because I (8) _have just arrived_ (just arrive), and they (9) _keep_ (keep) dancing. I generally (10) _go_ (go) into the kitchen to find something to eat. Usually, there (11) _are_ (be) several other people in the kitchen. They (12) _are sitting_ (sit) by an open window. We (13) _talk_ (talk) and (14) _laugh_ (laugh) for a while. Just when I (15) _is_ (be) almost always a knock at the door. I (17) _go_ (go) to answer it, and (18) _discover_ (discover) our neighbor, who (19) _is complaining_ (complain) about the noise. He (20) _asks_ (ask) us to turn the music down. We (21) _obey_ (obey), of course. And although the party (22) _gets_ (get) a little quieter, we generally still (23) _have_ (have) fun.

ANSWER KEY

Exercise 11 Answer will vary.

Exercise 12 Answers will vary. Tense choice should be similar to the possible answers given here: 1. I had never eaten hamburger./I thought everyone was rich.   2. I am homesick./I have done badly on a test.   3. snow before I visited Colorado./couples kissing in public before I came to the United States.   4. will be very happy./will be waving hello at the airport back home.   5. I don't have time to exercise./work is too crazy.   6. thought babies came from a factory./always pretended that I had my own horse.   7. was a student in high school./have been living in America.   8. have been thinking about my family./have been worrying about the next grammar test.   9. will get married./will find a good job./will go back to my country.   10. visited the Seychelles/bought a house

LESSON PLAN 2

EXERCISE 8 [15 minutes]

This exercise gives students the opportunity to use the past tense of verbs in different aspects. Although the time frame remains in the past tense, students will need to choose the appropriate aspect for each verb. This is a good review for students to check their understanding of the uses of the different aspects. The next two exercises (Exercises 9 and 10) are very similar, so it's important that students understand the correct usage of the aspects in this exercise first.

1. **Lead-In:** Begin with a quick show of hands by those who have a roommate. Next ask those students with a roommate if they have ever come home to find a party already in progress in their house or apartment. What was happening? How did they feel about it? Ask those students who don't have a roommate how they would feel about unexpectedly coming home to a party.

2. Have students read the passage without filling in any of the missing verbs. Ask the class to tell a little about what they think happened at this party.

3. Now have the students work individually to complete the story with the appropriate forms of the verbs.

4. When they finish, have them check their answers with a partner before sharing them as a class. See answers on LP page 22.

For more practice, use *Grammar Dimensions 3* Workbook page 7, Exercise 6.

EXERCISE 9 [10 minutes]

This exercise is very similar to Exercise 8 with a change in the time frame from past tense to present tense. Students should keep the same relationship between the verbs by maintaining the same aspects as in Exercise 8.

Have students work individually to fill in the blanks. You may want to let students continue on

and complete Exercise 10 and Exercise 11 before coming together as a class again to compare answers. See answers on LP page 22.

EXERCISE 10 [10 minutes]

Complete the paragraph one more time, this time using the future time frame. This exercise can be completed individually in class like Exercise 9 or it can be assigned to students as homework. See answers on LP page 22.

EXERCISE 11 [10 minutes]

In this exercise, students will get a chance to compare the last three exercises with a partner and discuss the choices they made. Have pairs report their observations to the class.

Note: The point of this discussion is to establish that aspect markers are basically the same in all three time frames. A situation that requires progressive aspect in present time frame will typically require progressive aspect in past or future time frames as well. This important priciple can emerge from student-student discussions, or you can lead the class as a whole by pointing out the parallel structures.

For more practice, use *Grammar Dimensions 3* Workbook page 7, Exercise 7.

EXERCISE 12 [15 minutes]

This exercise gets students to use a wide variety of verb forms to talk about themselves with a partner. After completing the exercises up to this point in the chapter, students should be more aware of the proper uses of the various aspects. This exercise should engage them enough to let them focus more on communicating.

1. Have students first complete the sentences about themselves.

2. When they have finished their own sentences, put students in to pairs or small groups to share what they have written.

3. When they have finished, have the pairs note the verb forms they used and any differences between them. Have volunteers share their observations with the class. See possible answers on LP page 22.

EXPANSION [20 minutes]

This expansion will allow students to continue their work from Exercise 12.

1. After students share a sentence about themselves with their partner or group, encourage the listeners to ask further questions about this topic.

2. Once the students have all finished sharing their sentences, ask them to circle those sentences that they found the most interesting to talk about with their partner or group.

3. Have students choose one sentence to develop further and write a paragraph as homework.

4. Collect homework in the next class. You may want to have the original pairs get together first and share their paragraphs before turning them in.

UNIT GOAL REVIEW [10 minutes]

Ask students to look at the goals on the opening page of the unit again. Refer to the pages of the unit where information on each goal can be found.

ExamView Test Generator For assessment of Unit 2, use *Grammar Dimensions 3 ExamView®*.

Use Your English

ACTIVITY 1 listening

CD Tracks
2, 3, 4, 5

Listen to the following conversations and put a check next to any statements that can be correctly inferred from each conversation.

Conversation 1

___✓___ (a) Mary doesn't want a roommate.

_____ (b) Mary doesn't have a roommate at the moment, but she's looking for one.

_____ (c) John doesn't want a roommate.

___✓___ (d) John doesn't have a roommate at the moment, but he's looking for one.

Conversation 2

___✓___ (a) Peter is looking the contract over at this moment.

_____ (b) Peter is not looking the contract over at this moment.

___✓___ (c) Denise is looking the contract over at this moment.

_____ (d) Denise is not looking the contract over at this moment.

Conversation 3

___✓___ (a) The janitor finished washing the floors before Angela's arrival.

___✓___ (b) He finished washing the floors after Angela's arrival.

_____ (c) The janitor emptied the trash before Angela's arrival.

___✓___ (d) He emptied the trash after Angela's arrival.

___✓___ (e) The janitor finished the windows before Angela's arrival.

_____ (f) He finished the windows after Angela's arrival.

Conversation 4

___✓___ (a) Bob works at the steel mill now.

_____ (b) Bob doesn't work at the steel mill now.

___✓___ (c) Dave works at the steel mill now.

_____ (d) Dave doesn't work at the steel mill now.

ACTIVITY 2 writing

Revise your descriptions of the photographs in the Opening Task on pages 12 and 13 by using the past time frame. Start your descriptions like this: *When this picture was taken . . .*

ACTIVITY 3 reading

Look at the front page of a newspaper. Find three examples of each of the three time frames (present, past, and future). They may be in the same article or three different articles.

ACTIVITY 4 speaking

Bring in three interesting photographs from a newspaper or magazine. Make a brief presentation about these photos to the class. Describe what is happening, what has happened, and what is going to happen. Then give three reasons why you think the photo is interesting.

USE YOUR ENGLISH

The Use Your English activities contain situations that should naturally elicit the structures covered in the unit. For a more complete discussion of how to use the Use Your English activities see To the Teacher on LP page xxii. When students are doing these activities in class, you can circulate and listen to see if they are using the structures accurately. Errors can be corrected after the activity has finished.

ACTIVITY 1 listening [10 minutes]

CD Tracks 2,3,4,5

Students will listen and make inferences based on the different aspects used in these short conversations.

1. Go over the directions with the class before you begin the audio. Be sure that students understand that they may put a check next to more than one true answer after each conversation.

2. Have students read over the statements for each possible answer in Conversation 1 before playing the audio.

3. Play the audio. If students are very unsure of the answers, you may want to play the conversation a second time.

4. Repeat steps 2 and 3 until you have completed all four conversations.

5. Let students check their answers with a partner. Circulate. If there is much discrepancy between answers play the audio again and let pairs discuss their answers again.

6. Go over the answers with the class, playing the audio in parts if you are able to highlight the aspects used (progressive, past, etc.) in the conversations. See answers on LP page 24.

ACTIVITY 2 writing [15 minutes]

This activity gives students the opportunity to revise their original descriptions of the pictures in the Opening Task on SB pages 12 and 13 with a shift in the time frame. The activity might also be assigned at the end of the lesson as a way to focus on the forms used in their original descriptions.

ACTIVITY 3 reading [20 minutes]

This activity, which can be completed after Exercise 1 on SB page 15, gives students a chance to survey a wide range of articles written in different time frames.

1. Either bring in some newspapers or ask students to do this on their own.

2. Ask students to look for examples of each of the three time frames.

3. Collect examples by asking students to put them in a list in their notebooks under the heading of present, past, or future. You may also wish to ask students to put their examples on the board.

EXPANSION [15 minutes]

You can expand on this search by having students find examples of different aspects. This can become a game that also develops scanning skills.

1. Give each student a newspaper with several articles in it.

2. Tell them that this will be a race to see who can find an example of the form that you call out.

3. Give students a chance to practice by starting out with a few samples. Call out a time frame (past, present, or future) or an aspect (simple,

progressive, perfect, perfect progressive). When they find an example of this form, have them circle it with a pencil and raise their hand. The first one with the correct answer gets a point.

4. As each example is given, you may want to list the examples on the board in groups or under headings.

Note: This activity can also be done by putting students into small groups or pairs and making it a team effort. However, each student should have a newspaper to scan. You can also have students take turns being the one to call out the forms or check the answers. Small prizes or bonus points can add excitement to the search.

ACTIVITY 4 speaking [20 minutes]

This activity encourages students to speak naturally about a topic without focusing too much on the forms as in a writing activity.

1. Ask students to bring in three photos. They may want to look in magazines, newspapers, or even their own photos.

2. Ask students to speak about the photos rather than read a prepared speech. You may want to put the questions for Activity 4 on the board (or better yet, on the wall in the back of the room) in order to guide the students in their presentations.

3. This can either be done in small groups or students can present only one photo each if the class is large and time is an issue.

4. You may want to take a few notes about errors or appropriate usage and bring them up after everyone has had a chance to speak.

ACCOMPLISHMENTS	GOALS	STRATEGIES
1.	1.	1.
2.	2.	2.
3.	3.	3.

STEP 1

Describe how your ability to communicate in English has changed since you began your studies. What kinds of things were you able to accomplish a year ago, and what can you do now that is different?

Examples:

1. *A year ago, I couldn't understand spoken English very well. My listening comprehension has improved a lot. I understand most things people say to me.*
2. *A year ago I needed to use a dictionary for almost every word. Now my vocabulary is much larger.*

Think of three areas where your skills have improved. Write sentences describing those things under the column marked Accomplishments in your chart.

STEP 2

Next, describe some things that you still can't do, but you want to be able to do. Think of at least three things you can't or don't do now, but want to be able to do by the end of this course.

Examples:

1. *I don't talk to my friends on the telephone because I have a hard time understanding them. I want to be able to talk on the telephone.*
2. *I can't do well on the TOEFL test. My scores on Part 2 are a little low. I want to get a good score on the TOEFL.*

Write sentences describing those skills under the column marked Goals.

STEP 3

Compare your accomplishments and goals to those of other people in the class. As a group, think of three strategies for increasing your language abilities and achieving your goals, and write them under the column marked Strategies. Present your list of strategies to the rest of the class.

ACTIVITY 5 writing/speaking

Describe a routine that you typically follow. Then describe one time when you did not follow that routine, and tell what happened. For example, perhaps you usually take the bus to school. What time do you get there? What are people on the bus doing when you get on? What happened on the day when you decided to walk to school because the bus was late, or on the day when your classmate offered to take you for a ride in his cousin's brand-new car?

ACTIVITY 6 research on the web

Do a keyword search in *InfoTrac® College Edition* under "protestors" and pick a recent article that seems interesting. Prepare a brief report on the protestors:

- What were they protesting?
- What actions did they take?
- Did the police become involved?
- Were arrests made?
- What had the protestors been doing that caused their arrest?

Prepare a brief presentation for the class, or write a short description of the protest, its causes and consequences.

ACTIVITY 7 language strategy/reflection

How are you progressing in English? In your notebook, create a 3-column chart, with sections for your accomplishments, goals, and strategies. Using the steps listed below, fill in the chart.

ACTIVITY 5 writing/speaking
[10 minutes]

This activity gives students practice in shifting time frames (present to past tense) and a chance for students to use the forms while writing and speaking about something that is based on their own lives.

1. Give the class an example of a typical routine by describing one in your own life or in the life of someone you know.

2. Now tell the class about a time that something happened to upset that routine. It can be something dramatic (a car accident), ordinary (not hearing your alarm clock go off), or even silly (losing a shoe in the subway).

3. Next, ask students to think of a routine they have and a time that they didn't follow that routine. Encourage them to take the time to really describe their usual routine before going into the day it changed. (The setting up of the habit makes the event show more contrast.)

4. When students are finished, you may find it interesing to have volunteers share their stories with the class or in groups.

ACTIVITY 6 research on the web
[40 minutes/homework]

Along with enhancing their technological skills, students will develop their research, reading, and vocabulary skills in this activity.

1. Have students look back at the first photo on SB page 12. Review the descriptions that were created earlier by students. Volunteers may want to share their descriptions again.

2. Ask students about their own experiences, *Have you ever seen or been a part of a protest? Where or when? Why did people protest? What did they do to protest? What happened as a result of the protest?*

3. Assign the students to research and write a report about a protest event. You will need to decide how much time and guidance should be given for an Internet research project.

ACTIVITY 7 language strategy
[15 minutes]

You can use this activity as homework at the end of the unit. This activity gives students an opportunity to analyze their progress in English and identify goals and strategies, while practicing using different tenses and time frames. This is also a good opportunity for you to get to know your students' strengths and weaknesses and help you tailor the course to meet their needs.

■ STEPS 1 AND 2   Have students reflect on and write responses to the questions.

■ STEP 3   After completing the first two columns in the chart, put students into groups to share their reflections. Have them help each other to complete the Strategies column.

EXPANSION 1 [20 minutes/homework]

This activity expansion can be used to allow students an opportunity to share their accomplishments and goals with their instructor in an informal letter.

1. Invite students to use the notes from Activity 7 to write a detailed letter to you sharing what they hope to attain in the class.

2. Collect and respond to students' letters. Suggest additional strategies for increasing their language abilities and achieving their specific goals.

EXPANSION 2 [15 minutes]

Use this activity expansion at the end of the unit to introduce students to the idea of a language log.

Have student bring a spiral notebook to use as a language learning log in addition to their regular binder. This activity allows students to keep track of their grammar progress and take control of the learning process.

1. For Section 1 of the language learning log, point out to students that when they log their mistakes and correct them, they are less likely to make them again. In class, have students look back at writing assignments from the unit, or recall corrections the teacher made, and start the language learning log.

2. For Section 2 of the log, explain that this is a unique opportunity for students to ask you grammar questions that there isn't time to discuss in class. Encourage students to be aware of grammar around them, in newspapers, TV, etc. and to ask about anything that is unclear.

3. Encourage or require students to submit the logs every week.

METHODOLOGY NOTE

Some students may not be accustomed to the idea of logging their errors and communicating with the instructor outside the classroom. Explain to students that doing so will allow them to fully take charge of their learning and track their progress.

3

ADVERBIAL PHRASES AND CLAUSES

UNIT GOALS

- **Identify phrases and clauses**
- **Correctly position adverbs**
- **Correctly position adverbial phrases and clauses**

OPENING TASK

Who? What? Which? Where? When? Why? How?

STEP 1

Newspaper reporters say that all basic news information about people and events can be summarized by asking and answering only the seven "Universal Questions" (Who? What? Which? Where? When? Why? How?). Summarize the following newspaper article by writing *Wh*-questions. Write as many questions as you need to in order to summarize all the important information.

Ski Mask Bank Robber Strikes Again

VANCOVER, BC— Columbia Savings and Loan was struck by a bank robber for the third time this year. An unidentified man in a blue ski mask entered the bank during the busiest time of the day and demanded money from the cashier.

Although three security officers were on duty, the thief was able to escape on foot. Bank officials estimate total losses of over ten thousand dollars. Police have been interviewing witnesses in hopes of getting a more complete description of the thief.

Similar robberies in other parts of the city have led police to suspect that the same person might be responsible for all three robberies. Authorities are concerned about the fact that robberies have increased a great deal in the last three months. As a result, bank officials say, they will begin to install metal detectors in order to prevent people from entering banks with guns.

STEP 2

Give your questions to a partner. Your partner should try to reconstruct the article by writing answers to your questions. Do the same with your partner's list of questions.

STEP 3

Compare your partner's answers with your questions and with the article. Your partner should do the same with your answers. Is any important information missing from your answers? Was there anything that you did not know how to ask about? Were there questions that you could not answer?

ADVERBIAL PHRASES AND CLAUSES

LESSON PLAN 1

UNIT OVERVIEW

Unit 3 reviews making *Wh-* questions along with using adverbial phrases and clauses. It goes on to focus on the basic order of adverbials and their position within a sentence.

GRAMMAR NOTE

Adverbials answer the basic questions of *how* (manner), *where* (place), *how often* (frequency), *when* (time), and *why* (purpose or reason). Adverbials modify and generally follow the verb phrase. When several adverbials are used in one sentence, they are placed in a basic order (see Focus 2). However, there are situations when adverbs, adverb phrases, and adverb clauses will not precede the main clause (see Focus 3) or will precede the main clause (see Focuses 4 and 5) rather than follow it.

UNIT GOALS

Some instructors may want to review the goals listed on Student Book (SB) page 28 after completing the Opening Task so that students understand what they should know by the end of the unit. These goals can also be reviewed at the end of the unit when students are more familiar with the grammar terminology.

OPENING TASK [30 minutes]

The aim of this activity is to give students the opportunity to form questions and answer them with adverb clauses. The problem-solving format is designed to show the teacher how well the students can produce the target structure implicitly and spontaneously when they are engaged in a communicative task. For a more complete discussion of the purpose of the Opening Task, see Lesson Planner (LP) page xxii.

Setting Up the Task

1. Write the seven "Universal Questions" on the board and ask the class to look at the photo and the article headline before you begin the reading.
2. Before reading the article, invite volunteers to suggest questions that they might have about this story based on only the headline. Put some of these on the board and assist with any problems in the formation of these questions.

Conducting the Task

■ STEP 1

Have the class read the article and then find a way to summarize the article by writing only questions. Circulate and assist as needed. Put any new vocabulary on the board.

■ STEP 2

1. Have students trade question lists with a partner and answer the list of questions.
2. Have students put their answers into complete sentences and on a separate piece of paper. This will help in Step 3.

■ STEP 3

Students should give back the question lists and the answers they wrote. Looking at their partner's answers, students should decide if this is a good summary of the article or if anything important was left out. If something was left out, have them refer to their list of questions and decide what other questions would help give a more complete story.

Closing the Task

1. Ask several volunteers to read out the summaries their partners wrote (just the page with the answers to their questions). Put a few sentences on the board.

2. Have the class decide what information was left out or could be added to make these summaries more complete.
3. Go over with the class any new vocabulary you put on the board.
4. Leave a few sentences from these summaries on the board for use in Focus 1.

GRAMMAR NOTE

Typical student errors (form)

- Incorrect word order in *Wh-* questions: * *What time be took the train?*
- Incorrect word order with negative adverbs of frequency: * *Seldom she was late.*
- Problems with the order of adverbial information: * *She jogs to lose weight at the gym regularly everyday.* * *He doesn't listen carefully always.*
- Problems moving adverbial clauses: * *Where we bought these CDs, there was a sale happening.*

Typical student errors (use)

- Use of too many adverbials following the main verb: * *She exercises with great determination at the gym near her house once a week in the early mornings in order to lose weight.*

FOCUS 1

Identifying Phrases and Clauses

Phrases are groups of related words.

EXAMPLES	EXPLANATIONS
(a) An unidentified **man in a blue ski mask** has been robbing city banks for several months.	**Noun phrases:** noun + determiner and modifiers. *Who, whom,* and *what* ask about noun phrases.
(b) An unidentified man in a blue ski mask **has been robbing** city banks for several months.	**Verb phrases:** auxiliaries + verb. *What . . . do . . .* asks about verb phrases.
(c) An unidentified man **in a blue ski mask** has been robbing city banks for several months.	**Prepositional phrases:** preposition + noun phrase. **Adjective prepositional phrases** *give more information about nouns. Which asks about adjective phrases.*
(d) An unidentified man in a blue ski mask has been robbing city banks **for several months.**	**Adverbial prepositional phrases** *give more information about verbs. Where, when, how, why, how long, how often, and how much ask about adverbial phrases.*

Clauses are groups of related words that contain both a subject and a verb.

EXAMPLES	EXPLANATIONS
(e) A man robbed the bank.	**Independent clauses** can function as sentences.
(f) Have you heard that a man robbed the bank?	**Dependent clauses** cannot function as sentences.
(g) A man robbed the bank that we visited yesterday.	**Adjective clauses** (also called relative clauses) give more information about noun phrases.
(h) A man robbed the bank before the police could arrive to catch him.	**Adverbial clauses** give more information about verb phrases.

The following chart shows how different kinds of *Wh*-questions focus on different parts of the sentences and can be answered with either phrases or clauses.

	WH-QUESTIONS	PHRASES	CLAUSES
Who/Whom	Who reported the crime to the police?	**The security manager did.**	**Whoever is responsible for security reported it.**
	Who(m) did the police arrest?	They arrested the old man.	They arrested the man who they found hiding in the alley.
What	What have you told the reporters?	I told them my experience.	I told them that the investigation is still not finished.
What . . . do	What did the police do?	They tried to catch the thief.	They hoped that they would find the criminal.
Which	Which teller was robbed?	It was the teller with the blonde hair.	The teller who was interviewed by the police was.
Where	Where did the thief go?	He went down the street, towards the park.	The thief went where the police couldn't find him.
When	When did they finish the investigation?	They finished it on Tuesday at 3:00.	They finished it when they had collected all the evidence.
How	How did the thief get away?	He got away on foot.	The thief disappeared as if he had become invisible.
How _____	How busy was the bank yesterday?	It was busier than usual.	It was so busy that nobody noticed the thief.
How long	How long has that officer been on the police force?	He's been a policeman for a long time.	He has been a policeman since he first moved to the city.
How often	How often has this bank been robbed?	It's been robbed from time to time.	It's been robbed as often as any other bank has been robbed.
How much	How much money did the thief take?	He took too much to count.	He took so much that they haven't determined the entire amount.
Why	Why did you go to the bank?	I went for some money. I went to the bank to cash a check.	I went to the bank because I needed money. I went to the bank so that I could cash a check.

ADVERBIAL PHRASES AND CLAUSES

LESSON PLAN 1

FOCUS 1 [20 minutes]

Focus 1 reviews what makes a phrase and a clause. It then goes on to give examples of how *Wh*- questions can be answered with either a phrase or a clause.

1. **Lead-in:** To review **phrases,** put the sentence used in examples a–d on the board or overhead transparency. Underline or circle the different phrases in this sentence as you go over the section on phrases. Use different colors of chalk or pen if you can.

2. Now contrast these examples of phrases with **clauses** by explaining that clauses use the following formula: **subject + verb.** Put the following sentence on the board to illustrate an independent clause:

    A man robbed the bank.

3. Add to this clause an adjective clause (example g) and then use an adverbial clause (example h). Be sure to note what each additional clause is modifying. (*adjective clause—noun phrase/adverbial clause—verb phrase*)

4. Because this unit will focus on adverbials, you may want to invite students to come up with several other options in place of the examples for adverb phrase and adverbial clause that are given.

5. As you go over the focus chart on SB page 31, let students point out the differences between the answers with phrases and those with clauses.

VARIATION

Before looking at the focus chart on SB page 31, photocopy it and cut up the example boxes into small strips. Mix them up and hand out one set of strips to each student. Students will then go around the room and try to find the other two students who have the matching question and answers. Students will end up in groups of three. These groups can be used as teams for Exercise 1.

FOCUS 2 | Basic Adverbial Position

Adverbials are words, phrases, and clauses that answer questions like *how, how often, how much, where, when,* and *why*.

EXAMPLES

EXPLANATIONS

(a) Biff **never** goes **downtown** anymore.

adverbs

(b) Biff exercises **as often as possible at the gym on Saturdays.**

adverbial phrases

(c) Biff works out **because he wants to improve his physique.**

adverbial clauses

Most adverbial information follows the verb phrase (verb + object) and usually appears in a basic order (some other variations are possible).

VERB PHRASE	MANNER	PLACE	FREQUENCY	TIME	PURPOSE OR REASON
what . . . do	how	where	how often	when	why
(d) Biff lifts weights	rigorously	at the gym	every day	after work	to fight stress.

Some adverbs can come before the verb or between the auxiliary and the main verb.

EXAMPLES

EXPLANATIONS

(e) Gladstone **often** goes on strange diets

Adverbs of frequency:
affirmative: *always, often, usually, sometimes*
negative: *seldom, rarely, hardly ever, never*

(f) He has **never** lost more than a few pounds.

(g) He has **rigorously** avoided sweets for more than a year.

Adverbs of manner:
rigorously, quickly, completely, etc.

(h) He **recently** lost fifty pounds.

Indefinite adverbs of time:
recently, typically, previously, finally, etc.

EXERCISE 1

There is a popular American TV quiz show called *Jeopardy*. Contestants are given answers, and they must provide a question for each answer. Play *Jeopardy* with a partner. Here are some answers. For each answer, decide what form it is (phrase or clause) and make up a suitable question.

Examples: Answer 1: *by studying (phrase):*

Question 1: *How can I get a good score on the TOEFL® Test*?

Answer 2: *once I get a good score on the TOEFL Test (clause):*

Question 2: *When will you begin your university studies?*

1. the president
2. He went to the movies.
3. I am.
4. in 2004
5. at noon
6. from Japan
7. for fun
8. after I finish school
9. because he needs money
10. because of the TOEFL test
11. by practicing
12. My sister can.
13. in order to learn English
14. to find a good job
15. the old man
16. until he passes the TOEFL test
17. to my brother
18. a book and a pen
19. too expensive
20. as long as I am a student
21. so he can buy books

EXERCISE 2

Each of these sentences consists of two or more clauses. Put brackets around each clause, as shown in the example.

Example: [Although John is a little homesick], [he still plans to stay in France for at least a year].

1. [Matt likes to get up early most days], [but he prefers to sleep late on weekends].
2. [Denise has a lot of work][that has to get done], [so she won't consider taking a vacation].
3. [Because they feel war is too destructive], [many people are opposed to military solutions for international problems].
4. [I once met a man][who looked just like a friend of mine].
5. [John is looking for an additional job][that he can do in his spare time][because he needs some extra money].
6. [I know an old lady][who swallowed a fly].
7. [Although I have many friends], [I still enjoy meeting people][that I've never met before].
8. [Last night after dinner Peter wrote to an old friend][who(m) he went to school with].

*TOEFL is a registered trademark of the Educational Testing Service (ETS). This publication is not endorsed or approved by ETS.

Exercise 1 Answers will vary. Possible answers include: 1. phrase; Who runs the government? 2. clause; Where is John? What did John do yesterday? 3. clause; Who is studying English? Who is taller; you or Rebecca? 4. phrase; When did you come to the United States? When did you start studying English? 5. phrase; What time is lunch? When does the bus leave? 6. phrase; Where is Michiko from? Where did you get that notebook? 7. phrase; Why do you go bike riding? Why does he watch TV? 8. clause; When will you start working? When will you get married? 9. clause; Why is John working after school? Why is he looking for a job? 10. phrase; Why can't you go to the movies tonight? 11. phrase; 12. clause; How can you improve your pronunciation? How can you improve your conversational skills? 12. clause; Who can bake a cherry pie? Who can tell when you aren't feeling happy? 13. phrase; Why are you in this class? Why are you reading this book? 14. phrase; Why are you reading the paper? What are you hoping to do after graduation? 15. phrase; Who left the party early? Who loves the old woman? 16. clause; How long will Juan study English? How long will he be in the language program? 17. phrase; Who did you give the money to? Where did you send that letter? 18. phrase; What do you need to bring to class everyday? What does he always forget to bring? 19. phrase; How much is that ring? Why didn't you buy me a Mercedes? 20. clause; How long will you continue studying? How long will you qualify for a discount at the bookstore? 21. clause; Why does he need money? Why did he go to the bookstore?

EXERCISE 1 [15 minutes]

This exercise asks students to identify phrases and clauses and then to create appropriate questions to match. You can either assign this for pairs to practice or, for a more competitive activity, use teams.

1. Begin by asking the class if they know the TV game *Jeopardy*. Explain the basic premise and then go over the examples for Exercise 1. You may want to supply a few more answers such as a classmate's name or a known location to get students practicing more (i.e., Johanna. Who was late for class today? or At Genki Sushi. Where can you buy Japanese food on campus?). Remind students that there may be more than one correct question. However, they will first need to state whether it is a phrase or a clause before they can give their questions.

2. If students are playing in pairs, let them work together. You may want one partner to keep his or her book closed as the other partner calls out the first few answers. They can switch roles after five questions.

3. If you are playing in teams as a class, explain how the points will work (for example, 1 point for correctly identifying phrase/clause and 5 points for making a correct question). Set a few rules. Everyone should have their books closed as you call out the answers. See possible answers on LP page 32. Feel free to mix them up in case students have already started looking at the list. Keep track of points and award prizes.

For more practice, use *Grammar Dimensions 3* Workbook page 9, Exercise 1.

EXPANSION [20 minutes]

You can use speaking/writing Activity 1 (speaking/writing) on SB page 42 to continue working on the formation of questions. In this activity, students will ask each other the seven Universal Questions, then write paragraphs or give presentations discussing the answers.

EXERCISE 2 [15 minutes]

This exercise asks students to identify clauses.

1. You can begin with a quick review of what makes a clause (see Focus 1).

2. Go over the example given and note the placement of brackets with the class. You may want to put another example on the board and invite volunteers to place the brackets.

3. Have students work individually and then compare answers with a partner. There may be two to three clauses in each sentence. See answers on LP page 32.

LESSON PLAN 2

FOCUS 2 [20 minutes]

This focus presents the basic order and the possible movement of three types of adverbial information.

1. **Lead-in:** Put the questions *how, where, how often, when,* and *why* across the board. You will use these as columns to present the basic order of adverbial information.

2. Go over the first chart, which distinguishes adverbs, adverbial phrases, and adverbial clauses.

3. Put the sentence provided in the second chart (*Biff lifts weights . . . vigorously . . . etc.*) on the board, lining up the adverbial information under the matching category (*how; where,* etc.). Add the corresponding meaning for each category (*manner, place,* etc.) to the chart you have created. This will match your book.

4. You may want to invite students to create a few more sentences to follow this chart (i.e., *Paul reads quietly on the patio every Sunday morning to relax.*)

5. As you move to the last chart in Focus 2, explain that the sentences created on the board are rather long and awkward with so much information following the verb phrase. Explain that some adverbs can come before the verb (or auxiliary). Go over the examples in the last chart.

6. Circle these three categories (adverbs that can move: *manner, frequency, time*) on the board. Invite volunteers to practice moving these around in the example sentences on the board.

7. Keep the chart on the board for Exercise 3.

EXERCISE 3

Read the following passage then follow these directions:

1. Circle the verb in every sentence.
2. Underline the adverbs, adverbial phrases, and adverbial clauses.
3. Decide whether the meaning of each adverbial is frequency, manner, place, time, or reason/purpose.

The first paragraph has been done for you as an example.

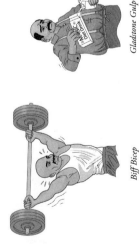

Biff Bicep   *Gladstone Gulp*

frequency

manner

Biff Bicep and Gladstone Gulp are close friends. (1) They (are) always (trying) to change the way they look because neither one is very pleased with his appearance, (2) but they do it differently.

Biff Bicep is a serious body-builder. (3) He (tries) to increase the size of his muscles by lifting weights at a gym near his house. (4) He usually (goes) there at the same time every day. (5) He (drinks) special vitamin supplements to gain weight and (6) (works out) vigorously twice a day—in the morning and in the afternoon. (7) He usually (starts out) on an exercise bike to warm up his muscles. Then he (moves) on to his exercises. (8) He (exercises) his upper body on Mondays, Wednesdays, and Fridays. (9) On Tuesdays, Thursdays, and Saturdays, he (does) exercises to develop the muscles of his lower body. (10) He never (works out) on Sundays, so his muscles can have a chance to rest.

Gladstone Gulp is a serious dieter. (11) He always (seems) to be trying to lose weight by going on special weight-reducing diets whenever he feels too heavy. (12) He usually (drinks) a special diet drink at breakfast and lunch. (13) Sometimes he (doesn't eat) anything after breakfast in order to save a few calories. (14) He also (tries) not to snack in between meals. (15) As a result, he (is) usually really hungry when he gets home, and (16) so he often (goes) directly to the kitchen to find something to eat. Although he (is) a serious dieter, he's not a terribly successful one. (17) He (has) never permanently (lost) more than a few pounds. (18) He (is) always looking for a magic way to lose weight without having to diet or exercise.

EXERCISE 4

Add the adverbials in parentheses to each sentence. There may be more than one possible position.

Example: He gains back the lost weight. (quickly) (usually)

He usually gains the lost weight back quickly.

Usually he quickly gains back the lost weight.

1. Gladstone Gulp goes on a new diet. (because he feels heavy) (every few months)
   Every few months Gladstone Gulp goes on a new diet because he feels heavy.

2. He uses diet pills. (to increase his metabolism) (regularly)
   He regularly uses diet pills to increase his metabolism.

3. He rides an exercise bicycle. (occasionally) (to use up calories) (very hard)
   He occasionally rides an exercise bicycle very hard to use up calories.

4. He trades diet plans. (with his friend Biff) (sometimes)
   He sometimes trades diet plans with his friend Biff.

5. He reads about every new diet. (in magazines) (carefully) (whenever he can)
   He reads carefully about every new diet in magazines whenever he can.

6. He doesn't follow their directions. (carefully) (always)
   He doesn't always follow their directions carefully.

7. He drinks a special vitamin supplement. (usually) (to make sure he gets proper nutrition) *He usually drinks a special vitamin supplement to make sure he gets proper nutrition.*

EXERCISE 5

Interview a classmate and find out something that he or she does:

1. every day
2. for his or her health
3. very well
4. before bedtime
5. outdoors
6. occasionally
7. better than anyone else in his or her family
8. automatically
9. with considerable difficulty
10. after class

Write complete sentences about these activities and report them to the class.

Exercise 3   The meaning of each adverbial is: 3. manner; place; place   4. frequency; place; time; frequency   5. reason   6. manner; frequency; time; time   7. frequency; place; reason; time; place   8. time   9. time; reason   10. frequency; time; reason   11. frequency; manner; frequency   12. frequency; time   13. frequency; time; reason   14. manner   15. manner; frequency; time   16. frequency; manner; place; reason   17. frequency; manner   18. frequency; manner

Exercise 5   Answers will vary. Possible answers are: 1. She goes to school every day.   2. She eats vegetables for her health.   3. He speaks English very well.   4. Joe always brushes his teeth before bedtime.   5. John plays tennis outdoors.   6. Ivan watches TV occasionally.   7. Maria sings better than anyone else in her family.   8. Steve automatically locks his car whenever he parks it.   9. Janet starts conversations with people she doesn't know with considerable difficulty.   10. Jacob usually does his homework after class.

LESSON PLAN 2

ADVERBIAL PHRASES AND CLAUSES

EXERCISE 3 [20 minutes]

This exercise reinforces the information on adverbial order and meaning presented in Focus 2.

1. Choose a sentence from the reading or one created in Focus 2 to put on the board as an example.

2. Go through the directions for Exercise 3 as a class and complete them step by step on your example sentence on the board.

3. Refer to the list of adverbial meanings from Focus 2 as you note the meaning of the adverbials in your example.

4. Go over the first paragraph as an example and assign the rest for individual work.

5. When finished, have students check their work with a partner and then go over with the class. See answers on LP page 34.

For more practice, use *Grammar Dimensions 3* Workbook page 9, Exercise 2.

EXPANSION [10 minutes]

You may want to use Activity 6 (research on the web) on SB page 45 as a follow-up to this exercise. In this activity, students use *InfoTrac® College Edition* to research diet and exercise.

EXERCISE 4 [15 minutes]

This reviews the basic order and placement of adverbials as described in Focus 2.

1. Go over the example. Write a few more of your own with possible adverbials for volunteers to place.

2. Review the basic order and guidelines for movement in Focus 2 (*frequency, manner,* and *time* can precede the verb).

3. Have students work individually to complete the exercise and then compare answers with a partner. Remind students that there may be more than one possible answer.

4. Invite the class to share possible answers. See possible answers on LP page 34.

EXERCISE 5 [15 minutes]

Students will use adverbials to ask classmates about their activities. This exercise can be done in pairs or as a whole class mixer.

1. Using the basic question format of *What do you do . . .?*, have students interview a classmate. You can also have students ask each question of only one student as they move around the room collecting information.

2. Students should record answers and write complete sentences when they are finished interviewing.

3. Put students into groups to share the information they learned (using the complete sentences). See possible answers on LP page 34.

Suggestion: Collect the sentences if you are unable to circulate enough to check on everyone's progress.

VARIATION

Have students interview only one person and then create an oral report on their findings to share with the class.

EXPANSION [20 minutes]

Follow up these classmate interviews by completing Activity 5 (speaking), on SB page 44. In this activity, students will interview each other again and report their findings to the class.

form

FOCUS 3

Position and Order of Adverbial Phrases

When there is more than one adverbial phrase in a clause, the order usually follows these guidelines.

EXAMPLES

(a) AWKWARD: He exercises vigorously at the gym every Monday, Wednesday, and Friday after work.

(b) BETTER: He exercises vigorously at the gym after work every Monday, Wednesday, and Friday.

(c) Many people frequently eat dinner in neighborhood restaurants in Toronto.

(d) NOT: Many people frequently eat dinner in Toronto in neighborhood restaurants.

(e) AWKWARD: He washes his car carefully in the driveway with a special soap once a week.

(f) BETTER: Once a week, he carefully washes his car in the driveway with a special soap.

EXPLANATIONS

Shorter adverbial phrases usually come before longer adverbial phrases. Since the frequency phrase is long, it is better to have it follow the time phrase.

When there are two adverbial phrases of the same kind (place, time, etc.), the more specific adverbial phrase always comes first.

It is not common to have more than two or three adverbials after the verb phrase. If there are several adverbials, then one is usually moved to the beginning of the sentence.

EXERCISE 6

Identify the meaning (*place, frequency, reason, time, etc.*) and form (*adverb, adverb phrase, adverbial clause*) of the underlined adverbials in the numbered sentences in the article on the next page. Tell why you think they appear in the order that they do. There may be several possible reasons, so discuss your ideas with a partner. The first one has been done for you as an example.

Example: (a) manner, adverb, (b) place, adverbial prepositional phrase, (c) time, adverbial clause, (d) time, adverbial phrase.

      Reasons: adverbials follow general manner, place, and time order.

Bizarre Attack by Wild Pigs on Rampage

Buttonwillow, GA—Mary Morris is a lucky woman tonight. (1) She is resting (a) comfortably (b) at her Buttonwillow home (c) after doctors released her from Button-willow Hospital (d) earlier this afternoon. Early this morning she was involved in one of the strangest automobile accidents in local history. Her car was attacked by a herd of wild pigs.

(2) "I was driving (a) on a dirt road (b) along the river, (c) just like I always do," she told reporters in an impromptu news conference at the hospital, (d) "when I hit a muddy patch of road. I got out of the car to try to push it out of the mud. (3) (a) While I was doing that a herd of pigs (b) suddenly came (c) out of the bushes (d) to attack me. There were so many of them that I was completely surrounded, but I was able to get back into the car. (4) I (a) finally scared them (b) back into the bushes (c) by blowing the horn. (5) Then I sat (a) there (b) for several hours (c) before I felt safe enough to leave the car and (d) could look for some help." Ms. Morris was treated for gashes on her legs and shock. She was given a tetanus shot, and released later in the day.

Scientists are a little puzzled as to why the pigs might have attacked in the first place. Animal psychologist Dr. Lassie Kumholm suggested that it may have been because one of the females in the herd could have just given birth near where the car got stuck. (6) (a) Sometimes pigs can (b) suddenly become aggressive (c) quite quickly (d) if their young are threatened. This herd of pigs is a well-known nuisance. (7) They have (a) repeatedly caused minor damage (b) in the area, (c) for the last several years, but this is the first time they have been known to actually attack humans. (8) (a) On several occasions local property owners have sent petitions (b) to county offices (c) to complain about the problem.

Exercise 6 2. (a) place, adverbial phrase; (b) place, adverbial phrase; (c) manner, adverbial clause; (d) time, adverbial clause; Reasons: The adverbial phrases of place are shorter than the clauses. 3. (a) time, adverbial clause; (b) manner, adverb; (c) place, adverbial phrase; (d) reason/purpose, adverbial phrase; Reasons: Adverbial clause connects the sentence to the previous one. The phrases follow the general order of place before reason/purpose. 4. (a) time, adverb; (b) place, adverbial phrase; (c) manner, adverbial phrase; Reasons: Manner comes at the end for clarity. 5. (a) place, adverb; (b) time, adverbial phrase; (c) time, adverbial clause; (d) time, adverbial clause; Reasons: Place comes before time, the shorter time adverbials come before the longer ones. 6. (a) frequency, adverb; (b) manner, adverb; (c) manner, adverb; (d) reason, adverbial clause; Reasons: These adverbials follow the usual order. 7. (a) manner, adverb; (b) place, adverbial phrase; (c) time, adverbial phrase; Reasons: These adverbials follow the usual order. 8. (a) time, adverbial phrase; (b) place, adverbial phrase; (c) reason, adverbial phrase; Reasons: These adverbials follow the usual order.

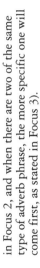

LESSON PLAN 2

FOCUS 3 [15 minutes]

Focus 3 explains the guidelines for moving adverbial information within a sentence.

1. **Lead-in:** Put an example of a sentence that uses several adverbial phrases (you may have generated these in Focus 2). Ask the class why this sentence appears to be awkward or strange. (*it's too long, there are too many adverbials,* etc.)

2. Go through the examples in Focus 3, noting why the first sentence in each row is awkward and how it is rearranged in the following sentence.

3. Return to your example on the board and invite volunteers to find ways to rearrange it with regards to the three examples in Focus 3.

VARIATION

For an inductive approach, put the pairs from Focus 3 on an overhead transparency or write them on the board. With books closed, ask the class to talk with a partner about what has been changed in each set of sentences. Then have the pairs create "rules" to explain what has been done to improve the awkward sentences.

EXERCISE 6 [15 minutes]

This exercise asks students to identify the meaning, the form, and then a possible reason for the placement of adverbials. Students will work on eight sentences within the article. Each sentence has three to four underlined adverbials to analyze.

1. Before assigning this exercise, review the five basic meanings of adverbials and their basic forms.

2. Go over sentence (1) a–d in the article with the class. On the board, first list the meaning and then the form of each underlined adverbial with the class. Once you have this information on the board, the reason for the order should become apparent (adverbials follow a basic order as stated

in Focus 2, and when there are two of the same type of adverb phrase, the more specific one will come first, as stated in Focus 3).

3. Have students complete the rest of the article on their own or with a partner.

4. Go over the exercise as a class. See answers on LP page 36.

For more practice, use *Grammar Dimensions 3* Workbook page 10 Exercise 3, and page 11, Exercises 4 and 5.

FOCUS 4

Putting Adverbial Phrases at the Beginning of a Sentence

form

use

EXAMPLES

(a) **Once a week,** Jeff carefully washes his car in the driveway with a special soap.

(b) **In the suitcase,** Matt found an extra wool sweater that had been knitted by his grandmother.

(c) NOT: Matt found an extra wool sweater that had been knitted by his grandmother **in the suitcase.**

(d) **Carefully and slowly,** Jeff carried the heavy tray of fragile glasses to the table.

(e) Matt and Jeff have a beautiful apartment. **Along one wall,** there are big windows with a marvelous view.

(f) Matt was born in 1965. **In 1988,** he moved to San Francisco.

(g) John became quite fluent in French. **As a result,** he was able to get a job with a company that exports computer parts to West Africa.

EXPLANATIONS

Most adverbials can also appear at the beginning of a clause or sentence for the following reasons.

• if there are several other adverbs or adverbial phrases, or if the object of the verb phrase is very long

• in order to emphasize adverbial information

• to show logical relationships between sentences.

Most adverbials can be placed at the beginning of the sentence without making other changes in word order, but some require a question word order when they are put at the beginning of the sentence.

EXAMPLES

Normal Position:

(h) Gladstone **seldom loses** more than a few pounds.

Emphatic Position:

(i) **Seldom does** Gladstone lose more than a few pounds.

EXPLANATIONS

• negative adverbs of frequency *(never, seldom, rarely)*

EXERCISE 7

Make these sentences more emphatic by moving the adverbial to the beginning of the sentence. Be sure to change the word order if necessary.

1. I have rarely seen such a mess.
2. Gladstone is often so hungry that he eats an entire cake.
3. He usually doesn't lose control.
4. We will never finish this project.
5. Steve seldom feels unhappy for very long.
6. Denise printed out the letter of complaint quickly and efficiently and sent it special delivery to Mr. Green.

FOCUS 5

Position of Adverbial Clauses

use

Most adverbial clauses appear after the main clause, but many can also come before the main clause.

EXAMPLES

(a) **As if it were the easiest thing in the world,** Biff did a triple backflip and ended with a handstand.

(b) **As soon as John got to the airport,** he began to have second thoughts about going to France.

(c) **Until Jeff moved to San Francisco,** he had never seen the ocean. He had never been to a disco or eaten Chinese food. He had never even fallen in love.

(d) **Whenever John thought about Mary,** he began to feel guilty. He would imagine her sitting sadly at home alone, writing him long letters. He felt that he wasn't missing her as much as she was missing him.

(e) I usually read the paper **before** I take a shower.

(f) **After** I read the paper, I usually take a shower.

(g) **If** you wash the dishes, **then** I'll dry them and put them away.

EXPLANATIONS

• to emphasize the adverbial clause

• to establish a context that applies to several sentences

• to show sequence

(Chart continued on next page)

ANSWER KEY

Exercise 7 1. *Rarely have I seen such a mess!* 2. *Often Gladstone is so hungry that he eats an entire cake.* 3. *Usually he doesn't lose control.* 4. *Never will we finish this project!* 5. *Seldom does Steve feel unhappy for very long.* 6. *Quickly and efficiently, Denise printed out the letter of complaint and sent it special delivery to Mr. Green.*

UNIT 3

LESSON PLAN 3

FOCUS 4 [20 minutes]

Focus 4 gives examples of adverbs and adverb phrases used at the beginning of sentences. However, students will see that there is a change in word order when placing the negative adverbs of frequency in the beginning of a sentence.

1. **Lead-in:** Put the awkward sentence (c) from the examples in Focus 4 on the board. Ask the class what is strange about this sentence. (Did the grandma knit the sweater while she was in the suitcase?) You may want to make up a few more awkward sentences.

2. Go over the examples and explanations in the charts. Explain that these are choices that writers make in order to make their sentences and paragraphs clearer.

3. For the section of the chart on negative adverbs of frequency, you may want to put examples on the board in order to give more practice for this difficult and less common structure:

    She rarely was late for work.

4. Circle the adverb to be moved. Now explain that the sentence will need to be changed to question word order (*she was* becomes *was she*) when a negative adverb of frequency is moved to the front of the sentence. Go through the changes on the board in steps until you have the final sentence (*Rarely was she late for work.*).

5. For more practice with this type of sentence put up a few more examples and have students make the necessary changes (note the changes in verb tense):

    She seldom spoke to anyone. (Seldom does she speak to anyone.)

    She has never missed a meeting. (Never has she missed a meeting.)

    He rarely calls his mother. (Rarely does he call his mother.)

    They seldom go to the theatre. (Seldom do they go to the theatre.)

    He never wanted to see her again. (Never did he want to see her again.)

EXERCISE 7 [10 minutes]

This will practice emphatic word order by moving adverbials to the beginning of sentences as explained in Focus 4. Have students complete this exercise immediately after covering Focus 4. Have them work individually and then compare answers with a partner. See answers on LP page 38.

For more practice, use *Grammar Dimensions 3* Workbook page 12, Exercise 6.

FOCUS 5 [20 minutes]

Focus 5 explains that some adverb clauses can occur at the beginning of a sentence for emphasis, to show a sequence or to establish context. These will take additional punctuation. Focus 5 also gives examples of adverb clauses that do not move to the beginning. Note that this focus is continued on SB page 40.

1. **Lead-in:** In order to prepare for Exercise 8, which follows, you may want to introduce Focus 5 by putting two category headings on the board: *Before Main Clause* and *After Main Clause.*

2. As you go through the three examples of putting an adverb clause **before** the main clause, write each reason under heading (*emphasis, establish context, show sequence*). Do the same for the three examples of putting the adverb clause **after** the main clause on SB page 40 (*adverb clauses of place, so that, for*).

3. Before turning to the last section of Focus 5 (punctuation, on SB page 40), have students look back at the examples on SB page 39 and note the

punctuation for them. Invite students to state the rule for this. Write this on the board. Look at the final section of Focus 5 as a class to check the rule.

4. Keep the two *Before* and *After* lists on the board to use in Exercise 8.

Certain adverbial clauses almost always appear after the main clause.

EXAMPLES	EXPLANATIONS
(h) Matt works out **where Biff works out.** (i) AWKWARD: **Where Biff works out,** Jeff works out. (j) **Wherever he goes,** Matt makes new friends and has wonderful adventures.	• adverbial clauses of place except those that begin with *wherever* or *everywhere*
(k) John worked all summer so (that) he would have enough money to study in France. (l) AWKWARD: **So that he would have enough money to study in France,** John worked all summer.	• adverbial clauses of result with *so that*
(m) Matt visited his grandmother for he knew she had been sick. (n) NOT: **For he knew she had been sick,** Matt visited his grandmother.	• adverbial clauses of reason with *for*

Punctuation of adverbial clauses depends on their position in a sentence.

EXAMPLES	EXPLANATIONS
(o) **After I took the examination,** I ate lunch. (p) I ate lunch after I took the examination. (q) **Since you don't have much money,** I'll pay for dinner. (r) I'll pay for dinner since you don't have much money.	Adverbial clauses before the main clause are followed by a comma. No extra punctuation is necessary if they appear after the main clause.

EXERCISE 8

Work with a partner to answer these questions about the sentences below. The first sentence has been done as an example.

a. Does the adverbial clause in these sentences appear before or after the main clause?

b. Decide which of the reasons listed in Focus 5 can be used to explain why the author chose to put the adverbial clauses in this order.

1. Because Biff enjoys vigorous exercise, he tends to pursue sports that build up his muscles.
   a. *before*   b. *to emphasize the adverbial clause*

2. On the other hand, Gladstone practices exercises like yoga because for him exercise is a means of relaxation.
   a. *after*   b. *order emphasizes the contrast introduced by "on the other hand"*

3. Both Biff and Gladstone want to lose weight because they want to feel and look better.
   a. *after*   b. *basic order—no special emphasis*

4. Because Mary Morris may have stopped her car too close to a newborn piglet, she became the victim of a bizarre attack.
   a. *before*   b. *emphasizes cause; underscores logical relation of cause and effect*

5. When the ski-mask robber entered the bank, he showed the teller a gun and demanded money.
   a. *before*   b. *follows the chronological order of events*

6. Columbia Savings and Loan had already been robbed three times when the ski-mask robber appeared yesterday.
   a. *after*   b. *basic order—no special emphasis*

7. The bank manager told the press about the robbery so that the public would become aware of the need for more security.
   a. *after*   b. *order expresses the logical relationship between cause and effect*

8. Since he first agreed to work on the project in 1985, he has spent more than twenty years trying to educate people about global warming.
   a. *before*   b. *follows the chronological order of events*

ANSWER KEY

Exercise 8   *There may be several possible explanations. Possible explanations are listed above.*

EXERCISE 8 [15 minutes]

Students will use the information in Focus 5 to identify the position and then explain the reasons for the placement of adverb clauses.

1. Go over the directions and the example. Refer to the lists of reasons you have on the board from Focus 5.

2. Have students work with a partner to identify and explain the placement of each adverb clause. You can also have students work individually and then discuss answers in a small group.

3. Go over this exercise with the class. Encourage students to share a variety of answers and discuss. See possible answers on LP page 40.

EXPANSION [30 minutes]

You may want to use Activity 3 (writing/speaking) on SB page 43 after this exercise.

UNIT GOAL REVIEW [10 minutes]

Ask students to look at the goals on the opening page of the unit again. Refer to the pages of the unit where information on each goal can be found.

ExamView®
Test Generator

For assessment of Unit 3, use *Grammar Dimensions 3 ExamView*®.

Use Your English

ACTIVITY 1 speaking/writing

■ STEP 1

Find out some basic information about another student in the class by asking some of the seven "Universal Questions" that were described in the Opening Task. Here are some suggested topics.

Who: name, family background
What: hobbies, special interests, plans for the future
Where: home town, current living situation
When: date of birth, date of arrival in this country, date of expected completion of English studies
How Long: length of time in this country, amount of previous English study
How Often: regular activities, hobbies
How Much: special skills, abilities, and interests
Why: reasons and goals for studying English, joining this class, leaving home

■ STEP 2

Report the information to the rest of the class in a short written paragraph or oral presentation.

ACTIVITY 2 speaking

An "ulterior motive" is a hidden reason for doing a good thing. For example, helping a friend who is in trouble is a good thing to do, but if your real reason for doing it is because you want that person to lend you money later, your motive may make your action a bad one.

■ STEP 1

In a small group discuss the following situations. For each situation identify some "pure motives"—reasons for doing the action that would make it a good or generous act—and some "ulterior motives"—hidden reasons that would make the act a selfish one.

- loaning someone money
- not telling a friend some bad news
- being friendly and obedient to a rich relative
- working harder than anyone else at your job

■ STEP 2

Based on your discussion decide whether people's actions should be judged by what they do (their actions) or why they do it (their motivations). Present your opinion and your reasons to the rest of the class.

ACTIVITY 3 writing/speaking

Which form of motivation is more common in your day-to-day activities: extrinsic motivation or intrinsic motivation?

Extrinsic motivation is **purpose**. You do something in order to achieve something else, such as studying business in order to get a high-paying job in the future.

Intrinsic motivation is **cause**. You do something because you like the activity itself, such as studying business because you love being a student and enjoy economic theory.

■ STEP 1

Decide whether your basic motivation for each of the activities listed below is extrinsic or intrinsic. Identify additional things you do because of intrinsic motivation. Make a four column chart in your notebook. In the first column in your chart, write three things you do because of intrinsic motivation.

studying English	watching TV	cleaning the house
driving a car	reading newspapers	doing homework
cooking	exercise	shopping

■ STEP 2

Interview three other students in the class to find out things they do because of intrinsic motivation. Write the information in the chart in your notebook. Use one column for each student.

■ STEP 3

Form a group with two or three other students whom you did not interview, and compare all the information you have gathered. As a group, decide on answers to the following question and present your ideas to the rest of the class.

What are the three most common characteristics shared by all things that people do because of intrinsic motivation? For example, do intrinsically motivated activities result in self-improvement? Are they pleasurable? Do people feel unhappy if they don't have an opportunity to pursue these activities?

USE YOUR ENGLISH

The Use Your English activities contain situations that should naturally elicit the structures covered in the unit. For a more complete discussion of how to use the Use Your English activities see To the Teacher on LP page xxii. When students are doing these activities in class, you can circulate and listen to see if they are using the structures accurately. Errors can be corrected after the activity has finished.

ACTIVITY 1

speaking/writing
[20 minutes]

You may want to use this activity after Exercise 1 on SB page 32 to continue practicing the formation of questions and answers.

■ STEP 1

1. Have students begin by using some of the topics listed to form interview questions. Circulate and assist as needed.

2. Put students into pairs or have them circulate around the room interviewing several classmates.

■ STEP 2
Give students time to put their notes into complete sentences. These can be turned into you for individual feedback or students can share with the class and you can use any common errors to give feedback to the class in general.

VARIATION

If students are already fairly familiar with each other, you can play the game of "Who am I?" Without letting the student see, tape, or pin the name of a famous person to the back of each student. Now, in order to discover the names on their backs, students must use the list of topics to prepare a list of questions that they will ask their classmates about themselves. For example, *Where was I born? When was*

I *born? What languages do I speak? What are my hobbies?* Students will ask all of their questions and then sit down and write down the name of the person they believe is noted on their back. Have students share their guesses with the class before they are told the truth. See how far off they are and what questions might have helped them.

ACTIVITY 2

speaking
[20 minutes]

This speaking activity gets students talking in groups. You may hear a variety of grammar used including adverbials of purpose.

Begin by putting the words *ulterior motives* and *pure motives* on the board. Use the example in the book and give a few other examples until the class understands the concepts. Better yet, set up a situation (giving money to a charity, bringing presents to your boss) and invite volunteers to suggest some ulterior and some pure motives.

■ STEP 1

1. Put students into small groups to discuss the listed situations.

2. Refer the class back to the examples you gave in the beginning.

■ STEP 2
Have the groups review their discussions. They may not be able to come to an agreement about judging others' actions. If not, have the class share a variety of opinions from all groups.

ACTIVITY 3

writing/speaking
[20 minutes/homework]

For this discussion activity, Step 1 can be assigned as homework. Students can then work on Steps 2 and 3 in class the next day.

Put the terms *extrinsic motivation* and *intrinsic motivation* on the board and give examples until the class understands their meanings.

■ STEP 1
Have students work on their own to read the chart and think about their own motivation for completing each of the tasks listed in it before making their own charts.

■ STEP 2
Have students move around the room talking to at least three other students and sharing a few of the things they put on their lists of intrinsically motivated activities with the class. They will be filling in their charts as they do this.

■ STEP 3

1. Ask students to get into groups with people they did not already talk with. They will discuss the questions and make some generalizations.

2. Have groups share their answers with the class or have students write up a short paragraph summarizing their discussion.

ACTIVITY 4 listening

CD Tracks 6, 7

STEP 1
Listen to the two recorded news broadcasts. Based on what you hear write as many questions as you can with *Who, What, Where, When Why* and *How* about each broadcast and give them to a partner to answer. You may need to listen to the broadcasts more than once in order to ask and answer the questions.

STEP 2
Compare your questions and answers with those of another pair of students. As a group try to write a summary of one of the news stories.

ACTIVITY 5 speaking

The world seems to be divided into two kinds of people: morning people (who do their best work early in the day) and night people (who are sleepy in the morning, and are most productive in the late afternoon or even late at night). Which kind are you? Interview a partner to find out which kind of person he or she is.

STEP 1
Find out **how** your partner does each activity in the chart below at the time of day listed. (Some examples have been provided.) Ask about two additional activities.

STEP 2
Decide on whether your partner is a morning person or a night person, and report your findings to the rest of the class.

WHAT? / WHEN?	EARLY MORNING: HOW?	AFTER LUNCH: HOW?	LATE AT NIGHT: HOW?
vigorous exercise	Slowly	Well, but not if he's hungry	Easily, but it keeps him awake
balancing your checkbook			
thinking up original ideas			
relaxed reading for pleasure			
concentrated reading for work or school			
social activity and conversation			

ACTIVITY 6 research on the web

Which means of weight control do you follow? The one used by Biff Bicep or the one used by Gladstone Gulp? Use *InfoTrac® College Edition*, to enter "diet and exercise" and scan a few articles to see which system the experts recommend for weight control. Prepare a list of the three advantages and three disadvantages of each approach and decide which one is most appropriate for your individual personality. Report your ideas to the rest of the class, or compare them with those of a partner.

ACTIVITY 7 language strategy

Language teachers recommend that students keep a journal or language learning log to record their progress, goals, and questions. Studies have proven that students who do this learn more quickly and effectively. Here is one example of a language learning log format. Fill out your log at least once a week during this course. Turn it in or discuss it with your teacher or with another student in the class.

> LANGUAGE LEARNING LOG
>
> Section 1. MISTAKES, CORRECTIONS, AND EXPLANATIONS
>
> Write down **five mistakes** that you made in either writing or speaking in the last week. For each mistake write the correct form. In your own words, explain what was wrong with your original sentence.
>
> **Examples:**   Mistake: *I exercise usually three times a week.*
>   Correction: *I usually exercise three times a week*
>   Explanation: *Usually must go before the verb.*
>
> Section 2. QUESTIONS
>
> Write **three questions** you have about any aspect of grammar that you have read, heard, or studied in the last week. Your teacher will return your journal with an explanation of your questions.
>
> **Examples:**   *Where do adverbial clauses usually appear?*
>   *How many adverbs can I use in a single sentence?*
>   *My friend said "Never have I seen such a mess!" Is that correct word order? Why does he use question word order?*

Activity 4 Answers will vary. Here are some possible questions. You should be able to determine the correct answers from the audio script.

Broadcast #1:   Who: Who toppled the government of Surinam? Who appeared on national television to announce the takeover?

What: What happened in Surinam? What did the coup leaders promise?

Where: Where did they announce the take-over? Where had normal holiday activities resumed?

When: When did the coup leaders say elections would be held? When did the coup take place?

Why: Why do people think that Desi Bouterse was responsible for the coup? Why did the U.S. and Dutch governments condemn the coup?

How: How did the coup take place? How was the change in government announced?

Broadcast #2:   Who: Who died yesterday? Who was Roosevelt Williams?

What: What did Williams die from? What was Williams known for?

Where: Where did he do his work? Where will memorial services be held?

When: When was he first diagnosed with AIDS? When will memorial services be held?

Why: Why was he well known? Why did some private organizations set up treatment programs?

How: How successful were his efforts at AIDS education? How did he help other people with AIDS?

USE YOUR ENGLISH

ACTIVITY 4 · listening
[25 minutes]

CD Tracks 6,7

This listening activity can be challenging for some classes. If so, you may want to just do one track rather than two. In this case, the second track focuses on only one person and may be a little easier for classes to create basic questions for.

STEP 1

1. Have students listen to the audio and write as many questions as they can. Remind them that they do not have to know the answers themselves as this point.

2. If you need to, play the audio again while students work again on creating questions. Remind them that they need to leave space for their partners' answers.

3. When they are ready, have students trade questions with a partner. Be sure that everyone reads and understands the questions before you play the audio again. Circulate as students look at their questions and encourage pairs to get clarification if needed. Look over the questions to get a general idea of what information students will be looking for.

4. Play the audio again, allowing time for students to answer questions. If possible, you may want to play the audio in parts. You may want to play it more than once.

STEP 2

1. When ready, put two pairs of students together to compare questions and answers.

2. If you have a very motivated class, they may want one last chance after the discussion to check their own and their classmates' answers.

3. Finally, answer any questions that students still are having trouble with as a class and put any difficult spellings or new vocabulary on the board.

You may also want to discuss where Surinam and the Bay Area are.

ACTIVITY 5 · speaking
[20 minutes]

This speaking activity can be used to expand on Exercise 5 on SB page 35. It can be done with a classmate or as an out of class survey.

STEP 1

1. After going over the directions, have students complete the interview in pairs.

2. If you have time, have students use a separate paper as they move around interviewing different classmates for Step 1.

STEP 2   You can do the reporting in Step 2 as a whole class activity or in smaller groups if you have a large class.

VARIATION

This can be used as a survey out of class. Have students interview people outside class about how they do the activities at each time of day. When finished, have students share their results in small groups. Are morning or night people more common? How about by age group? Which is more common?

ACTIVITY 6 · research on the web
[40 minutes/homework]

This activity encourages research and technology skills along with the reading skills of skimming and scanning for information. You may want to assign it after Exercise 3 on SB page 34.

1. Set this research assignment up by having small groups do a quick discussion of the weight control styles presented in the unit along with other ideas they may have used or have heard about from others.

2. Go over the assignment with the class and outline the number of approaches you would like them to compare in terms of advantages and disadvantages. Assign this either as a written report or an oral presentation and outline the length and any other guidelines.

3. If your students are not yet comfortable doing Internet research, go over the steps for using the *InfoTrac® College Edition* Web site.

4. When students are finished, you can have them report in pairs, small groups or to the whole class. If you are short on time, you can collect reports and give individual feedback.

ACTIVITY 7 · language strategy
[10 minutes]

This language log can be used throughout the term and students can turn it in to you each week. You can respond with written answers to each student or you can choose several questions each week to go over with the whole class in the next lesson. These can be a review as you begin the next week's lesson. These reflective language log entries help students focus on making progress in their development.

1. Go over the sample language log entries and have students set their own language log entries up in a similar way. They should have five entries like the example shown in *Section 1. MISTAKES* and three questions in *Section 2. QUESTIONS*.

2. If you have time after students have completed the activity, have them work in small groups to try and answer each other's questions before they turn it into you.

4

PASSIVE VERBS

UNIT GOALS

- **Review passive form and meaning**
- **Know when to include the agent**
- **Use *get* passives**
- **Choose between passive and active**

OPENING TASK

Has the Earth Been Visited by Beings from Outer Space?

Stonehenge is a circle of giant stones. It is located far away from anything else in the middle of a plain in southern England.

The Nazca Lines are a group of huge pictures drawn in the desert of western Peru that can only be seen from an airplane.

Certain structures around the world have very mysterious origins. Many people believe that these places are clear proof that beings from other planets have visited the Earth, because no one can explain exactly how or why they were constructed.

■ STEP 1

Two of the most famous of these mysterious structures are Stonehenge and the Nazca Lines. Read about one of them in the chart on the next page and then answer the questions.

How were they constructed?

STONEHENGE	THE NAZCA LINES
• The giant stones <u>were</u> transported from a great distance from an unknown place. • The stones are too heavy to be lifted upright or to be placed on top of each other. • A large number of people would probably <u>be required</u> to construct such a large structure, more people than were probably living in prehistoric Britain. • The distances between the stones are very precise, accurate to the millimeter.	• The pictures <u>can</u> only be seen from the air. The people who built the designs could not actually see them. • A large number of people would <u>be required to</u> construct such large pictures. There definitely isn't enough water for so many people there, because it is one of the driest places on earth. • The designs are very precise. One image is a perfect spiral, accurate to the millimeter.

Why were they constructed?

• Some stones seem to point to certain stars. • Some stones seem to have some connection with the position of the sun at certain times of year. • Some stones may have had some connection with human sacrifices.	• Some pictures seem to have some mathematical or geometrical meaning. • Some pictures represent flowers and animals that are not found anywhere near the location of the lines. • Some designs look like symbols that <u>are</u> used to direct modern aircraft.

When were they constructed?

• It <u>was</u> already <u>considered</u> to be a mysterious place when Britain <u>was occupied</u> by the Romans in the first century BCE. • There is no historical record of its construction.	• They weren't discovered until people started flying over the area in airplanes. • They predate Inca civilization by at least two thousand years.

■ STEP 2

Form a group consisting of one student who read about the same mysterious place as you did and two students who read about the other mysterious place. Compare your answers.

■ STEP 3

In your group discuss this question: Are these structures proof that the Earth has been visited by beings from some other planet? Why or why not? Share your ideas with the rest of the class.

LESSON PLAN 1

PASSIVE VERBS

UNIT OVERVIEW

Unit 4 reviews passive verb forms and meanings. The unit also gives practice in recognizing the agent and the receiver in a sentence, deciding when to include the agent, using the *get* passives, identifying verbs that have no passive forms, and choosing the passive versus the active voice.

GRAMMAR NOTE

Sentences in English are either active or passive. In a passive sentence, **the receiver**, not the agent, is the subject of a passive verb (example: **The cat was** chased by the dog.) The passive verb phrase is formed in English with **be + past participle**. The agent is then either not mentioned or introduced with **by + noun phrase.**

The passive can cause confusion because the receiver of an action is found in the subject position. Many students may depend on the importance of word order, which usually determines the agent and the receiver of a verb. However, altered word order for passive sentences can also cause confusion, as can the lack of an agent at all.

UNIT GOALS

Some instructors may want to review the goals listed on Student Book (SB) page 46 after completing the Opening Task so that students understand what they should know by the end of the unit. These goals can also be reviewed at the end of the unit when students are more familiar with the grammar terminology.

OPENING TASK [20 minutes]

The aim of this activity is to give the students the opportunity to use the form, meaning, and use of passive verbs as they consider some historical mysteries. The problem-solving format is designed to

show the teacher how well the students can produce a target structure implicitly and spontaneously when they are engaged in a communicative task. For a more complete discussion of the purpose of the Opening Task, see Lesson Planner (LP) page xxii.

Setting Up the Task

1. Ask students to look at the question above the pictures on SB page 46. Ask students to share whether they believe that the Earth has been visited by beings from outer space.

2. Now have the class look at the pictures on page 46 and read the captions for each one. Ask the class to share any knowledge they may already have about either of these places.

STEP 1

Assign half the class to read the purple column about Stonehenge on SB page 47. Assign the other half to read the orange column about the Nazca Lines. Ask each half to try to answer the three questions regarding *how, why,* and *when* their structure was constructed.

Conducting the Task

1. As students work, go around and make note of any difficulties students are having.

2. Offer help with vocabulary when needed and write any new or useful vocabulary on the board.

3. As you circulate, get an idea of students' current use and familiarity with the passive. Do they seem to understand the use of the passive in the reading? Are they attempting to use the passive in their writing? Note any common errors.

STEP 2

As students finish, put them into groups consisting of students from the Stonehenge group and from the Nazca Lines group. Ask them to compare answers.

STEP 3

1. As groups compare their answers, circulate through the classroom noting how comfortable students are using the passive voice in their discussions.

2. As groups finish comparing answers, write the following on the board: *Are these structures proof that the Earth has been visited by beings from some other planet? Why or why not?* Ask groups to discuss.

Closing the Task

Bring the class together and allow students to share any last thoughts on the final question on the board along with any interesting differences they found between the two structures. Listen for use of the passive.

EXPANSION [60 minutes/homework]

Assign the Activity 2 (writing) on SB page 62 as a follow-up to the Opening Task.

GRAMMAR NOTE

Typical student errors (form)

- Omitting the *-ed* from the regular past participle verbs: * *She was bother by the noise.*
- Omitting the *be* auxiliary: * *The Nazca Lines might destroyed by roads.*
- Problems with the irregular past participles: * *blowed* * *chose* * *waken*
- Misspelling the past participle form: * *written* * *riden* * *drawen*
- Problems forming questions (moving the auxiliary): * *When were built the Pyramids?* (See Focus 1.)

Typical student errors (use)

- Use of intransitive verbs in passive sentences: * *The aliens were disappeared long ago.* * *She was arrived last week.* (See Focus 5.)

FOCUS 1 Review of Passive Verb Forms

form

EXAMPLES

(a) The Nazca Lines **were discovered** by airplane pilots.

(b) They **weren't discovered** until the 1930s.

(c) How **were** such huge designs **built**?

(d) Stonehenge **was** constructed of rocks that came from many miles away.

(e) The Nazca Lines **were** made by removing soil and rocks to expose the different-colored soil underneath.

(f) Stonehenge **was** constructed long before Britain **was** invaded by the armies of Rome.

(g) The Nazca Lines **weren't** discovered until the 1930s because they **weren't** seen by people on the ground.

(h) Mysterious structures **are** found in a number of places in the world.

(i) Some **were** discovered this century.

(j) Perhaps the reasons for their existence **will be** discovered with further research.

(k) Many theories explaining their existence **have been** proposed.

(l) While they **were being** built, civilization was still very young.

(m) The Nazca Lines **may be** destroyed, if further protection **can't be** provided.

(n) Preservation efforts for all such mysterious structures **ought to be** started without delay.

(o) Both Stonehenge and the Nazca Lines **might have been** used to predict astronomical events.

EXPLANATIONS

be + past participle (+ *by* phrase)

Form all passive verbs in the same way. Only the *be* auxiliary changes form. There is often no information about who or what performed the action, but when there is, it appears as a *by* phrase.

Change *be* auxiliary to indicate:

• singular or plural

• affirmative or negative

• time frame (*present, past, future*) and aspect (*simple, perfect, progressive*)

• modal information (*prediction, ability, advisability, possibility*, etc.)

EXERCISE 1

Find eight examples of passive verb forms in the information provided on page 47 and underline them. Decide whether each form is:

a. singular or plural

b. affirmative or negative

c. present, past, or future time frame

d. simple, perfect, or progressive aspect

EXERCISE 2

Write the passive forms for the verbs provided below.

Example: construct (singular, present progressive) _is being constructed_

1. forget (plural, past perfect) _have been forgotten_

2. establish (singular, simple past) _was established_

3. manufacture (singular, simple present) _is manufactured_

4. obtain (singular, simple present) _is obtained_

5. require (plural, simple future) _will be required_

6. discover (plural, present perfect) _have been discovered_

7. make (singular, present progressive) _is being made_

8. leave (plural, past perfect) _had been left_

9. build (singular, simple past) _was built_

10. produce (singular, simple present) _is produced_

11. send (singular, future perfect) _will have been sent_

12. notice (plural, past progressive) _were being noticed_

13. need (singular, simple future) _will be needed_

14. forget (plural, present perfect) _have been forgotten_

15. study (plural, present progressive) _are being studied_

ANSWER KEY

Exercise 1 *See student page 47 for underlines. The passive verb forms are as follows: Stonehenge: were transported: plural, affirmative, past, simple; would be required: plural, affirmative, present, simple; was considered: singular, affirmative, past, simple; was occupied: singular, affirmative, past, simple The Nazca Lines: can be seen: pural, affirmative, present, simple; would be required: plural, affirmative, present, simple; are used: plural, affirmative, present, simple; weren't discovered: plural, negative, past, simple*

FOCUS 1 [20 minutes]

This focus reviews the passive verb forms. In the passive, the *be* auxiliary is shown to change in order to indicate singular/plural, affirmative/negative, time frame, aspect, and modal information.

1. **Lead-in:** Write the following sentences on the board:

   The Nazca Lines were created long ago.
   The Nazca Lines were discovered by airplane pilots.
   Some people think that Stonehenge was built by aliens.

2. Point out to the class that these are passive sentences. Underline the *be* auxiliary and the passive verb (*were created, were discovered, was built*).

3. Explain that in a passive sentence we often don't know who or what performed the action as in the first sentence. However, when we do know, we use a *by* phrase to show who performed the action as in the second and third sentences.

4. Have the class look at the sentences on the board from the Opening Task. Ask volunteers to point out which sentences use the passive construction.

5. Now write the following sentence on the board underlining the passive construction:
   The food is made in the kitchen.

6. Tell the class that the *be* auxiliary is very important in forming the passive because it will indicate singular/plural, affirmative/negative, time frame, aspect, and modal information.

7. Ask volunteers to take turns changing the new sentence on the board to different tenses and to use different aspects. For example: *was made, will be made, is being made,* etc.

8. Next, ask volunteers to change the sentence into the negative. Now suggest a few modals for volunteers to try adding to the original sentence on the board.

9. Go over Focus 1 on SB page 48. Note how the *be* auxiliary changes.

EXERCISE 1 [10 minutes]

Exercise 1 asks students to practice identifying examples of the passive verb forms in preparation to constructing them in Exercise 2. Students will look at the form of the passive.

1. Have students turn to SB page 47 again and have a student volunteer name one example of a passive verb form. Write the example on the board.

2. Now ask the class to decide whether this form is:
   singular or plural,
   affirmative or negative
   present, past, or future
   simple, perfect, progressive

3. Do as many examples together as a class as you feel necessary. For example:
   were transported = plural/affirmative/past/simple

   Ask the class to then find the remaining examples of passive verbs on SB page 47 from either the purple or the orange side and list the same points for each passive.

4. Let pairs check their answers together. Circulate to see how well students broke down the verbs into tense, aspect, etc. Keep a few examples on one side of the board to use in Exercise 2. See answers on LP page 48.

EXERCISE 2 [15 minutes]

This exercise builds on the work in Exercise 1 by asking students to add singular/plural, tense, and aspect to create passive forms for each verb.

1. Refer to one of the examples from Exercise 1. Tell the class that they will be working in the opposite direction to form verbs from the characteristics given. Tell the class that instead of deciding what tense and aspect a passive form is already in, they will now create a passive with an assigned tense and aspect.

2. Use one of the examples from Exercise 1. Write up an example of the passive as it appears in Exercise 2 on the other side of the board. For example:

Exercise 1:	Exercise 2:
were transported = plural/affirmative/past/simple	*transport (plural, simple past)* = *were transported*

3. Have the class now look at the example for Exercise 2 on SB page 49. Invite a volunteer to change this example to **plural**. Now ask another volunteer to change the example to **past progressive**. Call out a few more changes and ask volunteers to apply them to this example verb.

4. Have students work individually to complete Exercise 2. As they finish, have them check their work with a partner before going over the correct answers as a class. See answers on LP page 48.

For more practice, use *Grammar Dimensions 3 Workbook* page 13, Exercises 1 and 2.

EXPANSION [10 minutes]

You may want to review and reinforce the irregular past participle forms by creating a quick competition.

1. Divide the class into several teams. This depends on the size of your class.

2. Have each team decide on a team name and on a writer for their group.

3. Tell the class that you will call out the base form of a verb and that the team must decide on the past participle, which the writer will write down. When done, the team will raise their hands. The first team to get the correct past participle wins a point. Teams may want to rotate their writer as the game goes.

meaning

FOCUS 2

Passive Meaning: Agent Versus Receiver

Agent and Receiver in Active Sentences

SUBJECT	ACTIVE VERB	OBJECT	EXPLANATION
agent	action	receiver	The agent is the doer of an action. The receiver is the person or thing that is affected by the action. In active sentences the agent is the subject of the sentence. The receiver is the object.
(a) An employee	found	a wallet outside the office.	

Agent and Receiver in Passive Sentences

SUBJECT	PASSIVE VERB	(BY + NOUN PHRASE)	EXPLANATION
receiver	action	(agent)	In passive sentences the receiver is the subject and the agent is often not mentioned. When it is included, it occurs in a prepositional phrase with by.
(b) A wallet	was found outside the office.		
(c) The wallet	was found	by an employee.	

EXERCISE 6

Read the article on page 52 about the Nazca Lines. Underline all the passive constructions that you find. For each example of the passive that you can find, circle the receiver. If the **agent** is mentioned, draw a square around it. The first sentence of each paragraph has been done as an example.

EXERCISE 3

Use the information provided below to construct passive sentences.

Example: The Chinese invented gunpowder.

Gunpowder ___was invented___ in China.

1. Pakistanis speak Urdu, Punjabi, Sindhi, Baluchi, Pashtu, and English.

   Urdu, Punjabi, Sindhi, Baluchi, Pashtu, and English ___are spoken___ in Pakistan.

2. The people of Sri Lanka have mined gems for centuries.

   For centuries gems ___have been mined___ in Sri Lanka.

3. The French consider snails a great delicacy.

   Snails ___are considered___ a great delicacy in France.

4. People throughout Asia eat rice.

   Rice ___is eaten___ throughout Asia.

5. Argentineans consume more beef per capita than in any other country.

   More beef ___is consumed___ per capita in Argentina than in any other country.

6. Ancient Egyptians worshiped cats.

   Cats ___were worshipped___ in ancient Egypt.

7. The Japanese have developed a new system of high-resolution television.

   A new system of high-resolution television ___has been developed___ in Japan.

8. Americans invented the games of baseball and basketball.

   The games of baseball and basketball both ___were invented___ in America.

EXERCISE 4

Working with a partner, make up five additional passive sentences about products or accomplishments of a national or cultural group that you are familiar with.

EXERCISE 5

Choose eight verbs from Exercise 2. Make an original passive sentence for each verb.

Exercise 4 Answers will vary. Possible answers are: Batik is made in Indonesia. The best batik is produced by hand. The cloth is painted with wax and then it is dyed. The cloth is used for clothing and decoration. It is exported to many other countries.

Exercise 5 Answers will vary. Possible answers are: 1. The origins of the Nazca Lines have been forgotten. 2. Golden Gate University was established in 1901. 3. Batik is manufactured in Indonesia. 4. Lapis lazuli is obtained in Afghanistan. 5. Students will be required to take a test before they can enter the university. 6. New treatments for AIDS have been discovered in the last year. 7. Candy is being made next door. 8. The wallet had been left by mistake. 9. This house was built in 1952. 10. Oil is produced in many Middle Eastern countries. 11. By the time you get here, the results will have been sent to your office. 12. The symptoms were being noticed even before we went to the doctor. 13. More time will be needed if we want to do a good job. 14. We have been forgotten. 15. New designs for a bridge are being studied by the commission.

UNIT 4

LESSON PLAN 1/LESSON PLAN 2

EXERCISE 3 [10 minutes]

1. Write the following sentences on the board:

   Ben Franklin invented the lightening rod.
   The lightening rod _____ by Ben Franklin.

2. Tell students that they will now need to decide what the verb will be for the second sentence and then decide what the number, tense, and aspect will be in order to create a passive verb form.

3. Ask a volunteer to say what the verb will be for the example on the board. Ask another volunteer to say whether the verb should be singular or plural. Now ask someone to suggest the tense and aspect for this sentence.

4. At this point, you might ask a volunteer to come up to the board and write in the missing passive verb for the example. If this is not the correct answer, let another student come up and fix it.

5. Now either walk through the first sentences together as a class or have students complete Exercise 3 and check their answers together in pairs. See answers on LP page 50.

For more practice, use *Grammar Dimensions 3* Workbook page 14, Exercise 3.

EXERCISE 4 [10 minutes]

1. Take a few minutes to discuss the content of the sentences in Exercise 3 that are about the customs and accomplishments of different cultures.

2. You may want to put students from similar countries together to discuss the products or accomplishments of their own national or cultural groups.

3. If students need help coming up with ideas, encourage them to decide on a country or culture and then write about accomplishments or products using the following verbs as examples: *invent, develop, discover, build, make, manufacture, produce.*

4. When they are done, put groups or pairs together to share their sentences.

5. If you have time, you may want to ask a few volunteers to put their sentences on the board for examples. See possible answers on LP page 50.

For more practice, use *Grammar Dimensions 3* Workbook page 14, Exercise 4; and page 15, Exercise 5.

EXERCISE 5 [10 minutes/homework]

Exercise 5 can be done either in class or as a homework assignment. Sentences can be shared in class by asking students to write their most interesting sentence on the board, or they can be shared in groups. You may want to collect these sentences and give individual feedback on the form and use of the passive before continuing on with the unit. See possible answers on LP page 50.

For more practice, use *Grammar Dimensions 3* Workbook page 14, Exercise 3.

LESSON PLAN 2

FOCUS 2 [20 minutes]

This focus reviews the concepts of agent versus receiver. This is important to review in order to make sure that all students understand the difference between the subject of a sentence and the agent of an action. See the Grammar Note in the Chapter Overview on LP page 47.

1. **Lead-in:** Write the following sentences on the board (you may choose to write both the subjects in one color and both the objects in another color):

   The dog chased the tiger.
   The tiger chased the dog.

2. Point out that in these sentences the noun before the verb is the subject. These are **active** sentences and the subject is the **agent** or **doer** of the action. Now point out that the object in each of these active sentences is also the receiver of the action.

In these active sentences, we look at the **word order** to determine who is doing the action and who is receiving the action.

3. Now write the following sentence on the board:

   The cat was chased up a tree.

   Ask the class who the agent or doer of the action is now. At this point, you can point out that in a passive sentence the agent is often not mentioned. However, the receiver is placed before the verb in the subject position in a passive sentence.

4. Have the class look at the charts in Focus 2. The first chart illustrates the position of agent and receiver in an active sentence. The second chart illustrates the position of agent and receiver in a passive sentence. Tell students to note that the subject is simply a **position** in the sentence. The subject position holds the agent in an active sentence and the receiver in a passive sentence (the agent may or may not be mentioned in a passive sentence).

EXERCISE 6 [10 minutes]

1. Ask the class to look at the reading on SB page 52. Have a volunteer read the first sentence out loud.

2. Ask the class what passive constructions are in this sentence, then to point out the receiver of these verbs. They will notice that the passive is underlined and the receiver is circled.

3. Now ask students to look for an agent of these passive constructions. They will notice that the agent is in a square.

4. Move on to sentence (2). As you ask the class to find these structures again, have them underline the passive before marking the receiver (circle) and agent (square). Do sentence (2) together as a class. Have students work alone to finish the reading.

5. Have students work together to compare their answers. See answers on LP page 52.

For more practice, use *Grammar Dimensions 3* Workbook page 15, Exercise 6.

THE MYSTERY OF THE NAZCA LINES

(1) The Nazca Lines were not discovered until the 1930s, when they were first noticed by airplane pilots flying over Peru's Atacama Desert. (2) They consist of huge pictures, several kilometers in size, that were drawn in the desert. (3) They portray such things as birds, spiders, and abstract geometrical designs. (4) These pictures were made more than three thousand years ago by removing stones and dirt over large areas to expose the differently colored soil beneath.

(5) The amazing thing about the Nazca Lines is that none of these pictures can be seen by people on the ground. (6) They are so huge that they can only be seen from a great height. (7) The pictures were constructed with amazing precision. (8) How such measurements were made still hasn't been satisfactorily explained. (9) It seems impossible that the primitive construction techniques that existed three thousand years ago could have been used to create such gigantic, perfectly constructed designs.

(10) Why were these gigantic pictures made? (11) Were they intended as gifts for the gods, as some people have suggested? (12) Or, as others believe, were they created as "direction signs" for visitors from other planets? (13) No one knows. (14) One thing is known: The reasons and methods of their construction have been destroyed by time, but the pictures have been preserved for at least two thousand—and maybe even three thousand—years!

EXERCISE 7

Write one active sentence and one passive sentence for each set of agent, receiver, and verb.

Example: **Agent:** the maid; **Receiver:** the money; **Verb:** find
active: The maid found the money.
passive: The money was found by the maid.

1. **Agent:** pilots; **Receiver:** the Nazca Lines; **Verb:** discover
2. **Agent:** Ancient Romans; **Receiver:** Stonehenge; **Verb:** can not explain
3. **Agent:** Lee Harvey Oswald; **Receiver:** John F. Kennedy; **Verb:** assassinate
4. **Agent:** beings from outer space; **Receiver:** the Earth; **Verb:** visit
5. **Agent:** parents; **Receiver:** their children; **Verb:** teach good manners
6. **Agent:** society; **Receiver:** social minorities; **Verb:** discriminate against

---

FOCUS 3

When to Include the Agent

Because we most often use passive verbs to describe situations when the agent is not the primary focus, we usually do not include the agent (*by* + noun phrase) in passive sentences. However, sometimes it is necessary to include the agent.

EXAMPLES	EXPLANATIONS
	Include the agent:
(a) Many important scientific discoveries have been made **by women.**	• when the agent gives us additional new information.
(b) Radioactivity, for example, was discovered **by Marie Curie** in 1903.	• when information about the agent is too important to omit.
(c) This music was written **by a computer.**	• when the agent is surprising or unexpected.
(d) That picture was painted **by a monkey.**	

EXERCISE 8

Identify the agent in each of these sentences and decide if it is necessary. Correct any sentences by omitting unnecessary *by* phrases.

Example: That symphony was written by a composer in the nineteenth century.
Not necessary. (*That symphony was written in the nineteenth century.*)

1. The Nazca Lines were constructed by an unknown civilization approximately two thousand years ago.

2. The lesson was assigned by the teacher for next week.

3. This picture was painted by Picasso when Picasso was 12 years old.

4. My briefcase was taken by someone, but it was found and turned in to the Lost and Found Office by someone in my English class.

5. Many foreign students don't need scholarships because they are being supported by friends or relatives.

6. I would never guess that these poems were translated by children.

Exercise 7 Answers may vary. Possible answers are: 1. active: Pilots discovered the Nazca Lines in the 1930s. passive: The Nazca Lines were first discovered by pilots who flew over the area in the 1930s. 2. active: Ancient Romans couldn't explain the origin of Stonehenge. passive: Stonehenge couldn't be explained by the ancient Romans. 3. active: Lee Harvey Oswald assassinated John F. Kennedy. passive: John F. Kennedy was assassinated by Lee Harvey Oswald. 4. active: Beings from outer space have visited the Earth. passive: The Earth has been visited by beings from outer space. 5. active: Parents should teach their children good manners. passive: Children should be taught good manners by their parents. 6. active: Society often discriminates against social minorities. passive: Social minorities are often discriminated against by society.

Exercise 8 1. Not necessary. 2. Not necessary. 3. Not necessary. 4. Not necessary/Necessary. (second agent cannot be deleted—by someone in my English class is important information.) 5. Necessary. (agent cannot be deleted) 6. Necessary. (agent cannot be deleted)

LESSON PLAN 2

EXERCISE 7 [10 minutes]

Exercise 7 gives further practice in recognizing active versus passive sentences by asking students to take the same agent, receiver, and verb and to write both an active and a passive sentence for each group.

1. Keeping the active sentence on one side of the board and the passive sentence on the other side of the board, write the example sentences for Exercise 7 on the board using different colors to represent the agent and the receiver.

Active	*Passive*
The maid found the money.	*The money was found by the maid.*

2. Now ask the class to make active and passive sentences for sentence (1). Have volunteers write a sentence on the board in the appropriate column.

3. Have the class finish Exercise 7 individually and then compare answers with a partner. Circulate and make note of any errors or confusion students may have to address in debriefing. See possible answers on LP page 52.

FOCUS 3 [10 minutes]

Focus Chart 3 gives examples of when to include the agent in passive sentences. The agent is included when it gives new, important, or surprising information.

1. **Lead-in:** Have students close their books. Tell the class that sometimes a passive sentence has a *by* phrase telling us who the agent is and sometimes it doesn't. Ask them why we leave the agent out sometimes and when we need to include it. Write student ideas on the board.

2. Have students open books to SB page 53 and ask a volunteer to read the first example sentence in Focus Chart 3. Ask the class why this agent is important.

3. Continue in the same way with the next three example sentences.

4. Compare the explanations in the focus chart with those suggested by the students in the lead-in.

EXERCISE 8 [10 minutes]

This exercise focuses on finding the agent of a passive sentence and letting students make decisions about whether to include or omit the agent.

1. Have the class look at the example and suggest reasons why the agent should be omitted from this sentence.

2. Put students into pairs. Ask them to find the agent in each sentence and discuss together whether it should be kept or omitted.

3. Circulate through the class and listen to pairs present reasons to keep or omit the agent of each sentence. Some sentences are more controversial than others. Allow students time to discuss these together.

4. When they are finished, ask the class which sentences created the most discussion or confusion. Write these numbers on the board. As you address these sentences, ask the class to first volunteer any reasons to omit the agent. After listing these, ask for any reasons to keep the agent. Go over all the answers together. See answers on LP page 52.

For more practice, use *Grammar Dimensions 3* Workbook page 16, Exercises 7 and 8.

FOCUS 4

The *Get* Passive

form

use

Forming the *Get* Passive

EXAMPLES	EXPLANATIONS
(a) Matt rides to work with a neighbor who works nearby. He **gets picked up** at the bus stop every morning. (b) Matt **gets dropped off** in front of his office. (c) He **should be getting picked up** in a few minutes.	In spoken or informal English, we can use *get* instead of *be* as the passive auxiliary.
(d) **Did** Matt **get picked up** yesterday? (e) He **didn't get dropped off** at the usual place. (f) He **might not have gotten picked up** by the usual person.	Questions and negatives require *do* if the verb phrase does not contain a form of *be* or a modal auxiliary.

Using *Get* Passive Sentences

EXAMPLES	EXPLANATIONS
(g) George W. Bush **was elected** president by the electoral college after the Supreme Court ruled in his favor in 2000. (h) He **got elected** even though he did not get a majority of the popular vote. (i) The hospital **was built** in the 1930s. (j) NOT: The hospital **got built** in the 1930s.	The *get* passive is more common with animate (living) subjects, than with inanimate (nonliving) ones.
(k) Mariko **got married** last Saturday. (l) She **has** never **been married** before.	The *get* passive emphasizes the action rather than the state.

EXERCISE 9

Decide whether *be* or *get* is more appropriate in these sentences. Sometimes either form could be correct.

Examples: North America ___was___ settled by several European countries.

John's car ___got/was___ damaged, so he had to take public transportation.

1. The Nazca Lines ___were___ discovered in the 1930s.

2. Charlie ___got/was___ arrested on his way home from the football game.

3. New medicines are ___being___ developed that seem effective in fighting cancer.

4. That's really dangerous. If your leg ___gets___ broken, don't blame me.

5. I don't think John and Mary will ever ___get___ married. They're too different.

6. Don't put that fish in the same aquarium with the others. It might ___get/be___ eaten by the larger ones.

LESSON PLAN 2

FOCUS 4 [10 minutes]

The informal *get* passive is shown in Focus Chart 3. You may want to remind students that the *get* passive is generally found in informal, spoken English and it emphasizes the action.

1. **Lead-in:** Write the following sentences on the board.

   She got fired from her job last week.
   He got hit by a ball at the game.
   I got locked out of my apartment.
   Dave will get picked up at 10:00.

2. Ask the class what is different about these passives. (They all use *get* instead of the *be* verb.) Explain that sometimes we can use a *get* passive when we are speaking informally with someone. We don't usually use the *get* passive when we write or speak formally. In fact, we probably wouldn't hear the *get* passive on the news or see it in formal writing. It is also usually used for action verbs (in many cases a negative action, but not always).

3. Now ask the class how to make questions out of these sentences. Have students volunteer and write answers/suggestions on the board. Let the class suggest corrections.

   Did she get fired?
   Did he get bit?
   Did you get locked out?
   Will Dave get picked up?

4. Go over Focus 4 on SB page 54 with the class.

EXERCISE 9 [10 minutes]

This exercise asks students to consider whether a sentence or situation requires a *be* passive or whether it might also allow for a *get* passive.

1. Go over the examples with the class and ask volunteers to describe the differences between the two example sentences. Have students explain why the *get* passive is not suggested for the first example.

2. Let students work in pairs to decide whether *be* or *get* is better suited for each sentence. See answers on LP page 54.

For more practice, use *Grammar Dimensions 3* Workbook page 17, Exercise 9.

FOCUS 5

Special Cases: Verbs with No Passive Forms and Other Verbs with No Active Forms

EXAMPLES

(a) Few changes **have occurred** at Stonehenge over the years.

(b) The discovery of the Nazca Lines **happened** in the 1930s.

(c) Some Nazca lines **seem** to be in the shape of flowers.

(d) The purpose of the Nazca lines **has disappeared** under the sands of the Atacama Desert.

(e) NOT: A ceremonial function was had by these pictures.

(f) NOT: Some animals are resembled by the pictures.

(g) The drawing of the Nazca lines
| began
| was begun | more than 2000 years ago.

(h) Jeff **was born** in Kansas.

(i) NOT: Jeff's mother **bore** him in Kansas.

(j) The Nazca Lines **are located** (exist) in the Atacama Desert of Peru.

(k) They **located** (found) the Atacama Desert on a map.

EXPLANATIONS

Some verbs don't have a passive form because they do not take direct objects. This category includes verbs such as:

occur, happen, take place . . .

appear, seem, look . . .
emerge, vanish, disappear, appear . . .

Even verbs that take objects, when they describe states, do not occur in the passive.

Some verbs describe changes of state and can occur in the active in the past with a passive meaning.

A few passive verbs do not have active forms.

Some passive verbs have different meanings in passive and active.

EXERCISE 10

Here is a list of some verbs that do not have passive forms. Choose five verbs and write a sentence for each one. Compare your sentences with those of other students.

appear	consist of	seem	look	occur
take place	resemble	happen	collide	emerge
disappear	vanish			

FOCUS 6

Choosing Passive Versus Active

The active voice is more common than the passive, but in some situations, the passive form should be used.

EXAMPLES

(a) Denise's computer **was stolen** from her office.

(b) The new library **was finished** about a year ago.

(c) I had an accident yesterday. This other car went through a red light and hit me. My car **was** completely **destroyed.**

(d) Did you hear the news? Matt **was injured** slightly in the earthquake, but Jeff was O.K.

(e) Passengers **are asked** to refrain from smoking.

(f) The audience **will be encouraged** to participate.

(g) Something **should be done** about the drug problem.

(h) The present perfect tense **is used** to describe actions in the past that are related to the present in some way.

(i) Water **is formed** by combining hydrogen and oxygen.

EXPLANATIONS

Use passive instead of active:

• if the agent is unknown.

• if the agent is not the focus.

• if the agent is obvious from context.

• to focus on the receiver.

• to make general explanations, statements and announcements, or in scientific and technical writing.

EXERCISE 11

Why do you think the author used passive verbs in the following sentences? There may be more than one possible reason.

Example: No one is permitted to enter the office while the votes are being counted.
general announcement

1. Reagan was first elected president of the United States in 1980.

2. There is a lot of controversy about the Nazca Lines, especially about why they were built and how they were constructed.

3. They weren't even noticed until people started flying over the area in planes.

4. Was it John's brother who got arrested at the demonstration?

5. The house was broken into while the family was away.

ANSWER KEY

Exercise 10 Answers will vary. Possible answers are: John appeared suddenly./America consists of 50 states./This seems easy./She looks sad./A strange thing occurred at the party./It took place at the party./Jack resembles his mother./It happened at the laundromat./The car collided with the bus./A problem emerged./Patty disappeared./The bridge vanished in the fog.

Exercise 11 1. agent is obvious from context/agent is not the focus   2. agent is unknown/to make a general explanation   3. to emphasize receiver   4. to emphasize receiver/agent is obvious from context   5. agent is unknown

PASSIVE VERBS

FOCUS 5 [10 minutes]

Focus 5 illustrates examples of several special cases for the passive, which includes verbs that do not take the passive and verbs that have a different meaning in the passive.

1. **Lead-in:** You may want to make several lists of verbs that do not take the passive (because they do not take an object) or those that have no active forms (i.e., *was born*). Focus 5 has begun some of these for you (occur, happen, appear, seem, emerge, vanish, etc.). You may want to add to these lists.

2. Put these lists on the board or an overhead transparency. Ask the class to think about what defines each group. For example, what is similar about the verbs *appear, seem,* and *look?*

3. Remind the class that these lists are not complete and that they will simply need to learn the special cases as they come across them.

EXERCISE 10 [10 minutes]

Exercise 10 reinforces a list of verbs that do **not** take the passive.

1. Review the examples (a–d) in Focus 5. Ask the class if they can think of other verbs that do not take an object.

2. As the class works on Exercise 10, circulate and assist as needed. Tell students to use their dictionaries for any verbs that are unfamiliar, but remind them to create their own original sentences. Take note of these unfamiliar verbs for debriefing.

3. Let students share sentences in pairs. Based on your earlier observations, ask some students to put sentences on the board to share with the class. Again, remind the class that these are verbs that do not take an object and do not use the passive. See possible answers on LP page 56.

For more practice, use *Grammar Dimensions 3* Workbook page 17, Exercise 10.

EXPANSION [20 minutes]

You may want to use Activity 4 on SB page 62 after this exercise.

FOCUS 6 [10 minutes]

This focus explains when a passive might be used instead of the active voice. The examples and explanations in this focus chart will be very useful for reference, since the next few exercises will require students to explain why an author chose to use passive verbs.

1. **Lead-in:** Write the following sentences on the board and ask the class to think about why the passive is used in each sentence rather than the active voice.

My car was hit.
Only one prize was awarded this year.
Several people were arrested.
His leg was broken in the accident.
Cars will be towed from the reserved parking spaces.
A giant squid was found near Australia.

As students volunteer reasons for the passive in each example on the board, write notes next to each sentence.

2. When finished, as a class, go through the examples in Focus 6 on SB page 57. Ask volunteers to read each example sentence and the explanation for the use of the passive. Then ask the class if there is a similar example on the board. Continue through the list of examples, answering any questions as you go.

EXERCISE 11 [10 minutes]

This exercise asks students to focus on the use of the passive by explaining the reasons an author chose to use the passive. This exercise helps students to be able to talk about the choices writers make.

1. Ask the class to look at the example sentence and the reason given. Tell students that they may choose reasons from the right-hand column of Focus Chart 6 above for each of the sentences in Exercise 11. Remind them that there may be more than one reason for choosing the passive.

2. Have students work individually. When they finish, have them compare answers with a partner or in a small group.

3. Bring the class together and have volunteers explain a reason or reasons for using a passive to the class. See answers on LP page 56.

For more practice, use *Grammar Dimensions 3* Workbook page 18, Exercise 11.

EXPANSION [10 minutes]

Reinforce the explanations in Focus 6 by having students work in pairs to make their own example sentences for each explanation.

1. Put students into pairs and draw their attention again to the right-hand column of the Focus 6 chart. Ask students to work together to make up their own examples for each of these explanations.

2. Divide the board up into five sections with a brief heading for each based on the five general explanations.

3. Circulate around the classroom looking for good examples for each general explanation. Choose students to put specific sentences on the board.

4. Finish with a quick review of Focus 6.

EXERCISE 13

Decide whether active or passive forms should be used in these sentences, and write the correct form in the blank. There may be more than one correct choice.

The age of pyramid-building in Egypt (1) _____began_____ (begin) about 2900 BCE. The great pyramids (2) _were intended_ (intend) to serve as burial places for the Pharaohs, as the kings of Egypt (3) _were called_ (call). Construction on the largest pyramid (4) _started / was started_ (start) around 2800 BC for Khufu, the King of the Fourth Dynasty, or Cheops, as he (5) _is referred to_ (refer to) by Greek historians. It (6) ___is___ (be) 482 feet high and 755 feet long. The Pyramids as a group (7) _comprise_ (comprise) one of the Seven Wonders of the Ancient World. The other Six Wonders no longer (8) ___stand___ (stand), and modern archaeologists (9) ___know___ (know) of them only through the descriptions that (10) _were written_ (write) at the time they still (11) ___existed___ (exist).

EXERCISE 12

Read this excerpt from an introductory sociology textbook. Choose one paragraph, and underline all the passive constructions that you find. With a partner, decide why the author chose to use passive constructions.

> ### CHAPTER 3 SOCIAL MINORITIES AND DISCRIMINATION
> *INTRODUCTION*
>
> (1) In most societies, certain social minorities are sometimes discriminated against by society as a whole. (2) Discrimination may occur because of a group's race, religion, ethnic or cultural background, sexual orientation, or even the language that they speak in their homes. (3) Such groups are sometimes denied basic rights, legal protections, or access to the same facilities as the general public. (4) In many societies, discrimination is slowly being eliminated—at least in terms of legal and governmental policies. (5) But these changes have not come quickly or easily.
>
> (6) The United States, for example, has made a great deal of progress in eliminating discrimination against some of its social minorities. (7) As recently as the 1950s blacks and whites were not allowed to get married in many southern states. (8) They were forced to use separate drinking fountains, rest rooms, and even schools and libraries. (9) However, as a result of active protest and political demonstration such discriminatory laws were changed, and segregation based on race is no longer permitted.
>
> (10) But other groups have been less successful. (11) Women have made many gains in American society, but they are still paid less than men for the same kinds of work. (12) Gay people still face enormous legal and social discrimination. (13) They are not allowed to serve in the army or join organizations like the Boy Scouts; in many states they can be fired from their jobs if employers learn of their sexual orientation. (14) They do not have the same kind of basic legal protection for family relationships and property that the rest of society takes for granted. (15) Courts may still take children away from homosexual parents, or deny inheritance rights to lifelong partners when one partner dies.
>
> (16) Conditions for all minorities in the United States seem to be improving, although it will be a long time before social attitudes catch up with the progress that has been made in legal protections.
>
> P. 58   INTRODUCTION TO SOCIOLOGY SECOND EDITION

ANSWER KEY

Exercise 12 See above for underlined passive constructions. The reasons are as follows: (1) to focus on the receiver   (2) none   (3) to focus on the receiver   (4) to make a general explanation   (5) none   (6) none   (7) agent is unknown   (8) agent is unknown   (9) agent is unknown; agent is unknown   (10) none   (11) agent is unknown   (12) none   (13) agent is unknown; agent is obvious from context   (14) none   (15) none   (16) agent is unknown

EXERCISE 12 [15 minutes]

Exercise 12 provides an opportunity for students to see the use of the passive in an academic context. Students will then get practice discussing with a partner the use of the passive in academic writing.

1. Put students into pairs and have each pair first choose a paragraph to discuss.

2. Tell the class that they will work together to first underline all the passive verbs in their chosen paragraph and then discuss the reasons for each use of the passive. They may want to refer back to Focus 6 for guidance.

3. Have pairs check their answers. See answers on LP page 58.

EXPANSION [20 minutes]

You may want to use Activity 1 (reading/speaking) on SB page 61 after this exercise.

EXERCISE 13 [15 minutes]

This exercise gives students practice making choices about the use of the passive or active voice and then forming the verb construction. Form, meaning, and use are all considered in this exercise.

1. Have students first work individually and then compare their answers with a partner or in small groups.

2. Circulate as students compare answers and note any common errors or points of discussion to bring up during the debriefing. Let students negotiate their answers together. Do not correct them.

3. After all groups have discussed their answers, bring the class together and let students give

their answers along with the reasoning behind them. Give corrections or clarifications as necessary. See answers on LP page 58.

For more practice, use *Grammar Dimensions 3* Workbook page 19, Exercise 12 and Exercise 13.

Use Your English

ACTIVITY 1 reading/speaking

The article in Exercise 12 discussed discrimination against social minorities in the United States. Share your ideas and opinions about discrimination with other students.

■ STEP 1

Read the article again and discuss these questions with a partner or in a small group:

1. What is the main idea of this article?

2. What are some common reasons for discrimination mentioned in the article?

3. What examples does the article give of successful progress in eliminating discrimination in the United States?

4. What examples does the article provide about discrimination against women? Can you think of other examples?

5. The article discusses legalized discrimination and social discrimination. Name one example of each kind of discrimination against gay people.

Koreans in Japan
Turks in Germany
Arabs in France
Chinese in Southeast Asia
Jews in Eastern Europe
Hindus in Sri Lanka
Catholics in Northern Ireland
people with physical disabilities
people with certain political beliefs
people with certain physical characteristics (fat people, short people, left-handed people, etc.)

■ STEP 2

Listed below are examples of some other social groups that sometimes face discrimination. Identify one example that you are familiar with and describe that discrimination to another student.

■ STEP 3

With your partner think of one additional example and describe the discrimination that this group faces to the rest of the class.

■ STEP 4

Discuss whether there are situations in which legal or social discrimination can ever be justified. Report the results of your discussion to the rest of the class.

EXERCISE 14

Decide whether active or passive forms should be used in these sentences, and write the correct form in the blank. There may be more than one correct choice.

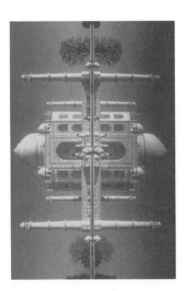

The Taj Mahal in Agra, India, (1) _was built_ (build) for the Moghul Emperor Shah Jahan. It (2) _was designed_ (design) to (3) _serve_ (serve) as a tomb for his beloved wife. Many people (4) _consider_ (consider) the Taj to be the most beautiful building in the world. The entire structure (5) _is made_ (make) of white marble and semiprecious stones. Shah Jahan originally (6) _intended_ (intend) for a second Taj (7) _to be located_ (locate) across the river from the first one. The second Taj was supposed to (8) _copy_ (copy) the original Taj in every detail except one: The second Taj, which Shah Jahan (9) _planned_ (plan) as his own tomb, was supposed to (10) _consist_ (consist) of black marble and semiprecious stones, instead of the same white marble that (11) _was used_ (use) for the first Taj. Shah Jahan (12) _was imprisoned_ (imprison) by his own son and (13) _died_ (die) before he (14) _got_ (get) a chance to (15) _implement_ (implement) his plan. His vision of two twin Taj Mahals, one white and one black, never (16) _was accomplished_ (accomplish).

UNIT 4

LESSON PLAN 3/USE YOUR ENGLISH

EXERCISE 14 [10 minutes]

This exercise gives students the chance to discuss making choices between using the active or passive voice. Conduct this exercise as in Exercise 13. Allow time for students to discuss their choices together before making any corrections. See answers on LP page 60.

work book For more practice, use *Grammar Dimensions 3* Workbook page 20, Exercise 14.

UNIT GOAL REVIEW [10 minutes]

Ask students to look at the goals on the opening page of the unit again. Refer to the pages of the unit where information on each goal can be found.

work book For a grammar quiz review of Units 1–4, refer students to pages 21–22 in the *Grammar Dimension 3* Workbook.

ExamView® Test Generator — For assessment of Unit 4, use *Grammar Dimensions 3* *ExamView®*.

USE YOUR ENGLISH

The Use Your English activities contain situations that should naturally elicit the structures covered in the unit. For a more complete discussion of how to use the Use Your English activities see To the Teacher on LP page xxii. When students are doing these activities in class, you can circulate and listen to see if they are using the structures accurately. Errors can be corrected after the activity has finished.

ACTIVITY 1 reading/speaking [20 minutes/homework]

You can use this activity after Exercise 12 on SB page 58. The preparation for this activity can be assigned as homework in advance of the group discussions.

The aim of this activity is to create an opportunity for students to use the passive when speaking about discrimination.

If you decide to complete the activity during class time, follow these steps:

■ **STEP 1** Allow students time to skim the article again and prepare to discuss the questions. Pair students up and give them time to discuss. Circulate around the classroom listening for the use of the passive in the discussion or any common errors to address. You may want to put a few examples on the board. Compare answers as a class.

■ **STEPS 2, 3, AND 4**

1. As the pairs/groups move through Step 2, 3, and 4, ask them to keep notes on their discussions. These notes will be used later to share with the whole class.

2. After giving the pairs/groups about 10 minutes to discuss, bring the class together and ask the groups to share the results of their discussion.

1. What was announced today?

2. When did Velasquez probably paint the portrait?

3. How did the painting get into the closet?

4. Why didn't officials know about the painting's existence?

5. Who authenticated the painting?

6. What is being done now, as a result of this discovery?

7. How much is the painting worth?

STEP 3 Compare your answers with a partner's. Listen to the news broadcast a third time to check answers that you disagree on or are unsure about. Share your final answers with the rest of the class.

ACTIVITY 5 research on the web

Go on the Internet and use a search engine like Google® or Yahoo® to find out how one or more of the common items listed below are manufactured. If you prefer, you can talk about some other item you are familiar with. Report your findings to the rest of the class.

glass   molasses   silicon chips   rope   porcelain   paper

ACTIVITY 6 reflection

Read a newspaper or listen to a national TV or radio news broadcast in English and write down three examples of passive verbs that you hear. Try to identify the receiver and the agent, if it is stated, and suggest why the passive form was used. If possible, have a partner listen independently to the same broadcast or read the same newspaper and then compare your answers.

ACTIVITY 2 writing

Go to the library, on *InfoTrac® College Edition*, or on the Internet. Use a search engine like Google® or Yahoo® and find enough information to write a brief report on the history of a famous structure or public monument. Include facts about its design, construction, and function, and why it is famous. Use the passive voice at least three times in your report. Pick one of these examples, or choose one of your own.

The Eiffel Tower (Paris)

The Golden Gate Bridge (San Francisco)

The Statue of Liberty (New York)

Angkor Wat (Cambodia)

The Parthenon (Athens)

Latin American Tower (Mexico City)

The Imperial Palace (Tokyo)

The Temple of Heaven (Beijing)

The Chunnel (between England and France)

The Sydney Opera House (Australia)

ACTIVITY 3 writing

Have you ever had a day that was so unlucky that it made you wish that you had never even gotten out of bed? What happened? Was it unlucky because of what happened to you or because of something you did? Were you the "agent" or the "receiver" of your unlucky events? Write a paragraph that describes what happened on that day.

ACTIVITY 4 listening

CD Track 8

STEP 1 Listen to the news broadcast and, in your notebook, write a one-sentence summary of what the news broadcast is about.

STEP 2 Read the following questions and then listen to the news broadcast again. Answer the questions in complete sentences.

ANSWER KEY

Activity 4 Answers will vary. Possible answers are: **Step 1:** A previously unknown painting by Diego de Velasquez has been found in a storage closet in the Ministry of the Interior in Madrid. **Step 2:** 1. A painting by Velasquez was discovered in a storage closet. 2. It was probably painted sometime between 1685 and 1700. 3. It had probably been put there during the Spanish Civil War. 4. It wasn't listed on any of the inventories of the ministry. 5. Experts at the Prado Museum authenticated the painting. 6. The ministry will do some "serious housekeeping." 7. The painting has been valued at over $1.5 million.

USE YOUR ENGLISH

ACTIVITY 2 writing [homework]

You can assign this activity as homework anytime after the Opening Task in order to give students time to begin working on the research.

1. Begin by reviewing the kind of information in the Opening Task about Stonehenge and the Nazca Lines. Note any references to their design, construction, and possible functions.

2. Now, as an example, turn the ideas of design, construction, and possible functions to the Eiffel Tower in Paris. Ask the class what they might already know and what they need to research. Encourage students to begin their research with questions in mind.

3. Because students may procrastinate on this project, it helps to have everyone commit to a topic before they begin the research. Remind the class that they will need to include at least three passive constructions in their reports. Give guidelines for the format, length, and any other requirements.

4. When they are finished, have students share, either in small groups or as a class. You may want to survey the class on what they found to be the best sources of information.

METHODOLOGY NOTE

Plagiarism can be a sensitive subject when doing Internet research, so be sure to outline what plagiarism is and ways to avoid it when assigning an activity like this. It will save you from potential misunderstandings later.

ACTIVITY 3 writing [20 minutes/homework]

Give students time to share their "unlucky day" stories with a partner or in a small group. Listen for examples of the passive to share with the class when finished.

ACTIVITY 4 listening [20 minutes]

Track 8

STEP 1 Play the audio through once. Have the class take a moment to write a one-sentence summary. Discuss what students wrote as a class.

STEP 2 Have students read through the list of questions in Step 2. They may not be able to answer any of the questions, but encourage them to write down a few guesses. Play the broadcast a second time and let them check or add to their answers.

STEP 3 Let students compare answers in pairs when they are ready. Before giving them the final answers, play the broadcast again and let the pairs check their own answers. You may want to pause after key phrases and let them decide whether their answers are correct. See possible answers on LP page 62.

METHODOLOGY NOTE

Students may feel uncomfortable guessing at answers. They may also feel frustrated by the speed of authentic speech. Because of these two factors, they may feel very insecure about taking risks and making a guess. Remind them that even when we listen to something in our native languages, we are always making little guesses to fill in the parts that we didn't hear clearly. Students need to understand that it's important for good language learners to be comfortable taking risks and making guesses sometimes.

ACTIVITY 5 research on the web [20 minutes]

1. Begin by having the class brainstorm examples of items that are manufactured. Several examples have been provided as a starting point. Have volunteers tell what they already may know about the manufacture of a few of these items. You may want to model the passive, by rephrasing some of the shared information. Each student will then choose an item to research.

2. Before students start doing the Internet research, you may want to ask volunteers to share strategies they use in doing searches.

3. Have students report their findings to the class.

ACTIVITY 6 reflection [homework]

This activity asks students to find examples of the passive on their own in natural contexts. Newspapers, TV, and radio news broadcasts are all natural places for the passive to be used. To encourage students to spend time searching, ask them to bring in a certain number of examples (e.g., 5–10). As the activity suggests, have students identify the receiver, agent, if it is stated, and tell why they think the passive was used. Have students share their findings with the class or in small groups. Have students write down their findings in their *Reflection Journal*.

5

ONE-WORD AND PHRASAL MODALS

UNIT GOALS

- Review modal forms and uses
- Identify and use one-word and phrasal modals
- Understand formal and informal uses of modals

OPENING TASK
Identifying the Pros and Cons of Immigration

Every year hundreds of thousands of people leave their native country and go to live permanently to another country. Some are political refugees; others hope to find better economic opportunities for themselves and their families. Some come to their new country legally, and others are forced to enter or stay illegally. But for everyone the move to a new country often involves a lot of difficulties.

STEP 1

Read this list of reasons why people immigrate to a new country and the list of difficulties people sometimes face after they immigrate. Check reasons why you would consider immigrating to another country and the difficulties that you think you might face. Then add one more reason and difficulty that are true for you.

REASONS	DIFFICULTIES
___ People can't make enough money to feed their families.	___ People have to learn a new language.
___ People aren't allowed to practice their religion.	___ People aren't able to forget their old customs.
___ People have to serve in the army for a long time.	___ Their children won't grow up the way they did.
___ People are expected to choose a profession or a spouse that their parents (or government) tell them to.	___ People have difficulty finding work or have to take low-paying jobs because they can't speak the language well.
___	___

STEP 2

Consider present immigrant unrest in countries like France or England and elsewhere. Do you think large-scale immigration is a good idea? What is the impact on the people who move to a new country and on the country itself? Discuss your ideas with several classmates. Decide on three reasons in favor of immigration and three reasons opposing immigration. Present your ideas to the rest of the class.

LESSON PLAN 1

UNIT OVERVIEW

Unit 5 reviews both one-word and phrasal modals. The focus of this unit is on the many uses and meanings of modals. Unit 5 gives practice in identifying and using modals for different uses and to change the meaning of sentences.

GRAMMAR NOTE

Modal auxiliaries and phrasal modals are used in English to change the mood of a verb. Modals can have many different meanings and uses.

One-word modals and phrasal modals can prove difficult for ESL students. This can be due to the fact that many languages do not have similar modals. Students from these language backgrounds may tend to treat one-word modals as verbs and inflect tense and agreement on them or use an infinitive (*to* + verb) following them. Phrasal modals can be confusing, because they, for the most part, take tense and agreement. Students can also have difficulty with the sometimes subtle changes in meaning and the wide variety of uses that modals offer.

UNIT GOALS

Some instructors may want to review the goals listed on Student Book (SB) page 64 after completing the Opening Task so that students understand what they should know by the end of the unit. These goals can also be reviewed at the end of the unit when students are more familiar with the grammar terminology.

OPENING TASK [20 minutes]

The aim of this activity is to give students the opportunity to use modals as they consider the issue of immigration. The problem-solving format is designed to show the teacher how well the students can produce a target structure implicitly and spontaneously when they are engaged in a communicative task. For a more

complete discussion of the purpose of the Opening Task, see Lesson Planner (LP) page xxii.

Note: Teachers should keep in mind that the difficulties faced in immigration can be a very sensitive topic for some students.

Setting Up the Task

1. Have students discuss with a partner the possible reasons that people immigrate to a new country. When finished discussing, ask the pairs to put a few reasons they came up with on the board.

2. Have the class look at the picture on SB page 64. Ask a volunteer to read aloud the caption below.

Conducting the Task

■ STEP 1

1. Give students a chance to read through the *Reasons* and *Difficulties* on SB page 65 and let them check the reasons they would consider moving and the difficulties they might face. Be sure students have time to add their own ideas to the lists.

2. Put students into small groups for discussion of Step 1. Note how comfortable students are using modals such as *have to, must, will, might,* etc.

■ STEP 2

Put the questions for Step 2 on the board:

Is large-scale immigration a good idea? What is the impact on the people who move to a new country? On the country itself? What are three reasons in favor of immigration? What are three reasons opposing immigration?

Have students discuss the questions in small groups or pairs. Listen for the use of modals as you record a few of these ideas.

Closing the Task

Have students write their ideas from Step 2 on the board. Create a chart on the board with each

question as a column head. Ask students to write their responses to each question under the head, and underline the modals. Point out that modals often appear in different forms—as one word, as phrasals with *be,* and as phrasals without *be.* You can leave this chart on the board as a reference to Focus 1.

VARIATION

Instead of having students complete a chart as the one discussed, you may wish to create one like the chart shown here:

Some new immigrants can't…
Some new immigrants aren't able to…
New immigrants have to…

As a lead-in to Focus 1, ask students to work with a partner on ways to complete the sentences.

GRAMMAR NOTE

Typical student errors (form)

- Putting tense and agreement on modals or verbs following a modal: * *He cans go with us.*
- Treating one-word modals like a verb or phrasal modal and using the infinitive: * *He must to go.*
- Forgetting tense and agreement on phrasal modals: * *She be able to go with us.*

Typical student errors (use)

- Using *must not* and *don't have to* similarly: *You must not smoke in here.* * *You don't have to smoke in here.*
- Confusing the many different uses and meanings of only a few modals: *You could take a taxi. It could rain tomorrow. Could you pass the salt? She couldn't keep up with us.*

FOCUS 1 — Review of Modal Forms

Many one-word modals correspond to one or more phrasal modals with a similar meaning.

ONE-WORD MODALS

can/could	may/might
will/would	shall/should
must	

PHRASAL MODALS

be able to	be allowed to
be going to	have to, have got to
ought to, be supposed to, had better	

MODAL	AFFIRMATIVE STATEMENTS	NEGATIVE STATEMENTS	QUESTIONS/ SHORT ANSWERS
One-Word Modals *can/could may/might will/would shall/should*	(a) Victor can speak Spanish.	(b) He cannot speak it at the school where he studies English.	(c) Where can he speak it?
			(d) Can he speak it at home? Yes, he probably can.
	(e) Victor should always speak English at school.	(f) He shouldn't speak Spanish with his classmates.	(g) Should he speak Spanish in school? No, he shouldn't.
Phrasal Modals with *Be* *be able to be going to be about to be supposed to be allowed to*	(h) Victor is able to speak Spanish.	(i) He is not supposed to speak Spanish in English class.	(j) Is he allowed to speak it at home? Yes, he probably is.
	(k) Victor was able to speak Spanish with his family.	(l) He wasn't supposed to speak Spanish at school.	(m) When was he allowed to speak Spanish? After class.
Phrasal Modals without *Be* *have to used to*	(n) Victor has to speak English in class.	(o) He does not have to speak it at home.	(p) Does he have to speak it at home? No, he doesn't.
	(q) Victor had to speak English with his teacher.	(r) He didn't have to speak it with his family.	(s) Where did he have to speak it? At school.
	(t) He used to speak only Spanish.	(u) He didn't use to speak English at all.	(v) Did he use to speak English? No, he didn't.

Continued

MODAL	AFFIRMATIVE STATEMENTS	EXPLANATION
have got to had better ought to	(w) He has got to speak English with his teacher.	These modals do not usually appear in questions or negative sentences. One-word modals are used instead.
	(x) He had better not speak Spanish in class.	
	(y) He ought to try speaking English at home, too.	

EXERCISE 1

Victor Sanchez immigrated to the United States six months ago and is busy trying to learn English. Read these sentences about Victor's study habits. The forms of the modals are incorrect. Identify the problems and correct the sentences.

Example: Has Victor to speak English?
Does Victor have to speak English?

1. Victor hasn't to do his homework.
Victor doesn't have to do his homework.

2. Does Victor able to speak Spanish at home?
Is Victor able to speak Spanish at home?

3. Can Victor speak Spanish? Yes, he can speak.
Can Victor speak Spanish? Yes, he can.

4. Where he is allowed to speak Spanish?
Where is he allowed to speak Spanish?

5. Why he can't speak Spanish at school?
Why can't he speak Spanish at school?

6. Ought Victor to speak Spanish at school?
Should Victor speak Spanish at school?

7. Had Victor better speak English at school?
Should Victor speak English at school?

8. Used Victor to speak Spanish?
Did Victor used to speak Spanish?

9. Does Victor allowed to speak Spanish in school? No, he doesn't allowed.
Is Victor allowed to speak Spanish in school? No, he isn't.

10. Why he should speak English in school? Why he shouldn't Spanish?
Why should he speak English in school? Why shouldn't he speak Spanish?

LESSON PLAN 1

FOCUS 1 [20 minutes]

This focus chart reviews both one-word and phrasal modals with examples of how they are used in affirmative and negative statements and in questions and short answers. The modals have been divided into groups within the Focus 1 chart in order to present modals with similar grammatical patterns together.

1. **Lead-in:** Refer back to the chart you created after the Opening Task. Write additional sentences like the following on the board to give examples of the four basic patterns these modals take:

Maria	should	do her homework everyday. (one-word)
She	is supposed to	do her homework everyday. (with BE)
She	had better	do her homework everyday. (used to/ought to)
She	has to	do her homework everyday. (with HAVE + to)

2. Let students take turns suggesting other modals to fit into the basic sentence structure.

3. Now change the subject of the basic sentence to *You* (*You are supposed to/You have to . . .*) Now ask volunteers to suggest other modals from the list in Focus 1 to go with this new subject. Then change the subject to *I* and have students make more sentences.

4. Go over the chart in Focus 1 and note the examples of negative statements and questions. Look back at the sentences on the board and ask volunteers to change some to negative statements or questions.

5. Leave some of these examples on the board. You may want them to refer to when going over answers to Exercise 1.

EXERCISE 1 [10 minutes]

This exercise draws students' attention to the correct formation of sentences and questions using modals.

1. Have students work individually to correct the errors in each sentence.

2. Let pairs work together to check their answers before going over the correct answers as a class. See answers on LP page 66.

3. It may be helpful to make a copy of the sentences on an overhead transparency and do the error correction in colored pen to highlight the changes.

work book

For more practice, use *Grammar Dimensions 3* Workbook page 23, Exercise 1.

Most basic social interactions use modals.

FOCUS 2

Social Uses of One-Word and Phrasal Modals

 use

USE	ONE-WORD MODALS	EXAMPLES	PHRASAL MODALS	EXAMPLES	SPECIAL NOTES
Making requests	would	(a) **Would** you open the window?			The one-word modals are listed here in order of most polite or formal to most informal.
	could	(b) **Could** you turn down the radio?			
	will	(c) **Will** you pass the salt?			
	can	(d) **Can** you loan me a dollar?			
Asking for, giving, or denying permission	may	(e) **May** I come in?	be allowed to	(h) You're **allowed to** bring a friend.	*May* is considered more polite than *can.*
	can	(f) Of course you **can**!			
	can	(g) You **can't** smoke here.		(i) You're **not allowed to** smoke here.	
Giving invitations	will	(j) **Will** you come for dinner?			
	would	(k) **Would** you like to join us?			
	can	(l) **Can** you come to my party?			
Making offers	will	(m) I'**ll** do the dishes.	would . . . like	(o) **Would** you **like** me to do the dishes?	Use *shall* to make offers of action by the speaker.
	shall	(n) **Shall** I help with the dishes?			

FOCUS 2

Social Uses of One-Word and Phrasal Modals

 use

Continued

USE	ONE-WORD MODALS	EXAMPLES	PHRASAL MODALS	EXAMPLES	SPECIAL NOTES
Making promises or expressing intention	will	(p) I'**ll** do it	be going to	(s) I'**m going to** finish this, I promise.	*Be going to* expresses a stronger intention than *will.*
	will	(q) I promise I'**ll** do it.			
	will	(r) I'**ll** do it, no matter what!		(t) I'**m going to** finish this whether you want me to or not.	See Unit 15, Focus 3, for more information on this difference.
Making suggestions	shall	(u) **Shall** we go out to dinner?			Use *shall* to suggest actions that involve both the speaker and the listener.
	could	(v) We **could** get Chinese food.			
	can	(w) You **can** try that new restaurant.			
	might	(x) Victor **might** try harder to speak English outside of class.			

LESSON PLAN 1

FOCUS 2 [20 minutes]

The Focus 2 charts on SB pages 68–70 have divided the modals up according to their uses in social interactions. Notice that one-word modals are listed in one column with examples following and phrasal modals are listed next with examples following. Be sure to clarify the points listed in the column under *Special Notes*.

1. **Lead-in:** Write the following sentences on the board and ask students what the differences are between them. If they are unable to say why the sentences are different, put the answers on the board (listed below in the correct order) in mixed up order and see if they can match the answer to the example sentence.

Could you close the window?	(making a request)
We could go to a movie.	(making a suggestion)
Can I smoke here?	(asking for permission)
Can you come to the movie with us?	(giving an invitation)

2. Have students look at the different sections of the focus chart on SB pages 68–70. Explain that several modals can be used in different ways. In the examples on the board, *can* and *could* are used for different purposes.

3. Go through the chart having students take turns reading the example sentences out loud. Clarify meanings and special notes as necessary.

Suggestion: You may want to use the Expansion that follows for a student-led presentation of Focus 2 in place of reading through the sentences in the chart.

GRAMMAR NOTE

Students can have trouble with the differences between *don't have to* and *must not*. They may use the two interchangeably. This misuse comes from the fact that *have to* and *must* can both be used to show necessity and obligation and *don't have to* shows a lack of necessity. However, *must not* has a completely different meaning showing prohibition. If students are having trouble, give an example of prohibition such as, *you must not steal*. Now explain how the meaning changes when you replace *must not* with *don't have to*. In this case, *you don't have to steal, but you can if you want*. Continue giving examples such as this until students see the difference.

EXPANSION [15 minutes]

This alternative to the teacher-led presentation makes small groups responsible for presenting parts of the chart to the class themselves.

1. Divide the class into eight groups (one for each modal use on the chart). You may want to divide the section on *expressing advice* into two groups because of the number of modals and special notes involved.

2. Inform the groups that they will be responsible for telling the rest of the class about one way that modals are used in social interactions as shown on the chart in Focus 2.

3. Assign each group a social interaction from Focus 2 (possibly two groups for *expressing advice*) and ask the groups to go over the chart together along with the section on special notes. Have each group create their own examples to represent their assigned modal use. You may want to give each group an overhead transparency sheet, on which they can write their examples to share with the class.

4. Let groups take turns presenting their use for modals, give a few examples, and explain anything extra mentioned in the *Special Notes* column.

5. If you have time, give the class a chance to ask questions of each group.

METHODOLOGY NOTE

Some students may not immediately see the value of learning through student-led activities like teaching and presenting. Explain the value of learning by doing and that they may encounter this type of learning in other classes.

FOCUS 2

Social Uses of One-Word and Phrasal Modals

use

USE	ONE-WORD MODALS	EXAMPLES	PHRASAL MODALS	EXAMPLES	SPECIAL NOTES
Expressing advice	could	(y) Victor could study harder.	ought to	(bb) You ought to do your homework every night.	These forms are listed in increasing order of necessity.
	should	(z) Victor should study every day.	had better	(cc) You had better start working harder if you want to pass this class.	*Ought to* is rarely used in negative statements or questions.
		(aa) He shouldn't speak Spanish at home.	had better not	(dd) You had better not skip class.	*Had better* is an emphatic form. It is often used as a threat. It is used in affirmative and negative sentences, but it is not used with questions. Notice that the negative form is *had better not*, NOT *hadn't better*.
			be supposed to	(ee) You're supposed to do your homework every night.	
				(ff) You're not supposed to ask your roommate to help you with the homework.	
Obligation, and necessity/ prohibition	must	(gg) We must leave before 5:00	have to	(ii) You have to leave before 5:00.	*Have to* and *must* have different meanings in negative sentences: *must not* = prohibition; *don't have to* = lack of necessity.
		(hh) You mustn't tell a lie		(jj) You don't have to work late if you don't want to.	
			have got to	(kk) You've got to stop spending so much money.	*Have got to* is not used in questions or negatives.

Continued

EXERCISE 2

Identify the social uses expressed by the modals in the sentences below the chart. Write the number of the sentences in the chart to show how it is being used.

For each modal use write one additional sentence of your own. The first three sentences have been identified for you as examples.

USE	FORM
Making requests Sentence #: _4, 11, 12_	Your own example _Can you help me with my homework?_ _Can you help me?/ Could you turn down the radio?_
Asking for, giving, or denying permission Sentence #: _1, 10_	Your own example _Can I bring a friend to the party?/_ _May I come in?_
Giving invitations Sentence #: _3_	Your own example _Could you come to my house for dinner?/_ _Would you like to come to my party?_
Making offers Sentence #: _2, 12, 17_	Your own example _I could do it for you./_ _Shall I help you?_
Making promises or expressing intentions Sentence #: _14, 15, 18_	Your own example _I'll be on time./_ _I'm going to do it for you._
Making suggestions Sentence #: _5, 6, 13, 16_	Your own example _We could try to sing./_ _Shall we have Chinese food?_
Expressing advice, obligation, necessity, or prohibition 7, 8, 9, 10, Sentence #: _16, 18_	Your own example _You ought to study harder./_ _You shouldn't be late for class._

1. May I have some cheese?
2. Shall I open a window?
3. Can you come to my party?
4. Would you join us for dinner?
5. We could have Chinese food tonight.
6. We might try the Hong Kong Café.
7. You mustn't forget John's birthday.
8. We don't have to study over the weekend.
9. You shouldn't stay up so late.
10. You ought to try harder in speech class.
11. Could you please turn down the radio?
12. Would you like me to help you with your homework?
13. Shall we go to Las Vegas for a vacation?
14. I'm going to pass the TOEFL® Test, no matter what it takes!
15. I'll pay you back next Tuesday.
16. You'd better not leave.
17. I can do that for you.
18. Victor can't speak Spanish in his English class.

ANSWER KEY

Exercise 2   Answers will vary. Possible answers are listed above.

LESSON PLAN 1

EXERCISE 2 [20 minutes]

This exercise gives students the opportunity to use the chart in Focus 2 to find examples of how modals are used in social interactions. They will then be able to write their own examples using a modal of their choice for the same use.

1. List the seven different categories for use from the orange box in Exercise 2 on the board or on an overhead transparency (which can then be used later in Exercises 4 and 5):

   Making requests
   Asking for, giving, or denying permission
   Giving invitations
   Making offers
   Making promises or expressing intentions
   Making suggestions
   Expressing advice, obligation, necessity, or prohibition

2. Go over sentences 1–3 below the orange box and note which category each sentence fits into. Continue through a few more sentences and have volunteers place each one in a category. Have the class decide whether these placements are correct and make other suggestions.

3. Once the class is comfortable attempting to place the sentences into a corresponding category, have students work individually to place all the sentences.

4. Let pairs check their work together before going over the correct answers with the class. See answers on LP page 70.

5. Next, ask students to write their own example sentence for each category. This can be assigned as homework and turned in at the next class for feedback. Alternately, sentences can be shared with a group and the group can give feedback to each other. See possible answers on LP page 70.

work book

For more practice, use *Grammar Dimensions 3* Workbook page 24, Exercise 2.

FOCUS 3 Common One-Word and Phrasal Modal Meanings

Continued

MEANING	ONE-WORD MODALS	EXAMPLES	PHRASAL MODALS	EXAMPLES	SPECIAL NOTES
Making predictions	could	(i) We could get our visas next week.	ought to	(n) It ought to take about a year to get the visa.	Listed in order of increasing probability. Ought to is rarely used in negative statements or questions.
	might	(j) It might take a little longer than that.	be going to	(o) It's going to take another month.	
	may	(k) We may have to wait a while			See Focus 4 and Focus 5 for more information
	should	(l) It should be ready in three months.			
	will	(m) It will be ready tomorrow.			
Making logical inferences	must	(p) People must get tired of waiting for their visas.	have to	(r) Getting a work permit has to be difficult!	These phrasal modals are not used in negative inferences or in questions
	must not	(q) Victor hasn't applied for a work permit; he must not need to work.	have got to	(s) Getting a visa has got to take a lot of determination!	
Describing abilities	can	(t) Victor can speak English now, but he couldn't speak it a year ago.	be able to	(u) Victor was able to ask his question in English, but he wasn't able to understand the answer.	Differences in meaning and use of these forms are discussed in more detail in Unit 24
Describing habitual actions in the past	would	(v) When Victor lived in El Salvador, he would dream of moving to Canada.	used to	(w) Immigrant visas used to be much easier to get.	Using would and used to implies that the situation no longer happens

---

Modals also express important meanings.

FOCUS 3 Common One-Word and Phrasal Modal Meanings

MEANING	ONE-WORD MODALS	EXAMPLES	PHRASAL MODALS	EXAMPLES	SPECIAL NOTES
Expressing general possibility	can	(a) Immigrating to a new country can be very difficult.			See Unit 17 for more information
	will	(b) Immigrating to a new country will usually require a lot of life-style changes.			
Expressing impossibility	can't	(c) It can't be easy to get U.S. citizenship!			See Unit 17 for more information
	couldn't	(d) You couldn't be thinking about going back home already!			
Describing future events	will	(e) Victor will get his green-card next year.	be going to	(g) Steve's going to move to Canada if the Republicans win the next election.	Shall is very formal in American English. Will is preferred
	shall	(f) We shall apply for an immigrant visa next year.	be about to	(h) He's about to apply for citizenship.	Be going to is discussed in Unit 15 Be about to is used to describe events in the immediate future.

ONE-WORD AND PHRASAL MODALS

LESSON PLAN 2

FOCUS 3 [20 minutes]

Whereas the Focus 2 chart outlined different ways that modals are used in social interactions, the chart in Focus 3 shows how modals can have different meanings.

1. **Lead-in:** Write the following sentences on the board and ask students what the differences are between them. If they are unable to say why the sentences are different, put the answers on the board (listed below in the correct order) in mixed-up order and see if they can match the answer to the example sentence.

> *Don't make plans, because it*
> *could rain tomorrow.*   (prediction)
>
> *She could dance very well*
> *when she was young.*   (ability)
>
> *Life can be difficult in a*
> *new country.*   (general possibility)
>
> *Emma can speak four*
> *languages.*   (ability)

2. Have students turn to Focus 3 on SB pages 72–73. Explain that several modals can have different meanings. In the examples on the board, *can* and *could* have different meanings.

3. Go through the chart having students take turns reading the example sentences out loud (examples a–w). Clarify meanings and any questions on the special notes as necessary.

Suggestion: You may want to use the Expansion suggested for Focus 2 for a student-led presentation in place of reading through the sentences in the chart.

EXERCISE 3

Identify the meanings expressed by the modals in these sentences. Write the number of the sentences in the chart to show how it is being used.

For each modal meaning, write one additional sentence of your own. The first three sentences have been identified for you as examples.

MEANING	FORM
General possibility Sentence #: 1	Your own example: *Getting an immigrant visa can be very tricky/ Tests can be very tricky./ English can be confusing.*
Impossibility Sentence #: 2, 10	Your own example: *It couldn't be 5:00 already!/ That can't be Mary! She's in Morocco.*
Future time Sentence #: 6, 13	Your own example: *I will be there next week./ I'm going to leave tomorrow.*
Prediction Sentence #: 5, 7, 11	Your own example: *I could be too busy to do it./ I may have to work.*
Logical inference Sentence #: 8, 12, 14	Your own example: *You must be tired from all that work./ They should be here by now.*
Ability Sentence #: 3, 9	Your own example: *I can speak Spanish./ I couldn't run fast enough to catch the ball.*
Habitual actions in the past Sentence #: 4, 15	Your own example: *I used to play the guitar./ We would pretend we were pirates when we were children.*

1. It can be quite rainy this time of year.
2. You couldn't be hungry! You just ate.
3. I couldn't understand American TV programs a year ago.
4. I used to get frustrated when I watched TV.
5. Those naughty children will misbehave if you give them a chance.
6. I will be there at 5:00.
7. I may have to leave early.
8. Antonio got A's in all his classes. He has to be very smart.
9. I've been able to make friends in every country I've lived in.
10. It can't be midnight already! It seems like we just got here.
11. We should be there in twenty minutes unless there's a traffic jam.
12. Naomi must not have to worry about money. She buys really expensive clothes.
13. I'll graduate next June.
14. It might be too late to call John. He usually goes to bed early.
15. I would always have trouble going to sleep on the night before school started when I was a child.

EXERCISE 4

How are the modals being used in each of these sentences? Decide whether they express: request, permission, invitation, offers, promises, suggestions, advice, obligation, necessity, possibility or impossibility, future time, predictions, logical inferences, abilities, or past habitual actions.

Examples: Can I ask you a question? _request_

Can you speak Spanish? _ability_

1. Will you open the door? _request_
2. Will the office be open tomorrow? _future time_
3. I can't hear you. _ability_
4. You can't smoke here; it's a church. _permission_
5. You shouldn't smoke; it's bad for your health. _advice_
6. You really ought to see a doctor. _advice/necessity_
7. The doctor has just finished with another patient; he ought to be ready to see you in just a minute. _prediction_
8. You walked twenty miles today? You must be tired! _logical inference_
9. You must leave at once if you don't want to miss the train. _necessity_
10. I may be late tonight, so plan on eating dinner without me. _prediction_
11. Can I speak to Dr. Martinez? _request_
12. You may not leave before the teacher tells you to. _permission_
13. I'm interested in buying that car, but it could be too expensive. _prediction_
14. Could you pass the butter? _request_
15. Could you read when you were 5 years old? _ability_

ANSWER KEY

Exercise 3   Answers will vary. Possible answers are listed above.

LESSON PLAN 2

EXERCISE 3 [20 minutes]

This exercise gives students the opportunity to use the chart in Focus 3 to find examples of how modals are used to express important meanings. They will then be able to write their own examples using a modal of their choice for the same use.

1. List the seven different categories for use from the orange box in Exercise 3 on the board or on an overhead transparency (which can then be used later in Exercises 4 and 5):

   General possibility
   Impossibility
   Future time
   Prediction
   Logical inference
   Ability
   Habitual actions in the past

2. Go over sentences 1–3 below the orange box and note which category each sentence fits into. Continue through a few more sentences and have volunteers place each one in a category. Have the class decide whether these placements are correct and make other suggestions.

3. Once the class is comfortable attempting to place the sentences into a corresponding category, have students work individually to place all the sentences.

4. Let pairs check their work together before going over the correct answers with the class. See answers on LP page 74.

5. Next, ask students to write their own example sentence for each category. This can be assigned as homework and turned in at the next class for feedback. Alternately, sentences can be shared with a group and the group can give feedback to each other. See possible answers on LP page 74.

For more practice, use *Grammar Dimensions 3* Workbook page 25, Exercise 3.

EXERCISE 4 [10 minutes]

This exercise is a review of the charts in Focus 2 on SB pages 68–70 and Focus 3 on SB pages 72–73. Students will choose from one of the 16 possibilities listed to explain how each modal is being used in these sentences.

1. You may want to use the overhead transparencies you created for Exercise 2 and Exercise 3 to remind students of all the possible uses and meanings that modals can carry.

2. Have students work individually to complete the exercise and then compare answers with a partner before going over the exercise with the class. See answers on LP page 74.

3. Circulate as pairs discuss their answers together and note any sentences that may need more attention during the class discussion.

For more practice, use *Grammar Dimensions 3* Workbook page 27, Exercise 4.

3. advice for a lazy student
4. something you know how to do well
5. a possible event in the future
6. something that is against school rules
7. something you don't know how to do

EXERCISE 7

Work with a partner. Use the phrasal modals below to ask your partner questions about daily life and activities. For each of the phrasal modals listed below ask:

a. one *yes/no* question.
b. one *wh-* question.

Report your partner's answers in full sentences.
The first one has been done for you as an example, using *have to.*

Example: have to: *Do you have to take the bus to get to school?*
No I don't. I get a ride with a friend.
What time do you have to leave home?
About fifteen minutes before class.
My partner doesn't have to leave her house until just before class because she gets a ride in a friend's car.

1. have to
2. be allowed to
3. be supposed to
4. be able to
5. be going to

EXERCISE 8

Restate the ideas you wrote about in Exercise 6 by using phrasal instead of one-word modals. Are there any modal meanings that cannot be expressed with phrasal modals?

Example: You should avoid foods that are high in fat.
You ought to avoid foods that are high in fat.

EXERCISE 5

Underline the one-word and phrasal modals in this paragraph. (There may be more than one modal in each sentence.) Then identify the meaning or use for each modal (permission, necessity, etc.—see Exercise 4 for options. The first sentence has been done for you as an example.

Example: (1) *necessity*

I'm not looking forward to this afternoon, because I <u>have to go</u> to the Immigration Office. (2) I have a problem with my work permit and I <u>can't get</u> a social security number. (3) I'm <u>supposed to be</u> there at three o'clock, and I <u>mustn't be</u> more than five minutes late, or <u>they'll cancel</u> my appointment. (4) So I guess I <u>had better leave</u> plenty of time to get there. (5) The bus is <u>supposed to come</u> every ten minutes, but it's often late. (6) I know that I <u>shouldn't be</u> nervous, but I really don't like the Immigration Office. (7) The officer is <u>going to tell</u> me that I <u>have to keep</u> better track of my documents. (8) I know that I'm <u>supposed to keep</u> a record of every visit, but sometimes I just <u>can't find</u> the time. (9) After my appointment I <u>won't be able to go</u> home for three hours, because I <u>have to go</u> back to my job. Here I am only a janitor at a chemical company instead of being a supervisory laboratory technician like I was in my country. (10) I know I'm <u>going to</u> be happy when I finally get my green card!

EXERCISE 6

Write a sentence with a one-word modal about each of the following topics:

Example: an activity to avoid if you want to be healthy
<u>You should avoid foods that are high in fat.</u>

1. a daily responsibility
2. the best way to keep in touch with friends far away

ANSWER KEY

Exercise 5 The modals are underlined above. The uses are as follows: (2) ability (3) obligation; obligation; future activity (4) advisability (5) advisability (6) advisability (7) future activity; necessity (8) advisability; ability (9) future ability; obligation (10) future activity

Exercise 6 Answers will vary. Possible answers are: 1. I must make my bed. 2. You should send e-mails frequently. 3. You should study harder. 4. I can play the piano. 5. I may have a party for my birthday. 6. You can't drink beer in class. 7. I can't water-ski.

Exercise 7 Answers will vary.
Exercise 8 Answers will vary.

ONE-WORD AND PHRASAL MODALS 77

UNIT 5

LESSON PLAN 2

EXERCISE 5 [20 minutes]

1. Initiate a discussion of students' experiences with immigration offices. You may want to put a general question on the board and ask small groups to share their experiences.

2. If you made overhead transparencies for Exercises 2 and 3, you can put them up for review while students work to complete Exercise 5.

3. Allow time after reviewing the answers in pairs and as a class for a quick discussion comparing this immigration office experience with the experiences shared earlier by the class. See answers on LP page 76.

EXPANSION [homework]

Ask students to write their own paragraph. This activity will give students the opportunity to use modals naturally in their own writing and build on the in-class discussion. You may want to assign a specific minimum number of modals that students must include in their paragraphs. Suggested topics:

1. Have students write a paragraph telling about an experience they had with an immigration office or another governmental office.

2. If students have moved from another country, have them write a paragraph explaining the steps involved in moving to this country.

Collect paragraphs and give feedback with particular attention to the use of modals.

EXERCISE 6 [10 minutes/homework]

1. Put the list of one-word modals on the board (see Focus 1 on SB page 66).

2. Go over the example with the class and ask volunteers to suggest other activities to avoid if they want to be healthy. You may want to ask a student or two to write the suggestions on the board.

3. Go over the suggestions you've collected on the board and comment on the use of the modals in both affirmative and negative forms.

4. Have students complete the rest of the exercise individually. When students finish, give them time to share their sentences in small groups or with the class. You can take this time to go around quickly checking student papers, or collect them and give feedback later. See answers on LP page 76.

EXPANSION 1 [homework]

You may want to follow up this exercise by asking students to choose a topic from Exercise 6 and to write a full paragraph to expand their previous response. You can ask students to practice by using a variety of modals in both affirmative and negative forms.

EXPANSION 2 [20 minutes]

Let students practice using modals by giving advice.

1. Begin by discussing with the class what an advice column is (you might want to bring in a sample from the local newspaper or from an online source). Give students a chance to practice giving advice out loud by starting with a sample problem and ask for volunteers to suggest answers. For example:

Jorge needs to find a part-time job to match his school schedule. What advice can you give him? (*Jorge should look in the school newspaper. He could ask his friends.*)

OR

Yoko is unhappy because her roommate is noisy and messy. What advice can you give Yoko? (*Yoko should find another apartment. She can try talking to her roommate.*)

2. Create a list of imagined "problems" that the students will address as writers of an advice column. You may make the list of problems up yourself, or you can ask students to work in pairs to create some problems.

---

3. Divide the class into small groups and assign each group 1–3 problems to discuss.

4. When they have finished their discussions, have the groups share their problems and advice with the rest of the class.

5. Follow up by having students individually write a letter with advice. You can have them use letter format or paragraph format for their responses. Collect papers for individual feedback.

EXERCISE 7 [10 minutes/homework]

After setting up Exercise 7, you can have students create their questions in class or as a homework assignment.

1. Begin the exercise by going over the instructions and the example with the class.

2. Create other questions about daily life and activities of your own using the phrasal modal *have to*. Go around the class asking students your *yes/no* and *wh-* questions. Encourage students to use full sentences for their answers.

3. Give students time to create their own questions for the rest of the exercise.

4. Put students into pairs and have them take turns asking and answering the questions they have created. Circulate through the classroom and listen for any common errors to address later. Be sure that students take notes of their partner's answers in order to report in full sentences later.

5. Give students time to write the full sentences for their partner's responses and then report these to the class or in small groups.

EXERCISE 8 [10 minutes]

After students complete this exercise, have the class discuss whether there were any cases of one-word modals that could not be expressed with a phrasal modal. Put these examples on the board. They will be used to lead into the next section in Focus 4.

FOCUS 4

Choosing One-Word Versus Phrasal Modals

 use

Certain modal meanings and uses can only be expressed by one-word modals.

USE	EXAMPLES	EXPLANATIONS
Requests	(a) **Would** you help me? (b) **May** I have some cheese? (c) **Can** you turn down the radio?	
Some predictions	(d) We **might** not have enough money. (e) We **could** fail the quiz if we don't study.	
Invitations	(f) **Can** you come to my party? (g) **Would** you join us for dinner?	
Suggestions	(h) We **could** have Chinese food tonight. (i) We **might** try the Hong Kong Café.	
Expressions of general possibility or impossibility	(j) A criminal **will** always return to the scene of the crime. (k) He **couldn't** have a TOEFL score of 600! He doesn't understand anything I say.	

In cases where both one-word and phrasal modals can be used, phrasal modals are preferred in the following situations.
To clarify modal meaning:

EXAMPLES	EXPLANATIONS
(l) Charlie **may not** bring a date.	This one-word modal has two possible meanings: It's possible that he **won't** bring a date. He **doesn't have permission to** bring a date.
(m) Charlie **isn't allowed to** bring a date.	This phrasal modal has only one possible meaning: He **doesn't have permission to** bring a date.

To combine two modal meanings in the same verb phrase:

EXAMPLES	EXPLANATIONS
(n) A teacher **must be able to** explain things clearly. (o) NOT: She **must can** explain things clearly.	Two one-word modals cannot be combined.
(p) Poor people **shouldn't have to** pay the same taxes as rich people. (q) I **may be able to** get some extra tickets.	We can combine a one-word and phrasal modal. In such cases the one word modal always comes first.
(r) A firefighter **has to be able to** carry at least 250 pounds. (s) You **ought to be able to** speak French if you want a job in Paris. (t) I'm **going to have to** leave in a minute.	We can also combine two phrasal modals.

EXERCISE 9

What are the duties of citizenship? Decide whether people in society (a) **should have to do** or (b) **shouldn't have to do** the things listed below. Add three more ideas of your own of what people should have to do and shouldn't have to do. Compare your sentences to those of a partner.

Examples: (a) *People should have to send their children to school.*

(b) *They shouldn't have to follow one particular religion.*

1. send their children to school
2. follow one particular religion
3. go to work wherever the government sends them
4. work without pay on community projects
5. always obey their leaders
6. be required to vote in elections
7. report criminals to the police
8. get permission to leave the country
9. serve in the army
10. pay taxes

Exercise 9 Answers will vary. Possible answers are: 1. People should have to send their children to school. 2. People shouldn't have to color one particular religion. 3. People shouldn't have to go to work wherever the government sends them. 4. People shouldn't have to work without pay on community projects. 5. People shouldn't have to always obey their leaders. 6. People should have to vote in elections. 7. People should have to report criminals to the police. 8. People shouldn't have to get permission to leave the country. 9. People shouldn't have to serve in the army. 10. People should have to pay taxes.

LESSON PLAN 3

FOCUS 4 [20 minutes]

The three sections in Focus 4 give further information and rules to help students understand the subtle differences when choosing between one-word and phrasal modals or when combining them.

1. **Lead-in:** Refer students back to any sentences the class found in Exercise 8 that could not be expressed with a phrasal modal or create one on your own. Explain to students that although many one-word modals have a phrasal modal counterpart, there are times when **only** a one-word modal will work.

2. Refer to the first section of the Focus 4 chart. Choose one of the examples you found in Exercise 8 or one of your own and write it on the board. Ask the class to find a similar sentence in this section of the chart. For example, from Exercise 6, some advice for a lazy student may have been:

   You could do your homework before you leave school each day.

   You would have students find that this example compares to examples (h) and (i) in the Focus 4 chart section labeled as *Suggestions* on SB page 78.

3. Go over the other examples of meanings that can only be expressed with one-word modals.

4. Continue to the next sections of Focus 4 (unclear meanings with one-word modals and combining two modal meanings in the same verb phrase).

   Suggestion: If you have time, have students make their own sentence for each example listed in the boxes for Focus 4 (examples a–t). If you are short on time, let students make their own example sentence for each *Use* in the first section of Focus 4 (five different uses) and one example for each *Explanation* in the next two sections of the chart (five different explanations).

EXERCISE 9 [10 minutes]

Exercise 9 has students combine the modals *should* and *have to*. Continuing with the topic of

immigration and citizenship, this exercise gives students practice expressing their own ideas about what people should or shouldn't have to do.

1. **Lead-in:** Begin with a short discussion of the "duties of citizenship." Ask the class for ideas about what they **should** and **should not have to do** to be a citizen of a country (the United States or another country).

2. Have the class spend a few minutes going through the list in Exercise 9 and decide for themselves whether each should or should not be required of a citizen. Ask them to also include three more ideas.

3. Put students into pairs and have them share their opinions. Ask them to use complete sentences in order to reinforce the use of these modals.

4. As students finish, have volunteers write a sentence of their choice on the board to share with the class. Point out the two modals in each sentence and again note the rules from Focus 4. See possible answers on LP page 78.

EXPANSION 1 [15 minutes]

You may want to assign Activity 1 (speaking) on SB page 82 as a follow-up to Exercise 9. In this activity, students will work as a committee to decide which of three candidates should be given a residence visa.

EXPANSION 2 [15 minutes]

Having students share opinions and look for the use of modals in the opinions of others demonstrates how modals can be used in context. Newspaper editorials can be a good place to find modals used to express opinions.

1. Bring several newspaper editorial sections to class. Have pairs look through the letters for examples of modals. They can underline or highlight any modals they find.

2. Have pairs write down five examples. They will then need to see if they can decide on the meaning of each modal, using the focus charts as a reference to state each modal's use or meaning. (Use the overhead transparency you created listing meanings and uses as a reference.)

3. Circulate and assist students. As students come across new vocabulary, you may want to put terms on the board to share with the class later.

4. Finish the exercise by either having pairs share their findings with the class or ask students for anything they noticed or were surprised by in this editorial modal search.

EXPANSION 3 [homework]

Have students practice using these modals by writing their own letter to the editor.

1. Brainstorm with the class about some problems they have found with the school or community they live in. These problems might include things such as parking issues, hours the library is open, difficulty getting into the classes they want, public transportation, etc.

2. Now explain that they will be writing their own letter to the editor (editorial), which will state a problem and then state some suggestions for change. These letters should include modals (you may wish to set a minimum number). Look again at the format of the newspaper editorials and answer any questions.

3. When students have finished, ask volunteers to read their letters to the class or in small groups. If you have a school newspaper, it can be very empowering for students to use their writing for real life and actually submit their letters to the school paper for possible publication.

EXERCISE 10

What modal meanings are being expressed by the following sentences?

Example: Don't leave your passport anywhere that the children are going to be able to reach. *(future activity, ability)*

1. We're going to have to leave the country if our government gets any more repressive.
2. If the immigration officer asks for another document, we aren't going to be able to get our visa today.
3. The customs agent isn't going to permit anyone to go behind the counter.
4. Most people have to be able to feel their private property is protected in order to live without worry.
5. Citizens have got to be allowed to vote if the government is going to stay legitimate.
6. Some people feel that anyone who wants to become an American citizen ought to be able to speak English.
7. Children under 18 years old aren't supposed to be allowed to immigrate without their parents' permission.
8. You don't have to be able to speak the language of a country in order to want to live there.

EXERCISE 11

Combine the modal meanings given below.

Example: You <u>might be allowed to</u> bring a guest. *(possibility, permission)*

1. Use a one-word and phrasal modal combination:
   a. I _____ speak with the visa officer. (necessity, permission)
   b. Noncitizens _____ to get drivers licenses. (advisability, permission)
   c. Students _____ speak English in class. (advisability, necessity)

2. Use two phrasal modals:
   a. A prospective immigrant _____ describe the system of government of the new country. (necessity, ability)
   b. I _____ come to the immigration meeting.
   c. In order for a society to be healthy, people _____ speak freely. (necessity, ability)
   d. You _____ speak French if you want a job in Paris. (advisability, ability)

EXERCISE 12

Pretend you are planning to immigrate to a new country. Make sentences that combine the following modal meanings.

Example: future possibility and permission

I may be allowed to run for political office after I get my new citizenship.

1. advisability and ability
2. necessity and ability
3. future possibility and ability
4. advisability and necessity
5. necessity and permission
6. advisability and permission

FOCUS 5   Formal and Informal Use of Modals

use

There are differences in the level of formality between some one-word and phrasal modals.

	MORE FORMAL	LESS FORMAL
Ability *be able to/can*	(a) I'm not able to speak to you now.	(b) I can't speak to you now.
Future activity *be going to/will*	(c) I will work a little longer.	(d) I'm going to work a little longer.
Necessity *must/have to, have got to*	(e) We must go.	(f) We have to go. (g) We ('ve) got to get out of here!
Advisability *should/ought to*	(h) You should tell your parents.	(i) You ought to tell your parents.

EXERCISE 13

With a partner, discuss the following topics using informal language. Compare the modals you used with those in your partner's sentences.

1. a daily responsibility
2. the best way to keep in touch with friends far away
3. advice for a lazy student
4. a possible event or occurrence next year

Choose one or two sentences and change them to more formal language to tell your teacher or the rest of the class.

ANSWER KEY

Exercise 10 1. future activity, necessity 2. future activity, ability 3. future activity, permission 4. necessity, ability 5. necessity, permission 6. advisability, ability 7. advisability, ability 8. necessity, ability

Exercise 11 Answers will vary. Possible answers are: 1. a. must be allowed to b. should/shouldn't be allowed c. should have to 2. a. has to/has got to be able to b. am going to be able to c. have to be able to d. had better/ought to be able to

Exercise 12 Answers will vary.

Exercise 13 Answers will vary. Possible answers are (informal/formal): 1. You gotta call your mother./You have to call your mother. 2. You oughta send them a tape recording./You ought to send them a tape recording. 3. You'd better not forget your homework./You must not forget your homework. 4. We gotta take a trip next year./We could take a trip next year.

LESSON PLAN 3

EXERCISE 10 [10 minutes]

1. Write the example sentence for this exercise on the board and ask volunteers to identify each of the **two** phrasal modals in the sentence. (*are going to = future activity, be able to = ability*) Go over the meanings of each. (You may want to again put up the overhead transparency you created earlier in the unit listing meanings and uses.)

2. Have students complete the exercise individually (remind students to look for two phrasal modals in each sentence) and then check over their answers with a partner or in small groups. See answers on LP page 80.

EXERCISE 11 [15 minutes]

1. **Lead-in:** Begin by listing the following uses for modals on the board:

necessity   permission   possibility   advisability   ability

2. Have students begin the exercise by suggesting both one-word and phrasal modals for each of these uses. (See the charts in Focus 2 and Focus 3 on SB pages 68–70 and 72–73.) Keep this list on the board for use again in Exercise 12.

3. After listing some of these modals, review the rules from Focus 4 on SB page 78 for combining one-word and phrasal modals.

4. Look at the first example in Exercise 11 and discuss how this example uses the modals of possibility (*might*) and permission (*be allowed to*) together. Ask the class what rules the example follows. (might + be allowed to = *one-word modals always come first*)

5. You may want to do the first sentence in Exercise 11 together as a class. Ask a volunteer to read the directions for the first three sentences. Ask another volunteer to read sentence (a) and the two modals uses that follow (*necessity, permission*). Now have the class look again at the list on the board for a combination of modals that would fit this.

6. Have students finish the exercise on their own. See possible answers on LP page 80.

For more practice, use *Grammar Dimensions 3* Workbook page 27, Exercise 5.

EXERCISE 12 [15 minutes]

1. **Lead-in:** Begin by asking the class what might change for them if they were to immigrate to a different country. You may want to give some suggestions (using future possibility and permission) such as *I may be able to get a better job. I may be able to afford a housekeeper.*

2. Refer back to the list of modals on the board from Exercise 11. Now have students imagine that they are planning to immigrate (or just move) to a different country and write six sentences using the suggested modal combinations for each sentence.

3. Let students share their sentences in groups. Have volunteers put their sentences on the board to share with the class.

FOCUS 5 [5 minutes]

Students can see from Focus 5 that although some modals have the same meaning, they may be used to show different levels of formality. Go over the chart with the class. Give examples of different situations that might require the more formal choices versus the less formal choices.

PRONUNCIATION NOTE

Teachers may want to take this opportunity to highlight the informality of some of the phrasal modals in the far right column. In American English, pronunciation of the informal phrasal modals *going to*, *have to*, *have got to*, and *ought to* can be demonstrated with the natural speed that comes with saying their shortened forms as in:

I'm gonna go now.
I hafta go now.
I've gotta go now.
I oughtta go now.

If you write these examples on the board to show the pronunciation of shortened forms, remind students that this is just to demonstrate and that these spellings are not used when writing these modals.

EXERCISE 13 [15 minutes]

Exercise 13 gives students the chance to use the informal choices from Focus 5 to speak informally with a classmate. Students then contrast their previous informal choices by choosing more formal language for the situation.

1. Put students into pairs and have them speak together on the four topics listed in Exercise 13. You may want to encourage them to use the informal shortened pronunciation (e.g., *I hafta clean my room each day*).

2. Circulate and listen to the informal modal choices. When students are finished discussing the topics listed, have volunteers put their informal sentences on the board.

3. Now have the class take a few of their own sentences from the discussion and have volunteers present sentences to the class using more formal modal choices. Have the class decide if these are appropriate. Let students take turns making the examples on the board more formal.

For more practice, use *Grammar Dimensions 3* Workbook page 28, Exercise 6, and page 29, Exercises 7 and 8.

UNIT GOAL REVIEW [10 minutes]

Ask students to look at the goals on the opening page of the unit again. Refer to the pages of the unit where information on each goal can be found.

ExamView®
Test Generator   For assessment of Unit 5, use *Grammar Dimensions 3* ExamView®.

Use Your English

ACTIVITY 1 speaking

Below are descriptions of three people who have applied for citizenship in a new country. In a small group, pretend that you are a committee who has to decide which one should be given a residence visa. (You can only choose one!) Follow these steps:

■ STEP 1   Examine the applicants' reasons for wanting to immigrate. Decide whether they will be able to fulfill the basic duties of citizenship in the new country.

■ STEP 2   As a group, decide which applicant most deserves the residence visa and which one least deserves it.

■ STEP 3   Present your decision and your reasons to the rest of the class.

APPLICANT A	APPLICANT B	APPLICANT C
• belongs to a religion that is discriminated against in his or her country and will probably be imprisoned or executed because of those beliefs	• wants to earn higher wages and send the money back to relatives in the home country	• was jailed for political activity in college and is now being threatened by the secret police
• plans on maintaining the family's religion and language	• has skills that are needed badly in the new country	• doesn't agree with the politics or government of the new country and doesn't believe in paying taxes
• will not allow children of the family to go to public schools in the new country	• does not intend to vote or become involved in the politics of the new country	• is engaged to someone from the new country
• has few job skills and may need to be supported by public welfare	• believes in obeying the law, but will try to avoid national service	• has skills that are badly needed in the new country

ACTIVITY 2 reading/speaking

The first requirement for many new immigrants is to find work in the new country. This is often difficult to do because of language and cultural differences. Below are three advertisements for jobs available in clerical administration, computer programming, and sales.

■ STEP 1   For each job, identify

1. the things that an applicant must be able to do.
2. the things he or she should be able to do (although may not be absolutely required).
3. some things that are neither required nor recommended, but are still characteristics that the "perfect candidate" might have.
4. what an interested candidate has to do in order to apply for the position.

■ STEP 2   Would any of these jobs interest you? Why or why not? Compare your ideas to those of other students in the class.

PROGRAM ASSISTANT

Provide clerical and admin. support to five public program coord. involved in developing educational materials and providing training for hazardous waste workers.

QUALIFICATIONS: exper. operating word processing software and laser-printer hardware. Skill in establishing and maintaining master computer and paper files of program information. Interpersonal skills required to commun. with numerous instructors and staff on various university campuses. Organizational skills to estab. priorities. Related exper. working in a public service/public program atmosphere pref'd. SALARY: $1799-2124/mo. with excel. benefits. Send detailed résumé to:

Personnel Office
Box 1012, 1066 Hastings St.
San Francisco, CA

LAW FIRM PROGRAMMER/ ANALYST

Exciting opportunities exist in our office as we continue to develop, install, refine, and enhance automated solutions to law firm information processing. If you are a professional with 5 years of programming experience, have a background in 4 computer languages, and have business software development exp., we'd like to hear from you. We seek individuals who strive for excellence in their work product, who prefer a challenging, fast-paced environment, and who are service oriented. Excellent communication skills are a must!

Send résumé and salary history to:

Human Resources
PO Box 7B-23R
San Francisco, CA

SALES CAREER OPPORTUNITY

College Textbook Sales McGruder-Hall Western Region Office has immediate openings for 2 Assoc. Sales Reps. These positions involve both office sales support & selling textbooks to professors on college campuses. Qualifications include:

* 4 yr. College Degree
* Exc. Communications Skills
* Strong Organization Skills w/ Ability to Prioritize Multiple Tasks
* Desire to Move into Outside Sales Position
* Strong Motivation to Succeed
* Willingness to Travel

We offer excellent salary & benefits package. Please send résumé to:

Sales Manager
McGruder-Hall Inc.
5561 Francisco St., Ste. 738
SF, CA 94133

No Phone Calls Please

USE YOUR ENGLISH

The Use Your English activities at the end of the unit contain situations that should naturally elicit the structures covered in the unit. For a more complete discussion of how to use the Use Your English activities see To the Teacher on LP page xxii. When students are doing these activities in class, you can circulate and listen to see if they are using the structures accurately. Errors can be corrected after the activity has finished.

ACTIVITY 1 speaking
[15 minutes/homework]

You can use this activity after Exercise 9 on SB page 79 to follow the discussion on the duties of citizenship. This activity asks students to discuss and come to a consensus in small groups. The discussion and explanation of the results should result in the natural use of modals.

■ **STEP 1** This step can be assigned as homework or you can go over the three applications together as a class in order to clarify any vocabulary or other information before breaking into groups. Let volunteers take turns reading bulleted points for each applicant out loud to the class and make clarifications as necessary. Encourage students to make their own choice and to clarify reasons why they think the person they chose should get the visa before beginning the group discussion.

■ **STEP 2** Put students into groups and have them discuss the applications and come to a consensus. Tell them they will present their choice to the class along with the reason they chose a specific applicant and decided against the other applicants.

■ **STEP 3** Let groups share their explanations either with the class or divide the groups up and have one member from each group form a new group in order to share results.

ACTIVITY 2 reading/speaking
[20 minutes]

This activity gives students experience in deciphering the language of want ads and the abbreviations that are found in many of these.

■ **STEP 1**

1. Begin with a discussion on job advertisements. What types of information would one expect to find in a job ad? Take notes on the board of suggestions. Explain that many job ads will list *required* qualifications along with *suggested* qualifications (things an applicant *must be able to do* versus *should be able to do*). Give a job example (e.g., police officer or nurse) and ask the class what would be *required* or *suggested* as qualifications.

2. Have the class look at the job ads on SB page 83. Go over the first ad as a class. Students should be able to make good guesses for the abbreviations used. On the board list:

   Must be able to . . .
   Should be able to . . .
   Might also be able to . . .
   Have to do to apply . . .

■ **STEP 2** Have students discuss which jobs would be of interest to them and why that is. Circulate and assist as needed.

ACTIVITY 3 — writing

Write your own want ads advertising the qualifications and skills necessary for these occupations. First decide on necessary and desirable qualifications, and then tell interested people what they should do in order to apply.

English teacher

firefighter

executive secretary/administrative assistant

United Nations translator

police officer

computer programmer

ACTIVITY 4 — reading/speaking

Look in the want ads of your local newspaper and find two examples of jobs that you think you would like. Describe the positions to the rest of the class, and tell why you think you would be a good candidate for the jobs.

ACTIVITY 5 — listening

CD Tracks
9, 10

STEP 1 Listen to the two following conversations. Write down the topic of each conversation. For each conversation notice any modals that the speakers used and the context for using them.

STEP 2 Listen to the conversations again and list at least two examples of modals that you heard in each conversation. What meanings did these modals communicate in Conversation 1? In Conversation 2?

STEP 3 Compare your findings to those of other students.

• What differences in level or formality could you hear?

• Based on what you heard, think of one question you want to ask your teacher about using modals in English.

ACTIVITY 6 — research on the web

Go to the Internet and log onto the Web site of the Migration Policy Institute (www.migrationinformation.org). Click on "Global Data" and choose a country whose migration patterns you are interested in finding out about. Browse through the statistics there and prepare a brief report about the migration patterns in that country. How have they changed over time? Are there any surprising features? Report your findings to the rest of the class.

ACTIVITY 7 — reflection

What does it mean to "speak another language"? Read the skills listed below and decide whether each skill is in category A or category B.

Category A: A person **must** be able to do this in a new language in order to say that he or she "speaks the language."

Category B: A person only **should** be able to do this if he or she is a native speaker of the language.

Write the letter of the category in the space provided, and for each category think of one more skill of your own.

1. _____ read a newspaper

2. _____ understand native speakers perfectly when they speak to each other

3. _____ understand native speakers when they speak to foreigners

4. _____ have a perfect accent

5. _____ never make mistakes

6. _____ discuss abstract philosophy

7. _____ take care of day-to-day needs

8. _____ read and understand literature and poetry

9. _____ speak correctly enough that people can understand what you mean

10. A _____

11. B _____

Based on your definition, do you consider yourself to be fluent in English? Explain.

ANSWER KEY

Activity 5 All modals are listed here.

Conversation 1

Topic: People arguing about a noisy TV   **Modals:** 1. Can you turn down the TV   2. I can't hear a thing   3. You don't have to shout   4. You can be so unpleasant   5. You could try sitting   6. We wouldn't have to go to deaf   7. I can't hear you   **Meaning:** 1. request   2. ability   3. necessity   4. general possibility   5. suggestion   6. hypothetical statement   7. ability

Conversation 2

Topic: Parents talking about their fighting children   **Modals:** 1. Will you tell Steve to stop   2. She's going to cry   3. Boys will be boys   4. She's got to toughen up   5. She's going to grow up   6. Boys have got to become more supportive   7. We had better start teaching   8. They're never going to learn   9. Why shouldn't they act that way   10. You must be joking   11. You can't be serious   12. I'm about to lose my temper

Meaning: 1. request 2. future activity 3. general possibility 4. necessity 5. future activity 6. necessity 7. advisability 8. future activity 9. obligation 10. logical inference 11. impossibility 12. future activity

USE YOUR ENGLISH

ACTIVITY 3 writing [homework]

Activity 3 can be used to build on the work done in Activity 2, which defines required and suggested skills needed for jobs and the written style of job advertisements.

VARIATION 1

1. Let students choose one of the listed job titles (or suggest one of their own) and write up their own lists of necessary skills, etc.

2. You may want to ask for a minimum number of modals to be used in the ads.

3. Collect papers and give feedback.

Give each student job ad a number. Have students post their job ads around the room and let the class browse the ads and choose one to "apply for." Let them write briefly on (a) which job ad they chose (by position and number), (b) why they chose it, and (c) why they might be qualified for this job.

VARIATION 2

Instead of posting the ads around the room, you may just have pairs exchange job ads. They can then write briefly on whether they would or wouldn't apply for this job and why.

ACTIVITY 4 reading/speaking [30 minutes/homework]

This activity allows students to identify real job advertisements in their own community. By finding jobs that interest them, students will be able to speak about and share their own interests and skills with the class.

Ask students to bring the ads to class with them and be prepared to share the following: describe the job and the necessary skills or qualifications, tell the class what skills or qualifications you have that match this job's requirements.

EXPANSION [15 minutes]

Have students use this as a chance to practice interview or presentation skills. Encourage them to speak clearly and professionally as they present their job information. Review topics such as eye contact and projection. You may even take the role of interviewer and begin each student's presentation with *So Mr./Mrs. X, what position are you interested in applying for?* Follow up with questions such as, *And why are you interested in this position? Why do you feel you are qualified for this position?* OR *What makes you a good candidate for this position?*

ACTIVITY 5 listening [20 minutes]

CD Tracks 9,10

This activity gives students the chance to hear modals used naturally in conversation.

STEP 1 Have students first listen globally for the topics of conversation.

STEP 2 Play the audio again, this time having students listen for specific examples of modals. Have students determine the meaning of the modals in use for both conversations.

STEP 3 Let students compare their answers with a partner before listening a final time. Have pairs then discuss the differences in formality.

ACTIVITY 6 research on the web [homework]

Assign this activity early in the unit and report as you finish the unit. This activity will encourage analytical skills and academic research skills as students browse statistics on migration patterns on the Internet.

1. Specify the format and length of the report they should write and be sure everyone is clear about finding the website and accessing the information.

2. Have students share with the class or in small groups. Collect the papers for individual feedback.

Suggestion: You might want to assign countries before they begin to ensure a wide range of reports. Have students suggest a few countries that new immigrants to the U.S. come from. What country do they think the most immigrants to the U.S. come from? Why? You may even encourage students to end their report with their own predictions for the future.

ACTIVITY 7 reflection [homework]

You can have students add this activity to their *Reflection Journals.* This activity asks students to reflect on what it means to "speak another language." Students will vary in their responses and their own perception of what it means to "speak the language" and what can only be expected of a native speaker. Note that several skills listed are difficult even for native speakers.

UNIT GOALS

- Review the form of infinitives and gerunds and the meaning of infinitives

- Understand and use sentences with verbs followed by infinitives

- Use infinitives as the subjects of sentences

OPENING TASK

The "To Do" List

Getting ready to go on a long trip requires a lot of preparation. In two days John Tealhome is leaving to spend a year studying in France. On the next page is his list of the things that he needs to do before he goes, the things that he would like to ask his girlfriend Mary to do and the things he wants his roommate Charlie to do for him.

TO DO	Check with Mary	Check with Charlie
• buy Mary a present	• Does she really understand why I'm going?	• remind about helping move boxes to Mary's garage?
• say good-bye to Prof. Monteigne	• Is she still planning to visit? When?	• check with landlord about cleaning deposit
• buy address book	• move boxes to her parents' garage	• clean the kitchen
• buy suitcase		• change name on the bill for the electric company
• buy new jacket	• drive me to airport?	
• get small gifts for my host family	• have farewell dinner? Where?	• get address of his old girlfriend (ballet dancer) don't tell Mary!
• have farewell dinner with Mom & Dad		
• get traveler's checks		• get money he owes me
• reconfirm ticket and get seat assignment		

STEP 1

Look at John's "To Do" list and discuss these questions with a partner.

- What things does John still need to do?
- What things does he want Charlie to do?
- What things does he need Mary to do?
- What thing does he want Charlie not to do?
- Has he forgotten to do anything?
- How ready do you think John really is?
- If he doesn't have time to get everything done, what things should he be sure to do, and what things could he decide not to do without creating problems?

STEP 2

Present your answer to the last question to the rest of the class.

Opening Task *What things does John still need to do? He still needs to buy a present for Mary. He still needs to buy a new jacket. He still needs to get small gifts for his host family. He still needs to have a farewell dinner with his parents. He still needs to get traveler's checks. He still needs to reconfirm his ticket and get his seat assignment. He still needs to decide where and when to have his farewell dinner with Mary.*

What things does he need Mary to do? He needs Mary to drive him to the airport. He needs Mary to understand why he's going to France. He needs Mary to make space in her parents'

garage for his boxes. He wants Mary to decide when she is going to visit him in France. What things does he want Charlie to do? He wants Charlie to help move boxes to Mary's parents' garage. He wants Charlie to clean the kitchen. He wants Charlie to change the name on the electric bill. He needs Charlie to pay him the money he owes him.

What things does he want Charlie not to do? John wants Charlie to not tell Mary about giving him the address of his old girlfriend. He wants Charlie to not forget about helping move boxes. Answers will vary for remaining questions.

LESSON PLAN 1

UNIT OVERVIEW

The focus of Unit 6 is on the form and use of infinitives. The unit presents three patterns that infinitives follow along with the use of infinitives with passive verbs and as subjects of a sentence.

GRAMMAR NOTE

Infinitives (to + verb) can be used as subjects, objects of verbs or prepositions, or with adjective phrases. Infinitives can also be active/passive, affirmative/negative, and simple/perfect/progressive aspect as in:

His bags needed to have been packed before the taxi arrived. = passive/perfect

He decided not to leave today. = negative

Because gerunds are used similarly, the infinitive is often taught alongside the gerund with time spent on memorizing which verbs require a gerund, which require an infinitive, and which can take both. *Grammar Dimensions 3*, after addressing the meaning, forms, and patterns of first infinitives (Unit 6) and then gerunds (Unit 7), will give students practice choosing which to use following another verb (Unit 7, Focus 7).

UNIT GOALS

Some instructors may want to review the goals listed on Student Book (SB) page 86 after completing the Opening Task so that students understand what they should know by the end of the unit. These goals can also be reviewed at the end of the unit when students are more familiar with the grammar terminology.

OPENING TASK [20 minutes]

The aim of this activity is to give students the opportunity to work with the form, meaning, and use of infinitives. The problem-solving format is designed to show the teacher how well the students can produce the target structures implicitly

and spontaneously when they are engaged in a communicative task. For a more complete discussion of the purpose of the Opening Task, see Lesson Planner (LP) page xxii.

Setting Up the Task

1. Begin by asking the class to look at the picture on SB page 86. Ask the class the following questions:

   What do you think of when you see this picture?

   What are a few things you usually need to do before taking a long trip?

   What would you need to do if you were going away for a whole year?

2. Now have a volunteer read the paragraph above the photo aloud to the rest of the class. Bring the class' attention to the *To Do* list on SB page 87 and notice that John has broken his list into three categories. Also note that some things have been crossed off.

Conducting the Task

■ STEP 1

1. Put students into pairs and have them begin discussing the questions. Make note of any difficulties students are having. You may hear the infinitive used after verbs and adjective phrases such as *need, want, forget, decide, be sure, be ready.* You do not need to correct errors in form at this point.

2. Offer help with vocabulary when needed and write any new or useful terms on the board. After the class has come together, take a moment to discuss the vocabulary on the board.

3. Listen for student examples that use infinitives or gerunds to put on the board for use in the Lead-in to Focus 1 on SB page 88.

■ STEP 2

Have students present their answers to the rest of the class. Be sure to have students explain why they think some things on John's To Do list are more important than others.

Closing The Task

1. On the board, create two column heads: one for the things John *should be sure to do* and one for the things John *could decide not to do.*

2. Bring the class together and allow students to share thoughts on how ready they feel John is for his trip.

3. Ask groups to suggest ideas to place in the *"be sure to do"* and *"decide not to do"* lists. Have volunteers write in their ideas.

4. Draw the class' attention to any new vocabulary on the board.

5. Use these sentences to lead into Focus 1 on SB page 88.

EXPANSION [15 minutes]

Assign Activity 1 (writing) on SB page 102 as an expansion of the Opening Task. In this activity, students will make another list, this time of things that they need to do in the two days before leaving on their own overseas trip. They'll then write a paragraph about their experience, offering advice to other travelers.

GRAMMAR NOTE

For the most part, errors made with infinitives occur because the incorrect pattern was used after a specific verb.

Typical student errors (form)

- Using a noun/object with verbs that should be followed directly by an infinitive: * *Dan hopes the plane to arrive soon.* (See Focus 4.)

- Omitting the noun/object pronoun between a verb and infinitive when describing a situation where the subject causes or influences the performance of the action: * *She encouraged to try our best.* (See Focus 5.)

- Omitting *for* with verbs that require it to use an infinitive: * *His office arranged Dan to fly home on Monday.* (See Focus 6.)

FOCUS 1 | Overview of Infinitives and Gerunds

form

Infinitives and gerunds are formed from verb phrases.

EXAMPLES

	EXPLANATIONS
(a) We need **to use** infinitives in certain situations.	Infinitives are formed by adding *to* before a verb (*to* + verb).
(b) Other situations require **using** gerunds.	Gerunds are formed by adding *-ing* to a verb (verb + *ing*).

Gerunds and infinitive phrases function like noun phrases.

EXAMPLES

	EXPLANATIONS
(c) **Using** gerunds and infinitives can be tricky.	They can be used:
(d) **To know** which form is correct requires some experience.	• as subjects
(e) Some verbs require **using** gerunds.	• as objects of verbs
(f) With other verbs, you'll need **to use** infinitives.	
(g) This unit and the following one will focus on **using** infinitives and gerunds.	• as objects of prepositions
(h) By the end, you should feel confident about **choosing** the correct form most of the time.	
(i) But once you understand the principles, it's not difficult **to decide** on the correct form.	• with adjective phrases

---

Underline the infinitive and gerund phrases in this passage. Tell how three of the forms you have identified are used in the sentence.

Example: Norman likes to collect stamps.

Used as object of verb likes

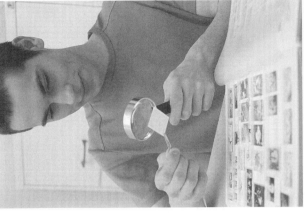

(1) Norman likes to collect stamps. (2) He likes getting them from anywhere, but he is particularly interested in collecting stamps from Africa. (3) He has tried to get at least one stamp from every African country. (4) This hasn't always been easy to do. (5) He has tried writing to the post offices of various countries, but they haven't always responded to his request. (6) A friend suggested looking in commercial stamp catalogs for hard-to-find stamps, and Norman has had pretty good luck finding rare or unusual stamps there. (7) He has also begun corresponding with stamp collectors in other countries and has asked them to send him stamps when they first come out. (8) They are usually happy to do it and have urged him to do the same thing for them. (9) He enjoys learning about other countries and finds that collecting stamps is a good way to do this.

ANSWER KEY

Exercise 1 (2) *object of verb likes; object of preposition* (3) *object of verb tried* (4) *adjective complement* (5) *object of verb tried* (6) *object of verb suggested; noun complement* (7) *object of verb begun; object of verb asked* (8) *adjective complement; object of verb urged* (9) *object of verb enjoys; subject of verb is*

LESSON PLAN 1

FOCUS 1 [15 minutes]

These boxes give an overview of the form and function of infinitives and gerunds.

1. **Lead-in:** Refer back to any examples on the board from the Opening Task and ask the class if they can spot any examples of the use of infinitives (or gerunds) in these sentences. Guide students to describe what an infinitive (or a gerund) looks like. How is a gerund different from a progressive verb? (*no be verb*)

2. Go over the examples and explanations in the first chart in Focus 1.

3. Write the following sentences on the board to use as examples of the functions of gerunds and infinitives:

   To help others is noble.
   Sam believes in helping others.
   Sam wants to help others.
   It's not always easy to help others.
   Helping others is noble.
   Sam enjoys helping others.

4. Ask the class to point out the gerunds and infinitives (you could also have volunteers come up and underline each gerund/infinitive).

5. Look together at the next chart in Focus 1 and have volunteers read the first two example sentences (c and d). Have the class find the two sentences on the board that also use gerunds or infinitives as subjects (*the first and fifth sentences*).

6. Continue going over each pair of examples (e–i) and asking the class to find similar examples on the board for objects of verbs (*the third and last sentences*), objects of prepositions (*the second sentence*), and used with adjective phrases (*the fourth sentence*).

EXERCISE 1 [15 minutes]

This exercise builds on the information in Focus 1 by asking students to find examples of the infinitive and gerund phrases and then to identify the functions of three of these examples.

1. Have students work individually to underline all the gerund and infinitive phrases in the passage.

2. Circulate through the class. As students finish up, if it appears that some students are missing many examples, tell the class the number of examples they should attempt to find. See answers on LP page 88.

3. Let pairs check their work together.

4. Have each student choose three underlined examples to tell their partner about. Each example chosen should be explained based on the functions listed in Focus 1.

5. Check answers as a class.

work
book

For more practice, use *Grammar Dimensions 3* Workbook page 30, Exercise 1.

FOCUS 2

Infinitives

form  meaning

EXAMPLES

(a) John wants **to study at the Sorbonne** while he is in Paris.

(b) He's afraid **to take the entrance examination** because he thinks his French isn't good enough.

EXPLANATION

Infinitives usually refer to the possibility of an action occurring. The action has not yet happened.

Infinitives can contain the same information as any verb phrase.

EXAMPLES

(c) John decided **to go** to Paris.
(d) Mary decided **not to go** with him.
(e) They want **to spend** John's last weekend in the country together so they decided **not to go** out with their friends.

(f) John needs **to pack** his clothes.
(g) His clothes need **to be packed**.
(h) John intends **to become** active in student government, and hopes **to be elected** to the student council.

(i) John would prefer **to have left** yesterday, but Mary would prefer next week.
(j) He hopes **to be studying** at the Sorbonne by January.

(k) Charlie plans **to have done** the things John asked him to do when John leaves for the airport. (He'll do the things before John leaves for the airport.)

(l) Charlie plans **to be doing** the things John asked him to do when John leaves for the airport. (Charlie will start doing the things just before or when John leaves.)

(m) Charlie plans **to do** the things John asked him to do when John leaves for the airport. (John will start doing them after John leaves.)

EXPLANATIONS

Affirmative/Negative
Affirmative infinitive: *to* + verb
Negative infinitive: *not to* + verb

Active/Passive
Active infinitive: *to* + verb
Passive infinitive: *to* + *be* + past participle

Perfect/Progressive Aspect
Perfect infinitive: *to* + *have* + past participle
Progressive infinitive: *to* + *be* + present participle

Aspect tells us when the infinitive happens in relation to the main verb.

EXERCISE 2

Complete the sentences by expressing the idea in the infinitive as a verb phrase. Be sure to include all the information about time, aspect, and active or passive in your verb phrase.

Example: I hope **to be elected** to the student council.

I hope _I will be elected to the student council_.

1. Charlie claims **to have paid** John the money he owes him.

Charlie claims that he _has paid John the money he owes him_ .

2. John expected Charlie **to have already talked** to the landlord.

John expected that Charlie _had already talked to the landlord_ .

3. Mary reminded John **not to forget** his passport.

Mary said, "_Don't forget your passport_ ."

4. John expected Charlie **to be cleaning** their apartment when he came home.

John expected that Charlie would _be cleaning their apartment when he came home_ .

5. Mary is never happy **to be left alone** on a Saturday night.

If Mary _is left alone on a Saturday night_ , she is never happy.

EXERCISE 3

Complete the sentences by expressing the underlined clause as an infinitive phrase. Be sure to include all the information about time, aspect, and active or passive in your infinitive phrase.

Example: John hopes that he will pass the entrance exam for the Sorbonne in two months.

He hopes _to pass the entrance exam in two months_ .

1. John has the hope that he will have finished all his tasks by his departure date.

John hopes _to have finished all his tasks_ by his departure date.

2. John's French teacher requires that all students stop talking when class begins.

John's French teacher requires all students _to stop talking when class begins_ .

3. The doctor told John: "Don't take this medicine more than twice a day."

The doctor reminded John _not to take this medicine more than twice a day_ .

4. John thought that Charlie would be cleaning their apartment when he got home.

John expected Charlie _to be cleaning their apartment_ when he got home.

5. When John is bothered while he is doing his packing, he doesn't like it.

John never likes _to be bothered while he is doing his packing_ .

FOCUS 2 [20 minutes]

In contrast to Focus 1, the Focus 2 charts focus specifically on infinitives, as will the rest of Unit 6.

1. **Lead-in:** Write the following sentences on the board:

   I hope to pass this class.
   I plan to visit my mom.
   I plan to have finished ESL classes by fall. (with perfect aspect)
   I decided not to take a math class. (with negative)
   I hope to be finishing ESL classes this summer. (with progressive aspect)
   I need to be picked up at 4:00. (with passive)

2. Let students read the first two sentences and then draw their attention to the first chart in Focus 2 on SB page 90. Point out that infinitives usually refer to things that have not yet happened or begun. These ideas are usually introduced with verbs such as *hope, plan, need, expect, want,* etc.

3. As you go through the second section of examples and explanations, have students find the matching example sentences on the board.

4. Finish up by summarizing the ideas in Focus 1 (SB page 88) and Focus 2. You can explain that Focus 1 showed that infinitives can function like noun phrases, and can be used as subjects or objects. Focus 2 shows that infinitives can carry the same information as a verb phrase including ideas of aspect, active/passive, and affirmative/negative.

EXERCISE 2 [10 minutes]

You will notice that Exercise 2 and Exercise 3 mirror each other in asking students to use the information in one sentence to create another sentence with the same meaning.

1. Put the following example sentence on the board:

   Mary hopes to see him soon.

2. Show the class how to express the infinitive in bold as a verb phrase:

   Mary hopes that she sees him soon.

3. Write a few more examples on the board and invite volunteers to make the changes.

4. Have students work individually to complete the exercise and then compare answers with a partner. Circulate and note any common errors to address before moving on to Exercise 3.

For more practice, use *Grammar Dimensions 3* Workbook page 31, Exercise 2.

EXERCISE 3 [10 minutes]

Use the same presentation to explain this exercise that you used for Exercise 2. This time you will need to use examples with a verb phrase and show how to express the verb phrase with an infinitive.

For more practice, use *Grammar Dimensions 3* Workbook page 31, Exercise 3.

FOCUS 3 Noun or Pronoun Plus Infinitive

EXAMPLES	IMPLIED MEANING	EXPLANATIONS
(a) Norman wants to collect foreign stamps.	Norman will collect the stamps.	Sometimes it is necessary to identify who is performing the action described by the infinitive.
(b) Norman wants us to collect foreign stamps.	We will collect the stamps.	
(c) Rare stamps are easy to identify.	They're easy for everyone to identify.	*to* + verb: The performer of the infinitive is usually the same as the subject of the main verb or "everybody."
(d) Rare stamps are easy for experts to identify.	They're only easy for experts to identify; not for other people.	*(for)* + noun phrase + *to* + verb: The performer of the infinitive can be a noun or an object pronoun (*him, us, etc.*).
(e) The stamp was difficult for Norman to obtain.	Norman had difficulty, but other collectors didn't.	

EXAMPLES		EXPLANATIONS
(f) Norman reminded us to give him the stamps.		Certain main verbs require using noun or pronoun + infinitive. (See Focus 5.)
(g) NOT: Norman reminded to give him the stamps.		
(h) Infinitives are difficult for students to understand.		With certain verbs (see Focus 6) and adjectives, the noun/pronoun + infinitive must occur with *for*.
(i) NOT: Infinitives are difficult students to understand.		

EXERCISE 4

Interview a partner to get two or three answers for each of these questions.

Examples: What things do your teachers expect you to do?
They expect me to speak up in class.
What things do your teachers expect you **not** to do?
They expect me not to copy my homework from other students.

1. What things does your partner's family expect him or her to do?
They expect me to study hard./ They expect me to do my best.
What things do they expect him or her **not** to do?
They expect me not to waste my time./They expect me not to forget to write them often.

2. How does your partner like **to treat** people he or she has just met?
I like to treat them politely./ I like to treat them in a friendly way.
How does your partner like **to be treated** by his or her teachers?
I like to be treated with respect./ I like to be treated in a friendly way.

3. What things do your partner's teachers expect him or her to do at the beginning of class?
They expect me to open my book./ They expect me to stop talking with my friends.
What things do teachers expect your partner **to have done** before the beginning of class?
They expect me to have done my homework before class./ They expect me to have studied the assignment.

4. What does your partner plan **to do** when school ends?
I plan to take a vacation./ I plan to go home for a visit.
What does your partner plan **to be doing** when school ends?
I plan to be taking a test./ I plan to be saying good-bye to my friends and teachers.

ANSWER KEY

Exercise 4 Answers will vary. Possible answers are listed above.

EXERCISE 4 [15 minutes]

This exercise works well to give students practice using the infinitive in natural speech with a partner. Have students close their books at first.

1. **Lead-in:** Begin setting up this exercise by asking students about their plans for the upcoming weekend or holiday.

   What do you plan to do this weekend/holiday?

2. Write a few answers on the board in complete sentences. The form should become clear as you continue asking questions and writing answers using the infinitive:

   Mari plans to see a movie. Thandi plans to visit friends.

3. Let students take a minute to ask their partner the same question and then you can ask students to tell the class what they learned about their partners' plans:

   My partner plans to sleep late this weekend.

4. Now have everyone turn to SB page 92 and go over the examples together. Take special note of the negative form used in the second example. Ask the class if they have any other answers to the question:

   What things do your teachers expect you not to do?

   This will give them practice forming the negative.

5. Direct the class to the first question in the exercise. Demonstrate by asking a student the first question in proper form and then writing the answer on the board:

   What things does your family expect you to do?
   My family expects me to work hard.

   Point out the changes to the original question and the format of the answer.

6. Have pairs complete the exercise together. As they do so, circulate, checking to see that students are making the necessary changes as they ask the questions and that they are writing their partners'

answers in the correct format. Have students share their findings with the class.

EXPANSION [homework]

You can expand this activity by having students go out and interview people outside of their class about future hopes and plans.

1. Have students make a form on which to write responses to the following questions. *What do you hope to do after you graduate? What do you plan to do after you finish this semester?* Then have them go out and interview ten people.

2. If you have time, put students into small groups and have them share their results with the group. Groups can create a chart or graph together to illustrate and present the results of their surveys.

LESSON PLAN 2

FOCUS 3 [15 minutes]

Focus 3 gives examples of the use of a noun (or pronoun) as an option before the infinitive to show that someone other than the subject is performing the action. As you go through the focus chart, be sure that the class can identify the performer of each infinitive.

1. **Lead-in:** Write the following sentences on the board. Underline the action in each sentence. For each sentence, ask the class to determine who is performing the activity, and list the performer on the board as the class goes through them.

   Norman needs to sign the papers. (Norman)
   Norman needs Anna to sign the papers. (Anna)
   The homework was easy for Anna to do. (Anna)
   The homework was easy to do. (everyone)

2. Go over the examples in Focus 3, along with their explanations. Note that when the performer is not stated, as in example (c), it will usually refer to "*everybody*".

3. You may want to go over examples (f–g) and point out that certain main verbs require the use of a pronoun or noun (in contrast to examples (a–b)). In addition, some main verbs and adjectives require the use of *for* before the noun/pronoun indicating the performer. These will be discussed in more detail in Focus 5 and 6.

EXERCISE 5

In these sentences identify who performs the action described by the highlighted infinitive.

Examples: Mary was expecting John **to be** ready before now.

John

Norman was asked **to bring** his African collection to the stamp club.

Norman

1. Norman claims **to be speaking** for the entire club.

   Norman

2. This airline requires people **to get** their seat assignments before going to the airport.

   people

3. Professor Montaigne requested her students **to bring** their books to class.

   her students

4. John's sister promised **to stay** after the party.

   John's sister

5. John intends **to pass** the entrance examination for the Sorbonne by Christmas.

   John

6. John asked his friend **to give** him his old girlfriend's phone number.

   his friend

7. Norman wasn't allowed **to stay up** late when he was a child.

   Norman

8. John's parents encouraged all their children **to study** in another country while they were in college.

   children

FOCUS 4

Verbs Followed by Infinitives: Pattern 1

Verbs Followed by Infinitives: Pattern 1

EXAMPLES	EXPLANATIONS
(a) **John decided to go** shopping but he **neglected to bring** his credit card.	With certain verbs the infinitive immediately follows the main verb.
(b) Charlie **tried to comfort** Mary, but she **refused to accept.**	
(c) Charlie **seemed to have** too much work, but he was only **pretending to be** busy.	

EXERCISE 6

There are seventeen Pattern 1 verbs in the following paragraph. Underline them and write the base verbs in the blanks.

(1) The Acme Stamp Company <u>agreed</u> to send Norman some stamps, but when he got them they didn't <u>appear</u> to be in good condition. (2) The company <u>claimed</u> to be reputable, but Norman still felt the stamps were bad. (3) He didn't <u>care</u> to pay good money for bad stamps and he felt that he <u>deserved</u> to get a refund. (4) So he <u>decided</u> to phone the company directly. (5) He <u>demanded</u> to speak to the manager. (6) The manager <u>pretended</u> to be concerned, but he <u>hesitated</u> to make any firm promises about refunds. (7) The company <u>offered</u> to exchange the stamps, but Norman <u>refused</u> to accept the offer. (8) All the stamps from that company <u>seemed</u> to be of poor quality. (9) The company also <u>tended</u> to be very slow in filling orders. (10) Norman has <u>learned</u> to make sure a company is reputable before placing a large order with them. (11) He <u>neglected</u> to do this with the Acme Stamp Company. (12) Norman still <u>hopes</u> to get a refund. (13) He is <u>waiting</u> to see if the company will give him one before he files a formal complaint with the post office.

agree	
appear	
claim	
care	
deserve	
decide	
demand	
pretend	
hesitate	
offer	
refuse	
seem	
tend	
learn	
neglect	
hope	
wait	

EXERCISE 5 [10 minutes]

This exercise asks students to identify the performer of an infinitive phrase. Students will notice that in some cases it is simply the subject of the sentence, and in other cases it is another noun or an object pronoun that precedes the infinitive.

1. Go over the example sentences as a class. Point out the infinitive phrase and then check to see whether the subject of the infinitive is a noun or object pronoun preceding the infinitive. If not, then decide whether the subject of the sentence is the performer of the infinitive.

2. You can either have students complete this individually or in pairs. Circulate and look for any common problems.

3. Check the answers as a class. See answers on LP page 94.

FOCUS 4 [15 minutes]

Focus 4 presents the first group of verbs, called Pattern 1 verbs (**verb + infinitive**). This contrasts with Pattern 2 verbs (see Focus 5), which require a noun phrase/object to follow, and Pattern 3 verbs (see Focus 6), which allow for an optional noun phrase/object:

Pattern 1 = verb + infinitive
Pattern 2 = verb + noun phrase + infinitive
Pattern 3 = verb (+ noun phrase) + infinitive

Repeated practice using these patterns through activities involving reading, writing, and speaking will help students to remember which pattern a verb takes.

Note: See Appendix A-7 for a list of other verbs that follow these patterns.

1. **Lead-in:** Write Pattern 1 formula on the board. Write a few example sentences using Pattern 1 on the board (see Appendix A-7 or Exercise 6 for verbs in this pattern). Some examples may include:

   Dana hopes to take biology next semester.
   Ali offered to help us.
   We decided to leave early.

2. Then go over Focus 4 with the class and note that there is nothing between the main verbs and the infinitives in these examples. The **main verb** determines this. Ask volunteers to point out the main verbs and the infinitives for each example sentence. Move directly into Exercise 6 below for more practice in this.

   Suggestion: Have the class work together in pairs or small groups to create a poster chart or page in their notebook that lists the main verbs used with Pattern 1. Go back through the focus chart and circle the main verbs that precede the infinitives. Put these on the Pattern 1 chart.

For more practice, use *Grammar Dimensions 3* Workbook page 32, Exercise 4.

EXERCISE 6 [15 minutes]

Exercise 6 gives students practice in identifying the main verbs that determine the use of Pattern 1 as seen in Focus 4.

1. After working as a class to isolate the main verbs that occur directly before an infinitive, have students work individually to find the remaining main verbs. Remind students to write these verbs in their base form only.

2. As students work, circulate to check that they understand the directions (students may mistakenly write the infinitives rather than the main verbs).

3. Have pairs check their answers together. Bring the class together and check that everyone has the correct answers. Again, point out that these verbs will follow the pattern of verb + infinitive. See answers on LP page 94.

FOCUS 5 — Verbs Followed by Infinitives: Pattern 2

Pattern 2: Verb + Noun/Object Pronoun + Infinitive

EXAMPLES	EXPLANATIONS
(a) Other stamp collectors have advised **Norman to order** stamps from catalogs.	Some verbs are followed by a noun/object pronoun plus infinitive. They describe situations where the subject causes or influences someone or something else to perform the action described by the infinitive.
(b) They **warned him not to spend** a lot of money unless he could **trust the stamp company to send** genuine stamps.	

Verbs that occur only with this pattern are:

advise	convince	hire	persuade	tell
allow	encourage	invite	remind	trust
cause	forbid	order	require	urge
command	force	permit	teach	warn

EXERCISE 9

Create sentences using the cues given.

Examples: (advise/study) *John's parents advised him to study French.*

(force/cancel) *The heavy fog forced the airport to cancel all flights.*

1. remind/pay
2. warn/not forget
3. convince/help
4. hire/work
5. require/pay
6. forbid/marry
7. invite/join
8. teach/speak
9. allow/leave
10. order/send
11. urge/vote
12. trust/spend
13. tell/eat
14. encourage/ask
15. force/leave

EXERCISE 7

Complete these sentences with infinitive phrases. Express your real opinion. Compare your answers with those of other students.

Example: An honest person should never pretend . . . . _to be something that he or she really isn't._

1. A good parent should never neglect _to give his child a good education_ .
2. Most children in elementary school learn _to read and write_ .
3. Most poor people can't afford _to take foreign vacations_ .
4. The world situation today seems _to be getting worse and worse_ .
5. Shy students sometimes hesitate _to raise their hands in class_ .
6. Selfish people rarely offer _to help other people_ .
7. A good friend should never refuse _to help a friend in trouble_ .
8. Criminals deserve _to be punished for their crimes_ .
9. Most children hope _to become wealthy and famous_ .
10. In general, good students tend _to think for themselves_ .
11. Most American teenagers can't wait _to become adults_ .
12. Most good teachers seem _to like and respect their students_ .
13. An honest person should never agree _to tell a lie_ .
14. Excellent athletes often appear _to perform difficult actions effortlessly_ .

EXERCISE 8

Interview a partner and find out about five of the following topics. Report your information to the rest of the class in full sentences.

Example: *My partner often neglects to do her homework.*

1. a responsibility he or she often neglects to do
2. something he or she learned to do in English class
3. something he or she can't afford to do
4. a kind of assistance that he or she would never hesitate to accept
5. something he or she would refuse to do, no matter how much he or she were paid to do it
6. a reward he or she thinks he or she deserves to receive
7. how he or she tends to behave in a room full of strangers
8. something he or she pretended to do as a child
9. how people in this class appeared to be on the first day of school
10. a famous person he or she would never care to meet

ANSWER KEY

Exercise 7 Answers will vary. Possible answers are listed above.

Exercise 8 Answers will vary. Possible answers are: 1. My partner often neglects to do her homework. 2. My partner learned to take lecture notes in English class. 3. My partner can't afford to go out to dinner every night. 4. My partner would never hesitate to accept help from a friend. 5. My partner would refuse to steal money from a friend. 6. My partner thinks he deserves to get an A in this class. 7. My partner tends to be shy in a room full of strangers. 8. My partner pretended to be a cowboy. 9. My partner thought they appeared to be nervous. 10. My partner would never care to meet Madonna.

Exercise 9 Answers will vary widely.

EXERCISE 7 [20 minutes]

1. Write the following sentences on the board:

   I never forget . . .
   Students should remember . . .

2. Go around the class and ask students to complete the sentences by asking *What is something that you never forget to do?* OR *What is something that students should remember to do?* As you collect answers, you may want to list them on the board in their infinitive forms.

3. Go over the directions and the example for Exercise 7 with the class. Show the class how to put the example statement into a question *What is something that an honest person should never pretend to do?* Have volunteers put the first few statements in the exercise into questions. Let other students suggest answers for these questions. Encourage students to answer in complete sentences that include an infinitive (students may try to place a noun phrase in these statements).

4. Have pairs work to complete the exercise. Bring the class together and have students share their most interesting answers with the class. See possible answers on LP page 96.

workbook
For more practice, use *Grammar Dimensions 3* Workbook page 33, Exercise 5.

EXPANSION [homework]

Have students practice using this infinitive verb pattern while working on their listening and speaking skills with other English speakers.

1. Have each student choose five statements from Exercise 7 that they think will generate interesting answers or conversation outside of class.

2. Students make an interview sheet for their questions with room to write the responses of five to ten people.

3. When finished, have them do the interviews. Later, put students into small groups and let them share their answers, any interesting experiences they had, and any ideas on the best ways or places to find people to interview.

4. Let students share their most interesting answers with the class. Discuss any answers that did not fit into the infinitive pattern.

EXERCISE 8 [15 minutes]

1. Look at the example in Exercise 8. Give a few examples of framing the topics into questions (*What is...?*)

2. Have pairs interview each other about at least five of these topics.

3. Have students report interesting answers in full sentences to the class or in small groups.

Suggestion: Look back at the main verbs used in Exercises 6, 7, and 8 and circle them. Are there any more Pattern 1 verbs that you can add to the poster or charts the class has created?

workbook
For more practice, use *Grammar Dimensions 3* Workbook page 33, Exercise 6.

EXPANSION [homework]

For homework, let students get further practice with these verbs and expand on the topics discussed by having students write their own opinions about the topics listed in Exercise 8. Assign specific topics you would like the whole class to write about or let students choose topics of their own.

LESSON PLAN 3

FOCUS 5 [15 minutes]

This group of verbs (Pattern 2) follows the pattern of **verb + noun/object pronoun + infinitive.**

Note: See Appendix A-7 for a list of other verbs that follow Pattern 2.

1. **Lead-in:** Write the following sentences on the board:

   My friend reminded me to study for our test.
   We hired musicians to play at our wedding.
   She invited me to come with her.

2. Again have students find the main verb and the infinitives following. Have students suggest what is different about this pattern as compared to Pattern 1. (*these sentences have nouns or object pronouns after the main verb*)

3. Go over Focus 5 and write the formula for Pattern 2 out on the board. Ask students if they remember the formula for Pattern 1.

4. Have the class note that these verbs are followed by noun/object pronouns because they are influencing someone or something to perform the infinitive action. Look at the other verbs in the box that follow Pattern 2. The class may begin to see the similarity in these verbs. They all show an influence the subject has on someone or something else.

Suggestion: Have small groups make another poster or a chart in their notebooks identifying the verbs that follow Pattern 2.

EXERCISE 9 [15 minutes]

1. Go over the example sentences together. Ask students to circle the main verbs, draw a rectangle around the infinitives, and underline the required noun or object pronoun between these.

2. Have students complete the exercise, creating their own sentences. Circulate and check for correct use and placement of verbs and nouns.

3. Choose students to write examples on the board. Review as a class.

4. Collect papers from the class to give individual feedback on all their sentences later.

workbook
For more practice, use *Grammar Dimensions 3* Workbook page 34, Exercise 7.

FOCUS 6 | Verbs Followed by Infinitives: Pattern 3

form

Pattern 3: Verb (+ Noun Phrase) + Infinitive

EXAMPLES	EXPLANATIONS
(a) John expects to leave in an hour, and he expects Mary to come with him. (b) Norman wants to get stamps from every country, and he wants us to help him.	Many verbs can be followed by either an infinitive or a noun phrase plus infinitive.
(c) Mary's father arranged for John to get a cheap ticket. (d) He never intended for Mary to be unhappy.	A few verbs of this kind must use *for* before the noun phrase. Verbs that follow this pattern are: *arrange, intend, consent, afford.*

EXERCISE 10

Interview other students in the class about one of the following topics. Report your answers in full sentences to the class.

Examples: *Jamal likes to do the dishes, but he prefers someone else to do the cooking.*

Hamdi needs to write a statement of purpose for her university application, but she needs a native English speaker to check over her grammar.

1. things they like to do versus things they like someone else to do
2. things they expect to do versus things they expect someone else to do
3. things they have asked to do versus things they have asked someone else to do
4. things they need to do versus things they need someone else to do
5. things they have arranged to do versus things they have arranged for other people to do

---

EXERCISE 11

Combine these sentence pairs by replacing *this* with an infinitive phrase made from the information in the first sentence.

Example: John will spend a year in France. Mary doesn't want this.
Mary doesn't want John to spend a year in France.

1. John will write a long letter once a week. Mary has requested **this**.
2. John might postpone his trip until next year. Mary would prefer **this**.
3. She will try to visit him while he's there. She has decided **this**.
4. She was upset by the news of his plans. He didn't expect **this**.
5. John got a very cheap ticket. Mary's father arranged **this**.
6. John didn't apply for a passport. He neglected **this**.
7. John will report to the police when he arrives. French law requires **this**.
8. Mary will begin to study French herself. John has encouraged **this**.
9. Mary feels hurt that John is leaving. John never intended **this**.

ANSWER KEY

Exercise 10 Answers will vary. Possible answers are: 1. My partner likes to do the dishes, but he prefers someone else to do the cooking. 2. My partner expects to study hard, and he expects his teacher to answer his questions. 3. My partner has asked to leave the room and he has asked me to go with him. 4. My partner needs to get a haircut, but he needs someone else to cut his hair. 5. My partner has arranged to leave on vacation right after school, and she has arranged for me to pick up her report card.

Exercise 11 1. Mary has requested John to write a long letter once a week. 2. Mary would prefer (for) John to postpone his trip until next year. 3. She has decided to visit him while he's there. 4. He didn't expect her to be upset by the news of his plans. 5. Mary's father arranged for John to get a very cheap ticket. 6. John neglected to apply for a passport. 7. French law requires John to report to the police when he arrives. 8. John has encouraged Mary to begin to study French herself. 9. John never intended for Mary to feel hurt that he is leaving.

LESSON PLAN 3

FOCUS 6 [15 minutes]

Pattern 3 verbs are presented here with an optional noun phrase by the formula: **verb (+ noun phrase) + infinitive.**

Note: See Appendix A-7 for a list of other verbs that follow Pattern 3.

1. **Lead-in:** Remind the class of the Pattern 1 verbs and the Pattern 2 verbs by writing the formulas on the board. Then add the formula for the Pattern 3 verbs:

   Pattern 3 = verb (+ noun phrase) + infinitive

2. Write a few examples on the board that follow Pattern 3. For example:

   I need to wash my car.
   I need someone to fix my car.
   David wants to get a job.
   David wants his wife to get a job.
   I arranged to work extra hours.
   I arranged for Sam to work my hours.

3. Have students take turns reading sentences out loud to the class and stating the main verb, the infinitive and the (optional) noun phrase in between. You may want to have students come up and circle, underline, and highlight these.

4. Go over Focus 6. Note the need to put *for* before noun phrases when using *arrange, intend, consent* or *afford.*

Suggestion: Have small groups make another poster or a chart in their notebooks identifying the verbs which follow Pattern 3. Make a special section for the verbs that will require *for* with a noun phrase.

EXERCISE 10 [15 minutes]

This exercise will give students a chance to practice using the verbs that follow Pattern 3. These verbs have the option to take a noun phrase between the main verb and infinitive.

1. Give the class a few sentences about the things that you prefer to do yourself and things that you prefer others to do for you. Some examples may include:

   I like to cook, but I like someone else to clean up.
   I like to go to the beach, but I like someone else to drive.

2. Have volunteers suggest things that they like to do and things that they like or prefer others to do. Then have the class go over the examples in the book for Exercise 10 and point out the placement of the noun clause in the second part of each example.

3. Have students interview a partner and write complete sentences for their answers. If you need to review putting these topics into questions for the interview see Exercise 7 on SB page 96. Circulate to see how the class is doing and to answer any questions student may have.

4. Let students share their most interesting answers with the class by writing interview responses on the board. Go over any problems. See possible answers on LP page 98.

For more practice, use *Grammar Dimensions 3* Workbook page 34, Exercise 8.

EXERCISE 11 [15 minutes]

Students will do sentence combining by taking information and adding it to another sentence as an infinitive clause.

1. Write the following sentences on the board:

   Hanna will leave tomorrow.
   Josh didn't expect this.

2. Ask for volunteers to combine these two sentences into one. Don't be surprised if you get a suggestion such as ** Josh didn't expect Hanna will leave tomorrow.* Remind the class that the main verb *expect* needs to be followed by an infinitive (with an optional noun phrase) as in:

   Josh didn't expect Hanna to leave tomorrow.

3. Let volunteers point out the main verb, the infinitive phrase replacing the word *this* in the second sentence, and the noun between them.

4. Do the same for the example sentence in the book. Point out that students' newly combined sentences should start with the second sentence in each pair. The word *this* will then be replaced with an infinitive phrase made from the first sentence. Students should include a noun between the two verbs if the two sentences have different subjects.

5. Let students work individually. Circulate and assist. As they finish and begin checking with a partner, have some students write their sentences on the board for the class to check. Remind them to check for any verbs that require the use of *for* before a noun phrase (see Focus 6 for this list of verbs).

For more practice, use *Grammar Dimensions 3* Workbook page 35, Exercise 9.

FOCUS 7

form

Using Infinitives with Passive Verbs

EXAMPLES

(a) People warned Norman not to pay a lot of money for stamps from unfamiliar companies.

(b) Norman was warned not to pay a lot of money.

EXPLANATIONS

Pattern 2 and Pattern 3 verbs (except those that require *for*) can be used in passive sentences.

EXERCISE 12

Complete these sentences with infinitives. Use real information that expresses your true opinion. Compare your ideas with those of other students in the class.

1. Most people can be trusted . . .
   to do the right thing.

2. Children should be allowed . . .
   to try different kinds of food.

3. All teachers should be encouraged . . .
   to help their students.

4. Noisy people should be told . . .
   to quiet down.

5. Teenagers should be warned . . .
   to say no to sex.

6. Students should be expected . . .
   to ask questions when they don't understand.

7. Guests should be invited . . .
   to make themselves at home.

8. Rich people should be required . . .
   to contribute to charities.

FOCUS 8

form

Infinitives as Subjects of a Sentence

AWKWARD	BETTER	EXPLANATIONS
(a) To collect stamps is fun.	(b) It's fun to collect stamps.	Infinitive phrases can be used as subjects in a sentence. We usually begin such sentences with *it* and put the infinitive phrase at the end of the sentence.
(c) To have been introduced to Professor Montaigne is an honor.	(d) It's an honor to have been introduced to Professor Montaigne.	
(e) For John to study in France is a good idea.	(f) It's a good idea for John to study in France.	

EXERCISE 13

Complete these sentences with ideas that express your true opinion. Compare your answers with those of other students.

1. It's always a good idea . . .
   to look both ways before you cross the street.

2. It's enjoyable . . .
   to sleep late on Saturday mornings.

3. It's never wise . . .
   to smoke marijuana in front of a policeman.

4. It's every parent's dream . . .
   to have a child become a doctor.

5. It's never a teacher's responsibility . . .
   to give up her weekends to tutor lazy students.

6. It's sometimes difficult . . .
   to understand native speakers.

7. It's usually necessary . . .
   to work hard if you want to succeed.

8. It's seldom easy . . .
   to learn a foreign language.

ANSWER KEY

Exercise 12   Answers will vary. Possible answers are listed above.

Exercise 13   Answers will vary. Possible answers are listed above.

FOCUS 7 [15 minutes]

Focus 7 gives examples of both active (a) and passive (b) sentences used with an infinitive. Note that only Pattern 2 and Pattern 3 (not those that require *for*) can be used in passive sentences.

1. **Lead-in:** Write the following sentences on the board:

    Colleges require students to take an entrance test.

    Students are required to take an entrance test.

2. Ask for volunteers to tell which sentence is active and which is passive. Ask for volunteers to underline the main verbs and the infinitives (*require/to take*). Ask students which pattern the main verb fits into. (*Pattern 2*) Once students have identified the main verb as a Pattern 2 verb, ask them what the verb is required to have. (*a noun/object pronoun/object/receiver of the action*) Note how the passive is formed in contrast to the active phrase (see Unit 4 to review) and how the receiver/noun has moved into subject position in the passive.

3. Go over the examples in Focus 7.

EXERCISE 12 [15 minutes/homework]

You can also assign this exercise as homework. Students can bring in their own answers and compare them with partners in class.

1. Begin by going over the directions as a class. Referring again to Focus 7, tell students that they will need to put their own opinions into these passive sentences using an infinitive phrase for each.

2. After the sentences have been completed, let students share in small groups. It works well for all members of the group to go around sharing their answers to number 1 before going onto number 2, etc.

3. Circulate as groups discuss and make note of any problems you see or hear. Bring these up in the debriefing.

For more practice, use *Grammar Dimensions 3* Workbook page 36, Exercise 10.

FOCUS 8 [15 minutes]

Although both infinitive phrases and gerunds can be the subject of a sentence, infinitive phrases usually sound too formal and awkward. Instead, they appear in a sentence beginning with *it*. Focus 8 gives examples of this.

1. **Lead-in:** Ask students to finish the sentence, *It's fun to . . .* Write several student suggestions on the board and point out the infinitive phrases. Now demonstrate how these infinitive phrases can be put at the beginning of a sentence as the subject (e.g., *To exercise is fun.*) Explain that although it is grammatically possible to use infinitives as subjects, we think that it sounds awkward and strange, especially when spoken.

2. Have students look at the examples in Focus 8. Examples (a) and (b) are similar to what you have already put on the board. Examples (c) and (d) show the use of a passive construction with the infinitive phrase. Examples (e) and (f) show that by adding *John* (the performer of the infinitive is now different than the subject of the main verb) we must now add *for*.

3. Write these sentence starter formulas on the board. Let students practice completing the sentences:

    It's important _____ (*infinitive*)

    It's important _____ (*for + noun*)

    _____ (*infinitive*)

4. Write a few responses on the board below the formulas. Keep this on the board to refer to as you begin Exercise 13 below.

EXERCISE 13 [15 minutes]

After students have practiced completing the sentence starters in Focus 8, they should now be ready to express their own opinions using similar sentence starters in this exercise.

1. Begin by putting the first sentence starter on the board. (*It's always a good idea . . .*)

2. Ask volunteers to complete the sentence with their own opinions. Try to get a variety of ideas, including those that use *for* + noun. Write some of these on the board. Keep doing this until students are consistently creating infinitive phrases without many errors.

3. Have students work individually to complete the exercise with their own opinions. Circulate and encourage students to use a variety of responses. Refer back to the formulas and examples on the board from Focus 8.

4. After the sentences have been completed, let students share in small groups. It works well for all members of the group to go around sharing their answers to number 1 before all going onto number 2, etc.

5. Have groups report their favorite answers to the class. See possible answers on LP page 100.

For more practice, use *Grammar Dimensions 3* Workbook page 36, Exercise 11.

UNIT GOAL REVIEW [10 minutes]

Ask students to look at the goals on the opening page of the unit again. Refer to the pages of the unit where information on each goal can be found.

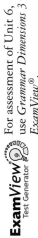 For assessment of Unit 6, use *Grammar Dimensions 3* ExamView®.

Use Your English

ACTIVITY 1 writing

In the Opening Task on pages 86 and 87 you examined the things on John Tealhome's mind a couple of days before his departure for a year overseas. Have you ever left for a long trip? How prepared and well organized were you two days before your departure?

■ **STEP 1** Make a list like John's that indicates the things you still needed to do, and some of the things that you needed other people to do for you. Compare your list and John's. Who was better organized?

■ **STEP 2** Write a paragraph describing your experience. Did you have a chance to do everything you needed or wanted to do? Was there anything you forgot to do? What advice would you give someone preparing for a similar trip?

ACTIVITY 2 speaking

Do parents treat boys and girls differently?

■ **STEP 1** Interview some classmates and find out what things children in their culture are taught to do when they are growing up.

	BOYS ARE ENCOURAGED TO . . .	BOYS ARE ENCOURAGED NOT TO . . .	GIRLS ARE ENCOURAGED TO . . .	GIRLS ARE ENCOURAGED NOT TO . . .
Examples	be brave defend their sisters	cry play with dolls	be neat and tidy play with dolls	play roughly get dirty
Student 1				
Student 2				
Student 3				

■ **STEP 2** Compare the responses of the people you interviewed. What differences are there? What might be the reasons for some of these differences? What things are taught to all children regardless of their gender or culture?

ACTIVITY 3 speaking

A **superstition** is a folk belief about lucky or unlucky events. For example, in some cultures the number 13 is considered to be an unlucky number. Friday the thirteenth is supposed to be a particularly unlucky day. Some people don't want to attend a party or sit at a table where there are thirteen people. Many buildings, especially hotels, do not have a thirteenth floor. Other superstitions still affect basic manners in society. Because of an old superstition, it is considered polite to say "God bless you" when someone near you sneezes, even to someone you do not know.

■ **STEP 1** Work with other students to develop a presentation for the rest of the class about some modern superstitions and how people act as a result of those superstitions. Identify some things that people try to do and some things they try not to. You may wish to compare the superstitions of several different cultures. Are there any superstitions that are universal? Why do you think superstitions come into being?

■ **STEP 2** Present your ideas to the rest of the class.

USE YOUR ENGLISH

The Use Your English activities at the end of the unit contain situations that should naturally elicit the structures covered in the unit. For a more complete discussion of how to use the Use Your English activities see To the Teacher on LP page xxii. When students are doing these activities in class, you can circulate and listen to see if they are using the structures accurately. Errors can be corrected after the activity has finished.

ACTIVITY 1 writing [15 minutes/homework]

This activity can be used after the Opening Task on SB pages 86–87 as writing homework.

Ask the class to think of a trip they have taken and how well prepared they might have been just two days before leaving. Let volunteers tell of a destination and get the class thinking about their own experiences. If students have never experienced this, ask them to pretend they have only two days to prepare for a trip they are about to take, and what they would need to do before leaving.

■ STEP 1   Ask the class to make a list like John's in the Opening Task. Let pairs take a moment to talk about their lists in comparison to each other's and John's.

■ STEP 2   For homework, have students write a paragraph as outlined in SB Step 2. Give parameters of length and possibly a minimum number of infinitives to include.

VARIATION

This variation of Activity 1 can be used as an in-class speaking activity or followed-up as written homework. In this variation, you will create an imaginary trip for the whole class to take in the near future.

1. Begin by having your class vote on a group destination for the upcoming vacation period. You may want to bring in a couple flyers from a local travel agency or the Travel section of your newspaper. You can then give the class three choices and let them vote.

2. Now ask pairs or small groups to begin preparations by brainstorming a list of all the things they need to do before they leave on this trip. Circulate and encourage them to make long and creative lists.

3. When the lists are complete, ask groups to respond to the following questions:
    What will you hope to do before you leave?
    What will you need someone else to do?
    What do you think you might forget to do?
    What things can you persuade someone else to do?

4. Have groups/pairs report their answers to the class or assign the questions as homework and collect papers at the next class.

ACTIVITY 2 speaking [15 minutes]

The infinitives are practiced through repetition of the interview questions. This activity is interesting for students because it can generate a wide variety of answers depending on the culture, age, and gender of those interviewed. If the students in your class are roughly the same age and background, you may want to take this activity a step further and have students interview people outside the class.

■ STEP 1   Have students move around the room interviewing at least three classmates for this activity. Be sure that they include the name of each person they interview. They should recreate the box in their notebook to fill it in, or set up their interview notes in a similar fashion.

■ STEP 2

1. When time is up, have students take a moment to look at their answers and make some generalizations in response to the questions on SB page 103.

2. Put students into small groups and have them share their responses to these questions. Let a writer for each group take notes on the answers to the Step 2 questions. Groups can then share their results with the class.

ACTIVITY 3 speaking [20 minutes]

Activity 3 asks groups of students to discuss superstitions and to make a presentation to the class about some of these.

Have volunteers read the section on superstitions out loud to the class. Ask for other examples of superstitions from students. Remind students that life events such as weddings, births, deaths, and celebrations are good places to look for superstitions along with ideas of health, luck, and general prosperity. Numbers, colors, and symbols can also be superstitious.

■ STEP 1   Ask students to share superstitions in groups. You may wish to organize the groups so that different nationalities are represented in each—many cultures have unique superstitions.

■ STEP 2   Have groups choose one or two superstitions to present to the class. Have them describe the basic superstition along with the things that people do or don't do in relation to the superstition.

Suggestion: You can encourage the use of infinitives simply by putting a few verbs on the board as suggestions for use in the presentations (e.g., *advise, cause, forbid, warn, remind, need, claim, hesitate, tend, seem,* etc.).

ACTIVITY 4 — listening

STEP 1

Read the questions below, and then listen to the conversation between two students for information to answer them in complete sentences.

STEP 2

Compare your answers with another student's. Listen to the conversation a second time to confirm or clarify any questions you're not sure of.

1. What information should the students expect to be tested on?

2. What were they told not to study?

3. What had the man been planning to do tonight?

4. Why wasn't the man in class yesterday?

5. What had he been told to do in order to improve his chance for graduate school?

6. Why doesn't he want a paid position at the library?

ACTIVITY 5 — research on the web

"Collectibles" can sometimes be worth a lot of money. In this unit you read about someone who collects stamps. There are many other kinds of objects that people like to collect, and they can sometimes command high prices. Go into *InfoTrac® College Edition* and type the keywords "treasures in the attic" or "collectibles." Scan articles to make a list of some of the other things that are considered "collectibles." Or, if you have a favorite collectible of your own, do some research to see whether your collection is worth much money. Present your findings to the rest of the class or write a short report for your teacher.

ACTIVITY 6 — reflection

STEP 1

Below is a list of some possible strategies for learning to speak English. Decide whether the listed strategy is something that language learners should try to do or something that they should try *not* to do in order to learn more effectively.

- Try to use new vocabulary in writing and conversation.
- Stop to look up every unfamiliar word in the dictionary.
- Be very careful not to make any mistakes.
- Guess at the meaning of unfamiliar words by using other clues in the sentence.
- Become discouraged if you don't understand 100 percent of everything you hear.
- Always think of your ideas in your own language first, and then translate them word-by-word into English.
- Listen for the general idea in conversations.
- Look for opportunities to speak English as often as possible.
- Go over your mistakes on homework and try to understand why you made them.
- Go over your mistakes on homework and write the correct answer.
- Find ways to punish yourself if you make a mistake.
- Don't speak unless you are sure the answer is correct.

STEP 2

List three more strategies language learners should try to use, and three strategies they should try not to do.

STEP 3

Compare your list with several other students', and present any interesting similarities and differences to the rest of the class.

ANSWER KEY

Activity 4 Answers will vary. Possible answers are: 1. anything in the second half of the book 2. anything in the first half of the book. 3. He had been planning on studying all night. 4. He had an appointment to be interviewed by the head librarian. 5. He had been told to try to get some practical experience. 6. He doesn't think he'd have much opportunity to get experience in all areas. The advisory board will give him a chance to learn about a variety of library issues.

Activity 5 One InfoTrac® article is "Treasures in the Attic: It Could Be at the Garage Sale Down the Street," from *Money Magazine, Dec. 1, 2005.*

USE YOUR ENGLISH

ACTIVITY 4

listening
[15 minutes]

CD Track 11

This activity gives students the chance to hear infinitives used in conversation and to use them in their answers.

■ **STEP 1**   Have students read the questions in Step 2 before listening to the audio. After listening to the audio, give students time to write down their answers in complete sentences.

■ **STEP 2**

1. Let students check their answers with a partner. Circulate and take note of any points of disagreement or particularly difficult questions to answer.

2. Play the audio again and have students check their answers or fill-in missed ones.

3. You may want to play the audio a little at a time as you go over the answers with the class.

ACTIVITY 5

research on the web
[10 minutes/homework]

● This Internet research activity can be used as a writing assignment, a presentation, or both. Be sure to set parameters for length and format when assigning a report or research project such as this. This will help give students focus and direction for their writing. You may want to have a small group discussion about collectibles before sending students out to begin research. Here are some ideas of topics to address in a prewriting discussion:

1. Do you or does anyone in your family have a collection?

2. If you could collect something, what would it be?

3. Did you collect anything when you were a child?

4. Why do you think people enjoy collecting things?

5. Why do you think people enjoy antiques?

6. What did you have as a child that might be considered an antique or something to collect now?

7. Do you have anything now that you think might be an interesting start to a collection?

ACTIVITY 6

reflection
[15 minutes]

Activity 6 can be used for students to reflect on their strategies as language learners by making them aware of the things they can choose to do to increase their skills in English. Students often feel that merely "soaking up" the language by attending class and doing homework will improve their language abilities. Letting students reflect on their own choices to improve their skills can help focus their energy.

■ **STEP 1**

1. Begin by having students read the list of strategies either silently or let volunteers read strategies to the class.

2. Give students time to divide the list up into things they should try or *not* try to do.

■ **STEP 2**   Encourage students to list three more ideas for each list.

■ **STEP 3**

1. Have small groups share their ideas and lists together.

2. Ask groups to share any interesting points with the class.

3. Have students write down their findings in their *Reflection Journals*.

UNIT GOALS

- **Understand the form and meaning of gerunds**

- **Understand and use sentences with verbs followed by gerunds**

- **Learn some basic principles about when to use an infinitive and when to use a gerund**

OPENING TASK

Leisure Time

How do you like to spend your free time? Researchers have found that most people fit into one of two categories: Do-ers and Be-ers.

DO-ERS like doing things during their free time. They have hobbies and activities that keep them busy. They plan their free time. A good vacation is one that lets them do many different things and have many new experiences.

BE-ERS prefer not doing things. They like to spend an afternoon relaxing, reading a magazine, or just doing nothing at all—sleeping, daydreaming. They don't plan their free time; they just let it happen. A good vacation is one that makes them feel relaxed.

◼ STEP 1

In this chart, list ways you spend your free time. Describe some things you do (or don't do) on a typical "day off." Two examples for each category have been provided. Add five more that are true for you.

ACTIVITIES I ENJOY DOING IN MY FREE TIME (I DO THEM, AND I ENJOY THEM).	ACTIVITIES I ENJOY *NOT* DOING IN MY FREE TIME (I *DON'T DO* THEM, AND I ENJOY NOT DOING THEM).	ACTIVITIES I DON'T ENJOY DOING IN MY FREE TIME (I DO THEM, BUT I DON'T ENJOY THEM).
1. *reading the paper*	1. *not getting up early*	1. *doing chores (cleaning and laundry).*
2. *talking with friends*	2. *not driving to work*	2. *taking work home from the office*
3.	3.	3.
4.	4.	4.
5.	5.	5.
6.	6.	6.
7.	7.	7.

◼ STEP 2

Describe the activities in your chart to a partner. Your partner should decide whether you appear to be a *do-er* or a *be-er*. What category does your partner seem to be in? Present your findings about each other to the rest of the class.

UNIT OVERVIEW

Unit 7 reviews gerunds and mirrors the previous unit on infinitives (Unit 6) by presenting three patterns and other places that gerunds are found. This unit concludes with explanations for and practice in choosing infinitives versus gerunds based on the difference in meaning between the two forms.

GRAMMAR NOTE
(see also the Grammar Note for Unit 6)

Gerunds (verb + *ing*) are basically nouns or noun phrases. Gerunds can be active/passive, affirmative/negative, and simple/perfect aspect as in:

*She hates **being told** what to do.* = passive

*He enjoys **not working** at night.* = negative

UNIT GOALS

Some instructors may want to review the goals listed on Student Book (SB) page 106 after completing the Opening Task so that students understand what they should know by the end of the unit. These goals can also be reviewed at the end of the unit when students are more familiar with the grammar terminology.

OPENING TASK [20 minutes]

The aim of this activity is to give students the opportunity to work with the form, meaning, and use of gerunds. The problem-solving format is designed to show the teacher how well the students can produce a target structure implicitly and spontaneously when they are engaged in a communicative task. For a more complete discussion of the purpose of the Opening Task, see Lesson Planner (LP) page xxii.

Setting Up the Task

1. Begin by asking the class what they enjoy doing in their free time on a "day off." Write these ideas on the board. Some may come as gerunds and some may not. Don't worry. You'll get a chance later to have the class try and change them all into gerunds.

2. Have volunteers read the captions below the pictures on SB page 106.

3. Now ask the class about the things they **enjoy not doing** on a day off. Give an example that is true for yourself (see Step 1 on SB page 107). Collect a few examples on a different section of the board.

4. Do the same for activities that they **have to do, but don't enjoy**. Get a few examples and put them on a third section of the board.

Conducting the Task

■ STEP 1

1. Now direct the class to the chart on SB page 107. Go over the headings and use examples from the board that match. Try to keep your directions and examples phrased with the key words "enjoy" or "don't enjoy," which will encourage your own use of gerunds naturally.

2. Now have the class put their own ideas under each heading. They should add five ideas to each column.

3. Circulate to see if students understand the headings. If they get stuck, direct them to some of the ideas on the board. Note whether they are naturally using gerunds or not. Don't worry if they don't use gerunds for all their ideas at this point. Errors can be corrected later.

■ STEP 2

1. When students have finished Step 1, put them into pairs to talk about their lists with each other and then decide whether their partner is a *do-er* or a *be-er*.

2. Have students share their findings about their partners with the class.

Closing the Task

Make a few observations about the things that your students enjoy and don't enjoy doing in their free time. Draw their attention to the use of gerunds following the verb *enjoy* and move onto Focus 1 on SB page 108. Keep the lists of activities on the board for later use.

EXPANSION [10 minutes]

You may wish to assign Activity 1 (speaking) on SB page 121 as an expansion of the Opening Task. In this activity, students are asked to form groups with classmates who are in the same category of *do-er* or *be-er* and decide on the best ways to spend a rainy afternoon.

FOCUS 1

Gerunds

form · meaning

EXAMPLES

(a) Norman enjoys **collecting stamps**. He doesn't mind **paying a lot of money for** rare ones.

(b) Mary isn't happy about John's **leaving for** a year.

(c) I hate **having** to do chores on the weekend!

EXPLANATIONS

Gerunds are nouns or noun phrases that are formed by adding *-ing* to the simple form of the verb. In general they refer to an action that is already happening or has been completed.

Gerund phrases can contain the same information as any verb phrase.

EXAMPLES

(d) I enjoy **staying in bed** on Sunday mornings.

(e) I like **not getting up early**.

(f) Peter likes **having a responsible job**, but he hates **not having enough free time** for his family.

(g) Matt and Jeff enjoy **inviting friends** for dinner.

(h) Matt and Jeff enjoy **being invited** to their friends' homes for dinner.

(i) Denise likes **giving orders**, but she hates **being told** what to do.

(j) Bambang was nervous about **taking** tests.

(k) Bambang was happy about **having gotten a good grade** on his exam.

EXPLANATIONS

Affirmative/Negative

Affirmative gerund: verb + *-ing*

Negative gerund: *not* + verb + *-ing*

Active and Passive

Active gerund: verb + *-ing*

Passive gerund: *being* + verb

Simple/Perfect Aspect

Simple gerund: verb + *-ing*

Perfect gerund: *having* + past participle

We don't often use perfect gerunds, and there is no progressive gerund.

EXERCISE 1

Complete the sentences by expressing the idea in the gerund as a verb phrase.

Example: I enjoy **not doing** anything on Sunday mornings.

I don't do anything on Sunday mornings, and I enjoy that.

1. I hate being asked to do laundry on the weekend.

When _____, I hate it.

2. I really appreciate your having cleaned the kitchen while I was taking my Saturday afternoon nap.

I really appreciate that _____.

3. Denise suspects Peter of sleeping on the job.

Denise suspects that _____.

4. We didn't plan for their having problems over the weekend.

We didn't plan for the fact that _____.

5. I think he resents not being invited to the picnic.

I think he resents the fact that _____.

EXERCISE 2

Complete the sentences by expressing the underlined clause as a gerund phrase. Be sure to include all the information in the verb phrase in your gerund phrase.

Example: I don't ever do any homework on Saturday nights, and I enjoy that.

I enjoy *not doing (never doing) any homework on Saturday nights.*

1. When I am asked for my suggestions about ways to improve my language skills, I like it.

I like _____.

2. Your teacher really appreciates that you have been so careful with this homework.

Your teacher really appreciates _____.

3. Mary suspected that John was planning to contact Charlie's old girlfriend.

Mary suspected _____.

4. The teacher didn't plan for the fact that the students had completely forgotten the grammar rules.

The teacher didn't plan on _____.

5. I think John is disappointed that he wasn't selected for the scholarship.

I think that John is disappointed about _____.

ANSWER KEY

Exercise 1 1. I am asked to do laundry on the weekend 2. you have cleaned the kitchen while I was taking my Saturday afternoon nap 3. Peter sleeps on the job 4. they would/might have problems over the weekend 5. he wasn't invited to the picnic **Exercise 2** 1. being asked for my suggestions about ways to improve my language skills 2. having been so careful with this homework 3. planning to contact Charlie's old girlfriend 4. the students having completely forgotten the grammar rules 5. not being selected for the scholarship

LESSON PLAN 1

FOCUS 1 [10 minutes]

Focus 1 introduces the form and meaning of gerunds. Although gerunds function similarly to infinitives, gerunds are used to refer to an action that has already been experienced. Gerunds can contain the same information as infinitives, but note that there is no progressive form for the gerund.

1. **Lead-in:** Refer back to the activities from the Opening Task. Ask students to point out a few gerunds. Ask students how gerunds are different from progressive verbs. (*no be-verb*)

2. Write the following sentences on the board:
   We enjoy speaking English everyday.
   They enjoy not doing anything on the weekends.
   She likes being invited to parties by her classmates.

   These will give you examples of using a simple affirmative gerund (first sentence), using a negative gerund (second sentence), and using a passive gerund (third sentence).

3. Have the class look at the first section of the chart in Focus 1 on SB page 108. Read the explanation out loud and have students read the example sentences. You may want to refer back to Focus 2 in Unit 6 on infinitives to point out the similarities between the two structures.

4. Move on to the second section of Focus 1 (examples d–k). Point out that gerunds work like nouns or noun phrases by showing how the sentences on the board using gerund phrases can be changed. You can underline each gerund phrase, and show how it can be replaced with the pronoun *it*.

5. Also point out that gerunds usually refer to things that have already been experienced or have begun. These ideas often include emotions about something that has already been experienced in the past and they are introduced with verbs such as *enjoy, appreciate, resent, mind*, etc.

6. As you go through the second section of examples and explanations, have students find the matching example sentences on the board.

7. Finish by summarizing the ideas in Focus 1. You can explain that, like infinitives, gerunds can function like nouns or noun phrases. Focus 1 also shows us that gerunds can carry much of the same information as a verb phrase including ideas of aspect, being active or passive, and being affirmative or negative.

8. Keep the three sentences on the board to refer to in Exercise 1.

EXERCISE 1 [15 minutes]

Exercises 1 and 2 focus attention on the content of the gerund phrase. In Exercise 1, students will take the content from a gerund phrase and create a verb phrase.

1. Refer students to the three sentences on the board that were used in Focus 1. If they are not already underlined, ask volunteers to identify again the gerund phrase for each sentence and underline it on the board.

2. Show the class how the gerund phrase can be written as a verb phrase and add an appropriate subject to make a complete sentence. As in:

   We enjoy speaking English everyday.
   We speak English everyday, and we enjoy it.

3. Do the same for the other two example sentences and check students' answers.

   They don't do anything on the weekends, and they enjoy it.
   She is invited to parties by her classmates, and she likes it.

4. Look at the example in Exercise 1. Although the second sentence is already completed, have students underline the gerund phrase in the first sentence (*not doing anything on Sunday mornings*). Point out that this information is used to create the verb phrase for the second sentence (*I don't do anything on Sunday mornings*).

5. Now look at number 1. Have students first underline the gerund phrase in the first sentence (*being asked to do laundry on the weekend*). Now ask them to take this information and create a verb phrase to put in the second sentence (*I am asked to do laundry on the weekend*).

6. Do another example if the class is confused. When they are finished, have them check answers with a partner and then go over the answers as a class.

For more practice, use *Grammar Dimensions 3* Workbook page 37, Exercise 1.

EXERCISE 2 [10 minutes]

Exercise 2 mirrors the previous exercise. Students will now take a clause (similar to the ones they created in Exercise 1) and create a gerund clause from that information.

1. Write the following sentence on the board:
   When I finish my homework early, I like it.

2. Ask a volunteer to come up and underline the first verb clause (*finish my homework early*).

3. Now begin a new sentence on the board with *I like . . .*

4. Ask another volunteer to come up and use the underlined verb phrase from the first sentence to make a gerund phrase to finish the second sentence (*I like finishing my homework early*).

5. Have students look at the example sentences. Point out that the underlined information in the first sentence is used to make a gerund clause with *not* (or *never*) used before the gerund.

6. Have the class take a moment to underline the verb clause in each sentence in Exercise 2. For example, in sentence 1, students should underline *am asked for my suggestions . . .* This will then become the gerund phrase *being asked for my suggestions . . .* in the new sentence.

7. Have students work individually and then discuss their answers with a partner before going over them as a class.

form

FOCUS 2

Noun or Pronoun Plus Gerund

	EXAMPLES	IMPLIED MEANING	EXPLANATIONS
(a)	Denise doesn't approve of **taking** time off.	She doesn't like anybody's doing it.	It is sometimes necessary to identify who is performing the action described by the gerund.
(b)	Denise doesn't approve of **Peter's taking** time off.	She doesn't like Peter to do it.	
(c)	Peter can't understand **being** so serious about work.	He can't understand why he or anybody should do this.	*verb + -ing:* The performer of the gerund is the same as the subject of the main verb or "everybody."
(d)	Peter hates **her complaining** about his absences.	Maybe he doesn't mind when other people complain; he just doesn't like it when she does it.	*possessive noun phrase + gerund:* The performer of the gerund is stated as a possessive noun (*Peter's* in (b)) or a pronoun in (d).

EXERCISE 4

In these sentences, underline the gerund and draw a line to the person who performs the action it describes. Circle that person.

Examples: Is there any way we can delay taking the test?

No politician will ever admit not having a solution to the budget problem.

1. Jeff enjoys playing with his puppy on the weekends.
2. I really appreciate your helping us get ready for the party.
3. Peter has considered looking for a job that has less stress.
4. Matt could never imagine taking work home from the office.
5. Mary resents John's spending a year overseas.
6. Denise will never excuse his having behaved so rudely.
7. John wanted to postpone leaving for the trip, but he didn't anticipate not being able to change his ticket.
8. We'll really miss Norman's singing and dancing in the stamp club talent show.

EXERCISE 3

Interview a partner and find out two or three things for each of these topics.

Example: Things your partner enjoys doing:

What things do you enjoy doing on Sunday mornings?

I enjoy reading the paper.

Things your partner enjoys not doing:

What things do you enjoy not doing on Sunday mornings?

I enjoy not getting up early.

1. Things your partner enjoys doing on the weekends.
   Things your partner enjoys not doing on the weekends.
2. Things your partner hates doing.
   Things your partner doesn't mind other people doing.
3. Things or services your partner likes giving to other people.
   Things or services your partner likes other people giving to him or her.
4. Things that attending a college typically requires **doing.**
   Things that attending a college typically requires **having done.**

Exercise 3 Answers will vary. Possible answers are: 1. What things do you enjoy doing on the weekends?/I enjoy sleeping late./I enjoy eating a fancy breakfast. What things do you enjoy not doing on the weekends?/I enjoy not getting up early./I enjoy not going to bed until late. 2. What things do you hate doing?/I hate doing grammar homework./I hate writing letters. What things do you not mind other people doing?/I don't mind other people helping me with my homework./I don't mind other people asking questions in class. 3. What things do you like to give to other people? I like giving help and advice to my friends./I like giving people silly presents. What things do you like other people to give to

you?/I like people giving me massages./I like other people giving me advice on my problems. 4. What things does attending a college typically require doing? Attending a college typically requires reading a lot of books./Attending a college typically requires studying several hours every night. What things do does attending a college typically require having done? Attending a college typically requires having scored well on the entrance exam./Attending a college typically requires having filled out an application.

EXERCISE 3 [10 minutes]

Exercise 3 moves away from a focus on the grammar and gives students practice using gerunds in a natural context as they interview their partner.

1. With student books closed, write the first example topic on the board (*things your partner enjoys doing on Sunday mornings*). Go around the classroom and ask students what things they enjoy doing on Sundays OR what things they enjoy not doing on Sundays.

2. Write several answers on the board (e.g., *Hing enjoys not getting up early on Sundays*).

3. Have students interview a partner about the topics listed. Students should be writing complete answers as they do the interview.

4. Circulate and check to see if students are having any trouble forming gerunds or negative gerunds. Address any of these issues when debriefing. See possible answers on LP page 110.

5. Bring the class together and let students share the most interesting things they found out about their partners. You may want to have some pairs write their most interesting sentences on the board as other pairs finish up their interviews.

Suggestion: To get students moving out of their seats, you can have students move around the room and ask each question of a different classmate.

For more practice, use *Grammar Dimensions 3* Workbook page 37, Exercise 2.

EXPANSION [homework]

You may wish to assign this activity as an out-of-class exercise.

1. Have students choose five topics and then create an interview form with clearly written questions before they head out.

2. Have students interview five to ten people (native speakers) and record their results.

3. After interviewing, you can ask students to either write a paragraph summarizing their results or present a summary of their results to a small group or the whole class.

FOCUS 2 [10 minutes]

This focus chart highlights the need to determine who is performing the action of a gerund. Focus 2 gives examples of gerund clauses with the same performer and then with a different performer than the subject of the sentence. Note that when the performer of the gerund is different from the subject of the sentence, a possessive noun or pronoun is used before the gerund.

1. **Lead-in:** Write the following sentences on the board:

    Emma enjoys singing.
    Emma enjoys Dave's singing.
    Emma enjoys his singing.

2. Point out that the first sentence can have different meanings. Does Emma enjoy singing herself or does she enjoy listening to singing? The second sentence tells us that Emma enjoys someone else's singing (*Dave's singing*). Dave is the performer of the gerund *singing*. Explain that we use a possessive noun (*Dave's*) or a possessive pronoun (*his*) when the subject of a sentence and the performer of a gerund are not the same.

3. Go over Focus 2 with the class. Note that example sentences (a) and (c) refer both to the subject or anybody in general. Also note that example sentence (d) uses the possessive pronoun *her*. (See the Grammar Note that follows.)

4. Keep the three example sentences on the board for use in Exercise 4.

GRAMMAR NOTE

Although the formal grammar rule says that a possessive pronoun or possessive noun (e.g., *his, our, their, Peter's*) is used to modify a gerund, native speakers will sometimes use an object form (e.g., *him, us, them, Peter*) in informal English. In addition, there are occasions when the possessive is awkward and can be let go (i.e., with a plural noun, more than one noun, or a long noun phrase) or when the possessive detracts from the meaning of the sentence. Students may notice this difference between their grammar books and native speakers or they may find that native speakers are unaware of the formal grammar rule.

EXERCISE 4 [10 minutes]

Students will practice identifying the performer of a gerund. This will help students to take note of whether the performer of the gerund is the same as the subject of the main verb.

1. Draw the class' attention back to the three example sentences on the board from Focus 2. Ask a volunteer to come up to the board and underline the gerunds in each sentence.

2. Now ask the class to think about who the performer of each gerund is. Have another volunteer come up and circle the performer of each gerund. The class will note that for the second and third sentences, the performers are not the subjects of the main verbs. In these cases, the possessive noun or pronoun is used.

3. Have a volunteer draw an arrow from the gerund to the performer.

4. Go over the example sentences for Exercise 4 and have students work individually to complete the exercise.

5. As you check answers in pairs or as a class, be sure to check for the use of the possessive nouns or pronouns when appropriate. (See preceding Grammar Note.) See answers on LP page 110.

For more practice, use *Grammar Dimensions 3* Workbook page 38, Exercise 3.

form

FOCUS 3 | Verbs Followed by Gerunds: Pattern 1

Pattern 1: Verb + Gerund

EXAMPLES

(a) Denise Driven can't help thinking about work all the time.

(b) Peter gave up bringing work home from the office because it took time away from his family.

EXPLANATION

Some verbs are followed immediately by a gerund.

EXERCISE 5

Underline the verbs in this passage that follow Pattern 1. The first two have been done for you.

LIVING THE LOW-STRESS LIFE

(1) Psychologists recommend reducing the amount of stress in one's life. (2) They suggest allowing time for activities you enjoy and avoiding activities that cause stress. (3) Some people deny having too much stress in their lives and would never consider changing their work habits. (4) Other people admit working harder than they would really like to. (5) But psychologists feel that everyone could benefit from the low-stress life, not only individuals themselves, but also their friends and families.

(6) Most people can't help having a certain amount of stress, no matter how relaxed they are. (7) But here are a few very simple, basic changes in daily activities that will greatly decrease the amount of stress in your life.

• (8) You can give up scheduling every minute of your day and keep some "open space" in your plans on a daily basis.

• (9) You should avoid making promises to do things you don't really want to do and quit doing activities that you don't find enjoyable.

• (10) You can practice making time each day for relaxation. (11) Such changes include not doing work activities on the weekend and spending time with loved ones or doing activities you enjoy instead.

(12) Initially these changes may be difficult, because we are taught to feel lazy if we aren't working, and you may resist changing old patterns. (13) But if you keep on following the basic principles listed above, it will get easier to keep doing it.

EXERCISE 6

Use five verbs that you found in Exercise 5 to describe some of your own leisure habits. Talk about things that you regularly avoid doing and things that you do regularly and intend to keep on doing.

form

FOCUS 4 | Verbs Followed by Gerunds: Pattern 2

Pattern 2: Verb + { Gerund / Noun Phrase + Infinitive }

EXAMPLES

Gerund

(a) Psychologists advise reducing stress in one's diet.

(c) They urge giving up activities that you don't enjoy.

Infinitive

(b) My psychologist advised me to reduce the level of stress in my life.

(d) He urged me to give up my weekends at the office.

EXPLANATION

Some verbs are followed by a gerund when referring to "everybody," and by an infinitive when referring to a specific person.

EXERCISE 7

For each of these Pattern 2 verbs listed below write two sentences—one with a noun phrase and one without. If you wish, you can write a single sentence that uses both patterns.

Example: advise

Most people advise taking a long hot bath if you want to relax but my doctor advised me to have a nice cup of tea instead.

Answers will vary. Possible answers include:

1. require

   Getting into a university usually requires doing well on the entrance exam.

   Bambang's university required him to get a score of 550 on the test.

2. encourage

   Health experts encourage getting regular exercise.

   I want to encourage you to study harder.

3. urge

   Doctors urge reducing fat in one's diet.

   My doctor urged me to lose weight.

4. advise

   Teachers often advise keeping a journal to improve your language ability.

   My teacher advised me to study harder.

5. forbid

   The government forbids selling drugs.

   My mother forbade me to stay up late when I was a child.

ANSWER KEY

Exercise 6 Answers will vary. Possible answers are: (1) recommend: I recommend following a stress-reduction program. Doctors recommend not exceeding more than eight hours of work a day. (2) suggest: My roommate suggests we get the house cleaning done early on Saturday so we can have the whole day to relax. (3) consider: In order to change your lifestyle, you have to consider changing your eating and exercise habits. (6) can't help: I can't help wishing that I had more free time. (8) give up: If you want to relax you have to give up trying to do everything. (9) avoid: I avoid taking on additional responsibilities at work. (11) include: My new stress-reduction plans include spending an hour a day exercising. (12) resist: I try to resist eating foods that are high in sugar or fat. (13) keep on: I plan to keep on working on this project until it's done; keep: It's important to keep trying, even if you sometimes don't follow your plan.

LESSON PLAN 1/LESSON PLAN 2

FOCUS 3 [15 minutes]

Focus 3 presents Pattern 1 verbs (**verb + gerund**). Unlike Pattern 2 and Pattern 3, these verbs are **not** followed by an optional noun phrase. To show the contrast, the three gerund patterns in this unit are:

Pattern 1 = verb + gerund

Pattern 2 = verb + gerund/noun phrase + infinitive

Pattern 3 = verb (+ noun phrase) + gerund

Repeated practice using these patterns through activities involving reading, writing, and speaking will help students to remember which pattern a verb takes.

Note: See Appendix A-7 for a list of other verbs that follow these patterns.

1. **Lead-in:** You can introduce this pattern of verbs by using several of them to give advice about a topic such as living a healthier lifestyle. Use a few verbs from the Pattern 1 list in the appendix A-7. You can write on the board *Advice for a Healthier Life.* Ask the class, "What do you think doctors recommend doing for a healthier life?" Write an example sentence on the board, such as *Doctors recommend exercising more often.* Encourage volunteers to add other suggestions. Then ask the class, "For a healthier life, what should people avoid doing?" (e.g., *People should avoid smoking.*) With the class, continue creating a list on the board of suggestions to encourage a healthier life using Pattern 1 verbs from A-7.

2. Go over the examples in Focus 3 and write the formula on the board.

VARIATION

You may begin instead by having students work on Exercise 5 before going over the focus box to check their understanding of the concepts prior to putting the formula on the board.

EXERCISE 5 [15 minutes]

1. Students will work individually to underline the verbs that precede each gerund.

2. When students are finished, have them check their work with a partner. Circulate and see how well students are distinguishing gerunds (i.e., that they are not confusing gerunds with progressive verbs). As students work together, you may want to tell the class how many verbs they should aim to have underlined (see answers on LP page 112). This will give them an idea of whether they have too many or too few and encourage some to check their work again.

3. As a class, go over the underlined verbs. Have a volunteer be the writer and write these verbs on the board.

4. Have students suggest more advice for a healthier life and add these to the list on the board from Focus 3.

For more practice, use *Grammar Dimensions 3* Workbook page 38, Exercise 4.

EXPANSION [homework]

You may wish to have students create a brochure as an out-of-class writing exercise. Have students research and write about their advice for *A Healthier Life.* This could also be assigned as an oral presentation or a group poster board presentation.

EXERCISE 6 [10 minutes]

Exercise 6 can be used as a speaking activity in small groups or pairs. It can also be used as a writing exercise. See possible answers on LP page 112.

For more practice, use *Grammar Dimensions 3* Workbook page 38, Exercise 5.

LESSON PLAN 2

FOCUS 4 [15 minutes]

This focus presents Pattern 2 verbs (**verb + gerund/noun phrase + infinitive**). These verbs take either a gerund (when referring to "everybody") or take a noun phrase + infinitive (referring to a specific noun). See appendix A-7 for more Pattern 2 verbs.

1. **Lead-in:** Referring back to the topic of *A Healthier Life,* list a few more ideas using Pattern 2 verbs to create pairs of sentences like those in the focus box. For example,

   Doctors advise eating more vegetables. (everyone)
   Doctors advise children to drink milk. (children specifically)

2. Go over the focus chart with the class. Put a few more of these verbs on the board and ask students to use them to give more advice on how to live a healthy life.

EXERCISE 7 [15 minutes]

This exercise gives students practice using Pattern 2 verbs to create sentences for both options: verb + gerund and verb + noun phrase + infinitive.

1. Have students work individually to make their sentences.

2. When they are finished, ask a few students to put sentences on the board to share.

3. Have other students switch sentences with a partner and check their work. Let them give each other feedback.

4. Go over the sentences on the board and invite others to read their sentence pairs to the class. See possible answers on LP page 112.

For more practice, use *Grammar Dimensions 3* Workbook page 39, Exercise 6.

FOCUS 5

form

Verbs Followed by Gerunds: Pattern 3

Pattern 3: Verb (+ Noun Phrase) + Gerund

EXAMPLES	EXPLANATION
(a) I don't mind being lazy on the weekend, but my roommate dislikes my doing so.	Many verb-gerund combinations can be used with or without noun phrases.
(b) I dislike doing chores on the weekend, but I don't mind your doing them.	

Common verbs that follow this pattern are:

anticipate	delay	don't mind	imagine	resent
appreciate	deny	enjoy	miss	tolerate
consider	dislike	excuse	postpone	understand

EXERCISE 8

Complete these sentences with true information. Use gerunds in your answers, and if the highlighted verb can be used with a noun phrase, try to use a noun phrase in your answer.

1. I usually **avoid** . . .
2. When I was a child I used to **imagine** . . .
3. My English teacher **recommends** . . .
4. I would like to **quit** . . .
5. I am **considering** . . .
6. Honest people shouldn't **tolerate** . . .
7. To be a good soccer player it's necessary to **practice** . . .
8. A teacher's **responsibility includes** . . .
9. Becoming a really good speaker of a foreign language **requires** . . .
10. I **appreciate** guests . . .

EXERCISE 9

Combine these sentence pairs by replacing "**this**" with a gerund phrase made from the first sentence.

Example: John will spend a year in France. Mary resents **this**.
Mary resents John's spending a year in France.

1. John sings a funny song whenever he sees her. Mary will miss **this**.
   Mary will miss John's singing a funny song whenever he sees her.

2. He wants to become really fluent in French. Mary doesn't really understand **this**.
   Mary doesn't really understand his wanting to become really fluent in French.

3. He applied to the program without consulting Mary. She resents **this**.
   Mary resents his having applied/applying to the program without consulting her.

4. She will not have a chance to talk with him every day. She's not looking forward to **this**.
   She's not looking forward to not having a chance to talk with him every day.

5. John is leaving in two weeks. He is quite excited about **this**.
   John is quite excited about leaving in two weeks.

6. John needs at least three weeks to get a passport. He didn't anticipate **this**.
   John didn't anticipate needing at least three weeks to get a passport.

7. This will make his departure even later than expected. John wanted to avoid **this**.
   John wanted to avoid making his departure even later than expected.

ANSWER KEY

Exercise 8 Answers will vary. Possible answers are: 1. eating fatty foods./staying up till dawn. 2. being an astronaut./becoming president. 3. reading an English newspaper for 20 minutes each day./doing homework carefully. 4. working on this project./borrowing money from friends. 5. going to another language program./changing my major. 6. other people stealing./being taken advantage of by unscrupulous salesmen. 7. running quickly./kicking the ball accurately. 8. helping students./knowing the material. 9. listening to native speakers./not being afraid to make mistakes. 10. helping with the dishes./not staying too late.

FOCUS 5 [15 minutes]

Focus 5 presents Pattern 3 verbs which allow for an optional noun phrase before the gerund as in the formula: **verb (+ noun phrase) + gerund.**

1. **Lead-in:** Begin by putting the following headings on two parts of the board: *I can't tolerate* and *I don't mind.* Tell the class about a few things that you can't tolerate and things that you don't really mind. Try to use noun phrases in several examples. Invite students to tell the class about their own opinions. Put a few of these under the appropriate heading on the board.

2. Go over the examples in the focus chart and look over the box below it with common verbs that follow this pattern.

3. Have volunteers come up and write a few more sentences using these verbs on the board under one of the headings.

GRAMMAR NOTE

You may find yourself "forgetting" to use the possessive form of the noun phrase before a gerund. See the Grammar Note for Focus 2 on LP page 111.

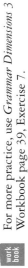

EXERCISE 8 [15 minutes]

By completing sentences with verbs that follow Pattern 3, students will become more familiar with this group of verbs and using noun phrases with them.

1. Use the first sentence starter as an example for the class. Write the sentence starter on the board and invite students to suggest ways to complete it.

2. Encourage the use of a noun phrase and assist with forming the possessive if necessary.

3. Have students complete the exercise individually and then share sentences in small groups.

4. Ask each group to put an example or two on the board.

5. Encourage any questions or comments from the class regarding the ideas on the board. See possible answers on LP page 114.

For more practice, use *Grammar Dimensions 3* Workbook page 39, Exercise 7.

EXERCISE 9 [15 minutes]

This sentence-combining practice asks students to make decisions about whether to include a noun phrase (a performer of the gerund other than the subject of the main verb).

1. Have the class look at the example sentence and circle the highlighted word *this*.

2. Now have the class underline the first sentence and draw an arrow over to the circled word *this*. Explain that the underlined information will be made into a gerund phrase to be put in place of *this*.

3. Ask the class what needs to be done to put the underlined section into a gerund phrase. (John becomes *possessive*, will *is dropped*, spend *becomes a gerund*)

4. Let the class take these steps to complete sentence (1) in the exercise. Ask for students to share their answers.

5. Have students complete the rest of the exercise individually and check answers with a partner. Go around and settle any differences that partners cannot agree on as they come up. See answers on LP page 114.

For more practice, use *Grammar Dimensions 3* Workbook page 40, Exercise 8.

FOCUS 6 — Gerunds in Other Positions in a Sentence

Gerunds can be used in other places in the sentence where noun phrases normally appear.

Subjects of a sentence

EXAMPLES	EXPLANATION
Gerund Subjects (a) **Collecting** stamps is fun. (b) AWKWARD: It's fun **collecting** stamps. **Infinitive Subjects** (c) It's fun **to collect** stamps. (d) AWKWARD: **To collect** stamps is fun.	Unlike infinitive subjects, gerund subjects usually begin a sentence and are not usually used with *it* constructions.

Objects of prepositions and two-word verbs

EXAMPLES	EXPLANATION
(e) John is excited about **moving** to France. (f) John is exhausted from **staying** up all night. (g) I'm exhausted from **staying** up all night. (h) I'm looking into **studying** overseas.	Gerunds can follow prepositions and two-word (phrasal) verbs.

EXERCISE 10

Complete these sentences with information that describes your true feelings about these topics. Compare your answers to those of other students in the class.

1. Talking to strangers . . .
2. Eating ice cream . . .
3. I'm nervous about . . .
4. I'm never afraid of . . .
5. My friends are concerned about . . .
6. I would like to give up . . .
7. Growing older . . .
8. I get tired of . . .

FOCUS 7 — Choosing Infinitives Versus Gerunds

There is a basic difference in meaning between infinitives and gerunds that can help us choose the correct form in many cases.

EXAMPLES	EXPLANATIONS
(a) I plan **to study** all weekend, so I guess I can relax this afternoon.	Infinitives usually refer to the possibility of an action occurring. The action has not happened yet.
(b) I don't enjoy **studying** all weekend, but we have a big examination on Monday.	Gerunds usually refer to an action that has already started or has already been experienced.
(c) I want **to swim** in the pool all afternoon. (d) I intend **to take** the TOEFL® rest at the end of the semester.	Verbs of desire (*hope, wish, plan, want,* etc.) imply that the speaker hasn't experienced the action yet, but may in the future. They are typically followed by infinitives.
(e) I enjoy **swimming** on warm Saturday afternoons. (f) I can't stand **using** my weekends to do chores. (g) I can't stand **to use** my weekends to do chores.	Certain verbs of emotion (*enjoy, appreciate,* etc.) imply that the speaker has already experienced the cause of that emotion. They are typically followed by gerunds. Other verbs of emotion (*like, love, hate, can't stand*) can be followed by gerunds or infinitives without much difference in meaning.

Some verbs have an important difference in meaning depending on whether they are followed by an infinitive or a gerund.

VERB	EXAMPLES	IMPLIED MEANING
forget	(h) I **forgot to meet** them.	I didn't meet them because I forgot about our appointment.
	(i) I **forgot meeting** them.	I met them, but I didn't remember that I did.
try	(j) We **tried to clean** the kitchen, but we ran out of soap.	We couldn't clean it.
	(k) We **tried cleaning** the kitchen, but there was still a bad smell.	We cleaned it, but that didn't solve the problem.
remember	(l) John **remembered to mail** the postcard to Mary.	He remembered, and then went to the mailbox.
	(m) John **remembered mailing** the postcard.	He mailed the postcard, and remembered it later.
stop	(n) Gladstone **stopped eating** bacon last month.	He doesn't eat it anymore.
	(o) Gladstone **stopped to eat** because he was so hungry.	Gladstone took a break and ate.

ANSWER KEY

Exercise 10 Answers will vary. Possible answers are: 1. is sometimes difficult./requires patience. 2. is a good thing to do on a hot day./can make people gain weight. 3. making friends in this country/having enough money to finish my studies. 4. meeting new people./making mistakes in English class. 5. passing the grammar test./my not having heard from my family. 6. smoking./working./exercising./doing homework. 7. means getting backaches/happens to everyone. 8. doing homework./eating American food.

FOCUS 6 [15 minutes]

This focus shows how gerunds can act as subjects and objects (of prepositions or two-word verbs).

1. **Lead-in:** Use gerunds to tell the class about activities you think are fun or interesting. Give examples, and invite students to make similar sentences about hobbies or activities they think are fun or interesting.

2. Have the class look at the examples of using gerunds and infinitives as subjects in the first section of the focus chart. As you read the sentences to the class, point out that, although it's possible for gerunds and infinitives to work both ways, gerunds tend to work better as subjects and infinitives work better with *it* constructions. Let students practice using both gerunds and infinitives as subjects or with *it* constructions as they continue suggesting activities that they enjoy.

3. Move onto the second section of the chart and ask students to circle the preposition in each sentence. Have students suggest things that they are nervous about or excited about. Answers may include *taking tests, going on vacation, meeting my girlfriend's parents, starting a new job,* etc.

EXERCISE 10 [15 minutes]

This exercise gives more practice using gerunds either as subjects or as objects of a preposition or two-word verb.

1. Before you have students work individually to complete the exercise, you may want to point out the two different types of sentences. Some sentences give the gerund as a subject and just need to be completed with an *it* construction while others need a gerund to be added. There may be a wide variety of answers.

2. After they have completed each sentence with their own opinions, put students into small groups and let them compare answers. See possible answers on LP page 116.

VARIATION

Have students move around the room and interview other students about their opinions. Put them into small groups when they are finished and have them talk about the most interesting or surprising answers they found.

For more practice, use *Grammar Dimensions 3* Workbook page 40, Exercise 9.

FOCUS 7 [15 minutes]

This focus gives students some insight into how to choose between infinitives and gerunds to follow a main verb by looking at basic differences in meaning.

1. **Lead-in:** Divide the board in half and begin two lists. In the first list write *hope, wish, plan, want, expect, intend, need.* In the second list write *enjoy, appreciate, don't mind, resent, tolerate.* Bring in a picture of people from a magazine or other source and ask the class to use vocabulary on the board to tell about the people.

2. Ask pairs to look at the picture and write about the people using any of the vocabulary on the board. Circulate and help with vocabulary, but let students negotiate the grammar together.

3. Invite pairs to share their sentences. Then ask the class which list has verbs that take gerunds and which list has verbs that take infinitives. Write these titles above the proper lists. Which list did students find they used more?

4. Go over the examples in the first section of Focus Chart 7. Add the words *possibility, already experienced, desire,* and *emotion* over the matching lists on the board.

5. Note that there are some very commonly used verbs that can take a gerund or an infinitive with no real difference in meaning. Put some of these examples in the middle of the board.

6. Note that, as shown in the second section of Focus Chart 7, a few special verbs can change meaning depending on whether a gerund or an infinitive is used. Write these four verbs on the board off to the side.

7. Use several examples of your own experiences or that of students' to make the changes in meaning clearer to the students and give some personal meaning to remember them by.

8. To review this last set of verbs quickly, have the class cover the Implied Meaning side of the second box with another paper, so that only the examples (h–o) are showing. Ask questions about the pairs of sentences such as *Which sentence means that I never did meet them?* (example h) *Which sentence means that we didn't really clean the kitchen?* (example j)

6. Ruth couldn't enjoy the movie because she forgot ___to bring___ (bring) her glasses with her.

7. Nowadays, children have stopped (a) ___playing___ (play) traditional children's games and seem (b) ___to prefer___ (prefer) (c) ___playing/to play___ (play) video games instead.

8. I'll try ___eating___ (eat) any kind of food once.

EXERCISE 13

Fill in the blanks with the correct form of the verbs in parentheses. There may be more than one correct answer.

Before the invention of radio and television, people spent much of their leisure time (1) ___doing___ (do) activities that required (2) ___doing___ (do) or (3) ___making___ (make) something. They practiced (4) ___playing___ (play) a musical instrument or studied (5) ___singing___ (sing). Most people learned (6) ___to keep busy___ (keep) busy by (7) ___trying___ (try) (8) ___to improve___ (improve) their abilities in some way or by (9) ___practicing___ (practice) a skill. People who couldn't afford (10) ___to spend___ (spend) much money on hobbies often started (11) ___collecting/to collect___ (collect) simple objects, such as matchbook covers or stamps, or even things like buttons or bottle caps. Of course, most people spent a lot of time (12) ___reading___ (read) and (13) ___writing___ (write) letters to friends. Children played games in which they pretended (14) ___to be___ (be) pirates or cowboys or people they remembered (15) ___reading___ (read) about in books. Many women were extremely clever at (16) ___making___ (make) and (17) ___decorating___ (decorate) articles of clothing. Men often kept busy by (18) ___making___ (make) toys for children or (19) ___carving___ (carve) small sculptures out of wood.

EXERCISE 11

In the chart below, review the basic patterns and common verbs in each pattern. Work with a partner and try to write as many additional verbs for each pattern as you can remember without looking through this unit. A few have been done for you.

VERBS THAT TAKE INFINITIVES

Pattern 1	Pattern 2	Pattern 3
appear	advise	expect
refuse	remind	arrange
seem	persuade	want
agree	urge	intend
claim	encourage	consent
care	convince	ask
deserve	force	need
decide	forbid	
demand	command	
pretend	order	
hesitate	allow	
offer	permit	

VERBS THAT TAKE GERUNDS

Pattern 1	Pattern 2	Pattern 3
can't help	encourage	appreciate
keep on	urge	anticipate
recommend	urge	dislike
suggest	forbid	don't mind
deny	allow	enjoy
consider	permit	resent
admit	invite	consider
give up	cause	delay
avoid	teach	postpone
quit		excuse
practice		imagine
include		miss

EXERCISE 12

Fill in the blank with the gerund or infinitive form of the word in parentheses. There may be more than one correct answer.

1. If you want to lose weight, you should try ___to avoid/avoiding___ (avoid) all sweets. That might be better than going on a diet.

2. I know Bambang was at the party, but I don't remember ___talking___ (talk) to him.

3. On his way home from the stamp club meeting, Norman stopped ___to pick up___ (pick up) a few things at the store.

4. Suddenly, all the people at the party began ___talking/to talk___ (talk) at the same time.

5. My sister has never been able to quit ___smoking___ (smoke).

EXERCISE 11 [15 minutes]

This exercise asks students to recall verbs according to which pattern they fit into.

1. If you already have posters or overhead transparencies of the patterns around the room, give students a chance to quickly review or check them before putting them away.
2. Put the formula for each verb pattern on the board in order to remind the class what each pattern stands for.
3. Have pairs recall as many verbs for each category as they can. You may want to set a time limit.
4. Have students form larger groups and let them share and add to their own lists before sharing with the class. See answers on LP page 118.

Suggestion: You could make this exercise a game or challenge and award prizes to pairs with the most correct verbs in each pattern list.

EXERCISE 12 [15 minutes]

In this exercise, students will choose between the gerund and infinitive depending on the meaning they want to convey.

1. Have students work individually to complete this review of Focus 7. They may want to refer back to the focus boxes as they decide between the meanings that will be expressed with an infinitive or gerund after certain verbs.
2. Put students into pairs or small groups and let them check their answers together.
3. Go over answers as a class. Ask students to volunteer answers and their reasons for choosing each form. See answers on LP page 118.

For more practice, use *Grammar Dimensions 3* Workbook page 41, Exercise 10.

EXERCISE 13 [15 minutes]

This exercise asks students to choose between gerunds and infinitives to fill in the blanks.

1. After students work independently to complete the exercise, put them into pairs and have them read their completed paragraphs out loud to each other. Some students may be able to hear their own mistakes more easily than they can see them on paper. Circulate and note any common difficulties.
2. Let pairs discuss their answers together before going over answers as a class. Remind students of the differences in meaning discussed in Focus 7.

Suggestion: It may be helpful to use a copy of this exercise on an overhead transparency as you go over the answers with the class.

VARIATION

As you go over the answers with the class keep running lists for the verbs found that take gerunds, infinitives, or both. Have students circle the main verbs that determine which to use as they complete the exercise. Look at the lists when finished and have the class make some general observations about the kinds of words in each (see Focus 7 for the differences in meaning).

For more practice, use *Grammar Dimensions 3* Workbook page 42, Exercise 11 and Exercise 12.

Use Your English

ACTIVITY 1 speaking

In the Opening Task on page 106 you were asked to decide whether you are a **do-er** or a **be-er** in the way that you spend your free time.

- **STEP 1** Form a group with other people who are in the same category as you. Together come up with a list of the five or ten best ways to spend a rainy afternoon.

- **STEP 2** Compare your list of activities with that of a group from the other category. What does this tell you about the differences between **do-ers** and **be-ers**?

ACTIVITY 2 speaking

Choose a partner that you know pretty well.

- **STEP 1** Describe two or three things you can't imagine him or her ever doing. Then identify two or three things you expect your partner to do on a routine basis. Explain your reasons. What is it about your partner that makes you think he or she would behave that way? Your partner should then do the same thing with you.

- **STEP 2** Were you or your partner surprised by any of the things you heard? For example, did your partner tell you that he couldn't imagine your doing something that you actually do quite frequently? Or perhaps your partner mentioned an expectation that you would never consider doing. Report any surprises to the rest of the class.

EXERCISE 14

Fill in the blanks with the correct form of the verbs in parentheses. There may be more than one correct answer, so be prepared to explain why you chose the answer you did.

Since the invention of radio and television, leisure-time activities have changed. Nowadays, people don't find it as easy (1) _____ to fill/filling _____ (fill) their time with such productive activities. Television has encouraged many people (2) _____ to stop _____ (stop) (3) _____ working on _____ (work) on their hobbies. Children are spending more and more time (4) _____ watching _____ (watch) TV or (5) _____ playing _____ (play) video games. As a result, traditional children's games that have been played for hundreds of years are beginning (6) _____ to be forgotten _____ (forget). Traditional skills such as embroidery, sewing, and woodcarving are failing (7) _____ to be passed _____ (be passed) on from parent to child. People seem (8) _____ to prefer _____ (prefer) activities that allow them (9) _____ to be _____ (be) passive observers rather than active participants. If these traditional forms of recreation keep (10) _____ disappearing _____ (disappear) at the current rate, many of the things that people used to enjoy (11) _____ doing _____ (do) will only be found on television documentaries about how people tried (12) _____ to spend/spending _____ (spend) their leisure time in the days before television.

EXERCISE 14 [15 minutes]

Exercise 14 is a review of Unit 6 and Unit 7. Like Exercise 13, students are asked to decide whether a gerund or an infinitive is the appropriate form to use. See Exercise 13 for a suggestion and a variation that could also apply to this exercise. See answers on LP page 120.

EXPANSION [15 minutes]

Have the class practice using gerunds and infinitives by creating and answering questions.

1. Depending on the time you have available for interviews in class, have students choose five to ten different verbs from the list of verb patterns in Appendix A-7.

2. They will then use these verbs with infinitive or gerund phrases following to create questions to ask their classmates. These verbs can generate some thoughtful questions such as *What do you anticipate doing five years from now? What do you hope to do by this time next year? What do you usually postpone doing? What would you recommend doing if I visited your hometown?*

3. Let students interview several different partners to get a few different answers to their questions.

4. Invite students to share interesting questions and the variety of answers they got.

5. Have students write a short paragraph summarizing what they found to be the most interesting or surprising things they learned from these interviews.

For more practice, use *Grammar Dimensions 3* Workbook page 43, Exercise 13.

UNIT GOAL REVIEW [10 minutes]

Ask students to look at the goals on the opening page of the unit again. Refer to the pages of the unit where information on each goal can be found.

For a grammar quiz review of Units 5–7, refer students to pages 44–45 in the *Grammar Dimensions 3* Workbook.

ExamView For assessment of Unit 7,
Test Generator use *Grammar Dimensions 3* *ExamView®*.

USE YOUR ENGLISH

The Use Your English activities at the end of the unit contain situations that should naturally elicit the structures covered in the unit. For a more complete discussion of how to use the Use Your English activities see To the Teacher on LP page xxii. When students are doing these activities in class, you can circulate and listen to see if they are using the structures accurately. Errors can be corrected after the activity has finished.

ACTIVITY 1 speaking [10 minutes]

You may wish to assign this activity after the Opening Task on SB pages 106–107 to give students the opportunity to share interests using gerunds.

STEP 1

1. After determining in the Opening Task which category they fit into, have students form into small do-er or be-er groups. You can help by first asking all the do-ers to stand up. Based on the number of students standing, put them into small

groups. Then ask the be-ers to stand up and do the same for them.

2. Ask the groups to choose a writer to record their group list of rainy day activities.

STEP 2
Have the groups come together to share lists or divide the board and ask groups to put their lists on the appropriate side of the board. Ask for general observations about the differences or similarities of the lists.

ACTIVITY 2 speaking [15 minutes]

This activity works well with a class made up of students who know each other fairly well. Let students choose their partners or put students together based on your own feelings about how comfortable they are with each other.

STEP 1

1. Begin with examples of things you might guess a friend or colleague of doing or not doing. Aim for a balance of both serious and slightly silly things.

2. Give students some time to make their own two lists about their partners: things they expect their partner to do regularly and things they can't imagine their partner ever doing.

3. After writing down ideas, have pairs share their lists with each other and explain their reasons.

STEP 2
When finished discussing, have students take a moment to write down a few things that surprised them in this discussion. Invite students to share these observations with the class.

ACTIVITY 3 writing

We all have bad habits that we would like to stop doing, and things that we know we should do, but don't. New Year's Eve is a popular time to make resolutions about ways to improve our behavior.

STEP 1

Make a list of "New Year's Resolutions."

What are some things you would like to stop doing? (For example, *watching so much TV*.) What are some things you would like to start doing? (For example, *getting more exercise*.)

STEP 2

Compare your New Year's Resolutions to those of other people in the class. Are there any common categories or characteristics?

ACTIVITY 4 speaking

Prepare a short talk for the rest of the class on one of these topics:

- Your likes and dislikes: activities that you don't mind, can't stand, love, hate, resent, and enjoy or things about other people that you can't stand but many other people don't seem to mind (for example: *I can't stand being too serious about their work, and having no other interests in life*), and things about other people that you don't mind, but many other people can't stand (for example: *I don't mind people being late*).

- Your future plans: activities that you anticipate doing or hope or intend to do—and things that would make you postpone or delay those activities or consider not doing them.

ACTIVITY 5 listening

STEP 1

Read the questions below. Then listen for the information to answer them from the radio program about leisure time in the United States.

CD Track 12

1. What amount of time per week are people expected to work in the U.S., Germany, and Japan?

2. What is the average amount of annual vacation for workers in the U.S., Germany, and Japan?

3. What do Americans typically do on the weekend?

4. What is the third reason mentioned for the decreasing amount of free time?

5. Give two examples of "working vacations."

STEP 2

Compare your answers with a partner's, and then listen to the program again to confirm any information you're not sure of.

ACTIVITY 6 research on the web

Go to *InfoTrac® College Edition* and type in the keywords "leisure time Americans." Choose an article and read it. Decide how similar American access to and use of leisure time is to your own. Are you similar to or different from "typical" Americans? Report three things that surprised you in the article. Compare your answers to those of two or three other students. Present your group's ideas to the rest of the class.

ACTIVITY 7 reflection

Work with two or three other students and make a list of at least five things that good language learners should try to do and at least five things that they should avoid doing when attempting to learn a new language. Present your ideas to another group and together come up with a list of "do's and don't's" for people trying to learn and practice a new language. You may want to work as a whole class to develop a poster to display in your classroom.

ANSWER KEY

Activity 5 1. 40; 38; 42 2. 11 holidays, 12 vacation days; 10 holidays, 30 vacation days; 20 holidays, 16 vacation days 3. one full day of household chores such as shopping, laundry, housecleaning, etc. 4. Americans are increasingly using their vacations for long-term projects. 5. collecting and cataloging plant and animal species in national parks; going on digs at archaeological sites; participating in community development projects

Activity 6 At press time, one sample *InfoTrac®* article is from *PR Newswire, Dec. 8, 2004*: "Different Leisure Activities' Popular Rise and Fall, but Reading, TV Watching and Family Time Still Top the List of Favorites; No Significant Change in Time Spent Working and Time Available for Leisure."

USE YOUR ENGLISH

listing things they like or dislike or their future plans. Encourage students to explain their reasons or tell what they do when faced with dislikes. This will make their presentation much more interesting for them and also the rest of the class.

METHODOLOGY NOTE

By giving students the opportunity to get to know their classmates and creating opportunities for students to come up to the front of the class in nonthreatening activities, you can help alleviate some of the nervousness students feel about speaking in front of the class. You could also have students speak and present in small, varied groups as often as possible, have the class give presentations from one side of the classroom (have the class be sure to face the speaker though) or let students sit on a stool or stand behind a podium. Allowing "props" such as posters or pictures is also a good way to help students forget about their fears.

ACTIVITY 3 writing
[10 minutes]

1. Begin with a discussion about "New Year's Resolutions." How many students have made them or know of others who have made them? Are there any other times that people make a kind of promise to start or stop doing something? (Ramadan, Lent, etc.) Note the difference between a shorter period of change and a New Year's Resolution to change which typically begins on New Year's Day and continues until a goal has been reached or is simply "broken" and not reached.

2. Put a variety of vocabulary from the unit on the board for students to work from such as *stop, quit, give up, avoid, keep on, continue, start, begin*, etc.

   ■ STEP 1 Let students create their lists.

   ■ STEP 2 Put students into groups and invite them to share their lists together and make observations about any similarities.

EXPANSION [homework]

Have students interview native English speakers about New Year's resolutions.

1. Have students make a list of questions to use. These may include things such as *Have you ever made any New Year's Resolutions? What were they? Did you keep them? How do you feel about making New Year's Resolutions?*

2. After interviewing native speakers, have students share their results with the class.

ACTIVITY 4 speaking
[30 minutes]

This speaking/presentation activity works best if students find a focus for their talk rather than simply

---

4. Give time for pairs to talk about what they found interesting or surprising in this radio program.

ACTIVITY 6 research on the web
[20 minutes/homework]

1. Begin with a quick class discussion to find out what the class thinks they might find out about the leisure time of "typical" Americans. Let the class make some guesses about what they may find in their research. Do they think that their findings will be very different from their own use of leisure time? Encourage discussion.

2. Students will then research and report their findings about "typical" Americans, the differences to themselves, and three things that surprised them in the article they found.

3. Have groups prepare some general observations to share with the class.

4. Review the pre-research guesses as a class.

ACTIVITY 7 reflection
[15 minutes]

1. Have students make a list of five things that good language learners should do and five things that they should not do.

2. Put students into small groups and have them share their lists.

3. Ask the groups to choose three things that good language learners should do and three things that they shouldn't do from their combined lists and put these on the board.

4. Use the "dos" and "don'ts" on the board to create a handout or a class poster to display in the classroom.

5. Have students write down their findings in their *Reflection Journals*.

ACTIVITY 5 listening
[15 minutes]

CD Track 12

■ STEP 1

1. First, have students read the questions in Step 1.

2. After listening to the audio, give students time to write down their answers.

■ STEP 2

1. Let students check their answers with a partner. Circulate and take note of any points of disagreement or particularly difficult questions.

2. Play the audio again and have students check their answers or fill-in missed ones.

3. As you check answers with the class, you may want to play the audio a little at a time.

INTENSIFIERS (*Very, Too, Enough,* Etc.) AND DEGREE COMPLEMENTS (*So That, Such That,* Etc.)

UNIT GOALS

- Use intensifiers such as *very, too,* and *enough*
- Use the word *not* with intensifiers
- Correctly form *so that* and *such that* clauses
- Use *too* and (*not*) *enough* plus infinitive phrases

OPENING TASK

How Much Is Too Much? Are You A Workaholic?

The word *workaholic* is used to describe people who like their jobs so much that they are "addicted" to them. They are not just very interested in their jobs; they're too interested in them. They often neglect other responsibilities (to their families, to their own physical health, etc.) in order to concentrate on their jobs and do them well. The word *workaholic* has an interesting history. It is derived from the word *alcoholic*, which is used to describe a person who is addicted to alcohol. And like alcoholics, an organization has been formed to help people recover from their addiction to work.

STEP 1

Read these questions developed by an organization called Workaholics Anonymous (based on the famous principles of Alcoholics Anonymous) and decide whether you or someone you know is a workaholic.

HOW DO I KNOW IF I'M A WORKAHOLIC?

1. Do you get more excited about your work than about family or anything else?
2. Are there times when you can change through your work and other times when you can't?
3. Do you take work with you to bed? on weekends? on vacation?
4. Is work the activity you like to do best and talk about most?
5. Do you work more than 40 hours a week?
6. Do you turn your hobbies into money-making ventures?
7. Do you take complete responsibility for the outcome of your work efforts?
8. Have your family or friends given up expecting you on time?
9. Do you take on extra work because you are concerned that it won't otherwise get done?
10. Do you underestimate how long a project will take and then rush to complete it?
11. Do you believe that it is okay to work long hours if you love what you are doing?
12. Do you get impatient with people who have other priorities besides work?
13. Are you afraid that if you don't work hard you will lose your job or be a failure?
14. Is the future a constant worry for you even when things are going very well?
15. Do you do things energetically and competitively including play?
16. Do you get irritated when people ask you to stop doing your work in order to do something else?
17. Have your long hours hurt your family or other relationships?
18. Do you think about your work while driving, falling asleep or when others are talking?
19. Do you work or read during meals?
20. Do you believe that more money will solve the other problems in your life?

© Workaholics World Service Organization 2005

STEP 2

In recent years the suffix *-aholic* has been applied to other things. Although you will not find these words in a dictionary, you may hear them in conversations or on television, or read them in popular magazines. In addition to workaholics, people can sometimes be *sportaholics* (too interested in sports), *shopaholics* (spend too much time and money shopping), *TVaholics* (too much watching television and not enough doing anything else), or even *chocaholics* (people who can't live without chocolate). What other kinds of "*-aholic*" people can you think of? You have read about workaholics. Work with a partner and invent at least one other term for people who carry their enthusiasm about something too far. Present your term and definition to the rest of the class.

UNIT OVERVIEW

Unit 8 reviews the form, use, and meaning of intensifiers and degree complements which answer the basic questions of *how much* or *to what degree*. Special attention is given to the use of *too* in different constructions to imply a negative degree of being excessive.

GRAMMAR NOTE

For this text, intensifiers refer to words that show the intensity or degree of an adjective or adverb. These intensifiers can range in degree from excessive (*it's too hot*) to insufficient (*it isn't hot enough*) with degrees in between (*it's fairly hot*). With the exception of *enough*, intensifiers are placed directly in front of the adjective or adverb. It's important to note that although intensifiers show a range of degrees, the excessive degree, *too*, is always a negative idea and not a good thing (*it is too hot for me to drink*). This is in contrast to a very high degree shown with intensifiers such as *extremely* or *very* (*it is very hot, but I can drink it*). In addition to degree, a few intensifiers can be used with *not* to create polite or indirect statements (*it's not very interesting* instead of *it's boring*).

Degree complements with *too* (*too* + infinitive phrase) also have the meaning of being excessive. The opposite meaning is created with *enough* (*enough* + infinitive phrase). Degree complements with *so* and *such* use a *that* clause to show the **result** of a very great degree.

UNIT GOALS

Some instructors may want to review the goals listed on Student Book (SB) page 124 after completing the Opening Task so that students understand what they should know by the end of the unit. These goals can also be reviewed at the end of the unit when students are more familiar with the grammar terminology.

OPENING TASK [20 minutes]

The aim of the Opening Task is to give students the opportunity to use the form, meaning, and use of intensifiers and degree complements. This task specifically uses the intensifier *too*. The problem-solving format is designed to show the teacher how well the students can produce a target structure implicitly and spontaneously when they are engaged in a communicative task. For a more complete discussion of the purpose of the Opening Task, see Lesson Planner (LP) page xxii.

Setting Up the Task

1. Begin with a brief discussion of the word *workaholic*. Do students know what it means? If not, ask students to think of what other English words the term "addicted" means. Ask if they know what the term "addicted" means.
2. Read the paragraph aloud as a class (or silently) and go over any new vocabulary or questions students may have.
3. Ask the class how they know if someone likes to work too much or how they know someone is a workaholic. List a few answers on the board.

Conducting the Task

■ STEP 1

1. Go over the instructions for Step 1 with the class and have students take out and number a piece of paper 1–20.
2. Put students into pairs to do the task and have them take turns reading out the questions to each other while at the same time marking yes/no answers on their papers for all questions. Remember, they can answer for themselves or someone else they know (a family member or friend).
3. As pairs work together on the questionnaire, circulate and assist with vocabulary or other questions.

4. As students finish the questionnaire, have them come to a conclusion about whether they are or know of a workaholic. Invite students to share.

■ STEP 2

Ask the pairs to create a new kind of "–aholic" and together to create a clear definition of what it means.

Closing the Task

1. Invite pairs to write their new terms on the board and to share the definitions they have created.
2. Keep these examples on the board for use in Focus 1.

EXPANSION [20 minutes]

See Activity 7 (research on the web) on SB page 145 to expand on this topic. In this activity, students will research workaholism and offer advice to persons suffering from it. They'll also do further research on the other types of –aholics they came up with.

GRAMMAR NOTE

Typical student errors (form)

- Misplacing the intensifier *enough* after the adjective or adverb: * *He doesn't work enough hard.*
- Using a gerund in place of the infinitive after degree complements with *too* or *enough*: * *I am too busy for relaxing.* * *She is old enough for driving.* (See Focus 3.)

Typical student errors (use)

- Confusing the use of *too* and *very* and using them interchangeably to show a very high degree: * *I am too happy to meet you.* (See Focus 3.)
- Using informal or slang intensifiers in more formal writing: * *The situation in Iraq is awfully serious.* * *The winter temperatures in Russia are way too cold.*

FOCUS 1

Describing How Much or To What Degree

meaning

We can answer *how* questions about degree or intensity with **intensifiers** or **degree complements**.

	INTENSIFIERS *very, too, quite, extremely, etc.*	DEGREE COMPLEMENTS *so/such...that...* *too/enough...to....*
How devoted is Denise?	(a) Denise is **extremely devoted** to her job.	(b) Denise is **so devoted** to her job **that** she spends her weekends at the office.
How hard a worker is she?	(c) She's **quite a hard worker**, and even spends her weekends at the office.	(d) She is **such a hard worker that** she has no time for a personal life outside her job.
How interested is Peter in his job?	(e) Peter is **extremely bored** with his job.	(f) Peter is **too interested** in other things **to** make his job the focus of his life.
How quickly does he work?	(g) He works **rather slowly**.	(h) Peter works steadily **enough to** avoid being fired.

EXERCISE 1

Underline the intensifiers in the following passage. The first sentence has been done for you.

(1) Denise Driven is a <u>very</u> dedicated employee, but she's <u>a little too</u> serious. (2) Although she's <u>extremely</u> hard working and <u>quite</u> efficient, she's <u>also rather</u> competitive and <u>not very</u> friendly. (3) She comes in to work an hour earlier than anyone else and is always the last one to leave. (4) At the end of the day she's <u>really</u> too tired for other activities. (5) She has no hobbies and few friends. (6) She's <u>actually</u> a bit dull, since she's <u>not really</u> interested in anything but her job.

(7) Peter Principle is a rather easygoing fellow. (8) Although he works <u>fairly</u> hard, and is <u>reasonably</u> serious about his work, his job is not the <u>most</u> important thing in his life, and he likes to have time to pursue other interests. (9) He lives a <u>fairly</u> normal life. (10) He likes spending time with his children, and he is <u>quite</u> active in the Lions Club. (11) He is also a <u>rather</u> accomplished musician. (12) He plays the clarinet in a jazz band with some of the other people from the office. (13) Peter and Denise <u>really</u> don't get along. (14) She thinks he's <u>a little</u> lazy and "<u>insufficiently</u> motivated." (15) He thinks she's a <u>rather</u> humorless workaholic who is "<u>not very</u> nice." (16) It's <u>somewhat</u> difficult to decide who's right.

EXERCISE 2

Underline the degree complements in the following paragraph. For each degree complement make a *how* question.

Example: Denise is too serious to be able to appreciate Peter's laid-back point of view.
How question: *How serious is Denise?*

Denise Driven and Peter Principle still aren't getting along. (1) Denise is so rushed at work these days that she doesn't have any free time. (2) She has too little energy at the end of the workday that she's too busy to make any close friends. (3) She's feeling a little lonely, but she's too busy to make any close friends. (4) Peter has suggested that she take some time off, but she always says that there's too much going on at work for her to take a vacation. (5) Nothing moves fast enough for her to feel satisfied. (6) Even her administrative assistant works too slowly to keep up with all the projects she is involved with. (7) Peter, on the other hand, still works hard enough to avoid being fired. (8) But, unlike Denise, he isn't so dedicated to his job that he is willing to give up everything else in order to get ahead. (9) He loves his family enough to make their needs his most important priority. (10) He's just not competitive enough about his job for Denise to consider him a threat to her authority.

ANSWER KEY

Exercise 2 1. How rushed at work is Denise these days? 2. How much energy does she have at the end of a workday? 3. How busy is she? 4. How much work does she say is going on? 5. How fast do things move? 6. How fast does her administrative assistant work? 7. How hard does Peter work? 8. How dedicated is he? 9. How much does he love his family? 10. How competitive is he?

INTENSIFIERS AND DEGREE COMPLEMENTS

FOCUS 1 [15 minutes]

Focus 1 gives students an overview of what intensifiers and degree complements are and how they are used.

1. **Lead-in:** You can refer back to any of the examples of –aholic definitions on the board from the Opening Task that used intensifiers or degree complements. Underline them. Here's an example definition:

   videoaholic: A person who plays videogames too much.

2. Go over Focus 1 with the class, pointing out that intensifiers and degree complements answer *how* questions about degree and intensity.

3. Put a few sentences on the board and have the class practice putting intensifiers or degree complements in them:

   Her job is boring.

   (Possible responses: *Her job is extremely boring. Her job is so boring that she wants to quit. Her job is too boring to discuss.*)

EXERCISE 1 [10 minutes]

Students begin by identifying examples of intensifiers as they are used in context.

1. Have students work individually first to underline as many intensifiers as they can.

2. After giving them a few minutes to complete the exercise, tell the class how many intensifiers they are aiming to find. Have them count their results and check their work one more time if they have too many or too few.

3. Put students into pairs and let them compare answers before going over the exercise as a class. See answers on LP page 126.

Suggestion: You may want to copy Exercise 1 and 2 onto an overhead transparency in order to review with the class.

For more practice, use *Grammar Dimensions 3* Workbook page 46, Exercise 1.

EXERCISE 2 [15 minutes]

Students will first identify degree complements in context. Then, they will need to create a *how* question for each underlined degree complement. Have the class refer back to Focus 1 for examples.

1. Go over the example with the class and note that the *how* question uses the adjective (and any optional noun phrase) along with the subject.

2. For another example, ask the class to find the degree complement in sentence (1) of the exercise and underline it. Invite volunteers to suggest a *how* question for this degree complement. See answers on LP page 126.

3. Have students work individually to first underline all the degree complements.

4. Next have them begin writing the *how* questions on a separate sheet of paper.

5. When finished, have pairs check both the underlined degree complements and the *how* questions or go over as a class (with the overhead transparency if you've created one).

EXPANSION [15 minutes]

See Activity 4 (writing) on SB page 144 for a writing activity based on what students have learned about Denise Driven and Peter Principle and their own ideas about work.

FOCUS 2 | Intensifiers

MEANING	MORE FORMAL INTENSIFIERS	LESS FORMAL (CONVERSATIONAL) INTENSIFIERS
An excessive degree	(a) That's too expensive.	(b) She's way too serious.
A great degree	(c) Denise is quite busy.	(f) Denise is really busy.
	(d) She's extremely dedicated.	(g) She works so hard!
	(e) She works very hard.	(h) She's awful(ly) serious.
	(i) He's a rather accomplished musician.	(n) Peter's pretty dedicated.
	(j) It's somewhat difficult to decide who is right.	(o) Denise is kind of depressed.
A moderate degree	(k) He's fairly hard-working.	(p) He's sort of easygoing.
	(l) He does his job reasonably well.	
	(m) He works hard enough.	
A small degree	(q) He gets slightly annoyed.	(t) He's a tad lazy.
	(r) She's a bit competitive.	
	(s) Work can sometimes be a little monotonous.	
An insufficient degree	(u) He doesn't work hard enough.	(v) Peter doesn't get paid near(ly) enough.

The position of intensifiers in a sentence

EXAMPLES	EXPLANATIONS
(w) Denise works extremely hard.	All intensifiers come before the adjective or adverb, except *enough*, which comes after.
(x) Peter works steadily enough.	
(y) Denise is a very dedicated worker.	In noun phrases, intensifiers come between the determiner (*a, the, some*, etc.) and the adjective, except for *quite*, which comes before the determiner.
(z) She is quite a dedicated worker.	

EXERCISE 3

Use the intensifiers from Focus 2 to describe the skills and activities listed below. After each example, make statements that are true for you.

1. **a skill you are proud of:** something you do well to a moderate degree
   Example: I'm a pretty good tennis player.

   I'm a pretty good baseball player. I'm rather a good violinist.

2. **a favorite food:** a kind of food you like to a great degree
   Example: I'm extremely fond of popcorn.

   I'm extremely fond of cake. I really like chocolate.

3. **something that is not enjoyable for you, but you don't hate:** an activity you dislike to a small degree
   Example: Doing homework can be slightly boring.

   Doing dishes can be slightly boring. Writing grammar books can be a little monotonous.

4. **an ability you want to develop:** a skill you have in an insufficient degree
   Example: I don't speak English fluently enough.

   I don't speak Spanish fluently enough. I don't read fast enough.

5. **a bad habit:** something you do to an excessive degree
   Example: I eat too much ice cream.

   I eat too much candy. I stay up too late on Saturday nights.

6. **a special talent:** something you do well to a great degree
   Example: I'm a really good musician.

   I'm a really good singer. I'm an awfully good dancer.

ANSWER KEY

Exercise 3   Answers will vary. Possible answers are listed above.

LESSON PLAN 1

FOCUS 2 [15 minutes]

The first section of the focus chart shows examples of both formal and informal intensifiers and the range of degrees they can express. The lower section of the chart points out the position of intensifiers and determiners along with exceptions for *enough* and *quite*.

1. **Lead-in:** Ask the class how they feel about Denise Driven or Peter Principle based on what they learned in Exercises 1 and 2.

2. Divide the board up into a chart made up of five sections for degrees like this:

Too Much	Great	Medium	Small	Not Enough

3. Using the sentences *Denise is hardworking* and *Peter is hardworking* ask the class to look at the chart in Focus 2 and suggest some intensifiers to discuss how hardworking each is. Write several suggested sentences on the board.

4. Point out the continuum of differences and the range of degrees along the chart you've created on the board. Write several of the intensifiers suggested by students in the corresponding sections of the chart.

5. If you haven't already, have students suggest examples using *too* and *not + enough*. Stress the **negative** meaning of both of these. (See Focus 3 for more on *too*.)

6. Point out the placement of the intensifiers in relation to the adjectives. Be sure to point out the fact that the placement of *enough* does not follow the pattern of the other intensifiers.

7. Changing the basic sentence used earlier, write *Denise is a hard worker* on the board and ask the class where they think the intensifier should go in this example. Note the placement of the determiner.

8. Save the less formal intensifiers for last and be sure to note that these are not used in academic writing or formal speech.

GRAMMAR NOTE

Be aware that the intensifiers that use an article, such as *a bit*, *a little*, or *a tad* can only be used before adjectives or adverbs.

EXERCISE 3 [15 minutes]

This exercise asks students to use information about themselves as they practice using intensifiers.

1. Encourage the class to look back at the intensifiers you've put on the board in the chart or in their books at Focus 2 as they work on this exercise. Have the class work individually to complete the statements.

2. Circulate as students work and check to see that they are using the appropriate degrees as listed. Students may already be more or less comfortable using some of these, so encourage them to use a wide variety as the exercise requires. See answers on LP page 128.

3. When finished, have pairs or small groups share their statements with each other.

4. Go around the room and have students tell the most interesting things they learned about their partners. For example: *Tran thinks that she talks on her cell phone too much. Mario said that he's quite a good soccer player.*

For more practice, use *Grammar Dimensions 3* Workbook page 46, Exercise 2.

VARIATION

Consider using this activity as an interview and have students create questions from the numbered list. Let students interview people outside the class to get practice hearing other speakers using the intensifiers in a natural context. Remind students that their interviewees may not always use the language they are studying. Encourage students to take special note of any new expressions and bring them to class to share.

meaning

FOCUS 3   *Too* Versus *Very*

VERY—A GREAT DEGREE

(a) This project is **very** difficult, but maybe I'll be able to finish it by the deadline.	
(c) Denise is **very** serious about her work. She's a good worker.	

TOO—AN EXCESSIVE DEGREE
(so much of something that it is not good)

(b) This project is **too** difficult. I can't finish it.	
(d) Denise is **too** serious about her work. She's a workaholic.	

EXERCISE 5

Complete these sentences using *too* or *very*.

1. We got there _____ *too* _____ late. All the other people had left.

2. I'm _____ *very* _____ busy, but I think I can finish the report for you.

3. Denise works _____ *too* _____ hard for her own good. She's going to get sick if she's not careful.

4. Denise works _____ *very* _____ hard because she's ambitious and wants to get ahead.

5. Don't bother to invite Denise to the party. She's _____ *too* _____ serious to have any fun!

5. She gave the instructions _____ *too* _____ quickly for me to hear well, but I'm _____ *very* _____ sure that she wanted this finished before the end of the day.

7. Children are growing up _____ *too* _____ quickly these days. They try to act like adults while they're still kids!

8. We arrived at the meeting _____ *very* _____ late, but there was still a little business to discuss.

9. I really like Peter. I think he's _____ *very* _____ intelligent and has a great personality!

10. I really don't like Denise. I think she's _____ *too* _____ serious about work.

EXERCISE 4

Are the following sentences written in formal or informal style? If they are in informal/conversational style, change the intensifier to make the sentence more formal. If they are in formal style, change the intensifier to make the sentence less formal. There are several possible answers, so be prepared to explain why you chose the answer you did.

Examples: That project is so hard! (*Informal*)

More formal: That project is very hard.

I'm rather busy at work, so I won't be able to attend your party. (*Formal*)

Less formal: I'm pretty busy. . . .

1. I'm feeling kind of sick today.
2. I'm somewhat confused by all your instructions.
3. She's really unfriendly.
4. He's quite annoyed about the missed deadlines.
5. I'm sort of busy right now.
6. It's rather hot in this office, don't you think?
7. Peter works pretty hard.
8. Denise is pretty serious.
9. That boss is awfully hard to satisfy.

ANSWER KEY

Exercise 4 Answers will vary. Possible answers are: 1. informal; more formal: I'm somewhat/rather sick today.   2. formal; less formal: I'm kind of/pretty confused by all your instructions.   3. informal; more formal: She's quite/extremely unfriendly.   4. formal; less formal: He's really/awfully annoyed about the missed deadlines.   5. informal; more formal: I'm somewhat/rather busy right now.   6. formal; less formal: It's sort of/a little hot in this office, don't you think?   7. informal; more formal: Peter works hard enough/pretty/reasonably hard.   8. informal; more formal: Denise is rather/quite serious.   9. informal; more formal: That boss is quite/very hard to satisfy.

LESSON PLAN 1/LESSON PLAN 2   INTENSIFIERS AND DEGREE COMPLEMENTS

EXERCISE 4 [15 minutes]

This exercise raises students' awareness of formal and informal language.

1. Begin by giving the class a sample of changing the feeling of a statement by using formal or informal intensifiers. For example, write the following sentence on the board: *That math class is hard.*

2. Now tell the class that they will use this when talking to a teacher. Invite students to use a formal intensifier (*extremely, very, quite, rather,* etc.).

3. Now tell the class that they are talking to another student. Ask them to use informal intensifiers for this (*way too, so, kind of,* etc.).

4. Go over the examples for Exercise 4 as a class.

5. Have students work independently to complete the exercise. Be sure they first decide whether each statement is formal or informal.

6. Let partners share answers and explain their choices for each statement. See answers on LP page 130.

GRAMMAR NOTE

You may want to point out that this list of informal intensifiers in Focus 2 is by no means complete. In fact, teenagers are always finding new ways to say *very.* This constant change is what makes slang terms so interesting, but difficult to keep track of. You can add to this list by bringing in a few slang intensifiers commonly used by teenagers in your area or some that you have heard on television. Ask students to suggest others they may know.

EXPANSION 1 [30 minutes]

This video activity will get students listening for intensifiers used in teenage dialogue and then using them in written descriptions of the characters.

1. Bring in an episode from a television comedy for teens or preteens (*That's So Raven, The Suite Life of Zach and Cody,* etc.).

2. Choose a scene and have the class watch it to get a sense of the characters. Put the class into pairs. Have pairs choose two of the characters from the scene and work together to write descriptions of these characters using intensifiers where possible.

3. Have students watch the scene again, this time listening for any formal or informal intensifiers the characters actually use in the scene. See who can hear the most.

4. Let the pairs add as much as they'd like to their previous descriptions. Circulate and assist as needed.

5. Have the pairs form larger groups and share their descriptions with the group.

6. Invite groups to write a few of their descriptions using intensifiers on the board.

EXPANSION 2 [15 minutes]

For more of a focus on the current use of informal intensifiers, use Activity 8 (reflection) on SB page 145. In this activity, students will discuss native slang intensifiers.

LESSON PLAN 2

FOCUS 3 [10 minutes]

This focus chart shows the important distinction between the intensifiers *too* and *very.*

1. **Lead-in:** Highlight the negative results for the use of *too* by using examples of your own. For example:

Rent in Boston is too expensive. She will move to another city.

Rent in Boston is very expensive, but she has a good job.

Boston is too cold in the winter. She's planning to move to Florida.

Boston is very cold in the winter, but she loves the fall.

2. Go over the examples in the focus chart together.

3. Be sure that students understand that *too* implies a negative result, whereas *very* will simply show a great degree. Ask the class a few questions to check their understanding: *Some people are very tall. Can someone be too tall? Describe a situation when someone might be too tall. Some people are very rich. Can someone be too rich?*

EXERCISE 5 [10 minutes]

Students will make choices about using either *very* or *too* based on whether or not there is a negative result.

1. Go over the first example together. Have a volunteer read the sentence out loud without filling in the blank.

2. Ask the class whether there was a negative result. If there is a negative result, then the missing word must be *too.* In this case *all the other people had left* is a negative result and this sentence does require the use of *too.*

3. Have students work independently to complete the rest of the exercise.

4. Have pairs check their work together. Be sure they talk about why they chose these answers.

5. Invite volunteers to explain their choices as you review the answers as a class. See answers on LP page 130.

For more practice, use *Grammar Dimensions 3* Workbook page 47, Exercise 3.

FOCUS 4

Using Intensifiers with *Too*

EXAMPLES

(a) It's way too difficult!
(b) It's really too hot.
(c) It's a little too expensive.
(d) It's a bit too late.

EXPLANATION

We use a few intensifiers with *too* to indicate how excessive something is.

EXERCISE 6

Complete these sentences, using an intensifier with *too*.

Examples: You just missed the plane. You _arrived a bit too late._

I can't quite reach the top shelf. It _is a little too high._

1. I don't have quite that much money. It _is a bit too expensive_ .
2. I wish she would smile sometimes. She _is much too serious_ .
3. There's no way I can help you finish that report. I _am really too busy_ .
4. Only a couple of students passed the test. The test was _way too difficult_ .
5. I can't drink that coffee. It's _way too strong_ .

EXERCISE 7

Pick five things from the list below that you don't like. Give reasons for your dislike, using *too* and an intensifier.

Examples: I don't like workaholics. They're really too serious.

I don't like dogs. They're a little too friendly.

babies	workaholics	doing homework
dogs	diamond necklaces	being away from my family
cats	summer weather	rap music
spinach	sports cars	police officers
liberals	conservatives	

FOCUS 5

Using Intensifiers with *Not*

These intensifiers (*too, very, so, really, quite*) can be used in negative sentences to "soften" a statement or make it more indirect or polite.

EXAMPLES

(a) Peter's new co-worker is not too bright.
(b) Sometimes Peter doesn't work very hard.
(c) Please don't drive so fast.
(d) She's not really interested in sports.
(e) I'm not quite sure I trust Denise.

IMPLIED MEANING

He's rather stupid.
Sometimes he's lazy.
You drive too fast.
She's somewhat bored with sports.
I distrust Denise.

EXERCISE 8

Make these sentences more polite by replacing or adding intensifiers that use *not*. There may be more than one way to "soften" your comment.

Examples: This movie's pretty boring. _It's not too interesting._

He dances rather badly. _He doesn't dance too well._

1. She's quite unfriendly.
   She's not too friendly.

2. The boss is somewhat unhappy with you.
   The boss is not so happy with you.

3. I hate homework.
   I don't really like homework.

4. Matt is a terrible cook.
   Matt isn't too good at cooking.

5. Denise dislikes listening to other people's problems.
   Denise doesn't really enjoy listening to other people's problems.

6. This office is too crowded for me.
   There's not too much space in this office.

ANSWER KEY

Exercise 6 Answers will vary. Possible answers are listed above.

Exercise 7 Answers will vary. Possible answers are: babies: They're a little too noisy. They're a bit too messy. dogs: They're a bit too dirty. They are too active. cats: They're much too independent. They are a little too aloof. spinach: It's much too healthy. It tastes much too bitter. liberals: They're far too altruistic. They spend way too much money. workaholics: They're really too serious. They're a bit too humorless. diamond necklaces: They're much too expensive. They're too easy to steal. summer weather: It's way too hot. It's much too humid. sports cars: They are driven way too fast. They're much too expensive. conservatives: They're way too rich. They're much too heartless. doing homework: It is too difficult. It takes way too long to finish. being away from my family: I'm a little too lonely. I get a bit too homesick. rap music: It's much too monotonous. It's far too sexist. police officers: They're a bit too threatening. They are too intimidating.

Exercise 8 Answers will vary. Possible answers are listed above.

LESSON PLAN 2

FOCUS 4 [10 minutes]

Focus 4 gives examples of how to use several intensifiers with *too*.

1. **Lead-in:** On a scale across the board, write the intensifiers that you would like the students to use to show degree with *too* (see the Grammar Note below for more).

2. Start at one end of the board with a lesser degree (*a bit, slightly,* etc.) and ask the class to think of something that they think would be a bit too heavy for you to lift (they can suggest serious or silly things). Then slowly move across the board letting students suggest things that they feel would be more and more difficult for you to lift.

3. As the class initially makes suggestions, model a sentence correctly using the intensifier with *too* and, as you move across the board, have them then suggest things only in full sentences.

4. Go over the focus chart together. Refer back to the list of intensifiers in Focus 2 and point out those that are **not** used with *too*.

GRAMMAR NOTE

Students may ask about using other intensifiers with *too*. Although the intensifiers listed in Focus 2 on SB page 128 do not all work in this position, you may find several others not listed in the chart for Focus 4 that may sound possible. These may include: *quite, extremely, somewhat,* and *slightly.*

EXERCISE 6 [10 minutes]

1. Go over the examples together before having students work individually on the exercise.

2. As you go over answers with the class, check that the intensity suggested in the exercise matches the intensity of the student answers. For example, sentence (1) suggests the use of *a little too* or *a bit too* rather than *way too.* Ask students to explain their reasons for their answers. See possible answers on LP page 132.

with the opposite meaning in a negative sentence. Then the sentences can be further softened by using an intensifier. Write these intensifiers on the board for students to reference: *too, very, so, really,* or *quite.*

4. Ask students to suggest adjectives with the opposite meanings for the four example sentences. Write the adjectives on the board next to each original sentence.

5. Now transform each sentence into a more polite form using a negative and the new adjective. Leave a space to put in one of the intensifiers:

His cooking is borrible.   *wonderful*
His cooking is not _____ wonderful.

6. Ask students to suggest one of the intensifiers to put in the blank. Note that there is more than one correct answer.

7. Do the same for the other example sentences and then go over the examples in the book.

For more practice, use *Grammar Dimensions 3* Workbook page 47, Exercise 4.

EXERCISE 7 [15 minutes]

1. Go over the examples with the class.

2. You may want to have a volunteer suggest something he or she dislikes and a reason for this using the intensifier + *too.*

3. Now have the students work individually to write statements of their own. Have them also write two sentences about things they dislike that are not included on the list.

4. Circulate and assist as needed. Put new vocabulary on the board and go over with the class later.

5. Let students share their statements in small groups or with the class. You may want to have some put their statements on the board. See possible answers on LP page 132.

Suggestion: If you still have the scale of intensifiers on the board from the Focus 4 activity, have students come up and write their topics along the scale. When they finish, go along the scale calling out topics and invite those who wrote the topics to share their reasons why they feel this way.

FOCUS 5 [15 minutes]

This focus chart gives examples of how to make statements more polite or indirect by using intensifiers with a negative sentence.

1. **Lead-in:** Write the following statements on the board and ask the class if they know how to say them in a more polite way.

His cooking is borrible.   She's very rude.
That painting is ugly.   That movie was boring.

2. Listen to the suggestions from the class and give them feedback on their skill at giving polite criticism.

3. Explain that it is also possible to make these sentences a little more polite by using an adjective

1. Notice that in the example *boring* becomes *not interesting* and *badly* becomes *not well.* Then the intensifier *too* is added to each.

2. Have students work individually to create more polite sentences.

3. Circulate and assist as needed. Note any problems with form or adjective choice to go over later.

4. Invite several students who finish quickly to put their polite sentences on the board.

5. Compare the sentences on the board with other suggestions. Note the differences that can occur while still keeping the grammar structures the same. See possible answers on LP page 132.

For more practice, use *Grammar Dimensions 3* Workbook page 48, Exercise 5 and Exercise 6.

EXERCISE 8 [15 minutes]

FOCUS 6

Degree Complements with *Too* and *Enough*

form

Too + infinitive phrase

	EXAMPLES
too + adjective	(a) Some teenagers are **too immature to make** really wise decisions.
too + adverb	(b) They grow **too quickly for** clothes **to fit** for very long.
too much/little + noncount noun	(c) They have **too much pride to ask for** advice from their elders.
	(d) They have **too little patience to wait for** complete freedom.
too many/few + count noun	(e) They have **too many people,** such as teacher and parents, telling them what **to do to feel** truly independent.
	(f) They have **too few chances to exercise** responsibility.
verb + *too much/little*	(g) Teenagers think they **know too much to listen** to their parents and **too little to be responsible** for their actions.

Enough + infinitive phrase

	EXAMPLES
adjective + *enough*	(h) Most teenagers are **responsible enough to do** a good job.
adverb + *enough*	(i) They work **hard enough to get** the same pay as adults.
verb + *enough*	(j) They have **learned enough to make** wise decisions.
enough + noun	(k) Parents often give their teenagers **enough responsibility to prepare** them for adult life.

EXERCISE 9

Restate each pair of sentences with a statement of degree using *too* or *enough*.

Examples: Denise is very serious about her career. She doesn't understand why Peter is so relaxed.

Denise is too serious about her career to understand why Peter is so relaxed.

Peter isn't terribly serious about his job. He doesn't want to spend every weekend at the office.

Peter isn't serious enough about his job to want to spend every weekend at the office.

1. Denise has lots of responsibilities. She can't take a vacation right now.
   Denise has too many responsibilities to take a vacation right now.

2. The pace of work is extremely hectic. Denise can't do her best work.
   The pace of work is too hectic for Denise to do her best work.

3. Denise's assistant works very slowly. Denise can't catch up on her correspondence.
   Denise's assistant works too slowly for Denise to catch up on her correspondence.

4. Mr. Green hasn't assigned Denise much additional support. Denise can't meet the contract deadline.
   Mr. Green hasn't assigned Denise enough additional support for her to meet the contract deadline.

5. Denise is very proud. She doesn't want to ask her boss for more help.
   Denise is too proud to ask her boss for more help.

6. Denise isn't nice to Peter. He won't offer to help her with the contract.
   Denise isn't nice enough to Peter for him to offer to help her with the contract.

7. There is always a little free time. Peter spends it on his friends, his music, and his family.
   There is always enough free time for Peter to spend on his friends, his music, and his family.

8. Peter plays the clarinet quite well. He could be a professional musician.
   Peter plays the clarinet well enough to be a professional musician.

9. He doesn't like Denise. He won't help her meet her contract deadline.
   He doesn't like Denise enough to help her meet her contract deadline.

10. Work is not that important. Peter doesn't make it the focus of his life.
    Work is not important enough for Peter to make it the focus of his life.

FOCUS 6 [20 minutes]

Focus 6 demonstrates how to make a degree complements using *too* or *enough*. Students will create sentences which state an excess by using *too* + infinitive phrase. They will also create sentences which state sufficiency by using *enough* + infinitive phrase.

1. **Lead-in:** Ask the class to suggest things that they feel a 10-year-old child is too young to do. They may suggest things like *drive, quit school*, etc. Write a few suggestions on the board.

2. Take one or two suggestions and create a sentence using the structure for Focus 6 (e.g., *Ten-year-olds are too young to . . .*). On the board above the suggested sentences, write the formula: *too* + **adjective** + **infinitive**

3. Now ask the class to suggest things that they have too little time to do. They may suggest things like *sleep, watch TV, study*, etc. Take notes and again make a few sentences with help from students (e.g., *We have too little time to . . .*). Then above these, write the formula: *too little/much* + **noncount noun** + **infinitive**

4. Next, ask the class to suggest things that 10-year-olds are old enough to do. Take notes and have the class help make sentences (e.g., *Ten-year-olds are old enough to clean their own rooms.*). Write the formula: **adjective** + *enough* + **infinitive**

5. Finally, ask the class to suggest things that they have enough time to do. Take notes and encourage volunteers to suggest sentences (e.g., *I have enough time to watch the news.*). Add the last formula to the board: *enough* + **noun** + **infinitive**

6. Go back and point out the four formulas on the board as you go over the examples in the focus charts on SB page 134 (note the differences for count and noncount nouns).

Suggestion: Ask students to create additional examples for each set of examples in Focus 6. Let them work in pairs in order to discuss the grammar structures as they go.

EXERCISE 9 [15 minutes]

Students will practice combining sentences to show an excess or sufficiency of something plus the result of that excess.

1. Put the following sentences on the board:

   Some teenagers are very immature. They can't make wise decisions.

2. Tell the class that you will be combining these sentences.

3. Demonstrate step by step how to combine these sentences into one by replacing *very* with *too*, cutting the repeated subject and modal, and using the infinitive *to make*. (*Some teenagers are too immature to make wise decisions.*)

4. Try another example and invite volunteers to talk the class through the steps:

   Some teenagers are not mature. They can't make wise decisions.

   (*Some teenagers are not mature enough to make wise decisions.*)

5. Go over the examples for Exercise 9 together and then have students work individually to complete the rest of the exercise.

6. Have students work with a partner to check their answers when finished.

7. Circulate to check for common errors. When students are finished, go over answers and common errors as a class. See answers on LP page 134.

For more practice, use *Grammar Dimensions 3* Workbook page 49, Exercise 7.

meaning

FOCUS 7

Implied Meanings of *Too* and *Not Enough*

The implied meaning of the infinitive phrase depends on which degree word we have chosen and the situation we are using it in.

EXAMPLES	POSSIBLE IMPLIED MEANINGS
(a) Mr. Green is too old to worry about losing his hair.	He doesn't worry about losing his hair. OR He worries about it, but he shouldn't.
(b) Mr. Green is not young enough to wear the latest fashions.	He doesn't wear the latest fashions. OR He wears those fashions, but he shouldn't.
(c) He is wise enough to listen to both sides in the argument.	He listens to both sides.
(d) He is wise enough not to take sides in the argument.	He doesn't take sides.

EXERCISE 10

Choose the correct implied meaning for these degree complements.

1. Teenagers are too young to buy alcoholic beverages.
   a. They can buy alcoholic beverages.
   (b.) They can not buy alcoholic beverages.

2. Peter does not work hard enough to be promoted.
   a. He will be promoted.
   (b.) He won't be promoted.

3. Mr. Green is wise enough to avoid taking sides in the argument.
   (a.) He avoids taking sides in the argument.
   b. He never avoids taking sides in the argument.

4. Teenagers think they are smart enough not to make mistakes.
   a. They think they might make mistakes.
   (b.) They think they won't make mistakes.

EXERCISE 11

Decide whether you agree with the following statements about teenagers. Use *too* or *enough* and an infinitive to give your opinion about things that 15-year-olds are old enough or too young to do.

Fifteen-year-olds are old enough . . .
Fifteen-year-olds are too young . . .

Examples: Fifteen-year-olds are old enough to drive.
Fifteen-year-olds are too young to live in their own apartments.

1. They should be able to drive.
2. They shouldn't live in their own apartments.
3. They can fall in love.
4. Schools should let them choose what classes they want to take.
5. Teachers should talk to them as adults.
6. They shouldn't be able to buy alcohol or cigarettes.
7. Their parents should give them some financial responsibility.
8. The law shouldn't treat them as adults.
9. They shouldn't be police officers or soldiers.
10. Society shouldn't give them total freedom.

EXERCISE 12

Do you have all the money or all the free time you wish you had? Are there some things you are **not** able to do because you don't have enough resources or time, or because you have too many responsibilities?

Write sentences that describe five activities you can't do, and what keeps you from doing them.

Examples: I don't have enough time to read novels.

I'm too poor to take a vacation this summer.

INTENSIFIERS (*Very, Too, Enough, Etc.*) AND DEGREE COMPLEMENTS (*So That, Such That, Etc.*)

Exercise 11 Answers will vary. Possible answers are: 1. They're (not) old enough to drive./They're too young to drive. 2. They're (not) old enough to live in their own apartments./They're too young to live in their own apartments. 3. They're (not) old enough to fall in love./They're too young to fall in love. 4. They're (not) old enough to be allowed to choose what classes they want to take./They're too young to be allowed to choose what classes they want to take. 5. They're (not) old enough for teachers to talk to them as adults./They're too young for teachers to talk to them as adults. 6. They're (not) old enough to be able to buy alcohol or cigarettes./They're too young to be able to buy

alcohol or cigarettes. 7. They're (not) old enough to be given some financial responsibility./They're too young to be given some financial responsibility. 8. They're (not) old enough for the law to treat them as adults./They're too young for the law to treat them as adults. 9. They're (not) old enough to be police officers or soldiers./They're too young to be police officers or soldiers. 10. They're (not) old enough to give them total freedom./They're too young for society to give them total freedom. **Exercise 12** Answers will vary, depending on the opinions of the student involved. Stressing the reason for the opinion will be appropriate for more advanced classes.

FOCUS 7 [10 minutes]

This focus chart gives examples of how the *too* + infinitive or *not enough* + infinitive structures can be confusing.

1. **Lead-in:** Put the following sentences on the board:

   They're not smart enough to go to Rydell High School.
   They're too smart to go to Rydell High School.

2. Now ask the class which sentence implies that the school is not a very good school. (*the second one*) Ask them which sentence implies the school is a very good school? (*the first one*) Ask students if they can tell what the first sentence says about the students (*they're not smart/they want to go to the school, but they can't*) versus what the second sentence says about the students (*they are smart/they don't want to go to the school/they are not fooled into going*).

3. You may have had different answers from the students. These structures can be confusing sometimes, because they are very subtle. The more students practice the structures, the more comfortable they will be with them. Go over the focus chart and note the possible implied meanings.

EXERCISE 10 [10 minutes]

1. Have students work individually to complete the exercise.

2. Let small groups check answers together and discuss if they disagree on any of them.

3. Go over the answers as a class. See answers on LP page 136.

Suggestion: After they finish, let students change each of these sentences to reflect the other or "wrong" answer for each pair of implied meanings. For example, change the first sentence like this: (1) *Teenagers are not too young to buy alcoholic beverages* = a. *They can buy alcoholic beverages.*

For more practice, use *Grammar Dimensions 3* Workbook page 49, Exercise 8.

EXPANSION [homework]

Assign Activity 3 (listening/speaking/writing) on SB page 143 for homework.

EXERCISE 11 [20 minutes]

1. **Lead-in:** Begin by asking the class how they feel about teenagers having their own cell phones or credit cards. Let them discuss these questions in pairs for a moment.

2. Now write the following sentences on the board:

   Teenagers should have cell phones.
   Parents should give their teenagers credit cards.

3. Invite volunteers to respond to the first statement using either *old enough* or *too young*. (You are aiming for a sentence like: *Teenagers are old enough to have a cell phone.*) Write student suggestions on the board and underline the infinitives.

4. Point out that the second sentence has a different subject (*parents*). Start the sentence for the class with:

   Teenagers are _____ a credit card
   (by their parents).

5. Ask volunteers to complete the sentence. If they need help, remind them to use *too young* or *old enough* plus the infinitive (*to be*), and because the subject is different they will also need to use the passive (*given*).

6. Go over the examples for Exercise 11 together.

7. Do the first sentence in the exercise together. Ask the class whether they believe that 15-year-olds should be able to drive. You will probably get both *yes* and *no* answers.

8. Ask for a volunteer to make a sentence to express their opinion as in the examples before. Write the sentence on the board and point out the infinitive used. Remind the class to use an infinitive for each sentence they make and to look for sentences that may need a passive. Have them complete the exercise individually.

9. Put students together in groups to share their opinions. Circulate and note any errors that should be addressed in debriefing. See possible answers on LP page 136.

EXERCISE 12 [15 minutes]

1. Tell the class about a few things that you can't do and why. Use *too* or *not enough* in your statements. For example, *I have too much homework to watch TV* or *I'm not strong enough to run a marathon.*

2. Ask the class about what they would like to do but can't. Ask students to tell you why they can't do those things. Encourage them to find a way to use *too* or *not enough*. Write these examples on the board. You may need to word them differently than students state them in order to get students to see the structures you're asking for.

3. Have students work individually and then share their activities in small groups. Circulate and note any common errors that should be addressed in debriefing.

EXPANSION [homework]

Ask students to interview six friends or family members about the things that they wish they could do and what keeps them from doing them. Have students write statements about their findings like those in Exercise 12. If you have time, let students share their results with a small group. Follow up by asking students to write a paragraph summarizing their group's results.

Working with a partner, ask and answer the following "foolish" questions. Answer the question with a *yes* or *no*, and give a reason for your answer using *too*. Then try to restate your answer using *enough*. Ask your partner five more "foolish" questions of your own.

Examples: Can you swim to Hawaii?

No. It's too far for someone to swim.

No. Nobody is strong enough to swim to Hawaii.

1. Do you have any great-great-grandchildren?
2. Can you walk 150 miles in a single day?
3. Is $50 a fair price for a cup of coffee?
4. Can dogs read?
5. Do banana trees grow wild in Russia?
6. Can one person lift a grand piano?
7. Can you learn to speak English fluently in a week?
8. Can a hundred-year-old woman still have babies?
9. Do you remember what you did on your first birthday?
10. Can you eat fifty hamburgers in a single meal?

Working with a partner, ask and answer these questions. Give your real opinions. Use *enough* in your answer. *Answers will vary.*

Example: Why don't some people do well on the TOEFL® Test?*

Because they don't know enough English to get a high score.

1. How much money do you need for a happy life?
2. How well do you speak English?
3. When should children move out of their parents' home?
4. When should people get married?
5. How quickly or slowly should a person drive on a turnpike or freeway?
6. What's an ideal age to retire?
7. What kind of person should be president?
8. What is an important characteristic for a basketball player?
9. Why can't monkeys learn to speak languages?

*TOEFL is a registered trademark of the Educational Testing Service (ETS). This publication is not endorsed or approved by ETS.

INTENSIFIERS (Very, Too, Enough, Etc.) AND DEGREE COMPLEMENTS (So That, Such That, Etc.)

Using this chart, interview a partner about what things he or she thinks people are old enough to do at the age of 15, and what things he or she thinks people are still too young to do. Then ask your partner to think of one other thing that people are old enough to do at age 15, and one more thing they're still too young to do. Report some of your partner's opinions and reasons he or she feels that way to the rest of the class. Some examples have been provided for you. *Answers will vary.*

ACTIVITIES	OLD ENOUGH OR TOO YOUNG?	WHY?
Marry and raise a family	too young	They are not mature enough to take that responsibility. They should be in their twenties.
Decide on a future career	old enough	They already know the kinds of things they like to do and the kinds of things they are good at.
Drive a car		
Go on dates without a chaperone		
Make wise decisions about life		
Live independently outside their parents' home		
Pay taxes		
Serve in the army		
Get a full-time job		
Get a part-time job		
Take care of young children		
Write poetry		
Be a professional athlete		
Vote in national elections		
Control their own money		
Become parents	too young	
	old enough	

Exercise 14 Answers will vary. Possible answers are: 1. No, I'm too young to have any./No, I'm not old enough to have any. 2. No, that's too far to walk./No, that's not enough time to walk that far. 3. No, that's way too expensive. 4. No, they're too stupid./No, they're not intelligent enough to read. 5. No, it's too cold in Russia for banana trees to grow wild./No, Russia isn't hot enough for banana trees to grow wild. 6. No, a piano is too heavy for one person to lift./No, one person isn't strong enough to lift a grand piano. 7. No, that's too little time to learn to speak English fluently./

No, that isn't enough time to learn to speak English fluently. 8. No, she's too old to still have babies./No, she's no longer young/strong enough to have babies. 9. No, I was too young to remember./No, that was too long ago for me to remember./No, I wasn't old enough to remember. 10. No, that's too many for me to eat./No, I would never be hungry enough to be able to eat 50 hamburgers in a single meal.

Five other "foolish questions" will vary.

LESSON PLAN 3/LESSON PLAN 4   INTENSIFIERS AND DEGREE COMPLEMENTS

EXERCISE 13 [20 minutes]

In this exercise, pairs will interview each other about the maturity of 15-year-olds. Have students do the exercise on a separate piece of paper in order to have enough space to record all the reasons why their partner feels the way that they do.

1. Go over the instructions with the class. Give students some time to review the activities. Everyone should have their own opinion on the topics before they begin the interview.

2. Put students into pairs. You may want to mix age groups, cultures, or sexes in order to put students with those more likely to express a different opinion and thereby create more discussion.

3. Have students fill in the box with their partners' reasons as they complete the exercise. This can take time, so partners should interview each other at the same time and write answers at the same time rather than one asking all the questions of one partner or the other first.

4. Circulate and assist as needed. Put any new vocabulary on the board to share with the class at debriefing.

5. When finished (be sure to set a time limit and give time warnings as needed to complete the task), let students share interesting responses with the class.

6. Put a few examples with the grammar structure on the board to highlight the use.

METHODOLOGY NOTE

This is an open exercise in the sense that students are not required to use the grammar structures. Students may find they are using the structures from Focus 6 naturally, or they may still be uncomfortable and find other ways to express their opinions. Don't worry too much about pushing students to use the grammar. Hearing their teacher and others use the structures is still building the language within them. As you invite students to

share their ideas, you can find ways to rephrase their ideas in a way that uses the grammar structures while still focusing on the idea and not just the grammar.

EXPANSION [homework]

Expand on this activity by having students use this chart to go out and ask actual teenagers for their opinions and the reasons for them. Bring the results to class and share in groups. How do these results compare to their in-class interviews?

LESSON PLAN 4

EXERCISE 14 [15 minutes]

Students will ask their partners wild questions and then use *to* or *enough* in their answers.

1. Begin by asking the class a "foolish" question similar to those in the exercise and write any responses on the board (e.g., *Do you have your own airplane? No, it's too expensive*). Encourage students to give a reason with their *yes/no* answers. You may need to remind them to use *too* or *enough* in their answers.

2. Go over the directions and examples for Exercise 14. Let students interview a partner and be sure to write down their partners' answers for each foolish question.

3. Circulate and encourage students to use *too* and to then rephrase their reasons again using *enough*.

4. Have students take a moment to make up five more foolish questions to ask their partners.

5. Invite students to share their most interesting answers with the class. See possible answers on LP page 138.

Suggestion: Have students move around the room asking only one question of each student and recording his or her answers. Encourage students to move quickly by setting a time limit and making this a quick and silly interview.

For more practice, use *Grammar Dimensions 3* Workbook page 50, Exercise 9.

work book

EXERCISE 15 [15 minutes]

This exercise is also an interview like Exercise 14. However, it asks for more serious answers than the previous exercise and focuses on the use of *enough* in the answers.

1. Ask the class a few real questions and invite students to respond using *enough/not enough* in their answers. Some examples might include:

   Why is the campus parking area always full?
   What do people need to have before they get a pet?

2. Write down some student answers and try to highlight the use of *enough* or ask for ways to reword an idea so that it includes the use of *enough*.

3. Give students a moment to read through the questions and form their own opinions before interviewing a partner.

4. Have students write down their partners' answers. Circulate and assist as needed.

5. If pairs finish quickly, ask them to put a sentence or two up on the board to share.

6. Finally, have students share interesting answers and go over the examples on the board. See possible answers on LP page 138.

FOCUS 8

form

Degree Complements with *So* and *Such*

So + Such + That clauses

	EXAMPLES
so + adjective	(a) Denise is **so serious** about her work that she rarely takes a vacation.
so + adverb	(b) Peter plays the clarinet **so well** that he once considered being a professional musician.
so + many/few + (count noun)	(c) Denise has **so many projects** that her assistant can't finish them fast enough.
	(d) She has **so few outside interests** that most people consider her rather boring.
so + much/little + (noncount noun)	(e) The project took **so much time** that Denise had to spend her weekend in the office.
	(f) They have **so little time** to get the job done that they'll have to spend the weekend in the office.
such + (a/an) + (adjective) + noun	(g) The disagreement between Peter and Denise has become **such a serious problem** that they are not speaking to each other.
	(h) Denise gives her assistant **such large amounts** of work that he is thinking about quitting.

In spoken English and less formal written English the *that* in *so/such* constructions can be omitted.

(i) I'm so busy **that** I could die.	OR	(j) I'm so busy I could die.
(k) Denise is such a serious person **that** she probably doesn't know how to have fun.	OR	(l) Denise is such a serious person she probably doesn't know how to have fun.

EXERCISE 16

Identify the degree complements in the following passage by underlining the result clauses where *that* has been omitted. The first paragraph has been done for you as an example.

Tall Tales

(1) In American English we use the term tall tale to describe stories that are so exaggerated they become funny. (2) No one really believes that they're true. (3) That's part of the fun. (4) The point of a tall tale is to tell such incredible lies everyone ends up laughing. (5) American folklore is filled with examples of tall tales.

(6) One famous tall tale is the story of the winter when the weather was so cold everything froze.

(7) Each day things got a little colder. (8) First, the usual things froze: water, plants, pipes, machinery. (9) Then it got worse. (10) It was such a cold winter dogs and cats froze when they went outside, and birds fell out of the sky, frozen solid. (11) Then it got even worse. (12) It got so cold people's words froze whenever they tried to talk. (13) You couldn't hear a single sound. (14) Of course, people like to talk, no matter how cold it is. (15) So people kept talking and their words kept freezing just as soon as they came out of their mouths.

(16) Then suddenly the cold weather came to an end. (17) One day it was so cold nobody could carry on a conversation because the words just froze right up, and the next day it was warm enough to wear shorts. (18) The change in weather was so great and so sudden everything became unfrozen all at the exact same minute, (19) All those frozen words thawed out at once, and the resulting noise was so loud everyone became deaf.

EXERCISE 17

Make statements of degree about the underlined items in the following pairs of sentences by using *so* and *such*.

Examples: There are **many plants** in the rainforest with possible medical uses. Scientists fear we may lose valuable medical resources if they are destroyed

> There are *so many plants* in the rainforest with possible medical uses *that scientists fear we may lose valuable medical resources if they are destroyed.*

1. The world's forests are being destroyed at a **rapid rate**.

   We can't ignore the problem any longer.

2. The world population is growing **quickly**.

   We can't continue our old habits.

3. We have **few alternative materials**.

   We haven't stopped using trees for fuel.

4. There has been a **rapid growth** in population.

   There are no other places for people to live except the rainforests.

(Exercise 17 is continued on Lesson Planner page 142.)

ANSWER KEY

Exercise 17 1. The world's forests are being destroyed at such a rapid rate that we can't ignore the problem any longer. 2. The world population is growing so quickly that we can't continue our old habits. 3. We have so few alternative materials that we haven't stopped using trees for fuel. 4. There has been such a rapid growth in population that there are no other places for people to live except the rain forests.

LESSON PLAN 4

FOCUS 8 [15 minutes]

These focus charts introduce the use of *so* or *such* with *that* clauses. Note the omission of *that* in spoken or informal English.

1. **Lead-in:** Write a few sentence starters on the board and ask students to think of ways to finish them. Here are sentence starters to illustrate each of the example types in Focus 8:

a. *She ran so fast that . . .*
b. *He is so tired that . . .*
c. *We have so few school holidays that . . .*
d. *They have so little money that . . .*
e. *I have such a small apartment that . . .*

2. Invite suggestions from students to finish each sentence. Then ask the class what these sentences have in common with each other (*so/such . . . that . . .*).

3. Circle or highlight the words *so* and *that* in each sentence. Next underline the words that come between them. Ask the class to say what part of speech these underlined words are and label them as you go (*a. adjective, b. adverb, c. few + count noun, d. little + noncount noun, e. a + adjective + noun*).

4. Go over the examples in Focus 8. Have volunteers read the examples and note the similar examples on the board.

5. Point out the omission of *that* in spoken or informal English and give an example of an expression, such as *I'm so hungry I could eat a horse!*

EXPANSION [15 minutes]

To give students additional practice in using *so/such . . . that . . .*, you may want to assign Activity 2 (speaking/writing) on SB page 143 after covering Focus 8. In this activity, students will talk about a time when they lost their temper, made a mistake or did something without realizing it, and what the result was.

EXERCISE 16 [15 minutes]

Students are asked to identify the degree complements that use *so/such* and then find the result clause in which *that* has been omitted. The context of a tall tale allows for the use of informal English.

1. Begin with a short explanation of what tall tales are (a distinctly American tradition usually associated with pioneer men who told exaggerated and often ridiculously untrue stories of their adventures in the wilds or of other people they had encountered) and ask the class if they have a storytelling tradition like this in their native language. Classic examples your students may have encountered in English before include Paul Bunyan, Pecos Bill, and Johnny Appleseed.

2. Remind the class that since tall tales are silly stories, they are usually told or written informally. Go over the directions for Exercise 16 together.

3. Have students work individually and then compare answers with a partner.

4. Go over the answers together, asking students to put each missing *that* back into sentences as they read them out loud. See answers on LP page 140.

EXPANSION 1 [20 minutes]

Students can see and use a wide range of degree complements by researching tall tales. Give the class a list of tall tales and have students choose one to learn about. Have them go out and research in the library and on the Internet to find information about their tall tale. Then have them summarize the story and share it with the class. Alternately, you can make storytelling groups with a variety of tall tales to share in each group. Let students vote on the most interesting or silliest tall tale.

EXPANSION 2 [20 minutes]

Use Activity 1 (writing) on SB page 143 to follow up with this exercise. In this activity, students will work with a group to come up with their own tall tale.

EXERCISE 17 [15 minutes]

Students will combine sentences using *so/such . . . that . . .* to create statements of degree. This exercise is continued on SB page 142.

1. Write sentences such as the following on the board:

   It's a cold day. My car wouldn't start.
   The line for tickets was long. I waited an hour.

2. Ask for volunteers to combine each of these sets of sentences into one sentence using either *so . . . that . . . or such . . . that . . .* If they need help, refer back to Focus 8 for examples of similar sentences. (*It's such a cold day that my car wouldn't start.* and *The line for tickets was so long that I waited an hour.*)

3. Go over the directions and examples for Exercise 17 together.

4. Have students work individually to complete the problems on SB pages 141 and 142 and then compare answers in pairs or together as a class. See answers on LP pages 140 and 142.

Use Your English

ACTIVITY 1 writing

STEP 1
In Exercise 16 you read an unbelievable story called a **tall tale**. Work with a group to invent a tall tale or unbelievable story of your own to tell to the rest of the class. The more unbelievable the story is, the funnier it will be.

STEP 2
The class should decide which group told the "tallest tale."

ACTIVITY 2 speaking/writing

Tell about a time when you or someone you know lost their temper, made a foolish mistake, or said or did something without realizing it. Here are some examples:

- The driver of the bus I was riding got so mad and shouted so loudly that his false teeth actually flew out of his mouth.
- My brother was so excited to get to Hawaii that he left his sweater and overcoat on the plane. He was pretty cold when he returned to Chicago.
- I was once in such a hurry to get to work that I left the house wearing one black shoe and one brown shoe.

Use one of the following situations, or think of some of your own:

- *I was once so happy that . . .*
- *My sister was so hungry that . . .*
- *A student I know once got so nervous in class that . . .*
- *When I was a child, I was once so frightened that . . .*
- *I once experienced such frustration that . . .*
- *I was once so angry that . . .*

ACTIVITY 3 listening/speaking/writing

When are adult children old enough to move away from home? Different cultures have different opinions about when (and if) this should happen. Interview people from three or four different countries. What is the average age at which people move away from home? What do other people think if someone leaves home at a much younger or much older age than the average? Are there different standards for men and women? Make a report on what you have discovered.

---

5. Some countries have <u>few other natural resources.</u>

They are forced to use the rainforests for economic development.

6. The problems appear <u>impossible</u> to solve.

Some countries haven't even begun to look for a solution.

7. The United Nations considers deforestation a <u>problem.</u>

They are trying to establish conservation programs throughout the developing world.

8. The loss of the rainforests is a <u>major global threat.</u>

The future of mankind may be at stake.

EXERCISE 18

Give true answers to these questions using *so/such.*

Example: What kind of student are you?

I'm such a good student that I always do my homework before class.

1. What kind of student are you?

2. How quickly or slowly do you walk or drive?

3. Have you ever wanted something a great deal? How badly did you want it?

4. Did you ever eat a huge amount of food? What happened?

5. How high are the Himalayan Mountains?

6. Did you have a good time on your first birthday?

7. How tall was the tallest person you've ever seen?

8. How hard is the TOEFL® test?

9. What happened in the most boring class you've ever been to?

10. How wonderful is your grammar teacher?

ANSWER KEY

Exercise 17 (continued from LP page 140) 5. Some countries have so few other natural resources that they are forced to use the rainforests for economic development. 6. The problems appear so impossible to solve that some countries haven't even begun to look for a solution. 7. The United Nations considers deforestation such a problem that they are trying to establish conservation programs throughout the developing world. 8. The loss of the rainforests is such a major global threat that the future of mankind may be at stake.

Exercise 18 Answers will vary. Possible answers are: 2. I drive so quickly that I get a speeding ticket once a week. 3. I once wanted a new bicycle so badly that I saved every penny of my allowance for over a year. 4. I once ate so much food that I got sick 5. They're so high that climbers have to carry oxygen with them when they climb them. 6. I was so young, I can't remember. 7. He was so tall that he had to buy his clothing at a special store. 8. It's so hard that some people try to cheat when they take it. 9. It was so boring that nothing ever happened. 10. My grammar teacher is so wonderful that I'm going to name my first-born child after her.

LESSON PLAN 4/USE YOUR ENGLISH   INTENSIFIERS AND DEGREE COMPLEMENTS

EXERCISE 18 [15 minutes/homework]

This exercise asks students to use *so/such . . . that . . .* in their answers. It could be used for individual work, pair work, moving pairs, homework, or for an interview outside the classroom.

For more practice, use *Grammar Dimensions 3* Workbook page 51, Exercise 10 and page 52, Exercise 11.

work book

UNIT GOAL REVIEW [10 minutes]

Ask students to look at the goals on the opening page of the unit again. Refer to the pages of the unit where information on each goal can be found.

ExamView® For assessment of Unit 8,
Test Generator use *Grammar Dimensions 3 ExamView®*.

USE YOUR ENGLISH

The Use Your English activities at the end of the unit contain situations that should naturally elicit the structures covered in the unit. For a more complete discussion of how to use the Use Your English activities see To the Teacher on LP page xxii. When students are doing these activities in class, you can circulate and listen to see if they are using the structures accurately. Errors can be corrected after the activity has finished.

ACTIVITY 1 writing [20 minutes]

You may wish to assign this activity after Exercise 16 on SB page 141 to expand on the informal exaggerating style of tall tales.

Suggestion: Encourage students to expand on their stories into more than one sentence to tell the story more completely. Have them explain what happened next.

ACTIVITY 3 listening/speaking/writing [homework]

This activity would work well after Exercise 11 on SB page 137. If your class does not have a wide mix of cultural backgrounds, you may want to have students interview outside the classroom.

1. Have students create an interview sheet with questions and space for answers to use. They will be asking the same questions of three or four people, so be sure their interview sheets are organized for this.

2. If the interview is done in the class, set a time limit and have people rotate or find a new partner. It may be necessary to form small groups to get at least one person from another culture represented within each group.

3. It can be helpful to have students share their final results with a partner and talk about ways to summarize the results before they write up their reports. This will help them to organize their thoughts before they write.

4. Reports can be turned in to you for individual feedback or presented to the class orally.

■ STEP 1

1. To get this activity going, read or have the students read another tall tale (a short version).

2. Have students get into groups to make up their own tall tale. Keep the groups small to ensure that all members get to take part in creating the story.

3. You may need to give students some ideas for story starters such as *"People say that many years ago there was a . . ."*

4. Have groups share their stories with the class.

■ STEP 2   As a class, discuss which group's tall tale was the best and why.

Suggestion 1: Check the Internet for other tall tale teaching ideas.

Suggestion 2: Although other countries have forms of tall tales, this can be seen as a very American storytelling style, so set the scene for your story presentations. These were originally told around a campfire with simple snacks and possibly some fiddle or banjo music along side ("Oh, Susanna," for example).

ACTIVITY 2 speaking/writing [15 minutes]

You may wish to assign this activity after Focus 8 on SB page 140 to give students practice using degree complements with *so/such . . . that . . . .*

1. Begin by going over the examples shown on SB page 143. Students will see that these stories can be serious or silly. You may have one or two of your own to add.

2. Point out that each of these uses the *so/such . . . that . . .* structure covered in Focus 8.

3. Have students use one of the sentence starters shown or simply begin with *"Once . . ."* Point out that several of the sentence starters use the word *once* to tell about an important memory.

ACTIVITY 4 — writing

Write a short (one-page) essay that describes how you feel about the importance of work in your life. Here are some questions you may wish to answer:

- Is work more or less important than other things in your life?
- Could you ever become a workaholic? Why or not?
- Who would you rather work with, Denise Driven or Peter Principle? Why?

ACTIVITY 5 — writing

There's a popular saying in America that it's not possible to be too rich, too good-looking, or too thin. Write a short (one-page) essay about the topic:

- Do you agree? Are there some qualities or characteristics that no one can have too much of? If so, what are they? Why do you feel that nobody can have too much of those qualities?
- Do you disagree? Is there a negative aspect to being extremely good-looking, wealthy, or fashionably slim?

ACTIVITY 6 — listening/writing

CD Track 13

STEP 1

Listen to the lecture on the destruction of tropical rainforests. Use the outline below to organize the information from the lecture.

I. Economic impact of rapid population growth
   A.
   B.

II. Result of economic impact on rainforests

III. Problems with reforestation

IV. Primary reasons to maintain existing rainforest areas
   A.
   B.

STEP 2

Write a one- or two-sentence summary of the lecture.

ACTIVITY 7 — research on the web

STEP 1

Using the Internet, go to the home page for Workaholics Anonymous (http://www.workaholics-anonymous.org). Read the information of the Web site under "About" regarding workaholism and decide whether you or someone you know is a workaholic. Based on what you read on the Web site, decide on three pieces of advice you would recommend to someone who is suffering from workaholism.

STEP 2

Use an Internet engine such as Google® or Yahoo® or Ask® and search some of the other -aholic conditions that were mentioned in the opening task (sportaholics, shopaholics, chocoholics). Which conditions are "serious" and have organizations like WA or AA to help sufferers, and which ones seem just for fun? Report your findings to the rest of the class.

ACTIVITY 8 — reflection

One way good language learners increase their vocabulary is by listening to how native speakers talk. Slang expressions change quickly and vary in usage by age. Intensifiers are one area where you can hear great differences between young and old and different regions of the same country. Slang intensifiers are popular with American teenagers. One current slang intensifier is "hecka" or "hella" to mean "very."

Listen to teenagers talking, either on TV or in real life and note the slang intensifiers that they use. Report one slang intensifier that you heard to the rest of the class. Tell where you heard it and how it was used. Your teacher may (or may not) be able to tell you the meaning. If you know any teenager, ask them what they think are the current styles for intensifiers.

Activity 6   Here is one version of the information from the lecture in outline and in summary forms.

I. A. Developing countries need foreign exchange—can get by selling wood from trees in rain forest. (export lumber)   B. Developing countries need more land for growing populations (land for agriculture)   II. Result of economic impact on rain forest   Many countries started to develop lands previously rain forest. Destruction happening so rapidly that in 20 years rain forests will be gone.   III. Problems with reforestation   Once rain forests cut down, don't grow back—too little fertility in soil.   IV. A. Rain forests contain many plants with possible medical uses; scientists worried species will be destroyed   B. Clear relationship between rain forests and climate, weather patterns of world. Rain forests disappearing so quickly scientists afraid of possible changes in planet's atmosphere, weather.   **Summary:** The destruction of the rain forests is a result of rapid population growth, which causes the need for export commodities and land for agriculture. If we can't halt the destruction of the world's rain forests we may lose scientifically valuable plant species and forever change the world's climate.

USE YOUR ENGLISH

ACTIVITY 4 — writing [15 minutes]

This activity would work well after Exercises 1 and 2 on SB pages 126–127. Have students take a moment to discuss the questions with a partner before they begin to write.

ACTIVITY 5 — writing [20 minutes]

1. Write the following on the board: *"You can never be too rich, too good-looking, or too thin."*

2. In small groups, have students discuss the meaning of this expression and whether they agree or disagree with it. Ask students to share their reasons.

3. Ask the groups to discuss whether there are any other things or characteristics that people can never have too much of or be too much of.

4. Have students write the essays on their own.

5. After students have finished the writing activity, put them again into small groups and let them share their paragraphs with each other.

ACTIVITY 6 — listening/writing [15 minutes]

CD Track 13

Before beginning, briefly review what an academic outline for a lecture would look like, the way information is presented, and general note-taking skills.

■ STEP 1

1. Have students go over the outline and note the missing information before listening to the audio. Ask the class what they think the lecture will be about, and why. Ask what kind of information they plan to listen for.

2. After listening to the audio, give students time to write down their answers.

3. Let students check their answers with a partner. Circulate and take note of any points of disagreement or problems with the note taking or vocabulary.

4. Play the audio again and have students check their answers or fill in missed ones.

Suggestion: You may want to play the audio a little at a time as you go over the whole outline to see how the information matches and is presented in this type of note-taking format.

■ STEP 2

Have students write a one- or two-sentence summary. You may decide to have them work in pairs or individually.

ACTIVITY 7 — research on the web [homework]

Assign this activity after the Opening Task on SB pages 124–125 and give a due date for research to be presented or turned in as you finish Unit 8. This activity can be used as a presentation or developed into a writing assignment.

■ STEP 1

1. Have students use the Internet to research *workaholism* on the home page for Workaholics Anonymous. Based on what they read, students should decide whether they know any workaholics.

2. They should then write three pieces of advice they would give to someone who is a workaholic.

■ STEP 2

1. Next, students should research the list of *-aholisms* listed in the Opening Task and decide which are serious and which are just made up.

2. Have students report their findings to the class or in small groups. Let students add to a master list of serious *-aholisms* on the board during the class.

ACTIVITY 8 — reflection [15 minutes]

You may wish to assign Activity 4 on SB page 130. By listening to native speakers and focusing on the language of teenagers, ESL students can learn popular slang and become more natural speakers. Slang can make up a large part of what non-native speakers of English hear outside of the classroom.

1. Before assigning this activity, give an example of slang that has changed across the country and with the younger generations through time.

   good = groovy, cool, rad, wicked, bad, sweet, fly, etc.

2. Ask for other synonyms students may have learned. Point out that teenagers will often invent or use new words for old meanings as a way to set themselves apart from their parents.

3. After the class has gone out and done their research, have them present the new intensifiers to the class. Again, you may need to make comments on what is appropriate to use in normal conversation.

4. Have students write down their findings in their *Reflection Journals.*

METHODOLOGY NOTE

Explain to your class that when they seek out new slang, they should also learn in what situation the new vocabulary is accepted and whether it might be considered rude or too informal to use in most situations.

UNIT GOALS

- Put adjective modifiers in the correct order

- Form and understand the meaning of present and past participle modifiers

- Use other noun modifiers in the proper order

OPENING TASK
Going to a Flea Market

Many Americans are fond of going to "flea markets" or "garage sales," where private individuals sell things that they no longer need. Such items are called "secondhand." People are attracted to these sales because it is often possible to find valuable antiques and collectibles for sale rather cheaply.

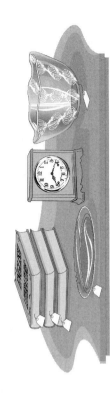

■ STEP 1

The objects shown here were were all found on sale at a flea market or garage sale. Match the objects with the descriptions, and guess how much the person who bought them paid for them.

- One slightly used, antique, blue Moroccan dish
- An interesting antique wooden clock
- A really beautiful old Italian glass bowl
- A fascinating collection of rare, used English textbooks

■ STEP 2

Think of two things you own that you don't want anymore. Write a short description of each thing. Show your descriptions to your classmates. Try to find classmates who want to buy your things, and find two things you want to buy from classmates.

UNIT OVERVIEW

Unit 9 focuses on the word order of adjective modifiers and other noun modifiers. The meaning, form, and use of past versus present participle modifiers are also reviewed.

GRAMMAR NOTE

Deciding on the order of two or more descriptive adjectives can cause problems for learners of English. Unlike many languages, English not only places all descriptive adjectives before the noun, it also keeps to a mostly fixed ordering of these modifiers. Language learners, therefore, may have trouble with this ordering because their native languages either do not follow such strict ordering, or do not require all adjectives to be placed before the noun (e.g., Arabic and French).

Present and past participle modifiers can also describe nouns. Learners can have trouble deciding which participle form to use when modifying nouns. As a rule, the present participle (-*ing* form) tells us about the noun it modifies (*an exciting movie* = the movie is exciting). Whereas, the past participle (-*ed*/-*en* form), tells us the noun is affected by something else (*an excited child* = the child is excited by something).

UNIT GOALS

Some instructors may want to review the goals listed on Student Book (SB) page 146 after completing the Opening Task so that students understand what they should know by the end of the unit. These goals can also be reviewed at the end of the unit when students are more familiar with the grammar terminology.

OPENING TASK [20 minutes]

The aim of this activity is to give students the opportunity to work with the use and order of noun modifiers. The problem-solving format is designed to

show the teacher how well the students can produce a target structure implicitly and spontaneously when they are engaged in a communicative task. For a more complete discussion of the purpose of the Opening Task, see To the Teacher, Lesson Planner (LP) page xxii.

Setting Up the Task

1. Begin by looking at the picture on SB page 146 and asking students about their experiences at similar types of markets for used goods. Did they find anything interesting? Can they describe it to the class?

2. Let the class look over the photograph on page 146. Does anything in the picture look like it could be a valuable antique? Which items?

3. Take note of the students' use of modifiers, but do not make corrections at this point.

Conducting the Task

■ STEP 1

1. Have the class look at the objects in the drawing on SB page 147 and work through Step 1 in pairs.

2. Go over the descriptions and talk about any new vocabulary with the class. Can they describe these items differently? Invite volunteers to do so.

Suggestion: Ask the pairs to describe two items from the photo on page 146 to each other. Have them describe one thing that they would never buy and one thing that they think might be a good gift for someone they know.

■ STEP 2

1. Tell the class that they will be creating a small classroom flea market and they will need to think of a few things they have that they don't want anymore.

2. Go over the Step 2 directions and give students time to write descriptions of things they would

like to sell. Remind them to describe their items well enough for others to imagine what they look like.

3. Have students move around the classroom looking for two items they are interested in buying.

Suggestion: You may want to have students tape their FOR SALE ads around the room and let the class move around looking for things to buy.

Closing the Task

After students have found items "to buy," bring the class together and invite students to describe the things they found and why they want to buy them. Put a few of these descriptions on the board and note the use of noun modifiers. Save the list of descriptions for Focus 1.

GRAMMAR NOTE

Typical student errors (form)
- Placement of the modifiers in relation to the noun: * *We have a bouse white.*
- Placement of modifiers in relation to each other: * *She has a red big nice apple.* (See Focus 2.)

Typical student errors (use)
- Confusing the use of present and past participle modifiers: * *The show was interested.* (See Focus 4.)

FOCUS 1

form

Overview of Word Order in Noun Phrases

A noun phrase consists of a determiner and noun plus all its modifiers. Determiners can be articles, demonstratives, possessives, or quantifiers.

TYPES OF NOUN PHRASES	PARTS OF NOUN PHRASES
determiner + noun	**Kinds of determiners**
(a) **the** books; **these** books	articles, demonstratives, possessives, quantifiers
(b) **my** books; **some** books	
determiner (+ modifiers) + noun)	**Kinds of modifiers**
(c) some **extremely interesting, really beautiful used** books	adjectives and participles (with or without intensifiers)
(d) some **interesting, really beautiful used grammar** books	other nouns
determiner (+ modifiers) + noun + (modifying phrases and clauses)	**Kinds of modifying phrases and clauses**
(e) some interesting, really beautiful used grammar books **with red covers**	prepositional phrases
(f) some interesting, really beautiful used grammar books **printed in China with red covers**	participle phrases
(g) some interesting, really beautiful used grammar books printed in China with red covers **that we studied last semester**	relative clauses

Although it is rare to have more than three or four modifiers for a single noun phrase, this is the usual order for different categories of modifiers.

DETERMINER	INTENSIFIERS	ADJECTIVES AND PARTICIPLES	NOUN MODIFIER	NOUN	MODIFYING PHRASES
the/a/an	really	old/new	stone	wall	next to the river
some/no	very	interesting	university	campus	described in the brochure
my/your	slightly	well-known			
each/every					
these/those					

EXERCISE 1

From the chart below, make five noun phrases that use more than one modifier. Then write a sentence for each noun phrase. You can use singular or plural forms of the nouns. Compare your sentences to the examples and to those of several other students.

DETERMINERS	INTENSIFIERS	ADJECTIVES AND PARTICIPLES	NOUN MODIFIERS	NOUNS
a	very	little	stone	teacher
some	rather	experienced	English	statue
your	extremely	cute	circus	animals
the	quite	famous	university	watches
this	wonderfully	relaxing	pocket	professor
those	really	expensive	three-week	vacation
	somewhat	good	grammar	
		pleasant		
		ugly		

Examples: I like this really expensive pocket watch.
Only your very experienced English teachers will know the answer.
Many very famous university professors are not very good teachers.

1. _____

2. _____

3. _____

4. _____

5. _____

ANSWER KEY

Exercise 1 Answers will vary. Check to make sure that intensifiers "match" descriptive adjectives and determiners "match" nouns. Example: "Some wonderfully pleasant stone statue" or "this rather gold grammar animals" would not be appropriate answers.

FOCUS 1 [15 minutes]

Focus 1 gives students an overview of the word order for noun phrases, including determiners, modifiers, and modifying phrases or clauses. The focus of Unit 9 comes from the second portion of the focus chart, which outlines the different categories of modifiers and their usual word order.

1. **Lead-in:** Write the following FOR SALE ad or your own on the board:

   I have some extremely beautiful antique blue glass lamps for sale.

2. Go over the first section of Focus 1 with the class.

3. Using the descriptions on the board generated in the Opening Task and your own FOR SALE ad, invite students to note any determiners used. Circle these in the examples on the board.

4. Now have the class note any modifiers used, including modifying phrases and clauses. Underline these on the board.

5. Now looking at their own FOR SALE ads, ask students to do the same for these. Circle the determiners and underline any modifiers.

6. Ask for examples, and make a list on the board of determiners students circled and some of the modifiers they underlined.

7. Go over the lower section of the Focus 1 chart. Looking again at the list of modifiers students underlined and are listed on the board, ask for examples that might fit into each of the categories (you've already completed a separate list for determiners).

the board. Note the need to keep these in the same order as the chart shows. If students do make errors in order, make note of the errors, but do not correct them at this point. Word order will be addressed in Focus 2.

2. Look at the example sentences and ask for suggestions of ways to put the noun phrases from the board into complete sentences.

3. Let students work individually to create their own sentences. Circulate and assist as needed. Note whether students are keeping to the order of these modifiers as they are laid out in the chart. Keep these errors in mind as you work on Focus 2, which focuses on word order.

4. Have pairs or small groups share sentences with each other. Did anyone create the same noun phrase? If so, how did their sentences differ? Note the comment in the Answer Key on LP page 148.

EXPANSION [10 minutes]

If students are comfortable with the exercise, ask them to add five more words to each category in the chart. Have students continue making noun phrases and sentences using these new words.

[work book]

For more practice, use *Grammar Dimensions 3* Workbook page 53, Exercise 1.

EXERCISE 1 [15 minutes]

This exercise asks students to mix and match to create their own noun phrases from a list of choices and then to make a sentence using their noun phrases.

1. After going over the instructions for Exercise 1, invite students to choose one word from each category to create noun phrases. Write these on

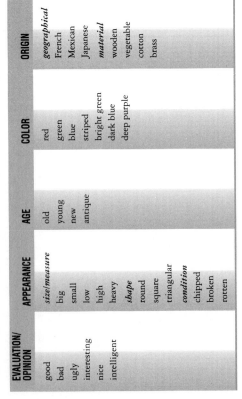

FOCUS 2

Order of Descriptive Adjectives

form

Different categories of descriptive adjectives **usually** occur in the following order.

EVALUATION/ OPINION	APPEARANCE	AGE	COLOR	ORIGIN
good	*size/measure*	old	red	*geographical*
bad	big	young	green	French
ugly	small	new	blue	Mexican
interesting	low	antique	striped	Japanese
nice	high		bright green	*material*
intelligent	heavy		dark blue	wooden
	shape		deep purple	vegetable
	round			cotton
	square			brass
	triangular			
	condition			
	chipped			
	broken			
	rotten			

Within a category there is some possible variation.

EXAMPLES

(a) a big, round, shiny apple
(b) a big, shiny, round apple
(c) a shiny, big, round apple

(d) a Japanese silk fan
(e) a silk Japanese fan

EXPLANATIONS

Adjectives of **appearance** usually follow the order in (a): size, shape, condition. But other orders are also possible.

Adjectives of **origin** usually follow the order in (d): geographical, material. But other orders are also possible.

EXERCISE 2

Put the descriptive adjectives in these noun phrases in the correct category in the chart below or your notebook. Not every category is used in each noun phrase. The first one has been done for you as an example.

Here are some things that were for sale at the flea market:

1. handsome, small, well-polished Italian leather shoes
2. a big shiny new red racing bicycle
3. a cute little brown puppy
4. some beautiful old Thai silk pajamas
5. a round antique brass tea tray
6. a painted Japanese wooden screen
7. an interesting recent French physics textbook
8. a funky, broken-down old chair

CATEGORY	1	2	3	4	5	6	7	8
EVALUATION/ OPINION	handsome	—	cute	beautiful	—	—	interesting	funky
APPEARANCE								
size	small	big	little	—	—	—	—	—
shape	—	—	—	—	round	—	—	—
condition	well-polished	shiny	—	—	—	painted	—	broken-down
AGE	—	new	—	old	antique	—	recent	old
COLOR	—	red	brown	—	—	—	—	—
ORIGIN								
geographical	Italian	—	—	Thai	—	Japanese	French	—
material	leather	—	—	silk	brass	wooden	—	—
NOUN	shoes	racing bicycle	puppy	pajamas	tea-tray	screen	physics textbook	chair

LESSON PLAN 1

FOCUS 2 [15 minutes]

Focus 2 outlines the usual word order for descriptive adjectives. This will be a chart that you will likely be referring back to throughout the unit.

1. **Lead-in:** Write the FOR SALE ad you used in Focus 1 on the board again:

   I have some extremely beautiful antique blue glass lamps for sale.

2. Ask a volunteer to underline the descriptive adjectives you used in this sentence (*beautiful, antique, blue,* and *glass*).

3. Now ask the class how we know what order to put these descriptive adjectives in.

4. After students have given a few answers, draw their attention to the focus chart on SB page 150.

5. List the categories across the board: Evaluation/ Opinion, Appearance, Age, Color, and Origin.

6. After going over these categories with the class, refer back to the underlined words in your sentence and invite volunteers to suggest which category each adjective belongs in. Write these on the board under the appropriate headings.

7. Explain that if you are using two adjectives within the **same category**, it usually doesn't matter which order they come in. However, the order is fairly strictly set **between categories.** Point out that some categories actually have subcategories within them, such as *appearance (size/measure, shape, condition)* and *origin (geographical, material)*.

8. Go over the examples in the lower section of the focus chart to show how variation can occur with adjectives within the same category and the usual ordering of these subcategories. (See the Grammar Note that follows.)

Suggestion: Create an overhead transparency listing the order of categories across it from left to right. You will refer to this for several exercises in this unit.

EXPANSION [10 minutes]

Referring back to the FOR SALE ad on the board, erase the four adjectives you used and have pairs create new descriptions for the lamps with the choices in the Focus 2 chart.

GRAMMAR NOTE

You may want to note that although it's possible to use more, English doesn't generally use more than three or four of these adjectives in one noun phrase.

When using two or more adjectives from the same category, commas are used to separate them, except for geographical and material adjectives, which do not require a comma between them. Two colors are conjoined with *and.*

EXERCISE 2 [10 minutes]

This exercise gives students practice identifying which category descriptive adjectives belong in. It's important for students to understand the differences between the categories in order to put modifiers into the correct word order.

1. Write the following noun phrases on the board:

   an ugly broken white ceramic dish
   a funny little metal car
   a pretty new blue rubber ball

2. Invite volunteers to place these descriptive adjectives in the appropriate categories in the box on SB page 151. Refer back to Focus 2 for help.

3. Go over the directions for the exercise with the class and let them work individually to complete the chart.

4. Have pairs compare answers and discuss any differences. See answers on LP page 150.

5. Go over answers as a class, asking pairs to volunteer answers and note where they disagreed.

Suggestion: To reinforce the word order of these categories, you may want to refer to the list of categories across the board from Focus 2 as you go over the answers for this exercise. Putting the categories across the board, rather than up and down as in the Exercise 2 chart, will highlight the left-right order for students who may have difficulties with this.

EXPANSION 1 [homework]

You may wish to assign Activity 1 (writing) on SB page 161 for students to complete as homework after Exercise 2. In this activity, students will go to a flea market and write descriptions of things they find there.

EXPANSION 2 [15 minutes]

You may also wish to assign Activity 2 (speaking) on SB page 161 after students finish Exercise 2. In this activity, students practice the order of noun phrases and modifiers by playing a game called *Adjective Tennis.*

EXERCISE 3

Add the modifiers in the correct order to the following passages. The first one has been done for you as an example.

My friend Wolfgang is a shopaholic. Whenever he goes out of the house he

returns with some (1) ___strange new___ (new, strange) "bargain." He rarely

buys any (2) _____ (useful, really) items. Once he came home with

some (3) _____ (bright, flannel, purple) blankets. "They match my

(4) _____ (pretty, French, new) curtains," he said. But those curtains were

still in their (5) _____ (plastic, original) wrappings. He was so busy

shopping that he hadn't had time to hang them up.

Fortunately, Wolfgang refuses to buy anything secondhand. I can imagine all

the (6) _____ (useless, incredibly ugly, antique) "art objects" he would

bring home. He already has (7) _____ (brand-new, European, expensive,

plenty of, brightly colored) shirts and sweaters. But that doesn't stop him from buying

more. He just piles them into his (8) _____ (little, dark, bedroom, over-

crowded) closet. He has some (9) _____ (Italian, nice, handmade) shoes

that I have never even seen him wearing.

He's running out of space to put things. He has such a (10) _____

(new, nice) apartment with lots of storage space, but his closets look like some

(11) _____ (old, poor) shopkeeper's (12) _____ (poor old) terrible,

(frightening, terrible) nightmare!

EXERCISE 4

Are these sentences correct or incorrect? If they are incorrect, identify the problem and correct it.

1. I bought a green, old, pretty vase at the flea market.
2. He's a university, brand-new dormitory resident.
3. It's an antique, genuine, black, old-fashioned umbrella.
4. Would you like some of these delicious, little, chocolate candies?
5. Would you like to hear about my summertime, exciting, vacation plans?

form

FOCUS 3   Participle Modifiers

EXAMPLES

(a) The **interesting** man told **fascinating** stories about his adventures in Sumatra.

(b) The **interested** woman listened carefully. She was **fascinated** by the man's stories about his adventures in Sumatra.

EXPLANATIONS

Present and past participles can be used like descriptive adjectives to describe nouns.

VERB	PRESENT PARTICIPLE	PAST PARTICIPLE
study	studying	studied
forget	forgetting	forgotten

EXPLANATIONS

Present participles are formed by adding -ing to the verb.

Past participles are formed by adding -ed to regular verbs or by using the third form (-en form) of irregular verbs. For a review of irregular past participle forms see Appendix 6.

ANSWER KEY

Exercise 3 Answers may vary in terms of order, as shown.   (2) really useful   (3) bright purple flannel   (4) pretty new French   (5) original plastic   (6) useless, incredibly ugly antique/incredibly ugly, useless antique   (7) plenty of brand-new brightly colored European   (8) overcrowded, dark little bedroom   (9) nice, handmade Italian   (10) nice new   (11) poor old   (12) terrible, frightening/frightening, terrible

Exercise 4   1. incorrect; I bought a pretty, old, green vase at the flea market.   2. incorrect; He's a brand-new university dormitory resident.   3. incorrect; It's a genuine antique old-fashioned black umbrella.   4. correct   5. incorrect; Would you like to hear about my exciting summertime vacation plans?

EXERCISE 3 [10 minutes]

Now that students have had practice identifying which categories that modifiers go into, this exercise will focus on the word order of those modifiers.

1. Go over the instructions and then have students work individually to fill in the missing words in the correct order.

2. Have students compare answers with a partner. Circulate and note any common errors. Pay special attention to these as you go over the answers together as a class. See answers on LP page 152.

Suggestion: If you created an overhead transparency for Focus 2, you can use it again here as you go over the answers.

For more practice, use *Grammar Dimensions 3* Workbook page 54, Exercise 2.

EXERCISE 4 [10 minutes]

This exercise asks students to identify the correct word order for descriptive adjectives.

1. You may want to begin this exercise with students closing their books. You can write an example of a sentence that is incorrect on the board and ask students how to fix it. Have students come up to the board to correct the sentence. Here's an example:

I have a metal yellow dented old lunchbox at home.
(I have a dented old yellow metal lunchbox at home.)

2. Next, let students open their books and check their guesses for word order with the chart in Focus 2. Discuss any problems.

3. Have students then work individually to complete the exercise and check answers with a partner. Go over with the class. See answers on LP page 152.

EXPANSION [15 minutes]

Have students make up five more sentences like these to test their classmates. They will need to make their own answer key on another piece of paper. Have everyone switch papers with a partner and try to find the "mistakes." When finished, have students check their partners' work with the answer key.

For more practice, use *Grammar Dimensions 3* Workbook page 54, Exercise 3.

FOCUS 3 [10 minutes]

Students will review the form of past and present participles and see them used as modifiers.

1. **Lead-in:** Quickly review what participles look like (verbs followed by *-ing/-ed/-en*) and show the class that they can also be used as descriptive adjectives. Use some commonly used participles in sentences to show this. Some examples include:

That movie was so boring that I fell asleep.
I wasn't very interested in the movie.
We were surprised by that very disappointing movie.

2. Invite volunteers to point out the participle modifiers and say whether they are present or past participles. (Keep these on the board to use in Exercise 5 later.)

3. Go over the examples and review the present and past participle forms in Focus 3.

Suggestion: You may want to review the irregular past participle forms while encouraging students to look at these as possible modifiers. This will not only be a review of the irregular forms, but it may also be a way for students to find new meanings for familiar words. Using the list in Appendix 6 (page A-10–A-11), ask students to see how many

different past participle modifiers work in sentence starters such as these:

He's a _____ man.
It's a _____ gift/chair/fruit/etc.

EXERCISE 5

Underline all the participles in the following passage, and tell what noun they describe. The first paragraph has been done as an example.

Examples: (1) revealing—present participle, describes "information"
(2) hidden—past participle, describes "emotions"
(3) widespread—past participle, describes "reactions"
(4) exciting—present participle, describes "situations"; increased—past participle, describes "heart rates"
(5) no participle modifiers in this sentence

Body Language

(1) Unconscious facial expressions and "body language" often give <u>revealing</u> information to other people. (2) Many people's "<u>hidden</u>" emotions are actually quite visible to anyone who knows how to read people's faces. (3) Some reactions are so <u>widespread</u> in all cultures that there seems to be a physical basis for them. (4) All people react in the same way to certain <u>exciting</u> situations by breathing more rapidly and experiencing <u>increased</u> heart rates. (5) Facial expressions of basic emotions, such as anger, surprise, and amusement, appear to be universal.

(6) Other reactions are not so universal. (7) Many, but not all, individuals respond to an embarrassing situation by blushing (when the face and neck turn bright red). (8) Some people show that they are bored by growing less active and becoming sleepy or inattentive. (9) Others respond to boring situations by becoming more active and showing such physical signs as jiggling feet or wiggling fingers. (10) But for other people, such reactions may be unintended indications of nervousness or anxiety, not boredom. (11) When someone experiences a confusing situation, he or she may unconsciously try to hide that confusion by smiling, thus making what is known as "the stupid grin." (12) But another person might respond by looking angry.

(13) There are not only variations in this "silent language" between different individuals, but there are also important differences between cultures. (14) Certain kinds of "silent language" give one particular message in one culture, but a conflicting message in another culture. (15) For example, eye contact (looking directly into the eyes of the person you are speaking to) has very different meanings in different cultures. (16) In American culture, if you do not look directly into someone's eyes while talking, the listener will think that you are dishonest. (17) If someone is described as "shifty-eyed" it means that he or she cannot be trusted. (18) But in many Asian cultures, avoiding eye contact is a sign of politeness and respect, and prolonged eye contact (which indicates sincerity in American culture) means aggression or hostility, and is seen as a threatening behavior. (19) Mistaken "body language" can often result in even more misunderstanding than using the wrong word or incorrect grammar.

ANSWER KEY

Exercise 5 (7) embarrassing: present participle, describes situation (8) bored: past participle, describes they (9) boring: present participle, describes situations; jiggling: present participle, describes feet; wiggling: present participle, describes fingers (10) unintended: present participle, describes indications (11) confusing: present participle, describes situation (14) conflicting: present participle, describes message (17) shifty-eyed: past participle, describes someone
(18) prolonged: past participle, describes eye contact; threatening: present participle, describes behavior (19) Mistaken: past participle, describes body language

---

FOCUS 4

Meanings of Present and Past Participles

EXAMPLES	EXPLANATIONS
(a) **a loving mother** (She loves her children.)	Present participles modify **agents**. The agents do or perform the actions described by the participle.
(b) **a well-loved mother** (She is loved by her children.)	Past participles modify **receivers**. The receivers are affected by the action described by the participle.

EXERCISE 6

Paraphrase these sentences by choosing the correct participle for the cues given.

Example: Most of my friends enjoy reading novels.
Most of my friends are ___interested___ (interest) in reading novels.
Novels are ___interesting___ (interest) to most of my friends.

1. The audience didn't understand the lecture.
   a. The audience was ___confused___ (confuse).
   b. The lecture was ___confusing___ (confuse).

2. The students didn't do well on the exam.
   a. The exam results were ___disappointing___ (disappoint).
   b. The students were ___disappointed___ (disappoint).

3. Children who watch scary movies may not be able to sleep afterwards.
   a. (Frighten) ___Frightened___ children may not be able to go to sleep.
   b. (Frighten) ___Frightening___ movies may keep children from sleeping.

4. That was quite a delicious snack.
   a. The snack was quite ___satisfying___ (satisfy).
   b. We were quite ___satisfied___ (satisfy).

5. Most students enjoy studying grammar.
   a. Most students are ___interested___ (interest) in grammar.
   b. Grammar is ___interesting___ (interest) to most students.

LESSON PLAN 2

EXERCISE 5 [20 minutes]

Students will identify participle modifiers and the nouns that they describe.

1. You may want to begin with a quick discussion of what body language is. Show some examples yourself. For example, try standing with your arms crossed across your chest and try to look grim and angry. Ask the class what your body is showing. Try tapping your foot impatiently and see what the class can guess about this gesture. Invite students to show other examples of body language and have others guess the meanings that they carry. Remind students that different body language means different things in different cultures.

2. Next, refer back to the example sentences you put on the board for Focus 3. Underline each participle modifier and ask the class what noun each one is describing. Go over the directions and examples for Exercise 5, which ask students to do a similar task.

3. Have students work individually, following the examples given.

4. Circulate and note whether students seem to be finding a majority of participles and making the right connections with their nouns. If they seem to be missing many participle modifiers, you can let the class know how many they should find in all. This will give them a number to aim for.

5. Have pairs quickly check their answers together and then go over them as a class. See answers on LP page 154.

Suggestion: You may want to copy this page onto an overhead transparency and use two colored markers (for modifiers and nouns) for easier review with the class.

For more practice, use *Grammar Dimensions 3* Workbook page 55, Exercise 4.

EXPANSION [20 minutes/homework]

After students have completed Exercise 5, you may wish to assign Activity 8 (research on the web) on SB page 165. For this activity, students will use the Internet to research body language and present their findings in small groups.

LESSON PLAN 2

FOCUS 4 [10 minutes]

Focus 4 explains the differences in meanings between past and present participles when used as modifiers. Students often have trouble with this difference and extra practice might be needed.

1. **Lead-in:** Give students several examples of the past and present forms of the same participles being used. Some examples may include:

   That movie was boring. We were bored.

   However, it was an interesting novel. I was interested in the story.

   We're excited to see the next movie. I hope the movie is exciting.

2. Ask students to suggest what they observe about any possible differences between the use of past and present participles in these examples.

3. Go over the examples and explanations for Focus 4 and note the difference between modifying agents or modifying receivers. A *by*-phrase is understood for past participle modifiers. For example, *We were bored (by the movie)*. See the Grammar Note that follows.

GRAMMAR NOTE

When modifying receivers that use a past participle, there is often a *by-* phrase that is understood. For example, *We were bored (by the movie)*. In many cases, the past participle modifiers refer to feelings caused by something else. For example, *She was confused (by what he said)*.

EXERCISE 6 [10 minutes]

This exercise gives students the chance to practice in choosing whether a past or present participle modifier is appropriate.

1. Go over the two example sentences and ask the class which participle is modifying an agent and which is modifying a receiver (*interested* = past participle which modifies the receiver/*interesting* = present participle which modifies the agent). Refer back to the examples in Focus 4 if necessary.

2. Let students complete the exercise individually and then compare answers with a partner. Encourage them to explain the reasons for their answers to each other.

3. Discuss the answers and students' reasons for choosing them as a class. See answers on LP page 154.

For more practice, use *Grammar Dimensions 3* Workbook page 55, Exercise 5.

EXPANSION [25 minutes]

You may wish to assign Activity 3 (speaking/ writing) on SB page 162 as an expansion of Exercise 6. In this activity students will use participles to discuss an emotion from their past and what caused it.

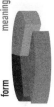

EXERCISE 7

Use present or past participles to complete these definitions.

Example: Information that reveals thoughts can be described as ___revealing___ information.

Emotions that people hide can be described as ___hidden___ emotions.

1. Situations that excite people can be described as ___exciting___ situations.
2. Temperatures that rise can be described as ___rising___ temperatures.
3. A situation that embarrasses people can be described as an ___embarrassing___ situation.
4. Results that people can prove in experiments can be described as ___proven___ results.
5. News that depresses people can be described as ___depressing___ news.
6. Individuals whom some bad news depresses can be described as ___depressed___ individuals.
7. A question that puzzles people can be described as a ___puzzling___ question.
8. People that are puzzled by a question can be described as ___puzzled___ people.

FOCUS 5   Adding Information to Participles

Noun + Participle

EXAMPLES	EXPLANATIONS
(a) a **man-eating** tiger (a tiger that eats people) (b) a **trend-setting** fashion (a fashion that sets a trend) (c) a **fire-breathing** dragon (a dragon that breathes fire)	Present participles usually describe the agent. You can also identify the receiver of the action by adding nouns.
(d) a **flea-bitten** dog (a dog that is bitten by fleas) (e) a **manmade** lake (a lake that was made by people) (f) a **male-dominated** society (a society that is dominated by males)	Past participles usually describe the receiver. You can add nouns to past participles when you want to identify the agent as well. Some noun-participle combinations appear without hyphens.

Adverb + Participle

EXAMPLES	EXPLANATIONS
(g) a **fast-moving** train (a train that moves fast) (h) some **homegrown** tomatoes (tomatoes that were grown at home) (i) a **much-visited** attraction (an attraction that is visited a lot)	You can add adverbs to both past and present participles to include important additional information to the participles. Some special cases appear without hyphens.

Special Cases

EXAMPLES	EXPLANATIONS
(j) a **blue-eyed** baby (a baby with blue eyes) (k) a **long-legged** ballet dancer (a dancer with long legs)	You can make "past participles" from some adjective-noun combinations to describe certain kinds of physical characteristics.
(l) a **barely concealed** dislike (m) a **deeply depressed** individual	Adverb-participle combinations, especially adverbs ending with *-ly* appear without hyphens.

LESSON PLAN 2

EXERCISE 7 [10 minutes]

Like Exercise 6, Exercise 7 asks students to choose between present and past participle modifiers. However, in this exercise, students must be able to clearly identify whether the participle is referring to the noun it modifies as an agent performing the action or a receiver affected by the action.

1. Give the class an example to highlight the difference between the use of past and present participle modifiers. For example, ask the class to use the participles of *excite* to fill in the missing blanks:

   Movies that excite people are described as _____ *movies. (exciting)*

   People who feel excitement from a situation are described as _____ *people. (excited)*

2. Go over the directions and examples for Exercise 7.

3. Have students work individually and then check answers with a partner. Ask them to discuss their reasons for each answer.

4. Go over the answers with the class and let students explain why they chose each answer. See answers on LP page 156.

For more practice, use *Grammar Dimensions 3* Workbook page 56, Exercise 6.

FOCUS 5 [15 minutes]

Focus 5 gives examples of ways to add information to participles by adding nouns or adverbs with or without hyphens. Focus 5 also notes special cases of adjective-noun combinations.

1. **Lead-in:** To see the difference between the use of the present participle and the past participle used in these two-word modifiers, write the following two groups of examples on the board:

a stomach-churning ride
some foot-tapping music
back-breaking work

some banana-flavored gum
a grief-stricken woman
a snow-covered mountain

2. You will be able to point out that in the first group of modifiers (noun + present participle), the modifier is directly caused by the noun it modifies (i.e., *the ride causes the stomach to churn*). Whereas in the second group (noun + past participle), the modifier is not caused by the noun it modifies (*the gum does not cause the banana flavor*).

3. Go over the examples in Focus 5. You can point out the difference between example (a) and example (d): *The tiger does eat the man, but the dog does not bite the flea.*

4. Go over the other examples (adverbs + participles and special cases) in Focus 5 and see if anyone can suggest any other examples.

EXERCISE 10

Choose the correct participle form for these sentences from the cues given. The first paragraph has been done for you as an example.

Problems in communication can happen when some of the conscious and unconscious actions of the (1) __nonspoken__ (nonspeak) part of a language are misunderstood. There can sometimes be (2) __confusing__ (confuse) situations between teachers and students in the classroom.

Teachers in American classrooms, for example, may often become (3) __annoyed__ (annoy) when students don't volunteer answers to general questions in class. Silence in American classrooms often means that the students are (4) __bored__ (bore), (5) __disinterested__ (disinterest), or (6) __uninvolved__ (uninvolve) in the class activity. Similarly, teachers interpret eye contact from students as a sign that the lesson is (7) __interesting__ (interest) and (8) __involving__ (involve) for them, and that they are actively (9) __engaged__ (engage) in the learning process.

Students are sometimes (10) __confused__ (confuse) about the best way to show that they are paying attention. In an American classroom, asking questions is one good way to do this, but students from other cultures may be (11) __embarrassed__ (embarrass) by having to admit that they are (12) __confused__ (confuse). Sometimes they feel (13) __worried__ (worry) that asking questions may be interpreted as (14) __teacher-challenging__ (teacher-challenge) behavior or as a somewhat (15) __insulting__ (insult) suggestion that the teacher has not explained things clearly enough.

The best way to solve these misunderstandings is to talk about them in class. Both American teachers and international students alike are often very (16) __surprised__ (surprise) to find out about their sometimes (17) __mistaken__ (mistake) assumptions about what classroom behavior means in different cultures.

EXERCISE 8

Use the information in these sentences to make participles.

Example: The story is loved very much. It's a __much-loved__ story.

1. In that incredible jump, the sky-diver defied death.
   The sky-diver made a __death-defying__ jump.

2. I bought this cake at a store.
   It's a __store-bought__ cake.

3. Gladstone Gulp bought a machine to reduce his weight.
   It's a __weight-reducing__ machine.

4. They trained the new employee well.
   She became a __well-trained__ employee.

5. That poor kitten is starved for love.
   It's a __love-starved__ kitten.

6. They filmed the movie with a camera that they held by hand.
   It was filmed with a __hand-held__ camera.

7. Look at that man with the long hair!
   Look at that __long-haired__ man!

8. Learning grammar can consume a lot of time.
   It can be a __time-consuming__ activity.

EXERCISE 9

Write original sentences that describe at least five of the following.

1. the most boring teacher you have ever had
2. the most self-satisfied politician you have ever heard of or read about
3. The most surprised reaction you have ever seen
4. The most amazing thing you have ever seen
5. The most worried person in your family
6. The most modern-thinking political leader you know
7. The behavior of the most bored student you have ever known
8. The most irritating habit your best friend has

ANSWER KEY

Exercise 9   Answers will vary.

MODIFYING NOUN PHRASES

LESSON PLAN 2

EXERCISE 8 [15 minutes]

This exercise asks students to create two-word participle modifiers out of the vocabulary found in the first sentence of each pair. Students will need to be able to identify whether the new participle is describing the agent or the receiver in order to decide whether to use the present or past participle form.

1. Begin by using the definitions in Focus 5 to create questions and invite students to supply the participle for each definition. For example, you can ask, *What do you call a dragon that breathes fire? (a fire-breathing dragon)*

2. Go over the directions and example for Exercise 8. Point out that the participle will be created out of either a noun + participle or an adverb + participle for this exercise. They will need to look for a verb to use as a participle.

3. You may want to go over the first problem together as a class. Ask the class what verb and noun or adverb can be used to describe the jump. Students may initially be misled by the adjective *incredible*, so point out that this is another way to describe the jump, but it does not use a noun or adverb + a participle.

4. When students seem fairly comfortable with the exercise, have them work individually to fill in the blanks.

5. Let students work with a partner to check their answers. Circulate and note any common errors. Go over answers as a class. Write these newly made modifiers on the board. See answers on LP page 158.

For more practice, use *Grammar Dimensions 3* Workbook page 56, Exercise 7.

EXERCISE 9 [10 minutes]

Exercise 9 reviews the participle modifiers presented in the unit and asks students to choose five to use in sentences followed by their own opinions.

1. Start the exercise by using a few of the participles from Exercise 9 in sentences of your own. For example, *The most boring teacher that I have ever had spoke very, very softly for the entire lesson. The most bored student that I have ever known would hide a comic book in his textbook to read in class.*

2. Ask students to write sentences using five different sentence starters from the list in the exercise.

3. When finished, let students compare their sentences in small groups. Invite students to share some with the class to close the exercise.

EXERCISE 10 [10 minutes]

This exercise is a review of participle modifiers. You may want to use it to see how well students can choose correct participles based on sentence clues.

1. Have students work individually to complete the exercise.

2. Rather than comparing answers with a partner, let students "grade" their own work either with an answer key provided by you or simply by having you call out the correct answers. See answers on LP page 158.

3. Find out which problems the most students missed (take a count of hands for each problem) and use this information to review if needed.

For more practice, use *Grammar Dimensions 3* Workbook page 57, Exercise 8 and page 58, Exercise 9.

FOCUS 6

Modifiers That Follow Noun Phrases

form

PARTICIPIAL PHRASES

(a) The man **speaking to John** told him some shocking information.

(c) The woman **surrounded by reporters** is a world-renowned expert on nonverbal communication.

PREPOSITIONAL PHRASES

(b) The man **with John** told him some shocking information.

(d) The woman **next to the window** is a world-renowned expert on nonverbal communication.

EXPLANATION

Prepositional phrases occur after the noun.

Participial phrases can occur before or after the noun, but there is a difference in function.

EXAMPLES

(e) The man **speaking to John** told him some shocking information.

(f) **Speaking to the man,** John found out some shocking information.

EXPLANATIONS

Participial phrases usually come after the noun if they identify the noun (tell which particular noun we are talking about).

They can come before the noun if that noun has already been identified and the participle describes more about the noun.

EXERCISE 11

Underline the modifying phrases in this article. Draw an arrow to indicate the noun each phrase modifies. Circle the noun. The first two sentences have been done for you as an example.

(1) One aspect of nonverbal communication frequently mentioned by researchers discussing cross-cultural differences is the varying size of the "conversation bubble" in each culture. (2) This bubble is the amount of physical distance maintained between people engaged in different kinds of conversation. (3) Americans having polite social conversations usually stand about an arm's length apart. (4) Closer distances are permitted only between people having a more intimate relationship. (5) Unless you are a very close friend or family member, moving closer than an arm's length is usually interpreted as overly aggressive (either socially or sexually). (6) People growing up in Latin cultures tend to have a smaller conversation bubble than people coming from Northern European cultures. (7) As a result, North Americans or Northern Europeans sometimes come across as a little cold or unfriendly to people raised in Latin countries such as Italy, Spain, or Latin America. (8) In general, Middle Eastern cultures tend to have the smallest conversation bubble, while Northern Asian and Northern European cultures tend to have the largest.

Use Your English

ACTIVITY 1 writing

Go to a flea market, thrift shop, garage sale, or even a department store. Write brief descriptions of things you find there that fit these categories:

- something really cheap
- something that costs more than $25
- something you might like to own
- something funny
- something ugly

ACTIVITY 2 speaking

Play *Adjective Tennis* with a partner. Here's how it's done:

▶ **STEP 1** One person thinks of a noun phrase (a noun plus a determiner) and a modifier.

▶ **STEP 2** The other person puts the modifier in its correct position and gives another modifier for the first person to add to the noun phrase. The modifier has to make sense. For example, if the noun is radio, intelligent is not an acceptable modifier.

▶ **STEP 3** The person who can't think of an appropriate modifier, or who puts it in the wrong place, loses. Keep going until one person puts an adjective in the wrong place or can't think of something new to add. You may want a third student to act as your referee.

Example:

Student 1: a ball . . . tennis
Student 2: a **tennis** ball . . . old
Student 1: an **old** tennis ball . . . rubber
Student 2: an old **rubber** tennis ball . . . dirty
Student 1: a **dirty** old rubber tennis ball . . . incredibly
Student 2: an **incredibly** dirty old rubber tennis ball . . . huge
Student 1: an incredibly dirty, **huge** old rubber tennis ball . . . etc.

EXERCISE 7 [15 minutes]

Students will make comparisons between two countries and create their own comparative statements based on the information provided for six different countries.

1. Have the class look at the three pairs of countries and the information provided for each. Invite volunteers to state any obvious comparisons for any of the pairs. Encourage the class to suggest an intensifier if the volunteered statement does not include one.

2. Next have students work individually to write comparative statements. You may want to ask them to create three or four comparative statements for each pair.

3. Have them refer back to Focus 2 for suggestions of intensifiers.

4. Let students share their statements with a partner or in small groups. Have groups share with the class. Review any common errors.

VARIATION

You can assign this as homework and ask students to write more comparative statements. You can require students to include statements showing more, the same, and less. You can also allow students to compare countries other than the ones they are paired with.

EXPANSION [25 minutes]

Use Activity 4 (reading/speaking) on SB page 181. In this activity, students will discuss economic and cultural differences.

EXERCISE 8 [20 minutes]

Students will interview each other and create their own comparative statements about themselves.

1. Go over the directions and the example. Note that the same information has been written in two different ways.

2. Invite volunteers to give an example of a complete sentence for each question to be asked.

3. Put students into pairs. Let students interview each other and record the answers.

4. Individually, students should create comparative statements based on the information in their charts and write them on the lines provided. Each answer needs to be written in two different ways. Circulate and assist as needed.

5. Let pairs check their statements with each other and then compare with another pair of students.

6. Have the class share together. Have students put a few of these sentence pairs on the board.

EXPANSION [10 minutes]

Have students create five more questions to ask their partner. These questions should ask *how many?*

FOCUS 3

Comparisons of Similarity and Difference: Noun Phrases

form · meaning

Comparisons can also be made in terms of **similarity** and **difference**, in addition to amount and degree.

EXAMPLES	MEANING	FORM
(a) Pakistan uses **exactly the same** official language as Bangladesh.	IDENTICAL: X = Y	X + VP + (intensifier) + *the same* NP *as* Y *(does)** X *and* Y + VP (intensifier) + *the same* NP*
(b) Pakistan and Bangladesh use **the same** official language.		*exactly* *precisely* } intensifiers
(c) Pakistan has **very much the same** life expectancy rate as Bangladesh (does).	SIMILAR: X ~ Y	X + VP + (intensifier) *the same* NP* *as* Y *(does)*. X *and* Y + VP + (intensifier) *the same* NP.*
(d) Pakistan and Bangladesh have **almost the same** growth rate.	great similarity ↕ small similarity	*very much* *basically* *almost* *somewhat* } intensifiers
(e) Bangladesh doesn't have **quite the same** population as Pakistan (does).	DIFFERENT: X ≠ Y	X + *not* + VP + (intensifier) + *the same* NP *as* Y (does).* X *and* Y + *not* VP + (intensifier) *the same* NP.*
(f) People in Pakistan and Bangladesh do not have **at all** the same culture.	small difference ↕ large difference	*quite* *nearly* *at all* } intensifiers
(g) Bangladesh has **a slightly different** growth rate from Pakistan.	small difference ↕ large difference	X + VP + (intensifier + *different* + NP *from/than* Y.* X *and* Y + VP + (intensifier) + *different* + NP*
(h) People in Pakistan and Bangladesh have **very different** cultures.		*slightly/a bit* *somewhat* *substantially/considerably* *much/very* } intensifiers

*NP = Noun Phrase   VP = Verb Phrase

EXERCISE 9

Underline the statements of similarity and difference in the following passage. For each comparative structure you find, (a) identify the **things** that are being compared, and (b) decide whether the comparison describes things that are **identical, similar, or different.** The first two sentences have been done for you as an example.

Example: 1. (a) *different kinds of English;* (b) *similar*
2. (a) *things like vocabulary and pronunciation;* (b) *different*

REGIONAL VARIETIES OF ENGLISH

(1) Although English is spoken in many countries, English speakers don't all speak quite the same kind of English. (2) Things like vocabulary and pronunciation are often substantially different. (3) The differences between some varieties of English are easy to identify. (4) No one would mistake Indian English for Australian English. (5) The pronunciation features of these two "Englishes" are quite different. (6) British English is substantially different from American English, not only in terms of accent, but also spelling and vocabulary—especially slang.

(7) But the differences between some regional varieties are more subtle. (8) For example, many people think that Canadian and American varieties of English are exactly the same, but in fact, there are some differences, and not all words are pronounced alike. (9) In America the vowel sound in the word *"out"* is pronounced differently from that in *"boot."* (10) But in Canada many people pronounce *shout* basically like *shoot.* (11) To most people Canadian English and American English seem very much alike. (12) But the careful listener will be able to find a number of examples of the ways Americans speak the language differently from their northern neighbors.

EXERCISE 10

Based on your own knowledge and the statistical information you read about in the Opening Task (pages 166–167), make statements about general similarities and differences between developing countries and developed countries. Describe one characteristic of developing countries that is likely to be (a) identical, (b) similar, (c) somewhat different, and (d) very different from developed countries.

EXERCISE 11

Interview a partner about how he or she typically likes to spend a vacation. Identify two things about your partner's vacation likes and dislikes that are (a) identical, (b) similar, (c) somewhat different, and (d) very different from yours.

Answers will vary.

Exercise 9 3. (a) some varieties of English; (b) different.   4. (a) Indian and Australian English; (b) different.   5. (a) the pronunciation features of these two Englishes; (b) different.   6. (a) British English and American English; (b) different.   7. (a) some regional varieties; (b) different.   8. (a) Canadian and American varieties of English; (b) different.   9. (a) the pronunciation of the vowel sound in out and boot in America; (b) different.   10. (a) the pronunciation of shout and shoot in Canada; (b) very similar.   11. (a) Canadian English and American English; (b) similar.   12. (a) the ways Americans speak and the ways their northern neighbors speak; (b) different.

Exercise 10 Answers will vary. Possible answers are: Developed countries can have the same land area as developing countries. Developed countries and developing countries can have the same number of official languages. Developing countries can have almost the same GDP as developed countries. Per capita incomes in developing countries are usually substantially different from those in developed countries. Per capita incomes in developing and developed countries are usually substantially different. Historical background of developed countries is often quite different from developing countries.

LESSON PLAN 3

FOCUS 3 [20 minutes]

Focus 3 presents examples of comparisons of similarity and difference with noun phrases. Like Focus 1 (differences of degree) and Focus 2 (differences of amount), the chart sets out patterns. However, this chart shows degrees of similarity or difference.

1. **Lead-in:** Explain to the class that Focus 2 gave us ways to show comparisons in amount. Now explain that Focus 3 will show ways to make comparisons in terms of whether things are identical, similar, or different.

2. Give examples to show: identical; similar; not the same; and different:

   I have exactly the same backpack as Sonja.
   I have basically the same backpack as Jake.
   I don't have quite the same backpack as Nina.
   I have a slightly different backpack than Nina.

3. Go over the chart for Focus 3 and point out that things can be **identical, similar, or not the same/different.** Match the example sentences from the board with the chart in Focus 3. Point out several different choices for intensifiers.

VARIATION

Before going over the focus chart, ask students to work with a partner and write their own sentences. They should go back to Exercise 7 on SB page 174 and find examples of things that are identical, similar, or different for these six countries. Divide the board into three parts (identical, similar, or different) and have students write sentences in the correct areas. Go over as a class and use these examples to move into the explanations in Focus 3.

EXERCISE 9 [15 minutes]

Students will identify statements of similarity and difference and then determine what is being

compared and whether it describes things that are identical, similar, or different.

1. Work on the first sentences together as a class. Have the class find the statements of comparison in sentences (1) and (2) and underline them. Then have them note the answers to (a) and (b) as listed in the directions.

2. Have students work individually to complete the rest of the exercise. Circulate and note any common errors to go over. Remind students that one sentence may have more than one statement of comparison.

3. Let pairs check their work together before going over the answers as a class. See answers on LP page 176.

For more practice, use *Grammar Dimensions 3* Workbook page 62, Exercise 5.

EXERCISE 10 [10 minutes]

Students will make statements about the differences and similarities of developing and developed countries based on the information in the Opening Task and their own knowledge. You may want to review the general statements students made during the Opening Task.

1. Have students work individually or in pairs to create statements about the ways that developing countries are (a) identical to, (b) similar to, (c) somewhat different from, and (d) very different from developed countries.

2. Put students into small groups to discuss and share their statements. Have groups decide which statements they will put on the board to share with the class.

3. Review any common errors. See possible answers on LP page 176.

EXERCISE 11 [20 minutes]

This exercise asks students to interview a partner and then state the differences and similarities between themselves and their partners.

1. Begin by asking students to think about what they usually enjoy doing during vacations. Invite volunteers to share a few ideas. This should get everyone ready to share ideas with a partner.

2. Put students into pairs and have them tell each other what they typically enjoy doing during a vacation. You may find that students will talk either about what they'd like to do or what they usually have to do. Encourage the discussion to continue long enough to ensure that everyone has enough information to make some comparisons.

3. Stop the discussion and ask students to compare their own vacation activities to their partner's and to individually write two statements for each:
   (a) identical, (b) similar, (c) somewhat different, and (d) very different.

4. Have pairs share their statements with each other and note how similar or different their statements are. Invite them to share these observations with the class.

FOCUS 4

Comparisons of Similarity and Difference: Verb Phrases

form ⟶ meaning

EXAMPLES

(a) Canadians pronounce most words **just the same as** American words (do).

(b) Canadians and Americans pronounce most words **very much the same.**

(c) Canadian English sounds **almost like** American English (does).

(d) American and Canadian English sound **very much alike.**

(e) Some Canadian words aren't pronounced **exactly like** American words (are).

(f) Australian English and Indian English **do not** sound **at all alike.**

(g) Canadians do not pronounce *out* **quite the same as** Americans (do).

(h) Americans and Canadians don't pronounce *out* **at all the same.**

(i) Canadians pronounce English **a bit differently** from Americans.

(j) Australians and Americans pronounce English **quite differently.**

MEANING

IDENTICAL OR SIMILAR

identical
↕
similar
↕
less similar

DIFFERENT

small difference ⟷ large difference

small difference ⟷ large difference

small difference ⟷ large difference

FORM

X + VP* + (intensifier) + *the same as* Y *(does).*
X *and* Y + VP + (intensifier) + *the same*

X + VP* (intensifier) *like* Y *(does).*
X *and* Y + VP + (intensifier) *alike.*

{ *exactly/just*
almost
very much
quite/much
somewhat }   intensifiers

X + *not* + VP* + (intensifier) *like* Y *(does).*
X *and* Y + *not* + VP* (intensifier) *alike.*

{ *exactly*
quite
much
at all }   intensifiers

X + *not* + VP* + (intensifier) *the same as* Y *(does).*
X *and* Y + *not* + VP* + (intensifier) *the same.*

{ *quite*
a bit
at all }   intensifiers

X + VP* + (intensifier) *differently from/than* Y
X *and* Y + VP* + (intensifier) *differently.*

{ *a bit*
somewhat
quite }   intensifiers

*VP = Verb Phrase

EXERCISE 12

Use the information you read in Exercise 9 and your own experience to make statements of similarity and difference using the cues below. Use intensifiers to indicate whether these differences are large or small.

Examples: Indians/Australians/pronounce English/like
Indians don't pronounce English at all like Australians.
Canadians/Americans/pronounce English/alike
Canadians and Americans don't pronounce English quite alike.

1. British/American/use slang expressions/differently
2. No two countries/speak a common language/the same
3. Spanish in Spain/in Latin America/differently from
4. The word *color*/in Britain/in America/is spelled/not alike
5. Many Canadians pronounce the vowel in *shout/shoot* /the same as
6. Grammar/in regional varieties of English/alike

FOCUS 5

Informal Usage of Comparisons

use

There are differences between formal (written) and informal (spoken) English when making comparative statements.

LESS FORMAL/CONVERSATIONAL STYLE	MORE FORMAL/WRITTEN STYLE
(a) The culture of Pakistan is **different than** Bangladesh.	(b) The culture of Pakistan is **different from** that of Bangladesh.
(c) Canadians pronounce certain words **differently than** Americans.	(d) Canadians pronounce certain words **differently from** Americans.
(e) Pakistan had **much the same** colonial history **that** Bangladesh **did.**	(f) Pakistan had **much the same** colonial history **as** Bangladesh.

EXERCISE 13

Change these informal comparisons to their more formal variations.

1. Canadian English follows the same grammatical rules that American English does.
2. My partner usually spends his vacations differently than me.
3. The social values of Korea are quite different than Kuwait.
4. Many people in developing countries have a lower per capita income than many people in developed countries.
5. My brother has almost the same hobbies that I do.

ANSWER KEY

Exercise 12 1. British and American speakers of English use slang expressions quite differently. 2. No two countries speak a common language exactly the same. 3. Spanish in Spain is spoken differently from Spanish in Latin America. 4. The word color is not spelled alike in Britain and in America. 5. Many Canadians pronounce the vowels in shout basically the same as the vowels in shoot. 6. The grammar in regional varieties of English is all basically alike.

Exercise 13 1. Canadian English follows the same grammatical rules as American English. 2. My partner usually spends his vacations differently from me. 3. The social values of Korea are quite different from those of Kuwait. 4. Many people in developing countries have a different per capita income from many people in developed countries. 5. My brother has almost the same hobbies as I do.

LESSON PLAN 3

FOCUS 4 [20 minutes]

Focus 4 presents examples of comparisons of similarity and difference with **verb phrases.** Like Focus 3 (similarity and difference of **noun phrases**), this focus chart shows the similarity and difference of **verb phrases.**

1. **Lead-in:** You can show the differences and similarities between the ideas in Focus 3 and Focus 4 by writing an example from each focus chart on the board such as:

   Omar works at the same company as Mona does. (Focus 3)

   Omar lives in a different city than Mona does. (Focus 3)

   Omar speaks English the same as Mona does. (Focus 4)

   Omar speaks Arabic differently than Mona does. (Focus 4)

2. Invite volunteers to point out the similarities and differences between the Focus 3 (comparisons of nouns) and Focus 4 (comparisons of verb phrases) example sentences.

3. Go over the Focus 4 chart as a class.

EXERCISE 12 [15 minutes]

Students will make statements of similarity or difference with verb phrases using the cues.

1. Refer the class back to the reading in Exercise 9 on SB page 177. What do they remember about the regional varieties of English? Invite volunteers to make any statements of comparison for review. Put a few on the board. For review, encourage students to add intensifiers to these statements. You may even get a statement using a verb phrase. Use this to help transition into Exercise 12.

2. Put the first example from Exercise 12 on the board: *Indians/Australians/pronounce English/like*

3. Let students volunteer a statement using these cues (they may just take this from the book, which is fine to start with).

4. Now change the word of comparison in this example (*like*) to other cues (*alike, the same, differently*) and invite volunteers to generate new sentences. Refer back to the corresponding chart section in Focus 4 if students are having trouble.

5. When they are ready, have students work individually to complete the exercise.

6. Circulate and look for any errors in formation or meaning. Note any problems with word order to go over in debriefing and remind students to choose intensifiers.

7. Have them share answers with a partner and check as a class. There will be differences in the intensifiers chosen. See answers on LP page 178.

For more practice, use *Grammar Dimensions 3* Workbook page 63, Exercise 6.

FOCUS 5 [10 minutes]

Students may have noted that Focus 3 and Focus 4 gave the option of using *different(ly) from/than.* This difference is explained in Focus 5 as a difference of formality. Although the focus charts have not suggested the use of *the same that,* students may hear it used informally by native speakers. You may want to put other examples on the board that are written informally and let students suggest a more formal version. This will lead naturally into the work to be done in Exercise 13.

EXERCISE 13 [10 minutes]

This exercise is practice for the concepts in Focus 5 and makes students more aware of the differences between formally and informally written comparisons as they rewrite the sentences.

1. Ask the class to look at the first sentence and, based on what they learned in Focus 5, underline what makes this comparison informal. Go over this first sentence and the changes that would be made with the class.

2. Again, referring back to the differences found in the examples from Focus 5, have students work individually to find ways to change these informal comparisons into the more formal variations. See answers on LP page 178.

Suggestion: You may want to put the first sentence on the board and have a volunteer come up and make the needed change.

For more practice, use *Grammar Dimensions 3* Workbook page 65, Exercise 7.

UNIT GOAL REVIEW [10 minutes]

Ask students to look at the goals on the opening page of the unit again. Refer to the pages of the unit where information on each goal can be found.

For a grammar quiz review of Units 8–10, refer students to pages 66–67 in the *Grammar Dimension 3* Workbook.

 For assessment of Unit 10, use *Grammar Dimensions 3 ExamView®.*

Use Your English

ACTIVITY 1 speaking

How can you tell if someone is from another country? What are some things people do differently when they come from another culture?

▪ STEP 1
Working with a partner from another culture, talk about how you know when someone is a foreigner. If you can, be sure to ask two or three Americans how they know when someone is from another country.

▪ STEP 2
Identify some general or universal differences in behavior, dress, etc. that are true for all cultures. Some examples of generic differences are: speaking with an accent, clothing styles, and so on.

ACTIVITY 2 writing/speaking

Have you ever met someone who reminds you of someone else? What characteristics and actions were similar? In what ways were the two people different? In a brief essay or oral presentation, tell about these two people.

ACTIVITY 3 listening

CD Track 16

Listen to the conversation between Kim and Bob about a class in Anthropology. See if you can get enough information to answer the questions on the quiz that Professor Jordan gave them the next day. If necessary you can listen to the conversation more than once.

Anthropology 112: Cultural Geography Quiz #3
1. Define "language family."
2. Define "culture family."
3. What two examples of culture families were mentioned in the lecture?
4. What is the relationship between culture and economic and political problems in developing countries?

ACTIVITY 4 reading/speaking

In this unit you have examined some information on the economic differences between developing and developed countries. Based on the information in this unit as well as your own knowledge, discuss the questions below in a small group.

- Which do you think is a more common source of conflict between nations: economic differences or cultural differences? Can you give examples to support your opinion?
- What do the differences and similarities between developed and developing countries mean for world peace and global development?

ACTIVITY 5 research on the web

Go onto the Internet and find the *Info Please Almanac* at http://www.infoplease.com/countries.html. Click under "Countries of the World" and find out information about two countries that you are interested in. Look for information about differences in population, geography, and economics and make a brief report that compares these two countries. You may also try looking for this information by using an Internet search engine such as Google® or Yahoo® and entering the key words, "countries of world". Your teacher will tell you whether the report should be written or oral.

ACTIVITY 6 reflection

Work with another student. Talk about your strengths and weaknesses as an English language learner. What skills are you particularly good at? What do you find most challenging? What about your partner's skills profile? Together, come up with at least three differences between you and your partner and three ways that each of you can use your strengths to assist your partner in strengthening his or her weak spots.

ANSWER KEY

Activity 3 Answers may vary. Possible answers are: 1. *groups of languages that have somewhat the same linguistic structure.*   2. *groups of cultures that have more or less the same basic values, attitudes, and beliefs.*   3. *European culture, Latin culture*   4. *Many developing countries were founded by colonial powers as political unions, not cultural ones. No matter how much their economic and political interest may be alike, cultures that think quite differently from one another may choose to act quite differently as well. The study of geography shows that political boundaries change much more frequently and more rapidly than cultural ones.*

USE YOUR ENGLISH

The Use Your English activities at the end of the unit contain situations that should naturally elicit the structures covered in the unit. For a more complete discussion of how to use the Use Your English activities see To the Teacher on LP page xxii. When students are doing these activities in class, you can circulate and listen to see if they are using the structures accurately. Errors can be corrected after the activity has finished.

ACTIVITY 1 speaking
[15 minutes]

Use this activity as a review of comparative structures throughout the unit.

STEP 1

1. Put students into pairs (or small groups) and ask them to discuss the first two questions in Activity 1: How can you tell if someone is from another country and what are some things people do differently?

2. Circulate and note any errors in comparative structures. Take notes to review later. Also note whether any discussions turn to negative stereotyping of groups rather than generalizations. This should be addressed either within pairs or with the whole class.

3. If possible, have pairs interview Americans.

STEP 2

1. When pairs have established their list of general differences that are true for all cultures, put them into larger groups and have them share together.

2. Draw the class together and ask groups to share any differences or similarities they discovered between pairs.

ACTIVITY 2 writing/speaking
[15 minutes/homework]

This activity can be used as a review for Unit 10.

1. Be sure to give students guidelines for the length and format of their essays or oral presentations. Assign the essays as homework.

2. Have students share their essays in small groups or collect papers and give individual feedback.

ACTIVITY 3 listening
[15 minutes]

CD Track 16

1. You may want to begin by inviting volunteers to guess what they think an Anthropology class might be about. What about Cultural Geography?

2. Have the class go over the questions for the quiz before they listen to the conversation.

3. Play the entire conversation and then give students time to write their answers. Remind students that recording things word for word is not as useful as writing the main ideas down.

4. You will probably want to play the conversation once more, give students time to work on their answers further and then let them share their answers in pairs.

5. Finally, play the conversation bit by bit if you can and go over the answers with the class. You may want to point out the differences between *a definition, an example* and *a relationship* when going over these answers. See possible answers on LP page 180.

ACTIVITY 4 reading/speaking
[25 minutes]

You may wish to assign this activity after Exercise 7 on SB page 174.

1. With the class, quickly review the country information presented in the charts on SB pages 166–167, 170–171, and 174.

2. Go over the discussion questions for Activity 4. You may want to give a few examples of possible sources of conflict to help get students started.

3. Put students into small groups and encourage them to use not only the information in the text, but to also share their own ideas. Circulate and assist any groups that are having difficulty understanding the questions.

4. Have one student in each group take notes. When they are finished, have them organize their answers as a group and present their results.

ACTIVITY 5 research on the web
[20 minutes/homework]

1. Set guidelines for the reports you would like them to write (length, format, etc.) and whether they will present their information orally. Set the deadline.

2. Have students do their research.

3. If giving an oral presentation, students may want to present their information with charts or visuals.

4. Collect reports and give individual feedback.

ACTIVITY 6 reflection
[20 minutes]

1. Begin by having all students write a list of their strengths and weaknesses as language learners in their *reflection journals*.

2. Put students into pairs and have them compare their lists together. Ask them to go over and discuss the questions in Activity 6.

UNIT 11

CONNECTORS

UNIT GOALS

- Correctly understand and use different coordinating conjunctions
- Correctly understand and use different sentence connectors
- Correctly understand and use different subordinating conjunctions

OPENING TASK

Improving Your Writing

Bambang Soetomo asked his English teacher to point out grammatical problems in his essay about culture shock.

STEP 1

With a partner, go over the essay and the teacher's comments. What suggestions would you give to Bambang in order to improve his writing? Can you correct his essay?

STEP 2

Compare your corrected essay to the sample with possible corrections in Exercise 1 on page 187.

My experience with culture shock

Every person has experience with culture shock. However I am no exception. And I have experience with culture shock. Although I have lived in the United States for almost 1 year. I still often feel homesick and I miss my family. When I first came to the U.S., I was very comfortable and because everything was new everything was interesting for me. I enjoyed my independence from my parents. I enjoyed to experience new food and making new friends. Everything was strange, nevertheless I enjoyed the new experiences.

Soon I got used to many differences. Even though I was used to them. Still I wasn't comfortable. Little by little I grew tired of the differences. Because the things in America weren't new to me anymore. The differences weren't interesting they were boring. However I began to miss things in Indonesia. For example, food, my friends, the warm climate. I became depress and homesick. I stayed in my room, because I was tired of speaking English all the time. Even though I studied however my grades weren't so good.

So I visited my advisor. He told me about culture shock. I learned that every person has this kind of experience and it can't be avoid. I learned that this culture shock is temporary but universal. My advisor told me I must to keep busy and talk about my culture shock with my friends. This was good advice, as a result, my culture shock became less and in spite I sometimes still miss my life in Indonesia. I don't feel depression the same as before.

Margin comments: FRAG; RUN-ON; RUN-ON; AWKWARD; AWKWARD; FRAG; FRAG; AWKWARD; RUN-ON; FRAG; RUN-ON; AWKWARD; RUN-ON; AWKWARD

UNIT 11

LESSON PLAN 1

UNIT OVERVIEW

Unit 11 reviews the meaning and use of coordinating and subordinating conjunctions, along with other sentence connectors and addresses common errors.

GRAMMAR NOTE

Connectors show the relationship between clauses within a sentence or the connection between sentences or even paragraphs. Connectors can be challenging for ESL students because they carry so much meaning and because many are found more often in formal contexts.

The connectors presented in Unit 11 are divided first into four groups by their meanings. They are then divided further by form as to whether they are used as coordinating conjunctions, sentence connectors, or subordinating conjunctions.

UNIT GOALS

Some instructors may want to review the goals listed on Student Book (SB) page 182 after completing the Opening Task so that students understand what they should know by the end of the unit. These goals can also be reviewed at the end of the unit when students are more familiar with the grammar terminology.

OPENING TASK [30 minutes]

The aim of this activity is to give students the opportunity to work with the meaning, use, and forms of connectors. The problem-solving format is designed to show the teacher how well the students can produce a target structure implicitly and spontaneously when they are engaged in a communicative task. For a more complete discussion of the purpose of the Opening Task, see To the Teacher, Lesson Planner (LP) page xxii.

Setting Up the Task

1. Begin by having pairs quickly discuss their experiences with culture shock.

2. Next, ask the class to look at the teacher's corrections on Bambang's essay. Have they seen these kinds of comments on their own essays before? Do they know what they mean?

3. Give an example of: a fragment; a run-on sentence; and a word form problem, such as:

    But we worked hard in the snow.

    Sara had a party it started at 8 o'clock.

    That movie was excited.

4. Invite volunteers to suggest which type of problem each sentence represents.

5. Write FRAG next to the first sentence, RUN-ON next to the second sentence, and circle the word excited in the third sentence.

6. Then ask for volunteers to come up to the board to make the necessary corrections.

Conducting the Task

■ STEP 1

1. Have students work in pairs to read and discuss the essay. The class should be discussing ways to improve the essay.

2. Next ask the pairs to try to make corrections to the essay. Circulate and notice how well pairs are finding and correcting problems. Don't worry about correcting errors at this time.

Closing the Task

■ STEP 2

1. When the class is ready, have students turn to Exercise 1 on SB page 187 and compare their answers with the revised essay.

2. Have pairs discuss how their changes are different from those in the revised essay. Remind the class

that it is possible to have different answers and not to worry about finding and correcting all the errors in this essay.

EXPANSION [homework]

You may want to assign Activity 1 (writing) on SB page 198, in which students write an essay describing their own experiences with culture shock.

GRAMMAR NOTE

Typical student errors (form)

- Creating fragments with connectors:
  * Even though he studied hard. (See Focus 5.)
- Creating run-on sentences with connectors:
  * We studied all night, however the test was too difficult. (See Focus 4.)
- Overusing connectors: * Although we loved Paris, but we left after only a week.
- Problems with punctuation: * Kana wanted to go but it was too late. (See Focus 3.)
- Using connectors with the wrong grammatical structures: * In spite of he grew up there, he didn't remember it. * Besides she is going to school, she is working nights. (See Focus 5.)

Typical student errors (use)

- Not understanding the meaning of connectors: Sue loved John. * Nevertheless, John loved Sue in return. (See Focus 1.)
- Confusing meaning by placing connectors in the wrong place: He was mean. Consequently, he was fired. ≠ *He was fired. Consequently, he was mean. (See Focus 4.)

Continued on next page

FOCUS 1 Overview of Connectors

form | meaning

Connectors show logical relationships between clauses in a sentence, between sentences within a paragraph, or even between paragraphs.

EXAMPLES	EXPLANATIONS
(a) Matt grew up in Kansas, but now lives in San Francisco. (b) Bambang not only misses his family, but he also wishes a few friends were in America with him.	There are three categories of connectors: Coordinating conjunctions connect two similar grammatical structures, such as noun phrases, prepositional phrases, or independent clauses.
(c) Matt grew up in Kansas. However, he now lives in San Francisco. (d) Bambang misses his family. In addition, he wishes a few friends were in America with him.	Sentence connectors show the logical connection between sentences.
(e) Although Matt grew up in Kansas, he now lives in San Francisco. (f) In spite of his homesickness, Bambang still tried to concentrate on his studies. (g) In addition to missing his family, Bambang wishes that a few friends were in America with him.	Subordinating conjunctions connect a dependent noun clause, a noun phrase, or a gerund phrase with the main clause.

Relationships expressed by these connectors can be divided into four general categories: additive, contrastive, cause and effect, and sequence. See the chart on pages 185–186.

MEANING	FORM		
	COORDINATING CONJUNCTIONS	**SENTENCE CONNECTORS***	**SUBORDINATING CONJUNCTIONS**
ADDITIVE			
Addition	(a) Bambang misses his family, **and** they miss him.	(b) Bambang misses his family, **too.** He **also** misses his friends. **In addition,** he is having culture shock. **Besides,** he's homesick.	(c) **In addition to** missing his family, Bambang misses his friends.
Emphasis/ Intensifying	(d) **Not only** does Bambang miss his family, **but** he is **also** experiencing culture shock.	(e) **Furthermore,** he's not doing well in school. **In fact,** he failed two midterms. **Actually,** he's quite depressed. **Indeed,** he's thinking about going home.	(f) **Besides** being depressed, he's having trouble in school, **not to mention** feeling lonely all the time.
CONTRASTIVE			
Contrast	(g) Everyone experiences culture shock, **but** it eventually passes.	(h) Some people have severe culture shock. Others, **however,** just feel a mild depression. Bambang's culture shock is almost over; yours, **on the other hand,** may just be beginning. Mild culture shock is a universal experience. Deep depression, **in contrast,** is not.	(i) Some people have severe culture shock, **while** others just feel a mild depression. **Whereas** some people have severe culture shock, others just feel a mild depression.
Concession (yes . . . but)	(j) The advisor told him culture shock can't be avoided, **yet** it is fortunately temporary.	(k) Bambang feels homesick. **Even so,** he will stay until he finishes his studies. Bambang studies hard. **Nevertheless,** he isn't getting good grades. **In spite of this,** he is still trying to improve.	(l) **Although** he feels homesick, Bambang will stay until he finishes his studies. He isn't getting good grades, **even though** he studies hard. **In spite of the fact that** he still experiences culture shock/**In spite of** experiencing culture shock, Bambang has decided not to go home.

* Need an example using *moreover.* See #23 on page 185.

LESSON PLAN 1

FOCUS 1 [30 minutes]

Focus 1 is broken into two parts. The first section (SB page 184) gives examples of how the three types of connectors (coordinating conjunctions, sentence connectors, and subordinating conjunctions) are formed. The second section (SB pages 185–186) focuses on meaning and also gives examples of the three different types of connectors for each meaning.

1. **Lead-in:** At the top of the board, write one basic example to show the difference between the three types of connectors. You can make up two sentences of your own, or use the following for an example:

Van grew up Vietnam. He lives in Seattle now.

2. Begin the focus chart on SB page 184 by going over examples (a) and (b) and the explanation regarding coordinating conjunctions. Ask the class to connect the sentences you wrote on the board (independent clauses) with a **coordinating conjunction.** Write the new sentence. (Note that there are several possible answers. One possible answer is *Van grew up in Vietnam, but he lives in Seattle now.*) Keep this new sentence up on one section of the board.

3. Move on to the second row in this chart, regarding **sentence connectors**, and go over examples (c) and (d). Ask the class how they might combine the original sentences from the board now with a **sentence connector.** (Possible answer: *Van grew up in Vietnam. However, he lives in Seattle now.*) Keep this new sentence up on another section of the board.

4. Next move on to the **subordinating conjunctions** in the last row of this chart. Go over examples (e–g), and ask the class how they might combine the two original sentences on the board with a **subordinating conjunction.** (Possible answer: *Although Van grew up in Vietnam, be lives in Seattle now.*) Keep this new sentence up on the last section of the board.

5. Take a moment to review the three different types of connectors in the examples on the board. Point out their positions (and their possible movements), any punctuation or capitalization needed, and the grammatical structures present.

Note: You may want to begin with a review of grammatical structures, such as noun phrases, prepositional phrases, gerund phrases, independent clauses, and dependent clauses. You can list an example of each of these in one column and list the structure names in a second column and ask students to match them up.

6. Briefly go over with the class how the focus charts on SB pages 185 and 186 are laid out, noting the main four groups of meanings (*additive, contrastive, cause/effect,* and *sequence*) before looking at the specific examples.

7. Make three columns based on your example sentences on the board and label them: *coordinating conjunctions, sentence connectors,* and *subordinating conjunctions.*

8. As the class goes through the four sections of the chart on SB pages 185 and 186, add examples to the appropriate columns. You may want to have three students (one responsible for each column) up at the board to record examples.

9. Keep in mind that the focus of these charts is on the meaning expressed in the connectors and thus it is best to go through the examples alphabetically across the chart. Covering the examples in this direction will focus on the meanings.

10. Keep the three lists on the board. You will add to them as you debrief after students have completed Exercise 1.

Suggestion: Have students keep a list of connectors in their notebooks to use and add to as they work through this unit.

EXERCISE 1

Identify the form and meaning of the highlighted connectors. The first sentence has been done for you as an example.

Examples: and—*form: coordinating conjunction; meaning: additive*
since—*form: subordinating conjunction; meaning: reason*

My Experience with Culture Shock

(1) Every person who has lived in a new culture has had some experience with culture shock, **and** I am no exception, **since** I, too, have had an experience with culture shock. (2) **Although** I have lived in the United States for almost one year, sometimes I still feel homesick, and still miss my family. (3) When I **first** came to the U.S., I was very excited. (4) **Because** everything was new, everything was interesting. (5) I enjoyed my independence from my parents; I **also** enjoyed experiencing new situations and making new friends. (6) **Although** everything was a little strange, I **nevertheless** enjoyed these new experiences. (7) **Eventually** I got used to many of the differences, **but even though** I was used to them, I still wasn't comfortable. (8) **In fact**, little by little I grew tired of the differences. (9) **Because** the things in America weren't new to me anymore, the differences weren't interesting. (10) **Indeed**, they had **actually** become boring. (11) **As a result**, I began to miss things about Indonesia, such as food, friends, and the warm tropical climate, more and more. (12) I **soon** became depressed and homesick. (13) I stayed in my room, **because** I was tired of speaking English all the time. (14) **Even though** I studied hard, my grades weren't good. I wanted to go home. (15) **Because of** these feelings, I decided to see my advisor, **so that** I could get some advice about returning home without finishing my studies. (16) He told me two important things about culture shock. (17) **First**, I learned that any person in a new culture has a similar kind of experience, **and** that culture shock can't be avoided. (18) **Furthermore**, I learned that culture shock is not only universal, but also temporary. (19) **As a result of** his advice, I realized that I should be patient, and that I shouldn't go home just yet. (20) My advisor **also** suggested that I try to keep busy and talk about my culture shock with my friends. (21) I followed this good advice, **and as a result**, my culture shock has become less troublesome. (22) **In spite of the fact that** I sometimes still miss my life in Indonesia, I don't feel as depressed as I did. (23) **Moreover**, I no longer want to return home before I finish my studies. I know that I can adjust to this new life.

Exercise 1 2. Although—form F: subordinating conj.; meaning M: contrastive 3. first—F: sentence connector; M: sequence 4. Because—F: subordinating conj.; M: cause and effect 5. also—F: sentence connector; M: additive 6. Although—F: subordinating conj.; M: contrastive. nevertheless—F: sentence connector; M: contrastive 7. Eventually—F: sentence connector; M: additive 8. In fact—F: coordinating conj.; M: contrastive. even though—F: subordinating conj.; M: contrastive 9. Because—F: subordinating conj.; M: cause and effect 10. Indeed—F: sentence connector; M: additive. actually—F: sentence connector; V: additive 11. As a result—F: sentence connector; M: result 12. soon—F: sentence connector; M: sequence 13. because—F: subordinating conj.; M: cause and effect 14. Even though—F: subordinating conj.; M: contrastive 15. Because of—F: subordinating conj.; M: reason. so that—F: subordinating conj.; M: reason 17. First—F: sentence connector; M: sequence. and—F: coordinating conj.; M: additive 19. As a result of—F: subordinating conj.; M: reason 20. also—F: sentence connector; M: additive 21. and—F: coordinating conj.; M: additive. as a result—F: sentence connector; M: result 22. In spite of the fact that—F: subordinating conj.; M: contrastive 23. Moreover—F: sentence connector; M: additive

Continued from previous page

	MEANING	FORM		
		COORDINATING CONJUNCTIONS	**SENTENCE CONNECTORS**	**SUBORDINATING CONJUNCTIONS**
CAUSE AND EFFECT	Reason	(m) Bambang went to see his advisor, for he was worried about his grades.	(n) Bambang was worried about his grades. **With this in mind,** he went to see his advisor.	(o) He found it difficult to concentrate, **due to** being depressed. **Because/Since** Bambang was worried about his grades, he went to see his advisor.
	Result	(p) He was depressed, **so** he went to see his advisor.	(b) Bambang was worried about his grades. **Accordingly,** he went to see his advisor. His advisor told him that culture shock is universal. He consequently felt much better about his depression. **As a result,** he decided not to go home early. He **therefore** canceled his plane reservation.	(r) **As a result of** feeling depressed, he decided to talk with his advisor. He made an appointment **so that** he could find out about leaving school early. **In order to** find out more about culture shock, he decided to read some articles about it.
	Conditional	(s) The advisor told Bambang to keep busy, **or (else)** he would become more depressed.	(t) Bambang didn't want to go home early. **Then** he would feel that he had failed. **Under such circumstances,** he might even feel worse than he had in America.	(u) His advisor told him to get a lot of exercise, **providing/if** he could do that without neglecting his studies.
SEQUENCE	Sequence	(v) He made an appointment, **and** he went directly to see his advisor.	(w) **First,** one must recognize culture shock. **Then** one must deal with it. **Eventually** everyone gets over it. **Soon** they start to feel more comfortable in the new culture.	(x) Bambang felt much better **after** he talked with his advisor. **When** he found out about culture shock, he was glad he hadn't decided to leave before talking with his advisor.

EXERCISE 1 [15 minutes]

Students are given connectors used in context and
will then identify the form and meaning for each
connector.

1. Referring back to Focus 1, ask volunteers to list
   the three forms of connectors. Ask other volunteers
   to list several of the meanings these can carry.

2. Go over the first two sentences in Exercise 1 with
   the class. The answers are given for form and
   meaning for the first sentence, but have students
   work out the second one on their own.

3. After reviewing these first few answers, have
   students complete the exercise individually, and
   then check answers with a partner.

Suggestion: As you go over the answers with the
class, you may want to add any new connectors to
the three lists you created in Focus 1. See answers
on LP page 186.

work
book

For more practice, use *Grammar Dimensions 3*
Workbook page 68, Exercise 1.

EXERCISE 2

Circle the appropriate connector from the options in parentheses. There may be more than one correct choice.

Both Canada and the United States have large minorities that speak languages other than English. Canada has a large French-speaking minority. The United States, (1) (on the other hand), furthermore, consequently, yet) has a large Spanish-speaking minority. (2) (But, However, So) the ways the two countries deal with this fact are rather different.

Canada has adopted a policy of bilingualism and has two official languages. All students study both languages in school. (3) (Moreover, Nevertheless, Therefore) all official government activities are conducted in both languages.

However, in the United States there is a movement to make English the only official language. (4) (So, So that, As a result,) some people may be officially discouraged from using languages other than English at work. In some parts of the country, there are very few facilities available to people who can't speak English, (5) (and, but, yet, so) (6) (under such circumstances, on the other hand, in addition to) Spanish speakers may be required to provide their own translators in such places as hospitals or government offices. (7) (In spite of, (Even though), Consequently) all students in the public schools are taught English, (8) (but, and, for, no connector) English-speaking students are not usually required to study Spanish.

These differences in bilingualism may result from geography. In Canada, the French speakers are actually a majority in certain parts of the country, primarily in the Province of Quebec. In the United States, (9) (however, on the other hand, in spite of this, therefore) Spanish-speaking communities are spread around the country. Large numbers of Spanish speakers are found in New York, Florida, New Mexico, and California. (10) (As a result, Under such circumstances, (In addition), (Besides) there are substantial numbers in many other states and large cities. (11) (Although, (However), In spite of) they do not constitute a majority in any single region.

EXERCISE 3

Complete these sentences using information provided in Exercises 1 and 2.

1. In addition to missing his family, Bambang . . .

2. In spite of sometimes still missing his family. . . .

3. Before he talked to his advisor about culture shock, ...

4. Bambang now understands that his depression was the result of culture shock. Because of this, . . .

5. Bambang sometimes does poorly on tests, even though . . . .

6. Bambang sometimes does poorly on tests, in spite of . . .

7. Canada has an official policy of bilingualism. The United States, however, ...

8. Canada has an official policy of bilingualism. Consequently, . . .

9. As a result of Canada's official policy of bilingualism, . . .

10. Canada's French-speaking minority is concentrated in a particular part of the country. Consequently, . . .

11. Canada's French-speaking minority is concentrated in a particular part of the country. Nevertheless, . . .

12. Since all government business is conducted in both languages, . . .

ANSWER KEY

EXERCISE 2 [15 minutes]

In Exercise 2, students are asked to choose an appropriate connector to complete the sentences. They will need to decide what meaning is needed and what grammatical form will fit.

1. Go over the directions with the class. You may want to do the first paragraph together before having students work individually.

2. Remind students to first decide what meaning is needed to connect and then decide what form works grammatically in the position. There may be more than one answer for some sentences.

3. Have students check answers with a partner. Then go over the possible correct options as a class. See answers on LP page 188.

Suggestion: You may want to have students add to their lists of connectors in their notebooks.

For more practice, use *Grammar Dimensions 3* Workbook page 69, Exercise 2.

EXPANSION [30 minutes]

You may want to assign Activity 5 (research on the web) on SB page 201 after this exercise. Students will use the Internet to conduct research on bilingualism.

EXERCISE 3 [20 minutes]

Students will show their understanding of the sentence connectors by completing these sentences. Sentences 1–6 refer to the reading in Exercise 1 (SB page 187) and sentences 7–12 refer to the information in the reading in Exercise 2 (SB page 188).

1. Explain to the class that this exercise focuses on the meaning of the connectors. Give a few sentence starters of your own to show how different connectors signal different information.

For example, have students find a logical place to put the following information into the sentences below (put them on the board): *she got very sick, she got a tan, she still felt stressed at work.*

> *Even though Mika vacationed in Hawaii, ...*
> *Mika vacationed in Hawaii. However, . . .*
> *Mika vacationed in Hawaii. Consequently, . . .*

2. Review the basic ideas presented in the readings for Exercise 1 (Bambang's culture shock) and Exercise 2 (bilingualism in Canada and the United States) with the class.

3. Have students work individually to complete the sentences with information from the readings. Circulate and help as needed. Note any common errors in form or use (in particular, check on answers to sentence 6).

4. When finished, have partners or small groups share their answers. Answers may differ, but the basic ideas should be the same. Go over possible answers with the class and discuss the reasons why some answers may not make sense. See answers on LP page 188.

form

FOCUS 2

Using Coordinating Conjunctions to Connect Parallel Forms

Unlike other connectors, coordinating conjunctions (*and*, *but*, *or*, *nor*, and *yet*) can join any parallel grammatical structures.

EXAMPLES

	STRUCTURES BEING JOINED
(a) **Jeff** and **Matt** are roommates and best friends.	nouns
(b) They **live** and **work** in San Francisco.	verbs
(c) They are **poor** but **hard-working** young men.	adjectives
(d) Every Saturday they clean their apartment **quickly** but **thoroughly**.	adverbs
(e) They hurry **down the street** and **around the corner** to do their shopping.	prepositional phrases
(f) They're always in a hurry **to go bike riding** or **to take their dog to the park**.	infinitives
(g) On Saturday nights they like **dancing at discos** and **going to nightclubs** to meet friends.	gerunds
(h) They enjoy **living together because they have many common interests**, and **it's cheaper than living alone**.	clauses

EXAMPLES

	EXPLANATIONS
(i) Jeff likes neither **dancing** nor **swimming**.	**Parallel Structure (correct):** In formal written English, structures joined by coordinating conjunctions should have the same grammatical form.
(j) Matt **is originally from** Kansas but now **lives in** San Francisco.	
(k) NOT: Jeff likes both **vacations** and **working**.	**Nonparallel Structure (not correct)**
(l) NOT: Matt **comes** originally from Kansas, but now **living in** San Francisco.	

EXERCISE 4

Circle the coordinating conjunctions in this passage and underline the elements that each one connects. The first paragraph has been done for you as an example.

(1) Matt (and) Jeff first came to San Francisco in 1990, after they had graduated from college. (2) Both of them had grown up in small towns. (3) Jeff was from Wisconsin, (and) Matt grew up in Kansas, (but) neither one enjoyed living in a small town. (4) There wasn't enough freedom (or) excitement for their tastes. (5) Each one decided to move to San Francisco because he had heard that it was a beautiful city, (and) that it was filled with interesting people.

(6) When they first met, they were surprised (and) delighted to discover how many things they had in common (and) how similar their interests were. (7) Jeff liked weightlifting, (and) so did Matt. (8) Matt loved opera, (and) Jeff did too. (9) Jeff wasn't entirely comfortable with "big-city" life, (nor) was Matt, (but) neither one missed living in a small town at all. (10) They both liked dogs (and) wanted to have one for a pet, so they decided to look for an apartment (and) live together. (11) They both thought it would be cheaper (and) more fun to have a roommate.

(12) However, when they moved in together (and) began living with each other, they found that there were also a lot of differences between them. (13) Jeff was very neat, (but) Matt wasn't. (14) He preferred to let the dirty dishes pile up until there were "enough" to bother with, (and) he did not pick up his clothes (or) keep things neat. (15) Jeff, on the other hand, always wanted things to be washed immediately, even if there were only one or two dishes. (16) Matt liked staying out late every Friday night, (but) Jeff always wanted to get up early on Saturday mornings to clean the house (and) to finish chores so they could spend the afternoon relaxing (or) playing with their new puppy in the park. (17) They soon realized that they would (either) have to start making compromises (or) start looking for separate apartments, which (neither) Matt (nor) Jeff wanted to do. (18) Fortunately, their similarities outweighed their differences, (and) they settled into a pleasant life together.

LESSON PLAN 2

FOCUS 2 [15 minutes]

Focus 2 gives examples of parallel forms used with coordinating conjunctions. Parallelism is a common problem for both native and non-native writers.

1. **Lead-in:** Put a few examples of sentences with nonparallel forms on the board. Students may or may not be able to see the problem at first. Simply tell the class that these are problem sentences and that you will come back to them later.

2. Go over the list of example sentences and structures being joined in the first chart of Focus 2. It may help to have students circle the connector used in each sentence and underline the two structures on either side of this connector. This will help to give a visual similar to a balanced scale.

3. If you have time, invite volunteers to replace the bold words in these examples with ones of their own.

4. Go over the second focus chart, with examples of parallel and nonparallel structures. Refer back to the problem sentences on the board and invite volunteers to make suggestions for change.

EXPANSION [10 minutes]

Practice the parallel forms with a quick back-and-forth competitive game.

1. Put students into pairs and write the following on the board:

   I like. . .

   I hate . . .

2. Player A will ask his/her partner to make a sentence using one of the structures from the list in Focus 2 and either "like" or "hate."

3. Player B will return with a complete and parallel sentence using "like" or "hate" and the suggested structure. For example:

   Player A: *"Gerunds and hate."*

   Player B: *"I hate exercising and cleaning."*

4. Players will get a point for every grammatical and parallel sentence. This works best if it's fast and points are only given if the returned parallel sentence is completed under a time limit (such as 15 seconds).

EXERCISE 4 [15 minutes]

Students will identify coordinating conjunctions used in context and the structures they connect.

1. After going over the directions and the examples in the first paragraph, have students complete the exercise individually.

2. After students have compared answers with a partner, you may want to go over the answers as a class and invite students to suggest what makes each pair of elements somehow parallel. This could be that they are parallel structures (nouns, gerunds, etc.) or that they are parallel clauses or that they are verb phrases that carry the same tense.

workbook

For more practice, use *Grammar Dimensions 3* Workbook page 69, Exercise 3 and page 70, Exercise 4.

EXPANSION 1 [homework]

Have students write a similar essay which compares two people they know. The essay could compare relatives, friends, themselves, or even movie stars. Modeling their essay after the one in Exercise 4, they will need to keep the ideas of parallel structures in mind as they write. If you have time, have students share their essays in small groups or with the class. Collect papers and give individual feedback.

EXPANSION 2 [15 minutes]

You may want to assign Activity 2 (speaking) on SB page 198 as an expansion of Exercise 4. In this activity, students will discuss the characteristics they desire in a potential roommate.

FOCUS 3

Problems Using Coordinating Conjunctions

form

use

REDUNDANT	LESS REDUNDANT	EXPLANATION
(a) Jeff enjoys cleaning, but he doesn't like to clean on Saturday mornings.	(b) Jeff enjoys cleaning, but not on Saturday mornings.	When using coordinating conjunctions, repeated information should be omitted unless doing so makes the meaning unclear.
(c) Jeff didn't like life in a small town, and Matt didn't like it either.	(d) Jeff didn't like life in a small town, and Matt didn't either.	
(e) Matt and Jeff get phone calls from their parents and from their friends almost every week.	(f) Matt and Jeff get phone calls from their parents and friends almost every week.	

EXAMPLES

EXAMPLES	EXPLANATIONS
(g) Bambang Soetomo studies hard, but he sometimes has trouble understanding assignments.	When coordinating conjunctions connect independent clauses, they must be preceded by a comma. Without a comma such sentences are called run-on or run-together sentences. They are considered incorrect in formal written English.
(h) NOT: Bambang Soetomo studies hard but he sometimes has trouble understanding assignments.	
(i) Jeff doesn't plan to leave San Francisco, nor does Matt want him to.	When clauses are joined with negative coordinating conjunctions (*nor, neither, not only*), the clause with the negative coordinating conjunction at the beginning must take question or inverted word order.
(j) Not only do the two have similar interests, but they also have similar personalities.	
(k) AWKWARD: I began to miss my family, and I was getting more and more depressed, so I decided to talk with my advisor.	In formal written English, using coordinating conjunctions to connect independent clauses is often considered to be awkward or poor style. Other kinds of logical connectors— sentence connectors and subordinating conjunctions—are more frequently used. In some cases, you may also wish to break up the run-on sentence into two or more sentences.
(l) BETTER: In addition to missing my family, I was getting more and more depressed. As a result, I decided to talk with my advisor.	

EXERCISE 5

Combine these pairs of sentences to make them less redundant. There is more than one way to combine most of the sentences.

Example: Jeff lives in San Francisco. Matt lives in San Francisco.

Jeff lives in San Francisco, and so does Matt.

Both Jeff and Matt live in San Francisco.

1. Jeff likes cleaning. Matt doesn't like cleaning.
2. Jeff may go home for a visit on his vacation. Jeff may travel to France on his vacation.
3. Matt doesn't plan to return to his hometown to live. Jeff doesn't plan to return to his hometown to live.
4. Jeff likes getting up early. Matt doesn't like getting up early.
5. Jeff always wanted to have a dog. Matt always wanted to have a dog.
6. Matt might take the dog to the park this afternoon. Jeff might take the dog to the park this afternoon.
7. Matt likes dancing at nightclubs. Matt likes meeting friends at nightclubs.
8. Matt comes from a small town in Kansas. Jeff comes from a small town in Wisconsin.

EXERCISE 6

Connect the numbered pairs of sentences this paragraph with coordinating conjunctions. Make any necessary changes to remove redundancy or to correct word order.

(1) Canada has a large French-speaking minority. The United States has a large Spanish-speaking minority. (2) Many people in Canada speak French. All government publications are printed in both languages. (3) Canada has two official languages. The United States discourages the use of languages other than English for official purposes. (4) In Canada, the French-speaking minority is found primarily in the province of Quebec. In the United States, Spanish-speaking communities are found in New York, Florida, New Mexico, and California.

ANSWER KEY

Exercise 5 Answers may vary. Possible answers are: 1. Jeff likes cleaning, but Matt doesn't. 2. Jeff may either go home for a visit or travel to France on his vacation. 3. Neither Matt nor Jeff plans to return to his hometown to live. 4. Jeff likes getting up early, but Matt doesn't. 5. Jeff always wanted to have a dog, and Matt did too. 6. Either Matt or Jeff might take the dog to the park this afternoon. 7. Matt likes dancing and meeting friends at nightclubs. 8. Matt and Jeff come from a small town in Kansas and Wisconsin, respectively.

Exercise 6 (1) Canada has a large French-speaking minority, and the United States has a large Spanish-speaking minority. (2) Many people in Canada speak French, and all government publications are printed in both languages. (3) Canada has two official languages, but the United States discourages the use of languages other than English for official purposes. (4) In Canada, the French-speaking minority is found primarily in the province of Quebec, but in the United States, Spanish-speaking communities are found in New York, Florida, New Mexico, and California.

FOCUS 3 [15 minutes]

Focus 3 addresses common problems that are found when using coordinating conjunctions.

1. **Lead-in:** Make up example sentences with problems that illustrate each of the four points listed in Focus 3 (redundancy, the use of commas, the position of negative coordinating conjunctions, and the use of too many coordinating conjunctions). Put these examples on the board or on an overhead transparency. Here are several examples with problems:

She went to Dallas, but she didn't go to Dallas to visit her sister. (redundant)

Mike wanted to ride his bike but it was raining. (comma)

Not only she forgot her keys, but she also forgot her wallet. (negative coordinating conjunction)

That country has strict laws and it has severe punishments, so the citizens are afraid to disagree with the government. (awkward)

2. As in Focus 2, tell students that these are problem sentences, and give them a moment to look for the problems before you move onto Focus 3 and go over the examples in the chart.

3. After going over the examples and explanations in the focus charts, give the class a moment to now find the problems with the examples on the board.

4. Invite volunteers to state the problems and others to suggest possible changes for them.

EXERCISE 5 [15 minutes]

Students will work on eliminating redundancy while doing a sentence combining exercise.

1. Before having students look at their books, you may want to put the first pair of sentences (1) on the board and invite volunteers to suggest different ways that these could be combined. See if students can figure out what can be used to combine the

sentences, and what information is repeated and can be left out of the new sentence.

2. Go over the directions and examples of sentence combining.

3. If students have been creating lists of connectors in their notebooks, they will want to refer to their lists as they work on this exercise (and Exercise 6).

4. When finished, put students into small groups to share answers. They may have different answers, but encourage the groups to decide if all the answers are correct.

5. Ask a few students to put a sentence on the board to share with the class. Go over other possible answers with the class. See possible answers on LP page 192.

Suggestion: You may want students to put their sentences on paper and collect these for individual feedback.

For more practice, use *Grammar Dimensions 3* Workbook page 71, Exercise 5.

EXERCISE 6 [15 minutes]

Like Exercise 5, this exercise asks students to combine sentence pairs and to remove redundancy. Students will need to be careful about the word order if they choose to use a negative coordinating conjunction.

1. Since this exercise is similar to Exercise 5, go over the directions and then have students work individually to complete the exercise. Although the sentences are longer than in the previous exercise, remind students that combining sentences will work in much the same way.

2. Circulate and assist as needed. Have pairs share their answers. See answers on LP page 192.

For more practice, use *Grammar Dimensions 3* Workbook page 72, Exercise 6.

EXPANSION [10 minutes]

Use the original text from Exercise 6 to practice using sentence connectors. Have students show the relationships between the pairs of sentences by placing sentence connectors into the paragraph (instead of coordinating conjunctions).

FOCUS 4

Problems Using Sentence Connectors

form

EXAMPLES

EXPLANATIONS

(a) I was getting more and more depressed. **As a result,** I decided to talk with my advisor.

(b) I was getting more and more depressed; **as a result,** I decided to talk with my advisor.

(c) NOT: I was getting more and more depressed, **as a result,** I decided to talk with my advisor.

Sentence connectors are used with sentences or independent clauses connected with a semicolon. Do not use them with commas to connect clauses. This produces run-on sentences.

(d) Jeff grew up in Wisconsin. **However,** Matt comes from Kansas.

(e) Jeff grew up in Wisconsin. Matt, **however,** comes from Kansas.

(f) Jeff grew up in Wisconsin. Matt comes from Kansas, **however.**

Sentence connectors normally occur at the beginning of a sentence, but some can also appear in the middle or at the end. See the chart in Appendix 4 (p. A–8) for more information.

(g) Living together has saved both men a lot of money. **Besides,** Matt likes having a roommate.

(h) NOT: Matt **besides** likes having a roommate.

(i) NOT: Matt likes having a roommate **besides.**

(j) Bambang put a lot of work into improving his writing. **Thus,** he was able to get an A in his composition class.

(k) He was **thus** able to get an A in his composition class.

(l) NOT: He was able to get an A in his composition class **thus.**

Other sentence connectors cannot occur in the middle and/or end of a sentence. See the chart in Appendix 4 (p. A–8) for more information.

EXERCISE 7

Correct these run-on sentences from Bambang's essay on page 187. You can correct the punctuation or make two sentences using a sentence connector of similar meaning. Compare your solution to other students' solutions.

1. I still often feel homesick and I miss my family.

2. Everything was strange nevertheless I enjoyed the new experiences.

3. The differences weren't interesting, they were boring.

4. I learned that every person has this kind of experience and it can't be avoided.

5. This was good advice, as a result, my culture shock became less but in spite of this I still miss my life in Indonesia.

EXERCISE 8

These sentences have problems with sentence connectors. Working with other students, identify the problems and correct them.

1. Every person has experience with culture shock. However, I am no exception.

2. Even though I studied however my grades weren't good.

3. In Canada all official government activities are conducted in both French and English. Under such circumstances, students also study both languages in school. Nevertheless, in the United States, there is no official bilingual policy in government operations. Besides, some local governments have policies that prohibit the use of any language other than English for official business.

Exercise 7 Answers will vary. Possible answers are: 1. I still often feel homesick, and I miss my family./I still often feel homesick. In addition, I miss my family.   2. Everything was strange. Nevertheless, I enjoyed the new experiences./Everything was strange, but I enjoyed the new experiences nevertheless.   3. The differences weren't interesting. They were boring./The differences weren't interesting. In fact, they were boring.   4. I learned that every person has this kind of experience and that it can't be avoided./I learned that every person has this kind of experience. Not only that, it can't be avoided.   5. This was good advice, and as a result, my culture shock became less. However, in spite of this, I still miss my life in Indonesia./This was good advice. As a result, my culture shock became less, but in spite of this, I still miss my life in Indonesia.

Exercise 8   1. Wrong meaning for the logical connector: The situation requires additive rather than contrastive meaning: Every person has experience with culture shock, and I am no exception.   2. Too many local connectors: Even though I studied, my grades weren't good./I studied. However, my grades weren't good.   3. Also is not needed. Wrong meaning for under such circumstances, nevertheless, and besides: In Canada all official government activities are conducted in both French and English. Accordingly, students study both languages in school. In the United States, on the other hand, there is no official bilingual policy in government operations. In fact, some local governments have policies that prohibit the use of any language other than English for official business.

FOCUS 4 [15 minutes]

Focus 4 addresses the danger of creating run-on sentences with sentence connectors and the possible movement of some sentence connectors.

1. **Lead-in:** Put a pair of sentences on the board to use as an example for sentence connectors. Here are a few examples:

The United States has no official language. Many people feel that English should be the official language.

Quebec is a French-speaking community. Schools are taught in French.

The United Sates has many Spanish-speaking communities. Schools are taught in English.

2. Review the lists of sentence connectors you created earlier or invite students to call out ones they remember from the charts in Focus 1. Write these on the board. Next, invite students to use some of these to connect the example sentences you have put on the board.

3. Remind the class that these sentence connectors are not used to combine sentences into one. Instead they are used to show the relationship between two separate sentences. They may connect sentences with either a semicolon or a period. However, stress that a semicolon can only be used between two sentences (where a period would otherwise be put).

4. For information on the placement of some sentence connectors, have the class check out Appendix 4 on SB page A-8. Using the example sentences on the board, let volunteers suggest a different placement for some of the sentence connectors they have used.

5. Go over the examples and explanations in Focus 4 and review any further questions.

EXERCISE 7 [15 minutes]

Students will find ways to correct the run-on sentences that were present in the Opening Task essay. Although the solutions may be different, students should be able to identify the problems.

1. Before they begin, remind students that a run-on sentence is basically two full sentences connected together that need to be separated.

2. Remind students that in general, if run-on sentences are connected with a coordinating conjunction, then either a comma may be added between them (see Focus 3, examples g–h) or a sentence connector may be used to separate them (see Focus 3, examples k–l). All other run-ons will need to be separated with a period or semicolon with a sentence connector.

3. Have students work individually to complete the exercise and then compare answers with a partner or small group. There may be differences in the solutions students find. Have students put different solutions on the board to share. See possible answers on LP page 194.

EXERCISE 8 [15 minutes]

Students will identify the misuse of sentence connectors. They will look for problems in punctuation or meaning.

1. Put students into small groups or pairs and have them work together to discuss any problems they find in the use of sentence connectors.

2. After they have found and discussed the problems of misuse, have groups make the necessary changes to these sentences.

3. Make each group responsible for putting one improved sentence on the board. Discuss these changes with the class. Are there other possibilities? See answers on LP page 194.

work book For more practice, use *Grammar Dimensions 3* Workbook page 73, Exercises 7 and 8.

FOCUS 5

Problems Using Subordinating Conjunctions

form

CORRECT SUBORDINATION

(a) **Because things were no longer new to Bambang, he began to miss his friends and family back home.**

(c) **Even though Bambang Soetomo studies hard, he sometimes has trouble understanding assignments.**

SENTENCE FRAGMENT

(b) NOT: **Because things were no longer new to Bambang. He began to miss his friends and family back home.**

(d) NOT: **Even though Bambang Soetomo studies hard. He sometimes has trouble understanding assignments.**

EXPLANATION

Subordinating conjunctions are used with dependent clauses, gerunds, or noun phrases. They cannot be used with sentences. This produces a **sentence fragment,** which is considered grammatically incorrect.

EXAMPLES

(e) **Besides missing his family, Bambang also misses his friends.**

(f) NOT: **Besides Bambang misses his family, he also misses his friends.**

(g) **Bambang sometimes doesn't do well on tests, in spite of studying carefully.**

(h) **Bambang doesn't do well on tests, despite his hard work.**

(i) **Bambang sometimes doesn't do well on tests, in spite of the fact that he studies carefully.**

(j) NOT: **Bambang sometimes doesn't do well on tests, in spite of he studies carefully.**

EXPLANATIONS

Some subordinating conjunctions cannot be used with dependent clauses. They function as prepositions and are used with gerund or noun phrases instead. Common subordinating conjunctions of this type are: *besides, in spite of, despite, regardless of, due to, as a result of.*

Adding *the fact that* to *in spite of* makes the error in (j) grammatically correct.

EXERCISE 9

Here are some problems with the form, meaning, or use of subordinating conjunctions that appeared in Bambang's essay. Identify the problems and correct them.

1. Although I have lived in the United States for almost one year, I often feel homesick and miss my family.

   Although is a subordinating conjunction and can't be used with an independent

   clause.

2. Even though I was used to them. Still I wasn't comfortable.

   Even though is a subordinating conjunction and can't be used with an independent

   clause.

3. However, I began to miss things in Indonesia. For example, food, my friends,
   the warm climate.

   However and for example are sentence adverbials.

4. In addition to he told me about culture shock, my advisor suggested that
   I should be patient.

   In addition to must be used with a noun phrase or a gerund phrase, not with

   a clause.

5. Besides I was homesick, I was also having trouble getting used to the way classes
   are taught in the United States.

   When besides introduces a contrastive clause, it should come after the main clause.

   If it precedes it, it should be used with a gerund or a noun phrase.

6. In spite of the fact that being homesick, I didn't want to go home without
   completing my education.

   In spite of is used with a gerund or a noun phrase; in spite of the fact that is used

   with a clause.

7. As a result of my conversation with my advisor. My culture shock got a little better.

   As a result introduces a clause; as a result of introduces a noun phrase.

8. Despite I was having problems, I didn't stop doing my best.

   Despite is used with a gerund or a noun phrase.

ANSWER KEY

Exercise 9 *Students should be able to identify the specific problem (written on lines above). However, the ways used to correct the problem may vary. Possible answers are listed above.*

LESSON PLAN 3

FOCUS 5 [15 minutes]

Focus 5 addresses the danger of creating sentence fragments when using subordinating conjunctions. This focus also addresses the subordinating conjunctions that require a gerund or noun phrase instead of a dependent clause.

1. **Lead-in:** If the class has made lists, review the subordinating conjunctions on them or invite students to call some out for you to write on the board.

2. Put the following sentence pairs on the board to use as examples and have students find ways to combine them by adding subordinating conjunctions:

   She felt homesick. She decided to stay here another year.
   He felt homesick. He decided to visit his family during his vacation.

3. Go over the first chart in Focus 5, then have students check for any sentence fragments in the sentences they created from the examples on the board.

4. Go over the second chart in Focus 5 and have students try using several of these subordinating conjunctions to combine the examples on the board. Invite students to share their sentences with the class.

Suggestion: Students may want to add a special section in the lists of connectors they are keeping in their notebooks for those subordinating conjunctions that take gerunds or noun phrases (such as *the fact that*).

EXERCISE 9 [15 minutes]

Students will identify problems in subordinating conjunctions, which were present in the Opening Task essay. Although the solutions may be different, students should be able to identify the problems.

1. Remind students to look for errors which may include: fragments, punctuation, and the use of subordinating coordinators which require gerunds or noun phrases.

2. Have students work individually or in pairs to find and correct errors.

3. Circulate and note any common problems to bring up later.

4. When finished, have students compare solutions in pairs or small groups. Circulate and check that students are finding the problems.

5. You may want to go over possible solutions with the class or collect student work and give individual feedback. See possible answers on LP page 196.

UNIT GOAL REVIEW [10 minutes]

Ask students to look at the goals on the opening page of the unit again. Refer to the pages of the unit where information on each goal can be found.

 For assessment of Unit 11, use *Grammar Dimensions 3 ExamView®*.

Use Your English

ACTIVITY 1 writing

Write a brief essay describing a personal experience with culture shock. Be sure to connect your ideas with logical connectors and avoid run-on sentences or sentence fragments. Then give it to your teacher. Ask your teacher to indicate places where there are grammatical problems. Follow the same procedure that you used for the Opening Task to analyze your problems and correct your mistakes.

ACTIVITY 2 speaking

What characteristics would you look for in a roommate? Make a list of things you would like in a roommate and things you would NOT want. Share your list with several other students and decide whether you would be able to get along with each other if you were living together in a new city.

ACTIVITY 3 speaking

Examine the different meanings that are implied by choosing one connector instead of another.

STEP 1

With a partner or in a small group, discuss these three groups of sentences. What are the differences in implied meaning?

1. (a) Indian food is spicy, and I love it.	2. (a) Although Indian food is spicy, I love it.	3. (a) Not only is Indian food spicy, but I also love it.
(b) Indian food is spicy, but I love it.	(b) Although I love Indian food, it's spicy.	(b) Because Indian food is spicy, I love it.
(c) Indian food is spicy, so I love it.		

STEP 2

The following sentences are illogical. With a partner or in a small group, discuss how the incorrect use of a logical connector makes the meaning of these sentences strange or unclear.

1. I love Indian food, and it is spicy.

2. I love Indian food, so it is spicy.

3. Since I love Indian food, it is spicy.

ACTIVITY 4 listening

CD Track 17

Silly Sally: A Game
Listen to the story about Silly Sally. Silly Sally likes and dislikes various things. There is one single, simple reason for all the things she likes or doesn't like. The purpose of the game is to discover this simple reason.

STEP 1

As you listen to the description of her preferences, follow along on the chart on the next page, and put a check in the appropriate column. One has been done for you.

STEP 2

Compare your answers with another student's and try to figure out the secret of her likes and dislikes.

STEP 3

With your partner come up with one additional example of something she likes and dislikes for each category. Your teacher will tell you if your examples are correct or not. If you think you know the secret of the game, don't tell other students. Just give more examples of the things that Silly Sally likes and doesn't like. Your teacher will tell you if you're correct.

ANSWER KEY

Activity 3 **Step 1:** Answers will vary. Possible interpretations are: 1. (a) That's why I love it. (b) I love it anyway. (c) That's the reason I love it. 2. There is a difference in emphasis. In sentence (a) the fact that I love Indian food is the most important. In sentence (b) the fact that Indian food is spicy is the most important. 3. (a) The two ideas don't share a strong logical cause-and-effect relationship. (b) The emphasis is on the cause-and-effect relationship. **Step 2:** Answers will vary. Possible explanations are: 1. The logical connector doesn't give information about the way these two ideas are related. Most teachers would consider this to be a run-on sentence. 2. This logical connector indicates result rather than cause. 3. This logical connector indicates cause rather than result.
Activity 4 Silly Sally only likes things that have double letters. She dislikes things without double letters. Hence she likes cooking, Greek food, Moroccan, etc., but dislikes eating, Chinese cuisine, Brazilian, and Japanese.

USE YOUR ENGLISH

The Use Your English activities at the end of the unit contain situations that should naturally elicit the structures covered in the unit. For a more complete discussion of how to use the Use Your English activities see To the Teacher on LP page xxii. When students are doing these activities in class, you can circulate and listen to see if they are using the structures accurately. Errors can be corrected after the activity has finished.

ACTIVITY 1 writing [homework]

You can either use this writing activity as a review of the concepts presented in this unit, or you can assign this activity after the Opening Task on SB pages 182–183. Students would revise their essays after completing the exercises in this unit. Be sure to give guidelines as to the format and length you will expect.

ACTIVITY 2 speaking [15 minutes]

You can either use this speaking activity after Exercise 4 on SB page 191 to practice using coordinating conjunctions and parallel forms or use it for a review of the concepts presented in this unit.

1. Before putting students into groups, have each student make two lists: things they DO want and things they DON'T want in a roommate.

2. Put students into small groups and have them discuss and share their roommate lists.

3. Ask the groups to work together and decide who might make the BEST roommates and who might make the WORST roommates in each group.

4. Have the groups share their results with the class.

ACTIVITY 3 speaking [15 minutes]

Students will determine the differences in meaning between sentences that vary only in the connectors used. Students should discover how the relationship between clauses changes depending on the connector that is used.

■ STEP 1 Put students into pairs or small groups and ask them to discuss how the sentences within each group are different. For example, how are sentences 1(a), (b) and (c) different from each other in their implied meaning?

■ STEP 2

1. Have groups discuss why these three sentences are strange.

2. Let groups share the results of their discussion with the class. See possible answers on LP page 198.

Suggestion: Before you begin the group activity, you might read the seven sentences out loud to the class giving some of the implied emphasis to key words along with pauses. You could read sentence 2(a) like this for example: *Although Indian food is spicy, I love it!*

ACTIVITY 4 listening [15 minutes]

CD Track 17

This activity can be used to review the unit. Students will listen to connectors used in context for likes and dislikes. They will then use these clues to find the key to what drives these likes and dislikes.

■ STEP 1

1. Go over the instructions for Activity 4 and Step 1 with the class.

2. Have the class look at the chart on SB page 200. Note that the lists are divided by categories. Students should put a check in either the LIKE or DISLIKE column as they listen to the story. One has already been done to illustrate (*likes tennis*). There are two blank lines at the end of each category. Later when they are finished, they will get directions explaining how they can add to each category.

3. Play the audio through. Circulate through the class and note whether students are having trouble keeping up. If it seems too fast for most of the class, play the audio a second time with pauses as needed.

■ STEP 2 After listening to the audio and filling out the box, have students read the directions for Step 2 and Step 3 and then work with a partner to check their work.

■ STEP 3

1. Circulate as students compare answers and try to figure out Sally's secret. Let them know if they have made a correct guess. Remind students not to tell others once they've figured out the game.

2. When students are ready, without telling the actual secret, ask volunteers to tell what they added to their category lists. See if these extra "clues" help any pairs who still haven't discovered the secret. Give the secret when ready. See answer on LP page 198.

ACTIVITY 5 research on the web

Go on the Internet and use an Internet search engine such as Google® or Yahoo® and enter the keywords "myths of bilingualism." Find a list of common misconceptions about bilingualism and its impact on children. Based on what you read, do you favor a political system that supports and fosters bilingualism, or one that promotes the use of a particular national language? Do you have personal experience with bilingualism yourself? What are the differences between a fluent speaker of a second language and someone who is bilingual in that language and another language? Discuss your ideas with two or three other students and present them to the rest of the class.

ACTIVITY 6 reflection

Think about ways that your first language affects how you express your ideas in a second language. What are some common connectors in your native language? How does "good style" affect their use? In this unit we learned that although it is grammatically possible to join sentences with coordinating conjunctions, it is not always considered to be "good writing." Think about the words you use to join ideas in your native language. Identify two situations where "good writing" may be different in your first language than it is in English. Present your ideas to the rest of the class.

Silly Sally's Likes and Dislikes

CATEGORY	LIKE	DISLIKE	CATEGORY	LIKE	DISLIKE
styles of food			**movie stars**		
cooking			Johnny Depp		
eating			Meryl Streep		
Greek food			Jennifer Lopez		
Chinese cuisine			Brad Pitt		
Brazilian			Denzel Washington	X	
Japanese	X		Whoopi Goldberg		X
Moroccan		X			
			dating		
sports			restaurants for dinner		
tennis	X		restaurants for lunch		
baseball			art gallery		
skiing			museum		
horseback riding			kisses		
hockey			hugs		
jogging	X		marriage		
walking		X	engagement	X	X
people			**vacations**		
queens			Greece		
princesses			Italy		
princes			inns		
kings			hotels		
Matt and Jeff	X		Philippines		
Peter and Denise			Indonesia		
John and Mary		X	travel in the summer	X	
			travel in winter		X
fruits and vegetables			**animals**		
beets			sheep		
carrots			goats		
apples			cats		
potatoes			dogs		
oranges	X		puppies	X	
cauliflower		X	kittens		X

USE YOUR ENGLISH

ACTIVITY 5 | research on the web
[30 minutes]

This activity can be assigned after Exercise 2 on SB page 188, with the presentations due at the end of the unit. Students will research bilingualism and discuss their results with the class.

1. You may want to begin with discussion in small groups. What is bilingualism? Is there a difference between being bilingual and being a fluent speaker of two languages? Do you have any personal experience with bilingualism? How do you think being bilingual affects children?

2. Next, go over the directions with the class and assign the research.

3. When they are finished, have students go over the discussion questions in Activity 5 and their opinions in small groups or with the class. You may want to rotate students into new pairs or groups.

ACTIVITY 6 | reflection
[20 minutes]

Students will reflect on ways in which they use connectors differently in their native language.

1. Read through the directions and questions with the class. You may want to invite students to suggest a few connectors in their native language to get them on the topic. The following may be good starting points:

What are some connectors in your native language?
Are any of these connectors more formal than others?
Is there a limit to how many you can use in a sentence?

2. Give students some time to go over the questions in Activity 6 and write their own answers in their *reflection journals.*

3. Then put students into small groups or have them share their thoughts with the class.

12 RELATIVE CLAUSES

UNIT GOALS

- **Understand restrictive and nonrestrictive modification**

- **Correctly form subject and object relative clauses in different parts of a sentence**

- **Correctly use or delete relative pronouns in different kinds of relative clauses**

- **Use *whose* in relative clauses**

OPENING TASK

Which One Is Which?

■ STEP 1

Read this article about twins who were separated at birth.

In 1953 two identical male twins were born in Ohio. Their mother was very young, so she gave the children up for adoption. They were separated the day after they were born, and grew up in different parts of the country. One grew up in Ohio and the other grew up in Oregon. Neither one knew he had a twin brother until the one twin moved back to Ohio, where the other twin was living. Then friends of the Ohio twin began to tell him that they had seen a man who looked exactly like him. The Oregon twin met several people who acted as if they knew him, even though he had never met them before. The two men each began doing research, and discovered their backgrounds and the fact that they were twins. They finally met each other in 1998, and the case was even reported on national television news programs.

Many researchers have been interested in this case because they want to see if the two men have any similarities even though they were raised in completely different environments. The researchers have found that there were, of course, many differences between the two men, but there are also some very interesting similarities: They had both married women with blonde hair and had had three children. They had both painted their houses yellow. They both had dogs and shared similar interests and hobbies. They both had jobs that called for a lot of travel.

■ STEP 2

Look at the list of differences on the next page between the twins, and use the information to answer the questions that follow.

Example: Which twin is married to Bernice?
The twin who has an old-fashioned home is married to Bernice.

Here is some information about one twin:

People call him "Rosey."

His house is a modern home.

He is married to a woman named Betty.

He has three children—all boys.

His children knew that he had been adopted.

He sells plumbing supplies.

He has a large dog named Prince.

His favorite sport is football.

He likes to listen to classical music.

Here is some information about the other twin:

People call him "Red."

His house is an old-fashioned home.

He is married to a woman named Bernice.

He has three children—all girls.

His children didn't know that he had been adopted.

He sells advertising space in magazines.

He has a small dog named King.

His favorite sport is basketball.

He likes to listen to jazz.

1. Which twin has children that are all girls?

   The twin who _____

2. Which twin owns a dog named Prince?

   The twin whom _____

3. Which twin sells plumbing supplies?

   The twin whose _____

4. Which twin likes classical music?

   The twin whose _____

5. Which twin prefers basketball?

   The twin that _____

6. Which twin lives in a modern home?

   The twin who _____

7. Which twin is married to a woman named Betty?

   The twin whose _____

8. Which twin's children didn't know that he had been adopted?

   The twin who _____

UNIT OVERVIEW

Unit 12 reviews restrictive and nonrestrictive relative clauses.

GRAMMAR NOTE

A relative clause is essentially a sentence embedded in a noun phrase and used to modify the noun. In English, a relative clause is placed directly after the noun it is modifying. The identical noun in the relative clause is then deleted and replaced with a corresponding relative pronoun (*that, which, who, whom, whose*), which is also moved to the front of the relative clause. The positioning, the use of a relative pronoun, and the deletion of the second identical noun are all features of the relative clause in English. Although relative clauses are found in other languages, those languages may or may not have these same features. For example, Japanese places relative clauses before the head noun and does not use relative pronouns to mark them. Arabic is an example of a language that does not delete the second identical noun. For these reasons, although they may not have trouble with the use of relative clauses, ESL students may have problems with the formation.

In addition, students may have some initial difficulties distinguishing which relative clauses are restrictive and which are nonrestrictive. This is an important distinction when it comes to punctuation (commas only in nonrestrictive relative clauses), the use of *that* (only in restrictive relative clauses), and the possibility for deleting relative pronouns (only in some restrictive relative clauses). Further problems are usually related to deciding whether a relative pronoun is to replace a subject or an object. This is important when deciding to use the relative pronoun *whom* (for objects) and when deciding whether the deletion of the relative pronoun is possible (only for objects and some subjects with *be* verb).

UNIT GOALS

Some instructors may want to review the goals listed on Student Book (SB) page 202 after completing the Opening Task so that students understand what they should know by the end of the unit. These goals can also be reviewed at the end of the unit when students are more familiar with the grammar terminology.

OPENING TASK [30 minutes]

The aim of this activity is to give students the opportunity to work with the meaning, use, and form of relative pronouns. The problem-solving format is designed to show the teacher how well the students can produce a target structure implicitly and spontaneously when they are engaged in a communicative task. For a more complete discussion of the purpose of the Opening Task, see To the Teacher, Lesson Planner (LP) page xxii.

Setting Up the Task

■ STEP 1

1. Have the class read the article. If you are short on time, you may want to assign the reading on SB page 202 as homework the night before you begin the unit.
2. Review the reading by asking volunteers to summarize the article into a sentence or two.

Conducting the Task

■ STEP 2

1. Read through the Step 2 directions with the class and the box at the top of SB page 203.
2. Go over the example given at the bottom of SB page 202. Ask the class which twin is called "Rosey," and which twin is called "Red." Write

answers on the board and select one with a relative clause and complete verb phrase to use as an example. Although you do not need to go over the grammar structure at this point, encourage the class to use your example on the board and the one in the book to base their answers on for Step 2.
3. If you want to have students work in pairs to complete Step 2, remind them that their answers can still be different. There are many possible answers.

Closing the Task

1. As you go over answers with the class, ask several students for answers to each question to show a wide variety of possibilities.
2. Keep one or two sentences on the board for use in Focus 1.

Note: So as not to cause any confusion, be sure to point out that the relative pronouns shown in each sentence starter are only suggestions. Students should not be worried about using the suggested relative pronouns (*whom, whose*). They may want to stick with *who* or *that* for all answers. Don't worry about these at this point. The use of all these relative pronouns will be explained later throughout the unit.

GRAMMAR NOTE

Typical student errors

- Not deleting the identical noun: * *Clara saw the man who she stole the money.* * *I love watching movies that they are suspenseful.* (See Focus 2.)
- Using *that* in a nonrestrictive relative clause: * *Seattle, that is where I grew up, is a beautiful city.* (See Focus 3.)
- Using *whom* for subjects: * *The friend whom gave me a ride lives nearby.* (See Focus 3.)
- Problems with commas: *Denise whom you met yesterday is my new roommate.* * *The man, who lives next door, drives a taxi.* (See Focus 3.)

FOCUS 1

Restrictive and Nonrestrictive Relative Clauses

EXAMPLES

EXPLANATIONS

(a) Which book do you want?
the one that's under the dictionary.

Restrictive relative clauses answer the question "what kind" or "which one."

(b) What kind of food do you like?
I like food that's not too spicy.

(c) Nitrogen, which is the most common element on earth, is necessary for all life.

Nonrestrictive relative clauses just provide additional information about noun phrases. They do not identify what kind or which one.

EXERCISE 1

Underline each relative clause in this passage and circle the noun phrase it modifies. The first two have been done for you as an example.

(1) My friend Charlie has fallen madly in love. (2) He told me he has finally met the (woman) that he has been looking for all his life. (3) He has always been attracted to (women) that are intelligent and independent and that have a good sense of humor and a love of adventure. (4) But (Amy), the woman that he has fallen in love with, has all those things and more. (5) Even though (physical appearance) isn't the most important characteristic that Charlie is looking for, he is quite happy his new friend is attractive and athletic. (6) She not only runs and skis, but also goes scuba diving, and has several other (interests) that Charlie also shares.

(7) Charlie was never completely happy with the (women) that he used to go out with. (8) There was always (something) that wasn't "right." (9) I used to tell him he was too choosy. (10) The ("ideal woman") that he has always been looking for just doesn't exist. (11) No real person can equal (the picture) that someone has in his or her imagination. (12) But I'm glad he has found (someone) that he thinks is perfect, because I've never seen him happier.

FOCUS 2

Forming Restrictive Relative Clauses

EXAMPLES

EXPLANATIONS

(a) I read a book [Charlie really liked *that* the book.] last week.

The relative pronoun [*that* in Example (a)] replaces the noun phrase in a relative clause in order to avoid repetition.

(b) I read a book [**that** Charlie really liked ⟋] last week.

When the relative pronoun is in the object position, it is moved to the front of the relative clause.

Relative pronouns can replace any noun phrase within the relative clause.

RELATIVE CLAUSE	UNDERLYING SENTENCE	FUNCTION
(c) I read the book **that** was published last year.	(d) **The book** was published last year.	subject
(e) I read the book **that** your professor wrote.	(f) Your professor wrote **the book**.	object
(g) I met the person **that** Charlie gave flowers to.	(h) Charlie gave **the person** flowers.	indirect object
(i) I met the person **that** Lin told me about.	(j) Lin told me about **the person**.	object of a preposition
(k) I read the book **that** was published last year.		Remember that the replaced noun or pronoun of the underlying sentence does **not** appear in the relative clause.
(l) NOT: I read the book that **it** was published year.		

FOCUS 1 [10 minutes]

Focus 1 explains the differences between restrictive and nonrestrictive relative clauses.

1. **Lead-in:** Looking back at the examples on the board from the Opening Task, underline the restrictive relative clauses and explain that the clauses answer the question of "which twin." This extra information is important because it explains which one we are talking about. This is called a **restrictive relative clause.** It restricts or explains which one we are talking about.

2. Go over the examples in Focus 1 that show restrictive relative clauses.

3. Now go down to point out the nonrestrictive relative clause and explain that a nonrestrictive relative clause is a clause that does not give information to tell which one or what kind. Point out that in example (c), there is only one kind of nitrogen and the relative clause is simply telling us more information about it. *Nitrogen* is one specific thing, whereas in examples (a–b) *a book* or *food* are not. We need to know *which book* and *what kind of food.*

4. Give a few more examples of restrictive and nonrestrictive relative clauses using information about students in the class. For example:

   The student who has a red bag is very quiet today.
   (restrictive)

   Anya, who has a blue bag, is also quiet today.
   (nonrestrictive)

EXERCISE 1 [15 minutes]

This exercise asks students to identify relative clauses.

1. Go over the directions and the examples. Students should be underlining relative clauses and circling the nouns they modify.

2. Let pairs check their work together before going over this as a class. Encourage them to notice the relative pronouns and the punctuation that are used.

3. To see how quickly you may want to move through this unit, invite students to explain why some relative pronouns and punctuation were used as you go over the exercise with the class. If students seem to be able to verbalize the rules, you can move through the unit more quickly. See answers on LP page 204.

For more practice, use *Grammar Dimensions 3* Workbook page 74, Exercise 1.

[work book]

FOCUS 2 [10 minutes]

Focus 2 reviews the basics of restrictive relative clauses. The choice of pronouns will be discussed in Focus 3.

1. **Lead-in:** Use the examples in the book or some of your own to show the step-by-step transformation of sentences into one with a restrictive relative clause (showing both a subject and an object being replaced by a relative pronoun). Here are some other examples:

   The movie [the movie won an award] was very good. =
   The movie that won an award was very good.
   The movie [we rented the movie] was very good. =
   The movie that we rented was very good.

2. Show how the repeated subject or object is replaced with a relative pronoun and how it will move to the front of the relative clause if it was previously in object position.

3. Looking at the lower chart in Focus 2, have the students practice breaking the sentences in the first column (examples c, e, g, i, k) into two separate underlying sentences. Ask the class to cover the middle underlying sentence column and then invite volunteers to state the two underlying sentences.

Write a few of these pairs on the board. Keep them up in preparation for Exercise 2.

4. Give special note to the examples (k) and (l). Students will need to be reminded to delete the replaced noun or pronoun.

meaning

use

FOCUS 3 | Relative Pronouns

The relative pronouns are *who*, *whom*, *which*, and *that*.

EXAMPLES	EXPLANATIONS
(a) The man **who** you told me about last week is over there.	Use *who* and *whom* to refer to humans. In formal written style, use *who* to refer to subjects in relative clauses and *whom* to refer to objects.
(b) The man **whom** you mentioned last week is here today.	
(c) The man **whom** you told me about yesterday is here to see you.	
(d) I read the book **which** Kevin had recommended.	Use *which* to refer to nonhumans.
(e) The man **that** wrote this book is a teacher.	Use *that* for humans or nonhumans, but only with restrictive relative clauses. (Review restrictive relative clauses in Focus 1, page 204.)
(f) The man **that** you told me about is a teacher.	
(g) I read the book **that** Kevin had recommended.	
(h) Abraham Lincoln, **who** was the sixteenth president of the United States, died in 1865.	Do not use *that* as a relative pronoun in nonrestrictive relative clauses. Use only *who*, *whom*, and *which*.
(i) NOT: Abraham Lincoln, **that** was the sixteenth president of the United States, died in 1865.	
(j) San Francisco, **which** is on the Pacific Ocean, has a very cool climate.	
(k) NOT: San Francisco, **that** is on the Pacific Ocean, has a very cool climate.	

EXERCISE 2

In the following article underline the relative clauses. Then restate each relative clause as an independent sentence. The first three have been done for you as examples.

Examples: (1) A new study may interest many people.

(2) *They conducted a survey with several thousand American women all around the country.*

(3) *These women have common attitudes about men.*

> ### Scientists Identify Today's "Prince Charming"
>
> (1) Sociologists at Mills College have released a new study that may interest many people, especially men. (2) They reported the results of a survey that they conducted with several thousand American women all around the country. (3) They wanted to examine common attitudes that these women have about men, so that they could identify important characteristics that women think are necessary in a good husband or boyfriend. (4) The study found a number of interesting results, which will probably not surprise most women, but may surprise some men.
>
> (5) The women in the survey generally seem to prefer men who can express their feelings. (6) Most women prefer husbands who they can talk to easily and that they can share their problems with.
>
> (7) There were also several other things that women consider important in a partner. (8) A man's character or personality is more important to many women than the job that he does for a living or the salary that he brings home. (9) Not surprisingly, most women want a husband that will take on an equal share of housekeeping and child-raising duties.
>
> (10) But the most important characteristic is this: Women want boyfriends who they can trust and husbands that they can depend on. (11) Unfortunately, more than 70 percent of the women who answered the questionnaires said they had husbands or boyfriends who lacked one or more of these important characteristics.

ANSWER KEY

Exercise 2 The relative clauses are underlined above. The restatements follow: (4) A number of interesting results will probably not surprise most women, but may surprise some men. (5) Men can express their feelings. (6) They can talk to their husbands easily. They can share their problems with their husbands. (7) Women consider several other things important in a partner. (8) He does the job for a living. He brings the salary home. (9) A husband will take on an equal share of housekeeping and child-raising duties. (10) They can trust boyfriends. They can depend on husbands. (11) The women answered the questionnaires and said their husbands or boyfriends lacked one or more of these important characteristics.

EXERCISE 2 [15 minutes]

Exercise 2 builds on Focus 2 by asking students to identify the underlying sentences in relative clauses.

1. With books closed, refer back to the underlying sentences you wrote on the board for Focus 2. If helpful, you may want to ask students to put them back together into relative clauses again. Write these on the board too. Note again the relative pronouns that are used to replace the nouns.

2. Have the class look at the paragraph in Exercise 2 and find the first underlined relative clause. Ask the class what the relative pronoun replaces, and how to write it as its original underlying sentence.

3. Do sentences (2) and (3) as a class.

4. Have students complete the rest of the exercise individually. Note that some sentences have more than one underlying clause replaced with relative clauses.

5. Check answers in pairs or as a class. You may need to write the answers to sentences that have replaced an underlying object (6, 7, 8, 10) on the board to help with any confusion in placing that original object. See answers on LP page 206.

For more practice, use *Grammar Dimensions 3* Workbook page 74, Exercise 2 and page 75, Exercise 3.

EXPANSION [15 minutes]

You can follow up this topic by assigning Activity 1 (speaking) on SB page 215 for groups to discuss. This activity can get students reviewing and using the grammar without thinking too much about it and focusing on the topic instead. This is a good activity for students who need more practice with fluency rather than accuracy.

FOCUS 3 [10 minutes]

Focus 3 presents the relative pronouns and their uses.

1. **Lead-in:** To explain the use of *who/whom*, put the following sentences on the board for students to combine using relative clauses:

> *The student is late.*
> *He is Anna's partner.*
> *I told you about him.*

2. Invite students to combine the first sentence with either of the next two sentences. (Possible answers include: *The student who/that is Anna's partner is late. The student who/that/whom I told you about is late.*) Point out that only when replacing the object pronoun *him* can you use the relative pronoun *whom.*

3. Go over the other examples in the focus chart and the rules for each. Pay special attention to examples (h–j) and (k).

VARIATION

If the class is not having trouble with the formation of relative clauses, use this focus chart as a quick review. Have students cover the right column (explanations). They can then look at the groups of sentences in the left column and work in pairs to prepare their own explanations of the "rules for relative pronouns".

EXERCISE 3

Combine these pairs of sentences by using a relative clause with *that*, *who*, *whom*, or *which*.

Example: I finally met the woman. Charlie has fallen in love with the woman.

I finally met the woman that Charlie has fallen in love with.

1. Last month Charlie fell in love with Amy. He had been introduced to her by some friends.

2. She had a number of positive characteristics. Charlie found these characteristics quite attractive.

3. She has a responsible position in a company. The company produces computer programs.

4. Information technology is a fast-growing field. Charlie is also interested in information technology.

5. Hobbies involve athletics and being outdoors. Both of them like these hobbies.

6. Charlie introduced the woman to his parents. He had been dating the woman for several weeks.

7. She has a wonderful sense of humor. This makes their times together relaxing and enjoyable.

8. From the first time they met, Charlie felt there was a "special understanding" between them. He was unable to explain this understanding.

EXERCISE 4

Answer these questions using a relative clause ("I like people who . . ."; "People whom I like . . ."). Compare your answers to those of a classmate.

1. What kind of people do you like?

2. What kind of people like you?

3. What kind of food do you like?

4. What kind of leisure activities interest you?

5. What kind of person do you want to marry?

6. What kind of person will want to marry you?

7. What kind of practice is useful in learning languages?

8. What kind of government is the best?

EXERCISE 5

The following sentences are incorrect. Identify the mistakes and correct them.

1. I read a book that ~~it~~ was published last year.

2. I saw an article that your professor wrote ~~it~~.

3. Jeff and Matt have been living in the city of San Francisco, ~~that~~ ^{which} is located in California, since 1990.

   (which must be used for nonrestrictive relative clauses, not that)

4. This is the person ~~to~~ whom Charlie gave ~~her~~ flowers.

5. I met the person who Charlie told me about ~~her~~.

6. The teacher that I studied with ~~her~~ has become quite famous.

7. The money that you loaned me ~~some~~ last week is there on the table.

8. The resort that we read about ~~it~~ in the newspaper is becoming more and more popular.

9. The people whom I visited ~~them~~ last year are coming here for a visit.

10. My father, ~~that~~ ^{who} lives in San Diego, loves sailing.

    (who must be used for nonrestrictive relative clauses, not that)

LESSON PLAN 1

EXERCISE 3 [15 minutes]

This exercise asks students to combine sentences using a relative clause. They will need to be able to identify which noun in the first sentence is being modified by the second sentence. They will then need to identify the noun or pronoun to be replaced in the second sentence and the proper relative pronoun to do this.

1. Write the example sentences on the board.

2. Ask the class which noun in the first sentence is being modified by the second sentence (*the woman*). Circle this on the board.

3. Next, ask the class to identify the same noun (or pronoun) in the second sentence (*the woman*). Circle this.

4. Now ask for a suggestion of a relative pronoun to use in place of this noun as you create a relative clause (*who, whom,* and *that* are possible).

5. Write the combined sentence on the board. Note all the relative pronouns that are possible.

6. Have students work alone or in pairs to complete the exercise. Depending on how comfortable students are with the exercise, you may want them to begin by circling the key nouns/pronouns as you did in the example.

7. You can either go over as a class or have them turn in their work for you to review. See possible answers on LP page 208.

EXERCISE 4 [15 minutes]

This activity can be in pairs or as a mixer. Students will share their opinions about a variety of topics such as the kinds of things and people they like.

1. You can start by randomly asking students a few of the questions for Exercise 4. If needed, put a couple answers on the board for students to see.

2. Have students either work in pairs or ask them to move around the classroom speaking to eight different people (as a mixer activity). In this case, you can either divide the questions among the

class, assigning specific questions to each student, or you can simply have students go through the list getting answers from different people.

3. Bring the class together and have students share interesting information about their classmates. Listen for any common errors. Make note of them and go over them before moving onto the next exercise. See possible answers on LP page 208.

EXERCISE 5 [15 minutes]

To review the information in Focus 2 and Focus 3, students will identify errors in sentences with relative clauses.

1. Have students work individually to find and correct the error in each sentence.

2. Put students into pairs. As they go over their answers, ask them to state the rule that has been broken in each case. In the end, students will find that only two different rules have been broken: (1) you must delete the underlying pronoun, and (2) you cannot use the relative pronoun *that* in nonrestrictive relative clauses.

3. If a pair of students finishes early, ask them to write their "rules" on the board.

4. Review with the class. See answers on LP page 208.

For more practice, use *Grammar Dimensions 3* Workbook page 75, Exercise 4.

form

FOCUS 4

Deleting Relative Pronouns

You can delete relative pronouns that function as objects in restrictive relative clauses.

EXAMPLES

	FUNCTION OF RELATIVE PRONOUNS
(a) I read the book **that** your professor wrote.	direct objects
(b) I read the book your professor wrote.	
(c) The lady **that** Charlie sent flowers to is on the phone.	indirect objects
(d) The lady Charlie sent flowers to is on the phone.	
(e) I read the book **that** Charlie was so excited about.	objects of prepositions
(f) I read the book Charlie was so excited about.	

You can only delete relative pronouns that function as subjects in restrictive relative clauses that contain *be* (either as a main verb or an auxiliary). In such cases both the relative pronoun and *be* are deleted.

EXAMPLES

	EXPLANATIONS
(g) I want a book **that was written** by an expert.	relative clauses with passive verbs
(h) I want a book **written** by an expert.	
(i) I think I know that woman **who is carrying** the blue suitcase.	relative clauses with progressive verbs
(j) I think I know that woman **carrying** the blue suitcase.	
(k) I tried to get an autograph from the baseball player **who is beside** the fence.	relative clauses with prepositional phrases
(l) I tried to get an autograph from the baseball player **beside** the fence.	
(m) Anyone **who is foolish enough** to use drugs should be free to do so.	relative clauses with adjective phrases
(n) Anyone **foolish enough** to use drugs should be free to do so.	
(o) Have you read the book **that made** Darryl Brock famous?	You cannot delete relative pronouns if they are subjects of a relative clause without *be*.
(p) NOT: Have you read the book made Darryl Brock famous?	

EXERCISE 6

Underline all the relative clauses in this passage. Make sure that you also include the ones that have deleted relative pronouns. The first paragraph has been done for you as an example.

The War To End All Wars

(1) When World War I, which was fought in Europe from 1914 to 1917, was finally over, it was called "the war to end all wars." (2) It was the most destructive war the world had ever fought until then. (3) Over ten million young men sent to battle from both sides were killed or permanently disabled.

(4) The war introduced powerful new weapons the world had never before seen. (5) The use of the airplane enabled armies on both sides to drop bombs with an effectiveness and precision that had been previously impossible. (6) Heavy casualties were also caused by the wide-scale use of a poison gas, called mustard gas, which permanently damaged the lungs of soldiers caught without gas masks.

(7) There were more than 8.5 million deaths. (8) Many people fighting this terrible war were killed in battles. (9) But many others died from intestinal diseases caused by the unsanitary conditions on the battlefield, or by infections that developed in lungs damaged by mustard gas, which was used by both sides.

(10) The peace established by "the war to end all wars" lasted less than a generation. (11) The most destructive war the world had ever known, like most wars, didn't solve the political and economic problems facing European governments at that time. (12) Less than twenty-five years after the conflict everyone hoped would bring world peace, Europe was again at war.

FOCUS 4 [20 minutes]

Focus 4 shows how relative pronouns can be deleted in restrictive relative clauses. This can only happen if the relative pronouns function as *objects* or if they are *subjects + be*.

1. **Lead-in:** For an inductive approach, put the following six sentence pairs on the board. Work with books closed to begin.

   I read the book. Your professor wrote the book.

   I read the book (that) your professor wrote.

   She did the homework. The teacher assigned the homework.

   She did the homework (that) the teacher assigned.

   I read the book. The book fell off the shelf.

   * I read the book fell off the shelf.

2. Ask the class why the last sentence is incorrect. Let them discuss the sentences together with a partner or in small groups if you wish. Let volunteers suggest rules.

3. Then go over the examples (a–f) in the focus chart on SB page 210 and compare these to the sentences on the board. Did the class discover the rule? (*Rule: relative pronouns can be deleted if they function as objects in restrictive relative clauses*)

4. Put the next six sentence pairs on the board and ask the class again (with books closed) if they can determine why the last sentence is incorrect. Again, invite suggestions of rules.

   I want the book. The book is sitting on the table.

   I want the book (that is) sitting on the table.

   I know that guy. That guy was on the bus.

   I know that guy (who was) on the bus.

   We saw the woman. The woman got off the bus.

   * I know that woman got off the bus.

5. Go over the second section of the focus chart (sentences c–p), which includes a good variety of examples to cover the deletion of subject relative pronouns with be. Did the class again discover the rule on their own?

EXERCISE 6 [15 minutes]

Students will identify relative clauses. They will also need to identify those that have deleted relative pronouns. After going over the directions and the example paragraph, have students work individually to identify and underline the remaining relative clauses.

1. Circulate and note how students are doing. If they seem to be missing several, you can tell them how many they should have found in all. This will encourage them to check again.

2. Have pairs check their work together. They may want to replace the missing relative pronouns (and missing *be* verbs where necessary) as they check. See answers on LP page 210.

Suggestion: Make a copy of this article on an overhead transparency to make the review easier.

Note: This exercise can be difficult for students. If your class is having trouble, have them complete the deletion work in Exercise 7 on SB page 212 first and then come back to this.

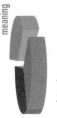

meaning

FOCUS 5

Whose in Relative Clauses

When a relative clause contains a possessive form, *whose* + noun can be used in the same way as relative pronouns.

	EXAMPLES	UNDERLYING SENTENCE	EXPLANATIONS
(a)	I met a man **whose house** was destroyed in the earthquake.	(b) I met a man. **His house** was destroyed in the earthquake.	*Whose* can be used with: • the subject of a relative clause
(c)	I got a letter from the man **whose house** we visited last week.	(d) I got a letter from a man. We visited **his house** last week.	• the object of a relative clause
(e)	I spoke to the man **whose party** we got an invitation **to**.	(f) I spoke to a man. We got an invitation **to his party**.	• the object of a preposition
(g)	I got a letter from the man **whose house** we visited last week.		You can never delete *whose* from a relative clause. It must always be used with a noun.
(h)	NOT: I got a letter from a man **house** we visited last week.		

EXERCISE 9

Combine these sentences using *whose*.

Example: I got a letter from a man. We visited his house last week.

I got a letter from the man whose house we visited last week.

1. Samira met a man. His brother is a well-known geneticist.

2. Jeff and Matt are roommates. Matt's nickname is "Akbar."

3. People may have similar personalities. Their genetic makeups are similar.

4. Nicole took a class from a teacher. She knew his wife in college.

5. Charlie's new girl friend would like to go to the lecture by the mountain climber. She read about his latest climb in *Adventure Magazine.*

6. Matt and Jeff have a dog. Its eyes are different colors.

7. I keep getting phone calls for some stranger. His last name is apparently the same as mine.

8. Charlie finally succeeded in meeting the artist. He had been admiring her work for years.

EXERCISE 7

Wherever possible, delete the relative pronouns in these sentences and make any other necessary changes.

Example: The kind of people **that** I like are usually people **who** have a good sense of humor.

1. I like people **who** think about other people's feelings.

2. I like people **who** are working to make the world a place **that** we can all share.

3. I like people **who** don't take the work **that** they do too seriously.

4. I don't like people **who** have no sense of humor.

5. I like people **who** don't worry about things **that** other people say about them.

6. I dislike people **who** try to hurt other people's feelings.

7. I dislike people **who** are very concerned with power and position.

8. I like people **who** question the things **that** they have been taught and the teachers **who** have taught them.

9. I like people **who** are like me.

10. I like people **who** like me.

EXERCISE 8

Write five sentences that describe the kind of people you like and five sentences that describe the kind of people you don't like. Compare your sentences with those of a classmate. Describe any common likes and dislikes.

The kind of people that I like are usually people who have a good sense of humor. I like people who take other people's feelings into account. I like people who are actively involved in making the world a better place. I like people who don't take themselves too seriously. I like people who think about important issues.

I dislike people who strive to be important and powerful without also trying to be kind, fair, and helpful. I dislike people who intentionally try to hurt other people's feelings. I dislike people who are too concerned with their own power and position. I dislike people who try to take power from other people by making them appear or feel bad. I dislike people who are shallow.

ANSWER KEY

Exercise 7 1. no deletion possible 2. I like people working to make the world a place we can all share. 3. I like people who don't take the work they do too seriously. 4. no deletion possible 5. I like people who don't worry about things other people say about them. 6. no deletion possible 7. I dislike people very concerned with power and position. 8. I like people who question the things they have been taught and the teachers who have taught them. 9. I like people like me. 10. no deletion possible

Exercise 8 Answers will vary. Possible answers are listed above.

Exercise 9 1. Samira met a man whose brother is a well-known geneticist. 2. Jeff and Matt, whose nickname is "Akbar," are roommates. 3. People whose genetic makeups are similar may have similar personalities. 4. Nicole took a class from a teacher whose wife she knew in college. 5. Charlie's new girlfriend would like to go to the lecture by the mountain climber whose latest climb she read about in *Adventure Magazine.* 6. Matt and Jeff have a dog whose eyes are different colors. 7. I keep getting phone calls for some stranger whose last name is apparently the same as mine. 8. Charlie finally succeeded in meeting the artist whose work he had been admiring for years.

EXERCISE 7 [15 minutes]

1. Put the example sentence on the board and ask the class whether either of the relative pronouns can be deleted (*that can be deleted, but who cannot*). Invite volunteers to explain their reasoning.

2. Have students work in pairs to complete the exercise. They should delete any relative pronouns that they can.

3. As pairs work together, have them verbalize the reasoning for the possibility or impossibility of the deletions. See answers on LP page 212.

4. Go right into Exercise 8 to follow up on this topic.

 For more practice, use *Grammar Dimensions 3* Workbook page 76, Exercise 5.

EXERCISE 8 [15 minutes]

Exercise 8 should be done directly after Exercise 7.

1. Have students work individually to write five sentences describing people they like and five sentences describing people they don't like.

2. When they are finished, put students into small groups and have them compare their answers with each other.

3. Groups should then discuss any common ideas and make general statements on these.

4. Have the groups present their findings to the class. Ask the class if they see any common likes or dislikes. Can any of the students make general statements about the likes or dislikes of the men or the women in class? Put any statements students come up with on the board. See possible answers on LP page 212.

EXPANSION 1 [15 minutes]

This fun and active relative clause game gets students moving similarly to musical chairs and is

sometimes called *Fruit Basket* in Japan. In this version, it is called *The Winds Are Blowing*.

1. Make a circle of chairs, one student sitting in each chair.

2. Write the following sentence starter on the board: *The winds are blowing for people who . . .*

3. Demonstrate the game by putting yourself in the middle of the circle to begin.

4. You will say, "*The winds are blowing for people who . . .*" Then you will finish the sentence with one relative clause which describes a portion of the students. For example:

> *. . . who are wearing jeans, . . . whose eyes are blue,*
> *. . . who have a pet, . . . who love English class,* etc.

5. After you complete the statement, all students who fit the description should get up quickly and race to find a different chair. At the same time, you will race to take one of the chairs that was just vacated.

6. One person will remain without a chair. The one left without a chair will take a turn to stand in the middle and call out a "the winds are blowing" statement. Again, a portion of the class matching this description will race to find a new chair and one will be left to take his or her place in the middle.

EXPANSION 2 [homework]

Expand on these sentences by assigning Activity 2 (writing) on SB page 215. Students will write a brief essay on personal characteristics they like and dislike in other people.

FOCUS 5 [10 minutes]

1. **Lead-in:** Begin by putting one of the examples of underlying sentences on the board to show the transformation from a possessive pronoun into a possessive relative pronoun. For example:

I met a man. His house was destroyed in the earthquake.

becomes

I met a man whose house was destroyed in the earthquake.

2. Put a few more pairs of underlying sentences using possessives on the board and invite volunteers to do the transformations.

3. Be sure to note that *whose* can never be deleted from a relative clause.

4. Go directly to Exercise 9 to practice this sentence combining with *whose*.

EXERCISE 9 [15 minutes]

1. Begin by putting the first two example sentences from the exercise on the board.

2. Ask the class to first decide what noun is being modified with information in the second sentence (*a man*). Tell the class that the relative clause will need to be placed directly after this noun. Remind students that this first step is very important.

3. Then circle both the noun to be modified in the first sentence (*the man*) and the possessive pronoun + noun (*his house*) in the second sentence.

4. Write the new combined sentence.

5. Now take students step by step again through the first example. Be sure that the class remembers to put the *whose* + noun phrase directly following the noun it is modifying.

6. Students should now be ready to complete the exercise individually.

7. Have pairs check their work together. They should have the same sentence. Let them discuss any differences. See answers on LP page 212.

 For more practice, use *Grammar Dimensions 3* Workbook page 76, Exercise 6.

EXERCISE 10

Combine the numbered pairs of sentences in this paragraph using relative pronouns or *whose*.

(1) Charlie wants to make some changes in his life. ~~These changes~~ involve both his *that* lifestyle and his social activities. (2) Charlie wants to find a new place to live. ~~The place~~ *that* has ~~to have~~ enough room for a dog. (3) He's looking at a new apartment. ~~The apartment~~ *that* has a balcony, so he can grow some flowers. (4) Charlie also wants to ge- married to *whose* someone. ~~Her~~ political beliefs are similar to his own. (5) He hasn't found anyone yet. ~~No~~ *who* ~~one~~ seems to share his interest in politics and sports. (6) He's thinking of putting a *that* personals ad in a paper. ~~A~~ lot of people advertise in ~~that paper~~ in order :o meet others with similar interests and backgrounds.

EXERCISE 11

Answer these questions, using relative clauses. Compare your answers with one of your classmate's.

Example: What kind of food do you like?

I like food that is not too spicy.

1. What kind of person do you want to marry?

_____

2. What kind of person should be the leader of a country?

_____

3. What kind of person makes the best teacher?

_____

4. What kind of television programs do you like to watch?

_____

5. What kind of place is the best for a vacation?

_____

6. What kind of house or apartment would you like to live in?

_____

7. What kind of books do you enjoy reading?

_____

8. What kind of students get the best grades?

_____

Use Your English

ACTIVITY 1 speaking

STEP 1

In Exercise 2 you read about some of the things that American women consider important in a husband. Divide into same-gender groups of men and women. In your group discuss the characteristics of "the ideal life partner." Prepare a list of five to ten statements like these: *The ideal partner is someone who takes an equal responsibility for raising the children./The ideal partner is a person whom I can always trust./ The ideal partner is someone whose sense of humor is well-developed.*

What ideals do you all agree on? Are there ideals that are controversial?

STEP 2

Present your statements to the other groups. Compare the ideals presented by women's groups and the ideals presented by men's groups.

STEP 3

Discuss these questions as a whole class or in mixed gender groups. What are the important similarities and differences between the statements of the two kinds of groups? Are there some ideals that all men share, no matter what culture they come from? Are there some ideals that all women share, no matter what culture they come from? Are there some ideals that both genders share?

ACTIVITY 2 writing

Write a brief essay describing personal characteristics in people that you like and dislike. You may wish to look at Exercise 7 for some ideas about the kinds of characteristics other students have identified. Here are some questions you should try to answer in your essay. What kind of people do you like most? What personal characteristics do you appreciate and respect in other people? What personal characteristics do you find distasteful?

ANSWER KEY

Exercise 11 Answers will vary. Possible answers are: 1. I want to marry someone who is rich./I want to marry someone who is intelligent. 2. The leader of a country should be someone who is honest./ The leader of a country should be someone who doesn't lie to the people about weapons of mass destruction. 3. The best teacher is someone who is intelligent./The best teacher is someone who cares about her students. 4. I like to watch a program that teaches me something./I like to watch a program that has a lot of action. 5. The best place for a vacation has a good beach./The best place for a vacation is a place that isn't too expensive. 6. I would like to live in a house that has a beautiful garden./I would like to live in an apartment that has a nice view. 7. I enjoy reading books that describe times long ago./I enjoy reading books with a suspenseful plot. 8. Students who work hard get the best grades./Students who are active in class get the best grades.

LESSON PLAN 2/USE YOUR ENGLISH

EXERCISE 10 [15 minutes/homework]

Exercise 10 is a review of Unit 12. Assign it as homework or give time in class for students to work together and then ask questions as they review. See answers on LP page 214.

EXERCISE 11 [15 minutes]

1. Have the class write down their own answers to the questions in the exercise. Circulate and encourage students to use complete sentences and to include relative clauses.

2. Put students into pairs (or small groups) and have them share their answers. Ask them to prepare to make some general observations to the class. See possible answers on LP page 214.

VARIATION

After reviewing the questions and types of relative clauses that should be present in the answers, have the class stand up and move around the room asking and collecting answers from as many classmates as they can. Then have students form small groups and share their answers with each other or simply ask students to volunteer interesting answers with the class.

For more practice, use *Grammar Dimensions 3* Workbook page 77, Exercise 7.

EXPANSION [20 minutes]

A fun way to review relative clauses is to play a version of the game *Password*. Put the class into teams of about five students. The first player will receive a list of words and they must get their team to guess the words they have. The player can only give clues to their team about their word and they cannot use any gestures, sound effects, or certain words in their clues. For example, if the player has the word *President Bush*, then the player can only give clues about this person but

may not say the words *president* or *bush*. Instead, the player may say things like, "It's the person who runs the *country. It's the person who lives in the White House.*" The team will get points for the number of words they get correctly in the time limit. They can shout out as many guesses as they want, but the other team(s) should not. Teams will take turns and the clue-giving player will rotate within the teams. Encourage students to form their descriptions with relative clauses such as, *someone who, something that, somewhere that,* etc.

UNIT GOAL REVIEW [10 minutes]

Ask students to look at the goals on the opening page of the unit again. Refer to the pages of the unit where information on each goal can be found.

For a grammar review quiz of Units 11–12, refer students of pages 78–79 in the *Grammar Dimensions 3* Workbook.

 For assessment of Unit 12, use *Grammar Dimensions 3 ExamView®*.

USE YOUR ENGLISH

The Use Your English activities at the end of the unit contain situations that should naturally elicit the structures covered in the unit. For a more complete discussion of how to use the Use Your English activities see To the Teacher on LP page xxii. When students are doing these activities in class, you can circulate and listen to see if they are using the structures accurately. Errors can be corrected after the activity has finished.

ACTIVITY 1 speaking [15 minutes]

You can use this activity after Exercise 2 on SB page 206.

STEP 1

1. Review the article in Exercise 2.

2. Put students into small same gender groups and ask them to share within the group their ideas of the characteristics of "the ideal life partner."

3. Ask the groups to prepare a list of the characteristics of the ideal partner. The list should include the characteristics that the groups agree on, but also controversial characteristics.

STEP 2 Combine groups of men and women together. Encourage these groups to share and compare the lists they made in the same sex groups.

STEP 3 Have the groups discuss and share their answers to the questions in Step 3.

Note: It's important to be able to encourage discussion while still ensuring that all students are comfortable expressing their own cultural ideas, including traditional or nontraditional attitudes. Be sure that everyone's opinion (no matter how traditional or culture specific) is accepted as valid in the class. Encourage all students to openly listen to others. This is an important skill for living, studying, or working in a multiethnic community.

VARIATION

If you don't have time for a full class discussion or the discussion doesn't seem to allow all to share their viewpoints equally, consider developing the discussion into a writing assignment.

ACTIVITY 2 writing [homework]

You can use this activity after Exercise 8 on SB page 212. Students can use the discussion they had in Exercise 8 to expand their own ideas into a brief essay. Be sure to go over any requirements of format or length with the class.

ACTIVITY 3   listening

CD Track 18

Listen to the lecture about "hawks" and "doves," and write definitions for the following terms based on the information you heard.

What is a pacifist?   *someone who doesn't believe in fighting wars*

What is a "hawk"?   *a person who is in favor of a particular war*

What is a "dove"?   *a person who is opposed to a particular war*

What is the difference between a war and a revolution?   *A war is a conflict that involves two different countries, and a revolution is a war between the people of a single country and their unjust government.*

ACTIVITY 4   speaking

Nicknames are additional names that are given to people to describe some physical characteristic or aspect of their personality.

STEP 1

Here is a list of some common American nicknames. Working with a partner, decide what characteristics would be likely for someone whose nickname is one of these:

Blondie	Doc	Sport	Cowboy	Tubby
Sugar	Gramps	Tiger	Honey	

STEP 2

Report your ideas by using sentences like these:

We think that someone whose nickname is Red is probably a person who has red hair. We think that someone whose nickname is Curly is probably a person who has curly hair (or perhaps someone who is bald). We think that someone whose nickname is Sunny is probably a person who has a cheerful, outgoing personality.

STEP 3

Discuss how nicknames are used in other countries. Do you have a nickname? Why do people call you that name?

ACTIVITY 5   research on the web

Some people use the Internet to meet potential partners. Would you ever consider that as a way to meet someone? Google "free online dating," and choose one of the free sites such as www.okcupid.com, www.plentyoffish.com or other Google® listings such as "Christian singles" or "Muslim singles". Be careful to choose a site that does not require you to register personal information, and reflects your interests. Click on "who's on-line" and scan a few of the profiles that you find there. Based on the profiles you have looked at, do you think that online dating would be a good way for you to meet a partner? What sorts of characteristics do peop.e mention there? You may want to do this activity with a classmate.

ACTIVITY 6   reflection

The word *daffy* means silly. A *daffynition* is a made-up definition for a word that doesn't really exist. In fact the word *daffynition* is itself, a made-up word.

STEP 1

Try to invent daffynitions for the made-up words below. Remember that many prefixes and suffixes in English are good indictors of meaning, so you can use that information as clues for possible meaning or what kind of word (noun, adjective, etc.) it is.

Example: Who or what is a murphler?

A murphler is someone who murphles. Murphling is a kind of sport.

- What are **parahawks**?
- What does **chemicophysiologicalistic** mean?
- What is **antinonsequitology**?
- Define **hypervoraciosity**.

STEP 2

Share your daffynitions with the rest of the class. Which one is the most believable? Which one is the most amusing daffynition for each term?

STEP 3

Make up some of your own imaginary words and provide definitions for them.

USE YOUR ENGLISH

ACTIVITY 3 listening [20 minutes]

CD Track 18

1. Go over the vocabulary to be defined. Activate students' background knowledge by asking them to make guesses about the topic of this lecture, through questions such as:

Will it be about birds? Why would the words "hawk" and "dove" be given in quotation marks? What would this have to do with war and revolution? What does pacifist mean?

2. Don't give any answers to these questions. You don't even need to tell students if their guesses are right or wrong. Simply leave them open for students to discover the answers within the lecture.

3. Play the lecture once and let students write their initial guesses to the definitions. Encourage all students to write something for an initial guess even if they are very unsure.

4. If students are having trouble with the listening, play the lecture again and let students correct their first guesses. Let pairs discuss their answers.

5. Play the lecture a final time and have pairs make any further changes as they check their answers together.

6. Debrief with the class and encourage a variety of answers which give the same meaning. Putting things in their own words can be more important than simply copying what they hear word for word. See answers on LP page 216.

ACTIVITY 4 speaking [15 minutes]

■ STEP 1 Introduce the topic of nicknames. As an example, share your own nickname or the nickname of a sports star or a well-known personality (e.g., David Ortiz who is also known as "Big Papi"). Then put students into pairs to go through the nicknames listed and work on Step 1.

■ STEP 2

1. After some discussion (you may want to encourage the class to be creative rather than predictable), pairs should write down their ideas.

2. Share these ideas with the class or in small groups.

■ STEP 3

1. You may want to use small groups (with mixed cultures) for the discussion in Step 3.

2. Circulate through the classroom to check quickly on how students are doing as they discuss Step 3. Listen for examples of relative clauses. Follow up by going over any common errors you heard with the class.

Suggestion 1: If you have time, ask pairs to make up nicknames for everybody in the class. Be careful that this doesn't turn into name-calling or hurt anyone's feelings.

Suggestion 2: Alternately, have everyone choose their own nickname and explain why they chose it. These can be put on slips of paper. You can then read the nicknames and reasons out loud and see if the class can guess who they belong to.

ACTIVITY 5 research on the web [20 minutes/homework]

Activity 5 asks students to do an Internet search for online dating services. Be aware that free online dating sites are not always able to censor postings immediately. If you feel uncomfortable assigning this activity, you may want to use the topic of newspaper personal ads instead.

1. Begin with a quick discussion of what online dating is and what the class already knows or feels about this type of dating. Ask the class what other ways there are to find a mate.

2. Be sure that everyone understands that registering information on one of these sites (including your email address) is not a good idea.

3. After students have had a chance to do their Internet search, have them come together in small groups and discuss their experiences. What are the pros and cons to these types of services?

4. This activity should encourage the use of relative clauses as students discuss and describe the kinds of people they found online.

ACTIVITY 6 reflection [20 minutes/homework]

You may want to begin with a few made-up words of your own. They can be like the word *daffynition* (a portmanteau, or combination of two other words) or simply a crazy made-up word. Encourage the class to find fun ways to define your new words.

■ STEPS 1 AND 2 Have students work alone or in pairs to create daffynitions and then share with the class.

■ STEP 3 As homework or in pairs, have students work on Step 3. Post these new words on the board for all to enjoy or make a handout for the class. Again, remind students that although these words are not real English, they are a great way to practice their knowledge of how English vocabulary works.

VARIATION

In place of the made-up words suggested, try using a section from Lewis Carroll's poem "The Jabberwocky." This poem is full of fun made-up words. Students will be surprised to find that they often will end up with very similar definitions. The context along with the combinations of the made-up words will cause this. Alternately, you could give a few of the made-up words alone and out of context and ask for definitions. Then give them the poem and see if they think their definitions still fit.

UNIT GOALS

- **Distinguish the use of progressive aspect from simple present**

- **Understand and use nondynamic or stative verbs**

- **Understand common uses of the present time frame**

OPENING TASK

Volunteers to the Rescue

STEP 1

Mary Rae is an account executive for a large advertising agency in New York, but at the moment she is working in New Orleans, participating in a program called "Citizens Care." Citizens Care assigns private citizens who volunteer to help with rescue and reconstruction efforts after natural disasters. Use the information in the chart on the next page to write a paragraph that describes at least five differences between Mary Rae's normal life and her life helping flood survivors of Hurricane Katrina.

Example: *Mary Rae normally spends her day as an account executive in a busy advertising firm, but with Citizens Care, she is spending twelve to fourteen hours a day in vigorous physical activity. In New York she supervises twenty-five employees, but in Louisiana, she is only supervising herself. . . . .*

MARY RAE'S LIFE IN NEW YORK	MARY RAE'S LIFE AT THE CITIZEN CARE CAMP
Occupation: advertising account executive; visits clients, supervises a 25-person office	Occupation: program participant; rows a boat through flooded streets, removes debris, looks for survivors, brings food to emergency shelters
lives in a small apartment	sleeps in a high school gymnasium, spends her days in a boat
often eats take-out Chinese food	eats in a Red Cross shelter
worries a lot about her career	worries a lot about people who are without food and water, not thinking about her career at all
doesn't get much exercise	rows her boat or hauls debris 12–14 hours each day
doesn't spend much time outdoors	doesn't spend any time indoors, except to sleep
often has trouble falling asleep	falls asleep almost instantly
doesn't feel challenged by her daily routine	feels very challenged by each day's activities
is somewhat bored with life	is excited about helping those in need
feels that she is not learning anything new	feels that she is learning something new every day
finds making new friends difficult	finds making new friends easy

STEP 2

Compare your paragraph with a classmate's. Did you both use the same verb tenses to describe Mary Rae's life in Louisiana compared to her life in New York?

STEP 3

Based on Mary Rae's experience, would you ever consider joining a volunteer rescue program? Why or why not?

LESSON PLAN 1

UNIT OVERVIEW

Unit 13 reviews ways to express the present time frame. The progressive aspect and simple present are contrasted along with their uses. A review of common nondynamic (stative) verbs is included.

GRAMMAR NOTE

In general, the simple present is used for facts, states, conditions, habits, and things that do not generally have a specific beginning or ending time frame. The present progressive, on the other hand, is used for more temporary situations that are in progress at the time and are in some way seen as temporary activities. Typical examples to show the difference would be: *I live with my sister* (a condition or fact that has no specific beginning or ending) versus *I am living with my sister* (a temporary situation in which the start or end points are of importance).

When stative verbs are used to describe a state or condition, they cannot be used with the progressive forms. The progressive is used for actions and not for states. There are times, however, when stative verbs are used in a way so as to have a dynamic or active meaning. Typical examples of this difference would be: *The flowers smell wonderful* (a condition or state) versus *The dog is smelling the flowers* (an activity which has a different meaning from the first example).

Besides the uses listed above, the present tense can be used in storytelling, reporting, or describing activities currently happening—to make the descriptions more immediate or interesting. Although many languages have similar forms, the variety of uses in English can cause some confusion.

UNIT GOALS

Some instructors may want to review the goals listed on Student Book (SB) page 218 after completing the Opening Task so that students understand what they should know by the end of the unit. These goals can also be reviewed at the end of the unit when students are more familiar with the grammar terminology.

OPENING TASK [30 minutes]

The aim of this activity is to give students the opportunity to work with the meaning and use of present progressive and the simple present. The problem-solving format is designed to show the teacher how well the students can produce a target structure implicitly and spontaneously when they are engaged in a communicative task. For a more complete discussion of the purpose of the Opening Task, see To the Teacher, Lesson Planner (LP) page xxii.

Setting Up the Task

You may want to begin with a quick discussion to find out what students know about Hurricane Katrina or another disaster which required rescue or reconstruction from a relief program, while being sensitive to the fact that some students may have had first-hand experience with a natural disaster such as an earthquake or tsunami. What are some ways in which private citizens were called on to volunteer?

Conducting the Task

■ STEP 1

1. Go over the directions for Step 1 with the class. Look over the chart on SB page 219 and note how the two columns contrast the same topics.

2. Have students write their paragraphs with comparisons based on the example on SB page 218.

3. Encourage students to make as many comparisons about the differences in Mary Rae's life as they can.

4. Circulate and note which verb tenses the class chose to use. You may find some students using the simple past to describe Mary Rae's life in New York. Remind the class that she still lives there and that she is only staying at the Citizen Care camp temporarily.

■ STEP 2

1. Have pairs compare their paragraphs and note any differences in verb tenses.

2. Ask a few students to put some sentences on the board.

■ STEP 3

Have the pairs or small groups discuss the questions.

Closing the Task

1. When finished, go over the examples on the board. Look over the use of verb tenses and comment on this. Did anyone use the simple present? Present progressive? Leave the examples on the board for later use in the discussion of Focus 1.

2. Don't worry about the wide variety of verb forms used. Some students may have used the simple present for everything. You may want to save some of these examples past Focus 1 and come back to them when you finish the unit to see how the class feels about the choice of verb tense then.

EXPANSION [30 minutes/homework]

You may want to assign the Activity 5 (research on the web) on SB page 229 at this time. Students can conduct their research as homework with a due date to turn it their work or presentations to be set for the end of this unit.

GRAMMAR NOTE

Typical student errors

- Using the present progressive to describe states or conditions or habits: * *Water is boiling at 100 degrees Celsius.* (See Focus 1.)

- Using the simple present to describe a temporary condition: * *She lives with her sister until she finds a job.* (See Focus 1.)

- Using stative verbs with the progressive: * *I am having a new car.* (See Focus 1.)

Using Simple Present Versus Present Progressive

use

USE SIMPLE PRESENT TO DESCRIBE:

- general statements about recurring habits and skills
  - (a) Mary Rae **works** in New York.
  - (b) She **lives in a small apartment.**
  - (c) She **sleeps** in a comfortable bed.
- timeless facts
  - (g) Hurricanes **cause** widespread flooding.
- permanent situations
  - (i) Mary Rae **lives** in New York.
- states and conditions
  - (k) She **thinks** the government should be more active in the rescue effort.
  - (l) She **has** a lot of job responsibilities waiting for her return.

USE PRESENT PROGRESSIVE TO DESCRIBE:

- actions in progress at the time of speaking
  - (d) She **is working** in New York.
  - (e) She **is living** in a high school gym.
  - (f) She's **sleeping** on the floor.
- situations in progress around the time of speaking
  - (h) The floods **are causing** many disruptions in basic services.
- temporary situations
  - (j) She's **living** in New Orleans until the project is over.
- actions
  - (m) She's **thinking** about ways to get other people to join the project.
  - (n) She's **having** a lot of fun!

EXERCISE 1

Choose the correct verb tense (simple present or present progressive) for these sentences. More than one answer may be correct.

1. Don't turn on the TV. I ___am talking___ (talk) to you!
2. My brother ___speaks___ (speak) a little Spanish. Let's ask him to help with hurricane victims that only speak Spanish.
3. Mary Rae ___is working___ (work) for Citizens Care in New Orleans, so I don't think she can come to the party.
4. She ___reports___ (report) for work about 7:30 every morning.
5. Volunteers ___are cleaning___ (clean) the big mess left by the flooding. Please go help them.

6. Mary Rae ___is doing/does___ (do) her best, but she still can't carry as many supplies as other stronger volunteers.
7. I ___am trying___ (try) to understand you, but you will have to speak more slowly.
8. Scientists ___are discovering___ (discover) that many severe floods are caused by human developments of coastal areas.
9. The frequency of hurricanes ___is getting/gets___ (get) worse every year.
10. Repairing hurricane destruction ___gets___ (get) easier when you have a lot of people helping.

EXERCISE 2

Write the correct form of the verb in parentheses (simple present or present progressive).

Ralph (1) ___isn't taking___ (not take) a vacation this summer, because he (2) ___thinks___ (think) that he (3) ___has___ (have) other more important things to do. He (4) ___teaches/is teaching___ (teach) computer skills to high school students, so he (5) ___gets___ (get) three months of vacation, but he (6) ___feels___ (feel) that teachers (7) ___have___ (have) a special responsibility. So he (8) ___is looking___ (look) for a temporary volunteer position for the period of his summer break. He (9) ___is trying___ (try) to find work as a computer programmer. But most relief agencies only (10) ___hire___ (hire) workers on a long-term basis. Ralph (11) ___is finding___ (find) that it is difficult to locate short-term volunteer positions. He (12) ___is getting___ (get) excited about the prospects of making a real difference in the lives of other people. No matter how hard he (13) ___searches___ (search), he (14) ___is beginning___ (begin) to realize that most programs are looking for long-term volunteers and he may have to take a vacation, whether he (15) ___wants___ (want) one or not.

EXERCISE 3

Describe your typical day starting from the time you wake up and ending with going to sleep at night. Write at least eight sentences about things you do on a regular basis. Now describe three things that you are currently doing differently than the way you normally do them, and why you may have changed your routine.

Example: *I'm living in a dormitory because I have moved to a new city to go to school.*

ANSWER KEY

Exercise 3 *Answers will vary. Possible answers are:* *I wake up at 7:00. I have breakfast and read the paper. I take a shower and get dressed. I drive to work. It usually takes about an hour. I usually exercise during my lunch hour, and I leave the office around 4:30 or 5:00. I watch the TV news when I get home, then I make myself dinner. I usually go to bed around 10:30 or 11:00 and read for a while before I fall asleep. I'm not eating breakfast these days, because I'm trying to lose weight. I'm not driving to work because my car is being repaired. I'm not exercising at lunch because my co-workers are workaholics and schedule meetings for every available moment of the day.*

LESSON PLAN 1

FOCUS 1 [15 minutes]

Focus 1 presents examples of the uses for the simple present in contrast with the present progressive. See Focus 3 in Unit 2 (SB page 17) for a quick review of the uses of the progressive aspect in general. Because students will most likely be familiar with this information, you can present this focus chart inductively at first by having the class explain the choice of verb forms for sentences.

1. **Lead-in:** Keep books closed to begin. On an overhead transparency or on the board, write a few examples that contrast a variety of uses of the simple present with the present progressive. For example:

Usually, I drive to work.

This week I'm taking the bus because my car is being repaired.

Water boils at about 200 degrees Fahrenheit.
The water on the stove is boiling.

This pineapple weighs three pounds.
She is weighing all the pineapples to see which one is the largest.

2. Put students into pairs and have them try and come up with a reason that explains why the simple present is used in some sentences whereas the present progressive is used in others.

3. Invite pairs to present their own "rules." You may want them to write the rules on the board.

4. Open books and turn to Focus 1 on SB page 220. Go over the examples in the chart. See how the "rules" the class came up with compare to the explanations in the focus chart. Did anything get left out?

Suggestion: Have pairs create their own example sentence for each explanation in the focus chart.

EXERCISE 1 [15 minutes]

Students will look at the context and then choose between simple and progressive verbs to place in the sentences.

1. Have students work individually and then check their work in pairs. Inform students that there may be more than one possible answer for some sentences.

2. Ask the pairs to refer back to the chart in Focus 1 to explain their choices to each other.

3. Go over the answers and explanations as a class.

For more practice, use *Grammar Dimensions 3* Workbook page 80, Exercise 1.

EXERCISE 2 [15 minutes]

This exercise is very similar to Exercise 1. However, it is a bit more difficult because students will need to understand the paragraph before they can make choices about the verb forms. Follow the steps given for Exercise 1. Again, be sure to inform students that some sentences may have more than one possible answer.

GRAMMAR NOTE

The first sentence in this exercise, *Ralph is not taking a vacation this summer*, can refer to the present or the future. Students may notice that the present progressive is sometimes used to refer to plans for the future. This is covered in the information on future time in Unit 15.

EXPANSION [10 minutes/homework]

Give more practice by assigning a writing topic that asks students to use the present progressive along with the simple present. This is modeled on the paragraph in Exercise 2.

1. Ask students to talk to a partner or small group about their current goals and the steps they are taking to attain these goals. They may be goals related to school, work, finances, projects, or personal improvement. You can model this by talking about a goal of your own (or a friend's) and the steps you are taking to achieve it. It could be a goal to get into better shape, finish your home improvements, etc.

2. Have students write an essay or paragraph describing their current goal(s) and the steps they are taking to attain it.

3. Collect papers and give individual feedback.

EXERCISE 3 [15 minutes]

This exercise asks students to use the verb forms to compare activities in their own lives.

1. Model this exercise by describing your typical day and contrasting that with a few current changes to your usual routine.

2. Encourage the class to think about any changes they have had to their usual routines.

3. Ask the class to begin the exercise by making a list of their usual activities using the simple present and any new activities using the present progressive. Circulate and assist as needed.

4. Put students into pairs or small groups and ask them to share.

5. Invite volunteers to tell the class about what they learned from their partners about their normal routines and any current changes to it.

Suggestion: This can be developed into a paragraph for homework.

FOCUS 2 | Nondynamic (Stative) Verbs

meaning

EXAMPLES

(a) I know that you are unhappy right now.

(b) NOT: I am knowing that you are unhappy right now.

EXPLANATION

Nondynamic or stative verbs do not take progressive forms when they describe conditions or states.

Common Nondynamic Verbs

SENSORY PERCEPTION	KNOWLEDGE & BELIEF	FEELING & ATTITUDE	LOGICAL RELATIONSHIP	
see	*agree/disagree with*	*love*	**Cause and Effect**	**Measurement**
hear	*believe*	*like*	*results in*	*weigh*
feel	*doubt*	*hate*	*requires*	*cost*
appear	*feel (believe)*	*dislike*	*depends on*	*measure*
look	*imagine*	*appreciate*	*means*	*equal*
seem	*intend*	*prefer*	**Possession**	**Inclusion**
smell	*know*	*want*	*belong to*	*contain*
sound	*recognize*	*need*	*possess*	*consist of*
taste	*realize*	*mind*	*have*	*include*
resemble	*remember*		*own*	
look like	*suppose*		*owe*	
	think (believe)			
	understand			
	consider			

EXERCISE 4

Work with a partner and ask W*h*-questions for the cues given. Your partner should give true answers, and then ask the same questions of you.

Example: which parent/resemble most
Which parent do you resemble most?
I resemble my mother more than my father.

1. what kind of fruit/taste best

2. what way/think/most effective to learn a foreign language

3. how/a sick person/appear

4. what/your MP3 player/contain

5. what/a handshake/mean

6. what activity/your family appreciate/your doing

7. what/learning another language/require

8. how many _____/you/own

9. who/that _____/belong to

10. what/not understand/American culture

EXERCISE 5

Report your partner's answers from Exercise 4 to the rest of the class.

Example: *Yoshiko resembles her mother more than her father.*

1. _____

2. _____

3. _____

4. _____

5. _____

6. _____

7. _____

8. _____

9. _____

10. _____

Exercise 4 Answers will vary. Possible answers are: 1. What kind of fruit tastes best with ice cream? Fruits that aren't too sweet taste best with ice cream. 2. What way do you think is most effective to learn a foreign language? The most effective way to learn a foreign language is to use it whenever possible. 3. How does a sick person often appear? He or she might appear flushed or feverish. Sometimes he or she might just appear tired. 4. What does your MP3 player contain? It contains all the music I like. 5. What does a handshake mean in your culture? It means that two people have reached an agreement about something. It's like an unwritten contract. 6. What activity do your parents appreciate your doing? They appreciate my studying hard. 7. What does learning another language require? It usually requires a lot of hard work. 8. How many neckties do you own? I only own five, but that's because I don't wear a coat and tie to work. 9. Who does that Mercedes belong to? I know it doesn't belong to our grammar teacher. She's too poor to own such a car. 10. What don't you understand about American culture? I don't understand how people become close friends in this country.

Exercise 5 Answers will vary. See previous exercise for possible answers.

FOCUS 2 [15 minutes]

Focus 2 is an explanation and list of some common stative (nondynamic) verbs. These can be difficult to remember, so the list is divided into groups. Students should be encouraged to refer back to this list as they continue working through the unit.

1. **Lead-in:** Because students may already have a feel for some of these verbs, you can introduce this focus chart inductively with books closed. On the board, write a few incorrect examples using stative verbs with the progressive. Be sure to note that these sentences are wrong.

   I'm having a new car.
   This suitcase is weighing too much.
   We are thinking that movie was terrible.
   It's smelling bad in here.
   That one is costing too much.
   She is knowing all the answers.

2. Invite volunteers to come up to the board and correct the errors (put them into the simple present tense).

3. Go over their corrections and then go over the explanation for Focus 2 on SB page 222. Review the groups of stative verbs and note the category headings that tie them together. Answer any questions students have about the meaning of any new vocabulary.

Suggestion: If you have time, extra practice with these verbs can be given by asking the class to write their own sentences with verbs from each group. Make it fun by getting the class to brainstorm a number of nouns such as people, places, and things. Write them across the board as they call them out (silly ones can be fun). Have the class use these in their sentences.

EXERCISE 4 [15 minutes]

Students will create *wh-* questions using a variety of stative verbs.

1. After looking over the example, have students work individually first to write questions using each set of cues.

2. Put students into pairs to check and compare their questions. Questions 8 and 9 will differ.

3. Have pairs ask and answer their questions. Be sure that they write the answers down. They will need them in Exercise 5.

Suggestion: If you have time, pairs can work together to create more questions by choosing verbs from the lists in Focus 2. Split the pairs and have them interview someone else.

For more practice, use *Grammar Dimensions 3* Workbook page 80, Exercise 2.

EXERCISE 5 [15 minutes]

Students will take their answers from Exercise 4 and write them in third person in order to present their results to the class.

1. Go over the example sentence as a class.

2. Circulate as students work to put their information into a similar format.

3. Give students the opportunity to present information to the class or in small groups.

Suggestion: Have the class or small groups make general statements about the most common answers. This can require a variety of stative verbs.

For more practice, use *Grammar Dimensions 3* Workbook page 81, Exercise 3.

meaning

FOCUS 3

Verbs with Both Nondynamic and Action Meanings

Some nondynamic verbs can also be used to describe actions.

VERB	NONDYNAMIC MEANING	ACTION MEANING
have	(a) Mary Rae **has** an important job in New York. (possess)	(b) She's **having** a great time in New Orleans. (experiencing)
mind	(c) She **doesn't mind** hard work. (object to)	(d) She's **minding** some lost children this afternoon. (taking care of)
see	(e) I **see** your point. (understand)	(f) Peter is **seeing** a specialist about his back. (consulting)
think	(g) I **think** you're right. (opinion)	(h) Be quiet! I'm **thinking**. (mental activity)
consider	(i) I **consider** money to be the cause of many problems. (opinion)	(j) I'm **considering** going to Hawaii for vacation. (mental activity)
depends on	(k) Athletic ability **depends on** strength and practice. (requires)	(l) I'm **depending on** you to help me move next week. (relying upon)
be	(m) She **is** a teacher. (identity)	(n) Those children are **being** very noisy. (behaving)
feel	(o) She **feels** that it's important to help the victims of the disaster. (believe)	(p) She's **feeling** a little sick today. (experiencing)

Other nondynamic verbs can indicate the **act of perception** or **measurement**, or the perceptions or measurements themselves.

VERB	PERCEPTION/MEASUREMENT (NONDYNAMIC MEANING)	ACT OF PERCEPTION/MEASUREMENT (ACTION MEANING)
smell	(q) The flowers **smell** wonderful.	(r) The dog is **smelling** the clothes of the missing boy.
taste	(s) That cake **tastes** delicious.	(t) Our host is **tasting** the soup to make sure it's not too salty.
feel	(u) My arm **feels** broken!	(v) The doctor is **feeling** my arm to see if it is broken.
weigh	(w) Joe **weighs** almost 100 kilos.	(x) The butcher is **weighing** that piece of meat.

EXERCISE 6

Decide whether the verbs indicated express an action meaning or a nonprogressive meaning and write the simple present or present progressive tense in the blanks. In some cases both answers may be correct.

1. This cloth ___feels___ (feel) really nice.

2. I ___am considering___ (consider) applying to Citizens Care.

3. Why did you ask that question? You ___are being/are___ (be) really rude!

4. I ___believe___ (believe) that Mary Rae ___is having___ (have) a good experience at the Citizens Care program.

5. I don't like this coffee. It ___tastes___ (taste) bitter to me.

6. I like people who ___mind___ (mind) their own business and don't try to tell others what to do.

7. Mary Rae ___doubts___ (doubt) that she will be able to return to New York right away.

8. It ___looks/is looking___ (look) as if the frequency of hurricanes is growing greater every year.

9. Mary Rae ___feels/is feeling___ (feel) a little guilty about leaving work for so long. But I'm sure they support her efforts to help the disaster victims.

10. Cleaning up after a hurricane ___requires___ (require) a lot of hard work.

11. These days the government ___is requiring/requires___ (require) people to take drug tests in order to get a government job.

12. The government ___is being/is___ (be) so slow! I wish someone would make them speed up the rescue operations.

LESSON PLAN 2

FOCUS 3 [20 minutes]

After practicing the nondynamic/stative verbs from Focus 2, students will see that some of them have an action meaning in some situations.

1. **Lead-in:** Begin by putting a pair of sentences on the board to illustrate both the nondynamic and the action meanings of a stative verb. You can use a pair from the charts in Focus 3 or some of your own. For example:

She thinks that sushi is disgusting. (opinion)

What are you thinking about? (mental activity)

He feels that this is a good school. (opinion/belief)

He is feeling sleepy today. (experiencing a feeling)

2. After explaining that some stative verbs have an action meaning too, have the class go over the examples in Focus 3.

3. Go over the second set of verbs, which shows verbs of perception or measurement.

Suggestion: Assign a verb or two to each pair of students and have them make their own pairs of sentences to show the differences in meaning. You can have students share their sentence pairs by passing around a piece of paper and asking each pair to print one pair of sentences neatly on the paper. After the paper has passed throughout the whole class, you should be able to make photocopies to pass around at the next class. Use these handouts to help draw attention to the special meanings of these verbs.

EXERCISE 6 [15 minutes]

Based on the context of each sentence, students will decide whether an action or nondynamic meaning is needed for the verb indicated.

1. Have students work individually to complete the exercise.

2. Put students into pairs and ask them to explain their reasons for the verb forms they chose. Remind them that in some cases both answers may be correct.

3. Go over as a class again asking volunteers to explain their choices. See answers on LP page 224.

4. Spend some time talking about the differences in meaning in those sentences that can take both.

For more practice, use *Grammar Dimensions 3* Workbook page 82, Exercise 4.

FOCUS 4

Uses of the Present Time Frame

use

EXAMPLES

EXPLANATIONS

(a) Supply **affects** demand in several ways. If supply **exceeds** demand, the cost of the commodity generally **decreases**. When cost **increases**, demand often **drops.** Decreased demand eventually **results** in decreased supply.

Use present time frame:
- to state general truths and relationships in scientific and technical **writing**

(b) Here's how we **make** cookies. First we **mix** a cup of flour and two eggs together in a bowl. Next, we **mix** in some sugar. A cup-and-a-half **is** probably enough, but if we **want** sweeter cookies, we **add** at least 3 cups of sugar.

- to describe actions as they are performed in live demonstrations

(c) Shimazu **throws** the ball. Martinez **hits** it. He **passes** first base. He's **making** a run to second base. He's **out**!

- for reporting in radio and television broadcasts such as sporting events

(d) One day I'm **walking** down the street. I **see** this guy talking on a pay phone. I **know** he's mad about something because I **can hear** him screaming all the way down the block. So, anyway, when I **get** next to the pay phone, he **stops** shouting and **asks** me if I have an extra quarter. I **tell** him, "Sorry, man," and all of a sudden . . .

- to tell stories orally in informal situations

EXERCISE 7

Here are reports of two scientific experiments. Change them into present time so that they are statements of general scientific principles, rather than accounts of specific experiments.

Example: *When baking soda is added to vinegar, a chemical reaction occurs.*

Experiment 1

(1) When baking soda was added to vinegar, a chemical reaction occurred. (2) The baking soda bubbled and CO_2 was produced by the combination of elements. (3) When a candle was put next to the container while the chemical reaction was taking place, the flame on the candle went out.

Experiment 2

(1) We wanted to determine whether gravity affected the rate of acceleration of objects falling through space. (2) Two objects of similar size and shape, but substantially different weights—a cannonball and a volleyball—were dropped from the same height. (3) We found that both objects hit the ground at the same time. (4) This indicated that the attraction of gravity was constant.

EXERCISE 8

Tell this story aloud, as if you were Mary Rae describing her own experience. Tell it in present time to make it more vivid and less formal. The first two sentences have been done as examples.

Example: *There I am, standing in dirty swamp water as deep as my waist, but I'm having a wonderful time! The boat we're rowing has gotten stuck on a log, so somebody has to get into the water and try to lift one end of it.*

There I was, standing in dirty swamp water as deep as my waist, but I was having a wonderful time! The boat we were rowing had gotten stuck on a log, so somebody had to get into the water and try to lift one end of it. I looked into the water. It looked really dark and dirty. I knew there were a lot of poisonous snakes in this area. I knew there were also toxic chemicals and horrible germs. All of a sudden, I realized that I wasn't afraid of any of these things. I had complete confidence in my ability to free the boat and to avoid getting some horrible infection. Without another thought, I jumped into the water and started to pull at the boat. At that moment I knew that there was nothing that I was afraid to do, and nothing that I couldn't do if I put my mind to it.

Exercise 7   Experiment 1: (1) When baking soda is added to vinegar, a chemical reaction occurs. (2) The baking soda bubbles and CO_2 is produced by the combination of elements. (3) When a candle is put next to the container while the chemical reaction is taking place, the flame on the candle goes out.   **Experiment 2:** (1) We want to determine whether gravity affects the rate of acceleration of objects falling through space. (2) Two objects of similar size and shape, but substantially different weights—a cannonball and a volleyball—are dropped from the same height. (3) We find that both objects hit the ground at the same time. (4) This indicates that the attraction of gravity is constant.

Exercise 8   I look into the water. It looks really dark and dirty. I know there are a lot of poisonous snakes in this area. I know there are also toxic chemicals and horrible germs. All of a sudden, I realize that I'm not afraid of any of these things. I have complete confidence in my ability to free the boat and to avoid getting some horrible infection. Without another thought, I jump into the water and start to pull at the boat. At that moment I know that there is nothing that I'm afraid to do, and nothing that I can't do if I put my mind to it.

LESSON PLAN 2

FOCUS 4 [20 minutes]

Focus 4 presents a variety of uses for the present tense (both simple and progressive). These uses range from the more formal statements of truth used in scientific and technical writing to a very informal oral storytelling style.

1. **Lead-in:** If possible, bring in a short factual reading about some topic of general interest (animals, nature, solar system, culture, etc.). This reading should be written in the present tense (*penguins walk for days to . . . /the Bedouin people of Egypt use camels for . . .*). Have a race to see who can find and circle all the present tense verbs first.

2. Discuss why this kind of information is written in the present tense. Ask the class what else they might find written in present tense.

3. Go over the examples in Focus 4. Have volunteers read the examples out loud. (Sports fans might add a little excitement to their reading of the baseball broadcast.)

4. Ask the class what words make example (d) seem so much more informal than the example you handed out or example (a). (*this guy, so, anyway, sorry, man*)

EXERCISE 7 [15 minutes]

Students will rewrite notes from two experiments using the present tense. This will create a general statement of fact.

1. Begin by asking the class for some general statements of scientific fact. Give an example or two (water boils at 100 degrees Celsius, etc.).

2. Go over the first sentence in Experiment 1 and the example. Have students work individually to put the two experiments into the present tense.

3. When finished, put students into pairs or small groups. After comparing their new versions of the experiment, ask them to discuss how this has changed the accounts (rather than representing one event in time, these now say that these

results are facts and will happen every time the experiment is done). See answers on LP page 226.

EXPANSION [25 minutes]

Add some science to your class by letting small groups do their own simple experiments and write up the notes from them. You can find many sites online for simple experiments with things found around the house. Here is one example:

1. What you need: paper plates, small amount of whole or 2% milk, food coloring, liquid soap, cotton swabs.

2. For each group cover the bottom of a paper plate with a shallow layer of milk.

3. Add a drop of each color of food coloring near the center of the plate (not touching each other though).

4. Touch the center of the plate with the cotton swab. What happens?

5. Now dip the cotton swab in liquid soap and coat it well. Touch it to the center of the plate again and keep it there. What happens? (The soap will cause the milk and food coloring to mix and move together, creating swirls of colors in the milk. This may continue for quite a while.)

6. Record your experiment and describe what happened. Use present tense.

Note: The actual scientific answer is that the bonds that hold the fat molecules in the milk together are separated and sent swirling by the reaction to the soap breaking these bonds.

EXERCISE 8 [15 minutes]

Students will change the story written in the simple past to the present tense. This will create an informal story to be told orally in small groups.

1. Have the class first rewrite the story making all the necessary changes (this can simply be done in their books if you don't have time for them to rewrite the whole story).

2. Put students into small groups or pairs and let them take turns giving dramatic readings of this story as if it has happened to them personally. Have students compete to see who can be the most dramatic storyteller.

VARIATION

If you have access to a lab or recording equipment, get students to record their stories. You can have students listen to each other and decide who is the most dramatic. Let students work on their pronunciation if they have the time to rerecord their stories in the lab.

For more practice, use *Grammar Dimensions 3* Workbook page 82, Exercise 5.

EXPANSION [20 minutes]

Let students tell their own dramatic stories and share them with the class. Encourage the class to think of a good story (it doesn't have to be true) and share it with the class. This is a great way to practice the use of the present tense in informal storytelling while sharing some very interesting stories. Keep in mind that this particular use of the present tense is generally only for oral storytelling and is not usually encouraged in written work.

UNIT GOAL REVIEW [10 minutes]

Ask students to look at the goals on the opening page of the unit again. Refer to the pages of the unit where information on each goal can be found.

ExamView For assessment of Unit 13, Test Generator use *Grammar Dimensions 3 ExamView*.

Use Your English

ACTIVITY 1 speaking

Give the class a demonstration of how to do something. This could be how to prepare a favorite food, how to perform some physical activity, or how to make some simple object. While you are demonstrating the activity, tell how it is done.

ACTIVITY 2 speaking

"How much does that cost?" "How much do you weigh?" "How old are you?" "How much money do you earn?" Most Americans think that these are rude questions to ask anyone who is not a very close friend. In other cultures, people don't consider these to be rude questions but they might hesitate to ask other kinds of questions, such as "How many daughters do you have?" "What do you do—what kind of job do you have?" or even "What kind of house do you live in?" Form a group and talk about what are considered to be rude questions in other cultures that you are familiar with. Make sure you use present time frame to discuss these ideas, since you are discussing general truths about different cultures. Present your findings to the rest of the class. Make a list of potentially rude questions in North American culture that you may want to avoid.

ACTIVITY 3 writing/speaking

We all learn our basic cultural values when we are very young. A first step in learning about different cultures is learning to identify some of these basic cultural values.

STEP 1

Write down at least five things your parents told you that were general truths when you were growing up. Make sure that these things are not orders or requests (such as: *My parents told me to clean my room*), but rather statements about things that are always true (*Big boys don't cry. Good manners are important.*)

STEP 2

Compare your list to the lists of several other students. Are any of the statements the same on all your lists? Are there any interesting similarities or differences based on different cultures? What does this tell you about the values your parents tried to teach you? Report your ideas to rest of the class.

ACTIVITY 4 listening

CD Track 19

STEP 1

Listen to Professor Freemarket's lecture for his Introduction to Economics class, and take notes. You may want to listen to the lecture a second time to make sure you understand the information he describes.

STEP 2

Use your notes to answer the questions that he asked the class on his weekly quiz.

STEP 3

Compare your answers to another student's to check the accuracy of your information and the grammatical correctness of what you wrote.

ECONOMICS 101—DR. FREEMARKET WEEKLY QUIZ #5 (25 POINTS POSSIBLE)
1.   (10 points) Define the Law of Supply and Demand.
2.   (10 points) How does transportation affect the Law of Supply and Demand?
3.   (5 points) What other forces affect the Law of Supply and Demand?

ACTIVITY 5 research on the web

Enter one of these words into the keyword search of *InfoTrac® College Edition*: *tsunami, earthquake, hurricane*. Scan the first twenty listings to determine information about the following: What is the most recent disaster of this sort? Where did it happen? Where do these kinds of disasters typically occur? What kind of relief efforts are being made to help the victims?

ACTIVITY 6 reflection

Listen to English speakers in conversation with one another and try to notice when they are using present progressive. List three examples of something you heard where the speaker is using present progressive. Decide why he or she chose to use present progressive instead of simple present. Compare your examples with those of another student, and report any interesting similarities or differences to the rest of the class.

ANSWER KEY

Activity 4 Answers will, of course, vary. One possible response would be: 1. According to classical economic theory, the law of supply and demand says that increase in demand raises prices, and increase in supply lowers prices. In classical economics this law is considered to be **the** major driving force in a free market economy.   2. Transportation has a fundamental impact on the law of supply and demand. Transportation means that the available supply of something can be moved around the country, and not just kept in one place. If there is too much in one area, the surplus can be sent someplace else. If there isn't enough, the supply can be increased from other places.   3. advertising, government regulations, and monopolies.

USE YOUR ENGLISH

The Use Your English activities at the end of the unit contain situations that should naturally elicit the structures covered in the unit. For a more complete discussion of how to use the Use Your English activities see To the Teacher on LP page xxii. While students are doing these activities in class, you can circulate and listen to see if they are using the structures accurately. Errors can be corrected after the activity has finished.

ACTIVITY 1 speaking [30 minutes]

1. Model a demonstration of a simple task such as making a peanut butter and jelly sandwich. Talk the class through the steps.

2. Number the steps you just completed on the board and ask for volunteers to recall what a person should do for each step.

Suggestion: For review, students can write up a paragraph describing the steps you demonstrated.

ACTIVITY 2 speaking [20 minutes]

1. Go over the directions. Point out that the questions in the text are examples of rude questions in North America.

2. Put students into groups of mixed cultures if possible. The groups will develop two lists: one list of rude questions in their own or other cultures, and one list of rude questions in North America.

3. Focus on the differences between the lists and have groups discuss this.

ACTIVITY 3 writing/speaking [20 minutes/homework]

You may want to assign Step 1 as homework the night before.

■ **STEP 1** Go over the directions for Step 1 with the class. You may need to give a few more examples.

■ **STEP 2** When students have their lists ready, put the class into small groups (mixed cultures and genders, if possible). Have them compare their lists and discuss the questions in Step 2.

ACTIVITY 4 listening [15 minutes]

CD Track 19

1. You may want to explain to the class that many introductory lectures or presentations are given using the present tense. This is because the information is usually given as a general truth. These ideas are the basic truths for this topic.

2. Ask the class what they already know about the topic of economics and have them go over the questions in the quiz. Can they answer any of them already?

■ **STEP 1**

1. Go over Professor Freemarket's quiz on SB page 229.
2. Play the audio and encourage the class to take notes as they listen.
3. Play the audio again.

■ **STEP 2** Give students time to write complete answers to the questions in the quiz.

■ **STEP 3**

1. Have students compare answers with a partner and discuss any differences or variations.

2. You can play the audio a third time and let the pairs work together to develop the best answers to the quiz questions.

3. When students are ready, review the answers as a class. See possible answers on LP page 228.

ACTIVITY 5 research on the web [30 minutes/homework]

1. Go over the directions and the information that students are asked to collect.

2. Decide whether you would like this to be reported orally or in writing. Give guidelines as to the length and format of the report.

Suggestion: In order to avoid too much repetition in oral reports, you may want to divide the class up into groups with different general topics for natural disasters: (1) tsunamis, (2) earthquakes, (3) hurricanes, (4) tornadoes, (5) floods, (6) wildfires, and (7) extreme weather (snowstorms, etc.).

Note: You may want to be sensitive to the possibility that there may be students in your class who have experienced a natural disaster personally, such as an earthquake or tsunami.

ACTIVITY 6 reflection [15 minutes/homework]

1. Tell the class that their reflection for this unit will require them to be language researchers. They will need to seek out and listen to English speakers. This can be done in the cafeteria, at work, or even just by watching TV.

2. They will need to list three examples they overheard of the use of present tense and then evaluate the reasons for using the present tense in these situations.

3. Have students bring their research to class and compare in small groups.

4. Let the groups share interesting findings with the class.

PRESENT PERFECT

Describing Past Events in Relation to the Present

UNIT GOALS

- Use the present perfect to understand and express past actions that are related to the present moment by time

- Use the present perfect to understand and express past actions that are related to the present moment by logical relationship or present result

- Understand and express meaning differences with present perfect progressive instead of present perfect tense

OPENING TASK

Identifying What Makes You Special

When American students apply to colleges and universities, they often have to write a personal essay about their individual character and achievements and explain what makes them different from the other people who are also applying to the school. Fill out the sample admissions application on the next page, and write a personal essay that identifies some of your characteristics, experiences, and achievements that might be of interest to a university admissions committee.

■ STEP 1

To get you started, here are the ideas that Aliona Fernandez used for her successful application to the North American Institute of International Studies. (Her personal essay has been reprinted in Exercise 1 on page 233.) For your essay identify at least one special characteristic, one experience that helped you develop that characteristic, and one achievement that this characteristic has enabled you to do.

	ALIONA FERNANDEZ	YOU
Characteristic	flexibility	
Experience	living overseas as a Peace Corps volunteer	
Achievement	she speaks other languages and understands different cultures	

■ STEP 2

Show your application and essay to another student and compare each of your special characteristics, experiences, and achievements. Decide whose essay would be most effective to use for a university application. Tell your opinion and your reasons to the rest of the class.

North American Institute of International Studies

Application for Admission

Applying for: _____ SPRING _____ SUMMER _____ FALL _____ WINTER 20 _____

Degree Objective: _____ Undergraduate _____ Graduate

_____ Major _____ Minor

Personal Data: Name _____

Address _____

Telephone _____ Birthdate _____

Sex _____ Ethnic Background _____

Educational Background:

List all secondary and postsecondary schools attended, including language programs.

Name and location of school   Dates of attendance   Degree granted   GPA

_____

_____

Personal Essay / Writing Sample:

All applicants must provide a writing sample. On another sheet of paper, write at least 200 words on the following topic. It must be handwritten, and written only by the applicant.

What are some characteristics that make you different from other people you know? How have your experiences in life shaped you as a person? What are some achievements that you have accomplished that you feel particularly proud of?

Signature _____ Date _____

All applications must be accompanied by official transcripts in English, proof of finances, and a nonrefundable $60 application fee.

LESSON PLAN 1

PRESENT PERFECT

UNIT OVERVIEW

Unit 14 reviews the meanings, uses, and differences between the present perfect, the simple past, and the present perfect progressive to describe events in the past and in relation to the present.

GRAMMAR NOTE

The present perfect expresses an event that happened in the past and yet is still relevant to the present (*I have lived here for 10 years, and I enjoy the neighborhood*). The present perfect progressive also expresses an event that happened in the past and is relevant to the present (*I have been living here for 10 years, but I hope to move soon*). However, the use of the progressive shows that it is still happening and it is considered to be temporary. In contrast, the simple past expresses an event that happened in the past and is completed (*I lived there for 10 years, and I was excited to move*).

UNIT GOALS

Some instructors may want to review the goals listed on Student Book (SB) page 230 after completing the Opening Task so that students understand what they should know by the end of the unit. These goals can also be reviewed at the end of the unit when students are more familiar with the grammar terminology.

OPENING TASK [30 minutes]

The aim of this activity is to give students the opportunity to use the present perfect as they write about events in the past with a relationship to the present. The problem-solving format is designed to show the teacher how well the students can produce a target structure implicitly and spontaneously when they are engaged in a communicative task. For a more complete discussion of the purpose of the Opening Task, see To the Teacher, Lesson Planner (LP) page xxii.

Setting Up the Task

1. You may want to have your class begin by assigning the essay on SB page 233 to read the night before. This will help them to understand the Opening Task and identify their own characteristics and life experiences.

2. To help students identify special characteristics they have, you may want to get the class brainstorming some admirable characteristics and put them on the board (*responsible, reliable, flexible, hard-working*, etc.). They can then take the next step and consider what life experiences they've had that have given or proven these characteristics. After that, they will need to identify what this characteristic has helped them to achieve.

Conducting the Task

STEP 1

You can either assign Step 1 and Step 2 as homework (for diagnostic purposes) or complete only Step 1 in class and move on to Focus 1. The essay will then be assigned as homework and due after going over the information in the first few focus charts.

VARIATION

If the "academic" format of the essay is not appropriate for your class, you may want to turn this into an application for a scholarship. These can be required by companies for advanced job training programs or by technical schools and community colleges.

STEP 2

Have students share Step 1 charts or essays with each other and give feedback based on the goals of the essay (job training, university entrance, scholarship, etc.).

Closing the Task

Invite volunteers to share some of their experiences and write them on the board in complete sentences. These are likely to require the simple past or present perfect tense. Keep these on the board for use in Focus 1.

EXPANSION [30 minutes]

Assign Activity 5 (research on the web) on SB page 243. This activity asks students to research and share advice on how best to write a personal essay like the one you will assign in this Opening Task. Students can then revise their essays from the Opening Task.

GRAMMAR NOTE

Typical student errors

- Confusing the use of the simple past and the present perfect: ** I have lived in Cairo when I was young. * I knew her since we were young.* (See Focus 1.)
- Using stative verbs with the present perfect progressive: ** I have been knowing about the changes for quite a while.* (See Focus 5.)
- Using the simple past rather than past participle to form the present perfect: ** We have knew each other for six years. * She has saw that movie before.*

FOCUS 1

Choosing Past Time Frame or Present Time Frame

use

We can use both past time frame and present time frame to talk about things that happened in the past.

PAST TIME FRAME	PRESENT TIME FRAME
Use past time frame (in the form of the simple past tense) to show that a **past event** has no direct, ongoing relationship to the **present.** The event was fully completed in the past or happened at a specific time in the past.	Use a present time frame (in the form of present perfect tense) to show that a **past event** is directly related to the **present.** The event happened in the past, but continues to influence the present in some way.
(a) I **lived** in Honduras as a very young child, but I **don't remember** much about it now.	(b) I **have lived** in four foreign countries, and as a result I am very aware of how cultural differences affect how we perceive reality.
(c) I **started** to fill out the application for the university, but I **didn't finish** it, because I realized I wouldn't be able to afford the tuition.	(d) I **haven't finished** the application for the university yet. I'm still working on the personal essay.

EXERCISE 1

Read the following personal essay written by a successful applicant to the North American Institute of International Studies. Underline the verb phrases and identify the tenses that are used. Then discuss these questions with a partner.

- Why did the author use present time in the first paragraph?
- Why did the author use past time in the second paragraph?
- Why did the author use present time in the third paragraph?

Personal Essay
by Aliona Fernandez

(1) One of the characteristics that makes me different from many people is my adaptability. (2) I am flexible and comfortable in new or unusual situations. (3) I think this is because I have had a lot of experience living in foreign countries. (4) This has given me a lot of opportunities to face unfamiliar situations and to learn about unfamiliar customs and beliefs.

(5) My first experience in a foreign country was as a Peace Corps volunteer. (6) I taught English in a small town in a rural area. (7) Life in my town was very simple. (8) Because there was no electricity and rather little contact with the outside world, my life was a lot like living in an earlier century.

(9) I have been to other countries since that first experience, and everywhere that I have traveled has been interesting and educational. (10) As a result of my experiences in other countries, I speak other languages and understand other cultures. (11) I have learned that relationships between people are very much the same, whether they have modern, busy lives, or old-fashioned, more peaceful lives. (12) I have learned to understand different ways of doing things and different ways of looking at the world. (13) Most of all, I have learned that "new" doesn't necessarily mean "better." (14) My experiences have made me adaptable, and this adaptability has allowed me to understand other people and cultures.

ANSWER KEY

Exercise 1 present; present (2) present (3) present; present present (4) present; present perfect
(5) past (6) past (7) past (8) past; past (9) present perfect; present perfect; present; present
perfect (10) present; present (11) present perfect; present perfect; present perfect
(12) present perfect (13) present perfect; present; present (14) present perfect; present
perfect

The author is talking about characteristics that she has now and where they came from.
She is referring to a time that ended in the past.
She is describing how she is today as a result of her previous experiences.

FOCUS 1 [10 minutes]

Focus 1 shows the differences between using the simple past or the present perfect tenses to talk about events in the past.

1. **Lead-in:** Put the following sentences on the board for the class to compare. What differences are there? Why?

   Josef worked in his father's restaurant last summer. (finished)

   Josef has worked in his father's restaurant every summer. (he may do it again next summer too)

   Mari taught Japanese. (She's finished now)

   Mari has taught Japanese. (She hopes to find a similar job soon.)

2. Discuss any sentences on the board from the Opening Task if they also use the simple past or the present perfect tenses. What are the differences between them? What does the simple past show? How is that different from the present perfect?

3. Go over the information in Focus 1 noting the differences between these two tenses.

VARIATION

For a more inductive approach, have the class do Exercise 1 first and then go back and review Focus 1.

EXERCISE 1 [15 minutes]

This exercise asks students to identify verb phrases and the tenses used. They will then discuss why they think the author chose different tenses for each paragraph.

1. This exercise can be done in pairs. They should consider the general reason for each paragraph. What is the topic for each paragraph and how does that relate to the verb tense?

2. Go over these ideas as a class. See answers on LP page 232.

Suggestion: If students will be working on their own essays for the Opening Task outside of class, encourage them to use this essay as a template and try to model their organization and use of tenses in a similar manner.

For more practice, use *Grammar Dimensions 3* Workbook page 83, Exercise 1.

Relationship to the Present: Still True (Present Perfect Tense) Versus No Longer True (Past Tense)

use

Past events relate to the present if they are still true at this time.

EXAMPLES	EXPLANATIONS
(a) I have lived in three foreign countries. I have learned how to adapt to the local culture.	**Present Perfect Tense:** Use the present perfect tense to show that something is still true now.
(b) I lived in Honduras for three years. I ate pupusas every day for lunch.	**Past Tense:** Use the past tense to talk about something that is no longer true now.

EXERCISE 2

Choose past tense or present perfect tense for the verbs in parentheses. More than one answer may be correct, so be prepared to explain why you chose the form you did. The first one has been done for you.

Bambang Soetomo (1) _came_ (come) to the United States last January to get a degree in mechanical engineering. Since he (2) _has been_ (be) in the United States, he (3) _has had_ (have) many new experiences. At home in Jakarta, servants (4) _cooked_ (cook) all his food. But here in the United States, Bambang (5) _has had_ (have) to prepare food for himself. In Indonesia, a lot of his university classes (6) _required_ (require) the ability to memorize large amounts of information. But here, Bambang (7) _has found_ (find) that memorization is not considered to be a very important skill in many of his classes. Of course, he (8) _was_ (be) ready for obvious differences in things like food and social customs, but he (9) _has not adjusted_ (not/adjust) to the subtle differences. He (10) _has learned_ (learn) that knowing about differences and dealing with them are two different things. In fact, he (11) _has been_ (be) rather homesick. In Jakarta he (12) _had_ (have) a large group of friends, but here in the States he (13) _has met_ (meet) only a few other Indonesian students, and none of them are in his department. When he (14) _was_ (be) planning his trip to America, he (15) _planned_ (plan) to go home for a vacation after his sophomore year, but he (16) _has changed_ (change) his mind since he (17) _got/has gotten_ (get) here. He (18) _has spoken/spoke_ (speak) with his father about the possibility of coming home during his first summer vacation. His father (19) _hasn't decided_ (not decide) whether that's a good idea or not.

Relationship to the Present: Until Now

use

Present perfect is used to describe things that began in the past but continue up to the present moment.

EXAMPLES	EXPLANATIONS
(a) I have visited Paris over a dozen times.	Use present perfect to describe: • the number of times something has happened
(b) I've eaten snake meat once, but I'll never do it again!	
(c) Your teacher has just left her office. Maybe you can catch her if you hurry to the parking lot.	• very recent events with *just*
(d) We've just been talking about your application. Can we ask you a few questions?	
(e) I've known Aliona since we were in high school.	Use present perfect in sentences: • with *ever, never,* or *since*
(f) I've never eaten snake meat. Have you ever tried it?	

EXERCISE 3

Work with a partner. Take turns asking each other these questions. Ask at least ten questions. You can use the suggested topics or make up questions of your own.

1. Have you ever . . . (ridden a horse, been in love, seen a flying saucer . . .)
2. How many times have you . . . (eaten Chinese food, taken the TOEFL® Test*, driven a motorcycle . . .)
3. Name three things you have never done, but would like to do.
4. Name three things you have done that you don't want to do again.

Then tell the rest of the class about your partner. The class should decide who has asked the most interesting or unusual questions.

*TOEFL is a registered trademark of the Educational Testing Service (ETS). This publication is not endorsed or approved by ETS.

ANSWER KEY

Exercise 3 Answers will vary. Possible answers are: 1. Yes, I have./ No, I haven't. 2. I've done it many times./ I've only done it once or twice./ I've done it, but I didn't inhale. 3. I've never been to Seychelles, but I'd like to go./ I've never become a movie star, but I'd like to./ I've never fallen in love, but I would like to. 4. I've served on a jury./ I've been in love with someone who didn't love me./ I've written a grammar book.

My partner has had an interesting life. She has visited seven foreign countries. She has flown an airplane. She hasn't been in a submarine, and she doesn't know how to swim. She hasn't begun her university study, but she is anxious to do so. She has taken the TOEFL® several times and wishes that she didn't have to take it again.

LESSON PLAN 1

PRESENT PERFECT

FOCUS 2 [10 minutes]

Focus 2 shows that the difference between simple past and present perfect is whether the event or action is still true now. *Simple past = no longer true. Present perfect = still true.*

1. **Lead-in:** Put several examples on the board to show the subtle distinction between these tenses. Ask pairs to discuss what they think the differences are. Some examples may lead to discussion as to their meaning. Here are a few examples (don't write the information in parentheses on the board):

I didn't finish that book.	(and I'm not planning to finish)
I haven't finished that book.	(but I'm still hoping to finish)
I worked all day!	(and I'm done now)
I've worked all day!	(and it's not over yet)
I lived in Seattle for two years.	(I don't live there now)
I've lived in Seattle for two years.	(I still live in Seattle)

2. Invite pairs to share their thoughts on the different meanings for each pair of sentences. What have they found is the general difference between the simple past and the present perfect?

3. Go over the explanations and examples in Focus 2 with the class.

EXERCISE 2 [15 minutes]

Exercise 2 can be used as a diagnostic before looking at Focus 2. Have students work individually and then go over answers as a class or in pairs. See answers on LP page 234.

For more practice, use *Grammar Dimensions 3* Workbook page 83, Exercise 2.

FOCUS 3 [10 minutes]

This focus concentrates only on the uses of the present perfect tense.

1. **Lead-in:** You can introduce this focus chart by simply putting a few questions on the board for students to answer that will encourage them to use the present perfect. (How many times have you visited Canada? What is something that you've never eaten? How long have you lived here?)

2. Go over the examples in Focus 3. If you have time, ask the class to write examples similar to those in the chart.

Suggestion: Review the irregular past participles in Appendix 6 on pages A10–11.

EXPANSION [20 minutes]

Give students more practice using the present perfect by describing activities that have just recently happened.

1. Bring in pictures of people or events from magazines or newspaper articles.

2. Let students choose a photo.

3. Ask the class to create stories for their photos. The stories should tell what happened just before the photo was taken.

4. Have students share their photos and stories in small groups. Circulate and listen for examples of present perfect. Put a few on the board to share with the class.

5. Invite volunteers to share stories with the class.

EXERCISE 3 [20 minutes]

1. Model the formation of the first two questions by asking students about things they have done (*Have you ever . . . ? How many times have you . . . ?*)

2. Have students work individually or in pairs to prepare their lists of questions before they begin the interviews. Circulate and assist as needed.

3. Put students into pairs (or with a new partner) and have them interview each other. If students take short notes during the interview, have them put their answers into complete sentences when they are finished for more practice.

4. Bring the class together and let students share interesting information about their partners. See possible answers on LP page 234.

EXPANSION [20 minutes]

The mixer called Find Someone Who . . . is a great game to practice the present perfect.

1. Based on your class, make up a handout with about 10–20 statements like the example below:

   Find Someone Who . . .

   has never eaten sushi. _____

   has tried to surf. _____

2. Give a copy to each student and tell them that they will be going around the room asking classmates questions until they find someone who matches a statement. Before they begin, students will first need to practice forming a question for each statement (*Have you ever eaten sushi?*) and then go around asking classmates these questions until they find a match (*No, I've never eaten sushi.*).

3. When they find a match, they will write that person's name down and then try to find a different classmate to match a different question.

4. Debrief by having students share what they found out about their classmates.

Suggestion: For even more conversational practice, have students ask follow-up questions once they find a match. For example, *When did you try surfing? Did you like it?*

EXERCISE 4

Choose past tense or present perfect tense for the verbs in parentheses. More than one answer may be possible. The first sentence has been done for you as an example.

My friend Bob is a very happy man. He *has* just (1) *found out* (find out) that he (2) *has received/received* (receive) a full scholarship to North American Institute of International Studies. He (3) *has applied* (apply) to several graduate programs in the last few years, but he never (4) *has gotten/got* (get) any scholarship offers until six months ago, when he (5) *was offered* (be offered) a partial scholarship to North Dakota State. Since then, apparently, the suggestions I gave him about improving his personal essay (6) *have changed* (change) his chances. He (7) *has gotten* (get) two other offers from his second- and third-choice schools. Most of the scholarship offers (8) *have been/were* (be) small until last week, when he (9) *got* (get) the letter from NAIIS offering him free tuition plus room and board. I wonder if he (10) *has thought about* (think about) doing something nice for the person who helped him with his essay.

FOCUS 4

Relationship to the Present: Present Result (Present Perfect Tense)

use

Another common way that past events relate to the present is if the past event continues to affect the present situation in some way. Use present perfect tense to describe past events that cause a result in the present.

The present result can be stated directly.

PAST ACTION	STATED PRESENT RESULT
(a) I have already seen that movie,	so I suggest we go see a different one.
(b) He has been wasting so much money	that I don't think we should give him any more.
(c) I have always felt that teachers were underpaid,	so I think we should suggest that our teacher ought to get a raise.

The present result can be implied.

PAST ACTION	IMPLIED PRESENT RESULT
(d) You have spilled juice all over my new tablecloth!	The tablecloth is dirty.
(e) John has obviously forgotten about our meeting.	He is not at the meeting.

The present result can also be the speaker's/writer's attitude.

NOT CONNECTED TO THE PRESENT (PAST TENSE)	CONNECTED TO THE PRESENT (PRESENT PERFECT TENSE)	EXPLANATIONS
(f) Did you find the article you were looking for?	(g) **Have you found the article you were looking for? Because if not, I think I know where you can find it.**	The event is connected to the present in the speaker's mind.
(h) The White House released new figures yesterday concerning the economy.	(i) **The White House has released new figures on the economy in the last quarter. These figures show that imports continue to exceed exports by more than 20%.**	Reporters often introduce news stories with the present perfect tense to emphasize the connection with the present.
(j) The historian Toynbee often observed that history repeats itself.	(k) **The historian Toynbee has observed that history repeats itself, and I believe that he is correct.**	A writer may mention a past event that has a connection to a point she or he is about to make.

EXERCISE 5

Choose the sentence that reflects the most logical continuation of the ideas expressed in the first sentence, based on the tense used in the first sentence. Both sentences are formed correctly.

1. I have told you that I don't like the color green.
   a. My brother didn't like that color either.
   ⓑ So why did you buy me a sweater in that color?

LESSON PLAN 1/LESSON PLAN 2

EXERCISE 4 [15 minutes]

Exercise 4 gives more practice with simple past versus present perfect.

1. Have students work individually and then compare answers with a partner or in small groups.

2. Encourage students to explain their reasons to their group for choosing simple past versus present perfect. Groups should work together to try to find some agreement on the correct answers. (Note that more than one answer may be possible.) See answers on LP page 236.

Suggestion: Copy the exercise onto an overhead transparency to make the review easier.

For more practice, use *Grammar Dimensions 3* Workbook page 84, Exercise 3.

(don't put the information in parentheses on the board):

She hasn't called him. (he's still waiting for the call)

The plane hasn't arrived. (it's late, but we're still waiting for it)

I've taken six classes at this college. (I may take more)

The teacher has assigned two essays this term. (I hope she doesn't assign any more)

2. Go over the examples in the focus charts and note that some connections are stated, some implied, and some show an attitude.

3. If you have time, give the class a chance to make their own examples based on those in the focus charts.

EXERCISE 5 [15 minutes]

This exercise can be a challenge for students because both choices are grammatically correct. It is continued on SB page 238.

1. Help by having students note the time frame for the first sentence and then choose the second sentence with a similar time frame.

2. When finished, have students discuss and compare answers with a partner before going over the exercise with the class. See answers on LP pages 236 and 238.

For more practice, use *Grammar Dimensions 3* Workbook page 84, Exercise 4.

LESSON PLAN 2

FOCUS 4 [20 minutes]

Focus 4 gives other examples of how the present perfect can be used to show the present result of a past action. The result can be stated, implied, or simply an attitude expressed by the use of the present perfect instead of the simple past tense. The subtle differences in meaning expressed with the present perfect can be difficult for students to see at first. Exercises 5 and 6 give more practice analyzing these differences.

1. **Lead-in:** You can begin by putting on the board a few sentences that imply a connection to the present. Then ask the class what they think the connection to the present might be. How would the meaning change if the sentences were written in the simple past? Some examples might be

FOCUS 5

Present Perfect Progressive Tense

use

EXAMPLES	EXPLANATIONS
(a) **I have been living** with my parents, but I hope to move out once I am accepted to your university. **(temporary)**	Use the present perfect progressive tense (*have/has been* + verb + *-ing*) instead of present perfect to describe something that is: • temporary rather than permanent
(b) **I have lived** with my parents since they became ill and needed me to help around the house. **(permanent)**	
(c) **I have been talking** to everyone about what to put in my essay, but I don't have a good plan yet. Do you have any ideas? **(repeated occurrence)**	• repeated rather than a single occurrence
(d) **I have thought** about the essay, and I have a good idea of what to write. **(single occurrence)**	
(e) **I have been working** constantly on my application for the last three hours. I don't know when I'll finish! **(continuous)**	• continuous rather than repeated or recurring
(f) **I have tried** several times to work on my application, but I keep getting interrupted. **(repeated)**	
(g) **I have been writing** my personal statement. I still have to proofread it and staple it together. **(uncompleted)**	• uncompleted rather than completed
(h) **I have written** my personal statement. Let's go celebrate! **(completed)**	
(i) Living in foreign countries **has required** a lot of flexibility.	Remember that nonprogressive verbs do not occur with the progressive aspect even when they refer to continuous states.
(j) NOT: Living in foreign countries **has been requiring** a lot of flexibility.	

2. Jeff met Matt at a party.
   a. They soon became the best of friends.
   b. They share an apartment in San Francisco.

3. Bambang Soetomo arrived in America about eight months ago.
   ⓐ He has been adjusting to American life ever since.
   b. He is living by himself in an apartment.

4. I have been trying to get in touch with my math professor since last week.
   a. I didn't do well on the last exam.
   ⓑ Whenever I go to her office, she isn't there.

5. I don't think that Denise likes Peter very much.
   ⓐ Have you ever noticed that she avoids looking at him when she speaks?
   b. Did she say anything about her feelings to you at the meeting last week?

EXERCISE 6

Discuss these questions about the short passages below with a partner and compare your ideas with those of other students.

• Why do you think the speaker chose to use the present perfect tense instead of simple past tense in these sentences?

• How is the past action related to the present: by time relationship, by present result, or by a combination of both?

1. Scientists have discovered a number of interesting similarities between the atmosphere on Earth and on Titan, one of the moons of Jupiter. They have found significant concentrations of water vapor and other chemicals common on Earth. As a result, they are hoping to send another space probe to Titan later this year.

2. If I have told you once, I've told you a hundred times: I hate broccoli!

3. Guess what? We've been invited to Liz's wedding. What should we get her for a gift?

4. Conservative politicians have often stated that welfare payments to poor families do not help reduce long-term poverty, but recent statistics show that this may not be true.

5. Shakespeare's reputation as a psychologist has grown in recent years. His plays have always reflected a deep understanding of human motivations.

6. Has Jill found a summer job? I was talking with my aunt, and she said her office might need a temporary computer programmer.

ANSWER KEY

Exercise 6 Possible explanations are: 1. There is a logical relationship to the present. The passage connects past discoveries with the current fact that scientists are planning another space probe in the future.   2. There is an implied logical relationship. This suggests that the speaker has just been offered broccoli.   3. There is a chronological relationship with this moment. The listener is now hearing the news for the first time.   4. Like the first passage, previous information is relevant to the current situation.   5. This seems to be connected with the present in the writer's mind. Perhaps the writer is going to make a new point about Shakespeare's understanding of psychology.   6. This is connected with the present in the speaker's mind. She has a job possibility for Jill at this moment.

LESSON PLAN 2

EXERCISE 6 [15 minutes]

This exercise asks students to think about and question the choices made to use the present perfect rather than the simple past. Students will see that a choice of tense and aspect (present perfect versus simple past) can carry quite a bit of meaning by relating a past event to the present.

1. Because students are asked to discuss the choices made in the passages, you may want to go over the first passage with the class.

2. Put key words for the two questions for discussion on the board to keep the discussion on track.

3. You can either have pairs continue working on the rest of the passages, or continue with the whole class discussion. See possible answers on LP page 238.

FOCUS 5 [20 minutes]

Focus 5 gives examples of the uses for the present perfect progressive tense. You may want to refer quickly back to Focus 3 in Unit 2 (SB page 17) for a review of the general meanings of the progressive aspect to show the contrast with the present perfect.

1. **Lead-in:** For a quick review, with books closed, ask the class if they can remember what the uses are for the progressive aspect (*temporary, repeated, continuous, and uncompleted*).

2. Go through the pairs of examples in Focus 5 that show the difference between the use of the present perfect and the present perfect progressive.

Suggestion: If you have time, have students make their own examples to show the differences. Assign one pair of examples—such as (a) and (b)—to a pair of students and have them work together to create their own examples.

Use Your English

EXERCISE 7

Choose the correct form, present perfect or present perfect progressive, for the verbs. More than one answer may be possible.

1. I (a) _____ (read) about the development of early forms of photography, and I (b) _____ (learn) some very interesting facts about it. I would like to continue my research next semester.

2. That baby _____ (cry) constantly since we got here. I wish its parents would do something to make it be quiet!

3. Bob's brother _____ (resent) his getting that full scholarship ever since he heard the news.

4. I _____ (try) to explain that for ten minutes. Aren't you listening?

5. I _____ (try) to explain that every way I know how. I give up!

6. I _____ (work) on this problem all afternoon. It's time for a break.

7. Aliona _____ (expect) the admissions committee to call about her application. That's why she wants to stay home this afternoon.

8. Bob _____ (tell) the committee that he doesn't want to accept the scholarship unless it includes room and board.

9. The college (a) _____ (try) to contact Bob about his scholarship. They (b) _____ (call) at least five or six times.

10. Bob (a) _____ (dream) going to NIIS ever since he read an article about their graduate program in public health. He (b) _____ (become) an expert on it.

EXERCISE 8

Decide whether the verbs in parentheses should use simple present, present progressive, present perfect, present perfect progressive, or the past tense. Write the correct verb form in the blanks. More than one answer may be correct.

Bambang Soetomo (1) _____ (speak) English quite fluently. I wonder where he (2) _____ (learn) it. He (3) _____ (study) mechanical engineering. He (4) _____ (plan) to go to graduate school once he (5) _____ (get) his B.S. degree. Bambang (6) _____ (think) about (live) by himself for the last few months. But he (7) _____ (miss) his friends back home a great getting a roommate. He (8) _____ (miss) his friends back home a great deal, and this (9) _____ (affect) his studies. He (10) _____ (hope) that his father will let him come home during the summer, but his father (11) _____ (nor decide) yet.

ACTIVITY 1 speaking

Find out what important changes your classmates have made in their lives.

STEP 1 Interview three classmates. Ask them the following:

- Have you changed any habits or routines recently?
- What kind of changes did you make?
- Why have you made the changes?
- How have the changes affected you?

STEP 2 Based on the changes your group has experienced, decide together whether you agree that changes in life are generally for the better. Present your group's ideas and reasons to the rest of the class.

ACTIVITY 2 speaking/listening

Experts in cross-cultural communication have found that North American culture tends to value individualism. As a result, many young children are taught to look for ways that they are different from other people. Most Americans can easily identify several personal experiences and characteristics that make them unique. What about people from other cultures?

STEP 1 Interview three or four people from various cultures and ask them these questions:

- What experiences have you had that most other people haven't?
- What things make you different from most other people?

STEP 2 Of the people you interviewed, who was able to think of the greatest number of individual differences?

ANSWER KEY

Exercise 7 1. (a) have been reading; (b) have learned 2. has been crying 3. has resented 4. have been trying 5. have tried 6. have been working/have worked 7. has been expecting 8. has told 9. (a) has been trying; (b) have called 10. (a) has dreamed/has been dreaming; (b) has become

Exercise 8 (1) speaks; (2) learned/has learned; (3) studying/studies; (4) is planning/plans; (5) gets; (6) has been living; (7) is thinking; (8) misses/is missing; (9) is affecting/has affected/has been affecting; (10) is hoping/hopes; (11) hasn't decided

LESSON PLAN 2/USE YOUR ENGLISH

EXERCISE 7 [15 minutes]

Use this exercise as a review for the information presented in Focus 5. Have pairs or small groups compare and discuss their answers. Remind students that more than one answer may be possible and go over these as a class. See answers on LP page 240.

For more practice, use *Grammar Dimensions 3* Workbook page 85, Exercise 5.

EXERCISE 8 [15 minutes]

Use this as a review for the ideas presented in this unit. Let pairs or small groups discuss their choices. Remind students that more than one answer may be possible and go over these as a class. See answers on LP page 240.

For more practice, use *Grammar Dimensions 3* Workbook page 85, Exercise 6.

UNIT GOAL REVIEW [10 minutes]

Ask students to look at the goals on the opening page of the unit again. Refer to the pages of the unit where information on each goal can be found.

ExamView®
Test Generator

For assessment of Unit 14, use *Grammar Dimensions 3 ExamView®*.

USE YOUR ENGLISH

The Use Your English activities at the end of the unit contain situations that should naturally elicit the structures covered in the unit. For a more

complete discussion of how to use the Use Your English activities see To the Teacher on LP page xxii. While students are doing these activities in class, you can circulate and listen to see if they are using the structures accurately. Errors can be corrected after the activity has finished.

ACTIVITY 1 speaking [15 minutes]

Students should use the present perfect and the simple past to discuss any changes they've made in their regular routines.

You may want to begin by describing a routine that you have changed lately. Put a few examples on the board if you can.

STEP 1

1. Put students into groups and have them discuss the questions in Step 1.
2. Have one student act as secretary for each group.

STEP 2

1. Ask the groups to look at their lists of changes and discuss Step 2.
2. Give the groups time to share their findings with the class.

Suggestion: Have the groups read off their lists of changes to the class. Has anyone else made the same changes?

EXPANSION [20 minutes/homework]

Students can turn the questions in Step 1 into an out of class interview for homework. Students may want to add or change a few questions (*Have you made any changes in your life lately?*) Ask them to look over

their completed interviews and find a way to summarize their findings in order to present them to the class or in small groups.

ACTIVITY 2 speaking/listening [15 minutes]

This activity assumes a multicultural classroom. However, if you do not have access to people various cultures, the exercise will still be an interesting survey of how people see themselves to be different. They can interview classmates or native English speakers out of class.

STEP 1

1. Students can work in pairs, in groups, move around the class, or use this as an out of class interview activity.
2. You may want to have students create an interview sheet which also has space for information such as age (*Age range: 15–25, 26–35, 36+*) and cultural backgrounds (*Where did you grow up?*) This will help students as they think about the question in Step 2.

STEP 2

1. As students prepare to answer Step 2, have them consider the differences in age or culture. Did older people or younger people list more differences?
2. Let students share with the class or in small groups.

INTERVIEW QUESTIONS	CANDIDATE 1 NAME: _____ PROGRAM: _____	CANDIDATE 2 NAME: _____ PROGRAM: _____
What makes you different from other candidates?		
What relevant experience do you have?		
What is an achievement that you're proud of?		

■ **STEP 3**

You and your partner should decide which student is a better candidate for admission. Tell your choice and your reasons to the rest of the class.

ACTIVITY 5 research on the web

■ **STEP 1**

Use an Internet search engine such as Google® or Yahoo® and enter the term "personal essay". You should find listed a number of Web sites of universities and other institutions that provide advice and guidance on writing personal essays for college applications. Visit at least three of these sites and summarize at least five pieces of advice that they provide to prospective applicants. Present that advice to the rest of the class.

■ **STEP 2**

Use the advice you find to revise the personal essay you wrote for the Opening Task of this unit. What changes did you make?

ACTIVITY 6 reflection

Bring in the front page of a daily newspaper and examine the articles with a partner or in a group. Find examples of sentences written in present time and past time. In what tense are headlines usually written? In what tense are the introductory paragraphs usually written? In what tense is the main part of the article generally written? Can you find a pattern? Why do you think the reporter chose one time frame rather than another? Discuss your ideas with your partner or group, and then present them to the rest of the class.

ACTIVITY 3 speaking

How do North Americans, as a group, compare to the students you interviewed for Activities 1 and 2?

■ **STEP 1**

Work with three different students than those you interviewed in Activity 1. Two of you should interview three or four North Americans, asking the questions that you used for Activity 1. The second pair should ask the questions you used for Activity 2.

■ **STEP 2**

Compare the responses of the North Americans to the responses of the students you interviewed in those activities.

■ **STEP 3**

Discuss these questions with your group and summarize your ideas for the rest of the class.

- Were there differences between the answers given by North Americans and those of your classmates?
- Were North Americans able to identify their individual differences more readily than people from other cultures?
- Did North Americans feel differently about change than people from other cultures?
- What do the similarities and differences between the answers of various cultural groups tell you about cultural differences?

ACTIVITY 4 listening/speaking

Which of these two people is most qualified to be accepted for admission to the North American Institute of International Studies?

CD Tracks 20, 21

■ **STEP 1**

Listen to the interviews with each candidate. Using the chart on the next page, identify what the candidates say about their most important accomplishment, their background and experience, and their special abilities.

■ **STEP 2**

Compare your chart with another student's, and listen to the interviews a second time to make sure you have heard all the important information.

ANSWER KEY

Activity 4 Candidate 1 Name: Aliona Fernandez; Program: Masters Program in Teaching English and a Foreign Language

What makes you different? more actual teaching experience overseas than some of the others

What relevant experience? been in the Peace Corps and worked in Taiwan and Japan

An achievement that you're proud of? speaks three languages/lived in other cultures/written a grammar book

Candidate 2 Name: John Teallhome; Program: International Business

What makes you different? just returned from spending a year studying in Paris

What relevant experience? worked in a bookstore in college

An achievement that you're proud of? high school class president/captain of the football team/received a scholarship to study in France

USE YOUR ENGLISH

ACTIVITY 3 speaking
[20 minutes/homework]

Because this activity assumes that your class is multicultural and that you live in North America, it may not be appropriate for all classes. If your students were not able to interview various cultural groups in Activity 1 and 2, then you may either need to modify this activity or skip it.

1. Review the questions the class used for interviews in Activities 1 and 2.

2. Explain that half the class will now go out and interview North Americans using the questions from Activity 1 and the other half will interview North Americans using Activity 2 questions.

■ **STEP 1** Divide the class in half (group 1 and group 2) and ask half of the class to use the questions from Activity 1 and the other half to use the questions from Activity 2 to go out and interview three or four North Americans as homework. Students should also bring these new interviews plus their previously completed interviews from Activity 1 and 2 to the next class.

■ **STEP 2** When students have completed their interviews, have them take a minute to compare their new interviews with the previous interviews they did in Activities 1 and 2.

■ **STEP 3** Put two group 1 and two group 2 students into one new group of four students. Have them work together to discuss the questions in Step 3.

Suggestion: You can put the questions from Step 3 on the board and let the groups come up and write up their answers as they finish their discussion.

ACTIVITY 4 listening/speaking
[15 minutes]

CD Tracks 20,21

Students will fill information in as they listen to interviewees talk about their achievements and past experiences using the present perfect and simple past.

Have students go over the chart on SB page 243 before listening to the audio. They should be comfortable with the topic of past experiences and accomplishments by now.

■ **STEP 1** Play the audio and have students complete as much of the chart as they can. Circulate and decide whether you feel they may need to listen again before comparing with a partner.

■ **STEP 2** Play the audio again and encourage pairs to make any changes before moving onto Step 3.

■ **STEP 3** Put the two candidate's names on the board and have the class vote for the best candidate. Invite volunteers to supply reasons for their choices and list them on the board. See answers on LP page 242.

ACTIVITY 5 research on the web
[30 minutes]

This is useful to assign before or as students begin writing their own personal essays from the Opening Task on SB pages 230–231. Students will practice locating pertinent information on the internet, scanning and making decisions on the usefulness of the information, and then reading and summarizing a variety of advice.

Review the personal essay on SB page 233. If your class has not yet finished writing their own personal essays (see the Opening Task), this research activity can get them started off on the right track.

■ **STEP 1**

1. After reviewing any guidelines you may have set up for Internet research, have the class complete Step 1. Depending on your goals for the class, you may want to ask that they not simply copy lists of helpful hints, but instead do their own summarizing from sites with longer text.

2. Have the class come together to present their pieces of advice.

■ **STEP 2** Narrow the key points down and have students keep these in mind as they write or revise their personal essays.

Suggestion: Copy the advice gathered by the class onto a handout for everyone.

ACTIVITY 6 reflection
[20 minutes]

Students will examine newspaper articles. They will look for patterns in the use of tenses.

1. Assign students to bring in their own front pages or bring in several Sunday papers yourself and hand out the front pages of different sections to groups of students.

2. You may want to divide up the questions in Activity 6 and have students begin by looking at the tenses of the headlines, introductory paragraphs, and main part. Then discuss the nature of headlines and how to expand them into their original longer versions.

3. Finally, have students discuss the remaining questions together: Can you find a pattern? Why do you think the reporter chose one time frame rather than another?

4. Have groups share their findings with the class.

15

FUTURE TIME

Using Present Tenses, Using *Will* Versus *Be Going To* Versus *Shall*; Adverbial Clauses in Future

UNIT GOALS

- Understand and use different verb tenses to express actions and states in future time

- Correctly use *will, be going to,* and *shall* and other modals to express future time

- Correctly express future time in adverbial clauses

OPENING TASK

Thinking About the Future

■ STEP 1

"Futurists" are people whose job it is to make predictions about the future and look at the way current trends might have unforeseen impacts in the future. They make "projections" of how things might be different in the future, based on things that are happening now. Based on some of the trends listed below, make a projection of how you think life will be different in a hundred years. Write a short paragraph answering the following questions: Do you think that life one hundred years from now will be better or worse than it is today? Why? Consider some of the current trends and issues listed below, and decide how they will affect the lives of people living one hundred years from now.

Positive Trends	Negative Trends
Technological improvements	Environmental problems (pollution, acid rain,
New medical treatments	global warming, decreasing natural resources)
Longer life spans	Population increase
Better food crops	New diseases
Growth of democratic governments	The growth of terrorism
Better communication	Increased traffic
More rapid transportation	Increasing government debt
Equal status for women	Changing family structures
More education	Increasing economic gap between the rich and
	poor

■ STEP 2

Exchange paragraphs with a partner, and decide which one of you is more of an optimist (someone who generally expects good things to happen) and which one is more of a pessimist (someone who generally expects bad things to happen) about the future of the world.

■ STEP 3

Report your decision and some of the reasons to the rest of the class.

Unit 15 — LESSON PLAN 1

UNIT OVERVIEW

Unit 15 reviews ways to express the future time frame. This unit shows how future time can be represented in a variety of ways including the use of the simple present tense, the present progressive, and modals. The use of adverbial clauses with future time is also covered.

GRAMMAR NOTE

In general, most students have not explicitly been taught the use of forms other than *will* or *be going to* to express the future. Using simple present and present progressive may initially be confusing for some. Students will often ask about the differences between *will* versus *be going to*. Because the difference between these two is rather small, in many cases the speaker/writer can show the degree of their own certainty by choosing to use one over the other.

The modals of prediction, like any modals, can cause problems for students from some language backgrounds due to the wide range of meanings and uses in English. See Unit 5 for more on this.

The future can also be expressed with *be + about to* and the quite formal *be + to*. These two examples are not covered in this unit, but they may arise in your class as students seek out written or oral examples of the future in the world around them.

UNIT GOALS

Some instructors may want to review the goals listed on Student Book (SB) page 244 after completing the Opening Task so that students understand what they should know by the end of the unit. These goals can also be reviewed at the end of the unit when students are more familiar with the grammar terminology.

OPENING TASK [30 minutes]

The aim of this activity is to give students the opportunity to use a future time frame as they are writing about events in the future. The problem-solving format is designed to show the teacher how well the students can produce a target structure implicitly and spontaneously when they are engaged in a communicative task. For a more complete discussion of the purpose of the Opening Task, see To the Teacher, Lesson Planner (LP) page xxii.

Setting Up the Task

Begin with books closed by writing the word *Futurists* on the board. Ask the class what they think a Futurist might be. Help by telling them this is a job. Put the following questions on the board: *How will life be different in 100 years? Will it be better or worse than it is today? Why?*

Conducting the Task

STEP 1

1. Have students read the information in Step 1 and briefly go over ideas with the class of what a Futurist might do.
2. Put students into small groups to discuss the questions on the board and add their own more specific ideas.
3. Circulate and note how students are choosing to express ideas in a future time frame. Which tenses or modals are they using? Use this information to guide how much time you will spend on the focus charts throughout the unit.
4. Assign the writing of the paragraph for Step 1 as homework or have students work on their paragraphs in class.

STEP 2

1. Put students into pairs and have them exchange paragraphs.
2. Students need to determine whether their partner is an *optimist* or a *pessimist*.

Closing the Task

STEP 3

1. Finish the Opening Task by inviting volunteers to come up and write a few of their own predictions on the board. Save these for use in Focus 1.
2. Have a show of hands for the pessimists and the optimists in the class!

Suggestion: Share the expressions "the glass is half full" and "the glass is half empty."

EXPANSION 1 [30 minutes]

Have students complete Activity 6 (research on the web) on SB page 255 to research further information about what Futurists are predicting.

EXPANSION 2 [30 minutes]

Use Activity 5 (speaking) on SB page 255 as a follow-up once your class has decided who the pessimists and the optimists in your class are.

GRAMMAR NOTE

Typical student errors (use)

- Using *be going to* for spur of the moment decisions or promises: Teacher: *Who can clean the board?* Student: * *I'm going to do it.* (See Focus 2.)
- Using *will* for the immediate future: *Look at those clouds!* * *It will rain any minute!* (See Focus 3.)
- The awkward use of shall or shan't: * *He shall arrive late.* * *He shan't be early.* (See Focus 4.)

Typical student errors (form)

- Using future time with adverbial clauses: * *When the pizza will arrive, we can eat.* (See Focus 6.)
- Using infinitives after a modal: * *I will to see him soon.*

FOCUS 1   Recognizing Future Time

We can use simple present, present progressive, and modals to talk about future time.

EXAMPLES

(a) The meeting **begins** at 10:00 every day.

(b) The conference on global warming **begins** in three weeks.

(c) The futurists **are having** problems with their study, so they are postponing their report.

(d) They're **presenting** their report next month.

(e) There's a package at the door. It **should** be their report.

(f) When they have finished analyzing the results, they **will present** their recommendations.

EXPLANATIONS

Simple present can describe present time.

It can also describe future time

Present progressive can describe present time.

It can also describe future time.

Modals can describe present time.

They can also describe future time.

EXERCISE 1

Do the verbs in these passages refer to future time or present time? Underline the verb phrases. Mark verb phrases that refer to future time with F. Mark verb phrases that refer to present time with P. The first sentence of each passage has been done for you as examples.

P

1. (a) School always <u>begins</u> in September in the United States. (b) This coming year, school begins on September 12. (c) Janet's <u>going</u> to start her third year of high school. (d) She's <u>taking</u> chemistry, history, English, and advanced algebra. (e) She <u>might take</u> a theater class, if she <u>can fit</u> it into her schedule.

F

2. (a) We're <u>having</u> a class picnic in just a couple of weeks. (b) As you know, school <u>ends</u> on June 15, and the picnic <u>will be</u> on the next day, so we're <u>already making</u> plans. (c) Most people <u>are being</u> really cooperative. (d) For example, Lucia <u>makes</u> great potato salad, so she's <u>bringing</u> some to the picnic. (e) There <u>should be</u> enough for everyone to have some. (f) But George <u>is being</u> difficult. (g) He <u>says</u> he <u>will come</u>, but he won't <u>bring</u> anything. (h) <u>Will</u> you <u>explain</u> something to me? (i) <u>Will</u> you <u>tell</u> me why George <u>is</u> so stubborn? (j) He really <u>should be</u> more cooperative. (k) Everyone else <u>is bringing</u> something. (i) Why <u>won't</u> he?

FOCUS 2   Present Tenses for Future Planned Events

EXAMPLES

(a) The conference **starts** on a Sunday next month.

(b) The futurist **is presenting** his findings next week.

(c) Next year **is** the fifth annual conference on global warming.

(d) **We will examine** the data if they can get it to us in time for the conference.

(e) There **might** be a surprising announcement.

EXPLANATIONS

Use simple present and present progressive tenses to describe future activities that are **already scheduled or planned** to take place in the future.

For future events that are **not already scheduled**, use *will* or other modals of prediction (*may, could, might*).

EXERCISE 2

Make at least five questions about things that will happen in this class at a future time and have already been scheduled. Ask your questions to another student.

Example: *When are we having our next grammar test?*

EXERCISE 3

Choose the best tense (present, present progressive, or a modal of prediction) for the verbs in the following sentences. Both forms may be grammatically correct, so be prepared to explain your choice.

Example: John *'s leaving* _____ (leave) for France in a week.

1. The bus _____ (leave) at 6:00 A.M. Don't be late.

2. Filipe _____ (have) a party on Friday. Have you been invited?

3. John doesn't know when he _____ (return) from France.

4. Peter is hoping that Denise _____ (stop) demanding that everyone work so hard.

5. Our teacher's birthday _____ (be) Friday, so we'd better buy her a gift.

6. Perhaps there _____ (be) a test next Friday.

7. There definitely _____ (be) a test next Friday.

8. I _____ (graduate) next June.

ANSWER KEY

Exercise 2 Answers will vary. Possible answers are: What time do classes start next Tuesday? When are we having our next grammar test? When does the semester end? Which unit do we study next? When do we have to make our speeches? When is the next grammar test?

Exercise 3 1. leaves/is leaving   2. is having   3. will return   4. stops/will stop   5. is   6. is/will be   7. is/will be   8. graduate/am graduating/will graduate

FOCUS 1 [10 minutes]

Focus 1 gives examples of how the simple present, the present progressive, and modals can be used not only to show present time, but also to show future time. These examples will be explained further and expanded on throughout the unit.

1. **Lead-in:** Have the class look at the predictions students put on the board from the Opening Task. Invite volunteers to explain what grammar we use when we talk about the future. You may get a variety of answers, but most classes will say that *will* and *going to* show the future. You can agree with this and ask if they can think of any other ways to show the future.

2. Draw the class' attention to Focus 1 and invite volunteers to read from this as you go over the chart. Note that each pair of sentences will show one expression of the present time and one expression of the future time.

Suggestion: If you have time, write the following on the board and ask the class (or pairs) to create their own examples for each: *Simple Past, Present Progressive, Modals.*

GRAMMAR NOTE

Students may ask why *be going to* is not listed in these examples for expressing the future. Remind students that this is a kind of modal (a phrasal modal or periphrastic modal) as discussed in Unit 5 (see Focus 2, SB page 69).

EXERCISE 1 [15 minutes]

Exercise 1 asks students to identify the time expressed in each verb phrase. This will give practice identifying the different uses of the simple present, present progressive, and modals from the context.

1. If students are comfortable with the information in Focus 1 and you are short on time, assign half the class to do each paragraph.

2. Students should work individually and then compare in small groups. See answers on LP page 246.

Suggestion 1: Copy the exercise onto an overhead transparency for whole class review/discussion.

Suggestion 2: Write the letters (a–i) on the board and let various students come up and write the verb phrases and times (*P* or *F*) for each.

For more practice, use *Grammar Dimensions 3* Workbook page 86, Exercise 1.

FOCUS 2 [10 minutes]

Focus 2 explains that the simple present and the present progressive show a planned event in the future, whereas the modals of prediction are used to show unscheduled events in the future. This is a key distinction between these future forms and can be difficult for students to recognize at first. Explain that it can be a writer's/speaker's choice in many cases and both can possibly be correct grammatically.

1. **Lead-in:** Contrast scheduled versus unscheduled events to the class with examples of your own on the board. For example:

   The movie starts at 8 P.M.

   The movie will start when everyone is seated.

   My writing class begins next Monday.

   The new ESL program will begin sometime in the fall.

2. Invite volunteers to suggest the differences between these pairs. You can put the words *scheduled* or *planned* on the board.

3. Go over the focus chart with the class and highlight the differences in these examples again. Remind the class that in many situations the difference is not about correct grammar, but it is

about choosing to express a sense of prior scheduling or planned intention.

EXERCISE 2 [15 minutes]

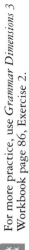

Students will practice using the simple present or present progressive in sentences that imply a planned or scheduled event.

1. It may help to put students into pairs and have them work together to create their questions.

2. Match students up with new partners as they ask their questions. See possible questions on LP page 246.

3. Bring the class together and let students ask you any unanswered questions. Give answers that express a scheduled or not already scheduled event.

   Student: *When are we having our final test?*

   Instructor: *Our final test is on December 15th.*

   or *We will have our final test sometime in December.*

Suggestion: If the students know each other fairly well, consider having them make sentences about planned events outside of class (*When is Maria moving into her new apartment?*).

EXERCISE 3 [15 minutes]

Students will need to choose the tense they think best fits each sentence.

1. Have students work individually. Remind them of the distinctions explained in Focus 2 if they need help.

2. Have pairs or small groups compare, negotiate, and explain their choices.

3. Go over the possible options as a whole class discussion. See answers on LP page 246.

For more practice, use *Grammar Dimensions 3* Workbook page 86, Exercise 2.

FOCUS 3

Will Versus Be Going To

use

Will

EXAMPLES

(a) I'm having trouble with my homework. **Will you help me?**

(b) I need some milk from the store. Oh, I'll get it for you.

(c) Denise **won't** go with us, no matter how much we ask her.

(d) I'm sorry I forgot the book. I'll bring it tomorrow, I promise.

(e) Plants **will** die if they don't get enough water.

EXPLANATIONS

Use *will*:
• for requests

• to express willingness or unwillingness

• to make a promise

• to express general truths

Be Going To

EXAMPLES

(f) I'm **going** to go to the party, whether you're there or not.

(g) We shouldn't go hiking this afternoon. It's **going to** rain any minute!

(h) Are you going to Grace's party? I can't. I am **going to** be out of town that weekend.

EXPLANATIONS

Use *be going to*:
• to talk about intentions

• to talk about the immediate future

• to talk about plans that have been made earlier

Will and Be Going To

EXAMPLES

(i) The weather will be fine for Reiko's wedding, and everyone's **going to** have a wonderful time!

(j) I'm **going** to paint my apartment. First, I'll get the paint and some brushes. Then I'll get to work. I **might** paint the walls green, but I haven't decided yet.

EXPLANATIONS

Use *will* and *be going to* to make predictions. When *be going to* is pronounced *"gonna"*, it is usually more informal than *will*.

Be going to usually introduces a topic. Following sentences often **use** *will* and other one-word modals.

EXERCISE 4

Decide which form, *will* or *be going to*, should be used in the following sentences. In some cases both answers may be correct.

1. I've got an extra ticket to the football game. (a) _____Will you go_____ (you go) with me? It (b) _is going to be/will be_ (be) a great game. Johnson (c) _is playing/will be playing_ (play) the quarterback. I'm sure he (d) _____will_____ (be) wonderful.

2. I don't know what to do for my vacation. Maybe I (a) _____will go_____ (go) to Mexico. I know the plane ticket (b) _is going to be/will be_ (be) expensive. Perhaps I (c) _____will take_____ (take) the bus to save some money. Your brother's taken the bus before, hasn't he? (d) _____Will you ask_____ (you ask) him how the trip was?

3. Lin (a) _is going to finish_ (finish) her assignment tonight, even if she has to stay up until dawn. It (b) _won't be/isn't going to be_ (not be) easy. She has to finish reading *War and Peace*, and then write a ten-page paper. She (c) _is going to probably be_ (probably be) up all night. Maybe her roommate (d) _will make_ (make) some coffee for her and do the dishes, so that Lin (e) _won't have_ (not have) to worry about anything else.

4. Different plants need different amounts of water. Too much water (a) _____will kill_____ (kill) certain kinds of plants. Other kinds require daily watering, and they (b) _____will die_____ (die) if they don't get it. Setting out a garden (c) _will require_ (require) some advanced planning to make sure that plants with similar water requirements (d) _____will be_____ (be) planted in the same areas.

FOCUS 3 [20 minutes]

Focus 3 gives examples of the distinctions between *will* versus *be going to.*

1. **Lead-in:** Divide the board in half and write the words *will* on one side and *be going to* on the other.

2. As you go over the focus chart examples with the class, write on the board the key words which define the use for each modal in the future on the appropriate side of the board.

   will   *be going to*
   requests   *intentions*
   predictions   *predictions*

3. Go over the pronunciation of *"gonna"* and the differences in formality.

4. Leave the charts on the board for students to refer to as they work on Exercise 4 and Exercise 5.

EXERCISE 4 [15 minutes]

Students will practice choosing between *will* and *be going to* depending on the context offered.

1. Have students work individually to complete the exercise as they refer back to the chart on the board from Focus 3.

2. When finished, have pairs or small groups discuss their reasons for their choices.

3. Go over the possible answers in a class discussion. See answers on LP page 248.

Suggestion 1: Copy the exercise onto an overhead transparency for class review/discussion. Otherwise, write the paragraph number and letters on the board and let various students come up and write their answers for each.

Suggestion 2: If you are short on time, divide the paragraphs up amongst the class and have these groups of students compare answers together when finished.

For more practice, use *Grammar Dimensions 3* Workbook page 87, Exercise 3.

FOCUS 5 — Other Modals in Future Time

Modals (*will, should, may, might, could*) that describe future events also tell about the **probability** of the event. See Unit 16 for more information and practice with predictions about future events.

EXAMPLES

		MEANING	FORM
(a)	There **will** be more people living on the earth in 100 years.	**certain** 100% probability	*will*
(b)	The average life span of most people **should** increase.	**probable** 65%–80% probability	*should*
(c)	There **may** be alternative energy sources, but people **may not** be able to afford them.	**quite possible** 35%–65% probability	*may* *may not*
(d)	The world **might** develop ways to reverse global warming, but they **might not** do it in time to prevent climate change.	**somewhat possible** 5%–35% probability	*might* *might not* *could*
(e)	It **could** rain before we get there.		
(f)	Life **won't** be the same as it is today.	**certain** 0% probability	*will not*

EXERCISE 6

Use a modal to give your opinion about the following questions. Give a reason.

Example: What will life be like one hundred years from now?

Life should be more complex one hundred years from now, because of so many technological developments.

1. Will there be enough coal and oil?
2. Will there be a decrease in air pollution?
3. Will the overall climate grow warmer?
4. Will the rate of population growth be greater?
5. Will there be increased use of automobiles?
6. Will there be political stability?
7. Will there still be large differences between developing and developed countries?
8. Will there be cures for cancer, AIDS, and other diseases?
9. What will be the problems that people face in the twenty-first century?
10. Will there still be wars between countries?

Make up three questions of your own and ask them to a partner. Compare your ideas about the future to those of your partner. Who is more optimistic about the future?

FOCUS 4 — Using *Shall*

EXAMPLES

(a) I'll go to the conference.
(b) (?) I shall go to the conference.
(c) I won't do it.
(d) (?) I shan't go.

(e) Shall I tell you my prediction?
(f) Should I answer the phone?
(g) May I help you?

(h) Shall we dance?
(i) Shall we begin with the first exercise?
(j) Let's go out for dinner.

EXPLANATIONS

Shall is not usually used in American English. Using *shall* to make statements about future actions sounds quite formal and old-fashioned to Americans. The negative contracted form (*shan't*) is almost never used.

Use *shall:*
- to make offers
  Should or *may* are often used in this context.

- to suggest activities that both speaker and listener will participate in.
  Let's is less formal and more common.

EXERCISE 5

Decide which forms (*will, be going to,* or *shall*) can be used in these sentences. In some cases more than one form may be possible, so be prepared to explain any difference in meaning or use communicated by the choice of a particular form. Discuss your ideas with a classmate and present them to the rest of the class.

1. ___Shall___ we go to a movie tonight?

2. When ___will/are you going to___ you graduate?

3. ___Shall___ I tell you the answer to the question?

4. He ___will___ not do it, even though his mother wants him to.

5. Water ___will___ not flow uphill.

Exercise 6 Answers will vary. Possible answers are: 1. There might be enough coal and oil if we can start to conserve them now. 2. There won't be a decrease in air pollution, because companies are unwilling to change their production techniques. 3. The overall climate may not get warmer because of continuing volcanic eruptions producing smoke and ash worldwide. 4. The rate of population growth will be greater, because the government is doing nothing about birth control. 5. There may be an increased use of automobiles if the government continues its lack of support for public transportation. 6. There might be political stability if the world economy stabilizes. 7. There

might not be large differences between developing and developed countries if a global economy continues to develop. 8. There will probably be cures for cancer and AIDS, but there will also probably be new diseases that mankind hasn't yet encountered. 9. People won't have to worry about health or economic problems, because science will solve all the problems. 10. There won't be any more wars, because we will have a single global government.

Additional questions: Will universities still require entrance exams? Will people still be writing grammar books? Will teachers still assign so much homework?

FOCUS 4 [10 minutes]

If you are short on time, you may wish to skip this section. Focus 4 addresses the use of *shall*. In general, *shall* is not commonly used in casual American English.

1. **Lead-in:** Write the words *statements about the future, offers,* and *let's* on the board. Refer to these as you go over the possible (or not recommended) uses of *shall* and the alternate modals.

2. Go over the three sections of the chart (as outlined on the board). You may want to circle the two possible uses (*offers* and *let's*) while crossing out the one not recommended (*statements about the future*) as you go over the chart. Note that this text does not advise students to use *shall* to express the future, but suggests that they recognize the possibility for its use.

GRAMMAR NOTE

Another common use for the word *shall* is its formal written use in legal contracts or technical requirements, as in *The signer shall agree to all terms and conditions.* This denotes a firm statement of intent or promise.

EXERCISE 5 [15 minutes]

Students will practice choosing between *will, be going to* or *shall* depending on the context offered.

1. Referring back to the charts on the board from Focus 3 along with the information covered in Focus 4, have students discuss the possibilities with a partner. They should discuss any differences as they go.

2. Invite pairs to share their answers with the class and explain their reasons for these choices. See answers on LP page 250.

For more practice, use *Grammar Dimensions 3* Workbook page 87, Exercise 4.

FOCUS 5 [15 minutes]

Focus 5 gives examples of other modals used to express future time and their meanings in terms of the degree of certainty or probability that each one expresses. This will be developed further in Unit 16, Focus 1.

1. **Lead-in:** Students should be somewhat familiar with these modals. Begin by creating a vertical line on the board with 100% probability at the top and 0% probability at the bottom.

2. Go over the column of the focus chart listing the forms and also their corresponding meanings along with the percent of probability.

3. Choose a volunteer to come to the board and record the forms in the focus chart next to a corresponding level of probability on the board. Let the class help out by calling out "higher" or "lower" as you call out the words to be placed.

4. After you go over the example sentences as a class, review the meanings of these modals again by asking the class whether they think *it might snow tomorrow* or some other possible weather change. Let them use the chart to find a modal of probability that fits their intention and suggest a full answer in response. (*It could snow tomorrow, but I doubt it.*)

5. Ask a few other questions about possible events in the future and invite students to answer with modals from Focus 5.

VARIATION

Have pairs ask each other questions about future events in the classroom and respond using modals from the chart.

EXERCISE 6 [15 minutes]

Referring back to the discussion and writing on predictions for the future, this exercise asks students to express their own opinions, which include a degree of probability from Focus 5.

1. Put students into pairs (or use this as a mixer to get students on their feet).

2. For some extra listening practice, have one partner close his or her book. The other partner will then ask the first five questions and take notes on his or her partner's answers. Switch roles for questions 6–10.

3. Circulate and encourage students to explain their opinions and reasons for each question rather than simply answering each question in a *yes* or *no* manner.

4. Have pairs create a few more questions about the future for each other, another pair, or a small group to discuss.

5. Have students decide whether their partners are optimists or pessimists and share their reasons with the class. See possible answers on LP page 250.

For more practice, use *Grammar Dimensions 3* Workbook page 88, Exercise 5.

FOCUS 6 | Future-Time Adverbial Clauses

In future time, adverbial clauses always use present tenses and not modal auxiliaries.

(a) I'll present the report tomorrow when I finish analyzing the evidence.

(b) NOT: I'll present the report tomorrow when I will finish analyzing the evidence.

(c) I'm going to watch TV as soon as I have finished my homework.

(d) NOT: I'm going to watch TV as soon as I will have finished my homework.

(e) Hani's planning to have a party while his parents are visiting relatives in Canada.

(f) NOT: Hani's planning to have a party while his parents will be visiting relatives in Canada.

EXERCISE 7

Join the second sentence in each of these pairs to the first sentence using the linking word in parentheses. Make sure to change nouns to pronouns where necessary.

Example: I'll go to the movies. I will finish my homework. (after)

I'll go to the movies after I finish my homework.

1. All my friends will be relieved. The semester will end in a couple of weeks. (when)
2. I'm going to go to the movies every day. I will have finished all the household chores that have been postponed all semester. (after)
3. It will be almost three weeks after the last day of class. Lin will finally get her research paper completed. (by the time)
4. I'm going to read that novel. I'll have some time after the exams. (when)
5. Bob's going to spend every day at the beach. The weather will be sunny. (while)
6. Matt and Jeff will be really tired. They are going to finish their 10-mile hike from the beach. (by the time)
7. Mark and Ann are leaving for Europe. They'll finish their last exam. (as soon as)
8. Doug and Elena are going to get married. They will be on vacation in Mexico. (while)
9. Even our teacher's going to take some time off. She will have finished grading the final papers and correcting the exams. (when)

Use Your English

 ACTIVITY 1 speaking/writing

What day and time is it at this moment? Imagine what you will be doing at **this exact moment** ten years from now, twenty years from now, fifty years from now. Describe these activities to a partner or write a brief essay about them.

 **ACTIVITY 2 speaking**

▪ STEP 1 Tell several other students about your vacation plans. Listen to their plans.

▪ STEP 2 Then answer these questions as a group.

- Whose plans sound like the most fun? Why?
- Whose plans sound like the most boring? Why?
- Whose plans sound like the easiest to arrange? Why?
- Whose plans sound like the best opportunity to practice English?

Decide on one additional category of your own.

▪ STEP 3 Report your answers to the rest of the class.

ACTIVITY 3 writing

Choose one of the three questions on the next page and write a paragraph or make a presentation expressing your ideas.

ANSWER KEY

Exercise 7 1. All my friends will be relieved when the semester ends in a couple of weeks. 2. I'm going to go to the movies every day after I have finished all the household chores that have been postponed all semester. 3. It will be almost three weeks after the last day of class by the time Lin finally gets her research paper completed. 4. I'm going to read that novel when I have some time after the exams. 5. Bob's going to spend every afternoon at the beach while the weather is sunny. 6. Matt and Jeff will be really tired by the time they finish their 10-mile hike from the beach. 7. Mark and Arn are leaving for Europe as soon as they finish their last exam. 8. Doug and Elena are going to get married while they are on vacation in Mexico. 9. Even our teacher's going to take some time off when she has finished grading the final papers and correcting the exams.

FOCUS 6 [10 minutes]

Focus 6 gives examples of the proper form when using adverbial clauses to express future time. Students need to be reminded to use the present tense with adverbial clauses in the future.

1. **Lead-in:** To help students remember to use the present tense in the adverbial clause for the future, put several example sentences on the board. Separate the clauses a bit by putting the main clauses on one side of the board and the adverbial clauses on the other side of the board.

2. Ask the class what they notice about these halves. Draw attention to the verb tenses used in each half.

3. Discuss the examples, the forms used, and the focus chart.

GRAMMAR NOTE

The present tense (simple present, present progressive, present perfect, etc.) is used in the adverbial clause referring to the future. The main clause will contain a future time marker (present progressive, *will, be going to*, etc.).

EXERCISE 7 [15 minutes]

1. Write the two sentences from the first example on the board and ask the class to combine them with a suggested conjunction of time (*before, after*, etc.).

2. Have students work individually to complete the exercise and then compare answers in pairs or as a class. See answers on LP page 252.

work book
For more practice, use *Grammar Dimensions 3* Workbook page 89, Exercise 6 and page 90, Exercise 7.

UNIT GOAL REVIEW [10 minutes]

work book
Ask students to look at the goals on the opening page of the unit again. Refer to the pages of the unit where information on each goal can be found.

For a grammar review quiz of Units 13–15, refer students to pages 91–92 in the *Grammar Dimensions 3* Workbook.

ExamView Test Generator — For assessment of Unit 15, use *Grammar Dimensions 3 ExamView®*.

USE YOUR ENGLISH

The Use Your English activities at the end of the unit contain situations that should naturally elicit the structures covered in the unit. For a more complete discussion of how to use the Use Your English activities see To the Teacher on LP page xxii. When students are doing these activities in class, you can circulate and listen to see if they are using the structures accurately. Errors can be corrected after the activity has finished.

ACTIVITY 1 speaking/writing [15 minutes]

This is mainly a speaking activity that asks students to make predictions about their futures (see Focus 3 or Focus 5). The time line markers (*10, 20, 50 years*) for this activity could be modified to *5, 10, 20* or even *1, 5, 10 years* for classes with older students.

1. To get students thinking about their own futures, draw a sample time line on the board. Mark the beginning for NOW and mark the rest of the line with the times to be described in the future. Have the class do the same on a piece of paper.

2. Have students write a few statements about their lives now below the marker and then write predictions about what their lives will be like in the following intervals marked along their lines.

3. Circulate and encourage students to make as many predictions as they can (no matter how wild or implausible). Note the use of future forms.

4. Have students explain their time lines in pairs or small groups.

EXPANSION [20 minutes]

Have students write horoscopes or fortune cookie slips. Collect these, put them in a bag, and let each student draw out a slip for themselves.

ACTIVITY 2 speaking [15 minutes]

This speaking activity asks students to talk about plans for a future vacation.

STEP 1 Put students into small groups and ask them to share their own plans for the next vacation. Everyone in the group should think of something to share, even if it is just "wishful thinking".

STEP 2 Have the groups discuss the questions in Step 2. Can the groups agree on the answers?

STEP 3 Let groups report to the class. Have the class decide on the most fun and best opportunity to practice English in the whole class.

ACTIVITY 3 writing [30 minutes/homework]

Have students choose a question and ask them to either write a paragraph or prepare a presentation, depending on how much time you have available in class.

Suggestion: Before they write, divide the class up into small groups and assign one of the three questions to each group for five minutes of discussion.

- What major **political and economic changes** are going to take place in your lifetime? Describe them and explain why you think they are going to happen.
- What major **social changes** are going to take place in your lifetime? Describe them and explain why you think they are going to happen.
- What major **scientific advances** are going to take place in your lifetime? Describe them and explain why you think they are going to happen.

ACTIVITY 4 listening/speaking

STEP 1

Listen to the two speakers talk about the future. As you listen, note each speaker's predictions and the reasons for those predictions in the chart below. Based on those predictions and reasons, decide whether each speaker is optimistic or pessimistic about the future.

CD Tracks 22, 23

Speaker 1

OPTIMISTIC OR PESSIMISTIC?	SPEAKER'S PREDICTION	SPEAKER'S REASONS
Public health and population		
Life expectancy and nutrition		
Energy and pollution		
Political and economic stability		

Speaker 2

OPTIMISTIC OR PESSIMISTIC?	SPEAKER'S PREDICTION	SPEAKER'S REASONS
Public health and population		
Life expectancy and nutrition		
Energy and pollution		
Political and economic stability		

STEP 2

Imagine that you are one of the speakers. Using the notes you took above, try to give a speech in your own words to a partner explaining why you are optimistic or pessimistic about the future. Your partner should do the same with the other speech. If you wish, add some ideas and reasons of your own.

ACTIVITY 5 speaking

STEP 1

Organize a debate between optimists and pessimists. Using the Opening Task on page 245, decide whether you are an optimist or a pessimist. Form groups of four or more. Try to have an equal number of optimists and pessimists in each group.

STEP 2

As a group, choose one category of world affairs (see Opening Task for examples). Discuss the current trends related to that category. Add one or two significant additional trends of your own. Optimists will then give reasons why they think the world will be better one hundred years from now. Pessimists will give reasons why they think the world will be worse one hundred years from now.

STEP 3

Present both sets of predictions to the other groups. As a whole class, decide who has presented the most persuasive reasons, the optimists or the pessimists.

ACTIVITY 6 research on the web

Go on *InfoTrac® College Edition* and enter the term "futurist". Skim at least ten articles quickly to determine what trends futurists are currently looking at and what predictions they are making about those trends. Choose three that you find interesting and report on these predictions to the rest of the class.

ACTIVITY 7 reflection

Find three written and three spoken examples of people talking about future activities. This can be in conversations with native speakers or from a radio or TV program, such as a weather report or a sports program. Written examples can come from newspaper horoscopes or any news article that talks about future trends. Identify the forms that the people used to talk about the future event. Did they use present tense or future tenses with *will* or *going to* or other modals? Report at least one example to the rest of the class.

ANSWER KEY

Activity 4 Speaker 1 Optimistic
Speaker 2 Pessimistic

USE YOUR ENGLISH

ACTIVITY 4 listening/speaking [20 minutes]

CD Tracks 22,23

Students will listen to and take notes on two speakers' predictions for the future. Based on these notes, students will then recreate one of the speeches and weave this with their own ideas into a similar speech.

STEP 1

1. Go over the directions in both Step 1 and Step 2 with the class. Students will then know that they are not only to take notes, but will eventually be giving a similar speech.

2. Go over the charts in Step 1 and note that there is a column for *predictions* and another column for *reasons*.

3. Use your usual steps for playing the audio, checking and playing again as needed while students take notes to fill in the charts.

4. Let students decide whether each speaker is an optimist or pessimist and then go over the information as a class or in pairs.

STEP 2

1. Divide the class in half and assign one to be Speaker 1 and another to be Speaker 2. If necessary, play the audio one more time once the class knows which part they are to play.

2. Give students time to prepare their speeches and be sure they include a few of their own ideas as they do this. Circulate and help as needed.

3. Have pairs give their speeches together, in a small group or as a pair in front of the class.

ACTIVITY 5 speaking [30 minutes]

Use this at any point after the Opening Task on SB pages 244–245 for fun interactive practice. This debate activity can be as simple or as elaborate as you like. You can plan an organized debate based on the format of (1) introductions, (2) major arguments, (3) initial questions, (4) responses, and (5) closing statements for the whole class. On the other hand, you can simply have small groups divided in half with each half presenting their arguments to the class along with an informal period for questions and responses. It helps to give each side a time limit and stick to it.

1. Write the debate question on the board: *What will life be like in 100 years?*

2. Give the students some information about how a debate works and explain that one side can win simply because their argument is more organized. There is never a definitive answer and a good debater can argue either side with skill.

STEP 1

Based on their results from the Opening Task in SB on page 245, divide the class into small groups of optimists and groups of pessimists. (If the groups are very uneven in numbers, you can divide the class in half and assign each half to be optimists or pessimists.)

STEP 2

As a class, choose a category of world affairs (medicine, food, education, etc.) for all groups to prepare arguments for. It works well to have each group present at least three points of support for their side. All groups of optimist and pessimists will prepare to convince the class why the world will be a better or worse place in 100 years.

STEP 3

1. Depending on your class size, you can either have groups present their arguments to the class or simply with another group representing the opposing side.

2. Come together as a class and discuss which sides had the most persuasive reasons, the optimists or the pessimists.

Suggestion: It might be fun to declare a winner based on which team was most persuasive.

ACTIVITY 6 research on the web [30 minutes]

You may want to assign this research activity after the Opening Task on SB pages 244–245. Like the *InfoTrac* searches in previous units, this activity gives students the chance to see and use the grammar in context and also practice reading and writing skills.

1. Give students guidelines as to how their findings should be presented (length and format/written or presentation). Be sure to remind students about putting their findings into their own words.

2. Collect papers and give individual feedback or have students present their results in small groups or to the class.

ACTIVITY 7 reflection [15 minutes/homework]

Students will seek out and collect written and spoken examples of the future being discussed. Students will then analyze what verb forms were used in these examples. Encourage students to bring in a wide range of examples rather than only newspapers or only from one television show.

16 MODALS OF PREDICTION AND INFERENCE

UNIT GOALS

- Understand and use different modals to express predictions in future time

- Understand and use different modals to express logical inferences in present time

- Correctly express predictions and logical inferences in past time

OPENING TASK
Solving a Mystery

STEP 1

Work with a partner. Choose one of the mini-mysteries on the next page to try to solve.

MINI MYSTERIES

MYSTERY #1

A man lives on the fortieth floor of a very tall building. Every day he rides the elevator down to the ground floor. When he comes home he rides the elevator to the twentieth floor, but he has to walk the rest of the way.

Why does he do this?

MYSTERY #2

In a room, a dead woman is hanging by a rope, more than three feet above the floor. There are no windows, and the door has been locked from the inside. The room is empty: no furniture, no ladder. The only thing in the room is a single piece of paper.

What happened to the woman?

MYSTERY #3

A police officer receives an emergency phone call about a terrible automobile accident. A boy and his father have both been very badly injured. The officer has to fill out the report and figure out what happened. The police officer takes one look at the boy and his father, and says "You'll have to find someone else to deal with this. I'm too upset. This boy is my son!"

How can the boy have two fathers?

■ STEP 2

Think of five possible explanations. Decide which ones are likely and which ones are not very likely.

■ STEP 3

Turn to page A-12 and read the additional clues. Then try to solve the mysteries.

ANSWER KEY

Opening Task Possible solutions include:

Mystery 1: The man must be too short to reach the highest button for the fortieth floor. He must not be able to reach the top button of the elevator. He must only be tall enough to reach the twentieth-floor button; that's why he has to walk the rest of the way.

Mystery 2: The woman must have killed herself by standing on a block of ice and then sliding it away or waiting for it to melt.

Mystery 3: The police officer must be a woman. She must be the boy's mother.

UNIT OVERVIEW

Unit 16 reviews modals of prediction (see also Unit 15—Future Time) and goes on to show modals of logical inference which reflect present or past time.

GRAMMAR NOTE

Modals typically are difficult to teach due to the very subtle meanings that they can carry and the wide variety of meanings that the same form can have. Modals of prediction (guesses about the future) and inference (guesses about the present or past) must be taught within contexts that show their meanings and the small differences between each modal. In this unit, modals used for prediction and inference are presented on a scale which then shows their degrees of possibility or probability. The formation of modals of prediction and inference in the past time can be especially challenging (see Focus 3) and may require a little more repetition and practice to get the form down correctly. In addition, the various negative forms and the possibility for contracting these forms can be tricky for students to grasp (see the Grammar Note following Focus 1).

UNIT GOALS

Some instructors may want to review the goals listed on Student Book (SB) page 256 after completing the Opening Task so that students understand what they should know by the end of the unit. These goals can also be reviewed at the end of the unit when students are more familiar with the grammar terminology.

OPENING TASK [30 minutes]

The point of this task is to give students the opportunity to make the distinction between making predictions versus logical conclusions/inferences as they perform a task. The problem-solving format is designed to show the teacher how well the students can produce a target structure implicitly and

spontaneously when they are engaged in a communicative task. For a more complete discussion of the purpose of the Opening Task, see To the Teacher, Lesson Planner (LP) page xxii.

Setting Up the Task

Begin by getting the class in the mood for a mystery. Ask if they enjoy mystery novels or movies or if they watch crime scene investigation shows on television. Discuss students' favorites to get them ready to take on the role of detectives.

Conducting the Task

■ STEP 1

Put the class into pairs and divide the mysteries up among the pairs. If you have time, let pairs work on all three mysteries.

■ STEP 2

Have pairs work together on creating a list of five possible answers to their mystery. Ask that students not go on to Step 3 until they have written their five possible explanations.

■ STEP 3

After students have completed Step 2, circulate and either ask students to check the extra clues on page A-12 or whisper the extra clues (see SB page A-12) to pairs as needed. If pairs finish their lists of possible answers early, have them try out another mystery.

Closing the Task

1. Put all the pairs that worked on Mystery #1 into a small group to compare their lists of possible answers. Do the same for the other mysteries.

2. Let the groups decide which answer is the most plausible. Have groups share their answers with the class. Verify the correct answers. See possible answers on LP page 256.

EXPANSION [15 minutes]

Bring in other mini-mysteries and ask the class to work in pairs or small groups to solve them. You can find these on the Internet or in books. They're fun, encourage reading and speaking skills, and get students using the target modals.

GRAMMAR NOTE

Typical student errors (use)

- Creating questions with modals other than will: * *Should we be finished by the end of the week?* * *May they need some extra time?* (See Focus 1.)
- Problems with the use of contracted versus non-contracted negative modals of prediction/inference: * *It should not be rainy tomorrow.* * *He mustn't be able to reach the top button.*

Typical student errors (form)

- Adding agreement to the verb following a modal: * *She may arrives late tonight.*
- Incorrect forms for inferences/predictions in the past: * *He might wanted to come too.* * *They must have saw the accident.* (See Focus 3.)

Modals of Prediction

meaning

use

Modals of prediction refer to future time. Use them to indicate how likely or possible it is that some future event will happen. (See Focus 3 for information about making predictions in the past time frame.)

EXAMPLES	FORM	MEANING/USE
(a) This class **will** end in an hour.	*will*	It will **certainly** happen. We can also use simple present or present progressive to describe these events.
(b) We **should** be able to finish the unit by the end of the week.	*should*	It is **likely** to happen. Using *should* for predictions sometimes sounds like advisability. If you aren't sure, use *will probably* to make your meaning clear.
(c) We **will probably** finish it in a couple of days.	*will probably*	
(d) We **may** need some extra time for review.	*may*	It will **possibly** happen.
(e) You'd better study tonight. We **could/might** have a surprise quiz tomorrow.	*might* *could*	
(f) We **may not** have one.	*may not*	It will **possibly not** happen.
(g) We **might not** have time for it.	*might not*	
(h) It **shouldn't** be difficult if you have studied the homework.	*shouldn't*	It is **not likely** that this will happen. Using *shouldn't* for predictions sometimes sounds like advisability. If you aren't sure, use *probably won't* to make your meaning clear.
(i) It **probably won't** take too long.	*probably won't*	
(j) We **won't** have a quiz tomorrow, because there's no class.	*won't*	It will **certainly not** happen.

EXAMPLES	EXPLANATIONS
(k) **Will** they finish the quiz by 5:00? Bambang **should** finish on time, but Reiko **might** be a little late.	To ask for predictions about future events, use only *will*, not other modal forms.

Make sentences from these cues using modals.

Example: certain: Andy/drive to New York for a vacation.

Andy will drive to New York for a vacation.

1. likely: Andy/decide what to do about his car next week.
2. certainly not: The car/work well enough for his trip to New York.
3. possible: Andy/get it repaired, if it can be done cheaply.
4. not likely: He/have trouble selling it.
5. likely: He/be able to get a good price.
6. possible: Andy's friend Paul/want to buy it.
7. possibly not: Andy/sell the car to Paul.
8. possibly not: The car/be in very good condition.
9. possible: Paul/expect a refund if he has troubles with the car.
10. certain: Andy/need the money to buy a plane ticket if he doesn't drive.

How likely is it that you will be doing the following activities next Saturday night at 8:00 P.M.?

doing English homework	taking a bath
watching TV	speaking another language
thinking about personal problems	sleeping
sitting in a movie theater	writing letters to my family
reading a magazine	having a good time with friends

Work with a partner. Ask questions with *will*. Answer questions with the appropriate modal of prediction.

Examples: *At 8:00 P.M. next Saturday do you think you will be doing English homework?*
I won't be doing homework on a Saturday night. I might be at a party.

Exercise 1 1. Andy should decide.... 2. The car won't work.... 3. Andy may/might/could get it repaired.... 4. He shouldn't have trouble.... 5. He should be able.... 6. Andy's friend Paul might/may.... 7. Andy might/may not sell.... 8. The car may/might not be.... 9. Paul could/might expect.... 10. Andy will need the money.... **Exercise 2** Answers will vary. All modals are possible in most situations, but likely answers are: At 8:00 P.M. next Saturday do you think you will be watching TV? I could/may/might/should be watching TV. At 8:00 P.M. next Saturday do you think you will be thinking about personal problems? I might be thinking about personal problems. At 8:00 P.M. next Saturday do you think you will be sitting in a movie theater? I could/may/might/should be sitting in a movie theater.

At 8:00 P.M. next Saturday do you think you will be reading a magazine? I may/might/could be reading a magazine. At 8:00 P.M. next Saturday do you think you will be taking a bath? I shouldn't/won't be taking a bath. At 8:00 P.M. next Saturday do you think you will be speaking another language? I could/might be speaking another language. At 8:00 P.M. next Saturday do you think you will be sleeping? I won't/shouldn't be sleeping. At 8:00 P.M. next Saturday do you think you will be writing letters to your family? I could/shouldn't be writing letters to my family. At 8:00 P.M. next Saturday do you think you will be having a good time with your friends? I will be having a good time with friends.

FOCUS 1 [20 minutes]

In Focus 1, modals of prediction for the future are presented in order of their strength of possibility. Illustrating these modals with a line of degree and percentage markers should help students who are having difficulties understanding the subtle differences between them.

1. **Lead-in:** Ask the class a few questions that should require a modal of prediction. Then put a few on the board. Some examples are:

   Will it snow tomorrow?

   Will you pass the next test?

   Will you take another ESL class next session?

2. Draw a line vertically on the board. Start at the top of one side of the line and write *100%* and *certain.* About halfway down, write *50%* and *possibly.* At the bottom, write *100%* and *certainly not.* Use this line as you go over the classes' answers to the questions on the board and write the modals used across from their corresponding degrees of likelihood.

3. As you go over the examples and modals in the focus chart next, add these modals to the board along the line of likelihood.

4. Ask a few more questions like the ones in the lead-in and note where on the line each student's answer is found.

5. Finally, note that when forming these questions of prediction for the future the modal *will* is used. See example (k).

6. Leave your chart on the board for use in Exercise 1.

VARIATION

Assign Exercise 1 as a diagnostic before going over Focus 1 to see how comfortable students are with these forms already.

GRAMMAR NOTE

Negative modals can be a problem for ESL students. You may want to point out that sometimes there can be differences in meaning between the full and the contracted negative modals (i.e., *should not* and *shouldn't*). In general:

(1) *shouldn't* is for predictions: *It shouldn't take long for him to finish.*

   should not is generally for negative advisability: *You should not be there.*

(2) *mustn't* is generally for negative necessity: *You mustn't go in there.*

   must not is for negative inferences (see Focus 2): *He must not have arrived yet.*

(3) *can't/couldn't* is for impossibility: *He couldn't be the killer.*

   Can not/could not is generally for negative ability: *I can not reach the top shelf.*

Furthermore, some negative modals *can not* be contracted. We do not use *may not* or *might not* with a contraction (* *mayn't/mightn't*).

EXERCISE 1 [15 minutes]

1. If you have left your chart (vertical line with meanings and modals) on the board from Focus 1, have students use this as they look for modals with the meanings listed in each cue for Exercise 1. There may be more than one possible modal.

2. Let students share their answers in small groups. They should note all possible answers as they check together. See answers on LP page 258.

For more practice, use *Grammar Dimensions 3* Workbook page 93, Exercise 1.

EXERCISE 2 [15 minutes]

1. Model a few questions for the class asking them about the possibility of future activities. For example:

   Do you think you will come to class tomorrow?

   Do you think you will pass the next grammar test?

   Do you think you will go to the beach this weekend?

2. Now get the class thinking about their usual activities on a Saturday night. Go over the directions and examples.

3. Let the class work together in pairs to take turns asking each other about the activities listed. See possible answers on LP page 258.

EXPANSION 1 [15 minutes/homework]

Have the pairs come up with a list of activities for a different time frame, such as 10:00 A.M. on a Monday morning. They should then create a survey form and interview native speakers outside the class. Students will need to listen for the modals people use and write them into the corresponding columns for meaning (see example below). Have the original pairs compare their results and report to the class.

Activity	certain	likely	possible	possibly not	not likely	certainly not
driving		will probably				
watching tv						

EXPANSION 2 [25 minutes]

Use Activity 2 (speaking/writing) on SB page 267. Students will make predictions about what they think friends or family in another country are doing at this moment.

meaning

FOCUS 2 | Modals of Inference

Modals of inference refer to the present time frame. Use them to express a logical conclusion, based on evidence. (See Focus 3 for information about making inferences in the past time frame.)

EXAMPLES	FORM	MEANING/USE
(a) The police officer **must** be the boy's mother.	*must*	There is no other possible conclusion from the evidence.
(b) There **should** be a good reason why the man walks the rest of the way.	*should*	This is a logical conclusion, based on the evidence we have, but it is possible that there is another conclusion.
(c) He **may** want the exercise.	*may*	This is one of several possibilities.
(d) The elevator **might** be broken.	*might*	
(e) He **could** want to visit people on the twentieth floor.	*could*	
(f) The officer **may not** be telling the truth.	*may not*	This is one of several possibilities.
(g) The man **might not** like to ride the elevator up so high so quickly.	*might not*	
(h) There **shouldn't** be any reason why the elevator wouldn't go up to the top floor.	*shouldn't*	This is not a logical conclusion, based on the evidence we have, but it could be possible.
(i) The man is so short he **must not** be able to reach the elevator button for the top floor.	*must not*	This is not a possible conclusion, based on the evidence we have.
(j) The officer **couldn't** be the boy's father.	*couldn't*	This is impossible.
(k) A person **can't** have two fathers.	*can't*	

EXERCISE 3

Write twelve true sentences about your plans for your next vacation using modals of prediction.

1. two things that you will certainly do

   I will go someplace warm. I will go some place with a beach.

2. two things that you will likely do

   I should get a nice tan. I should have a good rest.

3. two things that you will possibly do

   I might go with friends. I might travel there alone.

4. two things that you possibly won't do

   I might not go with friends. I may not have enough money to fly there.

5. two things that you won't likely do

   I shouldn't spend too much money if I go someplace cheap. I shouldn't have trouble finding a cheap airplane ticket.

6. two things that you certainly won't do

   I won't go anyplace cold. I won't stay anyplace really expensive.

EXERCISE 4

Write twelve true sentences about how you think life will be at the end of the next century using modals of prediction.

1. two things that will certainly be true

   Life will be more complex. There will be better communication.

2. two things that will likely be true

   Life should be more comfortable for most people. Communication between countries should be easier.

3. two things that will possibly be true

   Life may be better. Life may be worse.

4. two things that possibly won't be true

   The standard of living might not be better. Things may not have improved much compared to life today.

5. two things that won't likely be true

   The world shouldn't be less complicated. People's personal worries shouldn't be too different from the ones they have today.

6. two things that certainly won't be true

   I won't be alive. My parents won't be alive.

Exercise 3 Answers will vary. Possible answers are listed above.
Exercise 4 Answers will vary. Possible answers are listed above.

and *couldn't* do not have the opposite meanings from each other. Give a few more examples of the differences between *might/might not, may/may not* and *could/couldn't*.

EXERCISE 3 AND 4 [15 minutes/homework]

If you are short on time, Exercises 3 and 4 can be assigned as homework. Students can compare answers in pairs or small groups the next day. Students can then report any interesting findings to the class, such as the most common answers or the most unusual answers. See possible answers on LP page 260.

LESSON PLAN 2

FOCUS 2 [20 minutes]

Modals of inference refer to the present tense. They are based on looking at all the facts and making a conclusion. This focus chart looks at the kinds of inferences that would have been made in the Opening Task.

1. **Lead-in:** Refer back to the possible explanations students came up with for the Opening Task (or use examples from Focus 2). Put a few on the board:

   The elevator might be broken.
   The woman may have fallen.
   The man must not be able to reach the button.

2. Explain how inferences are different from predictions (present/future and based on what is possible or impossible/certain or uncertain to happen).

3. Create another vertical line on the board (next to the first one). The top will have *the only possible answer.* The bottom will have *completely impossible.* The middle will have *one of several possibilities.*

4. As you go over the chart, list the modals along the vertical line on the board.

5. Students should note that although most of the modals balance with their negative forms, *could*

EXERCISE 5

Make logical conclusions by filling in the blanks with an appropriate modal of inference. Decide whether the logical conclusion you express is:

- the only one possible (*must*) or impossible (*must not/can't/couldn't*)
- more likely than other possible conclusions (*should*) or less likely (*shouldn't*)
- or one of several possibilities (*could/may/might/may not/might not*)

There may be more than one correct answer, so be prepared to explain why you chose the form you did.

1. There's someone at the door. That (a) __should__ be my brother; I've been expecting him. But it (b) __could/may/might__ be the postal carrier, or it (c) __could/may/might__ even be a salesperson.

2. Someone is ringing the doorbell. It (a) __can't/couldn't__ (not) be my brother; he has a key. It (b) __shouldn't__ (not) be the postal carrier; he doesn't usually ring the bell. It (c) __shouldn't__ (not) be a friend; all my friends think I'm still in New York. It (d) __must__ be a salesperson. Let's not answer it!

3. I hope I can go to the movies with you tonight, but I (a) __might/may not__ (not) have enough money. I (b) __should__ have enough, because I cashed a check yesterday. But I won't be 100% sure until I buy groceries and see how much money I have left. I really hope I can go. Everyone who has seen that movie says it's really good. It (c) __should/must__ be very funny.

4. Martha looks pretty unhappy. She and George (a) __must__ be having another one of their fights. I don't know what the problem is this time. It (b) __could/may/might__ be because George is always working on his car. It (c) __could/may/might__ be because Martha wants them to spend every weekend at her mother's house. It (d) __can't/couldn't/shouldn't__ (not) be about money, though. That's the fight they had last week. They (e) __must not/can't__ (not) have a very happy marriage.

5. Where have I put my wallet? It (a) __must__ be somewhere! It (b) __can't/couldn't__ (not) just disappear by itself. It (c) __should/could/may/might__ be on my desk, since that's where I usually put it. But it (d) __could/may/might__ be in my briefcase, too. I sometimes forget to take it out when I get home.

6. Fiona (a) __must not__ (not) need money. She's always eager to pay when we go out for a night on the town. She never seems to have a job. It (b) __must__ be nice to have enough money without having to work.

7. Frank (a) __should__ have no trouble finding a job when he moves to California. It (b) __might/could/may__ take a while, but I know he'll find a good position. He seems unhappy in New York. He (c) __must not__ (not) like living there very much.

EXERCISE 6

Decide whether the following sentences are predictions or inferences and choose an appropriate modal. Compare your choices with a partner.

Examples: It __shouldn't__ (not) be very difficult to find a parking place today, because it's Sunday, and usually there aren't many people downtown.

Jack __must not__ (not) have much money, because he drives a 15-year-old car.

1. Traffic is getting heavy; rush hour __must/should__ be starting.

2. Commuters __must__ be getting really tired of driving to work in such awful traffic.

3. Experts tell us that traffic __will__ get worse every year unless we do something about the problem.

4. Some people think that traffic __might/could__ flow more smoothly if we increase the number of highways.

5. But most experts feel that the problem __won't/shouldn't/can't__ (not) be solved by building more highways.

6. That __will/should__ just increase the number of cars on the roads.

7. The traffic problem __will/should/might__ begin to improve once we have increased public transportation.

8. This city __must not__ (not) have a very efficient public transportation system, because people seem to drive everywhere.

LESSON PLAN 2

EXERCISE 5 [15 minutes]

Students can use the chart on the board from Focus 2 to choose modals of inference that show how possible their conclusions are based on the information available. Students will need to take the clues from what is written to decide how sure they are of their statements and whether there is more than one possible answer.

1. Go over the instructions for Exercise 5. Students will be choosing a modal that fits the blanks based on whether they feel there is only one or more than one possible conclusion. Refer back to the categories of modals you listed on the vertical line chart for Focus 2.

2. Have students work individually and then compare and discuss answers or work together with a partner and discuss answers as they go.

3. Go over the possible answers as a class. Invite volunteers to explain the reasoning behind these answers. See answers on LP page 262.

work book

For more practice, use *Grammar Dimensions 3* Workbook page 94, Exercises 2 and 3.

EXERCISE 6 [15 minutes]

Students now must decide whether each sentence refers to a prediction about the future or an inference about the present. They should note any time frame cues while working on this.

1. Go over the instructions and the examples with the class. Invite volunteers to explain which example shows a prediction for the future or an inference about the present (*shouldn't be very difficult* = prediction; *must not have much money* = inference).

2. Have students work together, first discussing whether each sentence refers to a prediction or an inference.

3. After making these decisions, have students work individually to complete the sentences with their choice of modals.

4. Compare answers as a class, first discussing whether each sentence refers to a prediction or an inference. Then invite students to share possible modals from Focus 1 or Focus 2. See answers on LP page 262.

FOCUS 3

Modals of Prediction and Inference in Past Time

You can make predictions and inferences about things that happened in the past time frame by using **perfect modals**.

form

Modal + *Have* + Past Participle

| The woman | must | have | committed | suicide. |

MODAL	EXAMPLES WITH PRESENT/FUTURE TIME	EXAMPLES WITH PAST TIME
must	Why won't the man ride to the top floor? (a) The elevator **must be** in working order, since he rides down from the top floor every day.	How did the woman die? (b) The woman's death **must have been** a suicide.
should	(c) There **should be** a logical explanation for all these mysteries.	(d) The woman **should have been** able to slide the block of ice out from under her feet.
may	(e) He **may want** exercise.	(f) She **may have been** mentally ill.
might	(g) He **might get** sick if the elevator rises too quickly.	(h) She **might have been** having problems.
could	(i) He **could be** nervous about elevators.	(j) She **could have been** fired recently.
may not	(k) He **may not** like elevators.	(l) She **may not have seen** any solution to her problems.
might not	(m) He **might not** want to ride all the way to the top floor.	(n) She **might not have had** anyone to talk to.
shouldn't	(o) He **shouldn't have** to walk up the rest of the floors.	(p) There **shouldn't have been** anyone else in the room with her, since the door was locked from the inside.
must not	(q) He **must not** be able to reach the buttons for the top floor.	(r) She **must not have wanted** to continue living.
couldn't	(s) That **couldn't be** the reason.	(t) The woman's death **couldn't have been** a murder.
can't	(u) There **can't be** any other explanation.	(v) She **can't have wanted** to go on living.

EXERCISE 7

Change this passage to the past time frame.

Example: Denise might not have enough time to finish the project today. That must be the reason why she isn't at the boss's birthday party.

Denise might not have had enough time to finish the project yesterday. That must have been the reason why she wasn't at the boss's birthday party.

(1) Frank might change jobs. (2) He should have no trouble finding a new job. (3) It might take a while, but he has excellent qualifications and lots of experience. (4) He must be really unhappy to want to move to a brand new company. (5) He must not like working in such a big company very much.

EXERCISE 8

Write the appropriate modal form in the blank. There may be more than one correct answer.

1. Someone called me up in the middle of the night. They hung up before I could answer the phone. It (a) _____ (not be) my brother; he doesn't have a telephone. It (b) _____ (be) someone I know, but why would they call in the middle of the night? It (c) _____ (be) a wrong number.

2. Where were you last night? I thought you were going to join us at the movies. You (a) _____ (have) enough money to go with us, because the tickets weren't that expensive. It's too bad you didn't come. I (b) _____ (be) able to lend you the money. Or perhaps Peter (c) _____ (pay) for your ticket. He's so generous. The movie was really funny. You (d) _____ (be) disappointed to miss all the fun.

3. Janet looked really unhappy as she was leaving Professor Brown's office. She (a) _____ (failed) another exam. I know she's already failed one midterm, and she had two more last week. It (b) _____ (not be) her chemistry test. I know she was really nervous about it. But it (c) _____ (be) her calculus exam. She's really good at mathematics, and I know she studied a lot for it.

4. Peter looked everywhere for the missing documents. They (a) _____ (not disappear) by themselves. He thought they (b) _____ (be) on the desk, where he usually put things he was working on, or they (c) _____ (be) in his briefcase, too. But when he looked, they weren't in either place. Then he remembered working on them at the office. He (d) _____ (leave) them there.

Exercise 8 is continued on LP page 266.

ANSWER KEY

Exercise 7 (1) Frank must have changed jobs. (2) He should have had no trouble finding a new job. (3) It might have taken a while, but he had excellent qualifications and lots of experience. (4) He must have been really unhappy to want to move to a brand new company. (5) He must not have liked working in such a big company very much. **Exercise 8** 1. (a) couldn't/must not have been; (b) could/might have been; (c) must have been 2. (a) should have had; (b) should/could/might have been; (c) could/might have paid; (d) must have been. 3. (a) must have failed; (b) could/may/might have been; (c) couldn't/shouldn't have been. 4. (a) couldn't have disappeared; (b) should/may/might/could have been; (c) may/might/could have been; (d) must have left

16 LESSON PLAN 2

FOCUS 3 [20 minutes]

Focus 3 uses both predictions (see Focus 1) and inferences (see Focus 2), but puts them into the past time frame using **modals + present perfect.**

1. **Lead-in:** Put a few sentences on the board from Focus 1 and 2 that use predictions or inferences. Show how these can be changed into the past tense by replacing the **modal + simple form of the verb with modal + present perfect form.**

2. Look at the chart in Focus 3. Go over several examples in both columns and then invite volunteers to change a few of the example sentences in the present/future column into the past. (*He must not be able to reach the buttons.* = *He must not have been able to reach the buttons.*)

Suggestion: Predictions in the past are generally more difficult to explain or understand than inferences. For more practice with predictions in the past, have students make statements about things that they may or may not have completed by 8:00 P.M. today. For example: *I may have finished my homework by 8:00 P.M. today, but I won't have eaten dinner yet.*

EXPANSION [15 minutes]

For a review of Focuses 1–3, use Activity 3 (speaking) on SB page 268. Activity 3 asks students to use modals of inference and prediction in the past time frame. Students will look at photos of household items that are no longer used to try to decide their use either in the past or in the present.

EXERCISE 7 [10 minutes]

Students will rewrite the five sentences using the past time frame.

1. Have students work individually.
2. Go over the answers in a class discussion. See answers on LP page 264.

Suggestion: Invite students who finish quickly to write a sentence on the board.

 For more practice, use *Grammar Dimensions 3* Workbook page 95, Exercise 4.

EXERCISE 8 [20 minutes/homework]

Students will need to choose an appropriate modal and then decide whether it needs to be put into a past time frame. If you are short on time, assign different students to each section or use this as a homework review. Remind students that there may be more than one correct answer. Exercise 8 is continued on SB page 266.

1. Assign the exercise. After students have finished, have them compare answers in pairs or as a whole class discussion.

2. As a class, encourage students to explain their choices and invite others to share alternate choices. See answers on LP pages 264 and 266.

Suggestion: Copy this exercise onto an overhead transparency to help during the whole class discussion.

 For more practice, use *Grammar Dimensions 3* Workbook page 95, Exercise 5.

Use Your English

ACTIVITY 1 writing

STEP 1
Watch a television program (comedy or drama) for a few minutes without turning on the sound. You should be able to see, but not to hear, what's going on.

STEP 2
Describe at least five interactions between characters. Describe exactly what happened, your interpretation of what happened, and your reasons for thinking so. Make a chart like this.

DESCRIPTION OF WHAT HAPPENED—WHO DID WHAT?	INTERPRETATION OF ACTION—WHAT WAS THE CHARACTER'S REASON OR PURPOSE?	REASON FOR YOUR INTERPRETATION— WHY DO YOU THINK SO?
Example: One man kept poking the other man in the chest with his finger.	He might have been trying to start a fight.	The other man's expression became more and more angry.
Interaction 1		
Interaction 2		
Interaction 3		
Interaction 4		
Interact on 5		

STEP 3
Write a paragraph that describes what you saw and what you think was happening. Be sure to distinguish between things that **might** have been going on versus things that **must** have been going on. Give reasons for all of your interpretations.

ACTIVITY 2 speaking/writing

Do you have friends or family living in another country? What time is it at this moment in that country? What do you think they are doing at this moment?

---

5. Who killed Judge Clarence? It (a) _____ (not be) his wife. She was in Switzerland learning how to ski. It (b) _____ (be) his accountant. Apparently there was some trouble with money. But nobody thought his accountant would do such a thing. There were a few clues. His wallet was missing. His brother's fingerprints were found on the candlestick that was used to kill the judge. The murderer (c) _____ (be) his brother, but Detective Grace O'Neill was not convinced. It all seemed too simple. The brother was rich and didn't need the money. The murderer (d) _____ (be) someone else, someone who was actually trying to get the brother in trouble with the law.

EXERCISE 9

Use modals of prediction and inference to give possible or probable reasons for these situations.

Examples: The window was open. The TV was gone.

A thief must have broken into the apartment.

The students are quiet. They're listening carefully.

They might be taking a test.

The teacher could be telling them about their final examination.

1. The parents are laughing. They're looking at a picture.
2. Mary's waiting at the corner. She's looking at her watch.
3. Altaz was smiling. A doctor was congratulating him.
4. The men were digging holes. They were looking at an old map.
5. A woman was crying. She had just received an envelope in the mail.
6. Denise stays late at the office every night. She tells her boss about it.
7. That man wears old clothes. He doesn't have enough to eat.
8. The police ran to their car. They drove quickly to the house.

ANSWER KEY

Exercise 8 Continued from LP page 265.   5. (a) couldn't have been; (b) could/may/might have been; (c) could/may/might have been; (d) must have been   **Exercise 9**   Answers will vary. Possible answers are: 1. It must be a cute picture of their baby. They could have gotten a funny photo in the mail.   2. She might be waiting for someone to arrive. The person she's waiting for might have gotten delayed.   3. He must have gotten some good news about his medical exam. He could be graduating from medical school.   4. They might have been searching for treasure. They could have been planting trees.   5. She must have gotten some bad news. She might have gotten a letter from her long-lost sister who had been kidnapped.   6. She must be trying to get a raise. She might be trying to get Peter in trouble with her boss.   7. He must be a homeless person. He must not have a family to take care of him.   8. They must have heard an alarm. There must have been a burglar.

EXERCISE 9 [15 minutes]

1. Using the information/clues given for the first two examples, invite volunteers to supply other inferences and predictions. Encourage students to be creative. Supply an inference or a prediction of your own if you need to get it started. (*It could be a hot day and the TV might be at the repair shop.*)

2. Remind students to note whether they may need to put their inferences or predictions into the past time frame.

3. Students can work individually or in pairs or you can assign this as homework to share in small groups the next day. See answers on LP page 266.

For more practice, use *Grammar Dimensions 3* Workbook page 96, Exercise 6.

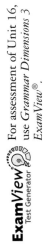

EXPANSION 1 [30 minutes/homework]

For a review of the unit, use Activity 1 (writing) on SB page 267.

EXPANSION 2 [30 minutes]

Have students create their own mini-mysteries individually or in pairs. Be sure students include the answers on another piece of paper. When finished, make copies of all the mysteries and hand them out to the class. Assign pairs to work on one or two and come up with their own lists of possible solutions. Then let them find the authors and check their answers.

UNIT GOAL REVIEW [10 minutes]

Ask students to look at the goals on the opening page of the unit again. Refer to the pages of the unit where information on each goal can be found.

■ STEP 3

1. You can assign Step 3 as a writing activity or simply use it as a speaking task for small groups to share their observations and interpretations.

2. If doing this activity in class, all students will have watched the same section of a movie. Have the small groups compare their interpretations and report any differences in these. Circulate and listen for the use of *might* and *must*.

Suggestion: If showing part of a movie in class, play the silent section again with sound for the class to see how their interpretations compare.

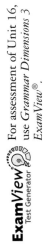

For assessment of Unit 16, use *Grammar Dimensions 3 ExamView®*.

USE YOUR ENGLISH

The Use Your English activities at the end of the unit contain situations that should naturally elicit the structures covered in the unit. For a more complete discussion of how to use the Use Your English activities see To the Teacher on LP page xxii. When students are doing these activities in class, you can circulate and listen to see if they are using the structures accurately. Errors can be corrected after the activity has finished.

ACTIVITY 1   writing [30 minutes/homework]

This activity asks students to watch a television program without sound and then interpret what was happening. You can have students complete Steps 1 and 2 either in class by showing part of a movie without sound or as homework.

■ STEP 1

1. This can either be assigned as homework or you can show part of a movie in class without sound.

2. Students should watch part of the program without sound for a few minutes or long enough to find five interactions.

■ STEP 2

1. Go over the example chart and explain the activity to the class. Students will need to take notes as they watch and keep track of five different interactions.

2. Have students create a chart like the one shown on SB page 267 and fill it in.

ACTIVITY 2   speaking/writing [25 minutes]

This activity will only work for those students who have family or friends living in another country. See the Variation below for other ideas.

1. As a class, decide what local time will be used as your time of reference for this activity. This will allow students to discuss the similarities and differences between families and their groups of friends later.

2. Decide whether this will be a writing or speaking assignment (or both) and give guidelines on the format and length you expect.

3. When finished with their preparations, have students share their ideas in groups. Try to create a mix in the groups as much as possible.

4. Have groups report any interesting similarities or differences to the class.

VARIATION

Have students come up with inferences about an absent classmate. What could have happened to him/her? What might he/she be doing right now?

ACTIVITY 3 speaking

Look at these pictures of six household items that are no longer used today.

a.

b.

c.

d.

e.

f.

■ STEP 1 Work with a partner and discuss what you think each object might have been used for. Give reasons.

■ STEP 2 Compare your ideas with those of other students in the class. See page A-12 for answers.

ACTIVITY 4 speaking

Number of Children
Love and Romance
Health
Wealth

Do you know how to predict people's future by looking at their palms? Here is a diagram of some of the important "lines" of the palm. If the line is deep and strong, the person should have favorable developments in those areas. If the line is weak or broken, this indicates that the person may have trouble in that area. Using this reference guide, choose a partner and examine his or her palm to make predictions about his or her future. Try to make at least two predictions about what will happen to your partner in the future and two inferences about his or her character or personality.

ACTIVITY 5 listening/speaking

CD Track 24

■ STEP 1 Listen to the conversation of a family trying to solve a mystery. Decide whether each person listed below is a possible suspect, a probable suspect, or not a possible suspect.

SUSPECT	LIKELIHOOD OF GUILT	EVIDENCE
Mom	could not be guilty	she discovered the cookies were missing
Dad		
Nancy		
Eric		
Diane		

■ STEP 2 Work with a partner to decide who the criminal is. Give reasons to support your decision. The thief must have been _____.

ACTIVITY 6 research on the web

Go to the Internet to investigate mysteries that have never been solved. Type in the words "unsolved mysteries" into a reliable search engine such as Yahoo® or Google®. Choose one of the mysteries there. Read about it and prepare a brief report about the mystery. Try to develop some possible and probable explanations for the mystery. Can you solve the mystery? Find another student in class who read about the same mystery you did and compare your ideas.

ACTIVITY 7 reflection

How do you distinguish between a prediction and a logical inference in your first language? Think about how you would indicate the difference between a possibility that you are guessing about and a logical conclusion that you have made on the basis of evidence. If there are other speakers of your language in class, work together with them to make a brief report about how these ideas are expressed in your own language as compared to the structures we use in English.

ANSWER KEY

Activity 3 The pictures show the following ingenious inventions: a. candle snuffer b. antique screwdriver c. cherry pit remover d. blender e. bread slicer f. meat chopper

Activity 5 *Step 1:* Dad: could be guilty; he's still full; there are crumbs on his mustache. Nancy: might be guilty/might not; she likes sweets; she was really hungry after school/she's been dieting Eric: could not be guilty; he hasn't been home at all Diane: could be guilty/might not be guilty; she once ate a whole chocolate cake/her mom was with her the whole afternoon *Step 2:* The thief must have been Dad.

USE YOUR ENGLISH

ACTIVITY 3 speaking [15 minutes]

Use this activity after Focus 3 on SB page 264 for more practice.

STEP 1

1. Put students into pairs or small groups and have them begin discussing the possible past uses for these objects.

2. Students should not check the answers in the back of the book (see SB page A-12) until all class discussion is finished. See answers on LP page 268.

STEP 2

Encourage pairs/groups to share their most likely and their most creative ideas with the class.

Suggestion: You may still need to explain the actual uses of these objects to the class and how each worked.

EXPANSION [15 minutes]

As a follow-up to this activity, have each student bring in one unusual object from home to share with the class. (Note that this version of Activity 3 does not require the use of modals in the past time frame.)

1. Set the objects up around the room and give each one a number.

2. Have students number their own piece of paper and then move around the classroom writing their own guesses for the use of each object next to its number.

3. When everyone has had a chance to write their guesses, put students into small groups to share their ideas.

4. Finally, ask the original owner to explain the object to the class.

ACTIVITY 4 speaking [15 minutes/homework]

This activity can be used after completing Focus 1 and 2.

1. You may want to poll the class (or have a small group discussion for a few minutes) and find out how many people may have had a "reading" of any sort in the past. Some may have had palms, tea leaves, tarot cards, aura, numerology, astrology or other forms of their "fortune" read for them. Ask students how they feel about these fortune readings and if they believe them.

Note: Be careful though, because for some students, this is a fun activity, while for others, it can be offensive to their religious beliefs. You may wish to assess whether this activity is appropriate for your class before beginning it.

2. With the diagram in the book, let pairs now practice "reading" each other's palm and talking about their findings.

Suggestion: Because this is quite fun for most students, if you are short on class time, let students read their own palms (or those of a friend/family member) as homework and share their findings in class or in writing the next day.

ACTIVITY 5 listening/speaking [15 minutes]

CD Track 24

Students will hear speakers using modals of inference in past time in the context of a family "mystery".

Important: To give students a chance to record their ideas about the likelihood of possible suspects, you will need to stop the audio just before the end of this section so as not to give the answer away before students have made their own guesses. Turn off the audio just when the mom says: *Oh, we can do that later. We're going to have dinner in a minute.*

STEP 1

1. Play the audio, stopping just short of the end as noted above.

2. Have students fill in their charts as to the likelihood of suspects.

3. Play the audio again (stopping short again) and have students revise or complete their charts.

STEP 2

1. Put students into pairs or small groups and let them share their opinions on the possible suspects.

2. Have the class vote on who they think is the most likely suspect. Invite volunteers to share their reasons.

3. Play the audio again without stopping this time. How many people were correct?

ACTIVITY 6 research on the web [30 minutes]

1. Set out the guidelines for this Internet activity as you have done for the past Internet activities.

2. Because many unsolved mysteries involve graphic descriptions of murder, you could direct students to report instead on missing persons, lost loves, or miscellaneous cases (see the Web site for the television series *Unsolved Mysteries*).

ACTIVITY 7 reflection [30 minutes]

1. Put students who share a first language together into groups if possible for this reflection activity.

2. If students are having trouble analyzing and isolating the structures in their native language, consider having them translate a few English sentences into their language.

17

HYPOTHETICAL STATEMENTS

UNIT GOALS

- **Correctly identify and understand sentences describing hypothetical or contrary-to-fact situations**

- **Correctly form hypothetical and contrary-to-fact statements in present, future, and past time frames**

- **Recognize and use various hypothetical constructions**

OPENING TASK
If I Ruled the World

Suppose that you had just been made Leader of the Entire World. Imagine that you had been granted the authority and resources to make any kind of changes in world affairs that you would like. You have the power and ability to change the world to fit your vision.

What actions would you take to:

- end world hunger?
- develop renewable energy sources?
- control population growth?
- protect the environment?
- abolish war?
- ensure political stability?
- maintain economic growth?
- _____?

■ STEP 1

Choose two or three of the areas listed above and think of one other area where you would like to see changes in the world (for example, access to health care, improving educational levels, ending disease).

■ STEP 2

For each general issue outline at least three actions you would take to achieve your desired results, if you had the power and resources to accomplish them.

Problem: _____
Actions: 1. _____
 2. _____
 3. _____

■ STEP 3

Report your plan to the rest of the class. The class will decide whom they would like to choose as President of the Entire World.

UNIT OVERVIEW

Unit 17 reviews hypothetical statements; their forms, meanings, and uses; and the underlying implied meanings of these statements. Also known as **unreal conditionals**, hypothetical statements describe conditions that are not true and in fact imply that the opposite is actually true.

GRAMMAR NOTE

Also known as unreal or Type II and III conditionals, hypothetical conditionals describe conditions that are not true and can imply that the opposite is actually true. Although most students should not have too much trouble with the forms, the meanings and uses can be difficult for students from non-Indo-European backgrounds (i.e., Chinese, Indonesian, and Arabic) who do not have the same variety of conditionals. However, since hypothetical speech is extremely common in English, and is used for strategies of politeness, indirection, and to indicate imaginary or hypothetical ideas, it is important that students master these fundamental meanings and uses through their use in a variety of contexts.

UNIT GOALS

Some instructors may want to review the goals listed on Student Book (SB) page 270 after completing the Opening Task so that students understand what they should know by the end of the unit. These goals can also be reviewed at the end of the unit when students are more familiar with the grammar terminology.

OPENING TASK [30 minutes]

The aim of this activity is to give students the opportunity to talk about hypothetical situations and use hypothetical constructions. The problem-solving format is designed to show the teacher how well the students can produce a target structure implicitly and spontaneously when they are engaged in a communicative task. For a more complete discussion

of the purpose of the Opening Task, see To the Teacher, Lesson Planner (LP) page xxii.

Setting Up the Task

1. This Opening Task can be presented in a more serious manner of running and winning a political election or in a more relaxed manner with the final presentation of a paper crown. Decide how the final vote will run and then present the task along those lines. There may even be a prize involved such as bonus points or some other "ruler for the day" type of award to motivate students in how creative they get with this task.

2. Explain how the election will run (choose areas to change, present ideas for change, vote for President of the World).

Conducting the Task

■ STEP 1

1. Once you have set the Opening Task up, you can assign the preparation for presentations as homework and then set aside at least three minutes per student for the presentation of their issues and plans for action.

2. Have students work alone or in pairs to develop ideas for the actions they would take for each of the issues listed.

■ STEP 2

1. Students should work individually to develop their plans for action.

2. Circulate and assist as needed. Note who is comfortable with the use of hypothetical statements, but don't worry about making corrections at this point. Remind students of the prize to encourage them to be creative in their plans.

■ STEP 3

1. Set up a sense of competition and formality to the presentations. Remind students that this is an election.

2. Give each student time to present their ideas in groups or to the class.

3. After presenting, each student should vote for the person who has the best ideas for change. Again, if you have a large class, this can be done in large groups rather than as a whole class activity.

Closing the Task

1. After the presentations, have students vote secretly on paper (they can not vote for themselves) and have a pair of students collect the votes and count them up while you review any new vocabulary or interesting points you noted during the presentations.

2. Share the voting results, have the winner stand, and present the prize (and/or crown).

VARIATION 1

Rather than running for President of the Entire World, set the Opening Task up to have students run for President of your school. Students will create and present a list of issues they would address for the school and the steps they would take to make changes. Continue with Steps 2 and 3. Then have the class vote for their new school President.

VARIATION 2

In place of the Opening Task, assign Activity 8 (research on the web) on SB page 293 for homework and begin the unit by having students discuss their answers to the most interesting hypothetical questions their group members brought in.

EXPANSION [30 minutes]

Assign Activity 8 (research on the web) to get the class thinking about the topic of hypothetical questions before moving on in the unit.

FOCUS 1

Overview of Hypothetical Meaning

meaning

There is an important difference between **hypothetical** and **actual** meaning

HYPOTHETICAL STATEMENTS	IMPLIED ACTUAL MEANING	EXPLANATIONS
(a) If I ruled the world, I would live in a luxurious mansion in Hawaii.	I don't rule the world, so I probably won't be able to live in a luxurious mansion in Hawaii.	Hypothetical statements describe conditions that aren't true or are impossible.
(b) If we were in Hawaii right now, we wouldn't have to study grammar. We could be lying on the beach.	We're not in Hawaii—we're in English class. We can't lie on the beach because we're studying grammar.	
(c) You should be happy with your life. If I were you, I wouldn't feel so sorry for myself!	You aren't happy with your life. I am not you, but I think you feel too sorry for yourself.	We use hypothetical statements to imply that the opposite situation is actually true.
(d) You could have done a better job on your homework. You should have avoided a lot of these careless mistakes.	You didn't do a very good job on your homework. You made a lot of careless mistakes.	

EXERCISE 1

Here are some more hypothetical statements. Choose the sentence that expresses their implied meaning:

1. If you had done your homework, you would have gotten an A.
   - ⓐ You didn't get an A because you didn't do your homework.
   - b. You did your homework, so you got an A.

2. You could have brought a friend to the party.
   - ⓐ You had permission, but you came alone.
   - b. You brought a friend.

3. You could have been more careful with your homework.
   - a. You did your homework carefully.
   - ⓑ You were careless with your homework.

4. You should have seen the doctor before you got so sick.
   - a. You followed my advice.
   - ⓑ You didn't follow my advice.

5. I would have been here early, but the traffic was terrible!
   - a. I arrived early.
   - ⓑ I arrived late.

6. I wish you had come to the lake last weekend.
   - ⓐ You didn't come.
   - b. You were there.

7. Let's pretend that we had a new president.
   - ⓐ We don't have a new president.
   - b. We have a new president.

FOCUS 1 [20 minutes]

Focus 1 presents an overview of hypothetical statements and their implied meanings. Students will next be asked to determine the implied meaning of hypothetical statements in Exercise 1.

1. **Lead-in:** Consider opening Focus 1 by playing any one of a variety of songs that include hypothetical statements ("If I Were a Rich Man," "If I Were You," "If I Had a Million Dollars," "If I Could Turn Back Time," "If I Had a Boat," etc.). Students can simply listen or you can put an example of a hypothetical statement on the board. (Use the same song later in Focus 3 with a fill-in activity to draw attention to the forms used in the song.)

2. You can go over the chart as a class or have students look it over individually and try to decide what hypothetical statements tell us. (*They tell us that a situation is not true, impossible, or that the opposite is actually true.*)

3. What can students learn from the words of the song you played?

VARIATION

Use Exercise 1 as a diagnostic to see how familiar students are with hypothetical meanings before going over Focus 1.

EXERCISE 1 [10 minutes]

Students will identify the implied meaning of hypothetical statements. You may want to use this exercise as a diagnostic to see how familiar students are with hypothetical meanings before going over Focus 1.

1. Students should keep in mind that hypothetical statements imply that a situation is not true or that the opposite is in fact true.

2. Have students work individually and discuss answers in small groups or pairs when finished. See answers on LP page 272.

Note: The photo is of Mt. Rushmore in the United States with four former presidents depicted (Left to right: Presidents Washington, Jefferson, T. Roosevelt, Lincoln)

For more practice, use *Grammar Dimensions 3* Workbook page 97, Exercise 1.

FOCUS 2 — Actual Versus Hypothetical Conditionals

ACTUAL VERSUS HYPOTHETICAL CONDITIONALS	IMPLIED MEANING
Actual Conditional: (a) If I have time, I always clean the kitchen before I go to work.	I always clean the kitchen when I have time.
Hypothetical Conditional: (b) If I had time, I would always clean the kitchen before leaving for work.	I don't usually clean the kitchen because I usually don't have time.
Actual Conditional: (c) If I don't have to work, I will come to your party.	I don't know if I can come, because there's a chance that I may have to work.
Hypothetical Conditional: (d) If I didn't have to work, I would come to your party.	I can't come because I have to work.
Actual Conditional: (e) If Denise was at the meeting yesterday, I'm sure she took very complete notes.	Maybe she was at the meeting and took notes.
Hypothetical Conditional: (f) If Denise had been at the meeting, I'm sure she would have taken very complete notes.	She wasn't at the meeting, so she didn't take notes.

EXERCISE 2

Match the statements in column 1 with their correct implied meanings in column 2.

STATEMENT	IMPLIED MEANING
1. If John has the money, he always stops for a cup of coffee on his way to class.	a. He doesn't usually do this, because he usually doesn't have the money.
2. If John had the money, he would always stop for a cup of coffee on his way to class.	b. He always does this whenever he has the money.
3. If I had to work, I wouldn't be helping you with your homework.	c. I may have to work.
4. If I have to work, I won't be able to help you with your homework.	d. I don't have to work.
5. If Bambang took the TOEFL® Test* yesterday, I'm sure he did very well.	e. Bambang didn't take the TOEFL.
6. If Bambang had taken the TOEFL, I'm sure he would have done very well.	f. Maybe Bambang took the TOEFL.

EXERCISE 3

Are these sentences hypothetical statements or statements about actual events? If they are hypothetical statements, state the implied meaning.

Examples: Those two are always together, so if she attended the meeting, he did, too. *statement about an actual event*

If the weather hadn't been so cold yesterday, the picnic would have been a lot more fun. *hypothetical statement. Implied meaning: The weather was cold yesterday, so the picnic wasn't much fun.*

1. I would come to your party if I didn't have to work.
2. If Juan went to Hawaii on vacation, he must have spent a lot of money.
3. If Tomas could afford to retire, I'm sure he would have done so by now.
4. I wouldn't tease that dog if I were you.
5. Suppose you had your own private jet. You could take me to Las Vegas for lunch.
6. If they left when they had planned, they should be here any minute.
7. If my brother needed money, he always asked to borrow it from me.
8. If I cook a big casserole for the party, do you think there'll be enough food?

*TOEFL is a registered trademark of the Educational Testing Service (ETS). This publication is not endorsed or approved by ETS.

ANSWER KEY

Exercise 2 1b; 2a; 3d; 4c; 5f; 6e

Exercise 3 1. hypothetical statement; implied meaning: I can't come to your party because I have to work. 2. prediction about a real event 3. hypothetical statement; implied meaning: Tomas can't afford to retire, so he hasn't done so yet. 4. hypothetical statement; implied meaning: It's not a good idea to tease that dog! 5. hypothetical statement; implied meaning: I know you don't have your own jet, but let's imagine that we do. In our imaginations, we can go to Las Vegas for lunch. (Notice that it's difficult to think of a way to restate this idea in nonhypothetical speech. That's how "ingrained" the pattern is in English.) 6. prediction about an actual event 7. statement about a recurring situation in the past 8. prediction about an actual event

FOCUS 2 [20 minutes]

Focus 2 gives pairs of sentences which show actual (sometimes taught as real or Type I) conditionals in contrast to hypothetical (unreal or Type II and III) conditionals. The pairs show examples of actual conditionals with results first in the present (a), then the future (c), and finally in the past (e) time frames. Hypothetical conditionals are shown with results in the present/future for (b) and (d) and in the past for (f). Because this unit focuses on hypothetical conditionals, the actual conditionals are simply used here to show the contrast.

1. **Lead-in:** For an inductive approach, ask students to work in pairs to identify what makes the actual conditional sentences different from the hypothetical conditional sentences (*hypothetical sentences use a modal of possibility in the main clause and hypothetical sentences do not use the present tense in the conditional clause*).

2. Put some examples of sentences with actual conditionals and hypothetical conditionals on the board. Invite pairs to share their observations about what makes these sentences different.

3. Go over the examples in the book in pairs (a–b, c–d, and e–f) and note their differences in implied meaning.

Suggestion: If you have time, have students work together to create their own pairs of sentences showing actual and hypothetical meanings.

EXERCISE 2 [10 minutes]

Like Exercise 1, students will again identify the implied meaning of statements. However, students will be challenged further because these statements are a mix of actual and hypothetical conditionals.

1. Have students work individually to match the statements with their implied meanings.

2. Students can check in pairs or you can go over these quickly as a class. See answers on LP page 274.

For more practice, use *Grammar Dimensions 3* Workbook page 98, Exercise 3.

EXERCISE 3 [10 minutes]

Students will again determine whether a statement is actual or hypothetical. They will then state the implied meaning for any hypothetical statements. This will require students to state what is not true for those statements. It can be difficult to do, which just shows us how useful hypothetical conditionals are in English.

1. Have students work individually. They should go through the sentences first to mark which are actual or hypothetical.

2. Circulate and check that students have done the first step correctly. Draw students' attention to any problem sentences to check again. You may find some are common errors for the whole class. Go over these before moving onto the next step.

3. Next have the class write their own versions of the implied meanings for the hypothetical statements.

4. Let students compare their work with a partner. See answers on LP page 274.

For more practice, use *Grammar Dimensions 3* Workbook page 97, Exercise 2.

form

FOCUS 3

Hypothetical Conditionals in Present and Future Time Frames

EXAMPLES

Conditions	Results
(a) If I had time,	I would always clean the kitchen before leaving for work.
(b) If I didn't have to work,	I would come to your party.
(c) If I won the lottery,	I would give you a million dollars.
(d) If I already spoke English perfectly,	I wouldn't need to read this unit.
(e) If we didn't have to go to school tomorrow,	we could stay up all night tonight.
(f) If John didn't plan to spend next year in France,	Mary might not be so annoyed with him now.

EXPLANATIONS

Use past-tense verb forms to describe present and future hypothetical conditions. Use *would/could/might* + verb to describe present and future results.

Using *were* in hypothetical statements

EXAMPLES

(h) If Mary **were** coming to the party, she could bring the potato salad.

(g) If my mother **were** here, she would want us all to wash our hands.

EXPLANATIONS

If clauses in hypothetical conditionals use *were* (rather than *was*) for singular subjects in formal English. *Was* is often used in informal situations.

EXAMPLES

Inverted Hypotheticals

Inverted Form	Regular Form
(i) **Were** I in charge of this country, I would make big changes.	(j) **If I were** in charge of this country, I would make big changes.

EXPLANATIONS

In formal English, in clauses with a *were* auxiliary, we can indicate hypothetical conditions by omitting *if* and using question word or inverted order.

EXERCISE 4

Change these statements of actual condition and result into hypothetical conditionals.

Example: Actual condition: I'm not the teacher. Actual result: We have too much homework.

Hypothetical condition: *If I were the teacher, we wouldn't have so much homework.*

1. I don't have a million dollars. I can't afford to buy you a new car.
2. I don't yet speak English perfectly. I still have to study grammar.
3. Doctors have to spend so many years in medical school. Medical care is quite expensive.
4. My mother doesn't know how I am living now. She's not worried about me.
5. I am not president of my country. I don't have influence on world events.
6. I have many good friends. My life is busy and rewarding.
7. The TOEFL Test is a difficult examination. Many people can't do well on it on the first try.
8. There aren't enough places in universities in other countries. Many students come to North America for university study.

EXERCISE 5

Here are some hypothetical conditions. Add hypothetical results that are true for you.

Example: If I could be anywhere in the world at this moment, . . .
I would be home in bed.

1. If I were going to attend any American university tomorrow, . . .
2. If I were president of the United States, . . .

(Exercise 5 is continued on LP page 278.)

ANSWER KEY

Exercise 4   Answers will vary. Possible answers are: 1. If I had a million dollars, I could afford to buy you a new car.   2. If I spoke English perfectly, I wouldn't have to study grammar.   3. If doctors didn't have to spend so many years in medical school, medical care wouldn't be so expensive.   4. If my mother knew how I am living now, she would worry about me.   5. If I were president of my country, I would have influence on world events.   6. If I didn't have many good friends, my life wouldn't be busy and rewarding.   7. If the TOEFL® Test wasn't a difficult examination, many people would do well on the first try.   8. If there were enough places in universities in other countries, many students wouldn't come to North America for university study.   **Exercise 5**   Answers will vary. Possible answers are: 1. I would be happy./I would be nervous about my English.   2. I would balance the budget./I would reduce military spending.

LESSON PLAN 2

FOCUS 3 [20 minutes]

Focus 3 on SB page 276 and 277 looks at the form of hypothetical conditionals in the present and future time frames (see Focus 4 for past time frames). Note that many students may have trouble using or recognizing the use of verbs in the **past tense** to describe hypothetical statements in the **present or future.**

1. **Lead-in:** You can again play a song which uses hypothetical conditionals. Use the song to focus this time on the form of the conditional. This can be done by using a gap fill-in for the missing verbs in each conditional sentence. Note that "If I Were a Rich Man" is a good song to illustrate the use of *were* as in examples (g) and (h) in Focus 3.

2. After going over the sentences and noting the two rules in the explanation column (use the past tense verb form and a modal + verb), have students practice mixing and matching hypotheticals from the *conditions* column with clauses from the *results* column.

   Suggestion: For more practice, have students create more sentences to illustrate the use of *were* and its inverted form.

VARIATION

Put a few example sentences on the board and let students work in pairs to create a rule or two for hypothetical conditionals in present/future time frame.

GRAMMAR NOTE

Note that the inverted hypotheticals in examples (i) and (j) are extremely formal. If you are short on time, you may want to wait until the end of the unit to go over these inverted hypothetical forms, along with Exercise 8.

EXERCISE 4 [15 minutes/homework]

Students will combine two statements of actual conditions into one hypothetical statement. For more advanced classes, you may want to skip this and move onto Exercises 5 and 6 if you are short on time.

1. Write two examples of actual statements about the class on the board. For example:

   It's not Tuesday. We don't have to take a test today. However . . .

2. Invite the class to make a hypothetical statement out of these two sentences. (*However,* **if it were** *Tuesday, we* **would** *have to take a test.*)

3. For advanced classes, move on and have students work individually or assign this (and Exercises 5 and 6) as homework.

4. If your class needs some extra assistance, take a moment and invite the class to point out each of the changes made in the second (hypothetical) sentence (these are in bold). Give a few more actual statements to combine and restate as hypothetical statements before having students work on their own to complete the exercise. See possible answers on LP page 276.

For more practice, use *Grammar Dimensions 3* Workbook page 98, Exercise 4.

EXERCISE 5 [10 minutes/homework]

Students can have fun coming up with their own results for hypothetical situations. Exercise 5 and 6 can be assigned as homework and then shared in pairs or small groups the next day.

1. Students can create their own results for these hypothetical conditions and then share with a partner or small group in the next class.

2. Pay particular attention to the form of the answers as you circulate during the sharing of answers. Note any common errors (verb tense, modals, etc.)

and go over these with the class later. See possible answers on LP pages 276 and 278.

3. If this exercise was completed in class, have students keep the same partner to work with for Exercises 7 and 8.

For more practice, use *Grammar Dimensions 3* Workbook page 99, Exercise 5.

EXPANSION [20 minutes]

Give students a chance to think quickly and talk hypothetically about what they might do with a variety of objects.

1. Paste photos of items on index cards (cut from magazines) and let students draw a card from your hand as you move through the class.

2. As a mixer, have students get up and circulate through the class telling other students what they would do if they won the item on the card. (*If I won a trip to Disneyland, I would . . .*)

3. As soon as they have spoken to one other person, they must then switch cards, think of something new to say about their new item, and find a different person to talk to.

4. This switching of cards and stating new hypothetical results to new partners will continue for several minutes.

5. Once students have spoken to each of their classmates, have everyone take their seats and then invite volunteers to share the most interesting or unusual hypothetical results they heard.

FOCUS 4 — Hypothetical Conditionals in Past Time Frame

form

EXAMPLES

	Conditions	Results
(a)	If Denise had been at the meeting,	I'm sure she would have taken very complete notes. She wouldn't have minded sharing them. She would have let you borrow them.
(b)	If William the Conqueror hadn't invaded England in 1066,	the English language would probably have many fewer words of French origin.
(c)	If I had been born in 1890,	I surely wouldn't be alive today.
(d)	If we hadn't saved enough money last year,	we wouldn't be able to take a vacation next summer.

EXPLANATIONS

Use past-perfect verb forms to refer to past hypothetical conditions. Use *would have/could have/might have* + verb to refer to past hypothetical results.

Use *would/could/might* + verb to refer to present or future hypothetical results.

Inverted Hypotheticals

EXAMPLES

Inverted Form

(e) Had I known that you were coming so late, I wouldn't have waited.

Regular Form

(f) If I had known that you were coming so late, I wouldn't have waited.

EXPLANATION

In formal English, in clauses with a *had* auxiliary, we can indicate hypothetical conditions by omitting *if* and using question word or inverted order.

---

3. If my teacher knew how I was studying now, . . .

4. If I were the teacher of this class, . . .

5. If I didn't have to worry about the TOEFL Test, . . .

6. If I went home next week, . . .

7. If I had all the money I needed, . . .

8. If I were the same age as my parents, . . .

EXERCISE 6

Here are some hypothetical conditions. Add hypothetical results that are true for you.

Example: I would take a vacation . . .

if I didn't have to get a bigger score on the TOEFL.

1. I wouldn't need to work . . .

2. I would bring my family here for a visit . . .

3. We wouldn't come to school . . .

4. We wouldn't need umbrellas . . .

5. I wouldn't be studying English . . .

6. I wouldn't have to take the TOEFL Test . . .

7. The world would be a much better place . . .

8. I would give my English teacher a thousand dollars . . .

EXERCISE 7

Work with a partner. Choose five sentences that your partner wrote for Exercises 5 and 6 and rewrite them in nonhypothetical language.

Examples: If I had a million dollars, I would give you a new car.

My partner doesn't have enough money to give me a car.

I would take a vacation if I didn't have to finish this project.

My partner has to finish this project, so she can't take a vacation.

My partner can't take a vacation because she has to finish this project.

EXERCISE 8

Look over the sentences that you and your partner wrote in Exercises 5 and 6. Which sentences can be rewritten as inverted hypotheticals?

Exercise 5 Continued from LP page 276. 3. she would worry about whether I was getting enough to eat./she would want me to study harder. 4. I would never give homework./I would give everybody an A. 5. I wouldn't be studying in this class./I would be happy. 6. I would bring everyone in my family a present./ I would make my family happy. 7. I would buy a new car every year./ I wouldn't have to find a part-time job. 8. I would probably be able to travel more./I would probably be as conservative as they are.

Exercise 6 Answers will vary. Possible answers are: 1. if I had all the money I needed./if my parents supported me. 2. if I had enough money./if they could all get visas. 3. if attendance weren't

required./if we already knew English. 4. if it never rained./if we never went outdoors. 5. if I weren't interested in earning it./if it weren't important for my future. 6. if I weren't applying to American universities./if I didn't care about my score. 7. if we didn't have to study grammar./if everyone followed the golden rule. 8. if she promised to give me an A./if pigs could fly.

Exercise 7 Answers will vary.

Exercise 8 Answers will vary.

EXERCISE 6 [10 minutes/homework]

This exercise works similarly to Exercise 5. Students will simply now add their own ideas of hypothetical conditions that would make the hypothetical results listed in Exercise 6 possible. Follow the same steps as Exercise 5. See possible answers on LP page 278.

EXERCISE 7 [15 minutes]

Students will rewrite five sentences they heard from their partner into statements of nonhypothetical facts similar to the statements shown in Exercise 4.

1. After students have shared their answers to Exercises 5 and 6, have students choose five sentences to rewrite.

2. Model this by asking for someone to share his/her partner's answer to one of the statements they heard and write the actual condition on the board. See the examples in the book.

3. Collect student work. Note any common errors and go over them as a class as needed.

EXERCISE 8 [15 minutes]

Students will practice the more formal pattern of inverted hypotheticals by changing any previously made sentences that include the *were* auxiliary. If you are short on time, save this more formal inverted order for the end of the unit.

LESSON PLAN 3

FOCUS 4 [20 minutes]

Focus 4 gives the forms for stating hypothetical conditionals in the past time frame. Just as the use of simple past tense to express the present or future (see Focus 3) can be confusing, the shift in tense to past-perfect to express the past can also cause difficulties. The addition of perfect modals (*would have/could have/might have*) can also be a source of errors.

1. **Lead-in:** Show the shift in tense and time frame by using an example of a hypothetical conditional in the present/future time frame. Put this on the board and illustrate the changes in verb tense and modals to put this into the past time frame. For example:

If I had time, I would clean the kitchen now.

If I had had time, I would have cleaned the kitchen last night.

If John didn't forget to do his homework so often, be might do better in this class.

If John hadn't forgotten to do his homework so often, be might have done better last semester.

2. After presenting the differences in form between past and present/future time frames, go over the first example in Focus 4.

3. Before presenting examples (b–d), point out that actions/conditions in the past can also have results in the present or future.

4. Again, if you are short on time, consider saving the more formal inverted hypotheticals for the end of the unit.

Suggestion: The differences between example (a) and examples (b–d) can be shown by putting a sentence starter with a condition in the past on the board and inviting pairs to create a variety of results both in the past and in the present/future (also see Exercises 11–13). For example:

If I had been born in 1950, ...

*. . . I **wouldn't have** gone to college.* (past result)

*. . . I **would be** a grandparent by now.* (present result)

EXPANSION [homework]

You may wish to use Activity 9 (reflection) on SB page 293 as follow-up to this focus chart. In this activity, students will use hypotheticals to describe how the world would be different had an historic event not taken place.

EXERCISE 9

Do these sentences indicate statements of past possibility, or hypothetical events that did not actually happen?

Examples: I didn't see him, but he could have been there. *past possibility*

If John had been at the concert, he would have been able to explain how the composer was able to get those effects. *hypothetical event*

1. My brother could have loaned me the money, but he's too cheap.
2. Assuming that the plane was on time, it should have landed a little while ago.
3. I don't know what the problem is. They should have been here by now.
4. You should have asked for a receipt when you bought those clothes.
5. Tiffany might have worked a little harder on this report. It's pretty careless.
6. The thief might have gotten in through the window. It's unlocked.

EXERCISE 10

Change these nonhypothetical statements of condition and result to hypothetical conditionals.

Example: I wasn't alive one hundred years ago. I have been able to fly all over the world.

If I had been alive one hundred years ago, I wouldn't have been able to fly all over the world.

1. My parents didn't speak English when I was a baby. I have to learn it in school.
2. English became a language of international business after World War II. Most developing countries require students to study it in high school.
3. Modern English developed from several different languages: French, German, Latin, Dutch, and even Norwegian. As a result, the grammar and spelling rules are very irregular.
4. England was invaded by France in 1066. Many French words replaced the traditional Anglo-Saxon ones.
5. English society changed a great deal after the French invasion. Modern English grammar is more similar to French grammar than to German grammar.

EXERCISE 11

Complete these sentences with past-time hypothetical results that are true for you.

Example: If I had been born one hundred years ago, _____

I wouldn't have had a chance to travel around the world.

1. If my family had used English at home when I was growing up, *I wouldn't have had to study it in high school.*
2. If World War II had ended differently, *the history of the twentieth century would have been very different.*
3. If the grammar of English hadn't developed from so many different languages, *it would have been much more like German than it is.*
4. If advanced computer technology hadn't been developed, *companies like IBM or or Microsoft would never have gotten so big.*
5. If I had never studied English, *I wouldn't have had to buy this book.*

EXERCISE 12

Add present or future time results to the following sentences.

Examples: If I had been born one hundred years ago . . .

I probably wouldn't be alive today.

my great-grandchildren might be entering the university in the next few years.

1. If I had been born in another country . . .
2. If World War II hadn't ended over fifty years ago . . .
3. If my parents hadn't wanted me to learn English . . .
4. If computers hadn't become so inexpensive and widely available . . .
5. If I had already gotten a score of 650 on the TOEFL . . .

EXERCISE 13

Here are hypothetical results. Add appropriate past-time conditions.

Example: I wouldn't have had a chance to travel around the world . . .

if I had been born one hundred years ago.

1. I wouldn't have asked you to join us . . .
2. I would not be studying English now . . .
3. English grammar would be much more regular . . .
4. Fax machines wouldn't be so popular . . .

(Exercise 13 is continued on LP page 282.)

Exercise 9 1. hypothetical event 2. past possibility 3. hypothetical event 4. hypothetical event 5. hypothetical event 6. past possibility **Exercise 10** 1. If my parents hadn't spoken English when I was a baby, I wouldn't have had to learn it in school. 2. If English hadn't become a language of international business after World War II, most developing countries wouldn't require students to study it in high school. 3. If modern English hadn't developed from several different languages— French, German, Latin, Dutch, and even Norwegian—the grammar and spelling rules would have been less irregular. 4. If England hadn't been invaded by France in 1066, many French words would not have replaced the traditional Anglo-Saxon ones. 5. If English society hadn't changed a great deal after the French invasion, modern English grammar would be less similar to French grammar than to German grammar. **Exercise 11** Answers will vary. Possible answers are listed above. **Exercise 12** Answers will vary. Possible answers are: 1. I wouldn't be studying English. 2. there wouldn't be such a high level of prosperity in Europe now. 3. I would probably have done it without their permission. 4. life wouldn't be as convenient as it is. 5. I wouldn't be studying this book. **Exercise 13** Answers will vary. Possible answers are: 1. if I had known you had to study. 2. if it hadn't been required for my education. 3. if it had been invented by a computer. 4. if their writing systems had been easier to transmit electronically.

LESSON PLAN 3

EXERCISE 9 [15 minutes]

Students will identify which statements imply a possible event and which statements imply events that are simply hypothetical and did not actually happen.

1. Give the class time to go over the sentences individually and decide whether each statement is *past possibility* or a *hypothetical event*.

2. Go over the examples as a class. Invite volunteers to explain the reasons for each answer. You may wish to do the exercise as a class also.

Suggestion: If the class is having trouble, simply turn each statement into a question (*Did my brother loan me the money?/Did the plane land a little while ago?*) If the answer is *no*, then this is simply a hypothetical statement. If the answer is *maybe*, then it is a possibility. See answers on LP page 280.

EXERCISE 10 [15 minutes]

This exercise is very similar to Exercise 4. Students will combine two statements of actual conditions into one hypothetical statement. Note that the time frames for the results can be either present/future or past. Follow the same steps as Exercise 4 for setting up the examples and completing the exercise. The following may be used as an example of the changes:

I wasn't born in the United States. I didn't speak English as a child.
If I had been born in the United States, I would have spoken English as a child.

See answers on LP page 280.

EXERCISE 11 [15 minutes/homework]

Like Exercise 5, students will create their own results for hypothetical situations in the past time frame. Follow the same steps as Exercise 5, but remind students that these results should be framed in the past (perfect modal + verb). If you

are short on time, this exercise can be assigned as homework.

1. To see if students are on track, invite everyone to give their own results to the first sentence starter. Put a few of these on the board to draw attention to the time frames and modal/verb forms.

2. Have students work individually in class or at home and then compare answers with a partner in preparation for Exercises 14–15. See possible answers on LP page 280.

For more practice, use *Grammar Dimensions 3* Workbook page 100, Exercise 6, Part A.

EXERCISE 12 [15 minutes/homework]

This exercise can also be used as homework. Remind students to frame their results in the present/future time. Have students work individually in class or at home and then compare answers with a partner in preparation for Exercises 14–15. See possible answers on LP page 280.

For more practice, use *Grammar Dimensions 3* Workbook page 100, Exercise 6, Part B.

EXERCISE 13 [15 minutes/homework]

This exercise is continued on SB page 282. Students will create their own conditions in the past time, rather than results as in Exercises 11–12. Have students work individually in class or at home and then compare answers with a partner in preparation for Exercises 14–15. See possible answers on LP pages 280 and 282.

5. America wouldn't be spending so much money on the military . . .
6. Transoceanic telephone calls wouldn't be possible . . .
7. There wouldn't have been such major political changes in Eastern European countries . . .
8. Modern antibiotics might not have been discovered . . .
9. Life today would be much more difficult . . .
10. I wouldn't have to answer this question . . .

EXERCISE 14

Look over the sentences that you and your partner wrote in Exercises 11, 12, and 13. Choose five sentences to rewrite as inverted hypotheticals.

EXERCISE 15

Work with a partner. Choose five sentences that your partner wrote for Exercises 11, 12, and 13 and rewrite them in nonhypothetical language.

Examples: I wouldn't have asked you to join us, if I had known you were going to be so rude.

I asked you to come because I thought you would be more polite.

If I had been born one hundred years ago, I wouldn't have had a chance to travel widely.

A hundred years ago people like me didn't have a chance to travel widely.

FOCUS 5

Mixing Hypothetical and Actual Statements

use

We sometimes combine actual conditions and hypothetical results.

ACTUAL CONDITION	HYPOTHETICAL RESULT
(a) I had to work last night.	Otherwise, I would have come to your party.
(b) Peter brought a doctor's excuse to explain his absence.	Otherwise, Denise would have accused him of being irresponsible.
(c) It's going to rain tomorrow.	Otherwise, we could have the luncheon outside.

HYPOTHETICAL RESULT	ACTUAL CONDITION
(d) I would have come to your party last night,	but I had to work.
(e) Denise would have accused Peter of being irresponsible,	but he brought a doctor's excuse to explain his absence.
(f) We could have the luncheon outside,	but it's going to rain tomorrow.

EXERCISE 16

Here are some actual conditions. State a hypothetical result by using *otherwise* or *but*.

Example: I'm not rich.

I'm not rich. Otherwise, I would loan you the money you asked for.

I would loan you the money you asked for, but I'm not rich.

1. I don't have a million dollars.
2. I don't yet speak English perfectly.
3. Doctors have to spend many years in medical school.
4. My mother doesn't know how I am living now.
5. My father is not the leader of my country.
6. I have many good friends.
7. Many students come to the United States for university study.
8. The weather forecaster has predicted heavy rain for tomorrow afternoon.

Exercise 13 *Continued from LP page 280.* 5. if I had been elected president./if the Republicans hadn't been in charge for so long. 6. if the telephone hadn't been invented./if communications satellites hadn't been put into orbit. 7. if the USSR hadn't collapsed./if their economies hadn't declined. 8. if scientists hadn't first developed penicillin./if there had been other effective disease-fighting drugs. 9. if TV hadn't been invented./if progress hadn't been made in most technological areas. 10. if I hadn't been called on by my teacher./if I had stayed home and not come to class.
Exercise 14 *Answers will vary.*

Exercise 15 *Answers will vary.*
Exercise 16 *Answers will vary. Possible answers are:* 1. Otherwise, I'd buy you a car. 2. I'd be in the university, but I don't yet speak English perfectly. 3. Otherwise, they wouldn't have enough expertise. 4. My mother would worry about me, but she doesn't know how I am living now. 5. Otherwise, I would still be at home. 6. I would have a bad case of culture shock, but I have many good friends. 7. Otherwise, universities wouldn't have special advisors for foreign students. 8. Otherwise we would hold the wedding outdoors.

EXERCISE 14 [15 minutes]

Students will practice making the more formal inverted hypotheticals by changing any sentences they or their partner made in Exercise 11–13 which include the *were* auxiliary. If you are short on time, you may wish to save this exercise for the end of the unit (along with Exercise 8).

EXERCISE 15 [15 minutes]

Students will work in pairs to practice rewriting hypothetical sentences in nonhypothetical language.

Note: The photos are of a stagecoach in the North American west (mid-1800s) and a flight boarding an Air Bus (2006).

For more practice, use *Grammar Dimensions 3* Workbook page 100, Exercise 7.

work book

LESSON PLAN 4

FOCUS 5 [20 minutes]

Focus 5 gives examples of actual conditions combined with hypothetical results. The chart shows two ways that this can be done (using *otherwise* or *but* depending on the order).

1. **Lead-in:** Divide the board in half under the headings *actual conditions* on one side and a *hypothetical results* on the other. List a few examples of each. Leave enough room on the board to also

write some examples of these conditions and results combined. For example:

actual conditions	hypothetical results.
I have to work today	*I would drive you to your class*
My car isn't working	*I would go to the beach*
My sister is visiting	*I would go with you to a movie*

2. Go over the examples in Focus 5 and then invite students to mix and match a condition with a result from the lists on the board using *otherwise* or *but*. (example: *I would go to the beach, but I have to work today*.)

3. Next, ask volunteers to change those sentences they've created on the board into the past tense (both the condition and result or only one or the other).

Suggestion: Take a moment to highlight the differences in *but* (a sentence connector) and *otherwise* (a conjunctive adverb).

EXERCISE 16 [15 minutes]

Students will use the actual conditions given and create their own hypothetical results using *otherwise* or *but* to combine them.

1. Have students take a moment and think of all the things they would do if they were rich. Write a few of these on the board.

2. Working from the example for Exercise 16, invite students to combine the actual condition, *I'm not rich*, with one of the suggestions on the board. They should try using *otherwise* or *but*. (Example: *I'm not rich. Otherwise, I would live in a mansion with a pool.*)

3. Have students complete the exercise individually and then share their answers with a small group.

4. Circulate as students share and note any errors to address during debriefing.

5. Have groups share their most interesting answers with the class. See possible answers on LP page 282.

For more practice, use *Grammar Dimensions 3* Workbook page 101, Exercise 8.

work book

FOCUS 6

Using Hypotheticals for Unlikely Possibility and for Sensitive Topics

use

Use hypothetical statements to indicate unlikely possibilities.

STATEMENT	IMPLIED MEANING
Likely Possibility (Nonhypothetical)	
(a) If we **get** some free time, we **can** go to the movies.	There is a strong possibility that we may get free time.
Unlikely Possibility (Hypothetical)	
(b) If we **got** some free time this weekend, we **could** go to the movies.	The possibility of free time is not strong, but we are discussing it anyway.
(c) If I **had** free time, I **would** go to the movies.	There is no possibility of free time, but this is what would happen if there were a possibility.

Use hypothetical statements to discuss potentially "sensitive" topics more easily and diplomatically.

STATEMENT	IMPLIED MEANING	EXPLANATION
Nonhypothetical		
(d) Will you ever leave your husband?	I think you might do this.	
Hypothetical		
(e) Would you ever leave your husband?	This is not a real situation, just an example. I don't really think that you would do this.	Using hypothetical indicates that the speaker does not believe the listener would actually consider doing the thing being discussed.

EXERCISE 17

Decide whether these statements are likely or unlikely possibilities for you, then make a hypothetical or nonhypothetical sentence that reflects that.

Example: marry someone from another country

  a. likely possibility—something that might actually be possible for me

  If I marry someone from another country, I will probably become a citizen of that country.

  b. unlikely possibility—something that I don't think I will ever be possible for me

  If I married someone from another country, my parents would be very disappointed.

1. go to Las Vegas for the next vacation
  a. likely possibility   b. unlikely possibility

2. pass the TOEFL Test the next time I take it
  a. likely possibility   b. unlikely possibility

3. become president of your country
  a. likely possibility   b. unlikely possibility

4. have eight children
  a. likely possibility   b. unlikely possibility

5. buy a new car within the next three months
  a. likely possibility   b. unlikely possibility

6. join the army
  a. likely possibility   b. unlikely possibility

7. get sick later today
  a. likely possibility   b. unlikely possibility

8. look for a new place to live
  a. likely possibility   b. unlikely possibility

9. have free time before class tomorrow
  a. likely possibility   b. unlikely possibility

10. win the lottery
  a. likely possibility   b. unlikely possibility

11. appear on television sometime in my life
  a. likely possibility   b. unlikely possibility

Exercise 17 Answers will vary. Possible answers are: 1. a. … I'll be sure to bring you a present when I come back. b. … that would mean that I had already been admitted to the university. 2. a. … I will begin my university studies right away. b. … I would be the happiest person in the world. 3. This is probably an unlikely possibility for all your students: If I became president of my country, I would make my grammar teacher the Minister of Education. 4. a. … I will probably need to have two jobs to earn enough money to feed and clothe them. b. … my family would be too large for us to travel anywhere in one car. 5. a. … I will have to renew my driver's license. b. … I would need to get automobile insurance. 6. a. … I will probably receive financial aid for college. b. … I would be the oldest recruit in boot camp. 7. a. … I won't come to class tomorrow. b. … I would know that this tuna sandwich has been sitting in the sun too long. 8. a. … I will consider living with a roommate. b. … I would start by checking the newspaper want ads. 9. a. … I'll write a letter to my parents. b. … I wouldn't have to do my homework tonight. 10. a. … I'll take you out to dinner. b. … I would buy you a car. 11. a. … I will ask my family and friends not to miss the program. b. … I would know that even people who aren't famous can get on TV.

HYPOTHETICAL STATEMENTS

LESSON PLAN 4

FOCUS 6 [20 minutes]

Focus 6 covers more advanced topics. You may need to assess whether your class is ready to cover them at this point. The same is true of Focus 7. If you feel your class is not ready to cover these topics yet, you may wish to save them for the end of the semester.

Hypothetical statements can be used to show likely/nonhypothetical possibility (with the present tense + modal of high possibility) or unlikely possibility (with the past tense + modal of lesser possibility). "Sensitive" topics can also be addressed by using hypothetical statements.

1. **Lead-in:** You can illustrate the differences that tense make (see examples (a–c)) by giving the class similar examples using different tenses and modals:

   If I have money, I'll visit my family during vacation. (not certain, but possible)

   If I had money, I could visit my family more often. (not likely, but things could change)

   If I had money, I would fly to Italy for the weekend. (no possibility)

2. Go over Focus 6. If you are short on time, you can skip the section on "sensitive" topics.

3. Go directly onto Exercise 17 to give students practice creating their own statements.

EXERCISE 17 [20 minutes/homework]

Students get the chance to make statements showing how likely or unlikely they feel the following statements are for them personally. They will also need to create a hypothetical or nonhypothetical result. This can be assigned for homework if you are short on time.

1. You can introduce this exercise by having students begin with books closed.

2. Write the words *likely* and *unlikely* on the board and then give the class a few statements (orally or written) such as the ones used in the example for Exercise 17 or others from the exercise. The class

should be able to tell you whether each statement is *likely* or *unlikely* and what tells them this.

3. After this practice, have students work individually to complete the exercise. They should first decide how likely each statement is for themselves. Next, students will create sentences reflecting their likelihood with an added result.

4. Let students share answers in small groups as you circulate and note any common errors to address in debriefing. See possible answers on LP page 284.

For more practice, use *Grammar Dimensions 3* Workbook page 102, Exercise 9.

FOCUS 7

Using Hypotheticals to Imply That the Opposite Is True

use

Use hypothetical statements to talk about things that didn't actually happen.

STATEMENT	IMPLIED MEANINGS
(a) You could have brought a friend.	You had permission, but you came alone.
(b) You could have been more careful with your homework.	You had the ability to be careful, but you didn't do it.
(c) You should have seen the doctor.	You didn't see the doctor.
(d) You might have cleaned the house before my mother got here.	The house was still dirty when she arrived.

EXERCISE 18

Restate these sentences in nonhypothetical language. Compare your answers with those of a partner.

Example: You should have been there.
You weren't there.

1. You shouldn't have gone to so much trouble!
You went to too much trouble!

2. We could have been seriously injured in that bus accident.
We're lucky that we didn't get hurt in that bus accident.

3. You might at least have invited her to the party.
Why didn't you invite her to the party?

4. You should be happy that I was able to come at all.
Why aren't you happy that I'm here?

5. She wouldn't have gone even if she had been invited.
It doesn't matter that you didn't invite her.

FOCUS 8

Using Hypotheticals with *Wish* and Verbs of Imagination

use

We use hypothetical statements with *wish* to talk about situations that are not true or not likely to become true.

STATEMENT	IMPLIED MEANING
(a) I **wish** you **had come** to the lake last weekend.	You didn't come.
(b) I **wish** you **liked** Chinese food.	You don't like it.
(c) I **wish** you **would come** to my party.	You refuse to come.

We use hypothetical statements with verbs that indicate imagination.

STATEMENT	IMPLIED MEANING
(d) **Let's imagine** that we **had** a new president.	We know this is not a real possibility.
(e) **Pretend** that you **could fly**. Do you think you **would** still own a car?	This is an impossible situation.
(f) **Suppose** we **went** to Europe next summer. How much do you think it **would** cost?	We are only talking about it now; we're not making an actual plan.

ANSWER KEY

Exercise 18 Answers will vary. Possible answers are listed above.

FOCUS 7 [10 minutes]

Note the comments for Focus 6.

Hypothetical statements can be used in English to show that something did not happen at all. Hypothetical statements such as these can be culturally confusing at first for students whose first language is not English. However, Exercise 18 will give students more practice. Go over the Focus 7 chart briefly before doing the following exercise as a class. Students will note that these sentences do not have an *If* statement and that the use of modals to state the opposite can be a difficult concept. Answer any questions students might have.

EXERCISE 18 [10 minutes]

Students will identify these as hypothetical statements that imply the opposite meaning. They will then restate these hypothetical statements to show their true meaning. You can go over these as a class or have students work in pairs. See possible answers on LP page 286.

For more practice, use *Grammar Dimensions 3* Workbook page 103, Exercise 10.

FOCUS 8 [10 minutes]

Focus 8 gives examples of the shift of verbs into the simple past (for wishes about the present time), *would/could* + simple form (wishes about the future), and past perfect (for wishes about the past or regrets). These hypothetical statements when used with the verb *wish* or with the verbs *imagine, pretend,* or *suppose* talk about things that are not true or are imaginary situations.

You may want to address the section on using *wish,* but skip the section on imaginary statements if you are short on time and your class is less comfortable with the topics presented.

1. **Lead-in:** You can begin with a few examples of things or situations you wish were true and then invite students to give their own wishes. Put a few on the board to show the structure. Note how these hypothetical statements are similar to (tense) and different from (*wish*/no *If* clause) the hypothetical conditions in Focus 3. Then invite students to shift the tense and make wishes about the past (these can be expressions of regret) or the future.

2. Go over the examples in the chart and move onto the section on imaginary conditions if you feel your class is ready for it.

Suggestion: You may want to give students practice making wishes in small groups and have everyone make a wish for their lives today or in the future (example: *I wish I had more time to relax*). Shift the tense and have everyone state regret about their past in the form of a wish in the past time frame (example: *I wish I had studied English more in high school*).

EXPANSION 1 [homework]

Use Activity 2 (writing) on SB page 290 to practice making wishes in the present and future or expressing regrets. In this activity, students will write a short essay using hypotheticals with *wish.*

EXPANSION 2 [20 minutes]

You may want to have students complete Activity 3 (writing/speaking) on SB page 290 as an expansion of Focus 8. In this activity, students are asked to come up with three wishes and compare them to those of a partner.

Use Your English

EXERCISE 19

Read the following paragraph. Underline the hypothetical statements. Rewrite the sentences using nonhypothetical language. The first hypothetical statement has been done for you as an example.

Example: *(3) For example, Sir Isaac Newton decided to take a nap under an apple tree, and as a result he was hit on the head by a falling apple.*

(1) Many important scientific developments have happened by accident. (2) Discoveries have often been made because someone was in the right place at the right time, or because someone made a mistake and got an unexpected result. (3) For example, <u>if Sir Isaac Newton hadn't decided to take a nap under an apple tree, he wouldn't have been hit on the head by a falling apple.</u> (4) It was this event that gave him the idea about the Law of Gravity. (5) <u>If Sir Alexander Fleming hadn't left a sandwich on a windowsill of his laboratory and forgotten about it, he wouldn't have discovered the fungus or mold that contains penicillin.</u> (6) <u>Had Christopher Columbus correctly calculated the actual size of the earth, he would never have tried to reach Asia by sailing west.</u> (7) <u>If that hadn't happened, the European discovery of the New World might have occurred in 1592, instead of 1492.</u>

ACTIVITY 1 speaking

We often use hypothetical language to discuss very controversial topics. Choose one of the following topics:

- Should drugs be legalized?
- Should people of the same sex be allowed to marry?
- Should human embryos be used for stem-cell research?
- Should doctors be allowed to assist people to commit suicide?

■ **STEP 1** Form a group with three other students in the class to discuss your opinions on the issues:

- What is your opinion? Pro or con? What are your reasons?
- What three things might happen if the government allowed it?
- What three things might happen if government didn't allow it?

■ **STEP 2** Based on your discussion, your group should answer these two questions:

- What is the strongest reason in favor of keeping the current policy?
- What is the strongest reason against?

Present your topic, your position, and your reasons to the rest of the class.

ANSWER KEY

Exercise 19 Possible nonhypothetical paraphrases are: (5) Sir Alexander Fleming left his sandwich sitting on a windowsill and forgot about it. That was how he discovered the mold that contains penicillin. (6) Christopher Columbus incorrectly calculated the actual size of the earth, and therefore tried to reach Asia by sailing west. (7) Because that happened, the European discovery of the New World occurred in 1492, instead of 1592.

HYPOTHETICAL STATEMENTS

EXERCISE 19 [15 minutes/homework]

Students will identify hypothetical statements in the past time frame and then rewrite them as actual conditions and results in the past. This can be assigned as homework if class time is limited. You may want to refer back to Focus 4 for more on hypothetical conditionals in the past time frame.

Note: The photograph is of Sir Isaac Newton.

For more practice, use *Grammar Dimensions 3* Workbook page 103, Exercise 11 and page 104, Exercise 12.

UNIT GOAL REVIEW [10 minutes]

Ask students to look at the goals on the opening page of the unit again. Refer to the pages of the unit where information on each goal can be found.

ExamView® Test Generator — For assessment of Unit 17, use *Grammar Dimensions 3* ExamView®.

USE YOUR ENGLISH

The Use Your English activities at the end of the unit contain situations that should naturally elicit the structures covered in the unit. For a more complete discussion of how to use the Use Your English Activities see To the Teacher on LP page xxii. When students are doing these activities in class, you can circulate and listen to see if they are using the structures accurately. Errors can be corrected after the activity has finished.

CULTURE NOTE

Students will find themselves, at some point, in the position to give their opinions on controversial topics. This is an important skill to develop in an environment such as the ESL classroom, which is more likely to be sensitive to the variety of student backgrounds. However, depending on the student population in your class, the topics listed in this activity may still be too controversial and cause discomfort for some students to discuss in class. It's important to take your students' backgrounds, ages, and familiarity with each other into consideration when assigning topics and creating groups or discussion in order to create a classroom environment that is comfortable for everyone to learn. Bring in a few alternate topics for your class if you feel those listed would lead to limited or strained discussions. For example:

Should libraries put limits on (censor) what they will carry?

Should _____ (a known law) be changed?

At what age should children begin schooling?

At what age should children be allowed to quit school?

When should teenagers be allowed to drive alone?

ACTIVITY 1

speaking
[30 minutes]

This activity asks students to use hypothetical statements to discuss controversial topics. (See Culture Note on this page.)

Begin by having students choose one of the given topics. You may want to have students prepare their opinions in advance to encourage more discussion in groups later.

STEP 1

1. Put students into small groups based on a single topic.

2. You may want to discuss ways that students can encourage others to share their opinions and ways that they can politely disagree. Put a few phrases on the board as reminders during the discussion. Some phrases might be: *What do you think? Do you agree? I see what you're saying, but I don't agree. I understand, but I think . . .*

3. Circulate and help groups to encourage all students to express their opinions and to acknowledge any differences with respect.

STEP 2

1. Groups should then answer the two questions.

2. Give the groups time to share with the class. They should be able to have reached an agreement on the two questions.

VARIATION

Turn this activity into an out-of-class interview. After students have completed their interviews, put them into small groups to share. Groups should report interesting findings to the class.

ACTIVITY 2 writing

There is a saying "Hindsight is 20/20," which means it's always easier to see things clearly and make the right decisions after something has happened and you can see the results. Think about some things that you would have done differently if you had known then the things that you know now. Choose one of the topics. Then write a short essay about this topic or make a presentation to the rest of the class.

- Things you wish you had done that you didn't do. For example: *I wish I had studied harder when I was in high school.*
- Things you wish you hadn't done that you did do. For example: *I wish I hadn't spent all my time watching television instead of exercising.*

ACTIVITY 3 writing/speaking

If you could have three wishes, what would they be, and why would you wish for them?

STEP 1 Write down your three wishes.

STEP 2 Compare your answers to those of someone else in class. What do someone else's wishes tell you about his or her life? What do your wishes tell someone else about you?

STEP 3 Make one statement about why you think your partner made the wishes that he or she did. Tell that statement to your partner, but not to the rest of the class.

ACTIVITY 4 reflection

Listen to native speakers talking to each other. (This can be a live conversation or something on TV or radio.) Identify three examples of hypothetical statements. Write down:

(1) the situation, (2) what was said, (3) the nonhypothetical meaning if there was one, and (4) why you think the speaker chose to use hypothetical in that particular situation. Share your examples with two or three other students, and together choose one to present to the rest of the class.

ACTIVITY 5 speaking

STEP 1 Think about what you would do if you were faced with the following problems.

- Your parents don't approve of the person you want to marry.
- Your friend and you both work at the same company. You feel very loyal to the company, but you discover your friend has stolen some of the company's money.
- You have fallen in love with the husband or wife of your best friend.
- Your best friend needs to borrow some money "for a serious emergency"—but he won't say what that emergency is. You had been planning to use that money to buy a birthday present for your boyfriend or girlfriend. Your friend needs the money right away, and the birthday celebration is also today. You can't get any more money: only what you have now.

STEP 2 Discuss your solutions in a small group. Together decide on one or two suggestions for what people can do if they are faced with any kind of difficult problem.

USE YOUR ENGLISH

ACTIVITY  2 writing
[homework]

You may wish to assign this activity after coverage of Focus 8 on SB page 287. Students will write about their wishes for the past/regrets.

1. Discuss the saying "Hindsight is 20/20." Does anyone have a saying like this in their native language?

2. If you have time, give students a chance to discuss the two topics listed with a partner to generate ideas.

3. Assign the writing as homework. Be sure to give guidelines for length or time and format based on whether it will be a writing assignment or a presentation.

VARIATION

If possible, have students interview a family member. Although the interview will most likely end up being done in another language, the final paper in English can end up being very insightful for many students.

ACTIVITY 3 writing/speaking
[20 minutes]

You can use this activity as an expansion of the topics covered in Focus 8 on SB page 287. Students will share three wishes with a partner and then make some guesses about why their partner chose these wishes.

Because this is based on the basic story of the magic lamp, you may want to briefly go over the story of Aladdin's Lamp to be sure that they are familiar with the idea.

■ STEP 1   Give students time to write down their three wishes before putting them into pairs to share.

■ STEP 2

1. Before students work on Step 2 together, invite volunteers to state what types of things one could learn about another person from his/her wishes. Students should share their wishes and circulate. Students should share their wishes and discuss what these wishes tell about their lives.

■ STEP 3   Students should try to decide why they think their partner made the wishes that they did. Give students time to either discuss their interpretations with their partner, or let them write their thoughts down.

Suggestion: Because these wishes can be fun to share, instead of putting students into pairs for discussion right away, have everyone mingle and share their wishes with as many people as they can in a short time. When you give the signal to stop moving around the room, have those people who are currently closest to each other sit down and begin work on Step 2 together.

ACTIVITY 4 reflection
[15 minutes/homework]

Students will seek out examples of the use of hypothetical statements in their environment and then analyze how and why it was used. See Variation below for classes outside North America.

1. Have students find and record examples of the use of hypothetical statements from TV, radio, or conversations they have overheard.

2. Students should also record information about the situation, possible reasons, and the underlying meaning of the statements and share this in a small group.

3. Ask each group to put one or two examples on the board to share along with any information about it.

4. When finished, discuss as a class. What general observations can the class make about the use of hypothetical statements?

VARIATION

If your students are not able to do this easily outside of class, use the audio from Activity 7 to analyze and record examples from.

ACTIVITY 5 speaking
[20 minutes/homework]

Students will work in small groups to share solutions to difficult situations. Hypothetical speech will be used to express ideas about what students would do if they personally experienced each situation.

■ STEP 1   Give students time to read through each of the four situations and formulate an answer for themselves before putting them into groups. This can be done for homework the night before.

■ STEP 2

1. As students work in small groups, circulate and encourage hypothetical discussions. (*What would you do? How would you feel?*)

2. Have each small group work on developing a few basic rules that they might use when confronted with any situation such as these. (Possible answer: *People should ask a friend for advice or sleep on it before they decide.*)

ACTIVITY 6 writing/speaking

Identify some things you would and wouldn't do for ten million dollars, and compare them to those of other people in class. Ideas to consider: Would you tell a lie? Would you betray a friend? Would you give a child up for adoption? Would you become a citizen of another country? Would you leave your family? What would you refuse to do, even if you were offered ten million dollars?

ACTIVITY 7 listening

CD Track 25

Listen to the conversation between Peter and Denise. Then choose the sentence that correctly describes the situations that they talked about.

1. ⓐ Peter didn't hear the announcement because he wasn't at the meeting.
   b. He heard the announcement because he was at the meeting.

2. a. The meeting wasn't important.
   ⓑ The meeting was important.

3. a. Peter thinks Denise did good work.
   ⓑ He thinks she was careless.

4. a. Peter finished the project in plenty of time.
   ⓑ He didn't finish it in plenty of time.

5. a. Denise told Peter that she hadn't gone over the figures.
   ⓑ Denise didn't tell Peter that she hadn't gone over the figures.

6. a. She didn't check the figures.
   ⓑ Maybe she checked the figures.

7. ⓐ There were many mistakes.
   b. There weren't many mistakes.

8. a. Denise said that she wanted to get Peter fired.
   ⓑ Denise said that she didn't want to get Peter fired.

ACTIVITY 8 research on the web

Go on the Internet and use a search engine such as Google® or Yahoo® and enter the keywords "hypothetical questions". You will find a number of Web sites that talk about hypothetical questions. Look at several of the sites and make a list of ten interesting questions you found there.

■ STEP 1   Work with a partner to choose three of the most interesting questions to report to the rest of the class.

■ STEP 2   With another pair of students try to develop a definition of what hypothetical questions consist of and how they might be useful in generating ideas or discussions.

ACTIVITY 9 reflection

What if Columbus had never sailed to America? What if Great Britain had never been a colonial power? What if communism had replaced capitalism worldwide? What if the United States had not decided to invade Iraq? Choose a famous event in history and decide what might have happened if that event had **not** taken place. How would life today be different? Write a paragraph or make a brief presentation to the rest of the class.

USE YOUR ENGLISH

ACTIVITY 6 writing/speaking
[15 minutes/homework]

Depending on your available time and your students' needs, this activity can be used in class as a speaking activity or as a writing activity for homework.

1. You can begin by putting the question on the board to get small groups talking or writers thinking: *What would you and what wouldn't you do for $10,000,000?*

2. At this point, have writers talk with a partner for a few minutes before assigning the writing guidelines for length and format.

3. For small groups, encourage the groups to list as many ideas as they can under the topics of *would do* and *wouldn't do.*

4. Give groups some time at the end of the activity to share a few of their ideas with the class.

VARIATION

This can also be an interesting out-of-class interview topic. Groups can create a list of activities and then go out as a group or individually to interview other students and find out about what they would or wouldn't do for so much money. They may want to simply keep tabs on the number of *yes* or *no* answers or they could add the extra element of marking male answers in blue and female answers in red. This would give information to compare and make generalizations about later as groups share their findings.

ACTIVITY 7 listening
[20 minutes]

CD Track
25

This listening activity gives students practice hearing hypothetical statements in context and then choosing a nonhypothetical statement to match.

1. Play the audio through one time.

2. Give students a moment to go through and circle the answers they think they know.

3. Play the audio a second time and let students look over their first answers and make any changes as they listen.

4. Circulate and note whether students are having a difficult time. If so, play the audio a third time with a few pauses.

5. Depending on how well students have done, you may want to simply go over the answers as a class or, if needed, give students a moment to compare answers with a partner and discuss any differences. See answers on LP page 292.

ACTIVITY 8 research on the web
[40 minutes]

This Internet search is generally fun for students due to the wide number of hypothetical questions they can bring to class. This activity can be an interesting way to start the unit off.

STEP 1 After assigning the activity, students will bring ten questions to class. In pairs, have students share their questions and narrow them down to only three or four.

STEP 2 Students can work in groups of four on Step 2. However, if you have time, give these small groups a chance to share and discuss the questions they have chosen with the group.

Suggestion: Collect the lists of hypothetical questions that students bring in and make copies for use as discussion topics for later or use them in interesting ways to start the unit in future classes.

VARIATION

In place of the Opening Task, assign this Internet search for homework and begin the unit by having students discuss their answers to the most interesting hypothetical questions their group members brought in.

ACTIVITY 9 reflection
[homework]

You may wish to assign this activity after Focus 4 on SB page 279. Like the paragraph in Exercise 19 on SB page 288, students will describe a hypothetical situation (in their own paragraph) about what would be different if some famous event in history had not happened.

1. Be sure to assign or look over Exercise 19 before starting this activity.

2. Give a few examples of other famous events in time and invite students to suggest what might have happened if these events had not taken place.

3. Before you assign the activity for homework, you may want to be sure that everyone has chosen a famous event in history. If presenting to the class, you may want to ensure that each student has chosen a different historical event (or not more than two students to cover one event).

4. You may want to require a minimum number of hypothetical results that students are to discuss in their paragraph or presentation.

UNIT 18

SENSORY VERBS, CAUSATIVE VERBS, AND VERBS THAT TAKE SUBJUNCTIVE

UNIT GOALS

- Correctly understand and use sentences with sensory verbs
- Correctly understand and use sentences with causative verbs
- Correctly understand and use sentences with verbs followed by subjunctive *that*-clauses

OPENING TASK

Parenting Techniques

Think about the way your parents raised you. How did they reward your good behavior or punish your bad behavior? What kind of responsibilities did they give you?

■ STEP 1

Complete the chart on the next page to identify some of the parenting techniques your parents used. Identify some things they saw you doing that they wanted to change or encourage. Decide whether their techniques were effective, and whether you would use (or are using) them to raise your own children. Examples have been provided.

Behavior	Parenting Techniques Your Parents Used	Effective? Yes/No	Would/Do You Use This Technique? Yes/No/Why
My mother heard me yelling at my younger brother.	**Discipline/Punishment** 1. sent to my room 2. 3.	1. no 2. 3.	1. No. My children have toys in their rooms so it's not really an effective punishment. 2. 3.
My father saw me helping my baby sister.	**Responsibilities** 1. gave me more chances to take care of her 2. 3.	1. yes 2. 3.	1. Yes. It was good practice for being a parent myself. 2. 3.
My mother caught me trying to feed my vegetables to the dog.	**Rewards/Motivations** 1. gave me ice cream and candy when I ate my vegetables 2. 3.	1. yes 2. 3.	1. No. I don't want to use food as a reward for good behavior. 2. 3.

■ STEP 2

Form a small group with three or four other students, and compare the information you have written in your charts. Based on your discussion, your group should make ten recommendations for parents. Start five of them with "Parents should have their children . . ." Start five recommendations with "Parents shouldn't make their children . . ."

■ STEP 3

Compare your group's recommendations to those of other groups. Compile a list of recommendations that the entire class agrees upon. Begin your recommendations with "Good parenting requires that . . ."

LESSON PLAN 1 SENSORY VERBS, CAUSATIVE VERBS, AND VERBS THAT TAKE SUBJUNCTIVE

UNIT OVERVIEW

Unit 18 focuses reviews the verb forms of a second action which follow sensory verbs, causative verbs, passive causative constructions, and verbs of urging with a *that*-clause. The focus charts in this unit show how the preceding are exceptions to the general rules. You may want to review Units 6 and 7 (the use of infinitives and gerunds) before beginning Unit 18.

GRAMMAR NOTE

This unit covers sensory and causative verbs because they both are exceptions to the rule of using either an infinitive or gerund form in the complement, or following a verb. **Sensory verbs** are followed by the simple form of a verb or a participle (which students may confuse with a gerund, because of the *-ing* ending) rather than an infinitive or gerund. In addition, a few **causative verbs** (*make, help, let, have*) are followed by the simple form of the verb rather than the infinitive like most other causatives. Passive causatives are yet another exception to the general rule by being followed by an infinitive rather than the base form of the verb. Finally, certain verbs of urging, which carry similar meanings to causative verbs, are followed by a subjunctive—*that* clause and the simple verb form. Because all of these structures are exceptions to general rules, you will find they can be challenging for students.

UNIT GOALS

Some instructors may want to review the goals listed on Student Book (SB) page 294 after completing the Opening Task so that students understand what they should know by the end of the unit. These goals can also be reviewed at the end of the unit when students are more familiar with the grammar terminology.

OPENING TASK [20 minutes/homework]

The aim of this activity is to give students the opportunity to use sensory verbs (*my mom heard me*

yelling), causative verbs (*parents shouldn't make kids eat*), and verbs that take the subjunctive (*good parenting requires that . . .*) as they perform a task. The problem-solving format is designed to show the teacher how well the students can produce a target structure implicitly and spontaneously when they are engaged in a communicative task. For a more complete discussion of the purpose of the Opening Task, see To the Teacher, Lesson Planner (LP) page xxii.

Setting Up the Task

Begin with a class discussion of the first questions about parenting techniques on SB page 294.

Conducting the Task

■ STEP 1

You can assign the chart in Step 1 as homework or give students time to work individually in class.

■ STEP 2

1. Once students have completed their charts, put them into small groups for discussion and sharing. If you have a variety of age groups in your class, try to mix them among the groups, noting that people who are parents may have different answers than those who are not.

2. Direct the groups to work together to create two lists to share with the class. Ask students to write a few of their recommendations on the board.

3. Circulate and note the use of the target grammar from the sentence starters in Step 2. Are students correctly using the simple forms or are they using infinitives and gerunds to complete the sentences?

Closing the Task

■ STEP 3

1. Go over any examples on the board and invite other groups to share their advice.

2. Put the sentence starter from Step 3 on the board after all groups have shared. Groups can work together to complete the sentence or a whole class discussion can lead to a few key points to use.

VARIATION

Have students write their answers to Step 2 and Step 3 group discussions on paper and turn them into you. Look them over and use these answers as a diagnostic for Unit 18. Address the grammar points within this unit as needed based on this diagnostic.

EXPANSION [homework]

You could assign Activity 9 (research on the web) on SB page 309 to follow the Opening Task.

GRAMMAR NOTE

Typical student errors (form)

- Inflecting verbs which follow a subjunctive— *that* clause with tense or agreement: * *The citizens demanded that the roads are repaired.* (See Focus 5.)
- Using infinitives after sensory verbs: * *I saw him to hit the child.* (See Focus 1.)
- Using infinitives after *let, make, have, help*: * *Parents should let kids to make their own choices sometimes.* (See Focus 3.)
- Using simple forms of a verb or infinitives after verbs of interception: * *We discovered the man to sleep in the library.* * *We caught her steal a camera.* (See Focus 2.)

Typical student errors (use)

- Using the causatives *get, have,* or *let* in passive constructions: * *Citizens should be let to leave work in order to vote.* (See Focus 4.)

FOCUS 2 | Sensory Verbs

EXAMPLES	EXPLANATIONS
(a) Mary **heard** the children **laughing**. (b) I **saw** the child **take** the cookies.	Sensory verbs use either a **present participle** (verb + *ING*) or the **simple form** of a verb to express the second action. Depending on which is chosen, the meaning differs.
(c) Bob **heard** the children **breaking** the bottles, so he called their parents. (d) I **saw** the child **leaving** school before class was over, so I ran to catch her. (e) The teacher **watched** the children **overturning** the chairs and **setting** them outside.	Use a present participle to describe actions that are: in progress (c) unfinished (d) repeated (e)
(f) Bob **saw** the children **take** the cookies and **put** them in their pockets. (g) I **saw** the child **leave** school before class was over, so I'm sure she's not coming to the conference with her teacher. (h) The teacher **watched** the children **overturn** the chair and **set** it outside.	Use the simple form of a verb to describe actions that are completed (f and g). or happen just once (h)
(i) I **saw** the child's bicycle **lying** by the side of the road. (j) NOT: I **saw** the child's bicycle **lie** by the side of the road.	Use present participles with verbs of position (*lie, stand, sit,* etc.), if the thing that performs the second action cannot move by itself.
(k) We **caught** the child **taking** cookies out of the jar. (l) NOT: We **caught** the child **take** cookies out of the jar. (m) We **found** the child **sleeping** in front of the TV. (n) NOT: We **found** the child **sleep** in front of the TV.	Use present participles with verbs of interception (*find, catch, discover,* etc.), where the second action is interrupted or not completed.

FOCUS 1 | Overview

The verbs that are dealt with in this unit are followed by simple verb forms or present participles that describe a second action.

TYPES OF VERBS	EXAMPLES
Sensory Verbs (*see, hear,* etc.)	(a) I **saw** the mother **spank** her child. (b) I **heard** the child **crying**.
Causative Verbs (*make, let,* etc.)	(c) My parents **made** me go to bed at 8:00 on school nights. (d) They **let** me stay up late on Fridays and Saturdays.
Subjunctive *that*-**Clause Verbs** (*demand, recommend,* etc.)	(e) Good parenting **demands that** parents be consistent with discipline. (f) Educators **recommend that** a parent **try** to explain the reasons for punishment to children.

EXERCISE 1

Underline the simple verb form or participle that **follows** the highlighted verbs in the passage below. The first one has been done for you as an example.

Ideas about the best way to raise children differ a great deal from culture to culture. In some cultures, if a mother **hears** her baby <u>crying</u>, she will immediately go to pick it up and try to **get** it to stop. But in other cultures people **insist** that a mother <u>ignore</u> her child, because they feel that if you don't **let** a baby <u>cry</u>, it will become spoiled. In some cultures, any adult who **sees** a child misbehaving will **make** the child <u>stop</u>, but other cultures **prefer** that only the parent be allowed to discipline a child. In some cultures, people **have** slightly older children help take care of their younger brothers and sisters, but in other cultures people rarely **let** children be responsible for their brothers and sisters unless they are at least twelve or thirteen years old.

In the United States, most parents prefer to get a child to behave by persuasion rather than force. You rarely **see** parents spank their children in public, and schools don't usually **let** teachers use physical punishment as discipline. Parents who are seen hitting their children may even be reported to the police. American child-care experts **recommend** that children be given responsibility from a relatively early age. As a result, many parents **let** their small children **make** their own decisions about what kind of clothes they want to wear, or what they want to eat. They prefer to get children to obey instead of **making** them obey.

FOCUS 1 [10 minutes]

Use Focus 1 as a brief overview leading into Exercise 1.

1. **Lead-in:** Refer back to the advice given in the Opening Task for more examples of these three types of verbs and the kinds of verbs that follow them. For a more inductive approach, invite volunteers to find examples of each type of verb in the Opening Task.

2. Let students create a few more examples for each type of verb (sensory, causative, subjunctive *that*-clause).

3. Move directly on to Exercise 1.

Suggestion: You may want to review Appendix 3 on SB page A-6 and A-7 before starting Focus 1. This will remind students of the patterns they previously looked at as they begin looking at a few exceptions to these patterns.

VARIATION

Alternately, you could use Focus 1 and Exercise 1 as a review at the end of the unit, rather than a preliminary overview.

EXERCISE 1 [15 minutes]

Students will identify the verb forms that follow sensory verbs, causative verbs, and subjunctive *that*-clauses. After students have found and underlined the verbs they needed to find, have pairs work together to check their work. Circulate and note any common errors (this will tell you how well they already know or have learned, depending on whether this is used at the end of the unit). See answers on LP page 296.

Suggestion 1: Make a copy on an overhead transparency for use in a class review.

Suggestion 2: After students have completed the exercise, make three columns on the board and as you go over the exercise with the class, list the verbs

in bold under each column as you find them. Add the verbs students underlined to these. When finished, note any patterns that are found in the verb complements for each column (i.e., *sensory verbs take the simple verb forms or a participle,* etc.).

For more practice, use *Grammar Dimensions 3* Workbook page 105, Exercise 1.

FOCUS 2 [20 minutes]

Focus 2 gives examples of the difference in meaning when a present participle or a simple verb form is used with a sensory verb. Show students how the present participle conveys the same meaning as progressive aspect (unfinished, in progress).

1. **Lead-in:** Consider having the class go over this focus chart in small groups and have the groups be responsible for explaining one section to the class. Assign three different groups to explain *the participle:* group 1 gets examples (c–e), group 2 gets examples (i–j), and group 3 gets examples (k–n). Assign the *simple form of the verb* to a fourth group. Each group should work together to talk over the points and give two examples in addition to those shown in the focus chart. These should be written on the board when it is their turn to present to the class.

2. Go over any main points of the focus chart that were missed or seemed confusing during presentations.

Suggestion: Consider following up this presentation of Focus 2 with Exercise 4, which asks students to recognize and choose between the participle and the simple verb form. If students have trouble with Exercise 4, go back and review Focus 2 more thoroughly before going on to Exercises 2 and 3.

3. Here is what I saw, heard, and felt during the hurricane. (a) The wind grew louder. (b) The windows and doors shook. (c) The trees swayed in the garden outside. I thought the house was moving. (d) A tree crashed against the house. (e) There was a sound of breaking glass upstairs. I went upstairs. (f) Rain was pouring through the broken window. (g) A strong wind blew into the room. (h) The wind howled louder and louder.

EXERCISE 4

Decide on which form of the verb to use, based on the context. Circle your answer. In some sentences both forms may be correct.

Example: I saw smoke (come/coming) from the storeroom, so I called the fire department.

1. I hear the phone (ring/ringing), but I'm not going to answer it.
2. Brian heard the phone (ring/ringing), but by the time he reached it, the person at the other end had hung up.
3. The principal watched the students (take/taking) the test, so she was sure there had been no cheating.
4. Matt felt himself (get/getting) angry as he and Jeff argued about who should do the dishes.
5. On my way to the store I saw Morris (ride/riding) his new bike.
6. As Mary listened to the radio (play/playing) her favorite song, she began to cry and hurried out of the room.
7. I heard the workers (leave/leaving) earlier today. I'm sure they haven't returned yet.
8. We could all smell something (burn/burning). Apparently somebody had tossed a lit cigarette into the waste paper basket.
9. As the hurricane grew stronger, they heard many branches of the big oak tree (snap/snapping) and (fall/falling) to the ground.
10. John was relieved when he saw his lost wallet (sit/sitting) next to his checkbook on the shelf.
11. Deborah heard Evan (cry/crying), so she went in to see what was wrong.
12. When we arrived we found the dog (wait/waiting) at the door for us.

EXERCISE 2

Answer these questions by using sensory verbs with a second action.

Example: What can you see at a disco?
You can see people dancing.

1. What can you hear at a concert? — You can hear musicians play music.
2. What can you see at a skating rink? — You can see people skating.
3. What can you smell at a bakery? — You can smell bread baking.
4. What can you hear at the beach? — You can hear the waves breaking.
5. What can you see at a shopping mall? — You can see people shopping.
6. What can you hear at a playground? — You can hear children playing.
7. What can you hear in an English class? — You can hear students talking about their ideas.
8. What can you see at a gym? — You can see people sweating.

EXERCISE 3

Restate the lettered sentences in these paragraphs as sensory verbs followed by a participle or simple form of a verb.

Example: Here is what Tom saw: (a) Three boys were swimming in the river. (b) They were splashing and playing. (c) One of them shouted that it was time to go. (d) They picked up their towels and left.

(a) Tom saw three boys swimming in the river. (b) He watched them splashing and playing. (c) He heard one of them shout that it was time to go. (d) He watched them pick up their towels and leave.

1. Here is what Doris observed: (a) A man came into the bank. (b) He got in line. When he reached the teller's window, he handed her a piece of paper and a brown paper bag. (c) The teller was putting money in the bag, when a loud alarm began to ring. (d) Guards rushed in, but the man had escaped through the side entrance.

2. When Mrs. McMartin looked out the window, this is what she saw: (a) There were a few children playing on the swings. (b) Others were climbing on the monkey-bars. (c) One little boy was running very fast around and around the playground. (d) Suddenly he fell down. (e) He screamed in pain. (f) All the other children looked around to see where the noise was coming from. (g) One child ran toward Mrs. McMartin's office.

Exercise 2 Answers will vary. Possible answers are listed above.
Exercise 3 Answers will vary slightly. Possible answers are: 1. (a) Doris observed a man come into the bank. (b) She saw him get in line. When he reached the teller's window, she saw him hand her a piece of paper and a brown paper bag. (c) She observed the teller putting money in the bag when a loud alarm began to ring. (d) She saw the guards rush in, but the man had escaped through the side entrance. 2. (a) Mrs. McMartin looked out the window and saw a few children playing on the swings. (b) She saw others climbing on the monkey-bars. (c) She watched one little boy running very fast

around and around the playground. (d) Suddenly, she saw him fall down. (e) She heard him scream in pain. (f) She saw all the other children looking around to see where the noise was coming from. (g) She saw one child running toward her office. 3. (a) During the hurricane I heard the wind growing louder. (b) I felt the windows and doors shaking. (c) I saw the trees swaying in the garden outside. (d) I heard a tree crash against the house. (e) I heard the sound of breaking glass upstairs. (f) I saw rain pouring through the broken window. (g) I felt a strong wind blowing into the room. (h) I heard the wind howling louder and louder.

LESSON PLAN 1 SENSORY VERBS, CAUSATIVE VERBS, AND VERBS THAT TAKE SUBJUNCTIVE

EXERCISE 2 [10 minutes]

Students will use a simple verb form or a participle as they answer questions using sensory verbs with a second action. Answers will vary since either form can be used in this exercise.

You can have students take turns with an open book to ask a partner these questions. Circulate and check for general oral comprehension and accuracy in grammar. This works best if only one student has an open book and then they switch. You can remind students that a variety of answers are possible. Go over a few possible answers with the whole class when pairs have finished. See possible answers on LP page 298.

VARIATION

You could also consider going over this with the class as you ask the questions (students should have their books closed) and call on students to give a variety of answers to each question. This will allow students to see the variation that is possible in verb forms and content.

For more practice, use *Grammar Dimensions 3* Workbook page 105, Exercise 2.

EXERCISE 3 [20 minutes/homework]

This exercise asks students to restate each sentence. To save time, the exercise can be assigned for homework or divided up among the class with students being responsible for only one of the three paragraphs.

1. This exercise can be a little difficult to explain to students. It can help to have students make a sentence (using a sensory verb followed by a participle or simple form of a verb) about something they witnessed in the class recently. For example:

   I saw Sanjay drop his bag on the floor.
   I heard Nina talking on her phone before class.

2. Now explain that they will write sentences to describe what other people saw, heard, or felt in these paragraphs.

3. Because answers will vary, give students a chance to hear from several students (in small groups or as a class). See possible answers on LP page 298.

For more practice, use *Grammar Dimensions 3* Workbook page 106, Exercise 4.

EXPANSION [homework]

Much like this exercise, students can work on creating their own paragraphs about observations made outside of class. Have students write similar paragraphs based on their own sensory observations while sitting in a public space (a mall, coffee shop, student union building, etc.). What do they see, hear, smell, feel, or taste? Have them describe the place in detail. See Activity 1 (writing/speaking) on SB page 305 for a similar task, but with eyes closed.

EXERCISE 4 [15 minutes]

This exercise is best done as a follow-up immediately after Focus 2. Alternately, you may wish to have students complete the exercise as a diagnostic prior to coverage of Focus 2.

1. After working individually, give students a chance to share answers in pairs or small groups. They should give reasons for their answers and decide which sentences allow for more than one answer.

2. Circulate as students discuss and encourage them to refer back to Focus 2 if they are having difficulty explaining their reasoning.

For more practice, use *Grammar Dimensions 3* Workbook page 106, Exercise 3 and page 107, Exercise 5.

form meaning

FOCUS 3 | Causative Verbs

Many causative verbs are followed by infinitives. But a few common causative verbs (*make, let, have, help*) are followed by the simple form of the verb. Causative verbs show how much force or persuasion is necessary to cause a person to perform an action. They are listed here from most forceful to least forceful.

CAUSATIVE VERB + INFINITIVE	CAUSATIVE VERB + SIMPLE FORM OF THE VERB
(a) Parents should **force** naughty children to **stand** in the corner.	(b) Parents should **make** naughty children **stand** in the corner.
(c) Parents should **get** their children to **read** instead of watching TV.	*no synonym or substitute for this form*
(d) Parents should **employ or hire** a doctor to **examine** their children at least once a year.	(e) Parents should **have** the doctor **examine** their children at least once a year.
(f) Good parents should **allow** their children to **play** outside on sunny days.	(g) Good parents **let** their children **play** outside on sunny days.
(h) Good parents **help** their children **to learn** good manners.	(i) Good parents **help** their children **learn** good manners. (*help* can occur with either form)

EXERCISE 5

Underline the causative verbs and circle the infinitive or base form of the verb that follows. One has been done as an example.

(1) Kilroy hated his life in the army from the very first day. (2) When he arrived at Fort Dix for basic training, a drill instructor had him (join) all the other new recruits on the parade ground. (3) The officers made them (stand) in the hot sun for several hours, while clerks filled out forms. (4) They wouldn't allow the new recruits to (joke), or (talk) to each other, or even (to move) their heads. (5) Then they had Army barbers (cut) their hair so short that Kilroy felt like he was bald. (6) An officer ordered Kilroy (to report) to a long building called Barracks B, along with about twenty other men. (7) The sergeant

---

at Barracks B had each man (choose) a bed. (8) He let them (put) their personal possessions in lockers next to each bed. (9) Kilroy helped the man in the next bunk (make) his bed, and that man helped Kilroy (to do) the same thing. (10) The sergeant then required the recruits (to sweep) the floors and clean the bathrooms. (11) Kilroy had wanted (to join) the army to learn how to be a soldier, but now he was beginning to worry that the army would only teach him how to be a janitor.

EXERCISE 6

Decide whether you think the policies suggested below are good ideas or not. Make statements with *should* or *shouldn't*. Then give a reason with *because*.

Example: *Parents should let their kids play actively every day, because vigorous physical exercise is important for growing bodies.*

CAUSER	CAUSTIVE VERB	DOER OF ACTION	ACTION
Example:			
parents	*let*	*kids*	*play actively*
1. parents	make	children	go to bed at 6:00
2. teachers	help	students	learn things by themselves
3. police	allow	people	break laws
4. people	have	a dentist	examine their teeth regularly
5. dog owners	let	pets	run around freely
6. a government	require	all citizens	take drug tests
7. a good manager	allow	employees	do whatever they like
8. a good manager	motivate	employees	do their best

EXERCISE 7

Match the verbs listed in Group A with the verbs in Group B which have the same or similar meaning.

GROUP A	GROUP B		
let	get	convince	assist	employ
help	make	hire	encourage	force
have		require	permit	allow

ANSWER KEY

Exercise 6 Answers will vary. Possible answers are: 1. Parents shouldn't make their children go to bed at 6:00, because that's too early. 2. Teachers should help students learn things by themselves, because then they will know how to learn independently. 3. Police shouldn't allow people to break laws, because that will make the society a bad one to live in. 4. People should have a dentist examine their teeth regularly, because that's a good way to prevent tooth decay or gum disease. 5. Dog owners shouldn't let their pets run around freely, because that might annoy people who don't like dogs. 6. A government shouldn't require all citizens to take drug tests, because this violates individual privacy. 7. A good manager shouldn't allow her employees to do whatever they like, because not everyone is a responsible worker. 8. A good manager should motivate his employees to do their best, because that's the best way to get people to do things.

Exercise 7 let—permit, allow help—assist have—employ, hire get—encourage, convince make—require, force

LESSON PLAN 2 SENSORY VERBS, CAUSATIVE VERBS, AND VERBS THAT TAKE SUBJUNCTIVE

FOCUS 3 [20 minutes]

Focus 3 gives examples of several exceptions to the pattern presented previously for verbs followed by infinitives (see SB page 97 Unit 6, Focus 5). You may want to review the verbs in Unit 6 that follow that pattern before presenting the causative verbs in this focus chart.

1. **Lead-in:** Put the causatives that are the focus of this section (*make, have, let,* etc.) on the board to draw attention to them. Ask the class a few questions about what teachers should *make, have, let* or *help* students do. Encourage a variety of answers. Some questions might include:

   What should teachers make students do to improve their English?

   What should teachers have students do when they miss a test?

   When should teachers let students watch movies in class?

   How can teachers help students learn better?

2. To clearly note the difference between causatives that take an infinitive and those that take the simple form of a verb, write one or two of your questions from the Lead-in on the board. Show how replacing the causative verb will change the verb following *to be* in the form of an infinitive (*What should teachers force students to do . . . ?*)

3. Go over the examples in the focus chart as a class, noting the parallel meanings between causative verbs and different complement forms.

Suggestion: Exercise 7 is a quick follow-up to the focus chart. However, Exercise 7 could also be used instead to introduce Focus 3.

GRAMMAR NOTE

When used as causatives the verbs *have* and *get* can be confusing for students who are not familiar with these uses. It can be useful to take a moment to point out these very common, but multifunctional,

verbs and their meanings. You can give several examples using them as causatives. However, remember that the meaning is further confused by the fact that they show only a medium sense of cause or force. A few examples include: *We should have Samuel give his presentation first. How can I get students to turn homework in on time? Let's have each group present their topic at the front of the class.*

EXERCISE 5 [15 minutes]

Students will identify a variety of causative verbs and then circle the infinitive or simple form of the following verb.

1. Invite students to volunteer some examples of causative verbs before you begin. Students can refer to Exercise 6 or Exercise 7 for this.

2. After students have worked individually to underline and circle the causatives and their following verbs, go over the answers as a class. See answers on LP page 300.

3. Review with an overhead transparency or by asking one student to record causative verbs on one side of the board (top to bottom of board) and another student to record the forms of the following verbs as students call them out during a whole class review.

Suggestion: To quickly review which causatives take the infinitive or simple verb form, make a game of it by quickly calling out a causative verb and see who can raise his or her hand and call out the correct answer first. This can even be done in teams.

For more practice, use *Grammar Dimensions 3* Workbook page 107, Exercise 6.

EXERCISE 6 [15 minutes]

Students will need to decide whether each causative will require the verb of action to be in the infinitive or simple verb form. They will also give their own

opinions with these causative statements using *should* or *shouldn't* and add a reason for this opinion.

1. Put the following words, as in the SB example, across the board:

   teachers—require— students— do more homework

2. Begin by asking the class whether they feel this sentence should take *should* or *shouldn't.* You may get different opinions. Choose one to use as an example.

3. Next, ask whether this causative takes the infinitive or simple verb form (*infinitive*).

4. Form the first part of the statement and invite volunteers to suggest reasons to support this statement. Ask a volunteer to add a reason to the end of the statement with *because.*

5. Review the steps and have students work individually to complete the exercise.

6. Have students review their sentences in small groups when finished. Circulate and check verb forms. See possible answers on LP page 300.

For more practice, use *Grammar Dimensions 3* Workbook page 107, Exercise 7.

EXERCISE 7 [5 minutes]

This exercise can be done as a review of verb meanings, directly after introducing Focus 3, or as a diagnostic before doing Focus 3. You can circulate quickly and check for common errors or simply go over this as a class review. See answers on LP page 300.

Grammar Dimensions 3 Lesson Planner   Unit 18: Sensory Verbs. Causative Verbs. and Verbs That Take Subjunctive   301

301

form

Passive Causative Verbs

The causative verbs *make* and *help* can be made passive, especially when the causer or agent of the action is obvious or not stated, or is a law or an institution. When the verbs *make* and *help* are passive, they must be followed by an infinitive, not the base form of the verb.

PASSIVE CAUSATIVE VERBS	ACTIVE CAUSATIVE VERBS
(a) Children should be made to brush their teeth before bedtime.	(b) Parents should make their children brush their teeth before bedtime.
(c) Children should be helped to learn good table manners.	(d) Parents should help their children learn good table manners.

Other causative verbs (*get*, *have*, *let*) cannot appear as passive verbs in causative sentences. If the agent is unknown or unimportant, we must express the passive sentence with another causative verb + infinitive that has the same meaning.

(e) NOT: Children should be gotten to read.	(f) Children should be inspired to read not forced.
(g) NOT: Teachers should be had to teach.	(h) Teachers should be employed to teach, not baby-sit.
(i) NOT: Children shouldn't be let to stay up too late.	(j) Children shouldn't be allowed to stay up too late.

Decide whether the causative verbs in these sentences can be made passive without omitting important information or being ungrammatical. If so, write the passive version of the sentence.

Examples: The law requires parents to send their children to school.

Parents are required to send their children to school.

The doctor got the patient to take the bitter tasting medicine.

No change possible

1. Tradition doesn't allow people to smoke in church.
2. Lack of time forced Kilroy to return to the barracks before the movie was over.
3. The law requires everyone who works to pay some income taxes.
4. People shouldn't let their dogs run free around the neighborhood.
5. We had the janitor clean up the mess.
6. When I was a child my mother didn't allow me to play in the street.

Use the chart below to make sentences about what governments should expect citizens to do and what citizens should expect governments to do. Choose three actions from each category and make sentences that express your real opinions. Write two sentences that express each opinion: one with a causative verb followed by a simple verb and one with a verb + infinitive.

Example: causer: government   doer: citizens   action: vote in regular elections

Governments should let their citizens vote in regular elections.

Governments should allow their citizens to vote in regular elections.

CAUSER	DOER	ACTION
government	citizens	pay taxes read any books and magazines they wish be of service to the nation meet national goals defend the country
citizens	government	be responsive to their wishes work without corruption establish national goals maintain law and order provide for basic defense

The government should:

make citizens pay/require citizens to pay taxes.

let them read/allow them to read any books or magazines they wish.

make them be/encourage them to be of service to the nation.

help them meet/assist them to meet national goals.

have them defend/require them to defend the country.

Citizens should:

make the government be/required the government to be responsible to their wishes.

make the government work/require the government to work with out corruption.

let the government establish/allow the government to establish national goals.

have the government maintain/expect the government to maintain law and order.

help the government provide/assist the government to provide for basic defense.

ANSWER KEY

Exercise 8 Answers will vary. Possible answers are listed above.

Exercise 9 1. People aren't allowed to smoke in church.   2. Kilroy was forced to return to the barracks before the movie was over.   3. Everyone who works is required to pay some income taxes.   4. No change possible.   5. No change possible.   6. When I was a child, I wasn't allowed to play in the street.

LESSON PLAN 2 SENSORY VERBS, CAUSATIVE VERBS, AND VERBS THAT TAKE SUBJUNCTIVE

EXERCISE 8 [15 minutes]

This exercise will test students' understanding of the subtle differences in meaning between causative verbs and the verb forms that will follow them. Students will create sentences using the suggested actions and their own opinions about the power of the government over the citizens and the power of the citizens over the government. You can suggest that students refer to the causative verbs listed in Exercises 6 and 7 for ideas.

1. Begin by pointing out that students will need to state three opinions about the power of the government on its citizens and three opinions about the power of citizens on their government. Beyond that, each opinion will need to be stated twice: once with a causative verb + infinitive and once with a causative verb + simple verb. All together, this will make 12 sentences.

2. Go over the examples with the class and note the addition of *should*, the choice of a causative verb, the correct form of the following verb to match, and that the same opinion has been stated once with a causative verb + infinitive and once with a causative verb + simple verb.

3. Have students work individually and circulate to check their progress.

Suggestion 1: Collect students' papers and use as a check to see how well they've understood this part of the unit. Go over any common errors in class the next day by putting a few sentences up on the board and having students find the problems and fix them. See possible answers on LP page 302.

Suggestion 2: If you plan to do Focus 4, you may want to save a few of the sentences generated in this exercise for use as examples of active causative sentences.

FOCUS 4 [20 minutes]

For more advanced classes, assign this for study at home. This will be a review of the formation of passive sentences and highlight the special characteristics of the passive causative. This focus

chart specifically presents the forms and uses of the causative verbs *make* and *help* in the passive.

1. **Lead-in:** To distinguish the active from the passive forms, divide the board in half and put the following category headings across each half:

   Active Causative: *agent— causative— receiver— action verb— object*

   Passive Causative: *receiver— passive causative action verb (infinitive form)—object*

2. Now go over Focus 4, making special note of the fact that the verbs *get, have,* and *let* are not used in passive causative and that for all passive causatives the action verb is put into the infinitive.

3. Take an active causative sentence (choose a few from Exercise 8) and line it up under the corresponding headings on the active side of the board. Some examples are:

   The government requires citizens to pay taxes.
   The government should help citizens get good medical care.

4. Now invite volunteers to create passive forms of these sentences to place under the headings on the passive side of the board. (*Citizens are required to pay taxes. Citizens should be helped to get good medical care.*)

VARIATION

If your class is more advanced, you can begin by having them take a few of the sentences created in Exercise 8 and try putting them into passive sentences. You can get them started by telling them that the first group of active sentences generated in Exercise 8 will have the "doer" (citizens) move to the front of the sentence as the receiver/subject and the "causer" (government) left out to create a passive sentence.

EXERCISE 9 [15 minutes]

Students will identify which of the following sentences can be made passive and then change those that they can. Unless you have just finished Focus 4,

---

review the causatives that cannot be used in the passive (*get, have, let*). Be aware that students may find a way to make every sentence passive by changing the causative verbs *get, have,* or *let* into other verbs that do allow the passive. Have students work individually or in pairs and then go over in groups or as a class. See answers on LP page 302.

For more practice, use *Grammar Dimensions 3* Workbook page 108, Exercise 8 and page 109, Exercise 9.

Use Your English

ACTIVITY 1 writing/speaking

Seeing is the sense that we rely on most. But when we are deprived of sight, our other senses become sharper. Test your other senses through the following activity.

STEP 1

Go to a place you know well. It could be this classroom, or a favorite room in your house, or someplace outdoors. Close your eyes and keep them closed for three minutes. Listen for the sounds that you can hear, both inside and outside. Are there any smells that you notice? Are they pleasant or unpleasant? What can you feel? Is it hot, cold? Make a list of things you have noticed about this place that you never noticed when your eyes were open. Try to think of at least three things for each of these categories:

I heard . . . I smelled . . . I felt . . .

STEP 2

Compare your list with several other people's lists. As a group, decide what other kinds of things escape your attention when you can rely on eyesight for information about the world around you. Present your ideas to the rest of the class.

ACTIVITY 2 speaking/writing

In the previous activity you had an opportunity to experience the world as a blind person does. How are blind people able to move around independently? In what ways do they compensate for lack of sight? How do they get information about where they are and where they are going? Consider deaf people, who cannot hear. How are they able to communicate with each other and the rest of the world?

In a small group discuss ways that people with sensory handicaps can compensate for those handicaps. Use your experience in the previous activity, and any other experiences you have had with people who are blind or deaf. Present your ideas in a written or oral report.

---

form

FOCUS 5

Verbs of Urging Followed by Subjunctive *that* Clauses

EXAMPLES

(a) The teacher **suggested** that the child **spend** more time on his homework.

(b) NOT: The teacher **suggested** that the child **spends** more time on his homework.

(c) The children **demanded** that their father **give** them candy.

(d) NOT: The children **demanded** that their father **gives** them candy.

EXPLANATION

Certain verbs of urging (*advise, ask, demand, desire, insist, propose, recommend, request, require, suggest, urge*) are followed by a *that* clause. The verb of the *that* clause must appear in simple form.

EXERCISE 10

Are these sentences correct or incorrect? For incorrect sentences, identify the mistake and fix it.

1. The students were got to do their homework.
2. The sergeant made the recruits to march for several hours.
3. A tailor was had to shorten my pants.
4. Parents shouldn't let their children watch too much television.
5. I had the waiter to bring the food to the table.
6. They encouraged all their children be independent.
7. We heard the protesters come closer and closer, so we left the area
8. Companies should be required to provide their employees with health insurance.
9. The baby sitter made the children to fall asleep by singing quietly.
10. Kilroy had his hair to be cut.
11. The judge demanded that he was punished.
12. The army requires that every new soldier gets his hair cut very short.
13. My parents heard our coming in late from the party.

Exercise 10 Ways to correct problems may vary. Possible answers are: 1. incorrect: got can't be made passive; The students were encouraged to do their homework. The teachers got the students to do their homework. 2. incorrect: made doesn't require to; The sergeant made the recruits march for several hours. 3. incorrect: had can't be made passive; A tailor was employed to shorten my trousers. I had a tailor shorten my trousers. 4. correct 5. incorrect: had doesn't require to; I had the waiter bring the food to the table. 6. incorrect: encouraged requires to; They encouraged all their children to be independent. 7. incorrect: unfinished actions should be described with V + ing;

We heard the protesters coming closer and closer, so we left the area. 8. correct. 9. incorrect: got can't be made has the wrong meaning for this sentence; The baby sitter got the children to fall asleep by singing quietly. 10. incorrect: to be is not correct; Kilroy had his hair cut. 11. incorrect: demand requires subjunctive; The judge demanded that he be punished. 12. incorrect: require requires subjunctive; The army requires that every new soldier get his hair cut very short. 13. incorrect: wrong pronoun form; My parents heard us coming in late from the party.

FOCUS 5 [20 minutes]

This focus chart gives examples of verbs that are similar in meaning to causatives, but are followed by a subjunctive *that*-clause. This group of verbs can be taught much like "vocabulary" items and should be reinforced by practicing their use in context.

1. **Lead-in:** Teach this section as you would teach new vocabulary. List the verbs from Focus 5 on the board, along with a sample sentence to show how the meaning changes by switching the verbs of urging (see underlines). For example:

   The customer asked that the manager return her money.

   The customer insisted that the manager return her money.

   The customer suggested that the manager return her money.

2. After going over the verbs in this group and their meanings, you can focus on the form of these sentences. Have the class work in pairs or small groups to make a list of "rules" for using these verbs (*they should include a that-clause, and the verb of the that-clause should appear in its simple form*).

EXERCISE 10 [15 minutes/homework]

This exercise can be used as a review for Unit 18.

1. This can be done individually in class or assigned as homework.

2. Students should note that some sentences may not have an error.

3. When finished, have students share the changes they made in pairs or small groups. They should be able to explain their reasons to each other for making any changes. See possible answers on LP page 304.

For more practice, use *Grammar Dimensions 3* Workbook page 110, Exercise 10.

---

2. When the three minutes are up, have students write as much as they can in response to the sensory questions in Step 1.

■ STEP 2

1. Have students discuss their observations as a group.

2. Each group should discuss the types of things that escape one's attention when relying on sight for information about the world.

ACTIVITY 2 speaking/writing [20 minutes]

This activity can be used as a small group speaking activity or as a written activity. Either approach can yield an oral report to the class.

1. Whether you use this as a speaking or writing activity, students should begin in small groups by discussing the ideas of compensating for and communicating with handicaps such as blindness or deafness. (See the Culture Note below.)

2. Circulate and note the use of sensory verbs. You can put examples on the board.

3. Give students time to organize their ideas and the main discussion points in order to present an oral report or to summarize a written report.

CULTURE NOTE

Some students may have very little knowledge or experience with the blind or deaf. Many countries still treat people with these handicaps as mentally handicapped. They are therefore isolated from and have very little interaction with mainstream society. Along those lines, their ability to communicate effectively is hindered by a lack of education. This communication or compensation can become an interesting topic for research if you are looking for an Internet activity.

UNIT GOAL REVIEW [10 minutes]

Ask students to look at the goals on the opening page of the unit again. Refer to the pages of the unit where information on each goal can be found.

For a grammar quiz review of Units 16–18, refer students to pages 111–112 in the *Grammar Dimensions 3* Workbook.

ExamView® Test Generator For assessment of Unit 18, use *Grammar Dimensions 3 ExamView®*.

USE YOUR ENGLISH

The Use Your English activities at the end of the unit contain situations that should naturally elicit the structures covered in the unit. For a more complete discussion of how to use the Use Your English activities see To the Teacher on LP page xxii. When students are doing these activities in class, you can circulate and listen to see if they are using the structures accurately. Errors can be corrected after the activity is finished.

ACTIVITY 1 writing/speaking [30 minutes]

This activity asks students to make statements with sensory verbs. You can choose to do this as a speaking activity, in which students will share their findings in small groups or you can use it as a writing activity, in which case you will skip Step 2 and collect students' writing instead. You can also use this after Exercise 3 on SB page 298, or at the end of the unit to check comprehension.

■ STEP 1

1. Explain the task and have students find a place to sit quietly for at least three minutes.

ACTIVITY 3 speaking/writing

There is a proverb in English that says: "You can catch more flies with honey than you can with vinegar." What do you think are the best ways to get someone to do something? Support your ideas by describing a situation when someone convinced you to do something you didn't want to do. How did that person convince you? Were you glad you did it or not?

ACTIVITY 4 listening/writing

Here are some general statements about human nature.

- People are usually in too much of a hurry.
- Children are spontaneous.
- Teenagers like to spend time together in groups.
- Older people are usually slower than younger people.

Do you think such generalizations are true or not? Test the validity of such generalizations by doing the following:

STEP 1 Choose a generalization that you want to test. It could be one of the statements listed above, or some other generalization. You may want to test a generalization that involves cultural differences, such as *North Americans are very outgoing* or *Asians are studious.*

STEP 2 Go to a place where you can watch lots of people. A shopping mall, a cafeteria, a busy corner—these are all good places. Watch how people behave. Look for examples of behavior that reflect the generalization you are testing. Find as many examples as you can that either support or contradict the generalization, and write a paragraph describing what you have observed. Here's an example:

They say that most people are friendly, and I have found that this seems to be true. At the mall yesterday I saw many people smiling at each other, I saw two people meet by chance. They must have been old friends because I saw them hug each other. I heard many people laughing and joking. I heard many of the salespeople say "Have a nice day" to customers. I saw one family arguing with one another, but strangers tended to be polite.

ACTIVITY 5 speaking

What routine jobs do you hate? Pretend that you don't have to worry about money. What things would you have other people do for you?

STEP 1 Decide on five to ten personal tasks that you would have someone else do, if money were no problem. (For example: *If money were no problem, I would have somebody else do my homework.*)

STEP 2 Compare your list to those of other students in class. Based on your discussion, decide what the three most unpopular tasks are that people have to do.

ACTIVITY 6 speaking

If you were the leader of the country, what things would you change?

- What laws would you establish for people to follow?
- What would you require people to do?
- What privileges would you allow people?
- What things would you not allow them to do?
- How would you get people to support you?

Think of at least three answers to each of these questions. Then tell the class why they should let you be their leader. Take a vote to see who is the most convincing candidate.

USE YOUR ENGLISH

ACTIVITY 3 speaking/writing [15 minutes]

This activity can be used as a whole class or small group discussion, or as a writing prompt. The discussion of ways "to get someone to do something" will require the use of a range of causative verbs and verbs of urging. You may need to restate or ask leading questions which require the use of vocabulary from the unit such as *force, make, demand, convince,* etc.

ACTIVITY 4 listening/writing [25 minutes/homework]

Students will use sensory verbs to describe observations they make while testing generalizations about human nature (a sort of scientific method approach).

■ STEP 1 Put the suggestions on the board and give the class time to choose one (or have each small group choose one generalization to work on and compare results together later). They will keep this generalization in mind as they observe a group of people outside class. They will test the truth of the generalization as they observe and write their observations.

■ STEP 2

1. Be sure the class understands the assignment before sending them out. This is actually great practice for any hypothesis testing they may encounter in other science or social science classes.

2. Have students write a paragraph describing their observations and whether these observations supported the generalization.

EXPANSION [10 minutes]

After the observations and recording, put students back into groups (original groups if they have the same topic) and give them time to share their findings. They should answer the following questions: *What was the generalization they chose? Did they believe it would prove true or untrue? Where did they go to test this generalization? What did they discover?*

Take a show of hands to discover how many students in the class found their generalization to be proven true. If you assigned papers, collect them and give feedback later.

ACTIVITY 5 speaking [15 minutes/homework]

This activity can involve the use of causative verbs or verbs of urging as students share the tasks they would like someone else to do. You may need to focus the discussion with questions that encourage the use of these verbs. This can be used as a discussion activity or a writing activity for homework.

■ STEP 1

1. Give students a chance to brainstorm a list of routine jobs with a group or partner.

2. Put the following questions on the board and have students take some time to create their individual lists: *If money were no problem, what would you have someone else do for you?*

■ STEP 2 Have students share their lists with each other in small groups and then determine the three most unpopular tasks to share with the class.

VARIATION

In pairs or small groups have students use these lists to negotiate a trade of tasks with each other rather than paying someone to do them. *What would you like to get someone else to do? What would you be willing to help someone else do?*

ACTIVITY 6 speaking [30 minutes/homework]

This review activity combines the use of the hypothetical (see Unit 17) with the use of causative verbs or verbs of urging.

1. Assign students to create their "platform," or answers to the list of questions, as homework.

2. Encourage students to be persuasive in their presentations in order to earn votes, by giving a prize to the one who gets the most votes (they cannot vote for themselves).

3. Have students present their ideas to the class and then give the class time to vote.

4. Collect students homework and give feedback.

Suggestion: Build up to the presentation and election with fanfare and a political feel: play patriotic music, drape crepe paper streamers on the board, and position a podium, if your class has one, at the front of the class.

ACTIVITY 7 — listening/speaking/writing

CD Track 26

In the radio, TV, and movie business the term "sound effects" is used to refer to the noises that are added to make the program or movie seem more real. You will hear some common sound effects that are used in radio and TV broadcasts or movies.

STEP 1

After you hear each sound, write a description of what you heard.

Example: *I heard a dog barking.*

STEP 2

Once you have identified all the sounds, compare your descriptions to those of another student to make sure you both interpreted the sound effects in the same way. Together, use your descriptions to write the story suggested by the sounds.

ACTIVITY 8 — listening

CD Track 27

Listen to the conversation between Matt and his doctor, and answer the following questions. You may need to listen to the conversation more than once. The first question has been answered for you as an example.

1. What does Dr. Wong recommend that Matt do? She recommends that he change his eating habits.

2. How does she suggest that Matt do this? She suggests that . . .

3. What is the problem Matt has with following her advice? His roommate Jeff, . . .

4. How does Jeff insist that food be cooked? He insists that . . . .

5. What does Dr. Wong urge that Matt demand? She urges that . . . .

6. What other solution does Dr. Wong suggest? She suggests that . . . .

ACTIVITY 9 — research on the web

Opinions on the best way to raise children vary widely from culture to culture and from family to family. Go to the Internet and use a search engine such as Google® or Ask® or Yahoo® to research this topic. Enter the term "child rearing" or "childrearing" and look for contrasting examples of how people think children ought to be raised. Some Web sites offer advice to parents about a variety of common problems parents have with their children. Find information about how children are raised differently in different cultures, or what the different viewpoints are regarding physical punishment. Prepare a brief report on a subject of interest for the rest of the class.

ACTIVITY 10 — reflection

STEP 1

What should a teacher do in order to help students learn to speak English? *Teachers should have students do homework every night. Teachers should help students guess the meaning of unfamiliar vocabulary, etc.* Think of at least five recommendations for teachers to help their students become more fluent.

STEP 2

Now think about things that students can do to help each other learn better: *Students should try to speak English with each other even outside of class. Students should work together to understand grammar, etc.* Think of at least five recommendations for students to help their fellow students become more fluent.

STEP 3

Compare your ideas with those of two or three other students and present two or three of the best suggestions to the rest of the class.

Activity 7 Sound 1: car driving up and stopping; Sound 2: car door slam; Sound 3: footsteps slowly climbing down stairs; Sound 4: knocking at door; Sound 5: creaky door opening; Sound 6: woman's screaming; Sound 7: gunfire; Sound 8: rapid footsteps running away; Sound 9: card door slam, car starts up, drives away; Sound 10: police sirens in the distance growing louder

Activity 8 Answers will vary. Possible answers are: 2. he started eating foods that are low in fat. 3. does all the cooking. 4. food be cooked with lots of butter. 5. Matt demand Jeff start cooking in a healthier way. 6. Jeff take over the cooking a couple of nights a week.

Activity 10 Answers will vary. Possible answers are: **Step 1:** Teachers should have students do homework every night. Teachers should help students guess the meaning of unfamiliar vocabulary. Teachers should let students talk about their lives in class. Teachers should get the students to talk as much as possible. **Step 2:** Students should get other students to practice English outside of class. Students should help other students understand grammatical patterns.

USE YOUR ENGLISH

ACTIVITY 7 — listening/speaking/writing [20 minutes]

CD Track 26

This activity gives students a fun way to use sensory verbs (to describe what they hear) and causative verbs (in the stories they create).

■ **STEP 1** Have students number a sheet of paper 1–10. Play the audio and have students write down a description of what they hear. There is no audio script for this particular listening, but the answers are listed on LP page 308.

■ **STEP 2**

1. Give students a second listen if needed and then put them into pairs or small groups to compare.
2. Once they have agreed on their descriptions, have each pair/group create a story based on the sound effects. The stories will consist of at least ten actions to match the sounds.
3. Give everyone a chance to share stories with the class or turn them in and give them feedback.

ACTIVITY 8 — listening [15 minutes]

CD Track 27

Students can hear and use the causative verbs in context.

1. Give students a chance to look the questions over before playing the audio.
2. Use your usual method for multiple listenings and pair review. See possible answers on LP page 308.

ACTIVITY 9 — research on the web [homework]

Students will get practice reading, writing, and speaking as they use the internet to research topics. You may wish to assign this after the Opening Task on SB pages 294–295.

1. Set this activity up as you would any Internet research activity.
2. Assign the final presentation of material as oral or written, to be completed at the end of the unit's coverage.

Suggestion: To focus students' topics early, you may want to have students choose a child-rearing topic of interest before they begin their search. This can be started by whole-class brainstorming of child-rearing differences across families or cultures. List the topics generated from this discussion on the board. For further development, you may want to put students into small groups for a quick discussion of what they think are some "hot" topics in child rearing and why they think so. For example, spanking or corporal punishment can be a hot topic, along with men staying home to raise kids or giving kids TV or video time.

ACTIVITY 10 — reflection [20 minutes/homework]

Students will use causatives or verbs of urging as they give real advice to teachers and students about ways to increase language learning.

Assign this as homework. Students should write at least five suggestions in response to each of the two questions.

Suggestion: As groups decide on their best recommendations for what students can do to help each other, have them create a small poster to display in the class.

UNIT GOALS

- Correctly distinguish generic and particular statements
- Correctly understand and distinguish specific and nonspecific reference in particular statements
- Use correct articles with specific, nonspecific, and unique nouns

OPENING TASK

Proverbs

A dog is man's best friend.

Other Common American Proverbs:

Time is money.

A fool and his money are soon parted.

Experience is the best teacher.

An idle mind is the devil's playground.

Absence makes the heart grow fonder.

The leopard cannot change its spots.

Actions speak louder than words.

Beauty is only skin-deep.

Every cloud has a silver lining.

Time heals all wounds.

Spare the rod and spoil the child.

Money is the root of all evil.

You are known by the company you keep.

STEP 1

Proverbs are well-known sayings that express general truths. On the previous page are some common American proverbs. Choose one that you agree with, and think of an example from your own life (or the life of someone that you know) that proves the truth of that proverb.

STEP 2

Write a paragraph about that example. Show why the proverb is true from your own experience. The first proverb has been done for you as an example.

A DOG IS MAN'S BEST FRIEND
I once had _a_ dog named Poppy. She was _a_ very faithful friend. Every afternoon when I came home, _the_ dog would greet me with kisses and _a_ wagging tail. I liked _the_ wagging tail, but I didn't enjoy _the_ kisses very much. Even so, she was always glad to see me, and I was happy to see her, too.
There was _a_ time in _my_ life when I was feeling very lonely. I didn't think I had _any_ friends. Every day I came home to _an_ empty house with _an_ empty heart. But Poppy was always at _the_ door waiting for me. She seemed to know whenever I was sad or lonely, and at _those_ times she would be extra friendly. _One_ time she even gave me _a_ "gift": _an_ old bone. Somehow she knew that I was especially sad. She must have thought _the_ bone would cheer me up.
Those bad times passed eventually, but they would have been _a_ _lot_ more difficult without _my_ faithful companion, Poppy. She proved to me that _a_ dog really is a wonderful friend.

Answers shown here are for Exercise 1 on SB page 313.

UNIT OVERVIEW

This unit provides an overview of the different categories of determiners and focuses on the use of definite and indefinite articles in particular. See Units 20, 21, and 22 for more on demonstratives, possessives, or quantifiers (in this order). In this unit, the distinctions between generic/particular statements, nonspecific/specific nouns, and indefinite/definite articles are used to work through steps in a flow chart allowing students to make an informed choice about which article to use. You may want to become familiar with Appendix 5 on Student Book (SB) page A-9 which presents the flow chart.

GRAMMAR NOTE

The proper use of articles can be equally tricky for ESL students to learn and teachers to explain. Although many languages do not use articles, many do mark the ideas of definite and indefinite in some way (i.e., word order, suffixes, etc.). In addition, many languages do not classify nouns in terms of being countable or noncountable like English does.

English has two types of articles: definite (*the*) and indefinite (*a/an*). The general ideas about choosing articles will be a review for students. However, possible new ideas may include the notion that *some* can be considered the plural form of *a/an* and that *Ø* can also be considered a possible determiner choice.

UNIT GOALS

Some instructors may want to review the goals listed on SB page 310 after completing the Opening Task so that students understand what they should know by the end of the unit. These goals can also be reviewed at the end of the unit when students are more familiar with the grammar terminology.

OPENING TASK [20 minutes/homework]

This task works best if begun in class and then assigned as homework to be collected and evaluated later. This would work well as a diagnostic to guide your choice of exercises and activities throughout the next several units or as a way to check progress at the end of the unit. For a more complete discussion of the purpose of the Opening Task, see To the Teacher, Lesson Planner (LP) page xxii.

Setting Up the Task

1. Begin with a brief discussion of proverbs. Go over the proverbs listed on SB page 310 and invite volunteers to paraphrase them.
2. If possible, have students share similar proverbs from their own countries.

Conducting the Task

■ STEP 1

From the proverbs listed, ask students to choose one that they agree with and think of an example of how it is true. Students should try to think of an example from their own life, or from the life of someone they know.

■ STEP 2

Read the example essay as a class. Have students write their paragraph about why the proverb they chose is true for them.

Closing the Task

1. If this is being used as a normal Opening Task and for possible diagnostic purposes, collect papers and note common errors to guide your teaching.
2. If the Opening Task is used as a review at the end of the unit, you can either collect papers for individual feedback or give students a chance to do some peer

editing and review. For this, students can work with a partner. After reading for general content and clarifying any questions, peer editing can be focused on articles by asking students to underline all nouns and to then go through and note the correct or incorrect use of articles with these nouns.

EXPANSION 1 [20 minutes]

Follow this Opening Task up with Activity 1 (speaking/writing) on SB page 329.

EXPANSION 2 [30 minutes/homework]

Follow-up with Activity 7 (research on the web) on SB page 331 for research task on proverbs.

GRAMMAR NOTE

Typical student errors (use)

- Using definite articles with a plural for generic statements: * *The lions can grow to weigh several hundred pounds.* * *She loves reading the books.* (See Focus 3.)
- Using definite articles for nonspecific nouns: * *I hope you have the wonderful vacation.* (See Focus 4.)
- Using indefinite articles for specific nouns:
  * *Did you see a same man that we saw yesterday?* (See Focus 4.)
- Omitting articles: * *I can't find book.*
- Using *some* when identifying part of a group:
  * *Ben and Maria are some teachers.* (See Focus 6.)
- Using articles with abstract nouns, proper nouns, or studies: * *The life is hard.* * *The English is a difficult language.*

FOCUS 1

Overview of Determiners

form

Most noun phrases in English require a determiner.

EXAMPLES	EXPLANATIONS
	Determiners can be:
(a) We need this pen. **That** pen is out of ink.	• **Demonstratives** (see Unit 20 for more information)
(b) **Peter's** information surprised us more than **his** appearance.	• **Possessives** (see Unit 21 for more information)
(c) Denise has **few** friends. She doesn't make **much** effort to meet people.	• **Quantifiers** (see Unit 22 for more information)
(d) Denise has **a** new position. She has **some** work to do. She feels **the** work is quite important.	• **Articles** (see Focus 2 for more information)
(e) NOT: Here is **a this** pen. (f) NOT: **That my** pen is green.	There is only one determiner of these types in each noun phrase.

Many nouns can have both a countable and a noncountable meaning.

NONCOUNT MEANING	COUNT MEANING
(g) They grow **coffee** and **tea** in Sumatra.	(h) We ordered **two coffees** and **a tea** in addition to dessert.

The form of most determiners depends on whether you think of the noun as being countable or noncountable, singular or plural.

EXAMPLES	EXPLANATIONS
one bottle/two bottles one dollar/two dollars one man/two men one chair/two chairs	If you think of a noun as countable then you must indicate singular or plural.
milk (one gallon of milk/two gallons of milk) money (one dollar/a hundred yen) furniture (two pieces of furniture)	If you think of a noun as noncountable then you must use a unit word in order to talk about specific quantities. Noncountable nouns have no plural form.

EXERCISE 1

Underline and identify the determiners in the sample paragraph of the Opening Task. Are they demonstratives, possessives, quantifiers, or articles? Are the nouns count or noncount, singular or plural? List them below.

_____

_____

_____

_____

_____

_____

_____

Exercise 1 See SB page 310 for underlined determiners. Note that a lot is used as an intensifier, not a noun phrase. The types of determiners are as follows:

Demonstratives: those, Those

Possessives: my, my

Quantifiers: any, One

Articles: A, a, a, the, the, a, an, the, a, an, the, the, a, a, a

Count: dog, friend, afternoon, dog, tail, kisses, time, friends, day, house, heart, door, times, time, gift, bone, bone, times, companion, dog, friend

Noncount: (none)

Singular: dog, friend, afternoon, dog, tail, time, day, house, heart, door, time, gift, bone, bone, companion, dog, friend

Plural: kisses, friends, times, times

FOCUS 1 [20 minutes]

Since most students have probably been introduced to determiners and count/noncount nouns before, consider using Focus 1 as a brief overview leading into Exercise 1.

1. **Lead-in:** If possible copy Focus 1 onto an overhead transparency. Cover the explanation side of the transparency and ask the class if they can state what the words in boldface (examples a–d) are called. Don't worry if they don't know the formal terminology for these. You can also simply ask students to open their books and cover the explanation half with a paper. Invite volunteers to also say what is wrong with examples (e) and (f) and state a rule for this.

2. When finished, note that the first three types of determiners listed in examples (a–c) will be covered in following units. This unit will focus on articles.

VARIATION 1

You can also consider doing Exercise 1 first; it can be followed by a review of Focus 1.

VARIATION 2

For more advanced classes, consider using one of the exercises (Exercise 11–13) at the end of the unit as a diagnostic before beginning the unit.

EXERCISE 1 [20 minutes]

Students will identify and name the determiners in the Opening Task paragraph.

1. A good way to list the determiners is to put the following column headings across the board and ask students to do the same on a piece of paper:

Demonstratives   Possessives   Quantifiers   Articles

2. Let the class go over the sample paragraph on SB page 311 and underline each determiner first. Then have them list these determiners in the corresponding column on their paper (or do this as a class activity on the board).

3. As they list each determiner, have students note whether each is count/noncount and singular/plural next to the determiner. This can be abbreviated (*dog – c/sing*).

4. Go over in pairs or as a class. See answers on LP pages 310 and 312.

Suggestion 1: Tell students how many determiners are in the paragraph to get them searching for more if you feel they haven't found them all.

Suggestion 2: Copy the paragraph onto an overhead transparency for an easier class review.

For more practice, use *Grammar Dimensions 3* Workbook page 113, Exercise 1.

FOCUS 2   Overview of Articles

form   meaning

There are two kinds of articles: definite and indefinite.

Definite Articles (used for specific reference)

EXAMPLES	EXPLANATIONS
the pencil/the pencils the information	There is only one form for definite articles: *the*. *The* can be used with any kind of noun: countable, singular and plural, and noncountable.

Indefinite Articles (used for nonspecific reference)

EXAMPLES		EXPLANATIONS
a book a church a hotel	a shiny apple a university	*a/an*: Used with singular count nouns. *A* precedes nouns (or their modifiers) that begin with a consonant sound.
an apple an honest man an easy lesson	an uncomfortable situation an hour	*An* precedes nouns (or their modifiers) that begin with a vowel sound.
(a) Please get me some pencils. (b) I've invited some friends for dinner. (c) I have some ideas about the party. (d) Would you like some rice?		*some*: Used with plural count nouns and noncount nouns. *Some* indicates a nonspecific quantity or amount.
(e) Some water got on my notebook. (f) I'm looking for some information.		
(g) Everyone needs friends. (h) Teachers want students to succeed. (i) Ideas can come from anywhere. (j) Rice is eaten all over Asia. (k) Water is necessary for life.		Use no article (Ø) with nouns that are nonspecific or generic. See Focus 3 for information in using Ø to make generic statements. See Focus 4 for information about nonspecific statements that do not refer to a quantity or amount and other rules regarding some versus Ø.
(l) I'm looking for information about public transportation.		

NOTE: See Appendix 5 for a chart that reviews the process for deciding how to choose the correct article for most situations in English.

EXERCISE 2

Decide which articles (*a, an, the, some, Ø*) can **NOT** be used with the following noun phrases.

1. pencils — *a, an*
2. water — *a, an*
3. apple — *a, Ø, some*
4. university professor — *an, Ø, some*
5. hourly employee — *a, Ø, some*
6. motherhood — *the, an*
7. bread — *a, an*
8. fast food — *a, an*
9. test — *an, Ø, some*

FOCUS 3   Using Articles in Generic and Particular Statements

use

There are different rules for using articles depending on whether we are making a **generic** statement or a **particular** statement. So the first step in choosing the correct article is to understand the difference between these two kinds of statements.

GENERIC STATEMENTS	PARTICULAR STATEMENTS
Generic statements describe concepts and ideas. They refer to general categories of things.	Particular statements describe real situations. They refer to individual members of a category.
(a) **Bicycles** are an excellent means of transportation. (a category)	(b) They went shopping for bicycles yesterday. (particular things they wanted to buy—they didn't buy all the bicycles in the world)
(c) **An angry customer** is a frightening sight. (a category of person)	(d) We saw **an angry customer** complaining about the high price of tickets. (a particular person—not all customers are angry)

Continued on next page

FOCUS 2 [20 minutes]

Focus 2 should be a review for most students. Note that you may need to review the concept of the "null article" symbol (Ø) with students before beginning this focus.

1. **Lead-in:** Exercise 2 on SB page 315 can be used to lead into this focus chart. It can be done in pairs, individually, or as a class activity. Depending on how well students answer, you can decide how much time to spend reviewing each of the sections in the Focus 2 chart.

2. For an inductive approach, have students cover the explanation side of their charts (or use an overhead transparency) and invite volunteers to tell the rule that is shown in each group of examples.

Suggestion: Refer students to the first flow chart in Appendix 5 on SB page A-9 showing how the forms of the noun lead to a choice of articles. You may want to make a copy of this appendix on an overhead transparency for reference throughout this unit.

GRAMMAR NOTE

Some issues of pronunciation can cause confusion with the rule for *an*. Although most students will be able to tell you the vowel rule for the use of the indefinite article *a* versus *an*, they may have trouble with those words in English which begin with a vowel but are not pronounced with a vowel sound. For example, the word *university* is not pronounced with an initial vowel sound in English and should, therefore become *a university*. However, many French speakers would pronounce *university* with an initial vowel sound (oo). This would lead many students to believe that it does begin with a vowel and then form *an university*.

EXERCISE 2 [10 minutes]

Through a process of elimination, students will identify which articles are NOT a possible match to each noun phrase. Students can work individually, in pairs, or as a whole class on this. Use this as a Lead-in or a follow-up to Focus 2. See answers on LP page 314.

FOCUS 3 [20 minutes]

Focus 3 introduces the key concepts of *generic* (general categories) and *particular* (individual members of a category) statements. This is the first step in the flow chart for "Reference" which will help students to make choices about articles.

1. **Lead-in:** Begin with two example sentences (choose a pair from Focus 3 or make two of your own) that highlight the contrast between generic and particular statements. Point out the differences between the sentences. Explain that recognizing these differences will help them to learn the rules for choosing articles.

2. Go over the example pairs in Focus 3 with the class. Note that the last section of the chart on SB page 316 describes only generic statements. Particular statements will be further addressed in Focus 4.

3. Follow this chart immediately with Exercise 3.

Continued from previous page

GENERIC STATEMENTS	PARTICULAR STATEMENTS
(e) **The lion** is found throughout Africa. (a category of animal)	(f) I saw **the lion** at the circus. (a particular animal—not all lions are in the circus)
(g) **Some people** never fall in love. (a category of people)	(h) **Some people** are joining us for dinner. (particular people, not a class of people)
(i) **Information** is increasingly communicated by electronic rather than printed media. (a category of things that are communicated electronically)	(j) Please give me **some information** on medical treatments for heart disease. (particular written or spoken facts)

Both definite and indefinite articles can be used to express generic statements. The following examples are listed from most common to least common.

EXAMPLES	EXPLANATIONS
(k) **Lions** are mighty creatures. (l) **Rice** is eaten throughout Asia.	Ø with plural count or noncount nouns is the most common way to make generic statements.
(m) **A lion** is a mighty creature.	A/*an* with singular count nouns is less common, but also acceptable.
(n) **The lion** is a mighty creature.	*The* with singular count nouns is also possible, but sounds very formal to most native speakers.

NOTE: Article usage in particular statements is explained in the rest of the focus boxes of this unit.

EXERCISE 3

Decide whether these sentences are (*G*) generic statements (describing classes or categories) or (*P*) particular statements (describing members of a category).

Examples:

G **Computers** are cheaper now than they were ten years ago.

P **Computers** for the new lab are being donated by a company in San Jose.

P 1. I wanted to buy **some mangoes** for the fruit salad, but they were too expensive!

G 2. **Mangoes** are a fruit found in most tropical places.

P 3. I saw **a doctor** about my cough.

G 4. **A doctor** is someone who has received training in medical science.

G 5. **Computers** have completely changed the way we live.

P 6. Don't go to that store for **computers**. They're cheaper at Radio Hut.

G 7. **Many people** don't like spicy food.

P 8. There weren't **many people** at Reiko's party.

P 9. If you really want to know how John is feeling, don't ask the doctor, ask **the nurses**. They will have better information.

G 10. There is a shortage of **nurses** in American hospitals today.

P 11. Raul is starting **a new company.**

G 12. **A company** needs to make sure that it is earning a profit.

EXERCISE 4

Write one generic statement and one particular statement for each of the cues listed here. The first one has been done for you as an example.

Examples: Generic: *Bicycles are a cheap and efficient means of transportation.*
Particular: *Bob Billy and his sister got bicycles for Christmas.*

1. bicycles
2. a new car
3. the English language
4. transportation
5. tea
6. salespeople
7. books
8. hard work
9. Chinese food
10. trouble

ANSWER KEY

Exercise 4 Answers will vary. Possible answers are: 2. *Generic*: A new car will make any man feel five years younger. *Particular*: My Dad just bought a new car. 3. *Generic*: English is spoken all over the world. *Particular*: We felt relieved when we heard the English language being spoken at the hotel. 4. *Generic*: We won't solve our pollution problems until we solve our transportation problems. *Particular*: I want to come to the party, but I don't have any transportation. 5. *Generic*: Do you prefer tea or coffee? *Particular*: Let's have some tea. 6. *Generic*: Salespeople may not know about the quality of the things they sell. *Particular*: If you want to know where the sale items are, you should ask the salespeople over there. 7. *Generic*: Books make good presents at Christmas. *Particular*: There are books all over this desk. 8. *Generic*: Hard work is good for you. *Particular*: Doing this exercise is hard work. 9. *Generic*: Chinese food is delicious and healthy. *Particular*: Let's get some Chinese food for dinner. 10. *Generic*: The upcoming grammar test means trouble for lots of students. *Particular*: I had some trouble doing this exercise.

LESSON PLAN 1

EXERCISE 3 [15 minutes]

Students will identify and label generic (G) and particular (P) statements. This activity can be done individually, in pairs, or as a class review of Focus 3.

1. If students are having trouble with the distinction from Focus 3, do this exercise as a class review and allow a lot of time for discussion and any questions.

2. If students are working individually or in pairs, give them time to compare answers and come to an agreement on any differences. When everyone is finished, go over the answers as a class. See answers on LP page 316.

3. It is important that students understand this basic difference in statements before you move on in the unit.

For more practice, use *Grammar Dimensions 3* Workbook page 113, Exercise 2.

EXERCISE 4 [15 minutes/homework]

After showing that they can identify both generic and particular statements in Exercise 3, students must create pairs of sentences of their own with the noun phrases given. The following are several variations for this exercise:

1. If your students have trouble creating sentences on their own, have them work in pairs or small groups.

2. You can also consider dividing the sentences up among the class and have each half of the class do five sentences or have students form groups and divide the sentences up among the group.

3. It can even work within groups to have some students writing only generic statements and others writing only particular statements. They will then come together and share in pairs. Everyone should agree as to whether they have a

good representation of each. See possible answers on LP page 316.

4. For more advanced students, you may wish to assign this exercise as homework.

FOCUS 4

Specific Versus Nonspecific Nouns

meaning

In particular statements, article use is determined by whether a noun is specific or nonspecific.

SPECIFIC NOUNS

	IMPLIED MEANING	EXPLANATION
(a) Please give me **the red pen.**	There is only one red pen.	Specific nouns require definite articles. Specific nouns refer to an identified object. **Both the** speaker and the listener know specifically which object is being talked about.
(b) Please pass **the tea.**	There is a teapot right here.	

NONSPECIFIC NOUNS

	IMPLIED MEANING	EXPLANATION
(c) Please give me **a red pen.**	There are several red pens. Any red pen is O.K.	Nonspecific nouns require indefinite articles. A noun is nonspecific when **either** the speaker or the listener or both do **not** know specifically which object is being referred to.
(d) Let's go to **a restaurant** and have **some tea.**	We don't know which restaurant it will be, or what kind of tea we will have.	

EXAMPLES

	IMPLIED MEANING	EXPLANATIONS
(e) I bought **a new car.**	You haven't seen it yet.	Use indefinite articles (*a/an, Ø, some*) when:
(f) I had **some cookies** with lunch today.	I know which cookies I had, but you don't.	• the speaker has a specific mental image of the noun, but the listener doesn't.
(g) There are **students** in my class who always do their homework.	I know which ones they are, but you don't.	
(h) I hear you bought **a new car.** What kind is it?	You know, but I don't.	Use indefinite articles (*a/an, Ø, some*) when:
(i) You said you were holding **some mail** that came for me.	You know what kind and how much mail there is, but I don't.	• the speaker doesn't have a specific mental image or idea, but the listener does.
(j) Mary tells you **secrets** that she never tells me.	You know which secrets, but I don't.	

Continued on next page

Continued from previous page

EXAMPLES

	IMPLIED MEANING	EXPLANATIONS
(k) I hope you have a **wonderful time** on your vacation.	We don't know what events will make it a wonderful vacation.	• neither the speaker nor the listener has a specific mental image.
(l) Let's get **some spaghetti** when we go out tonight.	We don't know what kind of or how much spaghetti we're going to get.	
(m) We're supposed to bring **dessert** to the picnic.	We haven't been told a specific kind of dessert to bring.	

EXERCISE 5

Decide whether the nouns in the sentences below are specific or nonspecific. Is the noun phrase identified for the speaker, the listener, or both? Write the number of the sentence on the appropriate line below. The first two have been done for you.

Both listener and speaker know which one: ___4___

Listener knows which one, but speaker doesn't: ___6___

Speaker knows which one, but listener doesn't: ___3, 2___

Neither listener nor speaker knows which one: ___5, 1___

1. Do you want to go to a movie tonight?
2. The O'Neills just bought a **beautiful new house.** You really ought to see it. I'm sure you'll think it's wonderful.
3. I want you to meet a **friend** of mine. You both have the same interests.
4. Did you have fun at **the party?**
5. Let's have **some friends** over for dinner on Saturday.
6. I heard Ali has a **new girlfriend.** What's she like?

EXERCISE 6

Choose the correct implied meaning for each of these sentences. (*I* refers to the speaker. *You* refers to the listener.)

1. The student from Japan is here to see you.
   a. There are several students from Japan who had appointments.
   b. There is only one student from Japan who had an appointment.
2. Let's go to a restaurant.
   a. We've already decided which restaurant to go to.
   b. Let's choose a restaurant.

Continued on next page

ANSWER KEY

Exercise 6   *Answers are circled above and are continued on LP page 320.*

FOCUS 4 [20 minutes]

Focus 4 focuses on the division in particular statements between specific and nonspecific nouns. It goes on to briefly mention the use of definite articles (examples a–b) for specific nouns, but the main focus of the remainder of the chart is to show examples of nonspecific nouns (examples c–m) and the use of indefinite articles. The three choices for indefinite articles are: *a/an, some, Ø.*

1. **Lead-in:** Use an overhead transparency or a large copy of the chart in Appendix 5. Use this chart to point out the different sections under *PARTICULAR STATEMENTS* as you work through the examples in Focus 4.

2. Point to the section of the A-5 chart labeled *Specific reference: Use definite articles.* Note to the class that these specific nouns require the definite article *the.* Go over the examples for *specific nouns* (a–b) in the focus chart on SB page 318. You may want to add a few more examples. Be sure students understand that specific nouns are known by **both** the speaker and the listener.

3. Next, point to the section of the A-5 chart labeled *Nonspecific reference: Use indefinite articles.* Show on the chart that the article choice is not as straightforward. We will need to make some choices for this path. The choices will be whether we are talking about *singular count nouns* (a/an) or *plural count & noncount nouns* (some/Ø). This information will determine the path taken down the A-5 chart.

4. Now, go over the examples for *nonspecific nouns* (c–d) in the focus chart on SB page 318. You may want to add a few more examples. Be sure students understand that nonspecific nouns are either **not** known by the speaker or the listener or both.

5. Continue looking at examples of nonspecific nouns by going over the examples (e–m), which continue on SB page 319. They are divided into groups illustrating who knows specifically what object they are speaking about (i.e., only the speaker knows, only the listener knows, neither knows). These divisions will be helpful as you work on Exercise 5 with the class.

6. Note that for each group of examples for nonspecific nouns, the article choices will be made on whether the noun is singular count (*a/an*) or plural/noncount (*some/Ø*).

Suggestion: Follow this focus immediately with Exercise 5 to give students practice identifying specific and nonspecific nouns.

VARIATION

Use Exercise 7 on SB page 320 as a diagnostic lead-in to this focus chart. In this way, you will be able to see in advance how well students are able to choose the appropriate article before going over the focus chart.

EXPANSION [15 minutes]

For more advanced classes, you can follow-up with Activity 5 (speaking) on SB page 330 for a speaking task to be used with a partner in the classroom. In this activity, students discuss what differences are implied when a definite or indefinite article is chosen.

EXERCISE 5 [10 minutes]

This exercise supports the examples given in Focus 4. Students will identify whether a noun is specific or nonspecific and further identify whether the nonspecific nouns are known by the speaker only, the listener only, or neither.

1. If you have noted the three groups of nonspecific nouns in Focus 4, this should be a perfect way to give students practice in identifying them.

2. Point out to the class that there are four categories listed in this exercise. They match the focus chart. The first category is a noun which "*Both listener and speaker know: . . .*" (a specific noun = uses definite article). The following three categories use the indefinite articles. Students will need to identify whether the speaker, the listener, or neither know the noun specifically.

3. Go over the first two sentences as a class and allow for questions from students. It's important that students grasp these distinctions.

4. Have students complete the rest of the exercise on their own. Have students share their answers in pairs or as a class. See answers on LP page 318.

EXERCISE 6 [10 minutes]

Students will look for the implied meaning of each sentence. From the implied meaning, students will determine who has specific knowledge of the noun. Have students complete this exercise in pairs or as a class review. Go over the answers in your usual manner. See answers on LP pages 318 and 320.

For more practice, use *Grammar Dimensions 3 Workbook* page 114, Exercise 3.

3. Some friends are coming to dinner.
   a. You know who's coming to dinner.
   ⓑ You don't know who's coming to dinner.

4. Let's invite the neighbors to dinner.
   ⓐ You know which neighbors will be invited to dinner.
   b. You don't know which neighbors will be invited to dinner.

5. You should see a doctor about that cough.
   a. I am thinking about a specific doctor.
   ⓑ Any doctor should be able to help you.

EXERCISE 7

Add the appropriate article (*a/an, the, some,* or Ø) in the blanks. There may be more than one correct answer.

1. I didn't bring ___the___ roses that you asked for. I completely forgot them.

2. Sally wanted to buy ___a___ new dress, so she's gone out to find one.

3. ___A___ teacher was here to see you. I think it was your English teacher.

4. Did you give ___the___ musicians a nice tip? They certainly played beautiful music for your party.

5. Would you like ___some/Ø/a___ cold iced tea?

6. How did you enjoy ___the___ Chinese food last night?

7. I have ___some/Ø___ problems that I don't want to talk about.

8. John sent Mary ___a___ card for her birthday, but she says she never received it.

9. (a) ___The___ bank where Dora works was robbed by
   (b) ___a___ masked man with (c) ___a___ gun.
   By the time (d) ___the/a___ police officer arrived, it was too late.
   (e) ___The___ robber had disappeared.

ANSWER KEY

Exercise 6 is continued from LP page 318. Answers are circled above.

FOCUS 5 | Using Articles in Discourse

use

EXAMPLES	EXPLANATIONS
(a) There once was a little old man who lived in a house by a river. **The shack** was rather dirty, and so was **the man**.	A noun is usually used with an indefinite article the first time it is mentioned because it is *nonspecific*: it is the first time the listener has encountered it.
(b) I once had a big black dog and a little white dog. **The black dog** kept itself very clean, but **the white dog** loved to roll in mud.	In later sentences the same noun is used with a definite article because it has become *specific*: both the speaker and the listener now know exactly which noun is being talked about.
(c) I had **a dog** named Poppy. Every afternoon when I came home **the dog** would greet me with **kisses** and a **wagging tail**. I liked **the wagging tail**, but I didn't enjoy **the kisses** very much.	A noun becomes specific: • by direct reference. (The noun is repeated.)
(d) If you have **a dog** as **a pet**, you can always look forward to going home because of **the kisses** and **the wagging tail** that are there to greet you when you arrive.	• by indirect reference. (The noun itself is not repeated, but the reference is still clear from the context.)
(e) I read **an interesting book**. **The author** suggested that all life came from visitors from another planet. **The first chapter** tells stories of visitors from outer space that are found in many different cultures.	

Exercise 6 is continued from SB page 319. See answers on LP page 320.

EXERCISE 7 [15 minutes]

Students will fill in the missing indefinite articles based on the context of the sentence.

1. Have students work alone or in pairs. You may want to refer them back to the flow chart in A–5 for review of choosing the appropriate article.

2. You may want to put the flow chart up again as you go over the answers and explain the process of making choices as you work your way through the chart for each sentence. See answers on LP page 320.

For more practice, use *Grammar Dimensions 3* Workbook page 114, Exercise 4.

FOCUS 5 [20 minutes]

Focus 5 outlines the general rule that the first time a noun is mentioned it is nonspecific. However, by *direct reference* when a noun is repeated, it is considered specific. Nouns can also be considered specific by *indirect reference*, which means that although they haven't been mentioned before, they are somehow already known and clear from the context (see Focus 7 on SB page 325 for more on this).

1. **Lead-in:** For an inductive approach, put only the examples (a–c) on the overhead transparency or have students cover the explanation side of their books with a paper. Let students work in pairs or small groups to answer why they think the articles change in the second sentences in examples (a–c). Invite pairs/groups to share their "rules" for these examples. Discuss them, but do not uncover the explanation side yet.

3. Ask pairs/groups to come up with a rule to explain examples (d–e). This will be more difficult, but it's good for students to attempt to make sense of the examples before you talk about it. Explain to students that Focus 7 will talk about some of these nouns.

use

FOCUS 6 Repeating the Indefinite Article

There are certain situations in which the usual rule of replacing an indefinite article with a definite article after the first time it is mentioned is not followed.

EXAMPLES	EXPLANATIONS
(a) There once was a little old man who lived in a house by **a river**. **The** house was rather dirty, and so was **the** man. Although **there was a river** right next to **the** house, **the** old man had to walk quite far to get clean drinking water.	• Sentences with *there is/there are*.
(b) I once had a dog. Her name was Poppy. She was **a** good dog. **Implied Meaning:** She was a member of the category "good dogs."	• Sentences that identify someone or something as a member of a category.
(c) You know John. He's **a** teacher. **Implied Meaning:** He's a member of the category "teachers."	
(d) John is a teacher. John and Fred are **some** teachers.	Do not use *some* for plural nouns that identify things as part of a group.
(e) NOT: John and Fred are **some** teachers.	
(f) Paris is a city. Paris, Rome, and Munich are **some** cities.	
(g) NOT: Paris, Rome, and Munich are **some** cities.	

EXERCISE 8

Write articles (*a/an, Ø, some, the*) in the spaces. More than one answer may be correct.

1. A fool and his money are soon parted. I have (a) ___a___ foolish friend who is really careless with (b) ___Ø___ money. He has

   (c) ___a___ good-paying job, but he doesn't even have

   (d) ___a___ bank account. He says he doesn't need one because he

   spends his salary right away. He gets (e) ___a___ paycheck once

   (f) ___a___ week. (g) ___The___ money is **always** gone

   before (h) ___the/a___ week is over. I can't tell you what he spends it on.

   And you know what? Neither can he!

2. You can't make a silk purse out of a sow's ear. I saw (a) ___an___

   interesting play last night. (b) ___The___ actors were excellent, and

   (c) ___the___ scenery was beautiful. However, (d) ___the___

   play itself was unfortunately really badly written, and actually rather stupid. Half

   (e) ___the___ audience left at intermission.

3. Spare the rod and spoil the child. Little Billy doesn't like (a) ___Ø___

   school. He's not doing well, and he's really rather lazy. He says

   (b) ___Ø/the___ teachers are boring. He doesn't like doing

   (c) ___Ø/the___ homework. He much prefers to watch

   (d) ___Ø___ cartoons on TV. As (e) ___a___ result, his

   teachers aren't very happy with (f) ___the___ way he performs in class.

   If he doesn't take (g) ___Ø/some/the___ responsibility for doing

   (h) ___Ø/the___ assignments, he may have to repeat

   (i) ___the___ same grade next year. Some people would say that he needs

   a good spanking.

LESSON PLAN 2/LESSON PLAN 3

EXERCISE 8 [15 minutes/homework]

This exercise differs from Exercise 7 because it looks at articles used in the context of a paragraph rather than simply one sentence. This allows for repetition of a noun and the possibility of direct or indirect reference. Students will practice the "rules" they just created in Focus 5. Students should show that they understand the basic rule from Focus 5 (a repeated noun goes from being nonspecific the first time to specific the second time) since Focus 6 will describe exceptions to this rule.

1. Give students time as homework or in class individually or in pairs to work on replacing the missing articles.

2. Review as a class. Refer to the Appendix 5 chart and the rules from Focus 5. See answers on LP page 322.

VARIATION

For more advanced classes, you can do this exercise as a diagnostic before going over Focus 5 or even at the beginning of the unit.

For more practice, use *Grammar Dimensions 3* Workbook page 115, Exercise 5.

LESSON PLAN 3

FOCUS 6 [20 minutes]

Focus 6 describes two exceptions to the rule described in Focus 5. The rule states that a noun is nonspecific the first time it is mentioned, but becomes specific thereafter. This would require a nonspecific noun to take the indefinite article (*a/an*, *some*, *Ø*) at the first mention and then the definite article (*the*) thereafter.

The first exception in Focus 6, however, states that the indefinite article is always used with *there is/there are*. It does not change to a definite article at second mention. Secondly, the indefinite article is always used when identifying a noun as part of a group or category.

1. **Lead-in:** This focus can be introduced deductively by simply reviewing the previous rule from Focus 5 and then stating the two exceptions to this rule as outlined above.

2. Go over the examples for each exception. Make special note of the rule that *some* is not used when identifying a noun as part of a group or category.

3. Here is another example to illustrate the exception of members of a group/category. You can put this on the board:

   My dog, Poppy, was always there for me. She was a great dog. She proved to me that a dog really is a wonderful friend.

EXPANSION [15 minutes]

Follow-up with Activity 4 (speaking) on SB page 330 for a speaking task to be used with a partner in the classroom. In this activity, students will come up with a story by looking at four pictures.

EXERCISE 9

Add the correct article to the blank spaces in these sentences.

I once had (1) __an__ experience that proved to me that (2) __an/the__ idle mind is (3) _____ devil's playground. Miss Kersell was my eighth grade science and math teacher. She was (4) __a__ very strict teacher and wouldn't allow any misbehaving in class. To my friend Billy, this presented (5) __an__ irresistible challenge. He found math and science very easy, so he was frequently bored in class. As (6) __a__ result, he would try to play (7) __Ø/some__ tricks on her without getting caught. It was (8) __a__ challenge that he could never resist, especially when he didn't have anything else to do. One day we were taking (9) __an__ arithmetic quiz. It was (10) __an__ easy quiz, but I have never been good at arithmetic, so it was taking me (11) __a__ long time. However Billy had finished (12) __the__ quiz in just (13) __a__ few minutes. I heard (14) __a__ strange noise coming from the back of the room. It was (15) __a/Ø__ noise like no other I had ever heard. Someone in (16) __the__ front of the class began to giggle. Then there were (17) __Ø/some__ giggles in the back. Soon there was (18) __Ø/some__ laughter everywhere. Miss Kersell was furious and looked everywhere to find out where (19) __the__ noise was coming from. Billy had found (20) __a__ way to make (21) __a/the__ strange noise by rubbing his foot against (22) __a/the__ leg of his chair.

FOCUS 7 | Unique Nouns

There are certain nouns that are specific for both the speaker and the listener the first time they are mentioned. These are called **unique nouns**.

EXAMPLES | EXPLANATIONS

EXAMPLES		EXPLANATIONS
(a) I hear someone knocking at **the** door.		Unique nouns are used with definite articles. We do not need to "introduce" them in a specific context.
(b) **The** sun is too hot. Let's sit in **the** shade.		
Unique Nouns	**Implied Meaning**	A noun can be unique:
(c) We were all having dinner. We were sitting around **the table**, and I asked my brother to pass **the butter**.	There was only one table and one dish of butter.	• because of a particular situation or setting.
(d) "How did you do on **the exam** yesterday?" "Terrible! **The questions** were really difficult!"	The speakers both know which test is being discussed.	
(e) I hope you remembered to ask **the neighbors** to pick up **the mail** while we're on vacation.	We've previously decided which neighbors we will ask to pick up the mail.	
(f) **The** sky is so beautiful tonight. **The moon** is bright.		• because it is a universal reference (there is only one).
(g) **The** street that John lives on is lined with trees.		• if it is immediately identified by a relative clause or prepositional phrase.
(h) First we went to a hotel where **the man** at **the desk** told us we had no reservations.		
(i) **The book** the teacher told us about is available at **the bookstore across the street**.		

LESSON PLAN 3

EXERCISE 9 [15 minutes/homework]

This exercise is another review of articles. You may want to use this after presenting Focus 7 as it brings up issues of unique nouns in addition to the concepts presented in Focus 5 and 6. Assign this exercise as you have time (homework or in class). Be sure to allow for alternate answers during a class review. See answers on LP page 324.

For more practice, use *Grammar Dimensions 3* Workbook page 115, Exercise 6.

workbook

FOCUS 7 [20 minutes]

Focus 7 describes another exception to the rule in Focus 5. Certain nouns are considered unique in English and are considered known by both the speaker and the listener due to this uniqueness. Therefore, these unique nouns are specific and do not need to be introduced at the first mention by an indefinite article. They will take the definite article. For further information on the use of definite articles with unique nouns see the Grammar Note on this page.

1. **Lead-in:** Since a classroom is a "particular situation or setting" as described in examples (c–e), you can begin with examples from a classroom. Some examples include:

   The teacher asked someone to write the answer on the blackboard. Then she asked if the exam was difficult as she closed the door.

2. Follow this with questions about whether any of these articles could be changed to the indefinite article (since they are all used to introduce a noun for the first time) as the rule states in Focus 5. Would it sound strange? Why? What makes these nouns specific even though they are mentioned only once?

3. Move to the examples in Focus 7 and go over the three explanations that describe unique nouns. Give other examples to support each of these descriptions. (Universal reference = there is only

one: *the stars, the devil, the Space Needle, the White House.* Particular setting = there is only one in our shared setting: *the mall, the parking lot, the police, the dinner table.*)

GRAMMAR NOTE

Although most proper nouns do not take an article, there are a few exceptions. A few proper nouns that do take the definite article include, but are not limited to: plural proper names or a person from a country (*the Johnsons, the German*), geographic names which describe a group (*the United States of America, the Republic of Ghana, the Great Lakes, the Alps*), singular geographic names which describe large areas (*the Mississippi, the Sahara, the Gulf of Mexico, the Pacific Ocean, the Middle East*), and proper names which include the preposition *of* (*the University of Washington versus Washington State University*). While these descriptions do overlap with each other in some ways, they also support each other and can be helpful for students to learn as they go through the unit on article use.

EXERCISE 10

Why do you think the highlighted nouns in the following sentences are unique? Decide whether they have been specified:

a. by being mentioned previously by direct or indirect reference (identify the reference)
b. by a specific context/situation (identify the context or situation)
c. by a universal context or situation
d. by being immediately identified by a relative clause or prepositional phrase (identify the modifier)

1. An idle mind is **the devil's playground.**
2. I saw a great movie last night. **The camera work** was fantastic.
3. **The newspaper** said it was going to rain tonight.
4. **The tallest mountain in the world** is on **the border** between Nepal and China.
5. **The place** we went last year is great for a vacation.
6. Let's go to **the club** for dinner tonight.
7. **The teacher** said we have to finish **the assignment** before Friday.
8. **The town** that I grew up in was quite small.
9. **The noise** Billy made was like no other noise I had ever heard before.
10. What did **the doctor** say about **the medicine** you've been taking?

EXERCISE 11

Write the appropriate article (*a, an, the,* or *Ø*) in the blanks. There may be more than one correct choice.

Peter Principle believes that every cloud has (1) __*a*__ silver lining. He is (2) __*a*__ very optimistic person. He thinks that (3) __*a*__ problem is really (4) __*an*__ opportunity in disguise. As (5) __*a*__ result, he is always happy and reasonably content with (6) __*the/Ø*__ things that (7) __*Ø*__ life has given him. (8) __*Ø*__ people like being around him, because he's (9) __*a*__ cheerful, positive person. Denise Driven is just (10) __*the*__ opposite. She always looks on (11) __*the*__ dark side of (12) __*Ø*__ things. If she encounters (13) __*a*__ problem, she sometimes blames it on (14) __*the*__ fact that she is (15) __*a*__ woman in (16) __*a*__ man's world. She believes that (17) __*the*__ world isn't (18) __*a*__ fair place, and she in particular has always had (19) __*Ø/some*__ bad luck. Although she's not

(20) __*an*__ optimistic person, she doesn't spend much time feeling sorry for herself. She rarely has time to listen to anyone's troubles or tell you about (21) __*the/some*__ troubles she is facing. But whenever (22) __*a*__ friend does something nice for her, she always suspects that the person actually has (23) __*a*__ hidden motive. She believes that every silver lining has (24) __*a*__ cloud.

EXERCISE 12

Write the appropriate article in the blanks. There may be more than one correct choice.

The tall person in this picture is one of (1) __*the*__ most beautiful people I know: (2) __*a*__ woman by (3) __*the*__ name of Big Sue. She proves (4) __*the*__ truth of (5) __*the*__ saying "Beauty is only skin deep." Perhaps people who don't know her well would say that she is not (6) __*a*__ beautiful person. I guess that compared to (7) __*a*__ movie star or (8) __*a*__ fashion model she isn't that attractive. But anyone who knows her well thinks that she has (9) __*a*__ beautiful and courageous spirit. Her beauty is in her personality. She has (10) __*a*__ deep, booming laugh that makes other people laugh with her. She's not self-conscious about her size. She makes (11) __*the*__ jokes about it. She was (12) __*the*__ person who invented (13) __*the*__ name "Big Sue." She says there are plenty of Sues in (14) __*a*__ few pounds she

world, but only one Big Sue. If she gains (15) __*a*__ few pounds she doesn't worry. She just says "There's more of me to love." She is (16) __*an*__ incredible dancer, and moves around (17) __*the/a*__ dance floor with (18) __*Ø*__ grace and style. She is (19) __*a*__ wonderful comedian. She can tell (20) __*Ø*__ stories in (21) __*a*__ way that (22) __*Ø*__ people falling down with laughter. She has (23) __*Ø*__ friends all over (24) __*the*__ world. She has turned down (25) __*Ø*__ dozens of proposals for marriage. People can't help falling in love with her, once they get to know her well. But she's not in (26) __*a*__ hurry to find (27) __*a*__ husband. She says "I'll wait till I'm old and skinny. Right now I'm having too much fun."

ANSWER KEY

Exercise 10 1. *c* 2. *a (a great movie)* 3. *c (there's only one newspaper in town)* 4. *d (in the world); b (there is only one border between the two countries)* 5. *d (we went last year)* 6. *b (we both know which club)* 7. *b (we both know which teacher and assignment)* 8. *d (that I grew up in)* 9. *d (Billy made)* 10. *b (doctor); d (you've been taking)*

LESSON PLAN 3

EXERCISE 10 [15 minutes]

This exercise asks students to decide by what reasoning each highlighted noun with a definite article is considered unique. There are four reasons to choose from which come either from the rule in Focus 5 or the exceptions to the rule listed in Focus 7.

1. Review the four choices (a–d) given to explain the reasons for these nouns to be considered unique. (Refer back to the focus charts if necessary.)

2. Have students work in pairs on this. Remind them that they will need to identify the context, reference, or modifier in some cases.

3. If you are short on time, have each half of the class do five sentences.

4. Go over the answers with the class and encourage discussion when needed. See answers on LP page 326.

For more practice, use *Grammar Dimensions 3* Workbook page 116, Exercise 8.

EXERCISES 11 AND 12 [30 minutes/homework]

The following two exercises are comprehensive practice in choosing articles in discourse based on the concepts presented throughout Unit 19.

1. You may assign one or both exercises as homework or have students work in pairs to complete them.

2. For more interaction and discussion, have individuals or pairs form groups and go over their answers together before going over with the whole class. Remind students that there may be more than one correct choice.

3. Be sure you give time in class to go over the answers with the whole class in order to provide time for the presentation of alternative answers as well as time for discussion and questions. See answers on LP page 326.

For more practice, use *Grammar Dimensions 3* Workbook page 116, Exercise 7.

Use Your English

ACTIVITY 1 speaking/writing

Describe an object that you found once, and what you did with it. Compare your story with the stories of other people in the class. Can you create a proverb that talks about finding objects, and what should be done with them? (For example, "Find a penny, pick it up, all day long you'll have good luck.")

ACTIVITY 2 speaking

A time capsule is a metal or concrete box (usually about one cubic meter) that is sometimes built into the floor or walls of a building. The designers of the time capsule fill it with objects that they think are important, or interesting, or characteristic of the time when the building was built.

■ STEP 1   Imagine that you are organizing a time capsule to be placed in a skyscraper being built today. The building is expected to remain standing for several hundred years. What objects would you place in the time capsule, and why would you choose those particular objects?

■ STEP 2   Work with several other people and decide on the contents of a time capsule that will not be opened for at least 500 years. Present your list of items and your reasons for choosing them to the rest of the class.

ACTIVITY 3 writing

What are three things that everybody needs? Write a short composition describing your three choices and why you think everyone should have them. Start your essay with: "*There are three things everyone needs:...*"

EXERCISE 13

Write the appropriate article in the blanks. There may be more than one correct choice.

When I first went to (1) __the__ university, I learned the truth of the proverb "Absence makes (2) __the/a__ heart grow fonder." It was (3) __the__ first time I had lived away from home. I was surprised to discover how homesick I got, even after just (4) __a__ few days. When I lived with my family, my brother and I used to fight about everything. He wanted to watch one TV program and I wanted to watch another. We fought about whose turn it was to do certain chores like feeding (5) __the__ dog, sweeping (6) __the__ garage, cutting (7) __the__ grass, and taking out (8) __the__ garbage. We argued about whose turn it was to use (9) __the__ car on Saturday night. (I was allowed to use it one week, and then he was allowed to use it on (10) __the__ other.) However when I moved away, I realized that there were (11) __a__ lot of things about my brother that I missed. I began to forget about all (12) __the__ tricks he used to play on me. I started to remember only (13) __the/∅__ happy times we had spent together. By (14) __the__ time (15) __the/a__ year ended and I went back to spend (16) __the/a__ summer at home, I was really anxious to see him again.

UNIT 19

LESSON PLAN 3/USE YOUR ENGLISH

EXERCISE 13 [15 minutes/homework]

The following exercise is comprehensive practice in choosing articles in discourse based on the concepts presented in Unit 19.

1. You may want to have students work individually, in pairs or assign this exercise as homework.

2. For more interaction and discussion, have individuals or pairs form groups and go over their answers together before going over with the whole class. Remind students that there may be more than one correct choice.

3. Be sure you give time in class to go over the answers with the whole class in order to provide time for the presentation of alternative answers as well as time for discussion and questions. See answers on LP page 328.

UNIT GOAL REVIEW [10 minutes]

Ask students to look at the goals on the opening page of the unit again. Refer to the pages of the unit where information on each goal can be found.

For assessment of Unit 19, use *Grammar Dimensions 3 ExamView* ®.

USE YOUR ENGLISH

The Use Your English activities at the end of the unit contain situations that should naturally elicit the structures covered in the unit. For a more complete discussion of how to use the Use Your English Activities see To the Teacher on LP page xxii. When students are doing these activities in class, you can circulate and listen to see if they are using the structures accurately. Errors can be corrected after the activity has finished.

ACTIVITY 1

speaking/writing
[20 minutes/homework]

This activity works well as a diagnostic and goes along with the theme of the Opening Task.

1. Begin by sharing a short story of your own. Get students thinking about what the message of your story might be.

2. If using this as a diagnostic, you can assign the writing topic as homework the day before starting Unit 19. Students will bring their stories to class to share in small groups.

3. After going over the Opening Task, they will work on creating their own proverbs to match their stories.

4. Collect the stories to evaluate and diagnose students' problems with articles.

ACTIVITY 2

speaking
[20 minutes]

Students will need to use a variety of determiners as they come up with a list of objects to place in a time capsule. This can be a fun group discussion to add variety at any point within the unit or used as an informal diagnostic at the beginning of the unit as you circulate and listen in on the groups or have them present their ideas to the class.

STEP 1

1. Begin with a discussion of time capsules. Make sure students know what they are used for.

2. Give students some time to individually think about objects to put into their time capsules and their reasons for choosing these items.

STEP 2

1. Put students into small groups and have them begin discussing which items they would put in a capsule not to be opened for at least 500 years. If possible, give each group an overhead transparency

sheet and pen to write their lists on. This will make it easier to share later.

2. Circulate and note the variety of determiners used and any common errors.

3. Give groups a chance to share their lists with the class and their reasons for these choices.

Suggestion: Consider giving a limit to how many items they can put in the capsule. This will force the groups to negotiate their lists based on reasons for their choices and encourage discussion.

ACTIVITY 3

writing
[homework]

This activity should be assigned as homework either as a review or diagnostic. Collect papers or consider having students share their papers in small groups before you collect them.

ACTIVITY 4 · speaking

Here are four pictures. What story do you think they tell? Tell your story to a partner or write it down for your teacher to correct.

ACTIVITY 5 · speaking

Think about the meaning differences that are implied when we use articles. For example, we would use "a Bible" to describe the physical book you can find in many motel rooms or bookstores in the United States, but "the Bible" when we refer in a more abstract way to the book Christians believe in. Similarly we distinguish between "a Koran" and "the Koran", the book Muslims believe in.

With a partner or in a small group consider some of these other distinctions. What difference is implied by choice of articles? Discuss when you would use one article rather than the other.

a law/the law	a truth/the truth	a government/the government

Present your ideas to the rest of the class.

ACTIVITY 6 · listening

Listen to the example and short conversations and then choose the statement from the pairs listed below that can be correctly implied from the conversation.

CD Tracks 28, 29, 30

Conversation 1
_____ There is one ACME sales representative.
_____ There are several ACME sales representatives.
_____ There is one vice president.
_____ There are several vice presidents.

Conversation 2
_____ There is only one snack bar in the building.
_____ There are several snack bars in the building.
_____ John has already decided what he is going to eat.
_____ John hasn't decided what he is going to eat yet.
_____ Mary already knows what snack John will bring her.
_____ Mary doesn't know what John will bring her from the snack bar.

Conversation 3
_____ This is the first time Bob and Betty have discussed the idea of a party.
_____ They've discussed the party before.
_____ They have already decided who they are going to invite.
_____ They haven't decided who they are going to invite.
_____ They have already decided which restaurant to go to.
_____ They haven't decided which restaurant to go to.

ACTIVITY 7 · research on the web

Every country has different proverbs. In America we say "Don't bite off more than you can chew," to remind people not to be too ambitious or try to do too many things at once. In Afghanistan the same idea is expressed by this proverb: "You can't hold two watermelons in one hand."

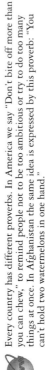

■ **STEP 1** Go on the Internet and use a search engine such as Google® or Yahoo® and type in the word "proverbs". You will find a number of Web sites that contain proverbs from many different countries. Find three pairs of proverbs from different cultures. Each pair should express the same idea in two different ways.

■ **STEP 2** Share each message and its two different proverbs with the rest of the class.

ANSWER KEY

Activity 6 These statements can be correctly implied from the conversation. **Conversation 1:** There is one ACME sales representative. There are several vice presidents. **Conversation 2:** There is only one snack bar in the building. John has already decided what he is going to eat. Mary doesn't know what John will bring her from the snack bar. **Conversation 3:** This is the first time Bob and Betty have discussed the idea of having a party. They haven't decided who they are going to invite. They haven't decided which restaurant to go to.

USE YOUR ENGLISH

ACTIVITY 4 · speaking
[15 minutes/homework]

This activity can be used in a variety of ways:

1. Use it in place of the Opening Task to get students talking and using articles.

2. Use it as a written diagnostic. Collect papers and evaluate for article usage.

3. Use it as a written review. Collect papers and evaluate for progress.

4. Use it for variety at the end of the unit. Assign the story as homework and then have students share stories in pairs or small groups. Students should note how differently their stories turned out.

VARIATION

Choose another photo or set of pictures for students to use in place of these. Any photo that gives the sense of a story (from a newspaper or journal) would spark a story.

ACTIVITY 5 · speaking
[15 minutes]

This activity asks students to discuss the distinction between the use of the nonspecific reference shown with an indefinite article and the specific reference shown with a definite article. This topic can be a difficult one for discussion and may work best for more advanced groups.

ACTIVITY 6 · listening
[15 minutes]

CD Tracks 28,29,30

Students will listen for the use of definite or indefinite articles and then decide what is implied by their use within each context. Note that Conversation 1 has two pairs of statements (students should make one check for each pair = 2 checks total). Conversations 2 and 3 each have three pairs of statements (students should make one check for each pair = 3 checks total for each).

1. Go over the two pairs of statements for Conversation 1 before playing the audio. Students must listen and decide whether there is one ACME sales representative or several sales representatives. They must then decide whether there is one vice president or several.

2. Play the audio for Conversation 1 again as necessary.

3. Go on to Conversation 2, giving students time to read the pairs of sentences before they listen. Play the audio and repeat as necessary.

4. Do the same for Conversation 3.

5. Go over answers with the class. You may want to play the audio one last time and pause just after each key article or point as you review the correct answers. See answers on LP page 330.

Suggestion: For more advanced listeners, play each conversation before giving them a chance to read the questions. This is better practice for global listening skills.

ACTIVITY 7 · research on the web
[30 minutes/homework]

Students will research and collect proverbs from different cultures. They will need to find pairs of proverbs that represent the same idea, yet are from different countries.

STEP 1

1. Begin by writing the example pair of proverbs given in the Activity 7 directions on the board ("Don't bite off more . . ." and "You can't hold two . . ."). Ask the class for other proverbs they know and see if you or other students can think of a matching one in English or from another country. Pair these up on the board.

2. Explain the assignment (much like you've just done with the class on the board) and have students do their research.

STEP 2

Students should organize their research and present it to the class. Each student will have three pairs of proverbs. They should also tell the basic underlying message for each pair of proverbs.

UNIT GOALS

- Correctly understand and use determiners and demonstrative pronouns

- Correctly understand and communicate differences in reference by using determiners

- Correctly understand and communicate differences in focus and emphasis by using determiners

OPENING TASK

This, That, or It?

■ STEP 1

Work with a partner. Read the dialogue on the next page and look at how the words *it*, *this*, and *that* are used in the first part of the dialogue. Discuss why you think one form is used rather than another. With a partner, replace the blanks in the dialogue with reference forms (*it*, *this*, and *that*). Finally, complete the last few lines of the dialogue.

■ STEP 2

Form a group with one or two other pairs of students. Compare your dialogues. Discuss any differences you had in choosing appropriate reference forms to fill in the blanks.

■ STEP 3

As a group, decide on three general observations about when to use *it* instead of *this* or *that*. Share your ideas with the rest of the class.

■ STEP 4

Finally, as a group, decide on the best way to end the dialogue and have two of your members perform the dialogue for the rest of the class.

Denise Driven: Mr. Green has informed me that you're not going to be here this afternoon. **That's** outrageous, Peter! What about the Davis contract? **It's** due first thing Monday morning.

Peter Principle: Well, my son's in a play at school. **It's** his first big role. He's one of the Three Wise Men.

Denise Driven: He certainly didn't learn **that** role from his father! Is some stupid school play more important than your job?

Peter Principle: You'd better believe **it!** Besides, I spoke with Mr. Green. I told him **it** would get done sooner or later.

Denise Driven: If he believes **that**, he'll believe anything. **That's** what makes me so annoyed, Peter. **This** isn't the first time you've left work early. You're always asking for permission to take time off, and I am left having to do all the work. I'm getting tired of _____ Peter. _____ **is** all I can do to keep this office running professionally!

Peter Principle: I'm sure Mr. Green would be happy to give you time off, too. Just ask for _____ Denise. _____ is all you have to do.

Denise Driven: _____'s not the point. _____'s true that most of us would probably rather be playing instead of working. But some of us have a sense of responsibility and a respect for hard work.

Peter Principle: _____'s true. My responsibility is to my son, and I respect the hard work he's put into learning his lines. _____'s not easy when you're only 8 years old.

Denise Driven: Don't give me _____ nonsense, Peter. I don't appreciate _____

Peter Principle: _____'s your trouble, Denise. You need a little nonsense in your life.

Denise Driven: _____

Peter Principle: _____

Denise Driven: _____

Peter Principle: _____

LESSON PLAN 1

REFERENCE FORMS IN DISCOURSE

UNIT OVERVIEW

Unit 20 continues the overview of determiners and focuses on the use of demonstratives as determiners for reference with *this/these* and *that/those*.

GRAMMAR NOTE

The concepts presented in this unit can be more difficult to explain due to their reliance on context. Rather than the physical uses of demonstratives, this unit puts emphasis on ways that demonstratives are used in place of other nouns and will refer back to or forward to information about these nouns. The unit also shows how demonstratives can be used to imply meaning. This is shown by placing stress on the verb with the use of *it* (*I don't believe it!*) or by placing the stress on the replaced noun with the use of *that* (*I don't believe that.*). You will need to show the differences through intonation and stress in cases like this.

UNIT GOALS

Some instructors may want to review the goals listed on Student Book (SB) page 332 after completing the Opening Task so that students understand what they should know by the end of the unit. These goals can also be reviewed at the end of the unit when students are more familiar with the grammar terminology.

OPENING TASK [20 minutes]

The aim of this activity is to build awareness of the reference forms (*it, this, that*) used in the dialogue and to give students the chance to discuss and make hypotheses about the use of these forms. The problem-solving format is designed to show the teacher how well the students can produce the target structures implicitly and spontaneously when they are engaged in a communicative task.

Students will be able to check these initial observations throughout the rest of the unit. For a more complete discussion of the purpose of the Opening Task, see To the Teacher, Lesson Planner (LP) page xxii.

Setting Up the Task

Begin by asking what the class can remember about the characters used previously in this text, Denise Driven and Peter Principle (see Unit 8, Focus 1).

1. Have students read through the dialogue on SB page 333 first for comprehension.
2. Before putting them with a partner, have students fill in the missing reference forms (*it, this, that*).

Conducting the Task

■ STEP 1

1. Have students work with a partner as they go over the dialogue to analyze the reference forms in bold and discuss why they feel these forms were used.
2. Working with a partner, have students fill in the missing reference forms (*it, this, that*) and complete the last few lines of the dialogue.

■ STEP 2

Have pairs get together with other pairs to share their choices for the missing forms and discuss any differences or reasons for these choices.

■ STEP 3

With the same group, have students complete Step 3. Discuss answers and rules as a class.

Suggestion: Record the group observations (their explanations for the use of *it, this,* and *that*) from Step 3 to use during the Unit Goal Review at the end of the unit.

Closing the Task

■ STEP 4

You can either have the groups agree on one ending or let each original pair perform their own ending for the class.

GRAMMAR NOTE

Typical student errors (use)

- Repeating demonstratives: * I told him about *that problem. That problem should be addressed soon.* (See Focus 1.)
- Confusing singular and plural forms: * *These book is from the library.* * *Can you give me five of this?* (See Focus 1.)

FOCUS 1

Overview of Demonstratives

form

meaning

use

Demonstratives can be used as determiners or as pronouns.

EXAMPLES

(a) Does **this** laptop belong to you?

(b) Yes, **that** is mine.

EXPLANATIONS

Demonstrative determiner

Demonstrative pronoun

The form of the demonstrative depends on whether the thing being referred to is singular or plural, and near or far.

	NEAR	FAR
Singular	(c) You take a look at **this** Web site.	(d) Does **that** laptop belong to you?
	(e) **This** is amazing.	(f) Is **that** yours?
Plural	(g) **These** problems aren't new, Peter.	(h) **Those** workers don't take time off the way you do.
	(i) If you want other examples of Peter's careless reports, look at **these**.	(j) **Those** are the sloppiest reports I have ever seen!

EXAMPLES

(k) Please sit in **this** chair (by me.) **That** chair (over there) is broken.

(l) I've been to dinner with two co-workers in the last week, but **this** one (today) with Peter is much more enjoyable than **that** party Denise had (a few days ago) at the club.

(m) What are we going to do about **this** budget deficit, Peter?

(n) I don't know, Denise. **That's** for you to worry about, not me!

EXPLANATIONS

Near and far distinctions can be determined by:
- physical distance.

- time distance.

- whether the speaker feels involved with the situation or distanced from it.

EXAMPLE

(o) There once was a workaholic who worked in an insurance company. Every day **this woman** would go to a file on her computer. **This** file was where she kept track of what time each of her co-workers arrived.

EXPLANATION

Use demonstratives with nouns that have been specified by being mentioned previously (see Unit 19 for more information).

A demonstrative is not usually repeated to refer to the same item. A personal pronoun (*be, it,* etc.) or a definite article (*the*) is used instead.

(p) Have you seen **these** figures? **They** are quite alarming.

(q) NOT: Have you seen **these** figures? **These** are quite alarming.

(r) **This** is the problem Denise was talking about. **It** will continue to get worse if we don't find a solution.

(s) NOT: **This** is the problem Denise was talking about. **This** will continue to get worse if we don't find a solution.

(t) I brought up **that** problem at the meeting. **The** problem was discussed but not solved.

(u) NOT: I brought up **that** problem at the meeting. **That** problem was discussed but not solved.

EXERCISE 1

Add appropriate demonstratives (*this, those,* etc.), personal pronouns (*be, it,* etc.), or articles (*a/an, the*) in the blanks. More than one answer may be possible. The first one has been done for you as an example.

1. When Denise came to Mr. Green with her complaints about Peter, he realized that they had talked about (a) ___these/those___ issues before. He told her there was no point in discussing (b) ___them___ any further.

2. I got these new file folders on sale. I'd like you to take a look at (a) ___them___. Which of (b) ___the___ red one or (d) ___these/the___ folders do you like better, (c) ___the___ the ___ green one? What about (e) ___the/these___ larger folders? Which do you prefer? (f) ___This___ one or (g) ___that/this___ one?

3. I got a new computer for my birthday. (a) ___It___ was a gift from my boss. I'm glad she got (b) ___this/that___ laptop instead of another kind. (c) ___It___ will be much more practical.

Exercise 1 is continued on LP page 336.

LESSON PLAN 1

FOCUS 1 [15 minutes]

Students will be familiar with the physical meaning of demonstratives (near and far), but the nonphysical uses may be new.

1. **Lead-in:** Put a few examples on the board or use a classroom object or a student to show examples of the basic physical meaning of the demonstratives *this/these/that/those*. This will be a review for students.

2. Put the first two examples on the board (a–b) and ask the class what the difference is between the demonstratives. (*one comes before a noun, one acts like a noun,* etc.) The demonstratives are different grammatically. Ask students if they know what to call the different types. (*demonstrative determiner and demonstrative pronoun*)

3. Go over the examples (k–o) with the class. Invite volunteers to give other examples to illustrate the various uses of demonstratives.

4. Finally, point out in the last examples (p–u) that demonstratives are not usually repeated when referring to the same noun.

Suggestion: Have students refer back to their explanations for use or hypotheses from the Opening Task and see if they would like to revise any of their explanations for the use of certain demonstratives based on any new information.

VARIATION

As a diagnostic, have students do Exercise 1 first and use Focus 1 to follow-up.

EXERCISE 1 [15 minutes]

This exercise can be used to review the concepts presented in Focus 1 or it can be used as a diagnostic before presenting Focus 1.

1. Assign this exercise to be completed individually or by pairs.

2. Put pairs together to compare answers in small groups. They should discuss whether there may be more than one correct answer.

3. Assign different groups to be responsible for presenting their results for one of the passages. See answers on LP pages 334 and 336.

VARIATION

If you are using this as a diagnostic, you may want to stop after step 2 above and go over Focus 1. After presenting the concepts in Focus 1, give the groups a few more minutes to prepare their answers and move on to step 3.

For more practice, use *Grammar Dimensions 3* Workbook page 117, Exercise 1.

Using a particular demonstrative form depends on whether it refers forward or backward in the text.

EXAMPLES

(e) **This** is why I didn't finish the report: I had a terrible case of the flu.

(f) I had a terrible case of the flu. **This** is why I didn't finish the report.

(g) I had a terrible case of the flu. **That** is why I didn't finish the report.

(h) Denise is a workaholic. **That** is why nobody wants to work with her.

EXPLANATIONS

This/these can be used to point both forward or backward.

That/those are usually only used for backward pointing reference (except with modifiers that follow a noun—see Focus 4).

EXERCISE 2

What do the demonstratives refer to in these sentences? Circle the demonstratives in these passages, and draw an arrow to what each one refers to. Is it an example of forward-pointing or backward-pointing reference? The first passage has been done for you as an example.

1. Most people find it difficult to sleep during the day and work at night. (**This**) is why people who work "swing shift" (as (**that**) work schedule is called) are usually paid a higher wage than (**those**) who work during the day.

2. We hold (**these**) truths to be self-evident, that all men are created equal, and have a right to life, liberty, and the pursuit of happiness.

3. Let me make (**this**) perfectly clear: No new taxes!

4. Frank said that he wanted to leave New York because he was tired of big city life. But I don't think (**that**) was the real reason for his move to California. The real reason was that his wife wanted to live in a place with warmer winters. At least, (**this**) is what Stuart told me.

5. (**These**) soldiers must report to Barracks B: Private Rebecca Adams, Private Mary Collins, and Corporal Marsha Powell. (**These**) soldiers have been assigned to patrol duty: Sergeant Kitty Westmoreland and Corporal Mary MacArthur. (**Those**) are your orders, soldiers.

6. The causes of the American Civil War were not very different from (**those**) of other wars that have taken place between different regions of any country. (**This**) is one of the things that can be learned by studying history.

7. The chemical composition of baking soda is similar to (**that**) of any compound containing sodium. (**This**) is what allows baking soda to enter into a chemical reaction with any compound containing acid, such as those (**found**) in vinegar or even orange juice.

8. Management techniques of many American companies now tend to resemble (**those**) used in Japan much more than they did a few years ago. (**This**) is due to the success (**those**) techniques have had in raising worker productivity.

---

4. The report that Peter submitted had to be done over. (a) _____ It _____ didn't follow any of the guidelines Mr. Green had explained when he had first assigned Peter to do (b) _____ the _____ report. (c) _____ The/Those _____ guidelines were not simple, but (d) _____ they _____ had to be followed in order to get the vice-president's approval on (e) _____ the _____ report. (f) _____ The/That _____ decision made Peter rather upset, but Mr. Green had made (g) _____ the _____ guidelines quite clear.

5. Where did you get (a) _____ this/that _____ fountain pen? (b) _____ It _____ is really beautiful. (c) _____ It _____ looks like (d) _____ it _____ came from Europe. Is (e) _____ it _____ silver?

FOCUS 2   Demonstratives for Reference

EXAMPLES

(a) Everyone started laughing. **This** made Denise very angry.

(b) I knew you were going to be late! **That's** why I wanted someone else to make the presentation.

(c) **This** is why I don't like Peter: He doesn't come to work on time, he doesn't check his work, and he takes no responsibility.

(d) I can use **these** kinds of software: Word, Excel and PowerPoint.

EXPLANATIONS

There are two kinds of demonstrative reference:

• **backward-pointing reference:** where demonstratives refer to information that has been previously mentioned.

• **forward-pointing reference:** where demonstratives refer to information that is about to be introduced.

ANSWER KEY

Exercise 1 is continued from LP page 334.

LESSON PLAN 1

Exercise 1 is continued from SB page 335.

FOCUS 2 [15 minutes]

Demonstratives can be used to refer back to information just mentioned or forward to information to come. *This/these* can point to information in either direction. However, *that/those* can usually only refer back to previous information. Although the basic concepts in this focus will not be new to most students, the presentation and terms may be new.

1. **Lead-in:** Put the first example sentence (a) on the board. Circle the demonstrative (*this*) and ask the class what it refers to (*everyone laughing*). Underline "*Everyone started laughing*." Do the same for example (d).

2. Now draw an arrow in example (a) from the demonstrative (*this*) back to the reference (*Everyone started laughing*) and explain that this is a **backward-pointing reference.** The demonstrative refers *back* to something.

3. Do the same for example (d) on the board. However, this is a **forward-pointing reference.** The demonstrative (*these*) refers forward to information (*Word, Excel and PowerPoint.*)

4. Go over the other examples in the focus chart and the rules for choosing demonstratives (examples e–h).

Suggestion 1: Keep these examples on the board for Exercise 2.

Suggestion 2: Have students refer back to their explanations for use or hypotheses from the Opening Task and see if they would like to revise any of their explanations for the use of certain demonstratives based on any new information.

EXERCISE 2 [15 minutes]

This exercise follows up on the concepts presented in Focus 2.

1. Refer back to the examples on the board from Focus 2. Students will do the same for demonstratives and the information that they refer to.

2. Go over the answers as a class review. See answers on LP page 336.

Suggestion: Copy the exercise onto an overhead transparency for easier class discussion and review.

For more practice, use *Grammar Dimensions 3* Workbook page 117, Exercise 2.

FOCUS 3

This/That Versus It

meaning

EXAMPLES

"Did you hear the news? Denise didn't get the promotion?"

(a) "I knew **it**! That woman is so unpleasant to work with." (*Implied Meaning:* I'm not surprised!)

(b) "I knew **that**. Mr. Green told me last week." (*Implied Meaning:* I'd already heard that news.)

They say that Denise is getting a raise.

(c) Has Peter heard about **this**? (*Implied Meaning:* Has this important information been told to Peter?)

They say that Denise is getting a raise.

(d) I don't *believe* **it**! (*Implied Meaning:* That's unbelievable!)

EXPLANATIONS

Both demonstrative pronouns (**this/that**) and personal pronouns (**it**) refer back to ideas or items in previous sentences, but there is often a difference in emphasis or implied meaning.

Using *this/that* emphasizes that the idea being referred to is the most important information in the new sentence.

Using *it* indicates that some other part of the sentence (the subject or verb) is the most important information. We do not generally use pronouns to talk about significant new information.

In some cases we **must** use *that* instead of *it*.

EXAMPLES

(e) Don't leave your laptop in the lobby. Someone might steal **it**.

(f) Don't worry. I'm smarter than **that**.

(g) NOT: I'm smarter than **it**.

(h) Denise is planning to file an official complaint about Peter.

(i) I was afraid of **that**! No wonder she was asking me what time he came in this morning.

(j) NOT: I was afraid of **it**!

EXPLANATION

This is especially true in cases where *it* could refer to a physical object (*the car* or *the dog*) rather than the general idea or situation.

EXERCISE 3

Decide which form, demonstrative pronoun (*this/that*) or personal pronoun (*it*), to put in the blanks. In most sentences, both forms are possible, but native speakers would tend to choose one form instead of the other to indicate a particular emphasis. Compare your choices with those of other students and your teacher.

1. Someone took your wallet? I was afraid _____ that _____ would happen!

2. I'm glad Peter's wife hasn't had her baby yet. She was afraid _____ it _____ would happen while her husband was out of town.

3. I'm sorry you had to spend such a beautiful, sunny Saturday in the office. _____ That/It _____ isn't really fair, is it?

4. I assume you have all heard the news about Denise. _____ This/That _____ is why I have asked you here to this meeting.

5. I love the wonderful California climate. _____ That _____ is why I moved here.

6. Did you say the Republicans are involved in another financial scandal? Are you completely sure of _____ that _____ ?

7. I just know Mary's dating someone else. I'm sure of _____ it _____ !

8. If you don't take advantage of this great opportunity, I know you'll regret _____ it _____ in the future.

9. Don't worry about making such a mess. _____ It _____ really doesn't matter.

10. Don't worry about making such a mess. _____ That/This _____ is why I put newspapers over everything.

11. **A:** You said "seventeen." Don't you mean "seventy"?

    B: Oh yes, _____ that _____ 's what I meant.

12. Don't complain to me. _____ That/This _____ is why we have a complaint department.

ANSWER KEY

Exercise 3 *Answers are listed above. While in most questions all three are grammatically possible, the best answer (based on native speaker responses) has been indicated. In some cases, more than one choice is equally acceptable.*

LESSON PLAN 1

FOCUS 3 [15 minutes]

This focus may be more difficult for students to grasp. Reading the sentences out loud to the class may help them to hear the differences in emphasis.

1. **Lead-in:** Explain that although both *this/that* and *it* can be used to refer back to ideas, they can sometimes give a difference in emphasis. Give a dramatic reading of the example sentences from the first section of the focus chart. You will give emphasis to the word *knew* in sentence (a) and emphasize *that* in sentence (b). Point out that in example (a) the use of *it* gives emphasis to the verb *knew* and shows that this person didn't know this particular information, but **knew** (or suspected) something like this might happen. Sentence (b), however, implies that this person knew **that particular information** (*that*).

2. Go over the explanations for example (c) noting that we use *this/that* to emphasize the idea being referred to: *I don't believe that!* = I don't believe what you've told me.

3. Whereas, in example (d), using *it* puts the emphasis on another part of the sentence (the verb or subject): *I don't **believe** it!* = It's amazing. I'm surprised.

4. The last examples (e–j) are more difficult and may take some time and a few more examples to make clear.

Suggestion 1: Follow this discussion immediately with Exercise 3, which should give more practice and shed more light on these concepts.

Suggestion 2: Have students refer back to their explanations for use or hypotheses from the Opening Task and see if they would like to revise any of their explanations for the use of certain demonstratives based on any new information.

EXERCISE 3 [15 minutes]

This exercise should be done immediately after presenting the concepts in Focus 3.

1. Work through the exercise as a class review allowing time for multiple correct answers and questions.

2. Alternately, you could have pairs work together and then compare their answers with the ones listed. See answers on LP page 338.

work book

For more practice, use *Grammar Dimensions 3* Workbook page 118, Exercise 3.

FOCUS 4

That/Those with Forward-Pointing Reference

use

EXAMPLES

(a) **Those who cannot learn from history** will repeat the mistakes made in the past.

(b) I'm not very fond of dogs, but **those that are well behaved** are O.K.

(c) The boss only gives raises to **those he really likes.** (whom has been omitted)

(d) This report is really confusing I can't tell the difference between **that which is supposed to be profit** and **that which is supposed to be loss.**

(e) Compare your paragraph to **that of another student** in the class.

(f) This problem will have to be solved by **those in charge.**

EXPLANATIONS

That and *those* can be used for forward pointing reference only when they occur with:

• relative clauses

• prepositional phrases

EXERCISE 4

Identify the demonstratives that are followed by modifying clauses or phrases in these passages. Not all sentences contain these structures.

1. There is an old proverb that says fate helps those that help themselves.
2. Please put those on Denise's desk.
3. My co-worker is very fussy about using certain kinds of computer programs. He won't touch these, but those he likes will be quickly downloaded onto his hard-drive.
4. Those in the stock brokerage business think that this is a bad time to invest.
5. One must learn to distinguish between that which is necessary and that which is only desirable.
6. Those who can't tell the difference between the colors teal and aquamarine shouldn't become interior decorators.
7. That is not my responsibility. You'll have to speak to those in charge of that part of the operation.
8. I read about that in the newspapers.

FOCUS 5

Special Uses of Demonstratives

use

Using *This/These* with Nonspecific Nouns

EXAMPLES

(a) I'm walking down the street, and I see **this** man on the corner. He's talking with **these** two other guys.

EXPLANATIONS

In very informal speech or written narratives we can use *this* and *these* in place of indefinite determiners (*a, an,* and *∅*) to introduce nouns for the first time.

Using *That* to Refer to Humans

EXAMPLES

(b) **That** man over there is married to **that** woman in the red dress.

(c) Were you talking to **that** boy again? I told you not to speak to him!

EXPLANATIONS

That is not usually used to refer to humans, except when the speaker is pointing to the person.

When *that* is used in other kinds of reference, it usually indicates the speaker is annoyed, or is insulting the person being referred to.

EXERCISE 5

Make this paragraph more informal by replacing the underlined articles with demonstratives. Are there some articles that can't be replaced with demonstratives? Decide which demonstratives are appropriate for the remaining blanks.

I went to (1) <u>a</u> party where I met (2) <u>some</u> rather strange people. They had all read (3) <u>an</u> article in <u>the</u> newspaper about (4) <u>a</u> new invention that was supposed to help people lose weight. Mary, the hostess, was the strangest of all. She went around the room, asking all the guests to put on (5) <u>some</u> very dark glasses. Apparently (6) _____ is supposed to help people eat less. Now I ask you: Why does a person go to all the trouble of giving (7) <u>a</u> party if she doesn't want her guests to eat? (8) _____'s Mary for you! She'll believe anything she reads in the paper.

ANSWER KEY

Exercise 4 Sentences 2 and 8 do not contain the structure. 1. those that help themselves
3. those he likes 4. Those in the stock brokerage business 5. that which is necessary; that which is only desirable 6. Those who can't tell the difference between the colors teal and aquamarine
7. those in charge of that part of the operation

Exercise 5 (1) this (2) these (3) this; this (4) this (5) these (6) this
(7) (no change) (8) That

LESSON PLAN 1

FOCUS 4 [10 minutes]

This focus presents the use of *those* (plural) and *that* (singular) for forward-pointing reference. This is the exception to the rule stated in Focus 2 (see examples g–h).

1. **Lead-in:** Put a few examples from your class on the board. Invite volunteers to come up and circle the demonstrative or underline the modifying phrases. Here are examples:

    Those who finished their homework can leave early.
    Can those sitting in the back of the class see the board well?

2. Go over the examples in the book and note that *those/that* point forward to their modifiers (relative clauses or prepositional phrases). *Those/that* replaces the noun being modified (i.e., **The those/that students** *who finished their homework . . . /***the ones** *sitting in the back . . .*).

3. Move immediately on to Exercise 4, which will give students a chance to identify examples of these structures on their own.

4. Keep these examples on the board for Exercise 4.

EXERCISE 4 [10 minutes]

Students will identify demonstratives *that/those* followed by modifying clauses or phrases. Note that sentences 2 and 8 do not contain examples of these structures.

1. Refer back to the examples on the board from Focus 4.

2. You can ask students to again circle the demonstrative in each sentence and underline the modifying phrase or clause. In each case, the arrow (as drawn in Exercise 2) should point forward. See answers on LP page 340.

For more practice, use *Grammar Dimensions 3* Workbook page 118, Exercise 4.

---

students a chance to tell a their own story using the informal *this/these*.

UNIT GOAL REVIEW [10 minutes]

Ask students to look at the goals on the opening page of the unit again. Refer to the pages of the unit where information on each goal can be found.

For a grammar quiz review of Units 19–20, refer students to pages 119–120 in the *Grammar Dimensions 3* Workbook.

ExamView Test Generator · For assessment of Unit 20, use *Grammar Dimensions 3 ExamView®*.

FOCUS 5 [10 minutes]

If you are pressed for time, you can simply note these two "details" or skip Focus 5 and Exercise 5 entirely.

1. **Lead-in:** Reading the informal example out loud to the class can make the concept clearer. You may want to go on and expand on this narrative.

2. Note the second concept gives two different uses of *that* when referring to humans. The first one requires the speaker to be physically present with the person he or she is referring to and to point the person out (with a finger or with his or her eyes or nod of the head which is more polite). However, the second example would be used when *that boy* is not physically present. This implies a negative feeling of distance from the boy. Using *that boy* in this situation is an insult.

GRAMMAR NOTE

Notice the use of the present time frame for the informal narrative. Refer back to Unit 13, Focus 4 on SB page 226 for a review of an explanation for this.

EXERCISE 5 [10 minutes]

In this exercise students will identify demonstratives. If you are short on time or students are more advanced, you may wish to skip this exercise. Have students share their answers with a partner. Because this special use of demonstratives is usually for informal speech, you may want to have volunteers "perform" their stories.

EXPANSION [15 minutes]

After practicing with the story in Exercise 5, you may wish to assign Activity 3 (speaking) on SB page 342 as an expansion of this topic. This activity gives

---

Use Your English

ACTIVITY 1 speaking/writing

Here is a puzzle. Can you punctuate it so that it makes sense?

that that is is that that is not is not is not that it is

There are four sentences in the correct answer. The solution is on page A-12.

ACTIVITY 2 writing/speaking

Write a dialogue like the one in the Opening Task on page 329. Work with a partner. First, decide what the argument will be about. Then write your dialogue. Try to use some of the phrases that Peter and Denise used. Perform your dialogue for the rest of the class.

ACTIVITY 3 speaking

Tell a story in informal spoken English. Use the present time frame and demonstratives (*this* and *these*) instead of indefinite articles. See Exercise 5 for an example to get you started.

ACTIVITY 4 research on the web

Go on the Internet and use a search engine such as Google® or Yahoo)® to find information about how common products differ from one country to another. For example: How does the coffee of Guatemala differ from that of Sumatra? How are automobiles from Japan different from those made in the United States? How does rice grown in India differ from that grown in China? Find comparative information on three different products and make a brief presentation in either written or spoken form.

ACTIVITY 5 listening

CD Track 31

Denise and Peter are arguing again. Listen to their conversation and answer the questions below in your notebook. You may need to listen to the conversation more than once. Use it or that in your answers. The first question has been answered for you as an example.

1. When did Denise finish the Davis contract?
   She finished it late last night.

2. What did Denise think of Peter's offer to help?

3. When did Denise write her official complaint to Mr. Green?

4. How does Denise react when Peter offers to show her pictures of his son's play?

5. What does Denise threaten to do with the computer terminal if Peter doesn't stop telling her to be less serious about work?

6. Why does Peter decide to leave the office to take his children to the beach?

7. What effect does Denise think that firing Peter would have on the class.

Compare your answers to those of another student in the class.

ACTIVITY 6 reflection

Discuss these pairs of sentences with a partner or in a small group. Can you identify a difference in implied meaning? Why do you think native speakers would use one form rather than the other? In what situations would one form be more appropriate than the other? What difference in intonation might be used in one sentence rather than the other? Can you think of a rule or strategy for learning and remembering which form is the correct one to use in each set of examples?

Try it. You'll like it.
Try this. You'll like it.

That's what she said.
It's what she said.

She really doesn't like that.
She really doesn't like it.

I can't believe you said it!
I can't believe you said that!

This is what's going to be on the test.
That's what's going to be on the test.

Present your ideas to the rest of the class. Pay special attention to the reference forms you are using in your presentation. Be sure to use all three reference forms in your presentation (for example: *This is what we decided about the first pair of sentences . . . That is the most important part of the sentence . . . It's difficult to decide . . . etc.*).

ANSWER KEY

Activity 5 Answers will vary. Possible answers are: 2. She thought it was too little and too late. 3. She wrote it before she finished the Davis contract. 4. She doesn't like it. 5. She threatens to throw it at him. 6. Denise told him to leave and said that she really meant it. 7. It would make this office so much more businesslike.

The Use Your English activities at the end of the unit contain situations that should naturally elicit the structures covered in the unit. For a more complete discussion of how to use the Use Your English Activities see To the Teacher on LP page xxii. When students are doing these activities in class, you can circulate and listen to see if they are using the structures accurately. Errors can be corrected when the activity is finished.

ACTIVITY 1 speaking/writing
[15 minutes]

This activity is a puzzle for fun. If students have not enjoyed this kind of puzzle in the past, you can skip this activity. Be sure that students work on finding ways to make sentences rather than just turning to the answer.

ACTIVITY 2 writing/speaking
[20 minutes]

Students will create an argument and then a dialogue together. This will give students the chance to use several of the expressions presented in the unit. In addition to looking at the Opening Task, encourage pairs to go through the focus charts looking for expressions or other concepts to use.

Give students the chance to perform their "argument" for the class. This can be a fun way to get students speaking in front of the group.

ACTIVITY 3 speaking
[15 minutes]

You may wish to assign this activity after presenting Focus 5 on SB page 341. Students will tell each other stories in informal spoken English.

Note: Some students really enjoy getting a chance to use informal structures (such as slang or reductions in pronunciation) in the safety of the classroom. For younger students, feel free to let them "ham it up" with other teenage mannerisms (". . . you know?" "And like . . ." or "It was like . . .").

ACTIVITY 4 research on the web
[30 minutes/homework]

This research activity will give students practice using demonstratives to refer to two different varieties of the same basic item. This will give them practice with a variety of concepts presented in Unit 20.

1. If you plan to use this as a review, you may want to assign this as a written report and collect papers to evaluate.

2. If you would like students to present their findings orally, have students present their results in small groups.

Suggestion: To engage those listening, have students prepare a chart like the one below and fill in the information as they listen to each other. Encourage students to take a few minutes after each presentation to ask clarifying questions of each presenter.

Student Name	Item	Country 1	Country 2	Differences

ACTIVITY 5 listening
[15 minutes]

CD Track 31

This activity gives basic practice in listening for specific information. Students' answers will include the demonstratives *it* or *that*.

1. If your students are more advanced listeners, play the audio before having them look over the questions. Then give them time to write as many answers as they can. Circulate and note how well students did. Play the audio again and let students revise their initial answers.

2. For less advanced classes, give students a chance to read through the questions before playing the audio. After playing the audio and giving the class time to write their answers, circulate and determine the need for further chances to hear the audio. Play as many times as needed.

3. Remind the class to use the demonstratives *it* or *that* in their answers.

4. Give students time to check with a partner (reminding each other to use *it* or *that*) and then go over with the class. If the class has had a difficult time with the listening, play the audio little by little as you go over the answers. See answers on LP page 342.

ACTIVITY 6 reflection
[20 minutes]

Students will analyze pairs of sentences and try to determine how they differ or may be used differently. Have students work in pairs for this activity. If you have time, once pairs have discussed the sentences, put them into small groups and see how their answers compare. Circulate and note any points of disagreement for a class discussion.

21
POSSESSIVES

UNIT GOALS

- Correctly identify and use possessive forms (possessive determiners, possessive pronouns, possessive phrases and, possessive nouns)

- Know when to use possessive nouns and when to use possessive phrases

- Correctly understand the various meanings of possessives

OPENING TASK

What's Wrong with This Picture?

How observant are you? How accurate is your memory? Look at the picture below for exactly thirty seconds, then cover the picture. There are at least fifteen strange things about the picture. For example, the legs of the table seem to be a person's legs. The little girl's hair is very unusual. Notice as many other strange things as you can, and then, without looking at the picture again, write complete sentences describing the strange things. When you are finished, compare your answers with a partner's, and then together check the picture to complete the list of strange things.

What's strange about . . .

the boy's hat? _____

the girl's hair? _____

the dog's tail _____

the dog's nose _____

the girl's tricycle _____

the girl's shoes _____

the boy's shoes _____

the hands of the clock _____

the fringe of the couch _____

the handle of the door _____

the top of the table _____

the cover of the book _____

the knobs of the TV _____

the drawers of the dresser _____

the legs of the table _____

POSSESSIVES

LESSON PLAN 1

UNIT OVERVIEW

Unit 21 covers the use of possessive forms in discourse. This unit can be completed in two lessons.

GRAMMAR NOTE

Although most students already have been introduced to possessive forms, they may not have studied the more complex issues of use and meaning. Concepts that may be new to students include the guidelines for choosing between the possessive noun or the possessive phrase (Focus 2), and the variety of meanings that can be conveyed through possessive forms (Focus 3). Students may have some questions about adding the possessive *'s* to words ending in *-s* or plural nouns. These issues are addressed in the Grammar Note following Focus 1. In addition, students may need a quick review of the pronunciation changes when adding the *'s*. This is addressed in the Pronunciation Note following Focus 1.

UNIT GOALS

Some instructors may want to review the goals listed on Student Book page 344 after completing the Opening Task so that students understand what they should know by the end of the unit. These goals can also be reviewed at the end of the unit when students are more familiar with the grammar terminology.

OPENING TASK [20 minutes]

The aim of this activity is to give students the opportunity to use a variety of possessive forms in an entertaining context. The problem-solving format is designed to show the teacher how well the students can produce a target structure implicitly and spontaneously when they are engaged in a communicative task. For a more complete discussion of the purpose of the Opening Task, see to the Teacher, Lesson Planner (LP) page xxii.

Setting Up the Task

1. Before having students open their books, set up the activity. Tell the class that they will open their books to SB page 344 at the same time when you tell them to do so, but not before.

2. Explain to the class that when they do open their books, they will have only 30 seconds to look at the picture on page 344 before you will then tell them to close their books. They will need to remember as many of the strange things they noticed about the picture as they can.

Conducting the Task

1. Now tell the class to open their books to page 344. Time them for 30 seconds. Tell them to close their books again.

2. On notebook paper, ask students to write down as many things as they remembered about the picture that were strange or unusual, using complete sentences. They should keep their books closed.

3. Put students into pairs when they've written as much as they can and have them compare their lists.

4. When ready, have students open their books and work with their partner to check their own lists and then to complete the list in the book on SB page 345 (using complete sentences again).

Closing the Task

Go over a few sentences students have as answers. There is no need to correct student errors at this time. Solicit a variety of possessive forms (i.e., possessive nouns, possessive phrases), and write them on the board. Leave a few of the examples on the board for use in Focus 1.

EXPANSION [20 minutes]

Play a similar game of description with the whole class. This will require students to use the possessive in their descriptions.

---

1. Have students work with a partner.

2. Each pair should set their chairs so that they are facing away from each other and their chairs are back to back. They should not be able to see each other when sitting in their chairs.

3. Pairs should begin by looking at each other for a moment.

4. Then have everyone sit down, facing away from their partners. Everyone should quietly change five things about their appearance. For example, a student might tuck in the bottom of his shirt, roll up the bottom of his pant leg, untie one of his shoelaces, take off his glasses, and remove his watch.

5. When everyone is ready, give the signal to turn the chairs around and now have partners face each other.

6. Pairs should now attempt to spot the five differences in the appearance of their partners.

7. You may want to award bonus points to those students who spot the differences the quickest (have them raise their hands when finished).

GRAMMAR NOTE

Typical student errors (use)

- Using possessive phrases with animate nouns:
  * *The shoes of the boy are dirty already.*
- Using possessive nouns with inanimate nouns:
  * *The house's roof was torn off in the storm.*
- Using possessive nouns with long nouns: * *The sad old man sitting at the bus stop's coat was wet.*
- Using more than one possessive noun: * *The man's daughter's car is green.*

Typical student errors (form)

- Omission of the possessive noun or phrase:
  * *My brother daughter is 16.*
- Incorrect use of the *'s* after a plural noun ending in *-s*: *I have five dogs.* * *My dog's collars are different colors.* * *My dogs' beds are too.*

form

FOCUS 1

Possessive Forms

EXAMPLES

(a) Their dog has a really long tail.

(b) His hair is covered by a cap, but hers appears to be made of snakes.

(c) The fringe of the couch looks like human fingers.

(d) The boy's shoes are swim fins, and the girl's have curly toes.

EXPLANATIONS

There are four kinds of possessive forms:

Possessive determiners:

(*my, your, his, her, its, our, their*)

Possessive determiners precede the noun.

Possessive pronouns:

(*mine, yours, his, hers, its, ours, theirs*)

Possessive pronouns can take the place of a noun phrase.

Possessive phrases:

(*the leg of the chair, the end of the story*, etc.)

Possessive phrases are formed by adding the preposition *of* to the noun phrase. Possessive phrases follow the noun.

Possessive nouns:

(*the student's answers, the children's laughter, those babies' cries, Elvis' cousin*, etc.)

Possessive nouns are formed by adding *'s* (pronounced **apostrophe -s**) to a noun, or simply adding an apostrophe to nouns or proper nouns ending in *-s.*

EXERCISE 1

Underline and identify all the possessive structures in the following passage. Then label each one: (a) possessive determiner, (b) possessive pronoun, (c) possessive phrase, or (d) possessive noun. The first paragraph has been done for you as an example. Do all the structures you identified describe possessive relationships?

(1) Have you ever tested <u>your memory</u>? (2) There have been many studies of <u>people's</u> ability to remember things. (3) These studies have found that there are two types <u>of memory</u>: short-term memory and long-term memory.

(4) Short-term memory depends on the "length" or number <u>of items</u> that someone needs to remember. (5) A <u>person's</u> ability to remember a series <u>of numbers</u> for more than a minute is limited to about twelve or fourteen digits. (6) An <u>individual's</u> ability to remember strings <u>of unconnected words</u> seems to average about eight items. (7) Most <u>people's</u> performance on such memory tests will drop quickly if they are tested again, even after only a few <u>hours'</u> time.

(8) Long-term memory seems to be determined by the <u>item's</u> usefulness to the person being tested. (9) For example, people do a better job of remembering one of Shakespeare's sonnets if they can apply the "message" <u>of the poem</u> to some part of their own lives. (10) The more important a piece of information is to a <u>person's</u> life, the longer and more accurately it can be retained.

1. <u>your memory</u> — possessive determiner
2. <u>people's</u> — possessive noun
3. <u>of memory</u> — possessive phrase
4. _____
5. _____
6. _____
7. _____
8. _____
9. _____
10. _____

ANSWER KEY

Exercise 1 4. possessive phrase 5. possessive noun/possessive phrase 6. possessive noun/ possessive phrase 7. possessive noun/possessive noun 8. possessive noun 9. possessive phrase/possessive phrase/possessive phrase/possessive phrase 10. possessive phrase/possessive noun

UNIT 21 LESSON PLAN 1

FOCUS 1 [15 minutes]

Focus 1 reviews the possessive forms. Although they will be familiar, students may not be able to name each form.

1. **Lead-in:** Put a few examples on the board or refer back to the examples you have from the Opening Task. Some examples include:

*The **girl's** hair is full of* (possessive noun)
snakes.

*The legs **of the table*** (possessive phrase)
look like feet.

*A dog is on the carpet. **His*** (possessive
tail is too long. determiner)

Her list has six things, (possessive pronoun)
*but **mine** has ten.*

2. Invite volunteers to point out the possessive forms and see if they can name the form. If they cannot name the forms, don't tell them. Wait until you have presented the focus chart.

3. Go over the focus chart and note the differences in each form.

4. Be sure to spend a few moments giving examples that show how to add the possessive to nouns which end in -s as explained under the section on Possessive Nouns (however, see also the following Grammar Note). Here are a few examples based on the rule supplied next to example (d). You may want to discuss the pronunciation of these:

It's my boss' car.

Our biology class' final exam is next week.

All of our classes' exams are next week!

That student's book is getting wet.

Those students' books are getting wet.

5. Go back to the examples on the board and see if anyone can name the forms now.

Suggestion: Give students some practice with the pronunciation of plural forms. See the Pronunciation Note on this page for ideas.

POSSESSIVES

Focus 1 reviews the possessive forms within the passage. Use this exercise immediately after presenting Focus 1 to review the four possessive forms presented.

EXERCISE 1 [15 minutes]

Students will identify and name the possessive forms within the passage. Use this exercise immediately after presenting Focus 1 to review the four possessive forms presented.

1. You may want to reinforce the grammar terminology by listing the four possessive forms across the board as listed in the instructions:
(a) *possessive determiners,* (b) *possessive pronouns,*
(c) *possessive phrases,* and (d) *possessive nouns.* Refer to these as you review the answers later.

2. Place the first few possessive forms done in the example paragraph under the corresponding heading on the board. (i.e., *your* goes under
(a) *possessive determiner*).

3. Have students continue with the following paragraphs. You can have them underline and then identify (a–d) the possessive forms in their books as the examples show.

4. Let students compare answers with a partner.

5. Go over answers with the class. If you have time, list the forms under the headings on the board as the class calls them out. This will visually help students to see the differences between forms. See answers on LP page 346.

6. Discuss the reasons for any structures that do not have a possessive meaning.

7. Remember that *use* will be discussed in Focus 2, and *meaning* will be discussed in Focus 3.

8. Note the variety of forms listed on the board or throughout the passage. Ask the student why or when we use each different form of the possessive. Use this discussion to lead into Focus 2.

work book

For more practice, use *Grammar Dimensions 3* Workbook page 121, Exercise 1.

GRAMMAR NOTE

The addition of **'s** (apostrophe *-s*) or simply **'** (apostrophe) to signal the possessive of a singular noun already ending in an *-s* can be a controversial topic in grammar circles. An example would be: *my boss' car* versus *my boss's car*. Although the traditional rule recommends adding only the apostrophe to any noun ending in an *-s* (singular or plural), many grammar guides now suggest adding the extra *'s* (apostrophe—*s*) to singular nouns such as these in order to more accurately reflect the pronunciation of these words—e.g., *my boss's car* (with an extra syllable in pronunciation).

Another point of confusion can come from the joint possession of something by two or more people or things. In this case, add the *-'s* or apostrophe to the last element only: *This is Sam and Sarah's daughter.* However, when two or more people or things possess something separately, add the *-'s* or apostrophe to each: *The Braves' and the Rangers' coaches are retiring.*

PRONUNCIATION NOTE

The pronunciation of the final *-'s* or *-s'* changes according to the final sound of the word it is added to. The rules are:

(1) after voiceless consonants it is pronounced /s/,

(2) after voiced consonants and vowels, it is pronounced /z/,

(3) after sibilants, it is pronounced /iz/ and takes on an extra syllable.

For practice, put several names (or other nouns) on the board (i.e., *Rick, Kurt, Mary, Kana, Grace, Jonas*). Then put three columns on the board with the following headings: /s/, /z/, /iz/. Students should be able to put each name into the correct column matching the plural pronunciation it would take (i.e., the /s/ column would take *Rick's, Kurt's*). Ask students to list five more names for each column. Go over as a class.

FOCUS 2

Possessive Nouns Versus Possessive Phrases

use

EXAMPLES

(a) **The little girl's hair** appears to be made of snakes.

(b) **The hair of the little girl** appears to be made of snakes.

(c) the boy's cap
NOT: the cap of the boy

(d) the dog's tail
NOT: the tail of the dog

(e) the razor's edge

(f) the train's arrival

(g) the moon's orbit

(h) the river's mouth

(i) the earth's atmosphere

(j) the top of the table
NOT: the table's top.

(k) the fringe of the couch
NOT: the couch's fringe

(l) the cause of the problem
NOT: the problem's cause

(m) the dog of a rather strange local family
NOT: a rather strange local family's dog

(n) the hat of the girl's older brother
NOT: the older brother's girl's hat

EXPLANATIONS

Possessive noun ('s) mean the same thing as nouns with a possessive phrase (of . . .), but one form is usually preferred over the other in specific situations.

Use **possessive nouns (with 's) for:**

• most animate (living) nouns

• objects that perform an action

• natural phenomena

Use **possessive phrases (with of + noun phrase):**

• for most inanimate (nonliving) nouns

• when the possessive noun phrase is very long

• when a multiple possessive is long

EXERCISE 2

For each noun + possessive, write the best possessive form in the blank in the sentence. Add articles where necessary.

Examples: hat/boy: _____ The boy's hat _____ has a propeller.

cover/Time magazine: Being on _the cover of Time magazine_ made Elvis Presley even more famous.

1. results/investigation: _____ were reported in the newspaper.

2. restaurant/Alice's mother: We had dinner at _____.

3. ability/individual: _____ to remember something depends on how important the information is.

4. rights/women: Suffragettes were early activists in the battle for _____

5. opening/novel: _____ begins with the famous words, "Call me Ishmael."

6. take-off/rocket: _____ was quite an amazing spectacle.

7. music/Elvis Presley: _____ has been heard all over the world.

8. discovery/penicillin: Sir Alexander Fleming was responsible for _____

9. children/a very famous American movie star: I went to school with _____.

10. rotation/earth: _____ is what causes night and day.

EXERCISE 3

Change the cues in parentheses to the correct possessive constructions. Add articles where necessary.

Last week Matt went shopping to get a present for his roommate, Jeff. It was (1) _____ (Jeff/birthday), and he wanted to buy a really "unusual" gift. He drove (2) _____ (Jeff/car) downtown. When he got there he realized that the (3) _____ (shopping district/center) was already quite crowded, and every (4) _____ (store/ parking lot) seemed to be full. He was in a hurry, so he decided to park in front of a hotel. He thought the (5) _____ (hotel/doorman) looked annoyed, but he wasn't really paying much attention. He visited several stores. In (6) _____ (one of the stores/window) he saw the perfect gift: a statue of a cowboy. In (7) _____ (cowboy/hand) there was a container for toothpaste, toothbrush, and razor. He thought that the statue would look perfect in (8) _____ (their apartment/bathroom). He bought it and

Exercise 3 is continued on LP page 350.

ANSWER KEY

Exercise 2 Although both forms are grammatically possible, the following are the most likely choices: 1. The results of the investigation 2. Alice's mother's restaurant 3. An individual's ability 4. women's rights 5. The opening of the novel 6. The rocket's take-off 7. Elvis Presley's music 8. the discovery of penicillin 9. the children of a very famous American movie star 10. The earth's rotation

Exercise 3 (1) Jeff's birthday (2) Jeff's car (3) center of the shopping district (4) stores' parking lot (5) doorman of the hotel (6) the window of one of the stores (7) the cowboy's hand (8) the bathroom of their apartment

LESSON PLAN 1

FOCUS 2 [15 minutes]

Focus 2 explains why and when the possessive noun versus the possessive phrase might be used.

1. **Lead-in:** Refer back to the passage in Exercise 1 or continue the discussion you began in step 8 of Exercise 1. Ask students why we use one possessive form over another, and if there is any difference in meaning between "the message of the poem" and "the poem's message." (*No*) Ask if it is preferred to use one form over another in some situations. (*Yes*)

2. Go on to Focus 2 examples (a–b).

3. Go over the general guidelines for using possessive nouns: animate, performs an action, or natural phenomena.

4. Go over the general guidelines for using possessive phrases: inanimate, has a very long noun phrase, has a very long multiple possessive.

5. Refer back to the previous passage and ask students to find a few examples to support some of these guidelines (i.e., *Shakespeare's sonnets* = animate = possessive noun).

Suggestion: Can students find possessive forms in the previous passage that do **not** match these guidelines? (i.e., *the item's usefulness*) Discuss some possible reasons for these.

EXERCISE 2 [15 minutes]

Students will use the guidelines presented in Focus 2 for choosing possessive nouns versus phrases.

1. Go over the example as a class. Ask students why the first example sentence takes the possessive noun. (*animate*) Why did the second sentence take the possessive phrase? (*inanimate*)

2. Have students work individually or in pairs to complete the exercise. They should be ready to explain their choices to the class. More than one answer may be possible.

3. Go over the possible choices with the class. See answers on LP page 348.

 For more practice, use *Grammar Dimensions 3* Workbook page 121, Exercise 2.

EXERCISE 3 [15 minutes]

This exercise works much the same as Exercise 2. Students will fill in the blanks with the correct possessive constructions adding articles as needed.

 For more practice, use *Grammar Dimensions 3* Workbook page 122, Exercise 3.

hurried back to where he had parked. The car was gone! At first Matt thought it had been stolen, but then he realized that it had probably been towed away. He called the police, and they verified that the car was at the station. When he got there, he found that (9) _____ (the car/front fender) had a dent, and there was a big scratch on (10) _____ (the car/side). Matt had to pay for the (11) _____ (repair/cost) and the towing charges. Jeff got a very expensive birthday present, and Matt got a long-overdue lesson about traffic laws and parking regulations.

FOCUS 3

Meanings of Possessive Forms

meaning

Possessive forms can be used to describe other kinds of meaning besides belonging to someone or something.

EXAMPLES	EXPLANATIONS
	We also use possessive forms to indicate:
(a) Please give me ten **dollars'** worth of unleaded gasoline.	• amount or quantity
(b) That leather coat cost me a **week's** pay.	
(c) This book represents three **years'** work.	
(d) The **index** of a book is the best place to start when you're looking for specific information.	• part of a whole
(e) The **team's** captain scored the goal.	
(f) Scientists are still trying to discover the **cause** of cancer.	• a general relationship or association
(g) The **streets** of New York can be dangerous at night.	
(h) **Margaret's** friend is blind.	
(i) We learned about the **exports** of Australia in our international business class.	• origin or agent
(j) **Joan's** conversation with the doctor caused her some concern.	

Exercise 3 Exercise 3 is continued from LP page 348. (9) the front fender of the car (10) the side of the car (11) cost of repairs
Exercise 4 The expressions are underlined above. The meanings conveyed are as follows: a. (none)
b. of Rock and Roll, of the first blues artists, of the United States, Elvis's, Presley's, of Rock and Roll
c. of the President of the United States, of Elvis Presley, of Rock and Roll, Presley's, of America, of
the first blues artists, of the United States, of an entire generation of teenage girls, Presley's, of

EXERCISE 4

By yourself: Read the following article about Elvis Presley and underline all the possessives or expressions with "of". The first paragraph has been done for you.

With a partner: Compare your answers. Find at least two examples of possessives that convey each of the following meanings, and write those examples in the space next to the meanings listed.

a. quantity or amount _____

b. part of a whole _____

c. general relationship or association _____

d. origin or agent _____

e. actual possession _____

f. phrases with *of* that should not be considered possessive _____

THE KING OF ROCK AND ROLL

(1) The most-visited residence in the United States is, of course, the White House, in Washington, D.C., the home of the President of the United States. (2) But the second most visited residence may surprise you. (3) It is Graceland Mansion in Memphis, Tennessee, the home of Elvis Presley, the "King" of Rock and Roll. (4) Presley's influence on the popular music of America was profound. (5) He was one of the first blues artists to make rock and roll popular with the middle class of the United States. (6) And Elvis's swinging hips and sexy voice made him the dream boyfriend of an entire generation of teenage girls. (7) Presley's historic appearance on a 1958 broadcast of The Ed Sullivan Show caused an uproar. (8) His singing could not be heard because of the screams of his adoring fans. (9) And Presley's famous swinging hips were not seen at all, because of the objections of TV broadcasters, who felt his wild movements weren't suitable for family television. (10) Presley rapidly became America's most popular male singer of all time. (11) He made dozens of records and many films. (12) Everywhere he went crowds of screaming, adoring fans showered him with gifts, love, and devotion.

(13) But his personal life was marked by tragedy. (14) By the time he died in 1977, everyone had heard the rumors of his troubles with alcohol and drugs. (15) They had read about his failed marriage in the movie magazines. (16) His suspicions about his friends' loyalties and motivations had made a "living nightmare" of his life. (17) He died a prisoner of his own popularity.

(18) In spite of his death, Elvis is still called "The King of Rock and Roll." (19) Graceland Mansion is visited by hundreds of adoring fans every day. (20) His records continue to be popular, and there are several radio stations that play nothing but Presley's music.

(21) Some people even believe that he is still alive and living in disguise. (22) There continue to be rumors that his mysterious death was just a trick to allow him to escape from the prison of his fame and his fans' adoration. (23) Many people still believe that he is living a quiet life with a new name and a thick beard to hide his famous face. (24) Today the Memphis post office still receives hundreds of letters addressed to Elvis at Graceland from fans who still await "The King's" return.

the Ed Sullivan Show, of his adoring fans, America's, of screaming, adoring fans, his friends', of Rock and Roll, of adoring fans, His, Presley's, his, Presley's, his, fans' adoration, "The King's" d. Presley's, of America, of the United States, of his adoring fans, of TV broadcasters, his, of screaming, adoring fans, his, of his troubles, of adoring fans, his, fans' adoration, "The King's" e. of Elvis Presley, of America, Elvis's, His, Presley's, his, his, of his troubles, his, His, his friends', of his life, of his own popularity, his, of his fame, his f. of course, of the screams, of the objections, of all time, of records

FOCUS 3 [15 minutes]

Focus 3 presents several different meanings that the possessive can have.

1. **Lead-in:** Remind the class that you have already discussed the **form** (Focus 1) and the **use** (Focus 2) of possessives. Now you will look at the **meaning** of possessives.

2. Ask the class to cover the explanation side of their focus charts (or use a copy on an overhead projector and cover that portion). Ask the class what the term *possessive* means. Does it only mean *ownership* or *belonging*? Look at the example sentences together and ask if anyone can identify the meaning for the possessive in these sentences? Help them by asking: *Does the team own the captain? Does the conversation belong to Joan?*

3. Uncover the explanations portion of the chart and ask the class to think of other examples to illustrate each meaning. Some other examples include: an amount (*one month's rent*), part of a whole (*the car's tires*), a general relationship (*the city's history*), origin or agent (*the author's purpose*).

EXERCISE 4 [15 minutes]

You may want to skip this exercise and do Exercise 5 immediately as a follow-up to Focus 3 and then come back to Exercise 4. Students will identify a variety of possessives along with other expressions using *of*. They will then need to find two examples that illustrate each of the meanings listed.

1. Ask students first to read through the article. This can be done individually or out loud as a class.

2. Students will then go through the article and underline each example of a possessive form along with any other expressions using *of*. You can encourage students by telling them how many underlined forms they should find.

3. Next, ask students to choose two examples to illustrate each of the meanings listed (a–f) in the exercise.

4. If you have time, put the article on an overhead transparency and go through it with the class, underlining forms as you go and inviting students to choose which meaning is being conveyed. See answers on LP page 350.

Suggestion 1: If you are short on time, simply ask students to read the article and look for two examples for each meaning listed.

Suggestion 2: To make it easier for you to respond to a variety of student answers, color code your answer key by highlighting all the examples for each meaning in the same color. For example, all the possessive forms that show (a) *quantity or amount* would be yellow and all the possessive forms that show (b) *part of a whole* would be pink, etc.

EXERCISE 5

Underline the possessive forms in the following sentences. There may be more than one possible interpretation. With a partner, discuss which of the following meanings the possessive forms indicate:

a. an amount or quantity
b. a part of a whole
c. a general relationship/association
d. an origin or agent
e. actual possession

Example: The streets of San Francisco are famous for their steep hills.
_(b)   (d)   (c)   (c)_

1. Scientists are studying the effects of alcohol on an individual's memory.
   _c/d_
2. The wines of France are among the best in the world.
   _c_
3. The teacher's assistant will hand back the homework.
   _b_
4. That concept was introduced in the book's first chapter.
   _b_
5. Chicago is four days' drive from Los Angeles.
   _a_
6. An investigation of short-term memory has shown that items of personal importance are more easily remembered.
   _c/d_   _b_
7. The top of the table looked like a small patch of grass.
   _c_
8. Matt's roommate likes ice cream.
   _c/d_
9. Beethoven's symphonies still thrill listeners.
   _c/d_

EXERCISE 6

Are these sentences correct or incorrect? If they are incorrect, identify the problems and correct them.

1. The fame of Elvis Presley spread across America.
2. The table's top was covered with grass.
3. The child of Bambang's classmate was sick with the flu.
4. Gladys' well-known next-door neighbor's dog's barking annoyed the entire neighborhood.
5. The scientists' studies' results indicate that memory is affected by such things as weather and time of day.
6. Memory's investigations have shown that the ability of people to remember things declines with age.
7. Rock and Roll's King died in 1977.
8. Elvis's death's circumstances are somewhat mysterious.

EXERCISE 7

Ask a classmate for his or her opinions on these topics, and the reasons for those opinions. Report your partner's answers to the rest of the class.

Example: best place to sit in a classroom
  You: *Where's the best place to sit in a classroom?*
  Your partner: *The front of the class is better if you're a good student, but the back of the class is better if you want to sleep.*

1. most important part of the semester (beginning, end, or middle)
2. favorite object that belongs to someone else
3. most important period of history
4. favorite piece of music

Ask two additional questions of your own that use possessive forms.

5. _____

6. _____

Exercise 6 1. correct. 2. possessive phrase with inanimate object: The top of the table was covered with grass. 3. correct. 4. long multiple possessive phrase/long possessive noun phrase: The barking of Gladys' well-known next-door neighbor's dog annoyed the entire neighborhood. 5. long multiple possessive phrase/inanimate object: The results of the scientists' studies indicate that memory is affected by such things as weather and time of day. 6. possessive phrase with inanimate object: Investigations of memory have shown that the ability of people to remember things declines with age. 7. possessive phrase with inanimate object: The King of Rock and Roll died in 1977. 8. possessive phrase with inanimate object/long multiple possessive phrase: The circumstances of Elvis' death are somewhat mysterious. **Exercise 7** Answers will vary. Possible answers are: 1. You (Y): Is the beginning, middle, or end the most important part of the semester? Your Partner (YP): The end is the most important because of final exams. 2. What's your favorite object of someone else? (YP) I like my friend's car because I don't have one. 3. What's the most important period of history? (YP) The time of the ancient Greeks was the most important for their art. 4. What's your favorite piece of music? (YP) My favorite is "Moonlight Sonata." 5 and 6. Answers will vary.

EXERCISE 5 [15 minutes]

This exercise asks students to look at individual sentences, identify the possessive forms, and then choose which meaning they feel each possessive form indicates. Depending on your class, you may want to do this exercise before Exercise 4.

1. Remind the class that there could be more than one possessive form in each sentence (see the example).

2. Have students work individually or in pairs to underline the possessive forms and then choose a meaning (a–e) to match. There may be more than one explanation for the meaning, but students should discuss their reasons for choosing these meanings with a partner.

3. Go over these with the class. Allow for some variation of answers in your discussion. See answers on LP page 352.

For more practice, use *Grammar Dimensions 3* Workbook page 122, Exercise 4.

EXERCISE 6 [15 minutes]

Students will identify errors in the use of possessive nouns versus possessive phrases. This exercise can be used for a diagnostic before Focus 2 or as a unit review.

1. Have students work individually to underline any problems in the use of possessive nouns or possessive phrases.

2. If you are using this as a diagnostic, you can circulate and note how well students found the errors. Before discussing the correct answers, go over the information in Focus 2. Then allow students some time to return to their original answers and work in pairs to make any changes based on the information presented in Focus 2.

3. If you are using this as a unit review, you can collect the answers on paper, go over them as a class review, or put students into pairs and direct

them to open their books to Focus 2 and check their work together. See answers on LP page 352.

For more practice, use *Grammar Dimensions 3* Workbook page 123, Exercise 5.

EXERCISE 7 [15 minutes]

Students will work with a partner to ask and answer questions based on cues. The questions and/or answers will most likely contain a form of the possessive. This can be used for pair work or as a mixer.

1. Have students write complete questions (based on the cues) on a piece of paper with room to write answers.

2. Put students into pairs or use this as a class mixer and have students move around the classroom speaking to different students.

3. Students should begin asking questions (of a partner or another classmate) and either take notes or write complete sentences for the answers.

4. If students are moving around the classroom, they may want to ask the same question of more than one student. This will take longer, but will give a wider variety of answers and possibly more possessive forms.

5. Invite students to share those answers that include possessives with the class for review. See possible answers on LP page 352.

UNIT GOAL REVIEW [10 minutes]

Ask students to look at the goals on the opening page of the unit again. Refer to the pages of the unit where information on each goal can be found.

ExamView Test Generator For assessment of Unit 21, use *Grammar Dimensions 3 ExamView*®.

Use Your English

ACTIVITY 1 speaking

Work with a partner to fill in the missing parts of the diagrams. Student A, look at diagrams A and C below. Student B, look at Diagrams B and D on page A-12. Diagram A contains elements not contained in Diagram B. Student A, help your partner complete Diagram B by verbally describing Diagram A. Student B should help Student A complete Diagram C, which is incomplete by verbally describing the diagram D. Student A should not look at Diagrams B and D. Student B should not look at Diagrams A and C.

Diagram A

Diagram C

ACTIVITY 2 writing/speaking

Check your short-term memory. Study the picture below for thirty seconds. Then close your book and describe to a partner what has happened to the car and its passengers. Your partner should look at the picture while you describe it and check your description for accuracy. Your partner should also check the accuracy of your use of possessive forms.

ACTIVITY 3 listening/speaking

CD Track 32

STEP 1

As you listen to the geometry class lecture, use the information to draw the diagram that is described by the speaker. Once you have finished, listen to the lecture again to check that you have completed your diagram correctly.

STEP 2

Compare your diagram with two or three others. As a group, decide on the correct answer to the two questions the speaker asks at the end of the lecture.

ACTIVITY 4 research on the web

Go to the Internet and use an Internet search engine such as Google® or Yahoo® to find information on a famous person who is no longer alive. Write a short description of that person. What are the things that made him or her famous? Be sure to describe his or her accomplishments, childhood, important experiences, and influence on society.

ACTIVITY 5 reflection

Write two paragraphs—one that describes some interesting things about your extended family (including grandparents, uncles, aunts, in-laws etc.), and one that describes your favorite room in your house. Compare your paragraphs with those of another student. Identify the possessive forms that you used in your description. Together, select five examples of possessive forms you used in your descriptions to present to the rest of the class. Tell why you used the form you did, and what meaning was communicated by the possessive (amount or quantity, part of a whole, a general relationship or association, an origin or agent, actual possession). If possible, pick one example for each possessive meaning.

USE YOUR ENGLISH

The Use Your English activities at the end of the unit contain situations that should naturally elicit the structures covered in the unit. For a more complete discussion of how to use the Use Your English Activities see To the Teacher on LP page xxii. When students are doing these activities in class, you can circulate and listen to see if they are using the structures accurately. Errors can be corrected when the activity is finished.

ACTIVITY 1 speaking [15 minutes]

This pair activity relies on students being able to clearly describe pictures out loud to their partners. The key to this activity lies in each partner looking only at their designated page.

1. Put the class into pairs. In each pair, one partner (Partner 1) will look only at SB page 354 Activity 1 while the other partner (Partner 2) will look only at page A-12 Unit 21 Activity 1.

2. Begin by having Partner 1 describe the picture they see in Diagram A on page 354. Partner 2 will look at their own picture of Diagram B on page A-12 and note any differences. Partner 2 should draw in any missing features as he or she listens to Partner 1's verbal description.

3. Next, ask Partner 2 to describe what they see in Diagram D. Partner 1 will listen and compare this description to his or her own picture in Diagram C. Partner 1 should draw in any missing features as they listen to Partner 2's verbal description.

4. When finished, have the pairs check their drawings by opening their books to both sets of diagrams (SB pages 354 and A-12). How well did they do? Which diagram was the most difficult? Why?

ACTIVITY 2 writing/speaking [10 minutes]

This activity works much like the one in the Opening Task. One partner will describe the picture (with book closed) while the other partner will check the accuracy of the description (with book open).

EXPANSION [15 minutes]

Look in the puzzle section of the newspaper, on the Internet, or in children's puzzle books for "Find the Difference" puzzles. These puzzles show two versions of the same scene. The goal is to find all the differences between the two pictures as fast as you can. Copy a few of these puzzles and pass them out to pairs. Each pair should be able to find and describe the differences between the two pictures within a timed period. Students will use phrases like, *The man's tie is shorter in this picture* or *The leg of the table is missing in this picture.*

ACTIVITY 3 listening/speaking [15 minutes]

CD Track 32

This listening activity works much like the information gap in Activity 1. However, this can be a bit tricky to follow. Students should listen to the audio and draw the geometric figure that is described to them.

■ STEP 1

1. You may want to pause the audio after the first instructions to draw a square. (The correct completion of the final figure relies on beginning with a good symmetrical square with straight sides.)

2. Play the audio two times and pause as needed for class to complete their drawings.

■ STEP 2

1. Have groups of students compare their drawings.

2. Students should then answer the two questions asked at the end of the audio.

3. To review, bring a student up to the board and play the audio again with pauses as he/she draws the figure on the board. Give any correction or assistance as you go through the audio. Then let the class count the triangles and squares and decide together on the answers to the two questions.

ACTIVITY 4 research on the web [15 minutes/homework]

Students will research a famous person and write a description.

1. You can begin by brainstorming for ideas of famous people and writing them on the board. You will have doubles, so encourage groups to try to replace any duplicates with a new name.

2. Assign the writing portion of the activity as homework.

ACTIVITY 5 reflection [20 minutes/homework]

1. Assign the two paragraphs. In order to give the class the opportunity for reflection, it is best **not** to point out the animate versus inanimate dichotomy in the paragraph topics.

2. After writing, put students into small groups or pairs to compare paragraphs and then identify the possessive forms used.

3. Next, have each pair/group select five examples of the use of the possessive and be ready to explain the reasons for and meanings of their use to the class.

Suggestion: Ask the class which meanings were the most commonly shown in the family paragraph. Which meanings were the most common in the room paragraphs? Why is this?

UNIT GOALS

- Correctly understand and use affirmative and negative quantifiers

- Correctly understand and use collective nouns

- Correctly understand and use collective adjectives

OPENING TASK

Statistics about International Education

The Institute for International Education publishes statistical information about international educational exchange. Work with a partner. Examine these charts on the enrollment of international students in educational institutions in the United States. Using that information and your own knowledge, answer these three questions:

- What fields of study do international students pursue in the United States?

- What kinds of locations do they choose to study at?

- Which parts of the world do students come from?

CHART A: FOREIGN STUDENTS BY FIELD OF STUDY

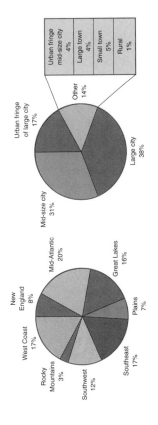

CHART B: FOREIGN STUDENTS BY DESTINATION

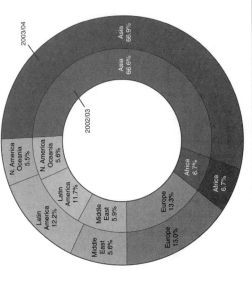

CHART C: FOREIGN STUDENTS BY ORIGIN

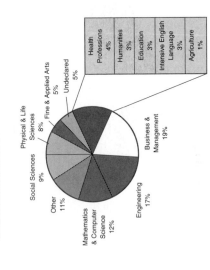

UNIT OVERVIEW

Unit 22 reviews the affirmative and negative meanings of quantifiers along with singular and plural forms. Collective nouns are also covered and include both collective nouns and collective adjectives.

GRAMMAR NOTE

Quantifiers can be difficult for ESL students. Students will need to learn the subtle differences in degree between quantifiers, which quantifiers are used only for count or noncount nouns, and the distinction between the affirmative and negative quantifiers. Collective nouns can cause confusion in terms of singular or plural agreement. Students should be told that for some collective nouns American and British English differ with American English preferring singular subject-verb agreement. At the same time, however, a writer or speaker can sometimes choose singular or plural agreement and in this way convey a sense of cohesion or division within the group. This can be difficult for students who prefer that grammar be straightforward with a "correct" answer given by the teacher.

UNIT GOALS

Some instructors may want to review the goals listed on Student Book (SB) page 356 after completing the Opening Task so that students understand what they should know by the end of the unit. These goals can also be reviewed at the end of the unit when students are more familiar with the grammar terminology.

OPENING TASK [20 minutes]

This aim of this activity is to give students the opportunity to use quantifiers while making generalizations and analyzing charts. This task can be done in pairs or small groups, orally or written. The problem-solving format is designed to show the teacher how well the students can produce a target structure implicitly and spontaneously when they are engaged in a communicative task. For a more complete discussion of the purpose of the Opening Task, see To the Teacher, Lesson Planner (LP) page xxii.

Setting Up the Task

Begin by having the class look over the charts and volunteer any observations. Write a few of these on the board. Avoid writing down statements at this point that directly answer the discussion questions.

Conducting the Task

1. Put the class into pairs or small groups and have them work together to answer the three questions in the Opening Task.
2. Circulate and note the current use of quantifiers. If students are having trouble, ask leading questions that require students to make generalizations, such as:

   What do most students choose to study?
   Which field has fewer students?

3. Have each group write down several sentences to answer each question. Remind the class that there is not just a single answer for each question.

Closing the Task

1. You may want to have a student from each group come up and write a sentence or two on the board. You can have one or two groups responsible for each question.
2. Discuss the answers as a class. You do not need to focus on the presence or absence of quantifiers at this point. However, if you do have examples of the use of quantifiers, keep these sentences on the board for use in Focus 1.

VARIATION

If you are short on time, use Exercise 15 on SB page 370 as a diagnostic in place of the Opening Task. If used as a diagnostic, collect answers. Otherwise, have students work together in small groups to check their own work. Do not give out the correct answers. Instead, go over Exercise 15 again at the end of the unit as a whole class review.

EXPANSION [30 minutes]

Building on the use of graphs to show a percentage, you may want to assign Activity 5 (speaking) on SB page 373, which asks students to create their own charts or graphs to represent the results of an in-class poll and make a presentation.

GRAMMAR NOTE

Typical student errors (use)

- Using *every* or *no* in place of a noun (*everyone/none/no one*): * *Did no student fail the test? No, no did.* * *Did every student pass the test then? Yes, every did.*
- Using specific reference for a nonspecific situation/overusing *most of the:* * *Most of the people have cars these days.*
- Using negative quantifiers in a negative sentence: * *Few people don't have a television in the United States.*

Typical student errors (form)

- Agreement problems with quantifiers *either, neither,* or *both:* * *She applied to two schools, but neither are nearby.*
- Using both singular and plural forms with one collective noun: * *The committee of volunteers wants their first meeting to be on Monday.*

FOCUS 1

form   meaning

Overview of Quantifiers in English

QUANTIFIERS
Listed in decreasing order from all (100%) to none (0%)

AFFIRMATIVE QUANTIFIERS

Used with count nouns	Used with noncount nouns	PHRASES OF QUANTITY AND AMOUNT WITH SIMILAR MEANING
all/any	all/any	the total number/amount
each/every		
almost all	almost all	the vast majority
most	most	the majority
a great many	a great deal of	a large number/amount
many	much	a substantial number/amount
lots of/a lot of	lots of/a lot of	
plenty of	plenty of	
a good number of	a good deal of	more than some
quite a few	quite a little	more than a few/a little
quite a number of	quite a bit of	
some/any	some/any	an indeterminate number or amount
a (certain/large/small) number of	a (certain/large/small) number of	
a few several	a little	a small number/amount

NEGATIVE QUANTIFIERS

Used with count nouns	Used with noncount nouns	
not all/every	not all	an unspecified number are not/do not
not many	not much	a small number/amount
few	little	an insufficient number/amount
hardly any	hardly any	the vast majority are not/do not
almost no/none	almost no/none	
no/none/not any	no/none/not any	the total number/amount are not/do not

---

EXAMPLES

(a) **Most** international students study business or technical subjects.

(b) **A few** study humanities or fine arts.

EXPLANATIONS

You can use quantifiers:
• as determiners with noun phrases
• in place of noun phrases to describe number or amount

EXERCISE 1

STEP 1 In the following passage, underline the quantifiers and circle the noun phrases they modify. The first sentence has been done for you as an example.

STEP 2 Are there quantifiers that do not appear with noun phrases? What sentences do they appear in, and what do they refer to?

Example: *Clause 1 of the first sentence has a quantifier that does not appear with a noun phrase: many. It refers to people or experts.*

Medical Education in the United States

(1) Even though American medical education is considered by many to be the best in the world, (2) there are relatively few spaces in American medical schools, and a substantial number of Americans are forced to go overseas to get their basic medical training. (3) As a result, not all the doctors practicing in the United States have received their training from American medical schools. (4) In fact, quite a few have been educated in other countries. (5) However, all physicians must have clinical experience and pass qualifying examinations in order to receive a license to work in the United States.

(6) Most doctors currently working in the United States have completed their practical training in an American hospital or clinic. (7) Every hospital in this country accepts a few recently graduated medical students each year, (8) including graduates from many foreign medical schools. (9) While some popular hospitals receive a great many applications for each available space, (10) a number of hospitals in rural areas may receive only a few. (11) This period of practical training is called a "residency," and most last for two years. (12) A few are longer; some are shorter, depending on the specialization of the doctor.

(13) Many doctors study for an extra year before they begin their residency in order to become a specialist in a particular area of medicine. (14) No doctor is an expert in every area of medicine, but some doctors have more than one specialty. (15) Each area of medicine has its own period of residency and its own qualifying examinations.

ANSWER KEY

Exercise 1 **Step 2:** (4) quite a few (doctors practicing in the United States) (10) only a few (applications for residency) (11) most (periods of residency) (12) a few/some (residencies)

FOCUS 1 [15 minutes]

Focus 1 gives a list of quantifiers divided into two groups: affirmative and negative. Within each group, the quantifiers are listed in decreasing order of amount. Although this should be review for most students, the division between affirmative and negative may be new. However, you do not need to focus much attention on this, as it will be discussed in greater detail in Focus 2.

1. **Lead-in:** Have students look over the list of quantifiers in Focus 1. Ask the class to point out any quantifiers used in the sentences on the board from the Opening Task. Invite volunteers to make statements about where quantifiers are used in a sentence (*before a noun phrase*) and what they mean (*to tell the quantity, amount or proportion and carry a positive or negative connotation*).

2. Point out the decreasing value of the quantifiers listed.

3. If you have time, call out a quantifier and have the class make sentences (they can be based on the charts in the Opening Task or on the student population in your class). Choose a few other quantifiers and do the same.

4. Point out that some quantifiers are affirmative (have a positive connotation) while others can be negative. Tell the class that this will be discussed more in Focus 2.

5. Follow this discussion with Exercise 1 for practice identifying and analyzing quantifiers in context.

EXPANSION [30 minutes/homework]

To build on this vocabulary and the work done in the Opening Task, you may want to assign Activity 6 (listening/writing) on SB page 373, which asks students to create and conduct their own opinion poll, create charts or graphs to illustrate their results, and make a presentation.

EXERCISE 1 [15 minutes]

Students will identify quantifiers in context and the nouns they modify. Students will also note quantifiers that appear without a noun. They will need to identify what noun these quantifiers are replacing.

■ STEP 1

1. Have students read completely through the passage first. They will need to refer back to this information in Exercise 2.

2. Students can work individually on Step 1. When finished, they can compare answers with a partner.

■ STEP 2

As students work together in pairs, they should list the sentence numbers, the quantifiers without nouns, and the nouns being referenced.

Suggestion: You may want to copy this passage onto an overhead transparency for the whole class review. See answers on LP page 358.

For more practice, use *Grammar Dimensions 3* Workbook page 124, Exercise 1.

meaning

FOCUS 2 | Affirmative and Negative Quantifiers

EXAMPLES	EXPLANATIONS
(a) Do **all** international students have similar educational backgrounds?	Affirmative quantifiers can usually be used in both affirmative and negative statements and questions.
(b) **Many** have different backgrounds. **Most** have graduated from high school, although **a few** haven't.	
(c) NOT: **Few** doctors **don't** have medical degrees.	Negative quantifiers have a negative meaning, and usually do not occur in sentences with negative verbs.
(d) BETTER: **Almost all** doctors **have** medical degrees.	

Negative quantifiers often imply that the amount or number is insufficient.

AFFIRMATIVE QUANTIFIERS (A Small Amount)	NEGATIVE QUANTIFIERS (Not Enough)
(e) **A few** doctors have studied non-Western medicine. (**Some** doctors have studied it.)	(f) **Few** doctors have studied non-Western medicine. (An **insufficient number** have studied it.)
(g) There's **a little** money left after the bills are paid. (There is still **some** money for other things.)	(h) There's **little** money left after the bills are paid. (There is **not enough** money for other things.)

EXERCISE 2

Based on the information you read in Exercise 1, write sentences that describe the training of medical doctors in the United States. Then write another set of sentences that describe medical training in a second country that you are familiar with.

1. Most doctors . . .
2. Not all doctors . . .
3. All doctors . . .
4. A few doctors . . .
5. No doctors . . .
6. Many doctors . . .

EXERCISE 3

Use quantifiers to paraphrase the highlighted phrases of quantity or amount.

Example: **The vast majority of students** pass their qualifying examination on the first try.

Almost all students pass their qualifying examination on the first try.

1. **The vast majority of medical students** in the United States already have bachelor's degrees.

2. **An indeterminate number of students** have more than one major.

3. There are **a small number of scholarships** for international students.

4. It takes **a large amount of money** to fund a university education.

5. **A small number of students** apply to only one university for admission.

6. **An unspecified number of applicants** don't achieve scores that qualify them for university admission on exams such as TOEFL® Test*, GRE, or GMAT.

7. **The majority of international students** apply for admission to more than one university.

8. **A large number of students** study English before they begin their academic studies.

---

*TOEFL is a registered trademark of the Educational Testing Service (ETS). This publication is not endorsed or approved by ETS.

ANSWER KEY

Exercise 2 Answers will vary. Possible answers are: 1. study both theoretical and applied topics. 2. are familiar with Western medicine. 3. try to cure patients as quickly as possible. 4. have advanced degrees from the United States. 5. are children. 6. have private practices in addition to working in government-run practices.

Exercise 3 1. Almost all medical students in the United States already have bachelor's degrees. 2. Some students have more than one major. 3. There are a few scholarships for international students. 4. It takes a great deal of money to fund a university education. 5. A few students apply to only one university for admissions. 6. Some applicants don't achieve scores that qualify them for university admission on exams such as TOEFL® Test, GRE, or GMAT. 7. Most international students apply for admission to more than one university. 8. Many students study English before they begin their academic studies.

EXERCISE 2 [15 minutes/homework]

1. Refer students back to the information they read in Exercise 1. If you have time, you can get students oriented by asking a few questions for review:

   What do you remember about the article?

   What kind of training do most doctors have?

2. Have pairs work on their sentences together.

3. Have students work individually to write sentences about medical training in another country.

4. Give time for students to share their sentences in small groups about other countries. Try to make groups with mixed students if possible. See possible answers on LP page 360.

Suggestion: Have students begin with statements about their own countries as homework first.

EXERCISE 3 [15 minutes]

This can be used as a review (or quiz) of the meanings outlined in the chart from Focus 1.

1. Go over the instructions with the class. They should replace the bold phrase with a quantifier showing a similar meaning.

2. Have students work individually or in pairs without looking at the chart in Focus 1.

Suggestion: If students are having trouble, you may want to list a variety of quantifiers on the board for students to choose from. Include a few that are not used in the answers for this exercise. Remind students that some quantifiers may be used more than once.

EXPANSION [20 minutes]

Students will work with the different meanings of quantifiers as they break the class down into different groups.

1. Put 12 different quantifiers on the board from the chart in Focus 1.

2. Have students work in pairs to make statements about the class using each of the quantifiers listed on the board once. For example:

   Quite a few students in this class have brown eyes.

   Hardly any students have green eyes.

   Every student has a backpack.

3. When they have finished, bring the class together and invite pairs to share sentences. Decide together if these are accurate statements.

Suggestion: If possible, have the class sit in a circle to start this activity so as to give everyone a chance to see each other.

FOCUS 2 [15 minutes]

This focus refers back to the quantifiers in Focus 1 that convey an affirmative or negative meaning.

1. **Lead-in:** Begin with a few sentences on the board illustrating the negative and affirmative meanings that various quantifiers can imply. For example, put sentences such as these on the board and ask the class in which sentences is the teacher happy or unhappy about the situation:

   Not many students completed the extra assignment.

   Several students completed the extra assignment.

   A few students arrived early.

   Few students arrived early.

   Hardly any students arrived early.

   Quite a few students arrived early.

2. Talk about the underlying affirmative or negative meaning conveyed by these and other quantifiers listed in Focus 1.

3. Then go on to Focus 2 and discuss the incorrectness of examples (c) and (d). You may want to list a few more negative statements on the board and give examples of the use of affirmative quantifiers rather than negative quantifiers (NOT: *Hardly any students **didn't** pass the test.* BETTER: *Most students **passed** the test.*).

4. Point out the differences shown in examples (e) and (f) in Focus 2 and also seen in the third and fourth examples on the board (*a few/few*).

5. Finally, go over the differences in Focus 2 examples (g) and (h).

EXPANSION [20 minutes]

To give students more practice with the subtle distinctions between negative and affirmative quantifiers, have them reword sentences.

1. Explain the idea of "the glass is half empty" pessimist and "the glass is half full" optimist.

2. Put several sentences on the board using affirmative quantifiers. Explain that these are statements from an optimist. For example:

   She has a little money left after the trip.

   Several friends came to his party.

3. Now ask students to reword these sentences using the pessimist view with a negative quantifier. The sentences above could then change to:

   She has barely any/little/not much money left after the trip.

   Few/Hardly any friends came to his party.

4. There will be more than one possible answer.

5. Put several "optimist" sentences on the board and encourage the class to be pessimists. If you have time, you could put several "pessimist" statements on the board and ask them to be optimists.

Suggestion: Put several negative sentences in the mix to remind students that they should not use negative quantifiers in a negative sentence (the sentence should be changed to the affirmative to allow for the negative quantifier).

form

Singular and Plural Quantifiers

EXAMPLES	EXPLANATIONS
(a) **All doctors know** basic first-aid techniques. **Most have studied** them in medical school.	Most quantifiers are used with plural count nouns, but *a few* have a singular form.
(b) **Every doctor knows** basic first-aid techniques. **Each has studied** them in medical school.	
(c) **Each student was** asked a question.	*Each* and *every* are only used with singular count nouns.
(d) **Every student wants** to do **his or her** best in this class.	
(e) **No student has** ever taken this test more than once.	*No* can be used with both singular and plural nouns.
(f) **No doctors** in this country **are** allowed to practice without a license.	
(g) When Bambang and Yanti took the TOEFL, **both students** got high scores on their first try.	*Both, either,* and *neither* are used in situations where there are only two nouns being described. *Both* is considered plural, but *either* and *neither* are considered to be singular.
(h) **Both were** worried about doing poorly on the exam, but **neither has** to take it again.	
(i) They applied to the same two universities; **both universities have** accepted Yanti, and Bambang is willing to go to **either** university that **accepts** him.	

Change these statements with plural count nouns to statements with *any, each,* or *every*. Remember to make any other necessary changes to preserve the meaning of the original sentence. More than one answer may be correct.

Example: *All doctors know basic first aid.*

Every doctor knows basic first aid.

Any doctor knows basic first aid.

1. All doctors must complete their residencies within two years.
2. All parents want their children to succeed in life.
3. Peter spends all free weekends at the beach.
4. All the people who came to the examination brought calculators.
5. A wise student takes advantage of all opportunities to gain practical experience.

ANSWER KEY

Decide whether to use *few* or *a few, little,* or *a little.* Compare your answers to those of a partner.

1. The students were discouraged because ___few___ people passed the examination.
2. Even very good students sometimes have ___a little___ difficulty gaining admission to a good university.
3. I can loan you some money, but I've only got ___a few___ dollars.
4. They were working in the laboratory for so long that now there's ___little___ time to get ready for the quiz.
5. There are ___few___ scholarships available for first-year medical students, so a medical education is expensive.
6. He put ___little___ effort into studying for examinations, and as a result, didn't pass on the first try.
7. The average medical student usually applies to at least ___a few___ places for residency.
8. Bambang had ___little___ trouble finding a university. Several schools were willing to accept him.

Using the following negative quantifiers, make true statements about the statistics on international education that you studied in the Opening Task on pages 356–357.

few	not all	little	hardly any	no

1. Few students come to the United States to study humanities. Few students come here to study agriculture.
2. Not all regions get the same number of foreign students. Not all international students come from Asia.
3. There is little foreign student demand for agricultural programs. There is little reason to come to the United States to study foreign languages.
4. There are hardly any foreign students in Montana. Hardly any students study agriculture anymore.
5. No student can escape culture shock. No student can study in two regions at the same time.

LESSON PLAN 1/2

EXERCISE 4 [15 minutes]

Use this exercise immediately following your presentation of examples (e–h) in Focus 2. Have students work individually and then compare answers with a partner. Go over quickly as a class. See answers on LP page 362.

For more practice, use *Grammar Dimensions 3* Workbook page 124, Exercise 2 and page 125, Exercise 4.

work book

EXERCISE 5 [15 minutes]

Students will return to the Opening Task and use negative quantifiers to make statements about the statistics. Because these quantifiers are not used as commonly as others, students probably won't have used them in their previous statements. This can be done orally since students will already be familiar with the information in the charts and will have made similar statements previously. See answers on LP page 362.

For more practice, use *Grammar Dimensions 3* Workbook page 125, Exercise 3.

work book

EXPANSION [20 minutes]

You can use Activity 9 (reflection) on SB page 375 after or in place of this exercise. In it, students will use quantifiers to discuss common errors made by people trying to learn English.

LESSON PLAN 2

FOCUS 3 [15 minutes]

This focus draws attention to some plural and singular forms of quantifiers.

1. **Lead-in:** Have students cover the explanation side of the chart in Focus 3. Ask the class if they can state whether each subject is singular or plural in these examples.

2. Put two headings on the board, *Singular* and *Plural*. As you go through the examples in Focus 3, write the highlighted quantifiers in the singular column, the plural column, or both. (Singular = *every, each, no, either, neither,* and *any*. Plural = *all, most, no,* and *both*.)

3. Uncover the explanation side of the chart and go over the information there.

4. Move immediately into Exercise 6 to reinforce the information in Focus 3.

EXERCISE 6 [10 minutes]

Students will need to make changes in agreement as they replace the plural quantifier *all* with singular quantifiers *any, each,* or *every*.

1. Go over the example sentences in Exercise 6 with the class. Ask the class what has been changed in the last two sentences in the example. (*know has been changed to knows*)

2. You can either go over the exercise as a whole class, or have students work in pairs to change the sentences.

3. If students work in pairs, as you circulate around the room, be sure to note any problems in verb-quantifier agreement. See possible answers on LP page 362.

For more practice, use *Grammar Dimensions 3* Workbook page 126, Exercise 5.

work book

EXERCISE 7

Complete these sentences with true information.

1. Each student in this class . . .
2. Every teacher I have had . . .
3. Any English class . . .
4. No student . . .
5. No teachers . . .

EXERCISE 8

Use each of the quantifiers *both*, *either*, and *neither* to make true statements about similarities between each of the following categories.

1. two students in your class
2. two other people that you know
3. you and a good friend

FOCUS 4 Using Quantifiers with *Of*

use

Quantifiers usually refer to nonspecific nouns (nouns that describe how many or how much, rather than identifying a specific item). But you can also use quantifiers with specific noun phrases, by adding *of* to the specific noun phrase. (See Unit 19 for more information and practice with specific and nonspecific reference.)

GENERIC/NONSPECIFIC REFERENCE	SPECIFIC REFERENCE
(a) **Any** TOEFL practice book will give you examples of the questions on the test.	(b) **Any of** the TOEFL practice books that our teacher has recommended will give us test-taking strategies.
(c) **Most** students want to get good grades.	(d) **Most of the** students whom Donna teaches have college degrees.
(e) **Several** teachers have studied overseas.	(f) **Several of the** teachers at this university have studied overseas.

Note that *all* can be used for generic reference and specific with or without *of*.

(g) **All students** hate to take tests.	(h) **All the students** in this class hate tests.
	(i) **All of the students** in this class hate tests.

Note *no* should be used for generic reference and *none of* for specific reference.

(j) **No books** will guarantee a passing score on TOEFL.	(k) **None of the books** that we have studied will guarantee a passing score on TOEFL.

EXERCISE 9

Decide whether to use a *quantifier* or *quantifier + of* for these sentences.

1. (All) ___All___ books and notebooks on your desk must be removed before beginning the examination.
2. (Almost all) ___Almost all___ students are anxious at examination time.
3. (Most) ___Most___ TOEFL practice books contain exercises.
4. You won't need (much) ___much of___ your warm clothing if you go to medical school in the Philippines.
5. (A great deal) ___A great deal of___ the population of China still believes in traditional medicine.
6. (Some) ___Some of___ the information in the report about international students studying overseas was incomplete.
7. Bambang doesn't need (any) ___any of___ my help.
8. Bambang wasted (little) ___little of___ the money his parents gave him for books on frivolous things.
9. The students at the café learned that (no/none) ___no___ classmates failed the test!

ANSWER KEY

Exercise 7 Answers will vary. Possible answers are: 1. is learning about English grammar./is hoping to pass the TOEFL®. 2. has told me to speak as much as possible./has taught me something. 3. will have students of different abilities./is boring. 4. likes homework./wants to fail this class. 5. sleep in class./ignore rude behavior.

Exercise 8 Answers will vary. Possible answers are: 1. Both Abdul and Chen like to study grammar. 2. Neither student has passed the TOEFL® but both of them hope to by the end of the semester. 3. Either my roommate or I will do the dishes before the party.

LESSON PLAN 2 QUANTIFIERS, COLLECTIVE NOUNS, AND COLLECTIVE ADJECTIVES

EXERCISE 7 [10 minutes/homework]

This exercise gives students practice with singular or plural agreement for the quantifiers *each*, *every*, *any*, and *no*. This can be assigned for homework and then gone over as a whole class, listening for any problems with agreement. See possible answers on LP page 364.

EXERCISE 8 [10 minutes/homework]

Students will compare students in the class and then create sentences which use *both*, *either*, or *neither* to describe the comparisons. This can also be assigned as homework. However, it would be good to give students a few minutes in class to look around the classroom and prepare some ideas of comparison.

1. If this is assigned for homework, have students share their sentences in small groups. Students should listen for correct agreement.

2. If this is done in class, you may want to have students work in pairs. See possible answers on LP page 364.

Suggestion: Make this into a contest and give bonus points for the most creative or unexpected comparisons. This will get students creatively thinking beyond the obvious and help eliminate duplicate sentences.

For more practice, use *Grammar Dimensions 3* Workbook page 126, Exercise 6.

FOCUS 4 [15 minutes/homework]

If you have not done Unit 19, it is probably better to skip this focus chart. This chart deals with specific and nonspecific reference. If you are short on time, this focus chart can be skipped or assigned as homework. In that case, go to Exercises 10 and 11 instead.

1. **Lead-in:** Have the class look at examples (a) and (b). Ask the class what identifies the noun in example (b) and makes it specific (*it's the book that our teacher has recommended*). Do the same for the next two pairs of example sentences (in (d) *they are the students whom Donna teaches and in (f) they are the teachers at this university*).

2. Explain that although we usually use quantifiers with nonspecific nouns (e.g., *several students*, *a few students*, *any student*), we can also use them with specific nouns. However, we need to add *of* to the noun phrase after the quantifier.

3. Have the class try a few other quantifiers with specific nouns (e.g., *A few of the students in this class are missing today. None of the missing students have turned in the assignment yet.*).

4. Point out that *no* can not be used with specific nouns and that all can appear with or without *of*.

Suggestion: If you are short on time, skip Focus 4 and Focus 5 or assign them for self-study at home.

EXERCISE 9 [10 minutes]

Students will identify whether a noun is nonspecific or specific based on the context clues in each sentence. They will then use the given quantifier and *of*, if appropriate.

1. Ask the class to consider the noun phrase in the first sentence in Exercise 9. Ask students if the noun is specific or nonspecific? Why? What identifies it as such?

2. Invite a volunteer to suggest the correct form of the quantifier for this sentence. Note that *all* can occur both with and without *of*.

3. Go over any concerns. If students have no questions, have them work individually to complete the exercise.

4. As students compare answers in pairs or as a whole class, be sure to have them note the reasons for each choice. See answers on LP page 364.

For more practice, use *Grammar Dimensions 3* Workbook page 127, Exercise 7.

How many Americans study at medical schools overseas?

6. How many Americans study at medical schools overseas?
7. How many foreign students are enrolled in American medical schools?
8. How many doctors are experts in every area of medicine?

EXERCISE 11

Choose the correct form in these sentences.

1. I feel sorry for Bambang. He's so shy and he has (few/a few/quite a few) friends he can talk to if he has problems.
2. Hardly any people (came/didn't come) to the meeting.
3. Your teacher went to (quite a bit of/a bit of/only a bit of) trouble to get those tickets, so you must remember to thank him.
4. (Not every/Not all/None of) students like to go dancing on Saturday nights.
5. Do you have (many/much/every) time to help me?
6. Sure I do. I've got (a lot/lots of).
7. Why are Bambang and Yanti so sad? (Both/Neither/None) passed the qualifying exam.
8. Learning English takes (several/a certain amount of/any) practice.

FOCUS 6 — Collective Nouns

form

One category of collective nouns refers to groups of people or animals.

EXAMPLES		EXPLANATION
a **troupe** of dancers two **teams** of ball players several **committees** of experts a **delegation** of officials	a **flock** of birds that **herd** of goats **packs** of dogs a **swarm** of insects a **school** of fish	These collective nouns function like other count nouns. You can use them alone or with *of* + *a noun phrase*. They can have both singular or plural forms.

FOCUS 5 — Quantifiers: Special Cases

use

EXAMPLES	EXPLANATIONS
(a) How **much** money do you have? (b) **Not much.** We'd better stop at the bank and get a little. Are there any banks around here?	*Much* is used in questions and negative sentences.
(c) I'm having **a lot of** trouble with finding a school. (d) NOT: I'm having **much** trouble with finding a school.	*A lot (lots) of* is usually preferred in affirmative sentences.
(e) **Much of the financial support** for study in the United States comes from the students themselves.	*Much* is **not** usually used in affirmative statements unless it is a specific reference (used with *of*).
(f) Is it true that **no students** failed the test? (g) That's correct. **None** did.	*No* cannot be used in place of a noun. *None* is used instead.
(h) Did **every student** pass the exam? (i) **Yes, every one** did. (j) NOT: Yes, **every** did.	*Every* cannot be used to replace a noun phrase without using *one*.

EXERCISE 10

Using the information in the article in Exercise 1, answer these questions with complete sentences, using quantifiers in place of noun phrases.

Example: Where are most doctors trained?

Most are trained here in America, but some study medicine overseas.

1. Do all doctors in the United States have to pass qualifying examinations?
2. How much money does it take to get a medical education in the United States?
3. How much competition is there for admission to American medical schools?
4. How many doctors have more than one specialty?
5. How many residency positions do most medical students apply for?

ANSWER KEY

Exercise 10 1. Yes, they do. All have to pass them. 2. It takes quite a bit of money to get a medical education in the United States./ It takes a lot of money to get a medical education in the United States. 3. There's a great deal of competition./ There's quite a bit of competition. 4. A few doctors have more than one specialty. 5. They usually apply for several residency positions./ They usually apply for a few residency positions. 6. Quite a few Americans study overseas./ Many Americans study overseas. 7. Some foreign students are enrolled in the United States, but not many. 8. No doctor is an expert in every area of medicine.

LESSON PLAN 2/3

FOCUS 5 [15 minutes/homework]

This focus covers special cases. If you are short on time, this focus chart, like Focus 4, can be skipped or assigned as homework. Then go onto Exercises 10 and 11.

1. **Lead-in:** For an inductive approach, write the following sentences on the board:

   How much time do we have?
   We don't have much time.
   We have much time.
   We have a lot of time.

2. Ask the class which of these sentences sounds awkward. (*the third sentence*) Then invite the class to suggest a few rules about the use of *much*.

3. Write the following four sentences on the board, and do the same for the use of *no* and *every*. Ask students which sound awkward (*the second and fourth sentences*) and if they can suggest a rule to explain this:

   It says that no cars are allowed in the garage at night.
   That's correct. No are.
   Did every car leave the garage already?
   Yes, every did.

4. Go over the examples and explanations in Focus 5.

EXERCISE 10 [10 minutes/homework]

Students will review a variety of quantifiers by answering questions in complete sentences.

1. Refer the class back to the article in Exercise 1 about doctor training.

2. Have students work individually (for homework) to create complete answers, which should include quantifiers (as suggested in each question).

3. Because this is a review of several points, it is best to finish with a class review. See answers on LP page 366.

EXERCISE 11 [15 minutes]

After students have worked individually to make their choices, have them compare answers with a partner or in small groups, be sure to go over the answers as a class. See answers on LP page 366.

 For more practice, use *Grammar Dimensions 3* Workbook page 127, Exercise 8.

LESSON PLAN 3

FOCUS 6 [20 minutes]

As this is a change in topic from quantifiers, you may want to begin the remaining portion of the unit on a new day. Students will review collective nouns and the issues of subject-verb agreement that can be confusing for some collective nouns.

1. **Lead-in:** If you are able, put together a sheet with pictures of animals and people in groups such as a group of kids, a troupe of dancers, a herd of cows, and a swarm of bees). Pass the pictures out to pairs and ask them to decide on a collective term for each picture. You can give them help by putting a few collective group terms on the board and have them match these up with a picture.

2. Turn to the first portion of Focus 6 on SB page 367 and go over the examples. Note that it is possible to have more than one collective group (i.e., *several committees* or *two teams of players*). Therefore, collective nouns can be singular or plural.

3. Contrast this first category of collective nouns with the second category (social and political groups) in the chart at the top of SB page 368. These nouns always occur in the singular form and require *the*.

4. The chart in the middle of SB page 368 shows that as collective nouns they can take either singular or plural agreement. However, the singular is favored in American English.

5. Finally, point out the importance of the agreement of pronouns once a collective noun is determined to be singular or plural as shown in examples (a–i) on SB page 368.

Suggestion: Prepare the class for Exercises 12 and 13 and show the class how collective nouns can be chosen by the writer to reflect a cohesive group (with singular agreement and pronouns) or reflect a group acting individually (with plural agreement and pronouns). Put the following sentences on the board and have the class choose singular or plural agreement to show whether the group is acting cohesively or individually.

The jury is/are fighting among itself/themselves on this issue.

The jury has/have come to a conclusion. It/They will return soon.

The media is/are waiting quietly outside the building.

The media is/are pushing each other as it tries/they try to interview the movie star.

EXPANSION 1 [20 minutes]

You could assign Activity 1 (speaking) on SB page 372 as an expansion of Focus 6. This is a fun activity based on the presentation of collective nouns.

EXPANSION 2 [30 minutes/homework]

You may want to assign Activity 8 (research on the web) on SB page 375, after presenting this focus on collective nouns.

A second kind of collective nouns refers to social or political categories.

EXAMPLES

the government
the middle class
the media
the opposition
the arts community

the administration
the aristocracy
the public
the establishment

EXPLANATION

They always occur with *the*. Their grammatical form is singular:
NOT: a public, a media
NOT: the publics of the United States

Although the form of this kind of collective noun is singular, it can be used with either singular or plural verbs and pronouns.

SINGULAR

Using singular verbs and pronouns implies that the group operates as a whole. American English tends to use singular forms with singular collective nouns.

(a) The committee of experts **has** decided to release **its** findings next week.

(c) The aristocracy **has** opposed any challenge to **its** economic privileges.

(e) **The middle class in America has** begun to protest the accelerating decline in **its** standard of living.

PLURAL

Using plural verbs and pronouns focuses on the individual behavior of the members of the group. British English tends to use plural forms with singular collective nouns.

(b) The committee of experts **have** decided to release **their** findings next week.

(d) The aristocracy **have** opposed any challenge to **their** economic privileges.

(f) **The middle class in America have** begun to protest the accelerating decline in **their** standard of living.

EXAMPLES

(g) The beginning class **likes its** teachers to give **it** lots of homework.

(h) The beginning class **like their** teachers to give **them** lots of homework.

(i) NOT: The beginning class **like their** teachers to give **them** lots of homework.

EXPLANATION

Although either singular or plural can be used, it is bad style to change from singular to plural within a single sentence or single reference.

EXERCISE 12

In the following sentences, underline each collective noun and any pronouns and verbs which refer to it. Decide why the author chose to consider the collective noun singular or plural.

Example: The French Revolution was caused in part by the refusal of the aristocracy to give up its social privileges.

Reason: Reference to a single social class—not a collection of individuals.

1. The victorious team all waved to their supporters while the crowd roared its approval.

2. The media is aware of the important role it plays in American presidential elections.

3. The herd of sheep bleated nervously to its shepherd as a pack of wolves made their way through the forest.

4. The military continues to fight further reductions in its funding.

5. The middle class is facing a greater tax burden than it has ever faced before.

6. A rash of new developments have made a great change in the government's priorities, and it is just beginning to respond to them.

EXERCISE 13

Decide whether the collective nouns in these sentences should be used with singular or plural verbs and pronouns, and choose the correct form. Although both choices may be grammatically correct, there may be a clear preference for one form instead of the other, so be prepared to explain why you have chosen the forms you did.

1. The staff took a vote about what kind of holiday party (it/they) (want/wants). (It/They) decided to rent a hall and hire a band.

2. The college administration (want/wants) a basketball team that (is/are) able to win enough games to place (itself/themselves) in the final play-offs.

3. The rowing team raised (its/their) oars as (its/their) boat crossed the finish line.

4. The advanced grammar class never like to turn in (its/their) homework right after a long vacation. (It/They) prefer(s) to finish all assignments before (it/they) leave(s) for vacation.

5. The crowd showed (its/their) approval by letting out a deafening roar.

6. The opposition voiced (its/their) disapproval of the policies the government had released in (its/their) latest report, by making more than three dozen speeches in Parliament.

ANSWER KEY

Exercise 12 The reasons for the number of the collective noun, as underlined above, are as follows: 1. Team members wave in different ways; the crowd behaved as a single entity. 2. an abstract single entity. 3. The sheep behaved more as a group, and the wolves behaved as individuals. 4. focus on whole group, not on individual members of the group 5. an abstract single entity 6. The author wants to keep the pronoun reference clear: developments—plural; government—single.

Exercise 13 Explanations for the choices circled above are as follows: 1. Singular sounds very British. 2. The team and the administration are each a single entity. 3. Oars in plural implies that we will talk about the members of the team, since each one has an oar. 4. It might be preferable for the first sentence, since it's the advanced grammar class, rather then Students in the advanced grammar class. However, the following sentences seem more natural with plural forms. 5. Both are possible. 6. By making government plural, pronoun reference is clearer.

EXERCISE 12 [10 minutes]

Students will identify collective nouns and the agreement and pronouns used in reference to these nouns. This can be done in pairs or as a whole-class exercise. It is best to do some form of whole-class discussion in order to allow time for questions and address points of confusion.

1. Go over the example as a class. Have students note the singular possessive pronoun and discuss the reason for the use of the singular in this example.

2. If students are having trouble with these, put the second sentence on the board and ask the class to find the collective noun and any pronouns or verbs that refer to it.

3. Invite a discussion of the reasons for these choices (possible reason: the team members waved in different ways to different directions and to different fans whereas the crowd roared as one). Refer students back to the general guidelines presented in Focus 6.

4. Go over the remainder of the exercise in a similar manner or have pairs of students discuss possible reasons the author made these choices. See answers on LP page 368.

Suggestion: Copy this and the following exercise on an overhead transparency for easier review.

For more practice, use *Grammar Dimensions 3* Workbook page 128, Exercise 9.

EXERCISE 13 [10 minutes]

Based on the context of each sentence, students will decide whether to use singular or plural verbs and pronouns for these collective nouns.

1. Assign this for individual or pair work. Be sure to encourage discussion if students are working in pairs or have students write down their explanations if working alone.

2. Give class time for a class review and allow for alternative answers. However, be sure that students support their answers with a reason. Ask the class which answers seem to fit better and why they feel that way. See answers on LP page 368.

For more practice, use *Grammar Dimensions 3* Workbook page 128, Exercise 10 and page 129, Exercise 11.

EXPANSION [20 minutes]

Use Activity 2 (speaking/writing) on SB page 372 to follow the work done in Exercises 12 and 13.

FOCUS 7   Collective Adjectives

form   meaning

EXAMPLES

(a) **The rich** get richer and **the poor** get poorer.

(b) These laws are designed to protect **the young** and **the helpless** from exploitation.

(c) **The elderly** are making **their** opinions a growing force in American politics.

EXPLANATION

The + adjective can be used to refer to a group that is defined by a particular characteristic. These structures are plural, and the verbs and pronouns reflect this.

EXERCISE 14

Rewrite each *the* + adjective construction below as a noun + relative clause.

Example: The French aristocracy didn't care about the poor.

the poor = people who were poor:

1. A few years ago, Britney Spears was very popular with the young.

2. Dear Abby writes an advice column in the newspaper for the lonely and the confused.

3. Nelson Mandela is an important hero for the oppressed.

4. Bambang and Yanti became doctors so they could help the sick.

5. The government should establish more comprehensive programs to help the underprivileged.

EXERCISE 15

Are these sentences correct or incorrect? If they are incorrect, identify the problem and correct it.

1. None of doctors are allowed to practice without a license.

2. I watched the flock of birds as it landed in the field across the road.

3. Few students never pass their qualifying exams.

4. The rich is always trying to avoid giving its money to pay taxes.

5. Quite a bit of time that doctors spend in their residencies is clinical training.

6. Students usually apply to several of universities for admission.

7. The herd of sheep was frightened by a pack of wolves, and it bleated nervously in their pen.

8. We had much trouble with the examination this morning.

9. A great many of traditional medicines are still used in rural areas.

EXERCISE 16

Circle the correct form of the underlined phrases below.

The Problem of Homelessness in America

(1) The homeless are/is an increasing problem in most American cities. (2) The homeless consist/consists of several different categories of people. (3) The first category consist/consists of the mentally disabled. (4) In the early 1980s the Reagan administration ended most of its/their funding for treatment programs for the mentally ill. (5) As a result, quite a few mental hospitals were released, and left to make its/their own way. (6) A substantial number have/has been unable to establish normal lives, and, as a result, it/they has/have ended up living on the streets.

(7) A second category of the homeless is/are the unemployed. (8) Typically, the unemployed is/are part of the homeless for a relatively short period of time—usually less than a year. (9) Some of it/them have/has lost its/their jobs; or the factories where it/they worked were closed without warning. (10) As a result, it/they didn't have enough money to pay rent. (11) Many of the unemployed has/have also ended up living on the streets or sleeping in its/their automobiles. (12) But the majority of the people in this category of the homeless is/are able to find housing again, once they have found other jobs.

(13) A third category of the homeless is/are the people who is/are addicted to drugs or alcohol. (14) Like the mentally ill, this category of homelessness represent/represents a persistent social problem. (15) The unemployed can hope for better times, and is/are usually able to escape from poverty and life on the streets, but the government has/have been very slow in giving its/their support to programs that help the mentally disabled or the addicted work on its/their recovery.

ANSWER KEY

Exercise 14   1. the young—people who were young   2. the lonely and confused—people who are lonely and confused   3. the oppressed—people who are oppressed   4. the sick—people who are sick   5. the underprivileged—people who are underprivileged

Exercise 15   1. No doctor is allowed to practice without a license.   2. Correct   3. Correct, but awkward: Most students pass their qualifying exams.   4. The rich are always trying to avoid giving their money to pay taxes.   5. Correct   6. Students usually apply to several universities for admission.   7. The herd of sheep was frightened by a pack of wolves, and they bleated nervously in their pen.   8. We had a lot of trouble with the examination this morning.   9. A great many traditional medicines are still used in rural areas.

UNIT 22 LESSON PLAN 3 QUANTIFIERS, COLLECTIVE NOUNS, AND COLLECTIVE ADJECTIVES

FOCUS 7 [10 minutes]

This focus chart gives examples of another type of collective group: collective adjectives (*the* + adjective), which represent a group defined by that adjective.

1. **Lead-in:** Put a few examples on the board. Some suggestions are:

   The school is collecting food donations for the hungry in our town.

   The rich are always looking for new tax credits.

   There is a special children's event for the disabled who are interested in sports.

   The deaf are becoming more active in the community.

   The ranchers herded the sheep along, but the young were too slow.

2. Point out the collective adjectives and their form. Explain that these work like collective nouns, and they describe groups of people (or animals) defined by the adjective. However, they are always considered plural.

3. Go over the examples in Focus 7 and follow up immediately with Exercise 14.

EXERCISE 14 [15 minutes]

Students will rewrite each collective adjective as a noun + relative clause to show the underlying meaning of each.

1. Refer back to the underlined collective adjectives in the examples on the board from the Lead-in in Focus 7. Ask the class what *the hungry* stands for. (*people who are hungry*)

2. Ask the same question for each of the examples written on the board ((2) *people who are rich,* (3) *children who are disabled,* (4) *people who are deaf,* (5) *sheep that are young*).

3. Go over the example and then do the exercise as a whole class. See answers on LP page 370.

For more practice, use *Grammar Dimensions 3 Workbook* page 129, Exercise 12.

EXPANSION 1 [20 minutes]

Ask pairs to discuss the following questions and then write complete answers to share:

   What do you think should be done to help the homeless?
   What do you think should be done to help the unemployed?
   What do you think should be done to help the elderly?

Have pairs present their suggestions to the class. This can be developed into a simple survey to do outside the class or even developed into a research project.

EXPANSION 2 [20 minutes]

Use Activity 3 (speaking) on SB page 373 as group work to follow the work done in Focus 7 and Exercise 14.

EXERCISE 15 and 16 [25 minutes/homework]

Exercise 15 and 16 are whole unit reviews.

1. Assign these as homework, use them as an in-class quiz, or simply use them for additional practice and review as pairs share and discuss their answers together.

2. Be sure to give time for a whole class review and allow for questions. See answers on LP page 370.

   Suggestion: Copy these onto an overhead transparency to make the review easier.

UNIT GOAL REVIEW [10 minutes]

Ask students to look at the goals on the opening page of the unit again. Refer to the pages of the unit where information on each goal can be found.

For a grammar quiz review of Units 21 and 22, refer students to pages 130–131 in the *Grammar Dimension 3* Workbook.

For assessment of Unit 22, use *Grammar Dimensions 3 ExamView®*.

Use Your English

ACTIVITY 1 speaking

English used to have many different collective nouns to refer to specific animals. These nouns usually indicated a quality or characteristic that these animals had: a *pride* of lions (because lions are proud), a *parliament* of owls (because owls are wise), a *leap* of leopards (because leopards leap).

Such collective words are rarely used in modern English. But sometimes for humorous reasons, people will invent collective words to apply to a particular group of people. Here are some examples: a sweep of cleaning ladies, a hustle of salesmen, a splash of swimmers.

Working with a partner, decide on some humorous collective terms for some of these categories of people:

flight attendants	English teachers	puppies/kittens	accountants
lawyers	magicians	computer programmers	real estate agents

ACTIVITY 2 speaking/writing

There is a joke that says, "A camel is a horse that was designed by a committee." Some management experts think that committees generate a product that is better than one made by a single individual. Others feel that committees tend to be inefficient and badly organized.

Based on your experience, identify the strengths and weaknesses of working in a committee. What are the advantages (Pro) of having a group work together on a single task? What are the disadvantages (Con)?

Example: Pro: *A committee is able to assign tasks to each member, so the work can be divided.*

> **Con:** *A committee doesn't reach decisions quickly because each member has to agree about the issue before they can take action.*

First decide how you are going to do this activity. By yourself or in a group? Then decide on at least three advantages and disadvantages and present your ideas to the rest of the class as a list of pros and cons.

ACTIVITY 3 speaking

Should the rich pay more taxes or higher penalties (for traffic tickets, etc.) than the poor? Why do you think so? Discuss your ideas in a small group, and present a report on your group's opinion to the rest of the class. Your report should use phrases like "Our group feels that . . ."

ACTIVITY 4 writing/speaking

Have you ever seen a political demonstration? Where and when did it occur? What was the demonstration about? What did the crowd do? What did the police do? Write a description of what happened.

ACTIVITY 5 speaking

■ STEP 1   Conduct a poll of your classmates to find out about their educational backgrounds. How many years of school do they have? What subjects have they studied? Did most of them enjoy school? Decide on two more questions to ask them.

■ STEP 2   Present your information by constructing pie charts similar to the ones in the Opening Task of this unit.

ACTIVITY 6 listening/writing

Conduct a public opinion poll on some aspect of current events.

■ STEP 1   In a group, choose some topic of current interest from the news, and develop a list of five to eight questions to determine how people feel about this issue.

(Continued on next page)

The Use Your English activities at the end of the unit contain situations that should naturally elicit the structures covered in the unit. For a more complete discussion of how to use the Use Your English Activities see To the Teacher on LP page xxii. When students are doing these activities in class, you can circulate and listen to see if they are using the structures accurately. Errors can be corrected when the activity is finished.

ACTIVITY 1
speaking
[20 minutes]

You may wish to assign Activity 1 after coverage of Focus 6 on SB pages 367–368.

1. Go over the directions with the class and put a few of the examples of collective animal groups on the board.

2. You may want to ask the class how many other collective nouns for other animal groups they know, such as a flock of birds, herd of cows, school of fish, or army of ants (check the Internet for some fun sites filled with these collective nouns). Put these on the board as well to help generate ideas.

3. Now go over the silly examples in Activity 1 and then ask the class to work in pairs to create their own humorous or creative collective terms for the listed groups.

Suggestion: If you have time, write the groups across the board. Then during your class review, as pairs share their ideas, write the suggested collective terms next to the groups they describe on the board.

ACTIVITY 2
speaking/writing
[20 minutes]

Assign this activity after Exercise 13 on SB page 369.

1. Begin by asking the class about the joke about the camel. Does anyone think that a camel is a poorly

designed animal? Does anyone feel that a camel is well designed? If your students are divided in their answers, then this illustrates the point of the joke. If your class is not divided then you may have to play "devil's advocate."

2. Explain to the class that they will need to list three strengths (pros) and three weaknesses (cons) to working on a project as a committee.

3. Students must first decide whether they would like to work alone or in a group on this activity. When finished, have them present their results to the class (in groups or individually).

Suggestion: You may want to summarize this activity by asking the class which side seemed to have a stronger argument: the pro arguments or the con arguments?

ACTIVITY 3
speaking
[20 minutes]

You may wish to assign this activity as an expansion of Exercise 14 on SB page 370.

1. Put students into small groups and encourage them to discuss the basic questions: *Should the rich pay more taxes? Should the rich pay higher penalties?* Groups should present some opinions from their discussion. They do not need to agree and can simply state, "Some people in our group feel that . . ."

3. Note any problems with collective noun agreement to go over when the presentations are finished.

ACTIVITY 4
writing/speaking
[homework]

This activity asks students to use collective nouns as they write about their experience with a political demonstration. If your students have no experience in this, you can either skip this exercise or remind students of the research they did in Unit 2 (SB page 26,

Activity 6) on "protesters" and have them write about this. The picture on SB page 12 can help remind them.

ACTIVITY 5
speaking
[30 minutes]

You could assign this activity after Focus 1 on SB page 358.

■ **STEP 1**   Have pairs create a survey sheet using the first three questions from Step 1 in the book along with two more they create on their own.

■ **STEP 2**   After polling their classmates, have pairs summarize their results in a pie chart and present their findings to the class.

Suggestion: Have the pairs also make general statements about their results in writing (without using percentages, fractions or numbers), so as to give more practice in using quantifiers.

ACTIVITY 6
listening/writing
[30 minutes/homework]

You could also assign Activity 6 after covering Focus 1 on SB page 358. This activity should be done over two days of class. On the first day, groups will create their surveys and poll the class. They will interview people outside of class either as homework or during class time and then in the following class, they will prepare their results and make a presentation. If you find you are short on time, you may wish to omit Step 5, the written report, from this activity.

■ **STEP 1**   Put students into small groups and ask them to choose a topic and develop five to eight questions to put on their survey. Each student should create a survey sheet.

Activity 6 directions are continued on LP page 375.

STEP 2 Poll your classmates, and also interview ten to fifteen people outside of class.

STEP 3 Devise a graphic representation of your results similar to the charts in the Opening Task of this unit.

STEP 4 Using your charts, make a presentation of your findings to the rest of the class. Report any interesting differences between the opinions of your classmates and the people you interviewed outside of class.

STEP 5 Make a short written report of your findings with your group. Have some members check the information and have others check the grammar.

ACTIVITY 7 listening

CD Tracks 33, 34, 35

STEP 1 Listen to the brief news reports and answer the following questions. You may need to listen to each report more than once.

Report 1

1. What happens every year on March 19th?

2. Who provides publicity about this event?

3. Who else arrives on March 19th besides the swallows?

Report 2

1. What did the Canadian government ask the committee to do?

2. What is being anxiously awaited by the press and the public?

Report 3

1. What is different about the theater company described in this report?

2. When was it founded?

3. What effect has the company had?

STEP 2 Compare your answers with a classmate's.

ACTIVITY 8 research on the web

Option A: Go to the Internet and find the home pages for several teams of a sport that you are interested in. It could be soccer, American football, baseball, hockey, or basketball, for example. Prepare a brief written or oral report that discusses the sport you have chosen. What are the strengths and weaknesses that most teams have in common? Which ones have a better chance of winning and why? What characteristics make some teams better than others?

Option B: Go on the Internet and find the home pages for several famous performing troupes or groups (for example, opera, drama, circus, dance, or orchestra). Prepare a brief written or oral report that identifies what characteristic(s) these troupes have in common that make them famous, and if you feel that reputation is justified.

ACTIVITY 9 reflection

Work with one or two other students and make a list of common errors that you hear learners of English making in their conversations. Try to identify some mistakes that all students make, and then mention other English language problems that many students might have trouble with, as well as problems that some have but others might not have trouble with. What is one feature of the English language that none of your classmates find difficult? Prepare a brief written or oral presentation about "The Troublespots of English" using both affirmative and negative quantifiers.

ANSWER KEY

Activity 7 Answers may vary slightly. **Report 1:** 1. A large flock of swallows returns to San Juan Capistrano Mission in southern California. 2. The city government in San Jan Capistrano provides publicity. 3. Flocks of tourists arrive at the Mission as well on March 19th. **Report 2:** 1. The Canadian government asked the committee to look into the effects of acid rain on the forests of North America. 2. The release of the committee's report is being anxiously awaited.

Report 3: 1. Most of the company cannot hear, and many members can only "speak" by using sign language. 2. It was founded nearly 30 years ago. 3. The troupe has played an important role in involving the disabled in the arts.

Activity 6 directions are continued from LP page 373.

■ STEP 2

1. Divide the class up into small groups with one member from the original group represented in each new group. Have these new groups poll the group members.
2. Assign the out-of-class portion of the poll as homework.

■ STEP 3 Students should now individually prepare a graphic to represent their findings.

■ STEP 4 Have students present their findings and charts to the class. Give time at the end of presentations for the class to discuss any interesting differences between surveys, findings, or charts.

■ STEP 5 Ask students to write a written report together with their original groups.

ACTIVITY 7 listening
[15 minutes]

CD Tracks 33, 34, 35

Students will listen to three news reports that use a variety of collective nouns and collective adjectives. Students will need to understand and use these as Students they respond to the comprehension questions.

■ STEP 1

1. Use your usual methods for using audio, and replay the recording as many times as necessary.
2. For classes who have more difficulty with the listening tasks, avoid problems with vocabulary by going over the questions before playing the audio. Be sure students understand the vocabulary used in the questions.

make in English. The presentation of a summary of this discussion will require the use of affirmative and negative quantifiers.

1. Have students work in pairs or small groups.
2. Groups will end up with three lists at the end of this discussion. You can get them organized by putting the three headings on the board: *Common Mistakes, Less Common Mistakes,* and *Very Rare Mistakes.*
3. Groups should make up their lists and then prepare to present their information to the class using both affirmative and negative quantifiers.
4. Listen for the correct usage of these quantifiers and note any problems to review with the class later.

■ STEP 2

1. Have students compare answers with a partner. You may need to play the recording one more time if students are having trouble or disagree.
2. Review answers with the class. See answers on LP page 374.

ACTIVITY 8 research on the web
[30 minutes/homework]

Use after Focus 6 on SB pages 367–368. Students will research either sports teams or performance groups and give a written or oral report. They will be reading about and using collective nouns in their research and presentation.

1. Have the class read the two assignment choices and decide which they would like to do.
2. To encourage brainstorming, you might have the class get into groups according to the option they have chosen and work with the group to create a list of possible teams or performance groups to research. Each student should leave the class with his/her own list of possible teams/groups to research.
3. Give the guidelines for the final report (written or oral).

Suggestion: If students are giving oral reports to the class, you can help engage the rest of the class by asking them to take notes on the main ideas of each report. This will involve listening for the collective nouns.

ACTIVITY 9 reflection
[20 minutes]

You may wish to assign this activity after Exercise 5 on SB page 362. Students will identify and discuss common, and not so common, errors that students

UNIT GOALS

- Use correct sequence of tenses in past time to indicate time relationships

- Correctly understand and use clauses with *when* and *while* in past time

- Correctly understand and use progressive and perfect aspect in past time

OPENING TASK

I'll Never Forget . . .

Everyone has had an unforgettable moment of one kind or another. Write a paragraph or tell a partner about a moment that you will never forget. You can tell about a time when you heard about or experienced an important world event or something more personal in your own life.

Examples:

- *I will never forget the moment I heard the newscast about the Berlin Wall being torn down.*

- *I will never forget the day my wife told me that I was going to become a father.*

- *I will never forget the day my father told me that my family wanted me to go overseas for my university education.*

Your description should include what you were doing at the time, what you had been doing, and how you reacted. You may want to read the example on the next page to help you organize your ideas.

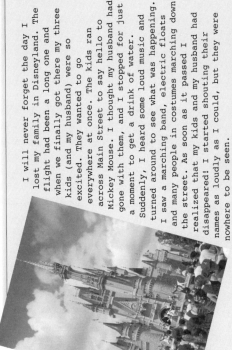

I will never forget the day I lost my family in Disneyland. The flight had been a long one and when we finally got there my three kids (and my husband) were so excited. They wanted to go everywhere at once. The kids ran across Main Street to say hello to Mickey Mouse. I thought my husband had gone with them, and I stopped for just a moment to get a drink of water.

Suddenly, I heard some loud music and turned around to see what was happening. I saw a marching band, electric floats and many people in costumes marching down the street. As soon as it passed I realized that my kids and my husband had disappeared! I started shouting their names as loudly as I could, but they were nowhere to be seen.

I knew I had to go find my family. I tried to catch up with the parade as quickly as possible. This wasn't easy, because the street was really crowded. I asked one of the cartoon characters if there was a lost children office. He told me where to go and when I got there, I saw several children but not my family. After several minutes, I heard my husband's voice calling my name. Our daughters were with him, but not our son. We finally found him watching a clown show by the Magic Castle. He hadn't even noticed the rest of us weren't with him. Now that we were finally back together, I made all of them promise to stay together, and for a little while the kids were keeping as close to me as they could, but they soon began to run around again. That's the last time I'm taking them to Disneyland until I can tie them together with a piece of rope!

UNIT 23

LESSON PLAN 1

UNIT OVERVIEW

Unit 23 reviews the use of sequence, adverbial clauses/phrases, and aspect in the expression of past time.

GRAMMAR NOTE

Non-native English speakers tend to overly rely on verb tense to express time rather than using sequence, adverbials, or aspect. Students, therefore, may need to be reminded of these other ways to indicate past time. This unit reviews some of the information introduced in Unit 2, concerning the meaning differences communicated by aspect and may work well as a review lesson or follow-up to Unit 2. Use the Opening Task as a written diagnostic with which to shape your choices for presenting the unit further. For advanced classes, it may not need to be presented in its entirety, but only as a response to student errors or questions. If so, choose and present only the focus charts that you feel are important for your particular class.

UNIT GOALS

Some instructors may want to review the goals listed on Student Book (SB) page 376 after completing the Opening Task so that students understand what they should know by the end of the unit. These goals can also be reviewed at the end of the unit when students are more familiar with the grammar terminology.

OPENING TASK [20 minutes]

Because this unit is generally a review, this task can be used as a written diagnostic. The aim of this activity is to give students the opportunity to use a variety of structures which express time in the past: time before the experience, time during the experience, and the time of the experience. The problem-solving format is designed to show the teacher how well the students can produce a target structure implicitly

and spontaneously when they are engaged in a communicative task. For a more complete discussion of the purpose of the Opening Task, see To the Teacher, Lesson Planner (LP) page xxii.

Setting Up the Task

1. Begin by asking the class to think of an experience in their lives that they will never forget. Go over the examples on SB page 376.
2. Put students into small groups or pairs and let them talk about an unforgettable experience or two. Encourage them to describe what led up to the experience, what they were doing when it happened, and how they reacted (see the instructions below the examples).
3. Circulate and note how comfortable students are using a variety of forms to express time in the past. Do not correct errors at this point.

Conducting the Task

The written portion of the task can be assigned as homework. Be sure that students read the example essay on SB page 377 (this can be done in class or at home).

Closing the Task

1. Collect papers or have students share their stories in small groups.
2. Review the essays and note the use of forms to express past time. You can use this information as you decide how much time to spend on the topics for the following focus charts.

GRAMMAR NOTE

Typical student errors (form)

Most of the errors mentioned in Unit 1 and 2 related to aspect and time are still pertinent here.

- Using adverbials in the same sentence as perfect aspect: * *Before we turned on the light, we had known it would be a mess.* (See Focus 4.)
- Using progressive aspect with stative verbs: * *People were believing that the earth was flat.*

Typical student errors (use)

- Using *when* and *while* interchangeably with simple past tense to represent the same time sequence: *When the phone rang, Jeff jumped.* ≠ *While the phone rang, Jeff was jumping. When the phone rang, Jeff jumped. When the phone rang, Jeff was jumping.* (See Focus 2.)
- Overuse of simple aspect: * *After the accident, Jeff tried to call, but the telephones stopped working.*

FOCUS 1

Overview of Time Relationships in Past Time Frame

use

EXAMPLES	EXPLANATIONS
(a) He walked up the stairs. He turned the knob, and opened the door.	Time relationships in past time can be indicated by: • sequence Things happened in the order they are mentioned.
(b) As he entered the room, he realized something was different. Before he had a chance to turn around, he knew something was missing. In a moment, he realized what it was.	• adverbial information Adverbial clauses and phrases describe the order in which things happened.
(c) The television had disappeared. The antenna wires were hanging from the wall. He had been watching TV a few hours ago, but now there was nothing there.	• perfect and progressive aspect Choice of a particular verb tense and aspect describes the order in which things happened.

EXERCISE 1

Work with a partner to examine how time relationships are indicated in these passages. Passage 1 has been done for you as an example.

STEP 1 List the highlighted verbs in the order that they occurred.

STEP 2 Tell how you think that the order was indicated (by sequence, adverbials, or using perfect or progressive verb tenses). Sometimes there is more than one indication. Passage 1 has been done for you on the next page as an example.

Passage 1

I'll never forget the day my apartment got broken into. As I **entered** the room, I **realized** something was different. Before I **had** a chance to turn around, I **knew** something was missing. In a moment, I **realized** what it was. The television **had disappeared**. The antenna wires **were hanging** from the wall. I **had been watching** TV a few hours ago, but now there **was** nothing there.

STEP 1 WHAT IS THE SEQUENCE OF EVENTS?	STEP 2 HOW IS THE ORDER OF EVENTS INDICATED?
1. I had been watching TV	1. perfect progressive; adverbial (a few hours ago) aspect
2. the TV had disappeared	2. perfect aspect
3. the wires were hanging from the wall	3. progressive aspect
4. there was nothing there	4. adverbial (now)
5. I entered the room	5. sequence aspect
6. I realized something was different	6. sequence aspect
7. I knew something was missing	7. sequence aspect
8. I had a chance to turn around	8. adverbial (before) aspect
9. I realized what it was	9. sequence, adverbial (in a moment) aspect

Passage 2

Jeff will never forget the time the earthquake hit San Francisco. He **was** still in his office. He **had been trying** to finish a project before he left for the day. Suddenly, the building **began** to move. Books **fell** off their shelves. People **were screaming**. Although it seemed as if things were moving for several minutes, the actual time was just fifteen seconds. Even before the building **stopped moving**, people were trying to get out as quickly as possible. This wasn't easy for people who **had been working** on the higher floors of the building. The electricity **had gone off** the moment the earthquake struck, so no elevators **were working**. Most people **ran** down emergency stairs in darkness and **got** out to the street.

Passage 3

Detective Smith will never forget the day he made the announcement of his first big arrest. Last Tuesday, he **reported** that he **had uncovered** a large amount of stolen property from a warehouse in the southern part of the city. The warehouse **had been** under surveillance for some time. A suspiciously large number of people **had been seen** going in and out of the building. Once Detective Smith **had obtained** a search warrant, he **entered** the warehouse in the middle of the night and **discovered** large amounts of electronic equipment and other supplies. He **announced** that this discovery **may lead** to the solution of a number of robberies.

Exercise 1 Steps 1 and 2, Passage 1 and 2, Passage 2: 1. people who had been working on the higher floors; perfect progressive 2. he had been trying to finish a project; perfect progressive 3. he was still in his office; sequence aspect, adverbial (suddenly) 4. the building began to move; sequence aspect, adverbial (suddenly) 5. the electricity had gone off; perfect aspect 6. books fell off their shelves; sequence aspect 7. people were screaming; progressive aspect 8. people were trying to get out; progressive aspect 9. the building stopped moving; adverbial (before) 10. no elevators were working; progressive aspect 11. most people ran down emergency stairs and got out; sequence aspect

Passage 3: 1. he reported that he had uncovered; sequence aspect 2. the warehouse had been under surveillance; sequence aspect, adverbial (for some time) 3. a suspiciously large number of people had been seen; sequence aspect 4. Detective Smith had obtained a search warrant; sequence aspect, adverbial (once) 5. he entered the warehouse in the middle of the night; sequence aspect 6. (he) discovered large amounts of electronic equipment and other supplies; sequence aspect 7. they had uncovered a large amount of stolen property; perfect aspect 8. police reported yesterday; adverbial (yesterday) 9. police announced that this discovery . . . ; sequence aspect 10. this discovery may lead to the solution of a number of robberies; future time

FOCUS 1 [15 minutes]

This focus is a good review of ways to indicate time relationships other than tense. Since this information is review, it may be best to present it in a straightforward manner.

1. **Lead-in:** Have the class look at the example sentences in Focus 1 and begin a class discussion by asking questions about the first two sentences. What tells us about the order in which these things happened? What tells us about the order things happened in example (c)?

   Have students identify the specific structures that provide the information about sequence (highlighted in the student texts).

2. Put the class into groups and assign each group to be responsible for explaining one area of the focus chart (*sequence, adverbial information,* and *perfect and progressive aspect*) to the class.

3. The groups should also turn to the essay in the Opening Task on SB page 377 and find examples in the essay which illustrate their area of the focus chart and use these as examples to support their explanation of ways to indicate past time.

4. Invite groups to share the information and examples they found for their area.

5. If possible, make a copy of the essay on page 377 on an overhead transparency and underline sentences as groups share their examples.

Suggestion: If students have completed their own essays, have them find examples in their own writing to share with their group.

EXERCISE 1 [20 minutes]

Students will identify the time relationship between the verbs used in each passage and then list them in order of time. They will then describe how the time relationship was indicated (sequence, adverbial information, or aspect) for each verb.

■ STEP 1

1. Go over Passage 1 with the whole class. You may want to draw a horizontal time line across the board and list the verbs in the time sequence they occurred as you go over the passage.

2. Now have the class work individually to list the order of events of the highlighted verbs in Passage 2 and Passage 3. They should list these events on paper, similar to the example.

■ STEP 2

1. Next, ask the class to decide how each time event was indicated. Which of the ways outlined in Focus 1 was used to indicate past time? Write these (*sequence, adverbials, perfect tense,* and *progressive tense*) below each point across the time line you created on the board for Passage 1. Be sure to point out that some verbs have more than one indication.

2. Have students return to their own lists from Passages 2 and 3 and state how the order was indicated for each verb they have down.

3. If you are short on time, put the class into groups and have some groups work on Passage 2 while others work on Passage 3. See answers on LP page 378.

For more practice, use *Grammar Dimensions 3* Workbook page 132, Exercise 1.

EXPANSION [15 minutes]

Use Activity 5 (reflection) on SB page 389 to follow the work in sequencing done in Exercise 5. Students will read their partner's stories from the Opening Task and construct a timeline.

FOCUS 2

When, While, and Progressive Aspect in Past Time

use

Using *when*

EXAMPLES	TIME SEQUENCE	EXPLANATIONS
(a) When the books fell off the shelf, Jeff hid under his desk.	First the books fell off the shelf; then Jeff hid under his desk.	If you use *when* to connect two clauses with simple past tense verbs, the action described in the *when*-clause happened before the action in the main clause.
(b) When the books fell off the shelf, Jeff **was hiding** under his desk.	First Jeff hid under his desk; then the books fell off the shelf.	Use past progressive with the main clause to describe situations where the action described in the main clause happened before the action described by the *when*-clause.

Using *while*

EXAMPLES	EXPLANATIONS
(c) While the books fell off the shelf, Jeff hid under his desk.	*While* indicates that the action was in progress at the same time as the action described by the verb in the main clause.
(d) While the books **were falling** off the shelf, Jeff **was hiding** under his desk.	We can use either past progressive or simple past, since *while* makes the meaning clear.

EXERCISE 2

Answer these questions about the example passage in the Opening Task on page 377.

1. What had the author been doing when she realized her children were missing?
2. What happened to the children when she left to get a drink of water?
3. What was happening in the park when she first couldn't find her children?
4. What did she do when she couldn't find them?
5. What happened when she reached the lost children office?
6. What was her son doing when they found him?
7. What happened when the family finally got together?

FOCUS 3

Other Uses of Progressive Aspect

use

EXAMPLES	EXPLANATIONS
	Use progressive aspect to express:
(a) When my kids disappeared **I was trying** to get a drink of water.	• actions that were in progress or uncompleted
(b) As soon as the parade passed **I was constantly calling** out the names of my children.	• actions that were repeated or continuous
(c) For the first hour after I found them, my kids **were keeping** as close to me as they could, they soon began to run around again.	• temporary situations

EXERCISE 3

Identify all the past progressive verb forms in the example passage of the Opening Task and tell why you think the author chose to use past progressive.

ANSWER KEY

Exercise 2 Answers may vary slightly. 1. She had been getting a drink of water. 2. They disappeared. 3. A parade was going down the street past her. 4. She shouted their names and she went to the lost children office. 5. She heard her husband calling her name. 6. He was watching a clown show by the Magic Castle. 7. She made all of them promise to stay together.

Exercise 3 was happening—already in progress
were keeping—duration over time

FOCUS 2 [15 minutes]

The use of *when* and *while* are contrasted. Many students have trouble with the differences in the time sequences they indicate.

1. **Lead-in:** For an inductive approach, put the following sentences on the board and let the class work in pairs to decide how the sentences differ in their sequence of events:

The students were laughing when the teacher entered the room.

The students laughed when the teacher entered the room.

The students were laughing while the teacher entered the room.

The students laughed while the teacher entered the room.

2. Lead a discussion as volunteers describe the differences in sequence of the events in each sentence. (First sentence: The students had started laughing before the teacher entered, and perhaps stopped when the teacher arrived. Second sentence: The students began laughing after the teacher came in. The third and fourth sentences have similar meaning and both indicate that the teacher's entrance and the students' laughter happened at the same time.)

3. Go over the similar examples and explanations in Focus 2. Did the class give similar explanations?

EXERCISE 2 [15 minutes]

Students will use the information in the Opening Task passage to answer questions using *when* to show the sequence of events.

1. If students did not read the passage as part of the Opening Task, be sure they read the entire passage for general comprehension before doing this exercise.

2. Be sure that students put their answers into complete sentences.

3. Give students time to review their answers in small groups as a review of reading comprehension.

4. Review answers quickly as a whole class and note the use of simple past or past progressive to indicate sequence. See answers on LP page 380.

FOCUS 3 [15 minutes]

This focus reviews the basic meanings of progressive aspect that were first presented in Unit 2 of this book (see Unit 2, Focus 3).

1. **Lead-in:** Put the three example sentences on the board (or make several of your own) and ask the class to come up with a list of what the progressive aspect expresses. *Why would we use the progressive aspect? What does it express?*

2. List these on the board and then compare them to the explanations listed in Focus 3. Keep these explanations on the board for use in Exercise 3.

3. Review the three explanations in Focus 3 and then move onto Exercise 3 for review and practice.

EXERCISE 3 [15 minutes]

Students will identify and explain the use of the past progressive in the Opening Task passage.

1. Students can work individually to underline all the examples of the past progressive.

2. When finished, have students work individually or in pairs to discuss the meaning of each example they have underlined. They should be able to refer to the explanations listed on the board from your presentation of Focus 3. See answers on LP page 380.

EXERCISE 4

Circle the appropriate form of the verbs in parentheses. There may be more than one correct choice. The first sentence has been done for you as an example.

The Search for the Northwest Passage

(1) The St. Lawrence Seaway, the waterway that (links/is linking) the Great Lakes of North America with the Atlantic Ocean, was discovered by explorers who (looked/were looking) for the Northwest Passage. (2) Geographers at that time (believed/were believing) that there was a water course that (connected/was connecting) the Atlantic and Pacific oceans. (3) Throughout the sixteenth and early seventeenth centuries, both England and France constantly (sent/were sending) one expedition after another to attempt to find the passage. (4) Early explorers (investigated/were investigating) every large inlet and river along the entire eastern coast of North America.

(5) Even though they never (found/were finding) the Northwest Passage, these early explorers (made/were making) a valuable contribution to the knowledge of North American geography. (6) While they (explored/were exploring) the coast they (made/were making) many other very useful discoveries. (7) Not only the St. Lawrence Seaway, but also Hudson Bay, Chesapeake Bay, the Hudson River, and the Delaware River all (were discovered/were being discovered) by explorers who actually (looked/were looking) for something else.

FOCUS 4

Using Perfect Aspect in Past Time Frame

use

You can use both **adverbials** and **perfect aspect** to indicate that a particular action happened before others.

ADVERBIALS	PERFECT ASPECT
(a) **Before** we left on the trip, we checked the car thoroughly.	(c) But we **had**n't **gotten** more than a few miles when we realized that we **had forgotten** something: We **had left** our suitcases on the front porch. We **had been worrying** so much about the mechanical condition of the car that we left without thinking about its contents.
(b) **After** we checked the oil, we made sure the tires had enough air.	

We don't usually use both adverbials and perfect aspect in the same sentence, and tend to avoid the past perfect tense if the time sequence is clear from other information.

EXAMPLES	EXPLANATIONS
	In general, we indicate time relationships with perfect aspect only when it is necessary:
(d) He **had seen** the movie, and therefore didn't want to go with us.	• to communicate a logical connection between the two events
(e) They **started** the project when I arrived, but they **had finished** it when I left.	• to clarify a time relationship
(f) I **had finished** all my homework before I went to Jane's party.	• to describe an action that was fully completed
(g) They told me that the doctor **had** just **left**.	• to change the time frame in reported speech.

EXERCISE 5

With a partner, examine how adverbials and aspect are used to indicate time relationships in the following passages.

• For each sentence, identify the verb phrases that happened **before** the verb phrases listed in the first column of the chart, and write them in the "Time Before" column.
• Then decide whether each time relationship is indicated by adverbials, by aspect, or by both. Record that information in the "How Indicated" column.
• Compare your answers with those of another pair of students.

The first two sentences in each passage have been done for you as examples.

1. I'll never forget our horrible vacation. (1) Before we left on the trip, we checked the car thoroughly. (2) After we checked the oil, we made sure the tires had enough air. (3) But we hadn't gotten more than a few miles when we realized that we had forgotten something: We had left our suitcases on the front porch. (4) We had been worrying so much about the mechanical condition of the car that we left without thinking about its contents.

VERB PHRASE	TIME BEFORE	HOW INDICATED
1. we left on the trip	we checked the car	adverb (before)
2. we made sure the tires had enough air	we checked the oil	adverb (after)
3. we realized that . . .		
4. we left without thinking about its contents		

Exercise 5 is continued on LP page 384.

ANSWER KEY

Exercise 5 *Passage 1: 3. we hadn't gotten more than a few miles/we had forgotten something/we had left our suitcases; aspect (past perfect)   4. we had been worrying so much; aspect and adverb (so/that)*

LESSON PLAN 1/LESSON PLAN 2

EXERCISE 4 [15 minutes]

This exercise can be used as a review or in place of Focus 3 if you feel your students are comfortable with the difference between the simple and progressive aspects.

1. Have students read the entire passage before selecting the correct answers.

2. Students should work individually. However, you may want to have small groups compare answers and discuss their choices when finished. See answers on LP page 382.

Suggestion: Use an overhead transparency for easier review.

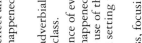

For more practice, use *Grammar Dimensions 3* Workbook page 133, Exercise 2.

LESSON PLAN 2

FOCUS 4 [15 minutes]

This focus shows that both the past perfect and adverbials can identify an event that happened before another in the past.

1. **Lead-in:** Go over the examples of adverbials and perfect aspect on SB page 382 as a class.

2. Invite volunteers to state the sequence of events. In other words, ask the class what happened first in examples (a–c). Then review the use of the adverbials and the perfect aspect in setting up the sequence.

3. Go over the rest of Focus 4 as a class, focusing on the explanation column that provides four situations when the past perfect might be necessary.

Suggestion: It would be better to not spend too much time on Focus 4. Move directly onto Exercise 5.

This should help clarify the points made in Focus 4 and give the class other examples in context.

EXERCISE 5 [20 minutes]

Do this exercise as part of your presentation of Focus 4. Students will identify the sequence of past events and the indicators for determining which event happened earlier.

1. Have the class read the first passage completely through before beginning.

2. Ask the class what happened first in sentence 1 and what tells them this. Read through the example at the bottom of the page to see if students were correct.

3. Go over the second sentence together with the class in the same manner. What happened before they made sure the tires had enough air? What tells you this event happened first? (*we checked the oil/adverb after*)

4. Put students into pairs and have them continue to work on Passages 1 and 2 (on SB page 384). Remind the class to read the whole passage before beginning the exercise.

5. Review as a class or have pairs check answers with another pair of students.

6. Circulate. If students are having problems or appear confused, do all of Passage 1 as a class. See answers on LP pages 382 and 384.

Suggestion: If you anticipate your class may need more assistance, be sure to bring a copy of Passage 1 on an overhead transparency to go over as a class. Then have the class work in pairs to complete Passage 2.

For more practice, use *Grammar Dimensions 3* Workbook page 133, Exercise 3.

VARIATION

If you would like more practice or feel that the content of Passage 2 would be a challenge for your class, you can use the passage in the Opening Task instead. After completing Passage 1 in Exercise 5, put the verb phrases listed below from the Opening Task on the board and ask the class to identify the verb phrases that happened before these and then state how this was indicated (the answers are given in parentheses).

my three kids (and my husband) were so excited . . . (*the flight had been long/aspect*)

I stopped for just a moment to get a drink of water . . . (*I thought my husband had gone with them/aspect*)

I realized that my kids and husband had disappeared . . . (*As soon as it passed/adverbial*)

I heard my husband's voice . . . (*After several minutes passed/adverbial*)

EXERCISE 6

Use past perfect in these sentences only if it is necessary to the meaning of the sentence. Otherwise use simple past or past progressive.

1. Peter (a) ___went___ (went) to talk with Mr. Green about the fight he (b) ___had___ (have) with Denise earlier in the day.

2. As soon as the building (a) ___stopped moving___ (stop moving), Jeff (b) ___tried___ (try) to call Matt, but the telephones (c) ___had stopped working___ (stop working).

3. It was too late to put out the fire because it ___had grown___ (grow) too big for anything to control.

4. I (a) ___looked___ (look) everywhere for my wallet, but I (b) ___didn't find___ (not find) it anywhere. It (c) ___had disappeared___ (disappeared).

5. Denise (a) ___went___ (go) to Peter's office to complain about his attitude, but he (b) ___had left___ (leave) early to take his children to the circus.

6. Mary (a) ___was___ (be) extremely worried about John since she (b) ___had not received___ (not receive) any letters from him in over a month.

FOCUS 5

Perfect Progressive Aspect in Past Time Frame

use

PERFECT PROGRESSIVE ASPECT

Continuous:
(a) I'll never forget our unlucky ski-trip. It had been snowing for three hours. Unless they cleared the roads soon, it was likely that we would have to spend the night in our car.

Uncompleted:
(c) I'll never forget the weekend I visited my aunt in New York. I had been visiting my aunt all morning when she suddenly became quite ill and asked me to drive her to the hospital.

PERFECT ASPECT

Repeated:
(b) I'll never forget our unlucky ski-trip. It had snowed several times since we arrived, but there still wasn't enough snow for skiing.

Completed:
(d) I'll never forget the weekend I visited my aunt in New York. I had visited my aunt all morning so I was free to spend the rest of the afternoon at the museum.

Use perfect progressive aspect instead of perfect aspect in past time frame to describe actions that are:
• continuous instead of repeated

• uncompleted instead of completed

---

2. European historians will never forget the impact of the Black Plague in the fifteenth century, which brought a new social and economic order to Europe. (1) By the end of the fourteenth century, the population of Europe was about a third smaller than it had been at the beginning of the century. (2) It was one of the few times in history when the population had actually decreased. (3) This smaller population was caused by repeated outbreaks of bubonic plague that had swept through the continent several times during the century, (4) and by the time the century had ended, this disease had caused some fundamental changes in society. (5) So many people had died that the traditional feudal landlords were forced to intermarry with wealthy merchant families instead of the aristocracy. (6) People who had previously only had the opportunity to make a living as farmers or serfs were able to become craftsmen and artisans. (7) The plague had killed so many people that the traditional social boundaries were wiped out, and this created a period of great social mobility and economic change.

VERB PHRASE	TIME BEFORE	HOW INDICATED
1. the population was one third smaller	than it had been at the beginning of the century	adverbial (By the end of the fourteenth century) aspect
2. it was one of the few times in history	the population had actually decreased	aspect (had actually decreased)
3. the smaller population was caused by repeated outbreaks of plague		
4. this disease had caused some fundamental changes in society		
5. landlords were forced to intermarry with wealthy merchants		
6. people were able to become craftsmen and artisans		
7. this created a period of great social mobility and economic change		

ANSWER KEY

Exercise 5 is continued from LP page 382. **Passage 2:** 3. that had swept through the continent several times during the century; aspect 4. the century had ended; adverbial (by the time) aspect 5. so many people had died; aspect/adverbial (so/that) 6. people who had previously only had the opportunity to make a living as farmers or serfs; aspect/adverbial (previously) 7. the plague had killed so many people that the traditional social boundaries were wiped out; aspect/adverbial (so/that)

LESSON PLAN 2

EXERCISE 6 [15 minutes]

Because native speakers tend to only use the past perfect when necessary, this exercise asks students to identify which sentences require the use of the past perfect.

1. Begin by reviewing the situations where the past perfect might be required. Can anyone remember one of the four situations as described in Focus 4 without looking back? Put these on the board.

2. Have students work in pairs and discuss their reasons for each choice as they work.

3. Pairs can compare their work with another pair or you can circulate and simply tell the pairs whether they need to check their work again (you can even note how many they have wrong without telling them which ones and they can check again). See answers on LP page 384.

For more practice, use *Grammar Dimensions 3* Workbook page 133, Exercise 4.

FOCUS 5 [15 minutes]

This focus reviews the basic meanings of perfect progressive aspect that were first presented in Unit 2 of this book (see Focus 5). You may be able to skip a formal presentation and go directly to Exercise 7. Refer students back to this focus if they have trouble with that exercise or feel they need additional review.

1. **Lead-in:** Put the following examples on the board and ask the class to state what differences in meaning they see between them (the answers are given in parentheses below):

When we arrived, we were told it had been snowing for three days already. (*it was still snowing/this was continuous*)

When we arrived, we were told it had snowed three days already. (*it had snowed three separate days/repeated, but not continuous*)

We had been driving to my sister's house when the earthquake struck. (*we were interrupted in our drive/this was uncompleted*)

We had driven to my sister's house when the earthquake struck. (*we were at my sister's house already/this drive was completed*)

2. As the class states the differences, list key words on the board.

3. Then go over Focus 5 as a class and move directly onto Exercise 7 for further review.

EXERCISE 7

Fill in the blanks with the appropriate form of the verbs (past perfect or past perfect progressive) in parentheses.

1. When the earthquake struck, Jeff was still in the office because he ___had been trying___ (try) to finish a project before he left for the day.

2. Denise ___had been looking___ (look) for a reason to complain about Peter even before he took time off from work to see his son's school play.

3. By the beginning of the fifteenth century, the bubonic plague ___had caused___ (cause) some fundamental social and political changes.

4. The police ___had kept/had been keeping___ (keep) the warehouse under surveillance for some time when they finally obtained a search warrant and investigated.

5. They first became suspicious because so many people ___had been going___ (go) in and out of the warehouse at strange hours of the day and night.

EXERCISE 8

Fill in the blanks with the appropriate form of the verbs in parentheses (simple past, past perfect, or past perfect progressive). More than one answer may be correct.

1. I (a) ___had been working___ (work) on my homework for about twenty minutes when I (b) ___overheard___ (overhear) the TV broadcast announcing Rabin's assassination.

2. Jeff (a) ___had experienced___ (experience) several minor earthquakes, but he (b) ___was___ (be) still surprised by the strength of this one.

3. Nancy (a) ___was___ (be) not really happy with what she (b) ___had been doing___ (do) so she (c) ___decided___ (decide) to look for another job.

4. European explorers (a) ___had been trying___ (try) to reach Asia, when they (b) ___landed___ (land) in the New World "by accident."

5. When Jeff (a) ___got___ (get) to the street, he (b) ___saw___ (see) that hundreds of other people (c) ___had left___ (leave) their offices and (d) ___were standing___ (stand) out on the street wondering what to do.

EXERCISE 9

Fill in the blanks with the correct forms of the verbs in parentheses (present, present perfect, simple past, past perfect, past progressive, or past perfect progressive). There may be more than one correct answer.

When George Washington was young
And full of energy,
He took his little hatchet
And chopped a cherry tree.

George Washington (1) ___was___ (be) the first President of the United States, and (2) ___served___ (serve) as the leader of American troops during the War of Independence. According to a famous story, when George (3) ___was___ (be) a young boy and (4) ___was learning___ (learn) how to use farming tools, his father (5) ___gave___ (give) him a hatchet for his birthday. George (6) ___was___ (be) anxious to use the hatchet, so he (7) ___ran___ (run) out of the house and (8) ___chopped___ (chop) down a cherry tree in his father's garden. When his father (9) ___discovered___ (discover) that someone (10) ___had chopped___ (chop) down the tree, he (11) ___was___ (be) very angry. He (12) ___demanded___ (demand) to know who (13) ___had chopped___ (chop) down his cherry tree. When little George (14) ___heard___ (hear) his father's angry shouting, he (15) ___went___ (go) to his father and (16) ___told___ (tell) him that he (17) ___had done___ (do) it with his new hatchet. He said, "I (18) ___am___ (be) sorry you (19) ___are___ (be) angry, and I (20) ___know___ (know) you will punish me, but I must admit my crime, because I cannot tell a lie." George's father (21) ___was___ (be) so impressed with his honesty, that he (22) ___decided___ (decide) not to punish the boy after all, and, in fact, (23) ___rewarded___ (reward) him by giving him a silver dollar. This incident actually never (24) ___happened___ (happen), but millions of American children (25) ___have read___ (read) this story in school. Parents and teachers (26) ___think___ (think) that it is a good way to teach children to always tell the truth.

LESSON PLAN 2

EXERCISE 7 [10 minutes]

This exercise will let you know whether students have grasped the meanings and uses of the past perfect and past perfect progressive.

1. For a quick comprehension check and review, have students do this individually.

2. Circulate quickly and check answers. Note whether students need further practice with this.

3. Go over the answers as a class. Be sure to ask students to give reasons for their choices. See answers on LP page 386.

work book

For more practice, use *Grammar Dimensions 3* Workbook page 134, Exercise 5.

EXERCISES 8 AND 9 [25 minutes/homework]

Exercises 8 and 9 are whole-unit reviews.

1. Assign these as homework, use them as an in-class quiz, or simply use them for additional practice and review as pairs compare and discuss their answers with each other.

2. Be sure to allow time for a class review and questions. See answers on LP page 386.

Suggestion: Copy Exercise 9 onto an overhead transparency to make the review easier.

work book

For more practice, use *Grammar Dimensions 3* Workbook page 134, Exercise 6.

EXPANSION [30 minutes]

Use Activity 2 (speaking/writing) on SB 388 for another whole unit review and to follow the story style shown in Exercise 9. Students usually enjoy the story in Exercise 9 and will be reminded of a similar story they were taught when young.

UNIT GOAL REVIEW [10 minutes]

Ask students to look at the goals on the opening page of the unit again. Refer to the pages of the unit where information on each goal can be found.

ExamView® Test Generator For assessment of Unit 23, use *Grammar Dimensions 3 ExamView®*.

Use Your English

ACTIVITY 1   writing

Form groups of three to five people. You are going to write a group story.

■ STEP 1   Each person should take a piece of paper and start a story with this sentence: "It was a dark and stormy night. Suddenly, (your teacher's name) heard a terrible scream." Then each person in the group should write for three minutes. When the three minutes is up, fold the paper so that only the last sentence or two can be read.

■ STEP 2   Pass your story to the person on your right, and take the paper of the person on your left. Then each person should write for three minutes to continue that person's story. Repeat the process until the papers have gone completely around the group.

■ STEP 3   Unfold the papers and read the resulting stories to each other. Which story is the funniest? Which story is the clearest? Choose the story you like best to read aloud to the rest of the class.

ACTIVITY 2   speaking/writing

Every country has famous stories in its history that all children learn about when they are growing up. In the United States, for example, all school children have heard the story of George Washington and the cherry tree (Exercise 5).

Do you know any similar kinds of famous stories about real people that you were told as a child? Write down your story or tell it to a partner or the rest of the class.

ACTIVITY 3   listening

CD Track 36

Listen to the story of one person's unforgettable experience and answer the questions below.

1. What was the speaker doing when she heard the news about John F. Kennedy (JFK)?
   She had been (was) studying in the library.

2. What did the speaker do when she heard the news about JFK?
   She left the library.

3. What were her classmates doing when they heard the news about JFK?
   They were taking a test.

4. What did they do when they heard the news about JFK?
   People began crying and all normal activities came to a halt.

ACTIVITY 4   research on the web

Go on the Internet to http://www.infoplease.com and search for "disasters", or use a search engine such as Google® or Yahoo® to find information on past or historical disasters.

Spend some time looking through the Web site and make a report about a historical disaster that occurred in a part of the world you are interested in. Write an "eyewitness" account of the disaster as if you had actually been one of the survivors.

ACTIVITY 5   reflection

Work with a partner. Read the story of your partner's unforgettable experience that was written for the Opening Task of this unit. Construct a time line of your partner's experience, identifying what he or she had been doing, what they did when the unforgettable thing happened, and what happened afterwards. Make suggestions about how to make the sequence of events clearer by using perfect aspect instead of adverbials. Ask your partner to do the same thing with your story.

ANSWER KEY

Activity 3   *Answers will vary. Possible answers are listed above.*

USE YOUR ENGLISH

The Use Your English activities at the end of the unit contain situations that should naturally elicit the structures covered in the unit. For a more complete discussion of how to use the Use Your English activities see To the Teacher on LP page xxii. When students are doing these activities in class, you can circulate and listen to see if they are using the structures accurately. Errors can be corrected after the activity is finished.

ACTIVITY 1
writing
[30 minutes]

This is a fun activity that gives the opportunity for creative and unstructured writing.

STEP 1

1. This can be done in small groups or as a whole-class circle. It will work well either way.
2. As students get their papers ready, put the opening line on the board, with or without the optional second line.
3. Have everyone put their name on their paper, copy the opening line onto their own paper, and then continue with the story from there.
4. Circulate. After about three minutes (or several sentences), have the class stop writing (you can decide whether you'd like them to stop completely or simply finish the sentence they were working on).

STEP 2

1. They should then fold their papers so that only the last line or two is showing and pass their paper to the person on their right.
2. Everyone should then read the lines visible and continue writing from there.

STEP 3
Continue in this manner for several more rounds and then stop and read the stories out loud to the group.

ACTIVITY 2
speaking/writing
[30 minutes/homework]

You may wish to use this activity as an expansion of Exercise 9 on SB page 387.

1. Begin by leading a discussion of legends such as the one about George Washington and the cherry tree.
2. If you are short on time, have students tell similar stories orally. Otherwise, assign this as a writing task for homework and have them share their stories the next day.
3. Students can share in small groups or in fluency circles (students tell their stories to a partner and then change partners as they continue around the circle of a small group).
4. If possible, give time for questions as students clarify confusing points in the story with the storytellers.
5. Circulate and note the use of past time indicators. Review any common errors as needed with the class after all stories have been shared.

ACTIVITY 3
listening
[15 minutes]

CD Track 36

Students will listen to one person's unforgettable experience and then answer questions. This is a good review of all the forms presented in the unit.

1. Use your usual methods for using audio. Repeat as necessary.
2. Have pairs or small groups review their answers together. Circulate and note whether students correctly understood the questions and used the correct indicators of past time in their answers. See answers on LP page 388.

ACTIVITY 4
research on the web
[homework]

Assign this activity after the Opening Task. Students may note that this activity is similar to the research done in Unit 13 (Activity 5). However, this will focus on an event in the past rather than the present.

Note: You may want to be sensitive to the possibility that there may be students in your class who have experienced a disaster personally and an "eyewitness" account may be a sensitive subject for some students.

ACTIVITY 5
reflection
[15 minutes]

This activity asks students to give each other feedback on the stories written as part of the Opening Task. If you did not assign the writing portion of the task, you can have students give similar feedback on another piece of writing done in this unit, such as Activity 2 or Activity 4. The time lines can still be created for one of these other writing topics. See the notes below for encouraging a positive peer review.

METHODOLOGY NOTE

Students often feel uncomfortable about what they see as "correcting" each other's writing when doing any kind of peer review. To avoid this be sure to focus students with a checklist of things to address. This will make the comments less personal. Comments will then be more helpful and less threatening. Be sure to encourage students to give positive feedback too.

UNIT GOALS

- **Correctly use *could*
  versus *was able to* to
  describe abilities in
  past time**

- **Correctly use *would*
  versus *used to* to
  describe habitual
  actions in past time**

- **Correctly use *would*
  versus *was going to* to
  describe future events
  in past time**

OPENING TASK

Identifying the Benefits of Growing Older

■ STEP 1

Think about these questions:

- In what ways are you different than you were in the past?

- What are some things that you used to do but don't do anymore?

- What are some things that you do now, but you couldn't or wouldn't do five or ten years ago?

- How do people change as they grow older?

■ STEP 2

Discuss your ideas with two or three other students in the class. Your group should decide on two general ways that people's lives change for the better as they grow older, and present those ideas to the rest of the class. You can read the paragraph below as an example of the kind of changes you may want to consider.

GROWING OLDER
Growing older makes people less worried about what other people think. In high school I used to be really shy. I would avoid talking to people, and I couldn't express my ideas in class without feeling very uncomfortable. I guess I was afraid that people were going to laugh at me, or that they would think I was strange. In high school people were supposed to "fit in." They weren't allowed to be different. So I used to wear the same kind of clothes and try to behave the same way as everybody else. I felt I had to be "one of the crowd." Now that I am older, I can stand up in front of other people and tell them what I think. I certainly couldn't do that in high school. I wear clothes because I like them, not because other people like them. I think I'm much more independent and self-confident than I used to be in high school.

MODALS IN PAST TIME

LESSON PLAN 1

UNIT OVERVIEW

This unit focuses on using modals to express ability, habitual action, and predictions about future events in past time.

GRAMMAR NOTE

Unit 24 might be presented after doing Unit 5 (a review of one-word and phrasal modals), Unit 16 (modals of prediction and inference), and/or Unit 17 (hypothetical statements). Although the forms will be familiar, the wide variety of meanings and uses for modals are always problematic. Therefore, it can be very confusing for students to find that a relatively small number of modals can have such a large number of meanings and uses. If students are comfortable using the phrasal modals, they will just as easily put them into their past time forms and, for the most part, find their meanings and uses in the past reflect those presented in Unit 5. However, the one-word modals do not all transfer uniformly into the past tense. There either is no past time counterpart and the phrasal modal is used instead, or the forms are found to have several other meanings and uses and can cause confusion. In this way, the use of modals in the past becomes especially challenging.

UNIT GOALS

Some instructors may want to review the goals listed on Student Book (SB) page 390 after completing the Opening Task so that students understand what they should know by the end of the unit. These goals can also be reviewed at the end of the unit when students are more familiar with the grammar terminology.

OPENING TASK [20 minutes]

The aim of this activity is to give students the opportunity to use modals to describe abilities or habits in the past time. The problem-solving format is designed to show the teacher how well the

students can produce a target structure implicitly and spontaneously when they are engaged in a communicative task. For a more complete discussion of the purpose of the Opening Task, see To the Teacher, Lesson Planner (LP) page xxii.

Setting Up the Task

1. Begin with a question to get the class thinking about the relationship between the present and the past:

   What benefits come from growing older?

2. Put students into pairs to quickly discuss the question on the board together.
3. Circulate and listen for the use of modals of ability or habits in the past time.

Conducting the Task

■ STEP 1

Have students look at the questions in Step 1 on SB page 390 and prepare their answers individually.

■ STEP 2

In groups, students should share their answers and prepare to present two ways that growing older has made their lives better (see SB page 391). They can read the paragraph on SB page 391 for some examples.

VARIATION

Have students read the passage on SB page 391 before their discussion if you feel they may need some ideas of specific examples before they continue.

Closing the Task

1. Bring the class together and have groups present their two benefits of growing older.

2. Listen for examples of modals in the past and write these down on the board as you hear them.
3. Draw attention to any example sentences and ask volunteers to identify the modals as you transition into the chart in Focus 1.

GRAMMAR NOTE

Typical Student Errors (use)

- Using past tense with *used to*, which is already in the past: * *She didn't used to drive to school. Now she does.* (See Focus 4.)
- Not using past forms of modals with past time frame: * *When I was young, I knew that I will grow up to be a teacher.* * *I thought I have to be there by noon.*
- Using *could* rather than *was/were able to* with statements of specific ability: * *We got there early, so we could get tickets.* (See Focus 3.)
- Using *would* rather than *used to* to describe habitual states in the past: * *When I was young, I would be shy.* (See Focus 4.)
- Using *would* rather than *was going to* to describe intentions that did not actually take place: * *I would call her, but she called me first.* (See Focus 5.)

FOCUS 1

Overview of Modals in Past Time Frame

MEANING/USE	ONE-WORD MODALS	EXAMPLES	PHRASAL MODALS	EXAMPLES
necessity			*had to*	(a) I **had to** do my homework before my parents would let me watch TV.
permission	*(No one-word modals for these uses.)*		*was allowed to*	(b) I **wasn't allowed to** watch TV until I finished my homework.
advice/obligation			*was supposed to*	(c) I **was supposed to** be in bed by 9:00 on school nights.
ability	*could* *couldn't*	(d) I **could** spend my summer vacations just playing with my friends.	*was able to*	(e) I **was able to** amuse myself by day dreaming.
habitual actions	*would* *wouldn't*	(f) When I was little I **would** pretend I was a pirate.	*used to*	(g) I **used to** be afraid of the dark.
future events in past time	*would* *wouldn't* *might* *might not (mightn't)*	(h) I hoped that I **would** grow up to be a famous person who **might** become president.	*was going to* *was about to*	(i) I **was about to** leave for college when I realized how much I **was going to** miss my family.

EXERCISE 1

Decide whether the modals in these sentences are requests in present time or questions about past habits and abilities.

1. Could you tell me how to improve my English?
2. Would you cry when your mother punished you?
3. Could you ride a bicycle when you were 5?
4. Would you mind putting out that cigar?
5. Do you think you could tell that joke without laughing?
6. When you were little, would you always do everything your parents wanted?

FOCUS 2

Expressing Necessity, Permission, and Advisability in the Past Time

EXAMPLES	EXPLANATION
	Use phrasal modals in the past time frame to describe:
(a) When I was a child, my brothers and sisters and I **had to** do a number of chores.	• necessity
(b) If we didn't, we **weren't allowed to** watch TV.	• permission
(c) I **was supposed to** wash the dishes on Mondays.	• advisability

EXERCISE 2

Make five statements about things you **were allowed to** do when you were a child.
Make five statements about things you **weren't allowed to** do.

EXERCISE 3

Work with a partner, and ask if he or she was allowed to do the things you talked about in Exercise 2.

Example: *When you were a child, were you allowed to stay out after dark?*

Identify one privilege that was the same for both of you, and report it to the rest of the class.

ANSWER KEY

Exercise 1 1. request in present time 2. question about past habit 3. question about past ability 4. request in present time 5. request in present time 6. question about past habit

Exercise 2 Answers will vary. Possible answers are: When I was a child, I was allowed to... watch TV late on Friday nights./stay over at friends' houses./read any kind of book I wanted./spend summers at my grandmother's house./have whatever I wanted for dinner on my birthday.

When I was a child, I wasn't allowed to... drink scotch./smoke cigars./hang out with unsavory characters./drive cars./go to the city by myself.

Exercise 3 Answers will vary. Possible dialogue might be: When you were a child, were you allowed to smoke? No, I wasn't. Oh, really? Neither was I. Neither Hortensia nor I was allowed to smoke when we were children.

FOCUS 1 [15 minutes]

This focus presents one-word and phrasal modals in past time and, like the presentation of modals in Unit 5, is organized according to meaning and use. Students will note that for the first three uses there is no equivalent past form of a one-word modal.

1. **Lead-in:** Refer the class to the examples you have put on the board from the Opening Task or put up a few of your own examples. Have the class add statements about the present for each statement (see the first example below). If some of the statements are already about the present, ask students to make a contrasting statement about the past (see the second example below). For example:

When I was younger, I couldn't stay out past 10:00 P.M.
(Now I can stay out as late as I like.)

Now that I have my own apartment, I have to cook for myself.
(When I was younger, my mom used to cook for me.)

2. Ask students to identify the modals and the time frame for each sentence as you add to them. Point out that this unit will focus on the use of modals in past time.

3. Present the focus chart as a review, but point out that each of these points will be covered in later focus charts. The less familiar uses of modals for past habitual actions and describing future events in past time will be covered in more detail in Focus 4 and Focus 5.

4. Move directly on to Exercise 1 or use the Expansion exercise that follows.

EXPANSION [15 minutes]

Continue giving focus to the use of modals in the past by having students ask questions of each other. Have pairs make up a list of questions to ask another pair of students. Ask them to use the modals in Focus 1 to create their questions. You can require that each pair makes five questions, but they cannot use a modal more than once.

EXERCISE 1 [10 minutes]

This exercise asks students to identify the time frame for questions using modals. Because the same modal forms are used in a variety of contexts, it's useful to make sure that students can distinguish the actual time reference despite the form being used. Use this to follow up your presentation of Focus 1.

Go over this as a whole class, asking volunteers to explain why they chose *present time* or *past habits and abilities* or have students do the same in small groups as you circulate. See answers on LP page 392.

work book For more practice, use *Grammar Dimensions 3* Workbook page 135, Exercise 1.

FOCUS 2 [10 minutes]

Focus 2 repeats the first part of the chart in Focus 1.

1. **Lead-in:** Write the following sentence starter on the board: *When I was a child. . .*

2. Point out the first three examples in the Focus 1 chart again and the similar examples to match in Focus 2.

3. Follow with more examples of your own beginning with the sentence starter. You should finish each sentence with an example of each meaning, such as *I had to. . ./I wasn't allowed to. . ./I was supposed to. . .* Put a few sentences on the board.

4. Now turn your sentences on the board into questions and show these changes on the board. Use these questions to ask the class about when they were children. Encourage them to use the same forms in their answers.

5. Leave your example sentences and questions on the board for use in Exercises 2 and 3.

EXERCISE 2 [15 minutes]

Students will write sentences about their childhood.

1. Have students write their own sentences based on the examples you just modeled in Focus 2. However, these statements should only express permission.

2. Students should have ten sentences in total about what they were allowed and not allowed to do when they were children.

EXERCISE 3 [15 minutes]

Students will turn the statements they created in Exercise 2 into questions about their partners' childhoods.

1. Have students look again at the example sentences on the board from Focus 2.

2. Students should turn their own sentences from Exercise 2 into questions.

3. Put students into pairs and have them ask each other these questions.

4. Pairs should identify what they discovered to be a similar privilege and share this with the class.

work book For more practice, use *Grammar Dimensions 3* Workbook page 135, Exercise 2 and page 136, Exercise 3.

EXERCISE 6

Fill in the blanks with *could* or *be able to*.

Example: ___Were you able to go___ to Joan's party?

No, I ___couldn't/wasn't able to___. But I ___was able to___ send her a birthday card.

1. Matt (a) ___was able to___ get tickets to the concert. However, he (b) ___couldn't___ (not) find them when it was time to go to the auditorium.
2. Peter (a) ___could___ convince his boss to let him do anything he wanted. As a result, he (b) ___was able to___ stay home from work last week.
3. Professor Katz (a) ___could/was able to___ speak Russian. Because of this, she (b) ___was able to___ translate the ambassador's speech to the United Nations last week.
4. Bambang (a) ___wouldn't/wasn't able to___ (not) get a high enough score on the TOEFL® Test*, so he enrolled in an English course. He still (b) ___couldn't/wasn't able to___ (not) get the score he needed last semester, but he succeeded this semester.

EXERCISE 7

1. Which of the following activities were you able to do ten years ago? Use complete sentences to identify things that you could do ten years ago and things that you couldn't do.

ride a bike _____	run a mile in eight minutes _____
speak fluent English _____	drive a truck _____
understand American films _____	support my family _____
play a musical instrument _____	shop for food in a foreign country _____
read and write English _____	swim _____
speak a second language _____	play soccer _____
drive a car _____	translate things into English _____

2. Describe two other things not listed below that you could do ten years ago and two other things that you couldn't do.

* TOEFL is a registered trademark of the Educational Testing Service (ETS). This publication is not endorsed or approved by ETS.

EXERCISE 4

Make five statements about things that you **had to** do when you were a child. Make five statements about things that you **were supposed to** do when you were a child but didn't always do.

EXERCISE 5

Work with a partner, and ask if he or she had to do the things you talked about in Exercise 4.

Example: *When you were a child, did you have to come home before dark?*

When you were a child, were you supposed to do your homework before you could watch TV?

Identify one responsibility that was the same for both of you, and report it to the rest of the class.

FOCUS 3

Ability in Past Time: *Could* Versus *Was Able To*

meaning

EXAMPLES	EXPLANATIONS
(a) I **could** amuse myself all summer long. (b) I **was able to** amuse myself all summer long.	In statements of general ability (skills that exist over time), there is no difference in meaning or use between *could* and *was able to*.
(c) Jeff **was able to** get two tickets to the concert. (d) NOT: Jeff **could** get two tickets to the concert.	In statements of specific ability (specific events or actions), use *was able to*.
(e) Matt stood in line for over an hour, but he **couldn't** get tickets. (f) Matt stood in line for over an hour, but he **wasn't able to** get tickets.	In negative statements of specific ability both *couldn't* and *wasn't able to* can be used.

Exercise 4 Answers will vary. Possible answers are: When I was a child, I had to. . . make my bed every day./clean my room every Saturday./help my sister with the dishes./watch after my little sister./practice the piano every night. When I was a child, I was supposed to. . . do my homework every night, but sometimes I told my parents I didn't have any./take care of my little brother, but sometimes I would hide from him so my friends and I could play without him./say my prayers every night, but sometimes I fell asleep in front of the TV./dry the dishes after dinner, but sometimes I said I had a stomach ache so I could go to my bedroom instead./take a bath every Saturday, but sometimes I just ran the water but didn't get in the tub.

Exercise 5 Answers will vary. See the answers from Exercise 3 for an example of the kind of dialogue that might result from this exercise.

Exercise 7 1. Answers will vary. Possible answers are: Ten years ago.. ./I could ride a bike./I couldn't speak fluent English./I couldn't understand American films./I could play the piano./I couldn't read and write English./I could speak a second language./I couldn't drive a car./I could run a mile in eight minutes./I couldn't drive a truck./I couldn't support my family./I couldn't shop for food in a foreign country./I could swim./I couldn't play soccer/I couldn't translate things into English. 2. Answers will vary.

EXERCISES 4 AND 5 [20 minutes]

Assign Exercises 4 and 5, which mirror the work done in Exercises 2 and 3. As before, bring the class together when students have finished the work. Invite volunteers to share a few statements and questions. If you have time, it can be interesting to take a class poll of yes/no answers to several of these questions.

 For more practice, use *Grammar Dimensions 3* Workbook page 136, Exercise 4 and page 137, Exercises 5 and 6.

VARIATION

Instead of interviewing partners, have students use the SB exercises as a mixer and move around the room talking to students. They can look for students who had similar privileges or responsibilities as a child.

FOCUS 3 [20 minutes]

Focus 3 presents the notions of general ability versus specific ability. While somewhat abstract, the difference in meaning between the two is critical to understanding which form to use.

1. **Lead-in:** Begin with a few examples of specific ability:

   We arrived early today, so we were able to get a good seat.

   He was able to get an appointment on Tuesday.
   The doctor was able to calm him down with an injection.
   She wanted to stay home, but they were able to change her mind.

   Contrast them with several examples of general ability:

   He could/was able to ride a bike before be was five years old!
   I could/was able to swim all day when I was young.
   I thought that be could/was able to jump higher than that.

2. Point out the differences between specific ability, which is shown at a specific time or in a specific situation, and general ability, which may be true over a general period of time or whenever in that situation.

3. Go over the examples and explanations in Focus 3.

4. Return to your examples on the board (or overhead transparency) and show that for the second set of examples it is possible to use either *could* or *was able to* in situations of general ability. However, point out that it sounds strange to use *could* in the first set of example sentences because they refer to specific ability at a specific time and might not be true at another time or in another situation.

5. Students should note that for negative statements, both *could* and *was able to* would be correct.

VARIATION

For a more inductive approach, simply put the example sentences on the board and ask the class what they perceive as the difference between sentences 1–4 and 5–7. See if they can develop a "rule" for this. Then go on to Focus 3 and have the class check their rule.

EXPANSION [15 minutes]

You may want to use Activity 1 (writing/speaking) on SB page 401, which asks students to use modals of past ability to describe the down side of growing older.

EXERCISE 6 [10 minutes]

Use this exercise as part of your presentation of Focus 3 to further illustrate the differences between specific and general ability and the use of negative statements of ability.

1. Do this in pairs or as a class review.

2. Be sure to give time for questions and note when there is more than one possible answer. See answers on LP page 394.

 For more practice, use *Grammar Dimensions 3* Workbook page 138, Exercise 7.

EXERCISE 7 [15 minutes]

1. Have students work in pairs or small groups as they discuss the things they could or couldn't do ten years ago.

2. Circulate and note the use of *could/couldn't* and *was able to/wasn't able to.* See possible answers on LP page 394.

VARIATION

Use this as a mixer and have students move around the class looking for other students who have five things in common. After putting a check after those activities that they could do, students should circulate around the room asking others, *Could you . . . ten years ago?* When they find someone who has five things in common, they can sit down.

EXPANSION [15 minutes/homework]

You may wish to expand this into a writing assignment. Have students write a paragraph or short essay about their abilities as a child in contrast to now. They should also explain any reasons why they have changed and give examples of these changes. For example, *I could climb very tall trees when I was young, but I'm too afraid of heights to do that now. I wasn't afraid to climb so high until I fell one day while I was. . .*

EXERCISE 8

Underline the structures that describe past abilities in these short passages. Why do you think the author decided to use the form he did?

1. (a) Matt stood in line for four hours, but he wasn't able to get tickets for the concert. (b) When he got home, Jeff could tell that he was frustrated and a little angry. (c) He wanted to cheer Matt up, but he couldn't do much to improve Matt's mood.

2. (a) Nigel was a genius. (b) He was able to do many things that other children his age couldn't do. (c) He could solve complicated mathematical equations. (d) He could write poetry and quote Shakespeare. (e) He was even able to get into college when he was only 14 years old. (f) But he couldn't make friends with other children his own age.

FOCUS 4 | Habitual Actions in Past Time: *Would* Versus *Used To*

use

EXAMPLES	EXPLANATIONS
(a) I **used to** live in Washington, D.C.	Habits and regular activities in the past are described by using *used to* and *would*. *Used to* is often used in the first sentence to establish the topic. *Would* is used in other sentences to supply the details.
(b) Every day I **would** go jogging past all the famous monuments.	
(c) No matter how hot or cold it was, I **would** run around the Tidal Basin and along the Mall.	
(d) When I was a child I **would** wait at the bus stop for my father to come home.	Habitual activities can be expressed by both *would* and *used to*.
(e) When I was a child I **used to** wait at the bus stop.	
(f) When I was a child I **used to** have lots of toys.	Habitual **states** must be expressed by *used to* or simple past tense. We do not use *would*.
(g) When I was a child I **had** lots of toys.	
(h) NOT: When I was a child I **would** have lots of toys.	

Exercise 9 *Answers will vary. Possible answers are: I used to be afraid of the dark. I used to be afraid of the dark. I used to play "cops and robbers" with my friends. I used to pretend to be able to fly. I used to cry when I was hurt. I used to spend the night at a friend's house. I used to have a secret hiding place. I used to enjoy going to school. I didn't believe in ghosts. I didn't ride a bicycle, because I was afraid. I didn't play with dolls. I didn't like going to the doctor. I didn't obey my older brother.*

EXERCISE 9

Below is a list of things many children do.

1. From this list choose five things that you used to do when you were a child.
2. Choose five things that you didn't used to do.
3. Think of three additional examples for each category.
4. Describe these activities in complete sentences. Be sure to use the correct form for verbs that describe habitual states rather than activities. You should create eight sentences describing things you used to do as a child and eight sentences about things you didn't used to do.

believe in ghosts	have a secret hiding place
be afraid of the dark	play with dolls
eat vegetables	like going to the doctor
play "cops and robbers"	enjoy going to school
pretend to be able to fly	obey older brother or sisters
ride a bicycle	cry when hurt
spend the night at a friend's house	

EXERCISE 10

Work with a partner, and ask questions about the things you described in Exercise 9.

Example: *When you were a child, did you ever pretend that you could fly?*

Report some of your partner's answers to the rest of the class.

Exercise 10 *Answers will vary. Possible answers are: When you were a child, did you ever pretend that you could fly? No, I didn't. But I pretended my bed could fly. When she was a child, Fiona used to pretend that her bed could fly.*

EXERCISE 8 [10 minutes]

This exercise gives more practice and discussion of the concepts presented in Focus 3.

1. Students should first work on underlining the structures of past ability.
2. Invite students to discuss the reasons the author had for choosing these forms either as a class or in pairs. See answers on LP page 396.

Suggestion: Ask students to identify places where an alternate structure of past ability could be used.

For more practice, use *Grammar Dimensions 3* Workbook page 138, Exercise 8.

LESSON PLAN 2

FOCUS 4 [10 minutes]

Focus 4 presents the concepts of habitual activities versus habitual states. Like Focus 3, the difference in meaning between the two is critical to understanding which form to use.

1. **Lead-in:** Because it comes up so often, you might want to begin this focus by addressing the common confusion between *used to + **verb*** and ***be used to + present participle***. Put several examples on the board which illustrate the difference:

Maria used to live in Ecuador. (Did Maria used to live in Peru?)

Maria is used to living in the United States now. (Is Maria used to living here now?)

Tomas used to drive his car to work everyday.

Tomas is used to walking to work now.

2. Once the difference is clear, erase sentences b. and d. from the board.
3. Point out to the class that sentences a. and c. both talk about habitual actions in the past. However, one sentence refers to a *habitual state* and one sentence refers to a *habitual action*. Ask the class to identify which is the state and which is the action and note these on the board. (*first sentence = habitual state and third sentence = habitual action*)
4. For sentence c., explain to the class that the past modal *would* can also be used to talk about habitual activities in the past (*Tomas would drive his car...*). However, *would* cannot be used to describe habitual states in the past in sentence a. (* *Maria would live in Ecuador*).
5. Go over the examples and explanations in Focus 4.

Suggestion: Ask the class to create four sentences describing habitual states in the past and four sentences describing habitual activities in the past. Have students share these with the class. You may want to divide the board in half (*states* and *activities*) and ask students to write sentences to discuss as a class.

EXERCISE 9 [10 minutes/homework]

Students will practice the forms for habitual activities and states in the past by describing their own childhood activities and interests. This exercise works well as a homework assignment to then share in class the next day (see Exercise 10).

1. Have students look at the list in Exercise 9 and choose five things they used to do and five more things they didn't use to do as a child.
2. Next, have students think of three more things that are not on the list that they used to do and didn't use to do as a child.
3. Students should now take these two lists of eight states or activities and write them down in complete sentences, being sure to use the correct forms for each. See possible answers on LP page 396.

VARIATION

Do Exercise 10 in pairs as a warm-up to this homework assignment.

For more practice, use *Grammar Dimensions 3* Workbook page 138, Exercise 9.

EXERCISE 10 [15 minutes]

This exercise can be done after students have completed the writing assignment in Exercise 9 or as a warm-up to Exercise 9, which can then be assigned as homework.

1. Put students into pairs or small groups.
2. Students should look at the list of activities and states in Exercise 9 and ask each other questions about childhood.
3. If you have time, encourage students to ask follow-up questions to interesting answers rather than just sticking with simple *yes/no* answers.
4. Have pairs or groups report the most interesting stories or findings to the class. For example, *Maria used to pretend that her bed could fly. Tomas used to hide in the washing machine.* See other possible answers on LP page 396.

EXPANSION [15 minutes/homework]

Have students choose one childhood memory of a habitual state or activity based on the discussion in Exercise 10 and develop it into a paragraph. You can use the following as an example:

When I was a child, I used to be very afraid of the dark. In fact, I was so afraid of the dark that I would try to keep the light in my room on all night. My parents used to sneak into my room after I was asleep and turn the light off, but usually I would wake up later and turn it back on.

FOCUS 5

Future in Past Time Frame

meaning

use

EXAMPLES

EXPLANATIONS

(a) My parents got married almost fifty years ago. In 1957 my father first met the woman that he **would marry** a few years later. From that very first day my father knew that he **was** eventually **going to marry** her.

The past time frame often includes references to future events. The actual time of these events may be in the past (in relation to **now**), but it is in the future in relation to our moment of focus. The moment of focus in Passage (a) is "that very first day" in 1957.

(b) Although Lincoln **wasn't to become** president until 1860, he started running for political offices quite early in his career. At that time he had no idea that he **was going to have** three unsuccessful attempts before he **would** finally **win** his first election.

In passage (b) the moment of focus is when Lincoln "started running for political offices." We use the one-word and phrasal modals for future activity in their past tense forms (*would, was/were going to,* and *was/were to*). See Unit 15 for more practice with these modals in the present and future time frames.

(c) Matt used to hope that he someday **would have** a job where he **might travel** around the world. Perhaps he **could** even have a chance to live in another country.

"Past tense" one-word modals (*might, would, could*) of future activity can be used to talk about future events in the past time frame.

EXAMPLES

EXPLANATIONS

(d) Elizabeth didn't have much time to get ready for the dance. She **was going to** do all her errands in a single afternoon. First she **would** pick up her dress. Then she **would** get her hair done. That **would** leave her the rest of the afternoon to get ready.

Was going to is preferred over *would*:

• to introduce a topic

(e) Yuri didn't want to leave the house. It **was going to** rain any minute.

• to indicate immediate future

(f) At first my parents **weren't going to** let me stay up late, but I convinced them to let me do it.

• to describe unfulfilled intentions—intended actions that did not actually take place

(g) Oh, here you are! I **was going to** call you. But now I don't have to.

(h) We **were going to** go skiing tomorrow, but there's no snow, so we'll just stay home instead.

EXERCISE 11

Underline all the modal structures that refer to future events or intentions in these paragraphs. The first sentence of each passage has been done for you as examples.

1. (a) When I was a child I used to dream that <u>I would have</u> a bright future. (b) I thought I was going to be a doctor or a movie star. (c) I <u>would have</u> a university medical degree. (d) I <u>would have</u> a job where I <u>could do</u> what I wanted, and <u>wouldn't have to</u> go to an office every day. (e) I was going to be famous, and I was definitely going to have lots of money. (f) I <u>would have</u> a big house in Hollywood and ten children.

2. (a) Nora was going to spend a month in Japan before she started her new job, which <u>was to begin</u> in six weeks. (b) She was going to fly to Japan last Monday, but a strange thing happened as she was about to leave for the airport. (c) Suddenly she had a strong sensation that she <u>shouldn't get</u> on the plane. (d) She had a strange feeling that there <u>might be</u> an accident or that there <u>would be</u> some other problem. (e) She knew that she could take a flight later in the week, so that's what she decided to do. (f) It's a good thing she did, because the plane she was going to take crashed into the ocean.

EXERCISE 12

Do these sentences describe unfulfilled intentions or future activities in the past time frame? In sentences that describe future activities, substitute *would* for *was/were going to*.

Example: Nora and Jim aren't here right now. They said they **were going to** be studying at the library.

> *It describes future activity. They said they would be studying at the library.*

1. I **wasn't going to** mention the money you owe me. But since you brought it up, I guess we should talk about it.

2. My teacher **wasn't going to** postpone the test, so we studied for the entire weekend.

3. The committee organized the refreshments for the party. Mary **was going to** bring cookies. John **was going to** take care of beverages.

4. I'm not finished painting the house. Jim **was going to help**, but I guess he had something else to do.

5. **Were you going to** send me a check? I haven't received it yet.

6. I never thought this party **was going to** be so much fun.

7. We **weren't going to** extend our vacation, but the weather was so nice that we decided to stay for a few more days.

ANSWER KEY

Exercise 12 1. unfulfilled intention   2. It describes future activity. My teacher wouldn't postpone the test, so we studied for the entire weekend.   3. It describes future activity. Mary would bring cookies, John would take care of beverages.   4. unfulfilled intention   5. unfulfilled intention   6. It describes future activity. I never thought the party would be so much fun.   7. unfulfilled intention.

FOCUS 5 [15 minutes]

Focus 5 presents *future events in the past time frame* and the use of modals to express this concept.

Suggestion: Do Exercise 11 as a class before going over Focus 5 in order to introduce the notion of future events or intentions in the past.

1. **Lead-in:** Be sure that the class first understands the idea of future in the past by providing a variety of paired examples to illustrate (you can put the second sentence in each pair on the board now, or put them up as a second step in your presentation):

   George knew that we were going to have a quiz yesterday.

   George knew that we would have a quiz yesterday.

   Tran hoped it wasn't going to rain on Saturday, but it did.

   Tran hoped it wouldn't rain on Saturday, but it did.

2. Point out that the time frame for these events is all in the past. However, *George knew* something about the future and *Tran hoped* something for the future.

3. Show the class how it is possible to use both the phrasal modal (*was going to*) and the one-word modal (*would*) to express the future in past time.

4. Show how other one-word modals can be used. For example, *Tran thought he could/might come with us, but he didn't.*

5. Go over the examples and explanations in Focus 5 with the class or assign it as homework. Be sure to note the section of the chart that outlines when *was going to* is preferred over *would*, especially when using unfulfilled intentions:

   Jan was going to call last night, but she forgot.
   * *Jan would call last night, but she forgot.*

GRAMMAR NOTE

Note that, in addition to actual events, *would* can also occur in hypothetical conditionals (see Unit 17, Focus 3, SB page 276 for more on this), which express a possible future event. These hypothetical events can be described in the past time frame. For example, *I thought that she would be angry if I told her the bad news.*

EXPANSION 1 [30 minutes]

You may want to use Activity 2 (speaking) on SB page 401 to give students practice with the use of modals to describe future events in the past. Students will discuss predictions that were made for past events.

EXPANSION 2 [30 minutes/homework]

You can Activity 6 (research on the web) on SB page 403. In this activity, students will research predictions that did not come true.

EXERCISE 11 [15 minutes]

This exercise asks students to identify references to future events or intentions and to underline the modals that signal these. This exercise can also be used before presenting Focus 5 to introduce the notion of future events in past time frame.

1. If you are short on time, assign half the class the first passage and the other half the second passage. Alternately, use the first passage as an example with the whole class and assign the second passage for students to do individually.

2. Especially if you are using this exercise as an introduction to the concepts in Focus 5, be sure to spend a few minutes discussing how the first sentence or two reflect future intentions and the modals that signal these.

3. Have students work individually to underline the modals and then compare answers in pairs or as a class review. See answers on LP page 398.

For more practice, use *Grammar Dimensions 3* Workbook page 139, Exercise 10.

EXERCISE 12 [15 minutes]

This exercise asks students to identify which sentences express unfulfilled intentions or future activities. Students should review the examples (f–h) in Focus 5 and again note that *was going to* is preferred in unfulfilled intentions.

1. Go over the example (*future activity*) and then go over the first sentence in Exercise 12 (*unfulfilled intention*) before assigning the rest.

2. Have students work individually or in pairs. Circulate and note any common errors or problematic sentences to go over as a class later.

3. As you review this exercise with the class, again point out that future activities can use either *was going to* or *would* and this exercise asks that students change these sentences to *would*. However, unfulfilled intentions should use *was going to* only. See answers on LP page 398.

4. Follow this exercise directly with Exercise 13.

For more practice, use *Grammar Dimensions 3* Workbook page 139, Exercise 11.

Use Your English

ACTIVITY 1 writing/speaking

■ STEP 1

In the Opening Task on page 387 you read about ways in which people change for the better as they grow older. Now think about ways that people change for the worse. Make a list of things that you can no longer do that you used to be able to do. These may be activities or privileges. If you wish, compare your list to those of other students in the class.

■ STEP 2

Write a paragraph or give a short speech to the rest of the class describing one general way that people's lives change for the worse as they grow older. Be sure to provide examples to support your ideas.

ACTIVITY 2 speaking

In 1989 political changes in Eastern Europe resulted in important changes in worldwide economics, politics, and military alliances. On September 11, 2001, the terrorist attack on the World Trade Center caused similar unexpected changes in world affairs.

What predictions did people make about world events before these changes occurred? What things are happening now that seemed impossible a few years ago? In a small group, develop two lists: *Things people thought were going to happen that no longer seem likely to happen* and *Things that are happening now that people never thought would happen. Present your lists to the rest of the class.*

ACTIVITY 3 writing

Write a short paragraph about one or more of these topics:

- Bad habits that you used to have, but don't have anymore
- A time when you were going to do something but weren't allowed or weren't able to do it
- How your life has turned out differently from your expectations (things you thought were going to happen that didn't, and vice versa)

EXERCISE 13

Decide which form, *would* or *was/were going to*, should be used in the following sentences. In some cases both answers may be correct.

1. As soon as Charlie heard about Maria's party he decided that he (a) _____ (not go). Sophie (b) _____ (be) there, and she and Charlie didn't get along. He was afraid that she (c) _____ (probably want) to tell everyone about how they used to be engaged to be married.

2. Last week Jeff stood in line for five hours to get a ticket to the opera, but he knew it was worth the long wait. It (a) _____ (be) a great performance. Pavarotti (b) _____ (sing) the part of Falstaff. Jeff had heard him before so he was sure it (c) _____ (be) wonderful.

3. Naomi didn't know what to do for her vacation. Perhaps she (a) _____ (go) to Mexico. The plane ticket (b) _____ (be) expensive, but she didn't want to travel by herself on the bus.

4. When I talked to Lin last Sunday night she wasn't planning on getting much sleep. Her project was already a week late, and she couldn't ask the professor for another extension. She (a) _____ (finish) her assignment, even if she had to stay up until dawn. It (b) _____ (not be) easy. She had to finish reading *War and Peace* and then write a ten-page paper. She (c) _____ (probably be) up all night.

5. We performed a very difficult experiment in our chemistry class the other day. I was very nervous because we had to put just the right amount of chemicals into a solution in order for the reaction to occur. Too much phosphorous (a) _____ (cause) the wrong reaction. If there was too little, nothing (b) _____ (happen) at all. If I (c) _____ (do) the experiment correctly, it (d) _____ (be) necessary to measure very, very carefully.

ANSWER KEY

Exercise 13 In cases where both answer are correct, the most likely answer is listed first.

1. (a) wouldn't go/wasn't going to go; (b) would be/was going to be; (c) would probably want

2. (a) was going to be/would be; (b) was going to sing; (c) would be/was going to be   3. (a) would go; (b) would be/was going to be   4. (a) was going to finish/would finish; (b) wouldn't be/wasn't going to be; (c) would probably be/was probably going to be   5. (a) would cause; (b) would happen; (c) was going to do; (d) would be

EXERCISE 13 [15 minutes]

Students should read each passage completely and then use *would* or *was/were going to* with the verbs given to complete each sentence. Have students work individually or in pairs and review as usual. See answers on LP page 400.

For more practice, use *Grammar Dimensions 3* Workbook page 140, Exercise 12.

UNIT GOAL REVIEW [10 minutes]

Ask students to look at the goals on the opening page of the unit again. Refer to the pages of the unit where information on each goal can be found.

ExamView®
Test Generator

For assessment of Unit 24, use *Grammar Dimensions 3 ExamView®*.

USE YOUR ENGLISH

The Use Your English activities at the end of the unit contain situations that should naturally elicit the structures covered in the unit. For a more complete discussion of how to use the Use Your English activities see To the Teacher on LP page xxii. When students are doing these activities in class, you can circulate and listen to see if they are using the structures accurately. Errors can be corrected when the activity is finished.

ACTIVITY 1 writing/speaking [15 minutes]

Use this activity after presenting Focus 3 on SB page 394. This activity refers back to the discussion and reading in the Opening Task on SB page 390. Students will now discuss the ways in which people change for the worse. This will involve using modals of ability in the past.

STEP 1

1. Have students refer back to the Opening Task on SB page 390 as they create their lists of changes for the worse.
2. If students are having trouble making a list, have them move around the room and ask at least five other people about any changes for the worse as they grow older.

STEP 2

1. After making the lists, students should use their lists to find one general idea to write about or speak about to the class. Encourage students to look at their lists and to find ways to generalize one idea about several examples. For example, students might have a list which includes (1) not being able to play video games all night, (2) not being able to hang out with friends as much, and (3) not having as much time to sleep. The general idea could be that the responsibilities of getting older limit our time for relaxation.
2. Have students prepare to present their findings either orally or in writing.
3. Give feedback on the use of the grammar forms presented in this unit.

ACTIVITY 2 speaking [30 minutes]

Use this activity after presenting Focus 5 on SB page 398. Students will use modals for describing the future in the past time frame as they discuss predictions for past events. You may want to begin with a brief class discussion of the world events listed in Activity 2. Ask students to consider what some of the unexpected changes in world affairs were due to these events.

1. Put students into small groups and have them work on making their lists as outlined in the activity.
2. When finished, have groups present their lists to the class. Be sure to have everyone use complete sentences to encourage the use of the target forms. For example, *We never believed that people would live in space stations.*

VARIATION

Have students write a paragraph as homework on one of these lists and share these in small groups the next day.

ACTIVITY 3 writing [15 minutes/homework]

Depending on which topic they choose, students will use modals of past habitual actions, past ability or permission, or describing the future in the past to write a paragraph.

1. Have students choose a topic and assign this as homework.
2. Give time in class for students to share their paragraphs when finished or simply collect the papers and give feedback as needed.

ACTIVITY 4 listening

STEP 1

CD Track 37

Listen to the short lecture on science fiction and match the predictions listed below to the authors who imagined them, by writing the initials of the author (JV—Jules Verne; HGW—H.G. Wells; GO—George Orwell; or AH—Aldous Huxley) next to the prediction. Then put a check by those predictions which have actually come true, and compare your answers with a partner's.

GO ✔ The government will control all aspects of people's lives.
GO ✔ Anyone who tries to disagree with the government will be put in prison.
JV Many people will own airplanes.
JV ✔ There will be exploration of the moon.
HGW People will be able to travel through time.
AH ✔ Children will be raised in state-run nurseries instead of in individual families.
JV There will be a single world language.
JV ✔ People will use solar power to get energy.
HGW Aliens from Mars will invade and conquer the Earth but will eventually die from common bacterial infections.
HGW Scientists will discover a way to make people invisible.
GO ✔ People will be watched by police, by hidden cameras, and by microphones.
AH ✔ Children will be born through artificial means.
AH There will be movies that are so realistic that people will think they are actually happening.
GO There will only be three or four huge governments, and they will constantly be at war with each other.
AH ✔ The use of mind-altering drugs will be widespread and encouraged by the government.

STEP 2

Based on the information you learned from the lecture, discuss the following question in a small group and present your opinion and your reasons to the rest of the class. Which writer did the most accurate job of predicting the future?

ACTIVITY 5 writing/speaking

First think about these questions: How has the social role of women changed? What things were your grandmothers not allowed to do, simply because they were women? What things wouldn't women consider doing fifty years ago that are commonplace today? Then write a paragraph or make a presentation to the rest of the class discussing the five biggest differences between women's lives fifty years ago and today.

ACTIVITY 6 research on the web

Go on the Internet and use a search engine such as Google® or Yahoo® to search for "mistaken predictions". You will find a number of articles that talk about events people thought would happen but didn't. Some topics focus on predictions about technological developments or medical breakthroughs that turned out not to have happened. There are even articles that discuss the most common predictions that turned out not to be true. Prepare a brief report that describes three mistaken predictions that interest you. Tell what people thought would happen and what actually happened.

ACTIVITY 7 reflection

How are you progressing in your English skills?

- Identify three mistakes that you used to make that you don't anymore. (For example: "I used to confuse *confusing* and *confused*.")
- Identify three concepts that you didn't used to be able to express that you now can. (For example: "I didn't used to be able to distinguish hypothetical from real statements.")
- Identify three "compensation" strategies that you used to use that you no longer need. (For example: "I used to avoid passive constructions.")
- Identify three things that you hoped you would be able to do by now that you are still not able to do. (For example: "I had hoped that I would be able to understand everything my roommate says without having to ask him to repeat it.")

Compare your answers with those of two or three other students. Identify common accomplishments and common goals you still want to achieve and report them to the rest of the class.

USE YOUR ENGLISH

ACTIVITY 4   listening   [20 minutes]

CD Track 37

Students will hear the modals from the unit used in context as they match the predictions to the authors. This can lead to an interesting discussion of science fiction.

1. You may want to begin this listening activity by first asking what the class knows about science fiction and if anyone enjoys science fiction novels or movies.

2. Then ask about the authors who will be discussed. Put the authors' names on the board and discuss what the class knows of them.

STEP 1

1. Play the audio and have students write the initials next to each matching statement. (See the following Variation.)

2. Play again as needed for students to check their work.

3. Give students time to mark those predictions that have actually come true.

4. Put students into small groups to check their work together. See answers on LP page 402.

STEP 2   Small groups should discuss the question in Step 2. If you have time, ask the groups to present their findings to the class.

Suggestion: Before listening to the audio, along with the authors' names on the board, put some of the authors' book titles up on the other side of the board (randomly mixed up) and see if the class can match the novel to the author (*War of the Worlds* (HGW), *Twenty Thousand Leagues Under the Sea* (JV), *Brave New World* (AH), 1984 (GO)). Make this a team competition and have teams correct their own answers after listening to the audio. Award bonus points to any team that gets all of the matches correct.

VARIATION

For variety and for those students who need more kinesthetic activities, copy the statements onto paper and cut them up into separate strips. Give one set of sentence strips to each small group. As they listen to the audio have them work together to arrange the statements into groups on the floor or a table according to authors.

ACTIVITY 5   writing/speaking   [25 minutes/homework]

Students will write about or discuss the changes in women's roles in the past 50 years. Students may prefer to write about women's roles in their home country. Assign this as written homework with the usual guidelines. Collect papers or have students present orally in class.

ACTIVITY 6   research on the web   [30 minutes/homework]

Use this activity after Focus 5 on page 398. In this activity, students will research predictions that did not come true. This will expose them to forms that discuss the future in the past time frame.

1. Because they are likely to come across Nostradamus at some point in this research activity, you may want to begin the assignment with a class discussion of who he was and what he did. Put his name on the board and ask the class what they know about him.

2. Assign the activity as a written assignment to collect and evaluate or as an oral presentation.

ACTIVITY 7   reflection   [30 minutes/homework]

Students will reflect on their progress in English. Students will use the forms presented in Unit 24 in their answers to the questions listed.

1. Assign the reflection activity as homework.

2. Have students compare answers in small groups the next day.

3. Each group should then list common accomplishments and common goals in complete sentences and share these with the class.

Suggestion: Each group can put their list on the board. Use these sentences to review the forms presented in Unit 24.

UNIT GOALS

- Correctly indicate meaning in statements of indirect quotation and reported speech

- Know when to make necessary changes in verb tenses and reference forms

- Correctly report statements questions and commands when using indirect quotation

- Distinguish between formal and informal patterns of quotation, paraphrase, and reported speech

OPENING TASK

What Are They Saying?

Look carefully at this series of pictures. It is a record of a conversation between Jack and Jean.

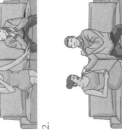
1.   2.

3.   4.

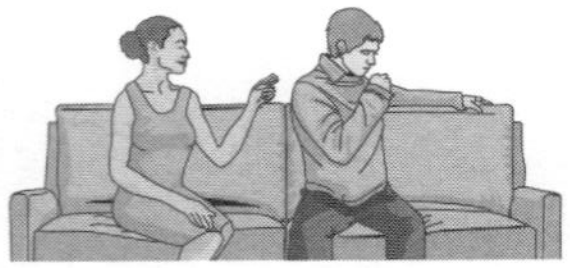

■ STEP 1

What do you think these people are talking about? Write down the exact conversation that you think occurred between them.

Picture 1

Jack: _____

Jean: _____

Jack: _____

Picture 2

Jean: _____

Jack: _____

Jean: _____

Jack: _____

Picture 3

Jean: _____

Jack: _____

Picture 4

Jean: _____

Jack: _____

Jean: _____

Jack: _____

■ STEP 2

Compare your conversation with that of another student. Discuss what you thought they were talking about in each picture and why you thought that. Your discussion might be something like this:

You: "In the first picture I thought that Jack was telling Jean that he had something important to tell her."

Your partner: "Oh really? I thought that he was trying to introduce himself for the first time. Why did you think he already knew her?"

You: "Because they're sitting rather close together."

■ STEP 3

Report the three most interesting differences between your two conversations (and your reasons for thinking so) to the rest of the class.

UNIT OVERVIEW

This unit reviews the use of indirect quotations to paraphrase and summarize the statements of others. This unit covers the formation of indirect questions, statements, and commands along with embedded questions. Due to its length, this unit has been divided into three lesson plans.

GRAMMAR NOTE

Indirect quotation, or reported speech, is used to report what someone else has said or written. It is extremely common in both written and spoken contexts, and is used for summarizing and paraphrasing. Many ESL students find indirect speech to be problematic due to the changes that need to be made in order to put direct quotations into indirect quotations, including time shifts of verbs and modals, shifts in reference, and changes in word order (see the Grammar Note at the end of this page). Reported questions can be the most confusing due to the additional change in word order. Complicating these rules is the reason that many native speakers do not use a shift in time frame in indirect quotations, especially when speaking casually.

UNIT GOALS

Some instructors may want to review the goals listed on Student Book (SB) page 404 after completing the Opening Task so that students understand what they should know by the end of the unit. These goals can also be reviewed at the end of the unit when students are more familiar with the grammar terminology.

OPENING TASK [20 minutes/homework]

The aim of this activity is to give students the opportunity to use direct and indirect quotations. The problem-solving format is designed to show the teacher how well the students can produce a target structure implicitly and spontaneously when they are engaged in a communicative task. Assign Step 1 of this task as homework the night before presenting Unit 25. For a more complete discussion of the purpose of the Opening Task, see To the Teacher, Lesson Planner (LP) page xxii.

Setting Up the Task

Begin with a quick discussion of body language (Unit 9, Exercise 5) and what the body language of the people in these pictures might suggest about their relationship.

STEP 1

1. Assign the conversation as homework. Alternately, you can have pairs work on creating the dialogue together in class.
2. Remind students to use quotation marks for the direct quotations in the dialogue of this first step. Circulate and assist if students are working together in class.

Conducting the Task

STEP 2

1. Once the dialogue has been prepared, either at home or in class, have students form pairs or have two pairs join together in order to share conversations.
2. Students or pairs can read their conversations out loud to each other. The more dramatic the reading, the more fun the activity.
3. As outlined in Step 2, students should discuss the differences between the two conversations. Circulate and note the students' current use of indirect speech.

Closing the Task

STEP 3

Bring the class together and ask students to share the most interesting differences between the two conversations. Students should also be able to discuss why they chose the ones they did.

Suggestion: Have students write the most interesting differences down. Collect these and use as a diagnostic to note common errors to address later in the unit.

EXPANSION 1 [30 minutes]

See Activity 1 (speaking/writing), on SB page 418 for a variation on the Opening Task. Students will act out their conversations in front of the class.

EXPANSION 2 [20 minutes/homework]

See Activity 8 (speaking), on SB page 420. Students will eavesdrop and report to the class on the conversations of strangers and report what they heard along with any indirect quotations the speakers used.

GRAMMAR NOTE

Typical student errors (form)

- Not changing the word order of reported questions: *Hana asked where am I going. (See Focus 6.)
- Not shifting the time frame of the modal in indirect quotations: *Jamal said that be will help us. (See Focus 2.)
- Not shifting the time frame of the verb in indirect quotations: *Jamal said that be went to the doctor last week. (See Focus 2.)
- Not changing pronouns or possessive determiners for clear reference in indirect quotations: *Ted said I gave Joe my book. (to mean Ted gave a book to Joe) (See Focus 3.)
- Not using an indirect object with reporting verbs that require one: *She told that she would come to the party.

FOCUS 1

Overview of Direct Versus Indirect Quotation

form | meaning
use

When we report information that was spoken, written, or thought at some time other than the current moment, we can use direct quotation or indirect quotation.

- **Direct quotation** is the **actual words** that were spoken, written or thought. Direct quotation occurs in informal spoken English and appears most commonly in fiction.

- **Indirect quotation** (also referred to as **"reported speech"** when we are reporting spoken language) expresses the **meaning** of what was said or thought or communicated rather than the actual words.

We can use these patterns to describe thoughts, ideas, and feelings of others that were thought but not actually spoken. Indirect quotation is most frequently used by reporters and writers in news reports and nonfiction writing.

DIRECT QUOTATION	INDIRECT QUOTATION
(a) Jack said, "I'm feeling really sick."	(b) Jack said that he was feeling really sick.
(c) Jean thought, "I wonder if Jack is OK because he doesn't look well."	(d) Jean wondered if Jack was OK because he didn't look well.
(e) A famous historian once wrote, "Western history shows repeated examples of great empires going into decline when uncontrolled military spending exceeds expenditures for other needs."	(f) A famous historian once observed that Western history showed repeated examples of great empires going into decline when uncontrolled military spending exceeded expenditures for other needs.
(g) So Jack's all, "Yeah, I guess I'm really sick," and he goes, "Okay I'm going to the doctor right away."	(h) So Jack admitted that he was really sick and promised that he was going to the doctor right away.

Direct quotation: In direct quotation, quotation word order changes depending on whether the quotation is a statement, a question or an imperative. In formal written English we use quotation marks (". . .") to indicate direct quotation. When the quotation follows the reporting verb, it is commonly preceded by a comma. In some contexts we can use a colon.

EXAMPLES	EXPLANATIONS
(i) The doctor told Jack, "I'm afraid we'll have to do more tests."	Direct quotation of a statement
(j) The doctor asked Jack, "Have you been having these headaches for a long time?"	Direct quotation of a question
(k) The doctor told Jack, "Take these pills three times a day, and please stop drinking coffee."	Direct quotation of a command or request

In casual spoken English we use can use reporting words such as *go* or *be like* to indicate direct quotation of something that has been spoken or thought.

EXAMPLES	EXPLANATIONS
(l) The doctor **goes**, "Well, buddy, I'm afraid we'll have to do more tests."	Casual spoken direct quotation of a statement
(m) And Jack **was like**, "Oh my gosh, have I got cancer or something?"	Casual spoken direct quotation of a question
(n) So the doctor **was all**, "Could you just relax? Put this thermometer in your mouth."	Casual spoken direct quotation of a command or request

Indirect Quotation: In indirect quotation, certain changes need to be made in time frame, reference forms, and word order, depending on whether the quotation is a statement, question, or imperative. These changes are outlined in the rest of this unit.

FOCUS 1 [20 minutes]

Focus 1 presents an overview of both direct and indirect quotations with special emphasis on the different kinds of direct quotations and the reporting verbs that indicate these. The rest of the unit will focus primarily on the changes that need to be made when turning a direct quotation into an indirect quotation.

1. **Lead-in:** Invite students to share a direct quotation from the Opening Task and put it on one side of the board. Explain that this is called a **direct quotation**. Point out the required punctuation for this.

2. Now rewrite this quotation as an **indirect quotation** on the other side of the board. Ask the class what has been changed to make this second sentence different from the first (*punctuation, speaker's name and a reporting verb added, shift in verb tense, shift in modal tense, change in pronoun forms, change in demonstratives or adverbials*).

3. Explain that both direct quotations and indirect quotes can refer to ideas that are spoken, thought, or written. See examples (a–f).

4. Explain that direct quotations can show a very casual and conversational tone as in examples (g) and (l–n). While this is not correct as written English, students should be able to recognize it as casual speech and slang when spoken.

5. Go over the examples of direct quotations used for statements, questions, and commands in examples (i–k).

6. Draw the classes' attention to the punctuation. Ask them to check their conversations in the Opening Task for proper punctuation. If you have time, circulate, check, and answer questions now before moving on with the rest of the unit.

Suggestion: Because this is just an overview that focuses more on the form of direct quotations, you can assign this to be reviewed by students on their own. Give the class time to ask questions about Focus 1 before moving on, however.

EXERCISE 1

Underline the indirect quotation patterns in the following passage that tell what the narrator heard or thought. The first one has been done for you as an example.

(1) When I was a child I often wondered <u>where babies come from</u>. (2) My parents always told me that <u>they had found me under a cabbage leaf</u>. (3) I knew <u>that probably wasn't true</u>, since I realized there were lots of new babies in my neighborhood and no cabbage plants at all. (4) For several years I thought <u>my parents had actually bought my younger sister at the hospital</u>. (5) I figured <u>hospitals were places that sold babies to any couple that wanted one</u>. (6) This was because when my mother came back from the hospital after giving birth to my sister, I heard her remind my father that <u>he had to be sure to pay the bill before that week was over</u>. (7) I was a little jealous of my new sister, and I hoped <u>my father would forget to pay</u> and that <u>the hospital would decide to take her back and sell her to someone else</u>. (8) It wasn't until several years later that I found out <u>babies were neither bought nor found</u>.

FOCUS 2

Indirect Quotation and Change of Time Frame

meaning

use

When using indirect quotation, because we are describing something that has already occurred (the speaking, thinking, or reporting), we use past time frame and modal forms of the verb phrases of what we are reporting.

To refer to present time frame: Use past verb forms instead of present.

DIRECT QUOTATION	INDIRECT QUOTATION
(a) Jack said, "I'm really sick. **I am having** terrible headaches. **I'm going to try to** see my doctor this afternoon, if **I can get** someone to drive me to her office."	(b) Jack acknowledged that he **was** really sick. He reported that he **was having** terrible headaches and **was going to try to** see his doctor yesterday afternoon, if he **could get** someone to drive him to the doctor's office.

To refer to past time frame: Use past perfect verb forms instead of past.

DIRECT QUOTATION	INDIRECT QUOTATION
(c) Last Tuesday Jean saw Jack. Here is what he said: "My headache **was getting** worse all the time, so I **went** to the doctor yesterday. She **took** my temperature. She **prescribed** some pills. My condition **has improved**, but I still **haven't gone** back to work yet."	(d) When Jean spoke to Jack last Tuesday he told her that his headache **had been getting** worse, so she **had gone** to the doctor the day before, on Monday. She **had prescribed** some pills. Jack felt that his condition **had improved**, but when Jean spoke to him he still **hadn't gone** back to work.

Modal forms in indirect quotation: Use past modal forms instead of present.

DIRECT QUOTATION	INDIRECT QUOTATION
(e) "I **will try** to see my doctor this afternoon, if **I can get** someone to drive me to her office."	(f) He said that he **would try** to see his doctor yesterday afternoon, if he **could get** someone to drive him to the doctor's office.

INSTEAD OF:	USE:
may	*might*
can	*could*
shall	*should*
will	*would*

EXERCISE 2

Here is the response Mr. Green made when he talked with Denise. Write a paragraph describing the outcome that reports all his statements. Start your paragraph with *Mr. Green decided that. . . .* Use *Mr. Green suggested that . . .* and *Mr. Green thought that . . .* later in the paragraph.

Mr. Green said, "The personnel officer will be asked to speak to Peter. If Peter can't get to the office on time, he will just have to take an earlier bus. He may not be crazy about getting up at 5:30, but he will have to do it if he wants to keep his job. Personnel won't talk to Peter about the other problems he may be having, though. One of Peter's friends in the office can deal with him directly about his lack of responsibility. Peter probably won't change much, but he may be more willing to listen to the complaints if he can get the information from someone he likes and respects."

ANSWER KEY

Exercise 2 Answers will vary. One possible answer is: Mr. Green decided that the personnel officer would be asked to speak to Peter. He also said that if Peter couldn't get to the office on time, he would just have to take an earlier bus. He might not be crazy about getting up at 5:30, but he would have to do it if he wanted to keep his job. Personnel wouldn't talk to Peter about the other problems he might be having, though. Mr. Green suggested that one of Peter's friends in the office could deal with him directly about his lack of responsibility. Mr. Green thought that Peter probably wouldn't change much, but he might be more willing to listen to the complaints if he could get the information from someone he liked and respected.

LESSON PLAN 1

EXERCISE 1 [15 minutes]

This exercise asks students to identify indirect quotations in a passage.

1. Go over the first sentence or two as a class and then have students work individually.

2. Circulate. After giving students some time to work, if it looks like students are missing several indirect quotations, you can call out the total number of indirect quotations that they should have found. This will encourage students to look again if they fall short.

3. When finished, go over as a class. Ask volunteers to note the reporting verb used to signal the indirect quotation. Put these on the board. See answers on LP page 408.

Suggestion: Have students keep a list of reporting verbs as they work through the unit.

For more practice, use *Grammar Dimensions 3* Workbook page 141, Exercises 1 and 2.

FOCUS 2 [20 minutes]

Focus 2 presents the basic concept of changing time frames to "more past" when using indirect quotations. Because this is a fundamental characteristic, be sure that students can make this time frame shift before continuing on.

1. **Lead-in:** Put a few direct quotations on the board and refer to them as you work through the three main concepts presented in this focus chart.

    Ana said, "Dinner is ready."

    James said, "It rained last night."
    Paolo said, "Alex will visit soon."

2. Explain that when using indirect quotations (reported speech), we need to shift the time frame into the past to report what has already been said, thought, or written.

3. To show that present time in indirect quotations should change to past time in indirect quotations, ask for a volunteer to put the first example sentence into an indirect quotation. (*Ana said that dinner was ready.*)

4. To show that past time should change to past perfect in indirect quotations, ask for a volunteer to put the second example sentence into an indirect quotation. (*James said that it had rained last night.*)

5. To show that present modal forms should change to past modal forms in indirect quotations, ask for a volunteer to put the last example sentence into an indirect quotation. (*Paolo said that Alex would visit soon.*)

Suggestion: You can have students review the information in Focus 2 on their own before or after your presentation. Move directly on to Exercise 2 or 3 to follow up this presentation.

GRAMMAR NOTE

Because reported speech does not typically make the required time frame shift when reporting very recent speech (*She said that she can't hear you*) or when reporting things that are still or always true (*She said that she doesn't like coffee*), having students report other students' utterances is not an effective way to introduce and practice this basic feature. See Focus 4 for more on this.

EXERCISE 2 [15 minutes]

This exercise works well as a check of the ability to shift time frames, because it focuses only on this shift.

The whole passage is a direct quotation, so students will put each statement into an indirect quotation using the reporting verbs listed in the directions. See a sample paragraph on LP page 408.

Suggestion: If you are using Exercise 2 as a diagnostic, collect students' paragraphs and go over any common errors in the next class.

For more practice, use *Grammar Dimensions 3* Workbook page 142, Exercise 3.

form

meaning

FOCUS 3

Other Reference Changes in Indirect Quotation

In indirect quotation we must change pronoun forms in order to keep the same meaning.

EXAMPLES

	IMPLIED MEANING
(a) Jack said, "**I** am sick."	Jack is sick.
(b) Jack told me that **I** am sick.	I am sick—nor Jack.
(c) Jack told me that **he** was sick.	Jack is sick.

Compare the pronouns in these two passages.

DIRECT QUOTATION

(d) Jack told me, "**You** will be happy to know that **my** condition has improved, but **I** still haven't gone back to **my** office yet."

INDIRECT QUOTATION

(e) He said that **I** would be happy to know that **his** condition had improved, but **he** hadn't gone back to **his** office yet.

If there is some confusion about what the pronoun or possessive determiner refers to, it may be necessary to substitute the actual noun.

DIRECT QUOTATION

(f) Jack said, "I asked **my** brother Peter to bring **his** wife to the party."

INDIRECT QUOTATION

(g) Jack asked **his** brother Peter to bring **his**—**Peter's**—wife to the party.

You may also need to change demonstratives and adverbials to keep the same meaning.

DIRECT QUOTATION

(h) On Saturday Maria said, "Please come **here** for lunch **this afternoon**."

(j) Jack said, "I went to the doctor **yesterday**."

INDIRECT QUOTATION

(i) On Saturday Maria asked me to go **there** for lunch **that afternoon**.

(k) Jack told me that he had gone to the doctor **(on) the previous day**.

Here are some examples of other common changes (→) in reference that may be required when reporting with indirect quotation.

this/these →	*that/those*
here →	*there*
today/tonight →	*(on) that day/that night*
yesterday →	*(on) the day before/the previous day*
tomorrow →	*the next day*
two days from today →	*two days from then*
two days ago →	*two days earlier*

EXERCISE 3

Denise Driven had a meeting with her boss, Mr. Green, to complain about Peter Principle's work in the office. Here are some of the complaints that Denise made about Peter. Report her complaints, using the cue given.

Example: "I've been getting more and more annoyed by Peter's behavior."

Denise reported that . . .

Denise reported that she had been getting more and more annoyed by Peter's behavior.

1. "Peter needs to be more serious about work."

Denise felt that . . .

2. "Peter came to work fifteen minutes late for the second time in a month."

Denise was angry that . . .

3. "Peter is going to leave the office early to see his child perform in a school play."

She complained that . . .

4. "He is always whistling in the office."

She didn't like the fact that . . .

5. "He has made rude comments about my personal life."

She was upset that . . .

EXERCISE 4

Here are other complaints Denise had about Peter. How do you think she stated her complaints? Use her probable actual words and direct quotation.

Example: She reported that she had been getting more and more annoyed by Peter's behavior.

"I have been getting more and more annoyed by Peter's behavior."

1. She observed that he didn't always finish projects on time.

2. She pointed out that he told too many jokes at staff meetings.

3. She complained that he refused to come into the office on Saturdays.

4. She reported that he had told her that he was going to miss an important meeting because he had promised to take his children to the circus.

5. She resented that he constantly allowed his personal life to interfere with his work obligations.

ANSWER KEY

Exercise 3 1. Peter needed to be more serious about work. 2. Peter had come to work fifteen minutes late for the second time in a month. 3. Peter was going to leave the office early to see his child perform in a school play. 4. he was always whistling in the office. 5. he had made rude comments about her personal life.

Exercise 4 Answers will vary. Possible answers are: 1. "I am annoyed that he doesn't always finish projects on time." 2. "I am unhappy that he tells so many jokes at staff meetings." 3. "I don't like the fact that he refuses to come into the office on Saturdays." 4. "I am upset that: he is going to miss an important meeting because he has promised to take his children to the circus." 5. "I am angry that he constantly allows his personal life to interfere with his work obligations."

LESSON PLAN 1/LESSON PLAN 2

EXERCISE 3 [10 minutes]

Students will change direct quotations into indirect quotations, focusing on the shift in time frame.

1. Since this is similar to the changes you had volunteers make to the example quotations in the presentation of Focus 2, have students work individually and then compare answers with a partner.

2. Circulate and assist as needed.

3. Because in each sentence only the main verb will change (shift into a more past time frame), it won't be necessary to put whole sentences on the board for review. See answers on LP page 410.

EXERCISE 4 [10 minutes]

This exercise works in the reverse of Exercise 2. Students will need to make a few changes, such as deleting the pronoun referring to Denise and the following reporting verb + *that*. Follow the steps outlined for Exercise 2. See answers on LP page 410. Note that while answers can vary slightly, the basic construct should be the same.

LESSON PLAN 2

FOCUS 3 [25 minutes]

Focus 3 outlines the changes in reference that are needed when changing from direct to indirect quotations. These include changes in pronouns, possessive determiners, demonstratives, and adverbials.

1. **Lead-in:** Put a few direct quotations on the board and refer to them as you work through the concepts presented in this focus chart.

   Ana said, "I'm not going to the party."
   James said, "You have my book in your car."

Paolo said, "I can return these books to the library tomorrow."

2. To show that pronoun forms should change in order to keep the same meaning in indirect quotations, ask for a volunteer to put the first example sentence into an indirect quotation. (*Ana said that she was not going to the party.*) Follow up by going over the first and second parts of the focus chart as a class.

3. Looking now at possessive determiners, have another student volunteer to do the same for the second example sentence, making the changes needed to keep the same meaning. (*James said that I had his book in my car.*) Go over the third portion of the chart as a class.

4. Finally, to show that demonstratives and adverbials should also change in order to keep the same meaning of reference, have a volunteer change the last example sentence into an indirect quotation. (*Paolo said that he could return those books to the library the next day.*) Finish the focus by covering the last part of the chart as a class. Note the box of other common changes.

Suggestion: You can have students review the information in Focus 3 on their own before or after your presentation. Move directly onto Exercise 5 to follow up this presentation.

FOCUS 4

When No Tense Changes Are Required in Indirect Quotation

In certain situations, English speakers do not always make the tense and modal changes we have practiced here. These situations occur when we are reporting in the following categories:

CATEGORY	DIRECT QUOTATION	INDIRECT QUOTATION
• things that are always true	(a) My father always used to say, "Time is money."	(b) My father always believed that time is money.
• things that are still true	(c) Jean told me, "Jack is still living with his parents after all these years."	(d) Jean observed (that) Jack is still living with his parents after all these years.
• hypothetical statements	(e) Peter said, "If I had the money, I would make a donation to the club, but I am a little short on cash this month."	(f) Peter admitted that if he had the money, he would make a donation to the club, but that he is/was a little short on cash this/last month.
• statements that were made only a very short time ago	(g) Bambang told me, "I can't understand a word you're saying."	(h) He just said that he can't understand a word I'm saying.
• future events that have not yet occurred	(i) Diane said, "I am going to Hawaii next month."	(j) Diane announced that she is going to Hawaii next month.
• casual speech using direct quotation with such words as be all, be like, go, etc.	(k) Jack thought, "This doctor's bill is way too expensive."	(l) So Jack was all this doctor's bill is way too expensive.

EXERCISE 7

Decide whether tense changes are required in the following sentences when they are stated as indirect quotation. If a tense change is not required, state the reason. Example: Shakespeare once observed, "Love is blind." *No change. Timeless truth—still true*

1. A student in my geography class reported, "Not all the people who live in China speak Chinese as their first language."

2. My brother told me, "I wouldn't need to borrow money from you all the time if I had a better paying job."

3. It was only a minute ago that I asked, "Are you paying attention?"

4. Jeff told Matt, "I couldn't get any tickets for the concert."

5. Yesterday Denise said, "If I were you, I would plan things a little more completely before you leave for vacation next week."

EXERCISE 5

Peter's co-worker had a conversation with him at the water cooler on Wednesday. The following Monday, he told Denise what Peter had told him. Report the things that Peter told him. Use the cues given.

Example: "My kids have an invitation for your kids."
Peter said that his kids had an invitation for my kids.

1. "My kids are having a birthday party at my house on Saturday." Peter said.
2. "My kids have invited your kids to come to their party." Peter said.
3. "I've asked my friend to bring her three girls." Peter added.
4. "I've hired a clown to entertain all our kids." Peter announced.
5. "While our kids are watching the clown, my wife and I can prepare the cake and ice cream for your kids." Peter predicted.
6. "I asked Denise's secretary to tell her about the party, because she wanted me to work all weekend." Peter mentioned.
7. "My family is more important to me than Denise's project." Peter admitted.

EXERCISE 6

Answer these questions using the information found in the direct quotations. Use indirect quotations in your answers.

Example: Ali told me: "I came here to get some groceries, but the store's closed until tomorrow."
Why didn't Ali buy groceries while he was out? *Ali said that he had gone there to get some groceries, but the store was closed until the next day.*

1. Peter told me, "I am coming to the meeting this afternoon."
Do you know if Peter is planning to be at this meeting?

2. Mary said, "My father may be able to take this letter directly to the Immigration Office later today."
When you saw Mary last week who did she say was going to take the letter and when would it get there?

3. Bambang announced, "I have already completed all the assignments I have for my classes this week."
How come Bambang was playing video games on Wednesday night?

4. The doctor said, "The results of your test will be here by tomorrow morning."
What did the doctor tell you the day before yesterday?

Exercise 5 1. Peter said that his kids were having a birthday party at his house that weekend. 2. Peter told me that his kids had invited my kids to their party. 3. Peter added that he had asked his friend to bring her three girls. 4. Peter announced that he had hired a clown to entertain all our kids. 5. Peter predicted that while their kids were watching the clown, he and his wife could prepare the cake and ice cream for our kids. 6. Peter mentioned that he had asked Denise's secretary to tell Denise about the party, because Denise had wanted him to work all weekend. 7. Peter admitted that his family was more important to him than Denise's project.

Exercise 6 1. Peter told me that he was coming to the meeting. 2. Mary said that her father might be able to take the letter directly to the Immigration Office later that day. 3. He told me that he had already completed all the assignments he had for his classes that week. 4. The doctor said that the results of my test would be there by yesterday.

Exercise 7 1. no change—timeless truth 2. no change—hypothetical statement 3. no change—statements occurred a very short time ago 4. no change—tense change would result in a change of meaning 5. no change—hypothetical statement

LESSON PLAN 2

INDIRECT QUOTATION

EXERCISE 5 [10 minutes]

Use this as a follow-up to your presentation of Focus 3. Students will change direct quotations into indirect quotations, focusing on making changes in pronouns, possessive determiners, demonstratives, and/or adverbials.

1. Since this is similar to the changes you had volunteers make to the example quotations in the presentation of Focus 3, have students work individually and then compare answers with a partner.

2. Circulate and assist as needed. Be sure that students note when to use nouns in place of confusing pronouns. See answers on LP page 412.

Suggestion: As students finish, invite them to write one sentence (indirect quotation) on the board to make the review quicker and easier. Allow time for questions and the possibility for alternative answers.

For more practice, use *Grammar Dimensions 3* Workbook page 143, Exercises 4 and 5.

EXERCISE 6 [10 minutes]

This exercise should follow Exercise 5. Students will answer questions by referring to the information in direct quotations to create answers using indirect quotations. This activity gives students a task that is very similar to what they will need to be able to do in real life conversations.

1. Go over the examples with the class. Explain that using reported speech to answer questions about what someone else said is one of the most common uses.

2. If your class is more advanced, go over these statements orally as a class. You can have students take turns reading the direct quotations aloud. You can then ask the question, and call on students to answer them aloud. See answers on LP page 412.

Suggestion: Have students put their answers on paper and collect these to evaluate progress.

FOCUS 4 [15 minutes]

Focus 4 describes situations when there is no need to shift the time frame of verbs or modals when using indirect quotations. Students may already have noticed the lack of a time frame shift while listening to native speakers, especially in the case of casual speech.

1. **Lead-in:** You can begin by asking the class a few questions that will not require a time frame shift when reporting the answers in indirect quotations later. For example:

    What is your favorite color?
    What kind of job do you have?
    What are your plans for the vacation?

2. Ask several students to answer these questions and put their names on the board next to the question they answered (if the class is paying attention, you shouldn't need to write each student's answer down).

3. Go over the categories in Focus 4 that give situations when the time frame does not need to change. When finished, ask the class if the questions on the board fit any of these categories and which ones.

4. Next, ask the class to report on the answers given previously by students. For example, you can ask *What is Chandra's favorite color?* In response, the class should write or answer orally *Chandra said that her favorite color is yellow.*

5. Immediately follow this focus with Exercise 7.

VARIATION

If your class is more advanced, this focus can be assigned for self-study outside of class along with Exercise 7. Be sure to review the reasons for NOT changing time frame in class the next day.

EXPANSION 1 [20 minutes]

In small groups, ask students to share good advice that they have heard through the years. They should be sure to state who gave them the wise advice. For example, students may recall, *My mother used to say that the best way to a man's heart is through his stomach.* Have the groups share the most useful pieces of advice in their group with the class.

EXPANSION 2 [30 minutes]

Have students interview each other and report on their findings, either orally or in writing. Interviews could focus on any number of topics, depending on the interests of your class, or you could do a simple survey of future plans for an upcoming vacation, ask hypothetical questions, or just find out about the likes and dislikes of other students. Each of these topics would not require a change in time frame when reporting and using indirect quotations.

EXERCISE 7 [15 minutes]

This exercise should be done as part of the presentation or self-study for Focus 4. Although the example implies that only those sentences needing a change in time frame should be rewritten, it would be better to practice the concepts presented in Unit 25 by having students rewrite all statements in indirect quotations. Students should still state any reasons for no change in time frame. See answers on LP page 412.

For more practice, use *Grammar Dimensions 3* Workbook page 144, Exercises 6 and 7.

FOCUS 5

Reporting Verbs and Indirect Quotation

Many reporting verbs used for indirect quotation have restrictions about what other information must be included.

EXAMPLES	EXPLANATIONS
(a) Jack **admitted that** he should have gone to the doctor before his symptoms got so bad.	Many reporting verbs are followed by *that* clauses. Verbs in this category include: *admit, announce, comment, complain, confess, explain,*
(b) The doctor **explained (that)** Jack had to take the medicine for a full two weeks, even if he began to feel better.	*indicate, insist, mention, point out, remark, reply, report, said, shout, state, swear, whisper.* That can usually be omitted without loss of meaning.
(c) Jack **replied** he would.	These verbs are not used with indirect objects.
(d) The doctor **assured Jack that** he would start to feel better soon.	Some reporting verbs require an indirect object to precede the *that* clause. Verbs in this category include *tell, assure, convince, inform,*
(e) Jean **reminded Jack that** he needed to take his pills with plenty of water.	*notify, persuade, remind.* Many of these verbs can also be used with infinitive constructions,
(f) Jean **reminded Jack to take** his pills on an empty stomach.	and verbs of this sort follow Pattern 2 (verb + infinitive constructions). (See Unit 6, Focus 5 and Appendix 3 for a review of these forms.)
(g) Jack **promised (the doctor) (that)** he would take the pills until they were finished.	Other reporting verbs can be used with or without indirect objects before the *that* clause. Verbs in this category include *advise,*
(h) The students **asked the teacher to give them** the answer.	*answer, ask, promise.*
(i) The students **asked that** the test be postponed until next week.	
(j) The doctor **recommended that** Jack take the pills before bedtime.	Some verbs of urging require the subjunctive *that* clause. (See Unit 18, Focus 5 for more information on these verbs.)

EXERCISE 8

Most of these sentences are incorrect. Identify the problem and rewrite them so that they are grammatical. Some of the sentences are correct. Which ones are they?

1. Peter admitted Mr. Green he and Denise didn't get along.

2. Mr. Green told he wanted both of them to try harder to cooperate.

3. He asked that they work together on another project.

4. He explained them how important the project was.

5. Mr. Green insisted them to work together.

6. He convinced them that working together would be beneficial.

FOCUS 6

Word Order and Indirect Quotation

In indirect quotation, different word order is used for reporting statements, questions, and imperatives.

EXAMPLES	EXPLANATIONS
(a) The doctor told Jack **(that)** he was afraid they would have to do more tests.	*That* introduces reported statements. *That* is often omitted in informal contexts and conversation.

Questions in indirect quotation require changes in word order: Indirect quotation uses statement word order, whether it is reporting a statement or a question.

DIRECT QUOTATION	INDIRECT QUOTATION
(b) "Am I late?"	(c) Peter asked **if he was late.**
(d) "Do you need money?"	(e) Jean wanted to know **whether I needed money.**
(f) "How much do you need?"	(g) She asked **how much I needed.**

Adding question markers: We use different patterns depending on whether the question being asked is a *yes/no* question or *wh*-question.

EXAMPLES	EXPLANATIONS
(h) Mr. Green wanted to know **if Denise could bring** her notes to the meeting.	*Yes/no* questions: We can use either *if* or *whether (or not)* to report *yes/no* questions. *If* is preferred for *yes/no* questions.
(i) He wanted to know **whether she could bring** her notes to the meeting.	
(j) He wanted to know **whether or not she could bring** her notes to the meeting.	
(k) I applied for a job. They wanted to know **where I had worked, when I worked there, how many years of experience I had,** and **what kind of previous experience I had** had in sales.	*Wh*-Questions: We use a *wh*-question word to report *wh*-questions.

Embedded questions:

(l) Can you tell me **what your zip code is?**	Direct *yes/no* and *wh*-questions sound more polite if they are embedded in a conversational frame such as "Do you know . . . ," or "Can you tell me . . . ," or "I wonder . . . ." It is not necessary to change the tense of the questions from present to past.
(m) Do you know **what time the store opens?**	
(n) I wonder **if Dr. Tang is able to come to the phone.**	

ANSWER KEY

Exercise 8 1. *Peter admitted to Mr. Green that he and Denise didn't get along.* 2. *Mr. Green told them that he wanted both of them to try harder to cooperate.* 3. *correct* 4. *He explained to them how important the project was.* 5. *Mr. Green insisted (that) they work together.* 6. *correct.*

LESSON PLAN 2/LESSON PLAN 3

FOCUS 5 [20 minutes]

Focus 5 gives information about the requirements that many reporting verbs have. This focus chart has divided reporting verbs into four general groups to show the patterns more clearly. Present the categories along with their patterns.

1. **Lead-in:** Consider using Exercise 8 as a diagnostic lead-in for this focus chart. Have students do the error-correction exercise before presenting the four types of reporting verbs outlined in Focus 5.

2. A useful way to present the information in Focus 5 would be to divide the board into four areas. As you go over the types of reporting verbs, put the corresponding pattern at the top of each section. Then list the suggested reporting verbs from Focus 5 under the matching pattern on the board. Your patterns could read: (1) verb + (to + indirect object) + *that* clause, (2) verb + indirect object + *that* clause, (3) verb + (indirect object) + *that* clause, (4) verb + subjunctive *that* clause.

3. If using Exercise 8 as a lead-in activity, have students work in pairs to check their previous answers. Otherwise, follow this presentation directly with Exercise 8.

GRAMMAR NOTE

It should be noted to students that the reporting verbs in the first category of the focus chart (verb + *that* clause) are, in fact, allowed to take an optional indirect object before the *that* clause. However, unlike the following categories, these indirect objects must be preceded by the preposition *to*, as in *She explained to the class that the test would be given in two parts.*

EXERCISE 8 [15 minutes]

Use this exercise either before or after your presentation of Focus 5. Have students work individually on the error identification and correction. They can then compare answers in pairs while

---

referring to the information presented in Focus 5 for their explanations. See answers on LP page 414.

For more practice, use *Grammar Dimensions 3* Workbook page 145, Exercises 8 and 9.

work book

LESSON PLAN 3

FOCUS 6 [15 minutes/homework]

Focus 6 outlines the question markers and the change in word order needed in order to put questions into indirect quotations. If you are short on time, this section can be assigned for self-study outside of class and then reviewed in class the next day.

1. **Lead-in:** Put a variety of direct quotations on the board (you may want to take these from things students have said or asked in the class). Ask the class to put each of the quotations into an indirect quotation. If you assigned Focus 6 as homework, students should be able to work this out on their own. If you did not assign Focus 6 yet, use this task for diagnostic purposes. For example, tell the class that these are direct quotes from a student named Kim and that they should report them using indirect quotations:

   "I'm never late to class."
   "Do we have any homework today?"
   "Is there a test today?"
   "Will there be a test tomorrow?"
   "What time did you call?"
   "When will the party start?"
   "Who took my pencil?"

2. Have students share their indirect quotations with a partner.

3. Pairs should then work out a few rules for making indirect quotations for *yes/no* questions versus *wh*-questions.

---

4. While pairs are working, ask a few students to put some indirect quotations on the board.

5. Ideally, you will have a variety of sentences on the board now and can refer to them as you go over the information in Focus 6.

6. Be sure to note that questions in indirect quotation require (1) statement word order, (2) the use of *if, whether,* or a *wh-* question to mark the *yes/no* or *wh-*question clause, and (3) the usual shift back in time frame (verbs or modals) to mark this as reported speech.

Suggestion: Save the section regarding embedded questions at the bottom of Focus 6 to present separately. Creating embedded questions is a very useful skill for students. Being able to ask questions in this more polite manner is important and should be emphasized. Remind students that there is no shift in time frame for these questions. Give students the opportunity to ask each other polite embedded questions using the three sentence starters shown. Use Exercise 11 for more practice.

---

use

FOCUS 7

Commands and Requests in Indirect Quotation

EXAMPLES

(a) Doctor to patient: "Take these pills."

(b) The doctor **told me to** take these pills.

(c) Jack: "Can you help?"

(d) Jack **asked Jean to** help with the dishes.

(e) The doctor told me **not to** stay up late or sit in a cold place.

(f) Jack asked Jean **not to** expect him at the party.

EXPLANATIONS

To report commands, use verbs like *tell* or *order* + infinitive. Many other reporting verbs of this sort follow Pattern 2 (verb + infinitive constructions). See Unit 6, Focus 5 and Appendix 3 for a review of these forms.

To report requests or invitations, use verbs such as *ask* or *invite* + infinitive.

Negative commands and requests are reported with *not* + infinitive.

EXERCISE 12

Rewrite these indirect commands and requests as direct quotations.

Example: On his first day in the army, Kilroy was told to report to the drill field by the master sergeant.

The master sergeant told Kilroy, "Report to the drill field."

1. Another officer assigned him to clean the area for nearly an hour.
2. The officers ordered all the new recruits not to talk to each other.
3. They were told to stand at attention until their papers had been processed.
4. Kilroy asked to go to the bathroom, but this request was denied.
5. Finally the processing was over, and they were ordered to return to their barracks.
6. Several other recruits invited Kilroy to join them in a game of cards.
7. He told them he was too tired, and asked them not to be too noisy since he wanted to sleep.

EXERCISE 9

Here is a list of interview questions that were common in American businesses thirty or forty years ago. Some of them are no longer asked by employers these days. In some cases the law prohibits asking such questions.

Restate the questions as statements about old-fashioned hiring practices by adding such reporting phrases as "A number of years ago employers used to ask . . . ," "They wanted to know . . . ," "They often asked prospective employees to tell them . . . ," and other similar phrases you can think of.

Which questions do you think are still being used?

1. Are you married or single?
2. Does your wife work outside the home?
3. How many children do you have?
4. Are you a Communist?
5. Do you go to church?
6. How old are you?
7. Why do you want to work for this company?
8. Do you use drugs?
9. What is your racial background?
10. How much experience do you have?

EXERCISE 10

Change this report of a job interview into the list of questions that the interviewer actually asked. The one underlined is done for you.

Example: *Where did you graduate from high school?*

Bob applied for a summer job as a computer programmer in a large company. (2) The head of the Personnel Office interviewed him. (3) <u>She wanted to know where he had graduated from high school</u>, and if he had ever studied in a college or university. (4) She wanted to know if he had ever been arrested, or whether he had ever needed to borrow money in order to pay off credit card purchases. (5) She wanted to know how fast he could type and what kind of experience he had had with computers, and whether he was more proficient in COBOL or BASIC. (6) She asked him what companies he had worked for in the past. (7) She wanted to know what his previous salary had been. (8) She wanted to know why he was no longer working at his previous job. (9) She asked him if he would voluntarily take a drug test. (10) He began to wonder if he really wanted to work for a company that wanted to know so much about his private life.

EXERCISE 11

Make these direct questions more polite by making them embedded questions using phrases such as "Do you know," "Can you tell me," or "I wonder."

1. What time does the test begin?
2. Is the bookstore open yet?
3. Can Peter come with us to the party?
4. How do I get to Carnegie Hall?
5. Where can I find a cheap apartment?

Exercise 12 Answers will vary slightly. Possible answers are:

1. Another officer ordered, "Clean the area for the next hour."   2. The officers commanded, "Don't talk to each other."   3. The officers said, "Stand at attention until your papers have been processed."   4. Kilroy asked, "Can I go to the bathroom?" But they told him, "No!"   5. The officers said, "Return to your barracks."   6. Several other recruits asked Kilroy, "Would you like to join us in a game of cards?"   7. He told them, "I'm too tired. Would you please not be too noisy, since I want to sleep."

ANSWER KEY

Exercise 9   Answers will vary.

Exercise 10   (3) Have you ever studied in a college or university?   (4) Have you ever been arrested?   (4) Have you ever needed to borrow money in order to pay off credit card purchases?   (5) How fast can you type?   (5) What kind of experience have you had with computers?   (5) Are you more proficient in COBOL or BASIC?   (6) What companies have you worked for in the past?   (7) What was your previous salary?   (8) Why aren't you still working at your previous job?   (9) Will you voluntarily take a drug test?

Exercise 11   Answers will vary. Possible answers are: 1. Do you know what time the test begins?   2. Can you tell me if the bookstore is open yet?   3. I wonder if Peter can come with us to the party.   4. Do you know how I get to Carnegie Hall?   5. Can you tell me where I can find a cheap apartment?

EXERCISE 9 [15 minutes/homework]

1. Go over the directions. Set up the context of interview questions by asking students whether they have ever been asked any of these questions during an interview.

2. Go over the reporting phrases given. Have students work individually to restate the questions in indirect quotations.

3. Have pairs or small groups compare their statments and then discuss their ideas about which of these questions they think might be used.

4. Circulate and check the indirect quotes. Go over any common errors with the class. See possible answers on LP page 416.

EXERCISE 10 [15 minutes]

Be aware that students may have difficulty shifting the time frame of each statement forward to recreate the original question. This exercise should be paired with Exercise 9.

1. Go over the directions with the class and show them how this works in the reverse of Exercise 9.

2. Go over the example question taken from the statement in the passage. Ask the class what changes were made to create the question. (*shift the time frame forward, use question word order and punctuation, and remove the reporting phrase*)

3. Have the class work individually or in pairs to create a list of questions (note that some sentences have more than one question in them).

4. Collect papers and evaluate or go over answers in class. See answers on LP page 416.

For more practice, use *Grammar Dimensions 3* Workbook page 146, Exercise 10.

EXERCISE 11 [15 minutes]

Use this exercise after your presentation of embedded questions if you chose to present it separately from the rest of Focus 6.

1. This can be done individually on paper or as a class review.

2. Give students more questions to embed if they need more practice. See possible answers on LP page 416.

Suggestion: Consider having students use embedded questions whenever they need to ask a question for a whole class period. Make it a contest, and award points.

FOCUS 7 [25 minutes]

Focus 7 presents the form for putting commands and requests into indirect quotations.

1. **Lead-in:** Have the class turn to Unit 6, Focus 5 and look for verbs which might be used to report commands or orders. Put these on the board as students call them out. Have the class note that these verbs follow Pattern 2 and are shown to need a noun/object pronoun + infinitive. Return to Unit 25, Focus 7.

2. Ask the class to supply some direct quotes using imperatives (commands) of things a parent might tell a child to do throughout the day. Put these on the board. Some examples might include (note that the imperative does not use a subject):

   Pick up your toys.

   Clean your room.

   Feed the dog.

   Stop hitting your sister.

3. Go over the rules in Focus 7 for putting commands into indirect quotations with the class. Be sure to point out that these verbs require a noun/pronoun and the use of the infinitive when they are used to express a command. Reported commands do not require a *-that* clause or other marker.

4. Give examples using a statement (*He told them that he wasn't feeling well*), using a question (*He asked if they were hungry*), and using a command (*He told them to turn the television off*) to show the difference.

5. Have students put the commands on the board into indirect quotations. Circulate and assist as needed.

6. Let students share their answers with the class. Discuss any problems.

7. Follow this presentation by giving the class more commands to put into indirect quotation or move directly on to Exercise 12.

EXERCISE 12 [15 minutes]

If students are comfortable putting commands into direct quotations, have them work on this exercise, which asks them to do the reverse (as in Exercise 10).

1. Go over the directions with the class and show them how this works in the reverse of the examples they did in Focus 7.

2. Go over the example given. Ask the class to underline the actual command in the first indirect quotation given. This will be put into quotes for the direct quotation of a command.

3. Have the class work individually or in pairs.

4. Collect papers and evaluate or go over answers in class. See possible answers on LP page 416.

For more practice, use *Grammar Dimensions 3* Workbook page 146, Exercise 11.

UNIT GOAL REVIEW [10 minutes]

Ask students to look at the goals on the opening page of the unit again. Refer to the pages of the unit where information on each goal can be found.

For a grammar quiz review of Units 23–25, refer students to pages 148–149 in the *Grammar Dimensions 3* Workbook.

For assessment of Unit 25, use *Grammar Dimensions 3 ExamView®*.

Use Your English

ACTIVITY 1 speaking/writing

Work with a different partner from the one with whom you worked on the Opening Task. Together, write a conversation that matches the photos in the Opening Task. Act out your conversation for the rest of the class. Other students should write a paraphrase of your conversation using reported speech.

ACTIVITY 2 listening/speaking/writing

Listen to a news broadcast on television. Report one story that you heard on that broadcast to the rest of the class. Start with some sort of statement like this: *I heard on the news that . . . , It was announced that . . .* , etc.

ACTIVITY 3 listening/speaking

Play a game of *"Telephone."* Here's how to play:

Form two or more teams of ten people each. Student 1 should make a statement to Student 2 very quietly, so that only Student 2 can hear what was said. Student 2 then reports what was said to Student 3 using reported speech (*Student 1 told me that . . .*). Student 3 tells Student 4 and so forth. When the last student receives the report, he or she should announce the message to the rest of the class. Compare how close that message is with what was originally said by Student 1. The team that has the closest and most accurate report wins a point. Student 2 starts the next round.

ACTIVITY 4 writing

Write a paragraph discussing some of the misconceptions about life that you had when you were a child. Describe what you thought, and why you thought it. See Exercise 1 on page 404 for an example.

ACTIVITY 5 writing

Tell about a time when you had an important conversation with someone. Perhaps you learned some important information about yourself or someone else. Perhaps you found out about a decision that had a big effect on your life in some way. Perhaps you got some valuable advice.

■ STEP 1   First, tell the **story** of the conversation. Write down who it was with and where and when it took place. Then try to write the conversation word-for-word.

■ STEP 2   Next, write a paragraph telling what you learned from this conversation, and why it was important for you. You may want to begin your paragraph with *When I was . . . , I learned that. . . .*

ACTIVITY 6 listening

CD Track 38

Based on the short news broadcast you hear, complete the following sentences with the actual words that were probably used by the speaker.

1. The Police Department representative announced, "_____

_____ "

2. He admitted, "_____ "

3. He predicted, "_____ "

Use the sentences you have written to perform the announcement.

ACTIVITY 7 research on the web

Go onto the Web and use an Internet search engine such as Google® or Yahoo® to research a common illness or physical complaint that is of interest to you. It could be something like "the common cold" or "asthma" or even "dry skin" or something that you might possibly consult a doctor about (like "losing weight" or "better sleep").

Visit three or four Web sites and summarize the recommendations you find there; imagine that you got these recommendations from a doctor and report to the rest of the class what the "Web doctor" told you to do.

ANSWER KEY

Activity 6 1. The rate of violent crime has decreased significantly over the last five months. 2. There has been a slight increase in thefts and burglaries, and the department will continue frequent patrols in all neighborhoods.   3. The budget will be finalized by the end of this week, and the accelerated hiring program may begin as soon as next Wednesday.

USE YOUR ENGLISH

The Use Your English activities at the end of the unit contain situations that should naturally elicit the structures covered in the unit. For a more complete discussion of how to use the Use Your English activities see To the Teacher on LP page xxii. When students are doing these activities in class, you can circulate and listen to see if they are using the structures accurately. Errors can be corrected when the activity is finished.

ACTIVITY 1 speaking/writing [30 minutes]

1. Have students work in pairs to create the conversation. This will likely involve using indirect quotations.

2. If you are short on time, consider putting pairs of students together into groups and have the pairs perform for their group rather than the class.

3. Be sure that students take time after each performance to take notes or write a summary of the conversation.

4. Collect the written paraphrases or have students give the paraphrase to the original performers and let them check the accuracy of the paraphrase. Students can then share their thoughts with the class about how well their audience summarized the performance.

ACTIVITY 2 listening/speaking/writing [20 minutes/homework]

1. Assign the report as homework.

2. Give guidelines as to how long the written report should be or how long of a news segment they should report on.

3. Give students time in class when finished to share the more interesting stories. They may have heard the same story and can often clarify each other's questions.

4. Collect written reports. Evaluate and give feedback as needed.

ACTIVITY 3 listening/speaking [20 minutes]

1. Write statements, questions, or commands onto separate slips of paper and use these as the original message to be relayed through the "telephone" line. Show the same slip to all Student 1's who will begin the game. They will then need to truly whisper so as not to help the opposing teams.

2. The whispering of the message will continue down the row until the final team member has heard it.

3. When every team has finished, the final team members should announce their indirect quotation to the class. The groups can then evaluate the accuracy of the statement.

ACTIVITY 4 writing [10 minutes/homework]

Be sure to have students review the passage in Exercise 1 on SB page 408 before beginning this activity.

1. Have students discuss in small groups other misconceptions they or their siblings may have had when they were younger.

2. Assign the writing as homework.

3. When finished, give time in class for students to share their paragraphs.

ACTIVITY 5 writing [30 minutes]

■ STEP 1

1. First, have students tell about the conversation.

2. Ask students to try to write down the story of the conversation, describing the place, time, situation, etc.

3. Next, students will write the actual conversation using direct quotes.

■ STEP 2   Have students write a paragraph about the conversation using indirect quotations to tell the story and telling why the conversation was important to them.

Have students turn in both the actual conversation and the paragraph describing this conversation. You will then be able to see how well the paragraph reports the conversation.

ACTIVITY 6 listening [15 minutes]

CD Track 38

1. Use your usual methods for repeating the audio as necessary.

2. Have students compare answers with a partner before reviewing as a class.

3. Invite volunteers to perform their announcements for the class. See answers on LP page 418.

ACTIVITY 7 research on the web [30 minutes/homework]

1. Give students time in class to brainstorm a list of common illnesses or physical complaints in small groups before assigning the research.

2. Students should research their chosen ailment on the Web, summarize the recommendations from three or four different sites, and prepare to report to the class on their findings. Students should use indirect quotations.

3. Give time in class for presentations.

ACTIVITY 8 speaking

To *eavesdrop* means to secretly listen to someone else's conversation. Go to a public place, like a restaurant, a shopping mall, or a bus station, and eavesdrop on someone's conversation. It's important not to let people know what you're doing, so pretend to read a book, study your English grammar, read a magazine in another language (people might think that you don't understand English), or pretend to write a letter.

■ **STEP 1**   Report what the people were talking about, and tell or write two or three things that they said to each other.

■ **STEP 2**   What reporting words did you hear people use? Did the people you listened to use casual direct quotation ("So he goes…" "I'm like…") ?

■ **STEP 3**   Report three interesting things about their lives, or about English, that you learned as a result of this experience.

ACTIVITY 9 reflection

Form a group with three other students. Discuss strategies that you use or could use to learn all the different forms that indirect quotation takes in English. Report to another group the strategies that came up in your group and say whose strategy it was.

Example: *Marco said that he memorized the different forms of modal verbs in the present and in the past.*

USE YOUR ENGLISH

ACTIVITY 8 speaking [homework]

This is a good activity to do in connection with cross-cultural discussions on body language and nonverbal communication as mentioned in the Opening Task on SB pages 404–405.

1. Be sure that you explicitly review eavesdropping "strategies" so that students can listen in on conversations unnoticed.

2. You may want to also share ideas as a class about where to do the best unnoticed eavesdropping (in a coffee shop, in the mall, in a busy restaurant or cafeteria, even someone chatting away on a cell phone, etc.).

■ **STEP 1** Students should write the main idea of the conversation they overheard and then a few specific things they heard. These can be direct or indirect quotes.

■ **STEP 2** Students should note the use of reporting words in the conversation, specifically casual reporting verbs.

■ **STEP 3**

1 Students are to think about what they learned about these people or about English, just by listening to this conversation.

2. Have students share their findings in small groups, in pairs, as a class, or simply collect papers and give feedback.

ACTIVITY 9 reflection [30 minutes]

This activity asks students to reflect and share their own learning strategies with the group. Hopefully, students by now are comfortable thinking and talking about the things they do to learn English. Here, students are again reminded that learning English is not something that simply relies on a teacher or a book; it also relies on a conscious effort supported by strategies. As students discuss the strategies suggested by the group, they will use indirect quotations.

APPENDICES

Appendix 1A

Present Time Frame: Use Present Time to talk about general relationships. Most scientific and technical writing is in Present Time. Anything that is related to the present moment is expressed by Present Time, so newspaper headlines, news stories, and spoken conversations, jokes, and informal narratives are often in Present Time.

FORM	MEANING	USE	EXAMPLE
SIMPLE PRESENT *I/you/we/they* + simple form of verb *he/she/it* + *-s* form of verb	true in the past, present and future	general relationships and timeless truths permanent states habitual and recurring actions	(a) Time **changes** the way people live. (b) Bob **has** two brothers and one sister. (c) Bob **works** in the library every afternoon.
PRESENT PROGRESSIVE *am/is/are* + present participle (verb + *-ing*)	already in progress now or around this time	actions in progress repetition or duration temporary states and actions uncompleted actions	(d) Bob **is studying** for a midterm at this moment. (e) Bob **is taking** a biology class this semester. (f) Bob's brother **is living** with his father for the summer. (g) **He is** still **looking** for a cheap apartment.

FORM	MEANING	USE	EXAMPLE
PRESENT PERFECT *have/has* + past participle (verb + *-ed* or past participle of irregular verbs)	began, in the past but related in some way to the present	past events related to now by time past events related to now by logical relationship	(h) Bob **has visited** Canada twice, so he won't join the tour to Quebec. (i) Bob **has gotten** very good at the computer, so he doesn't need to take another class.
PRESENT PERFECT PROGRESSIVE *have/has* + *been* + present participle (verb + *-ing*)	in progress before and including the present	repeated and/or continuous actions	(j) Bob **has been spending** his weekends at home since he started living in the dorm. (k) Bob **has been singing** in a chorus ever since he was in high school.

Appendix 1B

Past Time Frame: Use Past Time to talk about things that are not directly connected to the present moment. Most fiction, historical accounts, and factual descriptions of past events are in Past Time.

FORM	MEANING	USE	EXAMPLE
SIMPLE PAST verb + *-ed* or irregular past form	at a certain time in the past	states or general relationships that were true in the past habitual or recurrent actions that took place in the past specific events that took place in the past	(a) Tuberculosis **was** a common cause of death 50 years ago. (b) Robert Lee **worked** 12 hours a day for low wages. (c) Robert Lee **went** to work in a factory at age 14.

FORM	MEANING	USE	EXAMPLE
PAST PROGRESSIVE *was/were* + present participle (verb + *-ing*)	in progress at a certain time in the past	interrupted actions repeated actions and actions over time	(d) Robert **was studying** in high school when his father died. (e) Robert **was** always **trying** to get promotions at the factory.
PAST PERFECT *had* + past participle (verb + *-ed* or past participle of irregular verbs)	before a certain time in the past	actions or states that took place before other events in the past	(f) His father **had been** dead for several weeks when Robert quit school and started working to help his mother.
PAST PERFECT PROGRESSIVE *had been* + present participle (verb + *-ing*)	in progress until a certain time in the past	continuous versus repeated actions uncompleted versus completed actions	(g) Robert **had been working** for 12 hours when the foreman told him to go home. (h) Robert **had been hoping** to complete school when he had to find a job to help his family.

Appendix 1C

Future Time Frame: Use Future Time for anything that is scheduled to happen or predicted to happen in the future. Notice that two tenses (simple present and present progressive) that are used in Present Time Frame can also be used to talk about future plans or scheduled events.

FORM	MEANING	USE	EXAMPLE
SIMPLE PRESENT	already scheduled or expected in the future	schedules	(a) The plane **leaves** at 6:30 tomorrow.
PRESENT PROGRESSIVE		definite future plans	(b) **I am spending** next summer in France.
SIMPLE FUTURE one-word (*will/might/etc.*) or phrasal modals (*be going to*) + simple verb	at a certain time in the future	predictions about future situations	(c) Roberta is **going to take** a vacation on the moon. (d) She **will** probably **get** there by space shuttle, and she **might stay** on an observation platform.
FUTURE PROGRESSIVE future modal + *be* + verb + *-ing*	in progress at a certain time in the future	future events in progress	(e) 100 years from now Roberta **will be living** on the moon.
FUTURE PERFECT modal + *have* + past participle (verb + *-ed* or past participle of irregular verbs)	before a certain time in the future	events happening before other future events	(f) Scientists **will have visited** the moon long **before** tourists **will be** able to.
FUTURE PERFECT PROGRESSIVE modal + *have* + *been* + verb + *-ing*	in progress until a certain time in the future	repeated and/or continuous actions	(g) When Roberta retires on Earth she will probably not be used to the earth's level of gravity because she **will have been living** on the moon for several years.

APPENDIX 2   Passive Verb Forms

ASPECT:	SIMPLE	PROGRESSIVE	PERFECT	PERFECT PROGRESSIVE*
TIME: **Present**	TENSES: is/are studied is/are given	am/is/are being studied am/is/are being given	has/have been studied has/have been given	has/have been being studied has/have been being given
Past	was/were studied was/were given	was/were being studied was/were being given	had been studied had been given	had been being studied had been being given
Future	will be studied will be given	will be being studied will be being given	will have been studied will have been given	will have been being studied will have been being given

* Although perfect progressive passive forms are theoretically possible in English, such forms are **very** rarely found in speech or writing.

APPENDIX 3 Overview of Verbs Followed by Infinitives and Gerunds

VERB PATTERNS THAT ARE FOLLOWED BY INFINITIVES

(a) Norman **decided to specialize** in African stamps when a friend **offered to give** him some stamps from Ghana.	Pattern 1: verb + infinitive
(b) A friend **advised Norman to order** rare stamps from commercial companies, and **encouraged him to be** persistent.	Pattern 2: verb + noun phrase + infinitive
(c) Norman **likes to send** stamps to other people and also **likes other people to send** stamps to him.	Pattern 3: verb (+ noun phrase) + infinitive

VERB PATTERNS THAT ARE FOLLOWED BY GERUNDS

(a) Charlie **can't help falling** in love with a new woman every week. (b) The doctor told me that I've got to **quit smoking**.	Pattern 1: verb gerund
(c) Doctors **advise reducing** fats in one's diet. (It's good advice for everyone.) (d) The doctor **advised me to reduce** fats in my diet. (She gave this advice to me specifically.)	Pattern 2: verb { + gerund, + noun pharse, + infinitive }
(e) I don't **mind sleeping** late when I get the chance, and I don't **mind other people doing** it either.	Pattern 3: verb (+ noun phrase) + gerund

VERBS THAT ARE FOLLOWED BY INFINITIVES

Pattern 1
appear
refuse
seem
agree
claim
care
deserve
decide
demand
pretend
hesitate
offer
tend
learn
neglect
wait

Pattern 2
advise
remind
persuade
urge
encourage
convince
force
forbid
command
order
allow
permit
invite
trust
cause
tell
warn
teach
hire

Pattern 3
expect
arrange
want
intend
consent
ask
need

VERBS THAT ARE FOLLOWED BY GERUNDS

Pattern 1
can't help
keep on
recommend
suggest
deny
consider
admit
give up
avoid
quit
practice
include
resist

Pattern 2
advise
encourage
urge
forbid
allow
permit
invite
cause
teach

Pattern 3
appreciate
anticipate
dislike
don't mind
enjoy
resent
consider
delay
postpone
excuse
imagine
miss
tolerate
understand

MEANING CATEGORIES	BEGINNING OF THE CLAUSE	MIDDLE OF THE CLAUSE	END OF THE CLAUSE
ADDITION	*additionally* *also* *in addition*	*also* *in addition*	*also* *in addition* *too as well*
EMPHASIS/ INTENSIFYING	*actually* *as a matter of fact* *besides* *furthermore* *indeed* *in fact* *moreover*	*actually* *as a matter of fact* *furthermore* *indeed* *in fact* *moreover*	*as a matter of fact* *indeed* *in fact*
CONTRAST	*despite this* *however* *on the other hand*	*however* *on the other hand*	*despite this* *however* *on the other hand*
CONCESSION	*despite this* *even so* *in spite of the fact* *nonetheless*	*nonetheless*	*despite this* *even so* *in spite of the fact* *nonetheless* *regardless* *though*
REASON	*with this in mind* *for this reason* *therefore*	*therefore*	*therefore* *with this in mind* *for this reason*
RESULT	*accordingly* *as a result* *consequently* *thus*	*accordingly* *as a result* *consequently* *therefore* *thus*	*accordingly* *as a result* *consequently*
CONDITIONAL	*providing* *if* *then* *under such circumstances*		*under such circumstances*
SEQUENCE	*next* *then* *first, second, etc.*	*and* *next* *then* *first, second, etc.*	*next* *first, second, etc.*

1. What is the form of the noun? Noncount or count? Singular or plural?
2. Is the noun used to make a generic reference or particular reference?
    Does it describe a class of things or does it refer to a particular item?
3. If it refers to a particular thing, is the reference specific or nonspecific?

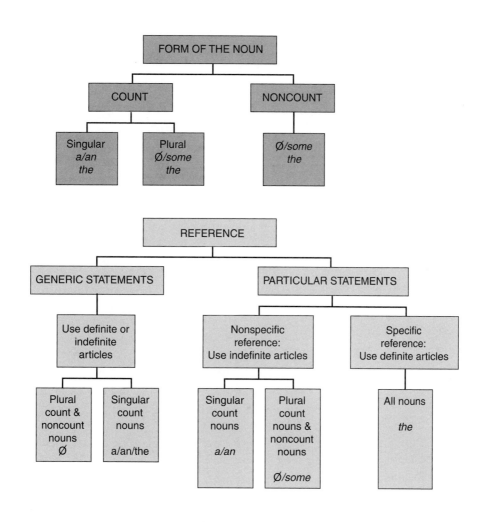

APPENDIX 6   Irregular Verbs

SIMPLE FORM	PAST TENSE FORM	PAST PARTICIPLE	SIMPLE FORM	PAST TENSE FORM	PAST PARTICIPLE
become	became	become	grow	grew	grown
begin	began	begun	hang	hung	hung
bend	bent	bent	have	had	had
bet	bet	bet	hear	heard	heard
bind	bound	bound	hide	hid	hidden
bite	bit	bit	hit	hit	hit
bleed	bled	bled	hold	held	held
blow	blew	blown	hurt	hurt	hurt
break	broke	broken	keep	kept	kept
bring	brought	brought	know	knew	known
build	built	built	lead	led	led
buy	bought	bought	leave	left	left
catch	caught	caught	lend	lent	lent
choose	chose	chosen	let	let	let
come	came	come	make	made	made
cost	cost	cost	mean	meant	meant
cut	cut	cut	meet	met	met
dig	dug	dug	put	put	put
do	did	done	quit	quit	quit
draw	drew	drawn	read	read	read
drink	drank	drunk	ride	rode	ridden
drive	drove	driven	ring	rang	rung
eat	ate	eaten	rise	rose	risen
fall	fell	fallen	run	ran	run
feed	fed	fed	say	said	said
feel	felt	felt	see	saw	seen
fight	fought	fought	seek	sought	sought
find	found	found	sell	sold	sold
fit	fit	fit	send	sent	sent
fly	flew	flown	set	set	set
forbid	forbade	forbidden	shake	shook	shaken
forget	forgot	forgotten	shine	shone	shone
forgive	forgave	forgiven	shoot	shot	shot
freeze	froze	frozen	shut	shut	shut
get	got	gotten	sing	sang	sung
give	gave	given	sink	sank	sunk
go	went	gone	sit	sat	sat
grind	ground	ground	sleep	slept	slept

SIMPLE FORM	PAST TENSE FORM	PAST PARTICIPLE	SIMPLE FORM	PAST TENSE FORM	PAST PARTICIPLE
slide	slid	slid	swing	swang	swung
speak	spoke	spoken	take	took	taken
speed	sped	sped	teach	taught	taught
spend	spent	spent	tear	tore	torn
split	split	split	tell	told	told
spread	spread	spread	think	thought	thought
spring	sprang	sprung	throw	threw	thrown
stand	stood	stood	understand	understood	understood
steal	stole	stolen	wake	woke	woken
stick	stuck	stuck	wear	wore	worn
sting	stung	stung	weave	wove	woven
strike	struck	stricken	weep	wept	wept
swear	swore	sworn	win	won	won
sweep	swept	swept	wind	wound	wound
swim	swam	swum	write	wrote	written

ANSWER KEY
(for puzzles and problems only)

UNIT 11

Answer to Activity 4 (page 199)

Secret: Silly Sally only likes things with double letters.

UNIT 16

Additional Clues for Opening Task (pages 256–257)

MYSTERY 1	MYSTERY 2	MYSTERY 3
The man is very, very short.	There's a big puddle of water in the room, and the paper is a delivery bill from an ice company.	The police officer is a woman.

Answer to Activity 3 (page 268)

(a) Candle snuffer; (b) Antique screwdriver; (c) Cherry pit remover; (d) Blender; (e) Bread slicer; (f) Meat chopper

UNIT 20

Answer to Activity 1 (page 342)

That that is, is. That that is not, is not. Isn't that it? It is!

UNIT 21

Activity 1 (page 354)

Diagram B

Diagram D

CREDITS

Photo Credits

p. 0: © Royalty-Free/Corbis

p. 1: (Top) © Brownie Harris/CORBIS, (Bottom) © Colin Anderson/Getty/RF

p. 12: (Top) © Frederic Larson/San Francisco Chronicle/Corbis, (Bottom) © SORBO ROBERT/CORBIS

p. 13: (Left) © STOCK IMAGE/Alamy, (Right) © Stockbyte/Getty/RF

p. 15: © Jim Sugar/CORBIS

p. 25: ©IndexOpen/RF

p. 28: © Photos.com/RF

p. 37: © Joe McDonald/CORBIS

p. 46: (Top) © Adam Woolfitt/CORBIS, (Bottom) © Charles & Josette Lenars/CORBIS

p. 55: © Michael Prince/CORBIS

p. 59: © Photos.com/RF

p. 60: © Photos.com/RF

p. 64: © Jeff Greenberg/Alamy

p. 76: © STOCK IMAGE/PIXLAND/Alamy/RF

p. 86: © Norman/zefa/Corbis

p. 89: © Virgo Productions/zefa/Corbis

p. 94: © Robert Fried/Alamy

p. 99: © IndexOpen/RF

p. 103: (Top Left) © IndexOpen/RF, (Bottom Left) PhotoObjects.net/RF, (Bottom Right) © IndexOpen/RF

p. 106: (Left) © Ingram Publishing/Getty/RF, (Right) © Stockbyte/Getty/RF

p. 110: © IndexOpen/RF

p. 113: © IndexOpen/RF

p. 120: © Royalty-Free/Corbis

p. 124: © Bruce Ayres/Stone/Getty

p. 130: © Digital Vision/Getty/RF

p. 137: © Yellow Dog Productions/Taxi/Getty

p. 146: © Steve Vidler/SuperStock

p. 156: (Top Left) © IndexOpen/RF, (Top Right) © Photos.com/RF, (Bottom Left and Right) © Photos.com/RF

p. 182: © Henry Westheim Photography/Alamy

p. 191: © Photos.com/RF

p. 202: © Seth Kushner/Stone/Getty

INDEX

WORKBOOK ANSWER KEY

Unit 1

Overview of the English Verb System

EXERCISE 1 [page 1]

(1) is   (2) are registering   (3) can't   (4) says
(5) owes   (6) knows   (7) paid   (8) shall/will
(9) has asked/asked   (10) is going to call/will call
(11) hopes/is hoping   (12) keeps/has kept

EXERCISE 2 [page 1]

1. simple present   2. present progressive   3. simple
present   4. simple present   5. simple present
6. simple present   7. simple past   8. simple future
9. present perfect/simple past   10. present
progressive/simple future   11. simple present/present
progressive   12. simple present/present perfect

EXERCISE 3 [page 2]

(1) have discovered   (2) tested/has tested   (3) switched/
have switched   (4) remained/have remained   (5) die
(6) is   (7) can occur/occur   (8) do not recommend
(9) focuses   (10) has already changed

EXERCISE 4 [page 2]

1. present   2. past/present   3. past/present   4. past/
present   5. present   6. present   7. present   8. present
9. present   10. present

EXERCISE 5 [page 2]

2. Every day people are discovering new uses for old
materials./Just yesterday I read a story about using old
tire tubes for floating down the river. The story said that
the old tubes could be used for a year or more./What
will they think of next?   3. For more than 30 years,
Dr. Simmons has been treating patients in the office on
the first floor of his home. He has mended broken bones
and delivered babies in this office./Recently, however,
the county medical association ordered him to move his
office to a separate building. The association insists
that the old office doesn't meet modem standards./
Dr. Simmons will probably retire and close his medical
practice rather than go through an expensive move.
What a loss this will be for the community!   4. I was
happy when I opened my mailbox yesterday. The mail
contained a letter from my family and my tax refund
check./What will I do with the money?/First, I need to
repair my car./Then I will hire someone to paint my
living room./I really don't like to paint.

EXERCISE 6 [page 3]

2. In the future   3. On January 1   4. The ancient
Greeks   5. in 1969   6. Paul Gauguin; Shortly after
he turned 40; today   7. first; later   8. Right now;
As soon as she completes 36 units of her major; Then
9. For more than five years   10. before she left for
her vacation overseas; for several days afterward.

Unit 2

Overview of the English Verb System

EXERCISE 1 [page 4]

(1) a   (2) a   (3) b   (4) b   (5) a

EXERCISE 2 [page 4]

1. keeps   2. was delivering; attacked   3. took
4. speaks   5. is still deciding   6. worries
7. proposed   8. remembered; left   9. snows
10. snowing

EXERCISE 3 [page 5]

(1) has graded   (2) spoke   (3) has visited
(4) lived   (5) had never worked   (6) immigrated
(7) had traveled only   (8) took   (9) flies   (10) has
been

EXERCISE 4 [page 6]

1. In the first sentence, the action was repeated for a finite period of time in the past. In the second, it is part of the dancer's professional experience.   2. In the first sentence, the speaker has finished his or her required chores for the week. In the second, the speaker is asserting that over a long period of time, he or she has fulfilled his or her housecleaning duties.   3. In the first sentence, the case is closed. In the second, there is still the possibility that the law will be changed.   4. In the first sentence, Matt keeps trying (and failing) to get a business off the ground. In the second, there is the implication that this is the first new business he has ever started.   5. The activity in the first sentence is an unusual occurrence, while that of the second is a habit.

EXERCISE 5 [page 6]

1. lectured/had lectured/had been lecturing   2. have eaten   3. has been trying; has been busy   4. has increased   5. have searched/have been searching   6. have changed   7. has stopped   8. will have lived   9. has been working   10. have been studying/have studied

EXERCISE 6 [page 7]

1. have been planning/have planned   2. learned   3. has rented/has been renting   4. convinced   5. have decided/decided   6. finish/have finished   7. have already selected   8. have met/met

9. made   10. can't   11. will need/are going to need   12. are looking

EXERCISE 7 [page 7]

(1) The first sentence talks about something in the past that is now over. The second describes an activity that started in the past and continues in the present.   (2) In the first sentence, the activity is happening at the moment of speaking. In the second, it started in the past and is still happening at the moment of speaking. In the third, the activity is a habit.   (3) The first sentence describes something that is happening right now; the second, something that has begun recently and continues into the present; and the third, something that happened in the past (once or numerous times) and is now over.   (4) In the first sentence, Tina tried once, failed, and left the bank, whereas in the second, she is perhaps still in the bank, or she has been back several times to try to cash her check.   (5) In the first sentence, the speaker is still driving. The second sentence describes an activity that ended in the past.   (6) The first sentence is about habit. The second is about a recently acquired habit.   (7) In the first sentence, Ms. Sideo still works for a bank, but in the second, her employment has ended (she's probably retired).   (8) The first sentence describes a habit; the second, an activity that is occurring at the moment of speaking.   (9) The first sentence describes something that happened at a specific time in the recent past, whereas the second is about Dr. Acosta's experience with a particular patient.   (10) The first sentence describes an ongoing activity. The second describes an action that occurred in the past.

Unit 3
Adverbial Phrases and Clauses

EXERCISE 1 [page 9]

1. How much   2. Where/How   3. How long   4. when   5. How   6. Why   7. How often   8. How   9. how long/how much time   10. When

EXERCISE 2 [page 9]

1. Usually (frequency) . . . where (place) . . . when workers can eat (time) . . . in the office (place).   2. At Worldwide Internet Company (place) . . . only in the kitchen area (place) . . . only at lunchtime (time) . . . on breaks (time).   3. . . . vigorously (manner) . . . to keep the office machines clean (purpose and reason).   4. once (time) . . . in the computer area (place).   5. . . . right away (time).   6. The next day (time) . . . on all the walls (place) . . . clearly (manner).   7. . . . only in the kitchen area (place) . . . only at specified times (time) . . . in order to reduce accidents (purpose and reason).   8. In the past

(time) . . . often (frequency) . . . on the computer keyboards (place).   9. Now (time) . . . always (frequency) . . . because no drinks are allowed (purpose and reason) . . . in the computer room (place).   10. These days (time) . . . often (frequency).

EXERCISE 3 [page 10]

Answers may vary. Check students' work for correct positioning of adverbials.   1. Belinda goes to the Bahamas every winter to make sure she gets to go snorkeling./ Every winter Belinda goes to the Bahamas to make sure she to go snorkeling.   2. Every day she swims two miles in the ocean to keep in shape./ To keep in shape, she swims two miles in the ocean every day.   3. Whenever she can, Belinda applies sunscreen to her skin./ Belinda applies sunscreen to her skin whenever she can.   4. Every day she eats fruit and fish because they are fresh./ She eats fruit and fish every day because they are fresh.   5. To lose weight, she recently

stopped eating beef and chicken./ Recently, to lose weight, she stopped eating beef and chicken.
6. When she goes home, she will continue to eat carefully./ She will continue to eat carefully when she goes home.

EXERCISE 4 [page 11]

Spoken skills pair/group work. Answers will vary.

EXERCISE 5 [page 11]

1. Jerry eats out in local restaurants on a regular basis. (*Place before time.*)   2. He recently discovered a Thai restaurant in his neighborhood in Hollywood. (*Adverbs can precede the verb if there is no auxiliary; the more specific adverb comes first when there are two of the same kind.*)

4. He will meet them in the lobby at 7 o'clock tonight. (*The more specific adverb comes first when there are two of the same kind.*)   5. Unfortunately, after looking at an old map, he gave them the wrong directions to the restaurant. (*Adverbials usually come after the verb phrase, which includes direct objects.*)   7. He's sincerely hoping that they look for the correct address in the phone book. (*One-word adverbials usually go between the auxiliary and the main verb; adverbials usually come after the verb phrase.*)

EXERCISE 6 [page 12]

1. Benjamin took on a second job so that he could afford to pay his car insurance.   3. The old man died after he entered the hospital.   4. I eat where the truck drivers eat.   6. First he washed the car, then he waxed it.   8. Sally got a job in the computer lab so that she could spend more time using the Internet.

Unit 4
Passive Verbs

EXERCISE 1 [page 13]

(1) are handed   (2) is collected   (3) are given   (4) was shown   (5) had been performed/was performed   (6) is being compared   (7) can be completed   (8) will be graded   (9) will be excused   (10) will be selected

EXERCISE 2 [page 13]

(1) are processed   (2) are given out   (3) are applied for   (4) is given   (5) is told   (6) be filled out   (7) was turned down   (8) had not been completed   (9) had been written/was written   (10) be redone

EXERCISE 3 [page 14]

Sometimes the coffee beans ~~age~~ **are aged** before they have been ~~roasted~~ **are roasted**. Americans, Germans, and Scandinavians <u>prefer</u> dark roasted beans. Light roasted beans ~~prefer~~ **are preferred** for blending. Coffee beans from Kenya and Ethiopia ~~use~~ **are used** both for blending and for their own flavors.   After the beans ~~have roasted~~ **have been roasted**, they ~~cool~~ **are cooled** and the batch ~~is being tested~~ **is tested**. If the batch is good, the beans ~~placed~~ **are placed** in bags, ~~sell~~ **sold**, and ~~ship~~ **shipped** to market.

EXERCISE 4 [page 14]

First, the oranges are picked and cleaned. Then, they are cut and the juice is squeezed out. The orange skins are thrown away or used for fertilizer.

Next, most of the liquid is taken out, and the result is that the juice is concentrated. Then, the juice is frozen and shipped to market. In the last step, water is added by the customer to make juice.

EXERCISE 5 [page 15]

Answers will vary.

EXERCISE 6 [page 15]

(2) are sighted (R = They)   (3) are described (R = UFOs)   (4) have been nicknamed (R = UFOs)   (5) was reported (R = saucer; A = a man)   (6) was followed (R = man; A = UFO)   (7) was given off (R = he; A = UFO)   (8) been reported (R = lights; A = others)   (10) have been abducted (R = people; A = ships)   (11) were examined (R = they)

EXERCISE 7 [page 16]

1. ~~by the translator~~   2. <u>by women</u>   3. ~~by a police officer.~~   4. ~~by a surgeon~~   5. <u>by Dr. Azarian</u>   6. ~~by someone~~   7. <u>by my grandmother</u>   8. ~~by computer users~~

EXERCISE 8 [page 16]

1. Agent cannot be deleted.   2. Agent cannot be deleted.   3. That car was built in Japan.   4. Agent cannot be deleted.   5. After Richard's car was stolen, it had to be replaced.   6. The pictures were taken at the wedding.   7. Agent cannot be deleted.   8. Agent cannot be deleted.

EXERCISE 9 [page 17]

(1) get   (2) be   (3) was   (4) was   (5) was   (6) was
(7) was   (8) was   (9) was   (10) get

EXERCISE 10 [page 17]

Only rewritten sentences are included below. All other sentences are *NC*.   1. The search for the missing child was conducted by the police.   3. The police accused a postal carrier.   6. The police arrested him anyway.   8. The police found the child in another state.   10. The police released the postal carrier from jail.   11. The police arrested the real kidnapper.

EXERCISE 11 [page 18]

1. were donated: a. *agent unknown*   2. were passed: a. *agent obvious*   3. have been reported: b. *emphasize the recipient*   4. is required: b. *emphasize the recipient*   5. should be done: d. *generic statement*   6. was awarded: b. *emphasize the recipient*   7. can be delivered: c. *connect ideas in two clauses*   8. has been made: a. *agent unimportant*   9. can be done: c. *connect ideas in two clauses*   10. has been attempted: a. *agent unknown*

EXERCISE 12 [page 19]

(1) is being built   (2) is living   (3) are being hung   (4) are being painted   (5) will arrive   (6) are being installed   (7) is being tested   (8) is supervising   (9) is paid/is being paid   (10) is doing

EXERCISE 13 [page 19]

(1) translate   (2) are written   (3) must think   (4) will be understood   (5) must be written   (6) will be performed   (7) can perform   (8) are used   (9) is interpreted   (10) will still be needed

EXERCISE 14 [page 20]

Did I ever <u>tell</u> you about the time my car **was hit** ~~hit~~ by a truck   Well, it <u>was</u> something! A large truck ~~was hit~~ the front of my car. All of the lights and the windshield **shattered/were shattered**. The left fender of the car **was crushed**. I <u>was</u> still in the car, and I <u>was</u> scared! My cousin ~~was~~ got <u>out</u>, but I **was** <u>trapped</u> inside the car. My cousin, Alice, <u>called</u> 911 and **was** <u>told</u> to go back to the car and <u>stay</u> with me.   When she <u>got</u> back, it **had** ~~been~~ begun to rain. The clouds <u>burst</u> open, and the temperature ~~was~~ <u>dropped</u>. When the ambulance <u>came</u>, the paramedic <u>discovered</u> that the impact **had** <u>brok**en**</u> my wrist when my hand ~~was hit~~ the steering wheel. At that moment I <u>promised</u> myself never to <u>rush</u> to work again!   (1) was hit   (2) was   (3) hit   (4) shattered/were shattered   (5) was crushed   (6) was   (7) was   (8) got out   (9) was trapped   (10) called   (11) was told   (12) got   (13) had begun   (14) burst   (15) dropped   (16) came   (17) discovered   (18) had broken   (19) hit   (20) promised

TEST PREP • UNITS 1–4 [page 21]

1. c	5. b	9. a	13. a	17. c
2. d	6. a	10. b	14. c	18. c
3. a	7. b	11. c	15. c	19. b
4. c	8. d	12. b	16. b	20. a

Unit 5

One-Word and Phrasal Modals

EXERCISE 1 [page 23]

1. Where is Claudia able to drive   2. Is Claudia allowed to drive on the highway   No, she isn't allowed.   3. Why can't she drive at night   4. Is Claudia able to see without her glasses   5. Should Bob get a driver's license   6. Did Juan used to drive a truck in his country   7. Is Carlos supposed to have car insurance   8. Should Carlos buy special car insurance for his new sports car   9. Barbara doesn't have to do housework.   10. Can Alice drive a truck   Yes, she can.

EXERCISE 2 [page 24]

New sentences will vary.

1. making offers/Shall I drive tonight   2. making suggestions/We could go to a movie instead.

3. expressing necessity or prohibition/He'd better not arrive late for the final exam.   4. making offers/Would you like me to fix lunch now   5. expressing advice/You ought to study harder.   6. giving invitations/Would you like to come to my graduation   7. denying permission/You're not allowed/supposed to chew gum in church.   8. giving invitations/Can you attend our party   9. expressing intention/I'll do it. I'll pick you up later.   10. expressing advice/You don't have to wash paper plates.   11. expressing prohibition/You'd better not drive fast near a police officer.   12. expressing intentions/I'm going to be a millionaire before I'm 30.   13. making requests/Could you please turn the TV off   14. expressing advice or obligation/We mustn't forget to shut the windows.   15. giving invitations/Can you come to my birthday party on Sunday?

EXERCISE 3 [page 25]

(1) impossibility   (2) prediction   (3) habitual actions in the past   (4) ability   (5) prediction   (6) general possibility   (7) future time   (8) habitual actions in the past   (9) logical inference   (10) impossibility   (11) prediction   (12) general possibility   (13) ability

EXERCISE 4 [page 27]

(1) use: necessity   (2) use: advice   (3) meaning: future   (4) meaning: inference   (5) use: permission   (6) meaning: ability   (7) meaning: past habitual actions   (8) meaning: possibility   (9) use: suggestion   (10) meaning: prediction   (11) use: request   (12) meaning: future time   (13) meaning: impossibility   (14) use: invitation   (15) use: promise

EXERCISE 5 [page 27]

(1) must   (2) should   (3) mustn't   (4) must   (5) shouldn't   (6) must

EXERCISE 6 [page 28]

Part A
You: will   You: must   FOB: should   You: not able to   FOB: should
Part B
Bob: have to, ought to   You: can't   Bob: can't, aren't going to

EXERCISE 7 [page 29]

1. necessity   2. ability, negative   3. necessity   4. inadvisability   5. necessity   6. ability

EXERCISE 8 [page 29]

(1) I   (2) F   (3) F   (4) I   (5) F   (6) I

Unit 6

Infinitives

EXERCISE 1 [page 30]

INFINITIVES: (3) to spend   (4) to make; to prepare   (5) to have   (6) to match; to represent   (7) to organize   (9) to learn; to finish   (10) to be completed   (11) to be named   (12) to prove; to pay   GERUNDS: (3) practicing   (8) Practicing   (13) Building; designing; paying for

EXERCISE 2 [page 31]

1. not to go—negative   2. to stay out—affirmative   3. to live—affirmative   4. not to drive—negative   5. to be cleaned—passive   6. to look—active   7. to be unpacked—passive   8. to unpack—active   9. to have gotten—perfect   10. to be finishing up—progressive

EXERCISE 3 [page 31]

1. is dropped off at a shopping mall   2. had been a princess   3. sign a computer-use policy   4. would have done the dishes   5. Don't forget to turn in your term papers   6. will be paid   7. are left alone   8. would be waiting

EXERCISE 4 [page 32]

1. Pauline will clean up after the party.   2. Mike will lose 10 pounds by July.   3. We will do more research on the Internet.   4. All students must return library books before they can get their semester grades.   5. The city government must resume funding the school lunch program.   6. Michael will pick the flowers in Mr. Johnson's front yard.

EXERCISE 5 [page 33]

Answers can vary. Italicized words are examples of extra information that may be added.   2. He needed to be told about the situation *before it was too late.*   3. We decided to leave earlier *than we had originally planned.*   4. They appeared to be happy.   5. Would you dare to swim during an *electrical* storm   6. Raphael sometimes hesitates to raise his hand in class.   7. She should never have agreed to send money *to her cousin.*   8. Sam refused to be nominated *treasurer of his class.*   9. Do you really want to know your future   10. Bill neglected to pay his rent last month, *and now he's in big trouble with his landlady.*

EXERCISE 6 [page 33]

Spoken pair work

EXERCISE 7 [page 34]

2. He warned *me* not to drive so fast.   3. He allowed *me* to go without giving me a ticket.   5. My mother

hired *a gardener* to trim the trees and cut the bushes.
8. Our speech teacher taught *us* how to introduce a topic in a natural way. 9. The state requires *car owners* to have car insurance.

EXERCISE 8 [page 34]

1. someone else will word process it for her 2. Beth to pay for the drinks 3. for someone else to write the invitations 4. someone else to arrange the flowers 5. to buy (herself) a new dress

EXERCISE 9 [page 35]

1. Kate's professor has requested her to keep detailed notes of her research. 2. The government requires Kate to get several vaccinations before she goes. 3. Her professor insisted that Kate study the language of the Amazon tribe that she will live with. (*"Insist" cannot be followed by an infinitive; it takes the English subjunctive.*) 4. Kate has decided to try to learn about

Amazon folk medicine. 5. Kate's professor has encouraged her to write a list of research questions. 6. Kate's family expected her to feel a little bit nervous before her trip.

EXERCISE 10 [page 36]

1. Kate was expected . . .
2. Kate was asked by her parents . . .
3. Kate was encouraged by her brother . . .
4. Maria was selected . . .
5. Maria was invited . . .
6. Stanford University is considered to be . . .

EXERCISE 11 [page 36]

1. It can be difficult to cook . . . 2. It's enjoyable to swim . . . 3. It's easier to learn . . . 4. It is my pleasure . . . 5. It's a good idea for Max . . . 6. It's a wise idea for . . .

Unit 7
Gerunds

EXERCISE 1 [page 37]

1. he is being spied on 2. most women are whistled at by men 3. you watered my garden 4. there would be an earthquake 5. I don't have to make the bed when I stay in a hotel

EXERCISE 2 [page 37]

Spoken activity

EXERCISE 3 [page 38]

1. I 2. Pete's 3. we 4. John's 5. Phil's 6. Jack's 7. Jack 8. Charles's

EXERCISE 4 [page 38]

(1) relaxing (2) enjoying (3) following (4) filling (5) mowing (6) trimming (7) painting (8) feeling (9) shopping (10) cleaning (11) sleeping (12) having (13) getting (14) letting

EXERCISE 5 [page 38]

Verbs that require gerunds (from Exercise 4): *recommend, resist, insist on, avoid, admit, help, try, consider, suggest*

EXERCISE 6 [page 39]

1. to take 2. giving up 3. to join 4. eating 5. to go 6. to sign up

EXERCISE 7 [page 39]

1. Katherine misses eating freshly made bread./ Katherine missed her sister's singing in the shower. 2. Benjamin understands needing time alone./ Benjamin understands his roommate's needing time alone. 3. I won't tolerate receiving torn magazines in the mail./ Patrick won't tolerate his mother's getting poor service. 4. Toshio postponed waxing his car./ Mr. Davis postponed his daughter's getting married. 5. Scott denied taking the last piece of cake./ The captain denied Anthony's taking a vacation.

EXERCISE 8 [page 40]

1. Matt's brother doesn't understand Matt's wanting to get a good job right away. 2. Matt wanted to avoid still having two term papers to write in his last semester. 3. Matt won't miss eating dinner in the cafeteria. 4. Matt's roommate Tom resents Matt's talking about returning to Hawaii. 5. Matt's parents are not looking forward to Matt's getting a new car. 6. Matt didn't anticipate having to pay for his own car insurance.

EXERCISE 9 [page 40]

1. Running   2. driving   3. worrying   4. spending
5. Relaxing   6. not smoking   7. Staying   8. watching
9. Collecting   10. not having

EXERCISE 10 [page 41]

(1) to watch   (2) playing   (3) to get   (4) spending
(5) to use   (6) to read   (7) being   (8) watching
(9) selecting   (10) to play/playing   (11) to imagine
(12) to practice/practicing   (13) to unplug   (14) to let

EXERCISE 11 [page 42]

1. a   2. b   3. b   4. a

EXERCISE 12 [page 42]

1. Jack quit smoking.   2. I always remember to lock
the front door.   3. The teacher tried to close the
window.   4. We tried turning on the heater.   5. I'd
forgotten taking these pictures.   6. He stopped to
think.   7. Penny stopped drinking coffee.

EXERCISE 13 [page 43]

1. talking   2. to do   3. to visit   4. listening   5. to
put/putting   6. to answer   7. to explain   8. to read

TEST PREP • UNITS 5–7 [page 44]

1. b	5. a	9. b	13. b	17. d
2. c	6. c	10. a	14. d	18. a
3. a	7. d	11. d	15. c	19. b
4. d	8. b	12. c	16. a	20. d

Unit 8

Statements of Degree: Intensifiers and Degree Complements

EXERCISE 1 [page 46]

(2) Recently, however, he hasn't received enough work.
(3) His partner told him that his new designs were
somewhat hard to understand.   (4) At first, Peter was
extremely upset by his partner's observation because he
had worked very hard.   (5) Later, he realized that his
designs really were too complicated for most city
buildings.   (7) First, he made the hallways slightly
wider to make it easier to deliver office equipment.
(9) This would provide quite a bit more light.
(11) is quite proud of his new design and is fairly
confident that it will be accepted.

EXERCISE 2 [page 46]

(1) too/very   (2) somewhat/rather/pretty/kind of/sort
of/fairly   (3) a little/slightly/a bit/a tad   (4) too/way
too   (5) a little/slightly/a bit/a tad   (6) very/really
(7) quite/very/extremely/really   (8) kind of/rather/
somewhat/sort of   (9) too/way too   (10) a little/
a tad/a bit/slightly

EXERCISE 3 [page 47]

1. too   2. very   3. too   4. very   5. too   6. too
7. very   8. too   9. too   10. very

EXERCISE 4 [page 47]

1. a little too/a bit too   2. a little too/really too
3. really too   4. a bit too   5. way too

EXERCISE 5 [page 48]

1. direct   2. softened   3. direct   4. direct   5. direct
6. direct   7. softened   8. direct   9. direct
10. direct

EXERCISE 6 [page 48]

3. This coffee isn't as strong as I'd like.   4. The seats
aren't quite big enough.   5. That story was not very
short.   6. The soup isn't very spicy.   8. Pauline
doesn't really like going to museums.   9. The new
delivery person is not very fast.   10. Janice isn't a very
good dancer.

EXERCISE 7 [page 49]

Intensifiers are in italics.
1. Mr. Green was worried *enough* about delays on the
new project to ask everyone to come in on Saturday.
2. Mr. Green is *too* cheap to provide free coffee for the

office workers.   3. Mr. Green is *too* busy at work to take a vacation.   4. Mr. Green has *enough* worries to keep him up at night.   5. Mr. Green's employees don't like him *enough* to have a birthday party for him.

EXERCISE 8 [page 49]

1. b.   2. a.   3. b.   4. b.   5. a.

EXERCISE 9 [page 50]

1. Betty has too much pride to ask her friend for a loan.
2. Teresa is too young/not old enough to get married.
3. The office is too noisy for Mr. Addison to concentrate on his work.   4. The cat weighs too much to catch mice.
5. Pedro bought enough photocopier paper to print his project.   6. Sam doesn't like his neighbor enough to water her plants while she is away.   7. The little boy is old enough to go to school.   8. I am too old/not young enough to join the army or police force.   9. Helen always has enough money to buy stocks and bonds.   10. Barbara has too many bills to be able to help me with mine.

EXERCISE 10 [page 51]

(1) so   (2) Such   (3) so   (4) such   (5) Such
(6) such   (7) so   (8) so   (9) Such   (10) so

EXERCISE 11 [page 52]

1. The Harrisons have purchased so many paintings that they can't show all of them at one time.   2. Paul has such an easy job that he can often leave work early.
3. The earthquake caused such heavy destruction that the chemistry building was no longer usable.   4. Carl ate so much pizza that he could hardly get up from his chair.   5. The college had so much success with the fundraising program that the program was expanded.
6. The carpet had become so dirty that it couldn't be cleaned.   7. The rabbits had so few natural enemies in Australia that they multiplied very quickly.   8. The rain caused such extensive flooding that the city streets had to be repaired and the lines repainted.

Unit 9

Modifying Noun Phrases

EXERCISE 1 [page 53]

1. a large new multistoried
2. some of that very old French
3. two rather spoiled little
4. six old-fashioned silver serving
5. several really fat wild
6. three slightly damaged

EXERCISE 2 [page 54]

(1) blue and white striped   (2) original store   (3) two very expensive wool   (4) old, knee-length wool   (5) big round white   (6) bright green wool   (7) shabby old hand-me-down   (8) ugly, worn-out   (9) brand-new designer   (10) well-polished Italian leather

EXERCISE 3 [page 54]

2. Patricia is planning her next month-long exotic cruise.   5. The entire family was living in a tiny, dark, one-room apartment.   6. The competition was held on the first floor of the brand-new government Department of Justice building.

EXERCISE 4 [page 55]

1. *Pressed*—PAST; *interesting*—PRESENT
2. *Enduring*—PRESENT; *contented*—PRESENT

3. *Interesting*—PRESENT; *revealed*—PAST; *reading*—PRESENT
4. *puzzling*—PRESENT; *exciting*—PRESENT
5. *growing*—PRESENT; *balanced*—PAST
6. *surprised*—PAST; *unexpected*—PAST

EXERCISE 5 [page 55]

1. damaging; damaged   2. embarrassing; embarrassed
3. depressing; depressed   4. disappointed; disappointing
5. terrified; terrifying

EXERCISE 6 [page 56]

1. enduring   2. interesting   3. interested
4. fascinating   5. annoying   6. worried
7. surprising   8. surprised   9. upsetting   10. boring

EXERCISE 7 [page 56]

1. a child who is in great need of attention
2. a museum that is visited by a lot of people   3. a salesperson who talks fast   4. traffic that is moving slowly   5. a story that is known by many people   6. a house that has been destroyed by fire   7. a millionaire who did not inherit his or her fortune   8. a steak that has been cooked thoroughly   9. a move that happens at a good time   10. food that was frozen quickly

EXERCISE 8 [page 57]

(1) disappointing	(2) expected	(3) worried
(4) frightened	(5) embarrassed	(6) confused
(7) insulting	(8) accused	(9) required
(10) expected	(11) frightened	(12) interested
(13) annoyed	(14) puzzling	(15) mistaken
(16) concerned	(17) uninvolved	(18) surprising
(19) terrified	(20) recommended	

EXERCISE 9 [page 58]

Spoken group work

EXERCISE 10 [page 58]

1. The price increase that was announced last week was the second in a year.   2. The reporter who was planning to break the story got a sudden surprise. 3. The criminal who was arrested last week will be tried in federal court.   4. The student who is speaking in front of the class is quite nervous.   5. The project that was mentioned in the first chapter took a year to complete.   6. The prize that will be given at the end of the week will be the largest in the club's history.

Unit 10
Comparatives

EXERCISE 1 [page 59]

1. X = lumber production in Canada
    Y = lumber production in the United States
    X > Y: large difference
    X = lumber use in Canada
    Y = lumber use in the United States
    X < Y: large difference
2. X = the population of the United States
    Y = the population of Canada
    X > Y: large difference
    X = the literacy rate of the United States
    Y = the literacy rate of Canada
    X < Y: small difference

EXERCISE 2 [page 60]

1. The number of castles in the United States is substantially smaller than that in France.   2. The number of castles in France is much higher than in the United States.   3. The land area of New Mexico is somewhat larger than that of Arizona.   4. The land area of Arizona is somewhat smaller than that of New Mexico.   5. The total size of Alaska is considerably bigger than that of Rhode Island.   6. The total size of Rhode Island is considerably smaller than that of Alaska.   7. Alaska achieved statehood slightly earlier than Hawaii.   8. Hawaii achieved statehood a bit later than Alaska.

EXERCISE 3 [page 60]

1. X = California
    Y = Connecticut
    feature: land area
    X > Y: large difference
2. X = Indiana
    Y = Kentucky
    feature: land area
    X < Y: small difference

3. X = Earth
    Y = Jupiter
    feature: number of moons
    X < Y: large difference
4. X = sherbet
    Y = ice cream
    feature: amount of fat in one cup
    X < Y: large difference

EXERCISE 4 [page 61]

1. New York City has many more immigrants than Fargo, North Dakota.   2. New York City has slightly less air pollution than Los Angeles.   3. An elephant is much heavier than a horse.   4. A plane ticket from Los Angeles to Paris is considerably more expensive than one from Los Angeles to San Francisco.   5. Catherine is not quite as tall as Marie.

EXERCISE 5 [page 62]

1. (a) one medicine and another;   (b) similar
2. (a) red wine and white wine;   (b) identical
3. (a) students who take the school bus and those who drive to school;   (b) different   4. (a) France and Italy;   (b) identical   5. (a) two ideas; (b) different   6. (a) his voice and his brother's voice;   (b) similar

EXERCISE 6 [page 63]

1. (a) family structures   (b) very different   (c) *from very different family structures*   2. (a) family structures (b) identical/very similar   (c) *from the same or similar family structures*   3. (a) patterns of behavior (b) somewhat similar   (c) *somewhat similar*   4. (a) a woman and a man   (b) identical   (c) *does not like his mother*   5. (a) family structure   (b) identical   (c) *the*

same type 6. (a) educational levels (b) somewhat similar (c) *very different* 7. (a) interests (b) somewhat similar (c) *similar* 8. (a) expectations (b) very different (c) *completely different* 9. (a) religion (b) identical (c) *the same* 10. (a) age range (b) identical (c) *the same*

EXERCISE 7 [page 65]

1. The eating habits of France are quite different from those of the United States. 2. Charles had much the same experience as José. 3. Europeans drive differently from Americans. 4. Patrick's writing style is not very different from mine. 5. Washington State has much the same number of rainy days as Oregon. 6. Health-conscious people eat differently from other people. 7. The typical age for marriage in North America is quite different from that in Africa. 8. I read the same report as Jeff.

TEST PREP • UNITS 8–10 [page 66]

1. d	5. b	9. c	13. d	17. a
2. d	6. b	10. b	14. c	18. d
3. d	7. c	11. b	15. a	19. c
4. c	8. d	12. b	16. a	20. c

Unit 11
Connectors

EXERCISE 1 [page 68]

Connector: Form, Meaning
(2) *First:* sentence connecter, sequence (3) *After:* subordinating conjunction, sequence (4) *but:* coordinating conjunction, contrast (5) *Consequently:* sentence connector, result (6) (none) (7) *Then:* sentence connector, condition (8) *Eventually:* sentence connector, sequence and coordinator addition (9) *As a result:* sentence connector, result (10) *However:* sentence connector, contrast (11) *Although:* subordinating conjunction, contrast (12) *In fact:* sentence connector, emphasis (13) *besides:* subordinating conjunction, emphasis (14) (none) (15) *Furthermore:* sentence connector, emphasis (16) *If:* subordinating conjunction; condition; *and:* coordinating conjunction, addition

EXERCISE 2 [page 69]

(1) but (2) on the one hand (3) on the other hand/however (4) In fact (5) if (6) However (7) but (8) Moreover/Furthermore (9) and (10) Besides

EXERCISE 3 [page 69]

(3) Janice cleaned her apartment until it was <u>shining</u> (and) <u>spotless</u>. (4) <u>She was going to get flowers,</u> (but) <u>she didn't have time</u>. (5) On her way to the airport, <u>she thought about making reservations</u> for dinner, (but) <u>she wasn't sure</u> whether her mother would prefer <u>Chinese</u> (or) <u>Thai</u> food. (6) She knew that her mother liked (neither) <u>pepper</u> (nor) <u>curry</u>. (7) Once she was on the road, Janice <u>turned on</u> the radio (and) <u>realized</u> that her mother was going to be late. (8) <u>The weather was good in L.A.</u> (but) <u>snow near Chicago had caused a delay.</u> (9) Janice had time <u>to go shopping</u> (or) <u>to sit</u> in a cafe (and) <u>read</u> a book. (10) An hour later, <u>Janice again headed toward</u> the airport, (and) <u>she took her time</u>. (12) Her mother had <u>heard about</u> the Chicago snowstorm (and) <u>decided</u> to take an earlier flight. (13) <u>She didn't have time</u> to call Janice, (but) <u>she knew</u> that Janice <u>was</u> careful (and) <u>would</u> arrive early to pick her up. (15) <u>Janice could have gotten</u> to the airport earlier, (but) she didn't. (16) <u>Her mother could have called</u> from the plane, (but) she didn't. (17) They were both <u>hungry</u> (and) <u>tired</u>. (18) <u>Janice offered</u> to take her mother to (either) a <u>Chinese</u> (or) a <u>Thai</u> restaurant, (but) <u>her mother</u> just <u>wanted</u> to <u>get</u> to Janice's apartment (and) <u>take</u> a nap!

EXERCISE 4 [page 70]

1. but 2. and 3. or 4. nor 5. but 6. or/and 7. but 8. and 9. nor 10. or

EXERCISE 5 [page 71]

Answers will vary. Possible answers are:
1. Karen likes to drink strong coffee, but Margaret doesn't./ Karen likes to drink strong coffee; however, Margaret doesn't. 2. Both Karen and Margaret want to go to Disneyland./ Karen wants to go to Disneyland, and Margaret does too. 3. Karen likes water skiing and diving./ Karen likes both water skiing and diving. 4. Margaret enjoys water skiing, but not when it's cold on the lake. 5. Karen likes getting visits from her friends and relatives every summer. 6. Margaret doesn't like meeting her relatives at the airport, and Karen doesn't either./ Neither Margaret nor Karen likes meeting her relatives at the airport.

EXERCISE 6 [page 72]

Answers will vary. Possible answers are:
1. Kate enjoys yoga but not judo. 2. Neither Kate nor Mary Jo goes home to change between work and her yoga class./ Kate doesn't go home to change between work and her yoga class, and neither does Mary Jo/Mary Jo doesn't either. 3. Kate doesn't eat before her yoga class, but Mary Jo does. 4. Both Kate and Mary Jo/Kate and Mary Jo both think that practicing yoga helps them

to reduce stress.   5. After yoga class, Kate usually wants to eat, but Mary Jo doesn't.   6. The instructor wants both Kate and Mary Jo to try the advanced yoga class.

EXERCISE 7 [page 73]

1. Although José wanted to return to his country, he didn't want to leave his job here.   2. Because he made a lot of money in the United States, he was able to send money to his family.   3. As a result of becoming more and more nervous about making a decision, José started

smoking again.   4. In addition, he started to drink heavily.   5. He eventually went to the doctor, but he ignored the doctor's advice.

EXERCISE 8 [page 73]

1. Besides I paid for: *Besides paying for*   2. pay. Mary: *pay, Mary*   3. In spite of she didn't pay: *Even though she didn't pay*   4. Due to she is cheap: *Because she is cheap*   5. mine. I: *mine, I*

Unit 12

Relative Clauses

EXERCISE 1 [page 74]

(1) Michelle has finally realized one of her lifelong dreams.   (2) She has always wanted to attend the cooking school that her mentor, Chef Troisgros, attended.   (3) The school, which is in Paris, accepts only 80 students every year. (4) The students who are accepted generally have at least three years of cooking experience.   (5) Michelle has five years of paid cooking experience in a restaurant. (6) The project that attracted the attention of Chef Troisgros, however, was a cake that Michelle made for a wedding.   (7) Chef Troisgras had never tasted a cake that was as light and creamy as the one that Michelle made. (8) He gave Michelle his card and invited her to cook pastries at his restaurant beginning the next month. (9) It was this invitation that began her career baking for a large restaurant.   (10) Right now, she is waiting for the plane that will fly her to Paris.   (11) There she will begin the same three-month course that Chef Troisgros attended.

EXERCISE 2 [page 74]

1. Michelle is attending the cooking course that she dreamed about.
2. The man whom she is cooking with is an experienced cook.
3. Michelle prefers to learn baking techniques that she can use back in the United States.
4. She met the man who is co-owner of the cooking school.
5. The school, which has received three blue ribbons, has been open since 1926.
6. Michelle was only recently introduced to the family whom she is now living with.
7. She bought the cookbook that was written by her teacher.
8. Every day, the students eat the food that they have prepared.

EXERCISE 3 [page 75]

1. Patrick took a course that is no longer offered at our school.   2. Kate bought a cell phone that had a good

calling plan.   3. Lawrence introduced me to the new friend with whom he had been jogging for two months. 4. Michelle has a friend who owns a restaurant just outside of Paris.   5. I want to visit the beach that was featured on a TV show.   6. The dog that was in my backyard belongs to my neighbors down the street.

EXERCISE 4 [page 75]

1. This is the person to whom David gave flowers. 2. My brother, who runs for two miles each morning, is in good physical shape.   3. Correct   4. The website that I read was interesting.   5. Correct   6. Correct

EXERCISE 5 [page 76]

1. Relative pronoun cannot be deleted.   2. She examined the menus ~~that~~ the chef had planned.   3. She wants to return home with a diploma ~~that was~~ signed by Chef Lyon.   4. The student ~~whom~~ she had dinner with last night is from Italy.   5. Relative pronoun cannot be deleted.   6. Michelle prefers to make friends with people ~~who are~~ studying at her school.   7. Chef Lyon tasted each cake ~~that was~~ baked by his students. 8. The prize ~~that is~~ awarded to the best student is a white chef's hat.   9. Relative pronoun cannot be deleted.   10. Relative pronoun cannot be deleted.

EXERCISE 6 [page 76]

1. . . . whose fur is long.   2. . . . whose sister she met at an Internet café.   3. . . . calls for a doctor whose phone.,,,   4. . . . whose window my son had broken. 5. . . . whose grade was . . .   6. People whose thinking styles are similar may vote alike.

EXERCISE 7 [page 77]

1. geRund   2. hEr   3. seLf   4. pAst   5. posT 6. actIve   7. neVer   8. sElect   9. Comma   10. deLete 11. dAffy   12. pUll   13. whoSe   14. hEad

1. c   3. d   5. a   7. d   9. c
2. b   4. c   6. d   8. d   10. a

11. a   13. d   15. c   17. a   19. b
12. a   14. c   16. c   18. c   20. a

Unit 13

Using Present Time

EXERCISE 1 [page 80]

1. plays   2. is speaking   3. is sleeping/sleeps   4. is having   5. goes/is going   6. is doing   7. are waiting   8. are still cleaning   9. speaks   10. is popping

EXERCISE 2 [page 80]

1. is doing   2. am living   3. makes   4. is working   5. want, have   6. tries, forgets   7. feels   8. is feeling   9. is searching   10. live

EXERCISE 3 [page 81]

Questions only are listed.
1. Which type of visa does the school require
2. What don't you like about winter   3. Who do you resemble most in your family   4. What does your wallet contain   5. How many shoes do you own   6. What does taking the test require
7. What kind of food do you prefer   8. To whom does that motorcycle belong   9. How much does that house cost   10. When did he realize he had a problem

EXERCISE 4 [page 82]

1. requires   2. tastes   3. is tasting   4. minds/is minding   5. is having   6. are being   7. am depending/depend   8. is weighing   9. weighs   10. is considering   11. smell   12. require

EXERCISE 5 [page 82]

(1) I push him back, and he falls down on the sidewalk. (2) When he gets up, he sees that his pants are torn. (3) He's really mad!   (4) He goes to get a policeman to arrest me.   (5) He crosses the street, and a cop gives him a ticket.   (6) The light was/is yellow, and this guy crossed/crosses anyway.   (7) Well, he tells his story to the cop, but the cop doesn't believe him. (8) The guy deserved it!

Unit 14

Present Perfect

EXERCISE 1 [page 83]

(3) was–(c)   (4) was born–(c) learned–(c) (5) translated–(c); went shopping–(c)   (6) has done–(b)   (7) has translated–(b)   (8) has helped–(b); have been–(b); have thanked–(b)   (9) has experienced–(b)   (10) has taught–(b)

EXERCISE 2 [page 83]

(1) applied   (2) has worked   (3) has looked (4) decided   (5) planned   (6) made   (7) reserved (8) didn't have to   (9) has worked   (10) has wanted (11) was canceled   (12) was   (13) quit   (14) has heard   (15) has been   (16) has just seen (17) brought in   (18) resolved

EXERCISE 3 [page 84]

(1) has just discovered   (2) has canceled/canceled (3) already made   (4) just returned/has just returned (5) opened   (6) read   (7) told   (8) has done (9) complained   (10) put   (11) hasn't changed

EXERCISE 4 [page 84]

1. a   2. b   3. b   4. a   5. a.   6. b

EXERCISE 5 [page 85]

1. has been painting   2. has been charging/has charged   3. has known   4. has been asking   5. has been running   6. has wanted/has been wanting; has called   7. has been trying   8. has resulted   9. has smelled/has been smelling   10. have been dreaming/have dreamed

EXERCISE 6 [page 85]

(1) has been considering/is considering   (2) is thinking   (3) has been   (4) enjoys   (5) likes   (6) was   (7) hasn't had   (8) started   (9) has begun/ is beginning

Unit 15
Future Time

EXERCISE 1 [page 86]

2. is bringing   (F)   3. might take   (F)   4. 's having (F)   5. tells   (P)   6. get   (F); 'll get   (F)   7. Look (P); could rain   (F)   8. 's staying   (P)   9. starts (F)   10. is wearing   (F); can't   (P)

EXERCISE 2 [page 86]

1. might/will graduate   2. is/will be   3. will go 4. might rain   5. is leaving   6. might/could win 7. going   8. is

EXERCISE 3 [page 87]

1. (a) will hurt   (b) will do   (c) is going to begin (d) won't/isn't going to include   2. (a) are you going to fix   (b) won't run   (c) won't be seen   (d) will buy 3. (a) is going to do   (b) will end   (c) won't have (d) is . . . going to say/will . . . say

EXERCISE 4 [page 87]

1. will   2. won't   3. Shall   4. are you going to 5. Shall

EXERCISE 5 [page 88]

Answers will vary. Possible answers are:
1. It will increase because its residents keep reproducing at the same rate.   2. They should, because it is a fast and efficient way of communicating. 3. It might, if enough citizens lobby for it.   4. I will have to take them at some other time.   5. I may not always have the same career because sometimes I am bored at work.   6. There could be a cure for cancer

someday.   7. She should like her present, because it's something she asked for.   8. The government won't get rid of taxes, because it is in debt up to its armpits.

EXERCISE 6 [page 89]

1. José and Maria are going to have a good time while they are on vacation in Costa Rica.   2. I'm going to go camping for three days once I finish all of my final exams.   3. Carl and Alicia are leaving for their new jobs as soon as they sell their house.   4. Even my boss is going to take time off when he finishes printing and checking the month-end report.   5. The cruise will be over before we realize how much money we spent. 6. It will be almost the next semester by the time Carol finally gets her research paper finished.   7. He's going to go skiing when he gets a book of discount ski lift tickets.   8. Janet will read her book while the baby is napping.

EXERCISE 7 [page 90]

(1) is going to/will travel   (2) returns   (3) gets (4) will have   (5) arrives   (6) will/is going to call (7) will/is going to go   (8) leaves   (9) will stop (10) will be sleeping   (11) ends/will end (12) touches   (13) will finally be

TEST PREP • UNITS 13–15 [page 91]

1. b	5. b	9. b	13. c	17. d
2. c	6. c	10. c	14. b	18. b
3. a	7. d	11. c	15. b	19. c
4. d	8. a	12. a	16. a	20. d

Unit 16
Modals of Prediction and Inference

EXERCISE 1 [page 93]

1. Pat should be able to decide where to go on vacation. 2. Pat won't want to take his mother-in-law along. 3. He might not even tell her about the trip. 4. His wife will tell her mother. 5. They may ask the mother-in-law to watch their house. 6. She might look in all of their closets. 7. It might/could rain heavily tonight. 8. That student won't be able to finish on time. 9. He shouldn't expect a tax refund. 10. That sick child will cry all night.

EXERCISE 2 [page 94]

1. (a) could/may/might (b) may/might/could (c) might/could 2. (a) should (b) couldn't (c) must/should (d) could 3. (a) might/may/could (b) should (c) can't (d) must

EXERCISE 3 [page 94]

1. a 2. b 3. a 4. b

EXERCISE 4 [page 95]

(1) Susan was late to the dinner party. (2) There may have been traffic on the way. (3) She could have called from her car phone. (4) The phone must not have been working. (5) She must have been frustrated.

EXERCISE 5 [page 95]

1. (a) must have been (b) may have been (c) should have arrived 2. (a) should have called (b) could have given (c) must have had 3. (a) could have taken (b) may have left (c) might have given (d) must not have been wearing

EXERCISE 6 [page 96]

Across: 1. perfect 11. should 13. must 15. used 16. blank 17. might
Down: 1. past 8. could 12. doubt 14. ok

Unit 17
Hypothetical Statements

EXERCISE 1 [page 97]

1. a 2. b 3. a 4. b 5. b

EXERCISE 2 [page 97]

1. I didn't live in Paris. 2. He didn't pay his share. 3. I won't come to your party. 4. He didn't ask me for help. 5. She didn't e-mail the report. 6. Bob lied.

EXERCISE 3 [page 98]

1. b 2. a 3. a 4. b 5. b

EXERCISE 4 [page 98]

1. If I had $40,000, I would be able to pay next year's tuition. 2. If my mother were here, she would cook for me. 3. If the manager weren't visiting our department, we wouldn't have to wear suits. 4. If my writing teacher returned essays on time, I would know how to improve my writing. 5. If Mary didn't have to study, she could have a part-time job. 6. If I could get a cheaper rate for my cell phone, I wouldn't have to switch to a new cell phone company.

EXERCISE 5 [page 99]

Answers will vary. Possible answers are:
1. if he didn't smoke. 2. if I had the time. 3. if she had a car. 4. if we already knew English. 5. if I visited them more often. 6. if I had a maid. 7. if people were more peaceful. 8. if people didn't commit violent crimes.

EXERCISE 6 [page 100]

Answers will vary. Possible answers are:
PART A: 1. . . . I would not have been born.
2. . . . he would be able to buy that new bike.
3. . . . I would have fixed you something to eat.
4. . . . he would have been out-of-pocket.
PART B: 5. . . . I wouldn't be taking it again this semester. 6. . . . more people could be studying now.
7. . . . I wouldn't be working in a mall.
8. . . . I wouldn't be living in a dormitory.

EXERCISE 7 [page 100]

Answers will vary. Possible answers are:
1. I can't go back to my country because I have to finish this term paper.   2. I didn't know he was so impolite when I invited him to the party.   3. I didn't attend this college 20 years ago when the tuition was cheaper.   4. Janice didn't pass her exam, so she's retaking the class in summer school.   5. He didn't get the job because he lied on his résumé.   6. She doesn't have a third ticket to give you.

EXERCISE 8 [page 101]

Answers will vary. Possible answers are:
1. Otherwise I would have gone to the movies with you.   2. Otherwise she wouldn't have given me this album.   3. I would drive the 200 miles to see you, but it's going to snow tomorrow.   4. Otherwise she could take you to the airport.   5. Otherwise they might never have left their home country.   6. Catherine wouldn't be so hard on Jack about his grades, but she doesn't know how hard he's studying.   7. Otherwise it would be finished by now.   8. I would go camping with you, but my boss asked me to work this weekend.

EXERCISE 9 [page 102]

PART A: 1. likely 2. unlikely 3. likely 4. likely
PART B: 5. hypothetical 6. nonhypothetical
7. nonhypothetical 8. hypothetical

EXERCISE 10 [page 103]

1. unlikely event 2. past possibility 3. unlikely event 4. past possibility

EXERCISE 11 [page 103]

1. not true 2. actual possibility 3. not true
4. actual possibility 5. not true

EXERCISE 12 [page 104]

1. b 2. a 3. b 4. b 5. b

Unit 18

Sensory Verbs, Causative Verbs, and Verbs That Take Subjunctive

EXERCISE 1 [page 105]

1. to be let in 2. to sit 3. to finish 4. be let outside

EXERCISE 2 [page 105]

1. SENSORY VERB: *watched*
OBSERVED ACTION: *The children skated on the lake.*
2. SENSORY VERB: *to feel*
OBSERVED ACTION: *The sun shines on Carol's face.*
3. SENSORY VERB: *heard*
OBSERVED ACTION: *The car crashed.*
4. SENSORY VERB: *observed*
OBSERVED ACTION: *The baby was crawling on the floor.*
5. SENSORY VERB: *smell*
OBSERVED ACTION: *The toast is burning.*
6. SENSORY VERB: *listened*
OBSERVED ACTION: *The customer complained about the cost of fixing his laptop.*

EXERCISE 3 [page 106]

1. play/playing 2. fix/fixing 3. mowing
4. leave/leaving 5. burning

EXERCISE 4 [page 106]

(1) I felt the house begin to shake.   (2) I heard the sound of the movement get louder.   (3) I saw the dishes fall out of the kitchen cabinet.   (4) I heard glass breaking. (5) I went under a table.   (6) I heard the sound grow fainter.

EXERCISE 5 [page 107]

1. fall/falling; break/breaking 2. sending
3. chase/chasing 4. burning 5. playing 6. arguing

EXERCISE 6 [page 107]

(1) Patrick started a new job last week.   (2) When he arrived, his <u>had</u> him sit next to the bill collector.
(3) The bill collector <u>made</u> Patrick dial all of his phone calls.   (4) Then he <u>forced</u> Patrick to listen.   (5) He <u>made</u> the people say they would pay.   (6) The next day, Patrick worked with the secretary.   (7) The secretary <u>got</u> Patrick to file all of her correspondence.   (8) She also <u>made</u> him photocopy old letters.   (9) Later Patrick <u>helped</u> her organize the files.   (10) On the third day, the boss <u>let</u> Patrick start his real job now that he understood the jobs of others in the office.

EXERCISE 7 [page 107]

Answers will vary. Possible answers are:
1. CAUSATIVE: *Cat owners shouldn't let their cats scratch guests.*
VERB + INFINITIVE: *Cat owners shouldn't allow their cats to scratch guests.*
2. CAUSATIVE: *Teachers should have students do research for term papers.*
VERB + INFINITIVE: *Teachers should require students to do research for term papers.*
3. CAUSATIVE: *A thief should not make a victim give up his iPod.*
VERB + INFINITIVE: *A thief should not require a victim to give up his iPod.*
4. CAUSATIVE: *Schools should have doctors examine students once a year.*
VERB + INFINITIVE: *Schools should require doctors to examine students once a year.*
5. CAUSATIVE: *Teachers should help students learn by example.*
VERB + INFINITIVE: *Teachers should get students to learn by example.*
6. CAUSATIVE: *The doctor should make Jack go on a diet.*
VERB + INFINITIVE: *The doctor should require Jack to go on a diet.*
7. CAUSATIVE: *Most people should have an accountant check their taxes.*
VERB + INFINITIVE: *Most people should get an accountant to check their taxes.*
8. CAUSATIVE: *Police officers should make drunk drivers pull over.*
VERB + INFINITIVE: *Police officers should force drunk drivers to pull over.*

EXERCISE 8 [page 108]

1. People are not allowed to drink and drive.   2. NO CHANGE POSSIBLE.   3. All adult men are required to enlist in the army.   4. Our tickets were taken by the attendant.   5. Wilson's report was prepared by his sister.   6. Children should be helped by their parents to learn good eating habits.

EXERCISE 9 [page 109]

(1) The boss required Patrick to answer the phone for several hours.   (2) When the phones were slow, he allowed Patrick to read the reports from last month.
(3) Later, the boss taught him to use the e-mail system.
(4) At noon, he allowed Patrick to go out to lunch.
(5) But the boss required him to bring back lunch for several people on the phone staff.   (6) He persuaded Patrick to pick up a newspaper and some rubber bands.
(7) At 5:00, the boss encouraged Patrick to work a few minutes extra.   (8) At 6:30, he allowed Patrick to go home.

EXERCISE 10 [page 110]

1. were gotten	*They got the children to be quiet.*
2. to redo	omit *to*
4. to be	omit *to be*
5. be	omit *be*
7. to borrow	omit *to*
8. was had	*He had a mechanic change the oil.*
9. has	*that every salesman have a cell phone.*
10. to write	omit *to*
11. was included	*that she be included*
12. was given	*that he be given a break*

TEST PREP • UNITS 16—18 [page 111]

1. c	5. c	9. d	13. c	17. a
2. b	6. b	10. b	14. b	18. c
3. b	7. c	11. a	15. c	19. d
4. b	8. c	12. c	16. b	20. c

Unit 19

Articles in Discourse

EXERCISE 1 [page 113]

1. The (article); his (possessive)   2. The (article); some (article)   3. That (demonstrative); the (article)   4. Few (quantifier); the (article)   5. Those (demonstrative); her (possessive)   6. their (possessive); the (article)

EXERCISE 2 [page 113]

1. generic   2. particular   3. generic   4. particular
5. particular   6. generic   7. particular   8. generic
9. particular   10. generic

EXERCISE 3 [page 114]

1. b   2. a   3. b   4. b   5. a

EXERCISE 4 [page 114]

1. the/some/ø   2. a   3. the   4. some/ø   5. The; a
6. a; the   7. A   8. the/a; the/an   9. the
10. ø/some

EXERCISE 5 [page 115]

1. (a) a (b) the (c) The (d) the (e) the (f) Some
(g) the 2. (a) Some/The (b) the (c) ø/the (d) the
(e) The (f) the/a 3. (a) ø (b) a (c) the (d) ø
(e) Some

EXERCISE 6 [page 115]

1. a; a/ø 2. ø 3. a; a 4. a; the 5. Some 6. a; a
7. a; a 8. a; an 9. a; a 10. a; ø

EXERCISE 7 [page 116]

1. the 2. the; the 3. a; the 4. The 5. an; the
6. a; the 7. the; the 8. the 9. the; the/an
10. The; the/a 11. the 12. a; a

EXERCISE 8 [page 116]

1. b 2. a 3. b 4. b

Unit 20

Reference Forms in Discourse

EXERCISE 1 [page 117]

1. These/Those; those/these 2. these; They 3. the/those 4. these; the/this; the/this 5. The; the 6. that/this; It; It; the 7. It; that; the/that; It 8. the; these

EXERCISE 2 [page 117]

2. Let me make this clear: No cheating!
3. These students are excused from the final exam: Robert Gonzales, Hosein Arifipour, and Carla Arnold.
4. The manager stated that he had received several expense reports that were not filled out correctly. These will be returned.
5. Louise said that she left her job because she wanted more free time. That doesn't sound correct to me.
6. These practices will be stopped immediately: sending personal e-mails and leaving early.
7. Smith will write the report and Wilson will word process it. Those are your assignments.
8. Our salaries will be reduced 5%. I don't like that.

EXERCISE 3 [page 118]

1. that 2. That/It 3. It 4. That 5. that/this
6. it 7. it 8. That

EXERCISE 4 [page 118]

Only sentences that contain a post-modifier are included below.
1. that of your partner 3. Those who cannot hear the difference between "t" and "th" 5. those who she thinks know the material 6. that which is genuine, that which is not

TEST PREP • UNITS 19–20 [page 119]

1. c	5. b	9. c	13. d	17. b
2. d	6. d	10. b	14. b	18. d
3. c	7. a	11. a	15. d	19. a
4. d	8. b	12. c	16. c	20. a

Unit 21

Possessives

EXERCISE 1 [page 121]

(3) his (a) (4) of each house (d) (5) his
(a) (6) Their (a) (7) of the condo (d); of the last
place (d) (8) of the day (d); Jerry's (c); Anita's
(c) (9) Their (a); theirs (b)

EXERCISE 2 [page 121]

1. Bob's friend's golf clubs 2. Beethoven's symphonies 3. the child's mouth 4. the child's

friend Sally/his friend Sally's child 5. The first page of a book 6. Administration Building's second floor
7. the son of a well-known French movie director
8. the seat of the chair 9. Susan's cousin's store
10. The cause of the dispute

EXERCISE 3 [page 122]

Spoken pair work.

EXERCISE 4 [page 122]

1. of the common cold (**c/d**)   2. Karen's (**e**)   3. of Freud (**d**); Professor Randolph's (**e**)   4. of Holland (**d**); their (**c**)   5. of his hikes (**e**); of Yosemite (**c**)   6. the book's (**b**)

EXERCISE 5 [page 123]

Only incorrect sentences are included below.
1. The roof of the house was damaged in the storm.
3. He was a prisoner of his own fame when he died.
4. The wool sweaters of England are famous for their quality.   6. The stepdaughter of a little-known singer's wife will be playing the guitar tomorrow night.

Unit 22

Quantifiers, Collective Nouns, and Collective Adjectives

EXERCISE 1 [page 124]

Underlined words are listed below.
(2) plenty of colleges; not all of them; every major field of study   (3) quite a few students; one college
(4) Most students   (5) Almost all schools; some assistance
(6) Many counseling departments   (7) Hardly anyone
(8) Quite a bit of the counselors' advice   (9) More than one counselor; most of the time   (10) Not many students   (11) A lot of students; three or four courses
(12) Some people   (13) A few students

EXERCISE 2 [page 124]

1. There are a few open seats left in that class.
2. Almost all parents worry about their children.
3. Some teachers work in the summer.   4. Most homeowners in the United States have some kind of homeowner's insurance.   5. All children in the United States must have vaccinations before they may start school.   6. It takes a lot of money to buy a house.

EXERCISE 3 [page 125]

Spoken pair work.

EXERCISE 4 [page 125]

1. little   2. a little   3. few   4. a little   5. few
6. little   7. Few   8. a little

EXERCISE 5 [page 126]

1. Every/Any/Each student wants to get a good grade.
2. Every/Each/Any postal carrier is warned about dogs.
3. Jack spends every/each paycheck on his car.
4. Every/ Each e-mail will be answered by the Customer Service department.

EXERCISE 6 [page 126]

1. Both   2. Both of them   3. Neither   4. both; either   5. either of them

EXERCISE 7 [page 127]

1. Some of my   2. Any   3. A little of the   4. No
5. Almost all   6. Most   7. hardly any   8. Several of the

EXERCISE 8 [page 127]

1. attended   2. every one   3. none   4. much
5. a lot   6. a few   7. a great deal of   8. every one

EXERCISE 9 [page 128]

Underlined words are listed below.
2. groups; a flock of pink birds; a gaggle of geese; a herd of goats; a flock of sheep; a swarm of bees
3. a committee of professors; herds of dairy cows; a delegation of dairy farmers   4. the government; the public; the media; a group of unhappy citizens; a team of media analysts

EXERCISE 10 [page 128]

1. has; its   2. are; their   3. are; their   4. their   5. is; is; its; its

EXERCISE 11 [page 129]

1. drink; their   2. has; its   3. has; its   4. were
5. has; its   6. are; their

EXERCISE 12 [page 129]

1. Fast bicycles and large pizzas are very popular with people who are young.   2. Very few well-paying jobs are open to people who can't read and write.   3. The shelters were opened to prevent people who don't have a place to live from dying.   4. Some hospitals in the United States specialize in diseases of people who are old.   5. Porsches and Ferraris are generally considered to be cars for people who are very wealthy.

TEST PREP • UNITS 21–22 [page 130]

1. c	5. c	9. d	13. d	17. d
2. a	6. d	10. b	14. b	18. b
3. d	7. c	11. d	15. b	19. a
4. b	8. a	12. d	16. a	20. c

Unit 23
Past Time Frame

EXERCISE 1 [page 132]

2. had been waiting; rang; aspect and adverbial (*when*)
3. returned; picked up; sequence
4. had not yet been deposited; didn't pay; aspect and adverbial (*yet*)
5. had been boiling; turned down; aspect and adverbial (*before*)
6. signed; ended; sequence

EXERCISE 2 [page 133]

1. b   2. a   3. a   4. b   5. a

EXERCISE 3 [page 133]

(1) was constantly looking   (2) was trying; returned
(3) went   (4) were having   (5) was looking; found; needed   (6) helped; left

EXERCISE 4 [page 133]

1. went; had registered   2. destroyed   3. was looking; found   4. heard; had received; called   5. noticed; had chewed/was chewing   6. was; hadn't gotten

EXERCISE 5 [page 134]

1. had been searching   2. had finished   3. had been raining   4. had been using   5. had gotten   6. had been waiting

EXERCISE 6 [page 134]

1. had been trying; discovered   2. wasn't; was running/had been running; took   3. had written; decided   4. had been training   5. got; had left
6. spent   7. went; exchanged   8. had been listening; realized

Unit 24
Modals in Past Time Frame

EXERCISE 1 [page 135]

1. (a)   2. (a)   3. (b)   4. (a)   5. (b)   6. (b)

EXERCISE 2 [page 135]

2. apple   3. wash   4. stay   5. chew   6. stand
7. cob   8. mind   9. type   10. answer

EXERCISE 3 [page 136]

Answers will vary. Possible answers are:
ALLOWED: 1. I was allowed to swim in the lake.
2. I was allowed to make the campfire.   3. I was allowed to stay up later than usual.   4. I was allowed to play all day.

NOT ALLOWED: 1. I was not allowed to cut school.
2. I was not allowed to go out on school nights.   3. I was not allowed to watch TV instead of doing my homework.
4. I was not allowed to stay up late.

EXERCISE 4 [page 136]

Answers will vary. Possible answers are:
1. I had to fill out a lot of forms.   2. I had to get certain vaccinations.   3. I had to prove that I would be studying here.   4. I had to send my passport to the United States embassy in my country.   5. Answers will vary.

EXERCISE 6 [page 137]

Answers will vary. Possible answers are:
1. Sabine was supposed to make her bed every day.
2. Sabine was supposed to watch her younger brother when her parents weren't at home.   3. Sabine was supposed to cook for the family once a week.   4. Sabine was supposed to do her homework every night.

EXERCISE 7 [page 138]

1. specific   2. general   3. specific   4. general
5. general   6. general

EXERCISE 8 [page 138]

1. was able to; couldn't   2. couldn't   3. was able to
4. couldn't

EXERCISE 9 [page 138]

(1) used to/would   (2) used to   (3) used to   (4) used to/would   (5) used to   (6) would/used to   (7) used to

EXERCISE 10 [page 139]

1. (a) wasn't able to open   (b) would work; had saved
(c) was . . . going to be
2. (a) ø   (b) would write up   (c) was . . . going to visit   (d) was to become

EXERCISE 11 [page 139]

1. (a) was going to   (b) would/was going to   (c) would /was going to
2. (a) was going to   (b) would   (c) would
3. (a) was going to   (b) would   (c) would

EXERCISE 12 [page 140]

1. was going to postpone   2. Were you going to send
3. correct   4. was going to

Unit 25

Indirect Quotation

EXERCISE 1 [page 141]

1. The teacher told me that my son needed to come to school on time.   2. She didn't like the fact that he often bothered other children.   3. Pauline was annoyed that the supermarket cashier had dropped her change.   4. The veterinarian explained that my cat needed more exercise.

EXERCISE 2 [page 141]

1. The manager said, "I am unhappy that we can no longer have free coffee."   2. The manager said, "I don't like the fact that there will be no more doughnuts at staff meetings."   3. The manager said, "I'm concerned that Mr. Romano didn't get any new contracts last month."   4. The manager said, "I'm concerned that two employees have left for other jobs."

EXERCISE 3 [page 142]

1. The teacher commented that Bill would probably need extra tutoring.   2. The bus driver admitted that he could have avoided the accident.   3. Jack's doctor stated that his father shouldn't continue eating so much sugar.   4. Patrick mentioned that the data files were ready to be sent.   5. The government official announced that the new tax rates would be released tomorrow/the next day.

EXERCISE 4 [page 143]

1. Jack said that his wife and your husband have a lot in common.   2. Jack's wife said that her husband thinks that she can read his mind.   3. Jack's brother said that his brother (Jack) and he often go hiking in the mountains.   4. Jack's mother said that Jack (her son) needed to visit her more often.

EXERCISE 5 [page 143]

1. Last week Mary told me that she had already taken all of the units she needed for her degree.   2. When Max saw his sister, he promised her that he would definitely be there for her graduation.   3. On Saturday evening, Peter mentioned that he could go to my concert after all.   4. When he stopped me, the INS agent said that he wanted to see my green card and my driver's license.

EXERCISE 6 [page 144]

1. Marilyn said that if she had known then what she knows now, her life would be very different.   2. Just five minutes ago the child asked if they were there yet.   3. Last month my roommate asked me if I minded if she copied my chemistry notes.   4. Paulette told us that Carol was still in the hospital recovering from her surgery.   5. Catherine warned her roommate that she would be up late typing her finishing her Internet search.

EXERCISE 7 [page 144]

The underlined passages are below.
1. Theresa called me to say that she had been nominated "Engineering Student of the Year." She told me that there were five finalists. She commented that she was the only woman of the five.   2. I told my mother that I knew where the North Pole was. I announced that I had written Santa a letter.   3. if you know how I can reach Mr. Zoltan; whether he's still teaching history; that I'm getting my M.A. in history.

EXERCISE 8 [page 145]

1. When I saw Tomoko last week, she mentioned that the counselor had told her that he wouldn't be able to help her get into ESL classes until the next day.
2. Yesterday the car mechanic informed me that he wouldn't be able to get the part he needed to repair my engine for another two days.
3. Last week the apartment manager promised me said that the apartment would be painted and that the plumbers were going to fix the pipes in the room above mine while I am on vacation. He also said that I would have to move all of my things out of my room by that night.
4. When I went to the embassy, the official pointed out that the papers had to be signed and returned by the next day at the latest.

EXERCISE 9 [page 145]

The underlined passages are below.
(2) Her coworker told her that they never chewed gum while sitting at the front desk.   (3) The woman who sold coffee from the coffee cart warned her that refills were not allowed.   (4) her boss reminded her that she couldn't leave early.   (5) her mother told her that there was no food in the refrigerator for dinner.
RESTATEMENTS: 2. Janice's coworker said, "We never chew gum while sitting at the front desk."
3. The woman who sold coffee from the coffee cart said, "Refills are not allowed."   4. On Friday, her boss said, "Remember, you can't leave early."   5. When Janice got home that evening, her mother said, "There's no food in the refrigerator for dinner."

EXERCISE 10 [page 146]

2. "How are your grades?"   3. "Have you had any speeding tickets or other problems with the law?"
4. "How are you planning to pay for your education?"

EXERCISE 11 [page 146]

1. Another advisor told her, "Get an e-mail account right away."   2. Akiko's new roommate said, "Take the bed near the window."   3. Akiko's host family asked, "Would you like to go to the mall with us?"
4. Akiko's English professor warned her, "Check your Internet sources carefully."   5. Akiko's friend asked, "Are you happy in your new school?"

TEST PREP • UNITS 23–25 [page 148]

1. b	5. a	9. b	13. c	17. b
2. c	6. c	10. a	14. b	18. d
3. d	7. d	11. d	15. a	19. a
4. b	8. c	12. a	16. c	20. b

AUDIO SCRIPT

(CD1 Track 1) Unit 1, Page 9, Activity 2

The foundation for Social Research today announced the winners of this year's Madison Award for distinguished work in the field of sociology. The award, one awarded posthumously, will provide $5000 to fund further research projects. This year's winners are Dr. Deborah Smith and Professor Sally Jones.

Dr. Smith has been a senior researcher at the Institute for Social Change since 1987. She is the author of several books on the welfare system, and has served on the President's Council for Welfare Reform for the last three years. Her research interests include the impact of welfare reform on the urban family and the effect of the Head Start programs on later academic performance of school-aged children. This is her first major award, and she says she will use the prize money to fund further research on the effect of poverty on family structure.

Professor Jones was the chair of the Social Welfare Department at Jordan College. She wrote extensively on economic patterns in rural America, and, in later years, researched the sociological profile of families involved in the home-schooling movement. In the last several months, she had been increasingly interested in the sociological impact of breast cancer. She received numerous awards throughout her long and distinguished career, including the Peabody Award and the Pulitzer Prize. Jordan College, which accepted the prize on her behalf, said that the money would be used for medical research, as Professor Jones had requested.

(CD1 Tracks 2, 3, 4, 5) Unit 2, Page 24, Activity 1

(CD1 Track 2) Conversation 1

John: What an interesting apartment. You don't have much space, do you?
Mary: No, not really. But actually it's OK because I live by myself.
John: Hmm. I'm living by myself, too, but it's really too expensive.

(CD1 Track 3) Conversation 2

Peter: I've looked over the Johnson contract, and everything looks fine.
Denise: Oh really, Peter? I've been looking it over too, and I can see at least three serious errors.

(CD1 Track 4) Conversation 3

Kathy: Did the new janitor do an OK job of cleaning up the office?

Angela: Yeah, I think he'll be fine. When I came in this morning he had done the windows and he was washing the floor.
Kathy: What about the trash? Did he empty the trash?
Angela: Yeah, he did it when I got there.

(CD1 Track 5) Conversation 4

Dave: Hey, Bob. Did you read in the newspaper that they're going to close down the steel mill?
Bob: Yeah, Dave, I saw it all right. I worked there for 15 years, and I must say, I'm not too sorry to hear about it.
Dave: That's fine for you, but I've been working there for five years, and I'm not really happy about having to look for another job.

(CD1 Tracks 6, 7) Unit 3, Page 44, Activity 4

(CD1 Track 6) Broadcast 1

An army-led coup on Christmas Eve toppled the two-year-old civilian government of Surinam. The coup was carried off without a single shot being fired, and, by today, normal holiday activity had resumed in the nation's capital. The leader of the country's military police appeared on national television to announce this takeover and promised that elections would be held within 100 days. However, the real leader of the coup is widely believed to be chief of the armed forces, General Bouterse was the dictator of the former Dutch Colony from 1980 to 1988, and has served as a commander of the armed forces since then. Although General Bouterse announced his own resignation from the army earlier in the day, he is reportedly still in charge of the troops. Bouterse carried out a similar coup in 1980, which toppled the previous civilian-led government. Both the U.S. and Dutch governments vigorously condemned the takeover.

(CD1 Track 7) Broadcast 2

Roosevelt Williams, a well-known educator and AIDS activist in Alameda County, died today from complications caused by AIDS. He was one of the world's longest-surviving AIDS patients. Since he was first diagnosed with the disease in 1980, he had been a tireless promoter of more education, support, and understanding for people with AIDS. He was widely known throughout the Bay Area for his inspirational appearances at local schools and churches, as well as on radio and television. He was a persuasive and eloquent speaker, and his efforts were so successful that a number of private organizations set up free treatment programs for the public. Memorial services will be held in several area churches on Sunday.

(CD1 Track 8) Unit 4, Pages 62 and 63, Activity 4

Officials in the Spanish Ministry of the Interior of Madrid announced today that a previously unknown masterpiece by Diego de Velasquez has been discovered in a storage closet at the Ministry. It seems clear that no one had opened the closet for at least 50 years, and officials have no idea how the painting got there in the first place. Officials believe that the painting, a portrait that was probably painted sometime between 1685 and 1700, had been stored away for safekeeping sometime during the Spanish Civil War, and then forgotten about.

Felipe Velasquez, a spokesman for the Ministry, who, in spite of having the same name, says that he is not related to the famous artist, theorized that officials at the time had no idea that the painting was particularly valuable. It isn't listed on any of the inventories of the Ministry, and, until yesterday, when it was authenticated by experts at the Prado Museum, nobody knew of its existence.

Diego de Velasquez, one of Spain's most famous artists, was very prolific, and painted dozens of portraits of many of the Court Nobility. The discovery of this portrait of a yet-to-be-identified middle-aged nobleman has led experts to wonder if there might not be other undiscovered masterpieces lying around in Ministry closets. "We'll be doing some serious house cleaning," said spokesman Velasquez, "to see what else is hiding in the attic."

The painting has been valued at over 1.5 million dollars.

(CD1 Tracks 9, 10) Unit 5, Page 84, Activity 5

(CD1 Track 9) Conversation 1

A: *(annoyed)* Can you turn down the television? I'm talking on the phone, and I can't hear a thing.
B: *(defensive)* You don't have to shout. Just ask nicely. You can be so unpleasant sometimes.
A: *(sarcastic)* You could try sitting in the same room as the TV. That way the rest of us wouldn't have to go deaf.
B: *(cold)* Sorry, I can't hear you. I'm watching TV.

(CD1 Track 10) Conversation 2

Mom: Will you tell Steve to stop teasing Nancy? She's going to cry in a minute.

Dad: Oh relax. Boys will be boys. Besides, she's got to toughen up if she's going to grow up to become a soldier in the army like her mom.
Mom: No, she doesn't. Boys have got to become more supportive and caring. Listen, we'd better start teaching them when they're little, or they're never going to learn.
Dad: Look, boys tease each other all the time. Why shouldn't they act that way with girls, too?
Mom: You must be joking. I mean, you can't be serious.
Dad: No, you're right. I was just trying to tease you, too.
Mom: Watch it, buster. You know, I'm about to lose my temper.
Dad: All right, Stevie! Stop teasing your sister!

(CD1 Track 11) Unit 6, Page 104, Activity 4

A: Were you in English class yesterday? What happened? Did the teacher say anything about the final examination tomorrow?

B: Well, he didn't exactly tell us what to study, but he did tell us what not to study. He said we could expect not to be tested on anything in the first half of the book.

A: Hey, that's good news! I was planning on studying all night tonight, but now it looks like I won't have to. I know the second half of the book really well.

B: So, where were you yesterday? You missed a good review session.

A: I'm trying to be selected for a position on the student advisory board for the library, so I had an appointment to be interviewed by the head librarian.

B: Student advisory board? That sounds like a chance you couldn't afford to pass up!

A: Well, I want to get a master's in library science and my advisor told me to try to get some practical experience. Successful applicants are expected to have first-hand knowledge of all areas of library operations.

B: Well, why don't you just get a job in the library? That way you have a chance to get paid while you're learning.

A: I don't think I'd have much opportunity to get experience in all areas. I'd probably just be expected to put books on the shelves, and I already know how to do that. The advisory board will give me a chance to learn about a variety of library issues.

(CD1 Track 12) Unit 7, Page 123, Activity 5

Narrator: Welcome to this week's edition of "Talk Talk," with our ever-popular host, Barry Roast.

Barry: In today's program we'll find out some surprising information about what experts are calling our latest endangered species: *free time*. We'll be hearing today from Doctor Belva Murphy, author of *Free Time: America's Vanishing Resource*. According to her study, Americans are having a hard time holding on to their free time. Dr. Murphy has discovered that the amount of leisure time in the U.S. has decreased by nearly 30 percent in the last 20 years. In a conversation with her in the studio earlier this week, I found out some interesting facts about our latest Vanishing Resource.

Barry [continues]: Doctor Murphy, you've stated in your book that Americans now have less leisure time than people in any other industrialized country in the world, and this amount will probably continue to decrease in the future. Where is this time going to?

Dr. Murphy: Well, employment practices in the U.S. are one cause. The average American company requires employees to work 40 hours per week. They are allowed to take 11 paid holidays, and have an average of 12 vacation days (about two weeks). Compare that to the Germans. They are required to work a 38-hour week, and get to enjoy a yearly total of 10 holidays and 30 days (six weeks) of paid vacation. Even the hard-working Japanese (who spend an average of 42 hours a week working at the office), are encouraged to take 16 paid vacation days, and have an additional 20 days of holidays. As you can see, the U.S. doesn't stack up too well in the time-off department.

Barry: But Dr. Murphy, work requirements aren't the only reason, are they?

Dr. Murphy: A second reason for this growing lack of free time comes from changing social patterns. Today, in most American families, both the husband and the wife need to work full-time outside the home. They are forced to postpone doing household chores until the weekend. Eighty-two percent of the people in my study said they need to spend at least one entire day of their weekend doing household chores, such as shopping for food, cleaning house, doing the laundry, and so forth.

Barry: But Dr. Murphy, you say vanishing free time isn't all the boss's fault. A surprisingly important cause of decreased free time is a way more and more Americans are using their free time.

Dr. Murphy: Yes Barry, there has also been a rapid growth in the popularity of "working vacations." Travel agencies can now arrange for people to work on scientific research projects, or to assist ecologists with collecting and cataloging plant and animal species in the national parks. Other popular "working vacations" include going on digs at archaeological sites, or participating in community development projects in other countries. Still other people enroll in travel-study courses in foreign languages, history, or geography.

Barry: For some Americans, their idea of a relaxing vacation is to take a 300-mile bicycle trip, or to spend a week climbing mountains in South America. But for all Americans one thing is certain: people have less free time than they did a generation ago, and the so-called labor-saving technological developments of the last 50 years have only made life faster—not easier! With Dr. Belva Murphy this is Barry Roast of "Talk Talk."

(CD1 Track 13) Unit 8, Page 144, Activity 6

Professor: In the second half of the twentieth century, there has been such a rapid growth in the population that many countries have started to develop lands that only a few years ago were uninhabited, dense tropical rain forest. Now, results of this population growth have had two economic impacts that have contributed to rapid deforestation. These developing countries need foreign exchange, which they can get by selling wood from the trees that grow in the rain forest, and they also need additional land for their growing populations. This need for lumber for export and land for agriculture has become so great that literally hundreds of square miles of tropical rain forest are now disappearing every day.

Now this process of destruction is happening extremely rapidly . . . so rapidly, in fact, that unless we can slow it down, all the world's rain forests—yes all of them—will be completely gone in just another 20 years!

Now why is this a problem? Why don't we just plant new trees to replace the ones that are being cut down? The problem is, that once the rain forests have been cut down, they don't just grow back. There is too little fertility in the soil of most tropical areas for the jungle to grow back at all. The original forests can never grow back again. This problem is so serious that scientists around the world and international organizations like the United Nations are all getting extremely concerned.

All right, so we can't replace the rain forests. Why should this be a problem? Why shouldn't we worry about it? We have many other resources like coal, and oil and minerals that can't be replaced. Why should rain forests be different from those?

Well, there are two primary reasons why the destruction of the rain forests poses a global threat. First, rain forests contain so many plants with possible medical uses that scientists are worried that many valuable species will be destroyed before we can find out how useful they are. But there is a second, more important reason why the destruction of the rain forests is too important to be ignored. There is a clear relationship between rain forests and the climate and weather patterns of the entire world. Rain forests are disappearing so quickly that scientists are afraid that this may already be causing changes in the atmosphere and weather of the planet. There are signs that it may already be too late for us to stop this process of global warming and climatic change. But further destruction of the rain forests will only make matters worse.

(CD1 Tracks 14, 15) Unit 9, Page 164, Activity 7

(CD1 Track 14) Conversation 1

Customer: (*Snobby tone*) Oh waiter, please give me a glass of cold water.
Waiter: Here you go.
Customer: No, I said I wanted cold water.
Waiter: Oh, I'm sorry. If you want cold water, I'll have to put ice in it.
Customer: Well, I didn't really want ice-water. If you have to add ice, then just make it an iced tea.
Waiter: I'll have to charge you for iced tea.
Customer: How much is it?
Waiter: A regular glass is 95 cents, and a tall glass is a dollar fifty.
Customer: Fine, I'll have a tall iced tea.
Waiter: Here you are.
Customer: You call that tall iced tea? The regular must be really small!
Waiter: Look, lady, I only work here. Would you like to talk to the manager?

(CD1 Track 15) Conversation 2

Young girl: Hello, Jocelyn residence.
Man: I'm trying to reach Dr. Jocelyn.
Girl: Well, which Dr. Jocelyn do you want? There are two here.
Man: I'm not sure. I'm calling for the Physics Department and I need to speak to the Dr. Jocelyn who is the retired physics professor.
Girl: Oh, then I think you want to talk with my grandmother, but she's a retired biology professor.
Man: Oh, I think she's the one. I'm calling about setting up a senior citizens lecture series.
Girl: Oh well. Are you sure you don't want to talk with her daughter, the other Dr. Jocelyn? She teaches physics.
Man: No, this is about a senior citizen's lecture series. I think I need to speak to the retired professor.
Girl: OK, I'll get her. Hey, Grandma! Phone call!

(CD1 Track 16) Unit 10, Page 180, Activity 3

Bob: Hi, Kim. I had to go to the dentist today. What did Professor Jordan talk about in Anthropology class?

Kim: She talked about culture.

GRAMMAR DIMENSIONS 3 LESSON PLANNER

Bob: Hmm. Is that like the "language families" she talked about last time?

Kim: Yeah, she said that just as there are large "language families"—you know . . .

Kim and Bob: *(reciting together as if by rote)* "groups of languages that have somewhat the same linguistic structure." *(they laugh)*

Kim: Yeah, well, she said that anthropologists are now trying to define and identify large "culture families," as well.

Bob: So now, what are culture families?

Kim: Hold on. Let me look at my notes . . . Oh here it is. Just as language families are made up of languages that share certain basic linguistic characteristics, culture families might be defined as groups of cultures that have more or less similar values, attitudes, and beliefs.

Bob: There's nothing surprising about that. I've traveled enough to know that one "European" culture—which, by the way, includes areas outside of geographical Europe, such as Australia and North America—has many of the same basic characteristics as any other European culture.

Kim: Yeah, well, the example she used in the lecture was the countries of Latin America. She said that in spite of being quite different from each other in terms of customs and social structures, people from Columbia probably think more like people from Venezuela than like people from Nepal. And a Nepalese and an Indian will be more alike than a Nepalese and an Austrian.

Bob: I'm confused. If no culture has exactly the same set of values as another culture—which is what she told us last week—how are they going to determine culture families?

Kim: Well, let's see here. According to my notes, she said one important unifying factor is religion. Another factor is a shared historical and political development. Cultures that have a shared historical background tend to have somewhat the same outlook on the world.

Bob: But wait a minute. Any student of geography knows that political boundaries change much more frequently and more rapidly than cultural boundaries. What about places like the former Yugoslavia, or in countries like Rwanda or Burundi?

Kim: Yeah, she mentioned that. She said that many of the problems in newly independent countries today are because these *developing* countries were founded by colonial powers as political unions, not cultural ones. But it is also important to remember that the differences between cultures can sometimes be more important than the similarities, no matter how much their economic and political interests may be alike, cultures that think quite differently from one another may choose to act quite differently as well.

Bob: Well, it doesn't sound like I missed anything terribly surprising. I think I already knew all that stuff.

Kim: Well, I thought it was pretty interesting, and she said it would definitely be on the midterm.

(CD Track 17) Unit 11, Pages 199 and 200, Activity 4

Narrator: Here are Silly Sally's likes and dislikes about styles of food.

Voice 2: Silly Sally loves cooking, but hates to eat. She likes Greek food but not Chinese cuisine. She won't touch anything from Brazil or Japan, but she likes Moroccan cooking a great deal.

Narrator: Now, here are Silly Sally's likes and dislikes about sports.

Voice 2: Silly Sally not only loves tennis and baseball, but also skiing. However, she hates horseback riding and hockey. She doesn't mind jogging, but she hates to walk.

Narrator: Now, here's what she thinks about people.

Voice 2: She likes queens and princesses, but neither kings nor princes. She loves Matt and Jeff, but she likes neither Peter and Denise, nor John and Mary.

Narrator: Now, here are Silly Sally's likes and dislikes about fruits and vegetables.

Voice 2: She's wild about beets, carrots, and apples, but she can't stand potatoes, or oranges, or especially cauliflower.

Narrator: Now, here are Silly Sally's likes and dislikes about movie stars.

Voice 2: She likes films with Johnny Depp and Meryl Streep, but not Marlon Brando or Elizabeth Taylor. She hates Denzel Washington, but loves Whoopi Goldberg.

Narrator: Now, here is what Silly Sally thinks about things to do on a date.

Voice 2: She likes going to nice restaurants for dinner, but not for lunch. She'll go to an art gallery, but not a museum. She loves to kiss, but she hates to hug. She wants to get married, but she doesn't want to get engaged. ideas about places to go for a vacation.

Voice 2: She loves Greece, but hates Italy. She likes inns, but she hates hotels. She'll go to the Philippines, but not to Indonesia. She'll travel in the summer, but not in the winter.

Narrator: And finally, here are Silly Sally's likes and dislikes about animals.

Voice 2: She doesn't mind sheep, but she's not fond of goats. She hates cats and dogs, but is fond of not only puppies, but also kittens.

(CD1 Track 18) Unit 12, Page 216, Activity 3

We use the term "pacifist to describe someone who doesn't believe in fighting wars. But there can be different kinds of pacifists. Most pacifists are opposed to war under any circumstances. They feel that armed conflict should never be used to solve disagreements. However, some pacifists believe that there is a difference between a war and a revolution. A war is a conflict which involves two different countries, and a revolution is a war between the people of a single country and their unjust government. Some pacifists feel that "revolution" is a justifiable conflict, but "war" is not. Whenever there is armed conflict, people will disagree about whether or not such a conflict can be justified.

All the recent examples of U.S. military involvement (such as the Vietnam War, the war in the Persian Gulf, or the war in the former Yugoslavia) have divided public opinion into two camps: "hawks" (the term we use to describe people who are in favor of a particular war) and "doves" (the term we use to describe people who are opposed to it). In American politics, disagreements between the "hawks" and the "doves" have been frequent and serious. Hawks and doves disagree about the role of the U.S. military should play around the world, and how much money the government should spend on military purposes. Hawks usually favor a strong army and large amounts of money for military purposes. Doves typically favor a small army and want less money spent on military purposes and more money spent on social programs.

(CD1 Track 19) Unit 13, Page 229, Activity 4

Good morning class. Today we're going to continue our discussion of the law of supply and demand. Remember last class we said that according to classical economic theory, supply and demand—remember that's the law that says increase in demand raises prices, and increase in supply lowers prices—well, this law in classical economics is considered to be THE major driving force in a free market economy. Well, modern economic theory states that there are a number of other forces at work too, so today we're going to take a look at what some of those other forces might be. The first thing we're going to look at is transportation. And in order to understand this, I'm going to tell you a little story. We're going to take a look at what happened about 100 years ago in the midwestern U.S., OK?

Now, about 100 years ago in the Midwest, there wasn't really a very good system of transportation. There wasn't really a very good way of transporting goods long distances, and getting things to market, so things were pretty much on a very local, region-by-region basis. So corn and wheat—which were the primary agricultural products, just as they are today—the price of corn and wheat were determined by the classic relationship of supply and demand that we talked about yesterday. Supply was determined by how much corn and wheat were available, and demand was determined by how many people needed to buy it. So, during the 1870s and 1880s, as the population increased, the demand for wheat

rose, and the price also rose. But then farmers responded to the price increase by producing more wheat, since they could get more profit on their investment of time and effort because of the higher prices. This made more corn and wheat available, so the competition to sell also increased, and the prices dropped.

Now this was really bad news. There were these continuous cycles of boom and bust, boom and bust. Prices would drop and farmers would go bankrupt. Then there wouldn't be enough corn and wheat, because nobody was growing it, and the prices would shoot through the roof. People couldn't buy bread or feed their livestock. It was really terrible.

Now what happened to change this? One thing: railroads. There was this explosion of railroad construction in the 1880s and everything changed. Railroads meant that you could move the available supply around the country, and not just keep it in one place. If you had too much in one area, you could send the surplus to someplace else. If you didn't have enough, you could increase the supply from other places. So the development of transportation had a really fundamental and significant impact.

So that's the first factor or force that affects the basic law of supply and demand. Next time we're going to take a look at some of the other forces: advertising, government relations, and monopolies. Any questions?

(CD1 Tracks 20, 21) Unit 14, Pages 242 and 243, Activity 4

(CD1 Track 20) Interview 1

Interviewer 1: Hi. Thanks for coming. We're glad that you're interested in the North American Institute for International Studies. Could you tell us your name, and which program you've applied for?
Candidate 1: Sure. Hi. My name is Aliona Fernandez, and I'm applying for the Master's Program in Teaching English as a Foreign Language.

Interviewer 2: Great! Well, why don't we get started by having you tell us why you think you'd be a good candidate for our program. I mean, what makes you different from other candidates?
Aliona: OK. Well, I'm not sure about the other candidates' background, but I suspect that maybe I've had more actual teaching experience overseas than some of the others. I've been in the Peace Corps and I've also worked in Taiwan and Japan.

Interviewer 2: Yes, we saw that on your application. Well, why do you want to go back to school, with so much experience?

Aliona: Well, I think that this experience has been really helpful, but I feel I really need some formal training to help me improve my skills.

Interviewer 1: That makes sense. Well, our time is a bit limited so we've only got time to ask you one more question. Can you tell us about an accomplishment that you feel particularly proud of?

Aliona: Gosh. Well, I guess this is not time to be modest, is it? Well, I speak three languages. I've lived comfortably in other cultures. And I've written a grammar book.

Interviewer 2: Really? Where was that?

Aliona: Oh, that was when I was a Peace Corps volunteer.

Interviewer 1: Well, our time's up. Thanks for coming.

Aliona: Thank you.

(CD1 Track 21) Interview 2

Interviewer 2: Thanks for coming. We're glad that you're interested in the North American Institute for International Studies. Could you tell us your name and which program you've applied for?

John: Sure. Hi. My name is John Tealhome and I'm applying for the International Business Program.

Interviewer 1: Great! Well, why don't we get started by having you tell us why you think you'd be a good candidate for our program. I mean, what makes you different from other candidates?

John: OK. Well, I've just returned from spending a year studying in Paris, and I'm really interested in using that experience to work in import-export.

Interviewer 1: Oh, a year in Paris, that's interesting. Have you had any experience in international business?

John: Well, not really. But I've made some good contacts that I hope to follow up on once I've gotten a little more training. Oh, and when I was in college here I worked in a bookstore.

Interviewer 2: Mmmm. Well, our time is a bit limited, so we've only got time to ask you one more question. Can you tell us about an accomplishment that you feel particularly proud of?

John: Let's see. Well, I was class president of my high school. I was captain of the football team. As you probably noticed on my application, I received a scholarship to study in France.

Interviewer 1: Yes, we did. Are you fluent in French?

John: Bien sûr! I made some really good friends in France and they taught me a lot.

Interviewer 2: Well, that's terrific, it was really nice to meet you. I'm afraid our time's up. Thank you very much for coming.

John: You're welcome. Nice talking to you.

(CD1 Tracks 22, 23) Unit 15, Page 254, Activity 4

(CD1 Track 22) Speaker 1

A hundred years from now will be a wonderful time to be alive. Certain things are already happening that will change human society and make the next century a wonderful time in the history of the world.

A hundred years from now there will be more people and they will be leading healthier lives. Most of the diseases that are common today will be wiped out. Scientists are already making progress in finding cures for AIDS, Alzheimer's disease, heart disease, and cancer. So people in the next century will be living longer and healthier lives.

In a hundred years people will have been eating more nutritiously for several generations; so, as we are already seeing in the countries like Japan and Thailand, human beings will, on the whole, be larger, stronger and more intelligent than they are today.

Another area of progress will be energy resources. Scientists will have discovered nonpolluting ways to produce cheap, clean energy. There are already alternative energy sources such as water power and solar energy, and as fuels such as gas, oil, and coal become scarcer and more expensive, then clean sources of energy will become cheaper to produce. So it is likely that by the end of the next century there will be much less pollution: no smog, no acid rain, and no fears about global warming.

Finally, 100 years from now will see greater political and economic stability. Global communication and global economic progress will improve the political situation. Changes such as the Internet are already making global communication available to everyone and will lead to increasingly international cooperation. By the end of the next century, the political changes that started in the late 1980s will remove forever the threat of nuclear war. People will be so used to thinking in global terms, and will have been doing so for so long that it will no longer even be necessary to have passports.

(CD1 Track 23) Speaker 2

A hundred years from now will be a terrible time to be alive unless the governments of the world begin to act now. If certain things don't begin to happen, the next century could be a very unpleasant period in the history of the world.

The population is increasing at a very rapid rate. Resources for health care, economic development, and even food cannot keep up with the enormous increase in population. In spite of this fact, many governments do not support birth control research or family planning programs. There will be more and more shortages of food as the population continues to grow uncontrollably and poor nutrition will affect more and more people. Lack of sufficient vitamins will make people weaker and less able to resist disease.

The growth of new diseases such as AIDS and Ebola Virus will continue, and all diseases will become harder to control. Such diseases as malaria and tuberculosis are already increasing. And common antibiotics have begun to lose their effectiveness against infectious diseases like pneumonia.

Supplies of fossil fuels such as coal, oil, and gas are almost finished, but governments are not supporting programs to develop alternative energy sources, such as solar power or wind-generated electricity. Massive deforestation is changing the world climates and increasing air pollution. And an increasing reliance on nuclear power will result in more nuclear accidents like Chernobyl.

In spite of increase global communication, countries are breaking apart. The small local wars in places like the former Yugoslavia or the former Soviet Union will become more widespread. This trend will continue around the world, as the economic gap between the rich and the poor continues to increase. War and revolution will be common in the next century.

(CD1 Track 24) Unit 16, Page 269, Activity 5

Mom: John, all the cookies I baked this morning have disappeared. I think one of those kids has been robbing the cookie jar. But which one is it?
Dad: Well, it could be any of them. You know how Nancy likes sweets. She could have eaten them when she came home from school today. But then again, it might have been Diane. Remember what happened to that chocolate cake you cooked for the bake sale? Of course, I suppose it could have been Eric, too. He's not that fond of sweets, but he is a growing boy.
Mom: Well, it couldn't have been Diane, because I was with her all afternoon. I don't think it was Nancy. She's been on a diet, so I don't think she could have done it. It must have been Eric.
Dad: Well, I think it could have been Nancy. She should have been really hungry after school if she's been dieting. She could have done it. Are you sure you were with Diane the whole afternoon? She might have taken them while you weren't looking.
Eric: Hi, Mom. Hi, Dad. Sorry I'm late. Basketball practice lasted longer than expected. What's for dinner? I'm starved.
Mom: Well, it must not have been Eric, I guess. He hasn't been home at all. It must have been one of the girls.
Dad: Let's check their rooms. That should tell us something. We might find some cookies still lying around.
Mom: Oh, we can do that later. We're going to have dinner in a minute.
Dad: Dinner already? I'm still full!
Mom: Full? Full from what, honey?
Dad: Um, err, uh . . .
Mom: Wait a minute—are those cookie crumbs I see on your mustache?

(CD1 Track 25) Unit 17, Page 292, Activity 7

Peter: Say, Denise, do you know if Mr. Green has announced the new projects?
Denise: Well, Peter, if you had been at the meeting, you would have heard the announcement. You couldn't have chosen a more important meeting to miss.
Peter: Yes, Denise, I know. But I was busy finishing up the contract. You know, you could have been more careful with the figures. I had to change several at the last moment.
Denise: You should have checked them before it got so close to the deadline.
Peter: And you might at least have warned me that you hadn't gone over them.
Denise: I might have gone over them, Peter. What makes you think I didn't?
Peter: If you had gone over them there wouldn't have been so many mistakes. We both know you are a careful worker. I think you left them there on purpose.
Denise: Now why would I do that?
Peter: Well, let's pretend you wanted to get me in trouble with Mr. Green. What would be an easy way to do that, I wonder?
Denise: Please, Peter. I've got better things to do. If I wanted to get you fired, I would have done it a long time ago.

(CD1 Track 26) Unit 18, Page 308, Activity 7

Story sound effects:

1. wind blowing
2. dog barking
3. owl hooting
4. gate creaking open
5. multiple footsteps walking
6. doorbell ringing
7. children giggling

8. Boy and Girl: "Trick or treat!"

9. rustling bags and papers

10. children giggling again

11. footsteps running, fading away

12. door shutting

13. wind blowing (fades out)

(CD1 Track 27) Unit 18, Page 308, Activity 8

Matt: Hi, Doctor Wong. How did the lab tests turn out?
Dr. Wong: Hi, Matt. I got the results this morning, and I'm afraid your cholesterol level is quite high. You really need to change your eating habits. You need to start eating foods that are low in fat.
Matt: Well, I try to eat healthy foods, but my roommate, Jeff, does all the cooking. He always cooks everything with lots of butter, and he won't do it any other way. He says that butter gives food more flavor.
Dr. Wong: Well, you could try to take over cooking a couple of nights a week, and then slowly start to introduce your roommate to more healthful ways to prepare foods.

Matt: I'm not sure he'd agree. He really loves to cook.
Dr. Wong: Then just demand that he start preparing foods in a healthier way. That's the best way. Good sensible eating habits require that a person take responsibility for his or her own body and the food that goes in it.
Matt: Well, I guess I could try that. Is there any other way?
Dr. Wong: Well, we could put you on medication to lower your cholesterol, but there might be side-effects. Anyway, it's better if we can correct the problem naturally, without having to use expensive drugs.

(CD1 Tracks 28, 29, 30) Unit 19, Page 331, Activity 6

(CD1 Track 28) Conversation 1

Denise: Hi, Dave. Were there any phone calls while I was away at the sales meeting?
Dave: Oh yes, Ms. Driven. The sales representative from ACME Publishing called. And a_vice president came by to talk with you. She left something for you on your desk.
Denise: OK, I'd better take care of that one right away.

(CD1 Track 29) Conversation 2

John: I can't concentrate on this any longer. I'm starving! Let's go down to the snack bar.
Mary: But we're almost done. Can't you wait just a little longer?

John: I'm going to get a quick snack. I promise I'll be back.
Mary: OK. Well, get a snack for me, too.

(CD1 Track 30) Conversation 3

Bob: Betty, it's my birthday next week, and I'm thinking about having a party.
Betty: I remembered that it was your birthday. I was thinking about inviting some friends over for cake and ice cream.
Bob: Hmm, I was thinking about going to a restaurant.
Betty: Sounds like fun. Chinese food is the cheapest choice for a lot of people.
Bob: Great! Let's do it.

(CD1 Track 31) Unit 20, Page 343, Activity 5

Peter Principle: Good morning Denise. Did the Davis contract get finished?
Denise Driven: It took some doing, but I got it done last night.
Peter: Well, I came in early to help out, just in case you needed it.
Denise: That's nice, Peter. Thanks for your concern and support. But, as usual, it's too little and too late.
Peter: Gee. I guess you don't need help with your official complaint to Mr. Green, either.
Denise: No, Peter. That's done, too. In fact, I did it before I finished the Davis contract.

Peter: Oh good, Denise. I'm glad you have your priorities straight. Would you like to see pictures of my son's school play?
Denise: Don't start that again, Peter. I'm warning you!
Peter: Come on, Denise. It won't hurt you to think about something besides work for just a minute.
Denise: If you bring that up one more time, Peter, I swear I'll throw this computer terminal at you.
Peter: That's very professional, Denise, very professional.
Denise: I think you had better leave right now, Peter. I really mean it!

Peter: Gee, Denise. Are you giving me the day off? That's really nice of you. I guess I can take my kids to the beach after all. Bye-bye, then. Have a nice day. And I really mean that!

Denise: That man is going to drive me crazy! If I could only fire him, it would make this office so much more business-like.

(CD1 Track 32) Unit 21, Page 355, Activity 3

Teacher: OK class, we're going to play a little game with geometry today. We're going to look at one of Euclid's laws that shows the fundamental relationship of squares and triangles. I would like you all to take out a piece of paper and draw a perfect square. If you need to use a ruler to make sure that all four sides of the square are the same length, go ahead. *(pause)* Has everybody done that? OK. Now draw a line from the upper left-hand corner of the square to the bottom right-hand corner. *(pause)* How many triangles do you have? Two, right? OK, now do the same thing from the bottom left-hand corner to the opposite corner of the square. *(pause)* You should now have a total of four isosceles triangles. All right, now here comes the tricky part: I want you to draw a mirror image of each triangle, with the base of each triangle being the line that you drew as the side of your original square. *(pause)* So, your diagram should now look like this: a square with an X inside it, inside another square, which is at a 45-degree angle to the first square. OK, now connect the top and bottom corners and the left and right corners of the new square with lines. *(pause)* So your original square should now be divided up into eight triangles, and the whole diagram should still be a perfect square. Now, here are my questions: How many triangles are there in your diagram, and how many squares have you drawn? Count carefully, ladies and gentlemen, because there are probably more of both than you think.

(CD1 Tracks 33, 34, 35) Unit 22, Page 374 and 375, Activity 7

(CD1 Track 33) Report 1

Every year on March 19 a large flock of swallow returns to San Juan Capistrano Mission in Southern California. No one knows how this flock manages to return every year on exactly the same date, but they have been doing just that for more than 200 years. The city government of San Juan Capistrano has been providing a great deal of publicity on the event for many years, and as a result, March 19 is also the day when flocks of tourists arrive at the Mission as well to watch the swallows return.

(CD1 Track 34) Report 2

A committee of scientists has been appointed by the Canadian government to look into the effect of acid rain on the forests of North America. They have been asked to present the results of their study by the end of the year. The press and the public are waiting anxiously for the committee to release its report.

(CD1 Track 35) Report 3

There is a very unusual company of actors, which is based in Washington D.C. Most of the company cannot hear, and many members can only speak by using sign language. The National Theater of the Deaf was founded nearly 30 years ago, and since then they have performed all over the U.S., and in dozens of foreign countries. The troupe has played an important role in involving the disabled in the arts.

(CD1 Track 36) Unit 23, Page 389, Activity 3

What was my unforgettable experience? Gosh— *(slight pause)* I think one has to be the day I hear that John F. Kennedy had been assassinated. I think any American who was alive at the time probably feels the same way. It's just something you can't forget. Even though it was more than 40 years ago, I can still remember everything about that day; it's amazing!

I was a junior in high school. I was studying in the school library at the time. Ordinarily, I would have been in class, but our teacher was giving a make-up examination. Since I had already passed the test, I had been excused from class and given permission to go to the library.

I can remember it just as if it were yesterday! The library door was open, and I heard a radio playing from one of the classrooms across the hall. At first I was kind of bothered by the noise. I wondered why they were playing that radio so loud when people were trying to study. Then all of a sudden I heard the announcer saying, "We have confirmed that President John F. Kennedy has been shot while traveling through Dallas, and that he is now dead. We repeat: President John F. Kennedy is dead." I was shocked. I couldn't believe it! I immediately left the library and returned to class I was so upset, I had to tell someone!

When I entered the room they were still taking the test. I was about to interrupt when I heard the school principal on the public address system announcing the horrifying news. Even before he finished talking, people began to cry. And when he was finished, all normal activities came to a halt. Of course we forgot about the test. No one could believe it. Our teacher turned on the television and for the rest of the day we watched the news reports instead of studying. *(slight pause)* Yeah—that definitely has to be one of my most unforgettable experiences, no doubt about it!

(CD1 Track 37) Unit 24, Page 402, Activity 4

Science fiction is a kind of literature that describes how things will be in the future. Writers of science fiction have been making predictions about the future for more than 100 years, and several famous writers have described how life would be at the end of the twentieth century.

It is interesting for us today to look at the works of some of these famous science fiction writers to see the sort of future that they predicted, and how accurate those predictions reflect our actual living conditions. There are four writers whose predictions about life at the end of the twentieth century are particularly famous: Jules Verne, H.G. Wells, George Orwell, and Aldous Huxley. Let's take a look at some of the things they expected would happen before the year 2000.

Jules Verne was a popular late nineteenth-century French writer. Although he wrote many novels, his most famous works are probably his science fiction novels, *From the Earth to the Moon*, and *Twenty Thousand Leagues Under the Sea*. The world that he portrayed in those books was surprisingly accurate. He predicted that many people would have their own personal airplanes. He also accurately predicted that there would be scientific exploration of the moon, and that people would use solar power to get energy. He also predicted, less successfully, that there would be a single world language. He undoubtedly thought that that language would be French, although today it seems that English is a more likely candidate for that title.

Our next author is H.G. Wells. Wells was an English writer of the late nineteenth and early twentieth centuries. His most famous books were *The War of the Worlds, The Invisible Man*, and *The Time Machine*. In *The War of the Worlds* he described a frightening invasion from Mars, where aliens conquered the earth,

but eventually became victims of simple nonserious earth diseases such as the common cold. His other famous novels, as their titles suggest, predicted worlds where scientists created inventions that would allow people to travel through time, or would make people become invisible.

Two more famous English authors wrote in the second half of the twentieth century about times that they thought would be here very, very soon. Instead of writing about the world 100 years later, they wrote about a future that was less than 50 years away.

In the 1930s, George Orwell wrote his most famous novel, *1984*. In it he portrayed a gloomy and frightening world of three or four all-powerful governments that were constantly at war with each other and with their own people. Orwell pessimistically predicted that the government would control all aspects of people's lives, and that people would be watched by secret police, by hidden cameras, and microphones. He also feared that anyone who tried to disagree with the government would be put in prison.

Aldous Huxley's predictions in *Brave New World* were somewhat more optimistic, but he hardly expressed the optimism of Jules Verne or H.G. Wells. He portrayed a world where children would be born through artificial means and raised in state-run nurseries, instead of by individual families. He thought that there would be movies that were so realistic that people would think they were actually happening. He also thought that the use of mind-altering drugs would be widespread, and encouraged by the government.

As we can see, all four nations had an intriguing mix of right and wrong guesses about the ways we would actually be living today.

(CD1 Track 38) Unit 25, Page 419, Activity 6

At last month's press conference, a representative of the Metropolitan Police Department announced the rate of violent crime had decreased significantly over the last five months. He admitted there had been a slight increase in thefts and burglaries, and that the Department would

continue frequent patrols in all neighborhoods. When asked about the budget being discussed with the Mayor's Office, he predicted that it would be finalized by the end of the week, and the accelerated hiring program might begin as soon as the following Wednesday.